Communications in Computer and Information Science 1221

Commenced Publication in 2007
Founding and Former Series Editors:
Simone Diniz Junqueira Barbosa, Phoebe Chen, Alfredo Cuzzocrea,
Xiaoyong Du, Orhun Kara, Ting Liu, Krishna M. Sivalingam,
Dominik Ślęzak, Takashi Washio, Xiaokang Yang, and Junsong Yuan

More information about this series at http://www.springer.com/series/7899

Paolo Mori · Steven Furnell ·
Olivier Camp (Eds.)

Information Systems Security and Privacy

5th International Conference, ICISSP 2019
Prague, Czech Republic, February 23–25, 2019
Revised Selected Papers

 Springer

Editors
Paolo Mori (ORCID)
IIT-CNR
Pisa, Italy

Steven Furnell
Plymouth University
Plymouth, UK

Olivier Camp
MODESTE/ESEO
Angers Cedex 2, France

ISSN 1865-0929   ISSN 1865-0937 (electronic)
Communications in Computer and Information Science
ISBN 978-3-030-49442-1   ISBN 978-3-030-49443-8 (eBook)
https://doi.org/10.1007/978-3-030-49443-8

This Springer imprint is published by the registered company Springer Nature Switzerland AG
The registered company address is: Gewerbestrasse 11, 6330 Cham, Switzerland

Preface

The present book includes extended and revised versions of a set of selected papers from the 5th International Conference on Information Systems Security and Privacy (ICISSP 2019), held in Prague, Czech Republic, during February 23–25, 2019.

ICISSP aims at creating a meeting point for researchers and practitioners to address both technical and social issues of security and privacy challenges concerning information systems, especially in organizations. The conference welcomes papers of either practical or theoretical nature, presenting research or applications addressing all aspects of security and privacy, that concern organizations and individuals, thus creating new research opportunities.

ICISSP 2019 received 100 paper submissions from 32 countries, of which 18% were included in this book.

The papers were selected by the event chairs and their selection was based on a number of criteria that included the classifications and comments provided by the Program Committee members, the session chairs' assessment, and also the program chairs' global view of all papers included in the technical program. The authors of selected papers were then invited to submit a revised and extended version of their papers having at least 30% innovative material.

The papers selected for inclusion in this book address various topical research issues within the field of information security and privacy. These include a range of technical contributions, including new approaches for attack modeling and prevention, incident management and response, and user authentication and access control, as well as business and human-oriented aspects such as data protection and privacy and security awareness. The discussions also span a variety of application areas, including social networks, mobile devices, and the Internet of Things.

We would like to express our thanks to all the authors for their contributions and also to the reviewers who helped to ensure the quality of this publication.

February 2019

Paolo Mori
Steven Furnell
Olivier Camp

Organization

Conference Chair

Olivier Camp   MODESTE/ESEO, France

Program Co-chairs

Paolo Mori   CNR, Italy
Steven Furnell   University of Plymouth, UK

Program Committee

Carlisle Adams	University of Ottawa, Canada
Ja'far Alqatawna	Higher Colleges of Technology, UAE
Mario Alvim	Federal University of Minas Gerais (UFMG), Brazil
Thibaud Antignac	CEA/DRT/LIST, France
Alessandro Barenghi	Polytecnic University of Milan, Italy
Montserrat Batet	Universitat Rovira i Virgili, Spain
Carlo Blundo	Università di Salerno, Italy
Chiara Bodei	Università di Pisa, Italy
Christos Bouras	University of Patras, CTI&P Diophantus, Greece
Francesco Buccafurri	University of Reggio Calabria, Italy
Ismail Butun	Chalmers University of Technology, Sweden
Olivier Camp	MODESTE/ESEO, France
Nancy Cam-Winget	Cisco Systems, USA
Luigi Catuogno	Università di Salerno, Italy
Hervé Chabanne	Idemia, Télécom ParisTech, France
Rui Chen	Samsung Research America, USA
Thomas Chen	City University London, UK
Feng Cheng	Hasso-Plattner-Institute at University of Potsdam, Germany
Hung-Yu Chien	National Chi Nan University, Taiwan, China
Stelvio Cimato	Università degli Studi di Milano, Italy
Gianpiero Costantino	CNR, Italy
Rafael de Sousa Junior	University of Brasilia, Brazil
Hervé Debar	Télécom SudParis, France
Mingcong Deng	Tokyo University of Agriculture and Technology, Japan
Andreas Dewald	Friedrich-Alexander-Universität Erlangen-Nürnberg, Germany
Oriol Farras	Universitat Rovira i Virgili, Spain
Mathias Fischer	University of Hamburg, Germany

Benjamin Fung	McGill University, Canada
Steven Furnell	University of Plymouth, UK
Alban Gabillon	Laboratoire GePaSud, Université de la Polynésie Française, French Polynesia
Clemente Galdi	Università di Salerno, Italy
Debin Gao	Singapore Management University, Singapore
Bok-Min Goi	Universiti Tunku Abdul Rahman, Malaysia
Mario Goldenbaum	Bremen University of Applied Sciences, Germany
Ana González-Tablas	University Carlos III of Madrid, Spain
Gilles Guette	University of Rennes, France
Martin Hell	Lund University, Sweden
Guy Hembroff	Michigan Technological University, USA
Jin Hong	The University of Western Australia, Australia
Fu-Hau Hsu	National Central University, Taiwan, China
Danny Huang	Princeton University, UK
Dieter Hutter	German Research Centre for Artificial Intelligence, Germany
Mariusz Jakubowski	Microsoft Research, USA
Jens Jensen	STFC Rutherford Appleton Laboratory, UK
Anne Kayem	Hasso Plattner Institute, Germany
Christoph Kerschbaumer	Mozilla Corporation, USA
Zubair Khattak	Mohi-Ud-Din Islamic University, Pakistan
Hiroaki Kikuchi	Meiji University, Japan
Ansgar Koene	University of Nottingham, UK
Nicholas Kolokotronis	University of Peloponnese, Greece
Elisavet Konstantinou	University of the Aegean, Greece
Hristo Koshutanski	Atos, Spain
Nadira Lammari	Conservatoire National des Arts et Métiers, France
Gianluca Lax	University of Reggio Calabria, Italy
Gabriele Lenzini	University of Luxembourg, Luxembourg
Shujun Li	University of Kent, UK
Konstantinos Limniotis	Hellenic Data Protection Authority, Greece
Flamina Luccio	Università Ca' Foscari Venezia, Italy
Ilaria Matteucci	Istituto di Informatica e Telematica, CNR, Italy
Catherine Meadows	US Naval Research Laboratory, USA
Francesco Mercaldo	CNR, Italy
Mattia Monga	Università degli Studi di Milano, Italy
Paolo Mori	CNR, Italy
Kirill Morozov	University of North Texas, USA
Roberto Nardone	University of Reggio Calabria, Italy
Paliath Narendran	State University of New York at Albany, USA
Vivek Nigam	Federal University of Paraíba, fortiss, Brazil
Mehrdad Nojoumian	Florida Atlantic University, USA
Aida Omerovic	SINTEF, Norway
Carles Padro	Universitat Politecnica de Catalunya, Spain
Yin Pan	Rochester Institute of Technology, USA

Mauricio Papa	University of Tulsa, USA
Günther Pernul	University of Regensburg, Germany
Wolfgang Reif	University of Augsburg, Germany
Karen Renaud	cyber4humans, UK
Roberto Rojas-Cessa	New Jersey Institute of Technology, USA
Christophe Rosenberger	Ensicaen, France
Neil Rowe	Naval Postgraduate School, USA
Antonio Ruiz-Martínez	University of Murcia, Spain
Nader Safa	Coventry University, UK
Rajeev Sahu	Universite libre de Bruxelles, Belgium
Hossein Saiedian	University of Kansas, USA
David Sanchez	Universitat Rovira i Virgili, Spain
Antonella Santone	University of Molise, Italy
Andrea Saracino	Istituto di Informatica e Telematica, CNR, Italy
Michael Scott	Certivox Ltd., Ireland
Gaurav Sharma	Université libre de Bruxelles, Belgium
Qi Shi	Liverpool John Moores University, UK
Nicolas Sklavos	University of Patras, Greece
Boris Skoric	Eindhoven University of Technology, The Netherlands
Angelo Spognardi	Sapienza Università di Roma, Italy
Paul Stankovski Wagner	Lund University, Sweden
Rainer Steinwandt	Florida Atlantic University, USA
Hung-Min Sun	National Tsing Hua University, Taiwan, China
Iraklis Symeonidis	Snt-APSIA, University of Luxembourg, Luxembourg
Nadia Tawbi	Université Laval, Canada
Cihangir Tezcan	Middle East Technical University, Turkey
Pierre Tournoux	Université de la Réunion, Reunion Island
Yuh-Min Tseng	National Changhua University of Education, Taiwan, China
Raylin Tso	National Chengchi University, Taiwan, China
Yasuyuki Tsukada	Kanto Gakuin University, Japan
Udaya Tupakula	The University of Newcastle, Australia
Sylvestre Uwizeyemungu	Université du Québec à Trois-Rivières, Canada
Bîrjoveanu V. Catalin	University of Iasi, Romania
Adriano Valenzano	CNR, Italy
Gilles Van Assche	STMicroelectronics, Belgium
Rakesh Verma	University of Houston, USA
Luca Vigano	King's College London, UK
Bing Wu	Fayetteville State University, USA
Ching-Nung Yang	National Dong Hwa University, Taiwan, China
Alec Yasinsac	University of South Alabama, USA

Additional Reviewers

Haohan Bo	McGill University, Canada
Ziya Genç	University of Luxembourg, Luxembourg

Kallol Karmakar   The University of Newcastle, Australia
Miles Li   McGill University, Canada
Pegah Nikbakht Bideh   Lund University, Sweden
Alexander Schiendorfer   University of Augsburg, Germany

Invited Speakers

Bill Buchanan   Edinburgh Napier University, UK
Roberto Di Pietro   Hamad Bin Khalifa University, Qatar
Gerald Quirchmayr   University of Vienna, Austria

Contents

SPROOF: A Decentralized Platform for Attribute-Based Authentication

Clemens Brunner$^{(\boxtimes)}$, Fabian Knirsch, and Dominik Engel

Center for Secure Energy Informatics, Salzburg University of Applied Sciences,
Puch bei Hallein, Austria
{clemens.brunner,fabian.knirsch,dominik.engel}@en-trust.at

Abstract. Paper documents are still very common for all types of records of personal achievements, ID cards and many other types documents issued to an individual or a company. These paper documents, however, often come at the cost of expensive printing and issuing, loss of data or malicious counterfeits. The origin and integrity is often hard or even impossible to be verified. Digital signatures solve some of these issues, however, this still requires centralized trusted infrastructures and still does not allow for easy verification or recovery of lost documents. Furthermore, attribute-based authentication is not possible with traditional signature schemes. In this paper, we present a decentralized platform for signing and verifying digital documents that is based on the previously presented SPROOF platform and additionally supports attribute-based authentication. This platform allows for issuing, managing and verifying digital documents in a public blockchain. In the proposed approach, all data needed for verification of documents and issuers is stored decentralized, transparent, and integrity protected. The platform is permissionless and thus no access restrictions apply. Rather, following principles of the Web of Trust, issuers can confirm each other in a decentralized way. Additionally, scalability and privacy issues are taken into consideration.

Keywords: Blockchain · Certificate · Privacy-friendly · Digital document · Pseudonym

1 Introduction

Educational certificates, employment certificates and other records of personal achievements are still most commonly issued as a paper document with a handwritten signature. These paper documents can often be easily manipulated, lost or also destroyed and are hard to verify. To verify if such documents are not altered and are issued correctly, e.g., for a job application, one has to manually contact the issuing institutions for verifying the integrity and validity of the paper document and the printed records. Issuing – and reissuing such paper documents in case they get lost – can be a cost and labor intensive process and is impossible if the issuing institution does not exists anymore. While documents

© Springer Nature Switzerland AG 2020
P. Mori et al. (Eds.): ICISSP 2019, CCIS 1221, pp. 1–23, 2020.
https://doi.org/10.1007/978-3-030-49443-8_1

can be signed digitally, this only solves some of the problems and requires a centralized and trusted infrastructure that has – in the past – already shown to be unreliable in some circumstances [10]. Additionally, traditional digitally signed documents do not allow for easy verification or recovery of lost documents and especially do not support the completeness feature which is introduced below. Another problem that traditionally signed documents face is that providing evidence for a single attribute requires to share the data of the entire document. For instance, given that someone wants to provide evidence for the date of birth, sharing a driver's license or passport will also reveal attributes such as the name. In order to protect privacy in such circumstances, attribute-based authentication can be used.

In this paper, a decentralized platform for signing and verifying digital documents via a public blockchain is presented. This work extends the platform SPROOF originally presented in [4] with the ability to support attribute-based authentication. In this paper, the architectural building blocks of SPROOF are presented, the detailed protocol that uses a blockchain and a distributed storage for signing and verifying is discussed, and the concept of attribute-based authentication and how it integrates in SPROOF is described.

As a document, we define a digital file that is granted from an issuer to a receiver, e.g., a diploma granted from a university to a student or records of achievements granted from an company to a employee. Such a document can represent any data that has an issuer and a attributed-based receiver. The proposed approach uses a blockchain for sealing hash references of data storing in a distributed hash table. The blockchain acts as a decentralized, transparent, and integrity protected log of hash references. The corresponding raw-data contains all events, e.g. issuing and revoking a single or multiple documents at once. The approach is fully permissionless and does not allow single entities to gain control over issued documents or to prevent others to verify documents. Furthermore, validation is easy and can be automatized for a large number of documents from different issuers and for different subjects.

The contribution of this work is manyfold: It is shown how documents can be issued, received and verified while being fully decentralized, permissionless and transparent. In addition, the ability to group related documents from the same issuer is outlined and the concept of attribute-based authentication is presented. For evaluating the proposed protocol, scalability and privacy issues are taken into consideration. Attributed-based authentication on a decentralized platform and the describtion of the proof of concept is the new contribution of this extension.

For issuing, receiving and verifing documents in SPROOF the following roles are defined:

Issuer. The issuer of a document can be a company, an educational institution or basically anyone who wants to grant a document. The platform itself poses no limitations on issuers and there is no central third party to control issuers.

Receiver. The receiver of a documents can be a student for an educational certificate, an employee or even a company. Similar to issuers, there is no control over receivers.

Verifier. The verifier represents anyone who wants to view and verify the validity of documents. A verifier also wants to authenticate the identity of an issuer or a receiver. Authentication is fully decentralized and follows the principles of the Web of Trust (WoT). This role can be assumed by, e.g., an employer.

These participants interact via a platform for storing and verifing digital documents at low cost, with a simple verification feature, and with a reliable storage of data. We define the following desired properties:

Decentralization. The platform is completely decentralized and especially allows the verification of data without a single trusted third party. Furthermore, verification of past documents must be possible even if the issuing institution is not existent anymore.

Permissionless. The platform is permissionless and thus no single entity has control over the participants. Any participant has full access and can add new or has the possibility to revoke own issued documents without being required to register at a third party.

Integrated Issuer Verification. The platform provides built-in mechanisms to verify the identity of issuers. Thus, no additional or centralized channel is needed.

Transparency. The platform is transparent and every participant has read access to validate a given document. Privacy of documents is preserved by not revealing details of the receiver or sensitive content of a digital document, such as the name, without the consent of the receiver.

Completeness. Issuers have the ability to group documents and verifiers can check whether a group of documents is complete or not, i.e., if some document are intentionally hidden by the receiver (e.g., verifying a Bachelor's diploma includes verifying all related courses). This can be enforced by the issuer at the time of granting documents and is explained in detail in Sect. 4.

Attributed-based. Receivers have the possibility to share selected attributes of their documents, e.g, only the name or the date of birth.

The rest of the paper is structured as follows: Sect. 2 compares SPROOF to state of the art approaches in the field of educational certificate management and with respect to the stated requirements. Section 3 describes the basic building blocks of this work and the proposed protocol. Section 4 then describes the roles and the SPROOF protocol in detail. The proof of concept is described in Sect. 5. Section 6 conducts a security analysis of the proposed protocol and Sect. 7 summarizes this work and gives an outlook to future research.

2   Related Work

In this section, related work in the field of blockchain-based digital document management is presented. Table 1 shows a comparison of such approaches in the field of educational certificates. The related work is evaluated with respect to our

Table 1. Comparison of related work with respect to decentralization, permission management, transparency, support for integrated issuer verification, completeness and attributed based authentication of receivers.

	Decentralized	Permissionless	Transparent	Integrated Issuer Verification	Completeness	Attribute-based
University of Nicosia	✓	✓	✓	✗	✗	✗
Blockcerts	✓	✓	✓	✗	✗	✗
LLP	✓	✗	✓	✓	✗	✗
uPort	✓	✓	✓	✗	✗	✓
Sovrin	✗	✗	✓	✓	✓	✓
SPROOF	✓	✓	✓	✓	✓	✓

initial requirements, which are decentralization, permission management, transparency, support for integrated issuer verification, completeness and attribute-based representation of receivers, as described in the previous section.

The University of Nicosia[1] was the first (2014) to register academic certificates for an online course on the Bitcoin blockchain. A hash of an index document, which contains a list of hashes of all certificates for a specific semester is registered on the blockchain. Hence, attribute-based authentication is not supported. Their approach is decentralized, permissionless and transparent, but does not allow for integrated issuer verification and for validating the completeness of issued academic certificates.

The MIT Media Lab is working on a project called Blockcerts[2]. Their approach is similar to the one implemented by the University of Nicosia, i.e., registering the root hash of a Merkle tree of hashes of documents on a public blockchain. This approach is decentralized, permissionless and transparent. The project is not attempting to map the digital identity to the real identity of an institution and thus does not allow for integrated issuer verification and validation. Additionally, verifying the completeness of issuing documents and attribute-based authentication is not possible.

By Gräther et al. (2018), an approach for a Lifelong Learning Passport (LLP) is presented which is very similar to the approach of *Blockcerts*. Their approach is decentralized, transparent and additionally they support a mechanism for issuer verification. However, they use a hierarchical scheme for issuer accreditation and therefore it is not fully permissionless. Verifying the completeness of issuing documents and attribute-based authentication is not possible.

uPort[3] is a service that allows users to register and set up their own identity. The platform is based on the Ethereum blockchain and uses smart contracts. The

---

[1] https://digitalcurrency.unic.ac.cy/free-introductory-mooc/self-verifiable-certificates-on-the-bitcoin-blockchain/academic-certificates-on-the-blockchain/   [retrieved: August 16, 2018].

[2] https://www.blockcerts.org/ [retrieved: August 16, 2018].

[3] https://www.uport.me/.

proposed scheme does not provide integrated issuer verification to the extent it is covered by this work and does not provide a completeness feature.

Sovrin [20] is a protocol and token for self-sovereign identity and decentralized trust. It allows attribute-based authentification and integrated issuer verification. However, the proposed scheme is built on top of its own token and does not allow to use arbitrary blockchains. Furthermore, it is not fully decentralized and permissionless due to the managing Sovrin Foundation that must approve all new nodes and is therefore able to restrict access to unwanted participants.

We are not aware of any scheme that meets all of the initial stated requirements and, in particular, resolves the completeness issue in a decentralized, permissionless, and transparent way, which is one of the main contributions of SPROOF.

3   Building Blocks

This section introduces the fundamental building blocks for SPROOF. First, the concept of public storage and blockchain is introduced, and the advantages and challenges for using such a technology are briefly discussed. Second, the principles of key management in HD wallets are explained. The latter is crucial for the completeness feature.

3.1   Public Storage

By Nakamoto (2008), *Bitcoin* is proposed as a decentralized, permanent, trustless public ledger. The proposed approach is the first to reliably solve the double spending problem[4] and sets the foundations for the concept of decentralized, permissionless append-only databases, commonly referred to as *blockchain*. In general, a blockchain can be seen as a global state machine where updates are performed by conflicting-free, authenticated transactions. Following the initial approach by Nakamoto (2008), many implementations have been proposed in recent years, also for fields other than financial transactions, see e.g., [6,16,17].

For SPROOF we use a public permissionless blockchain, e.g., Bitcoin or Ethereum [23], in order to create a platform where nobody, not even a selected consortium, has the right to exclude data or participants [25]. SPROOF is built on top of a public blockchain and does not intend to develop a new blockchain for this purpose. The blockchain is used by SPROOF in order to have a verifiable global state of ordered pieces of data in a decentralized, transparent manner and without the need of a single trusted platform operator. The use of a blockchain in SPROOF comes with two main issues: scalability and storage costs.

Blockchain implementations often come with limitations on the scalability [7], i.e., the number of transactions and the amount of data that can be stored or processed within a certain amount of time. Polkadot [11,24] proposes a strategy for solving these scalability issues by decoupling the consensus architecture from

---

[4] The problem that two conflicting transactions spend the same funds twice.

the state-transition mechanism. This means that all data is accepted to become part of the blockchain, i.e., the data is stored and distributed, but the semantics of that data and thus the actual validity are processed independently and off-chain. For SPROOF we only need the blockchain to register chronologically ordered pieces of data and thus the consensus is built off-chain by processing data with a publicly known rule set separately, the SPROOF protocol.

Storage on a public blockchain is often limited in terms of size (e.g., 80 Bytes of data in Bitcoin) or expensive [21]. To avoid this problem, SPROOF only adds hashes of data to the blockchain within a transaction. The corresponding raw data is then stored in a distributed hash table (DHT). Data stored in such a DHT inherits the immutability and ordering property from the blockchain if a cryptographically secure hash function is used to calculate the hash that is sealed in the blockchain. In order to create a fully decentralized platform, also the DHT needs to be managed in a decentralized way. For example, established DHTs such as IPFS [2] or Swarm[5] can be used.

Blockchains use public-private key cryptography [9] to represent a user and to sign transactions. The public keys can be seen as pseudonyms, because they can be created offline and without the need of an authentication process. However, this does not provide full anonymity, since public blockchains are transparent. If an attacker knows that a pseudonym is linked to an identity, the attacker also has the possibility to see all transactions which have been recorded in the blockchain since the beginning and are linked to that pseudonym [19]. A solution to this traceability problem is to generate a new key pair for each transaction, hence to use an address only once. One method to generate keys out of a single seed is explained in the next section.

3.2   Key Management

In most blockchains, users are represented by a unique ID derived from a public-private key pair using the Elliptic Curve Digital Signature Algorithm (ECDSA) [15]. In order to solve the traceability problem, a new key pair for each transaction is created. A key derivation function (KDF) is therefore used to derive one or more private keys from a single password[6], master key or a pseudo random number, a so-called *seed* S. In the following, a method to deterministically derive hierarchically structured pseudorandom public-private child keys $(Q_1, d_1), (Q_2, d_2), \ldots, (Q_n, d_n)$ out of a single master key pair $(\hat{Q}, \hat{d})$, is explained and illustrated in Fig. 1. Each child key can be used as a new master key, hence it is possible to build an infinite hierarchical tree. This concept is called a hierarchical deterministic (HD) wallet.

---

[5] http://swarm-gateways.net/bzz:/theswarm.eth/ [retrieved: August 23, 2018].
[6] Deriving a key from a password is not recommended [22].

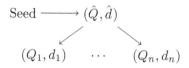

Fig. 1. Representation of a HD wallet, where child key pairs $(Q_1, d_1), \ldots, (Q_n, d_n)$ are derived from a parent key $(\hat{Q}, \hat{d})$ and a seed S [4].

The ECDSA is based on (the assumed hardness of) the elliptic curve discrete logarithm problem (ECDLP), which is denoted as follows: $E(K)$ denotes an elliptic curve over a field K. A generator of the elliptic curve is referred to as $P \in E(K)$ with an order p. These parameters are publicly known. With the private key $d \in K$ it is easy to calculate the public key $Q \in E(K)$, which is a point on the elliptic curve, using the formula $Q = dP$. Recovering d by only using Q and P constitutes breaking one instance of the ECDLP. Although there exists no formal proof, the ECDLP is commonly assumed to be hard to invert if the underlying elliptic curve is properly chosen [15].

The KDF of an HD wallet uses a cryptographically secure hash function $\mathcal{H}(\cdot)$ which maps an index i and a public key $Q \in E(K)$ to an element of K. The index is the number for the child key pairs (Q_i, d_i), which is calculated as follows:

$$d_i = \hat{d} + \mathcal{H}(i, \hat{Q}) \qquad (\mod p) \qquad (1)$$

$$Q_i = d_i P \qquad (2)$$

One of the main properties of HD wallets is that each child public key Q_i can be calculated without using (and needing to know) a private key, by $\hat{Q} + \mathcal{H}(i, \hat{Q})P$. This is called *master public key property*.

A known vulnerability of HD wallets, however, is that it is possible to calculate the master private key $\hat{d}$ with the knowledge of the master public key $\hat{Q}$ and an arbitrary child private key d_i, by using the derived formula $\hat{d} = d_i - \mathcal{H}(i, \hat{Q})(\mod p)$. This vulnerability can be bypassed by allowing so-called hardened child keys, where also the public keys are derived from the master private key, instead of the master public key. Such keys lose the master public key property. Another approach for HD wallets that tolerates key leakage is presented by Gutoski and Stebila [14].

In SPROOF, HD wallets are used to derive key pairs out of a single seed to generate pseudonyms, which are then used for receiving documents. The use of multiple pseudonyms allows to release only a selected subset of documents to a verifier.

4 SPROOF

In this section, we describe SPROOF, a decentralized, permissionless, integrity-protected and transparent platform for granting, storing and verifying digital documents. There are three basic roles in the upkeep of SPROOF: issuer, receiver and verifier.

For the communication between the users representing these roles, two distinct channels are needed: a public and a private one. The public channel is used for publicly available data that is stored on a blockchain, i.e., the issuing of a document. The private channel is needed to transfer non-publicly available and direct personal or sensitive information required for issuing and verifying documents.

Any information sent over the public channel is denoted as an *event*. Events are the only way to add information to the publicly available data set of SPROOF. Events are signed by the issuer and are sealed and integrity protected with the help of the blockchain and a DHT.

In the following, we first describe the processes to create an issuer, then ways to trust an unknown issuer, the generation of a privacy-friendly representation for receivers and finally, necessary steps to verify a document.

4.1 Issuer

The role of an issuer represents any organization or person who wants to grant documents, e.g., a university. Issuers need to be publicly known, trustworthy and verifiable.

In order to create a new account, an issuer establishes a public-private key pair. The public key is the representation of the issuers public profile P_P in SPROOF and the private key is needed to sign events triggered by the issuer. The key pair itself provides no information about the organization or person behind and is thus pseudonymous. However, issuers need to be identifiable and therefore P_P needs to be linked to the issuers organization. This can be done by adding a new $E_{Identity\ Claim}$ event. This event includes all necessary data to address the issuer, e.g., the name of the company or organization. Since the platform is permissionless and decentralized there are no restrictions for generating such identity claims and there is no single trusted third party to verify the correctness of the provided claims. To increase the trustworthiness of an issuer, additional $E_{Identity\ Evidence}$ events can be provided. These events, also created by the issuer, provide additional evidence by connecting the SPROOF account with already established central trusted platforms, e.g., social media accounts or known public key infrastructures. To link a social media account, the issuer needs to add an $E_{Identity\ Evidence}$ event including a reference to a publicly accessible message, e.g., a post in an online social network, which contains P_P. To link an X.509 certificate, the issuer needs to add an $E_{Identity\ Evidence}$ event including the certificate and a signature over P_P created by the confirmed private key of the X.509 certificate. Note that this process is possible for all types of PKI certificates. This allows to connect several, already established central trusted infrastructures, to P_P. There is no limitation in the number of $E_{Identity\ Evidence}$ events, hence an issuer can add multiple $E_{Identity\ Evidence}$ events to strengthen its P_P.

While the methods to increase trustworthiness of an issuer described above are based on central trusted authorities, this is used as bootstrapping to build a decentralized confirmation network which borrows concepts from the WoT [5]. In a WoT others must be able to confirm the identity of the issuer, by sending a $E_{Confirm}$ event. The purpose of a confirmation is that the sender verifies the receiver's identity claim. Confirmations are linked to the identity claim that was added last. This is to rule out the possibility of an issuer to maliciously rename itself after collecting some confirmations. Before an issuer confirms another issuer it needs to verify P_P and the provided identity claim.

This can be done based on the identity evidence events or also outside SPROOF, e.g., during a personal meeting. This means that – in return – an issuer may lose its reputation if it confirms a fake issuer. A confirm event contains a boolean value, either a positive or negative trust indicator and arguments to justify the decision. Confirmations can thus be used to create networks of issuers. Given such a network, newly added issuers can quickly gain reputation by a confirmation from a well-known and established issuer. As an example, consider a network of universities. While a newly established university sets up relationships with well-established institutions for research and teaching collaborations it can – in the same way – gain confirmations in SPROOF after a while. Once one or more major institution confirmed the integrity of the new university, this sets up a WoT.

4.2   Receiver

A receiver of a document is, analogously to an issuer, represented with a public key. This public key is used together with the corresponding private key to prove the ownership of a document to a verifier. Reusing the same pseudonym for all documents that a receiver gets would lead to the receiver being only able to share all documents ever received at once to a verifier, which would not be privacy-friendly and also impractical for the receiver. Once a third-party knows the pseudonym, it would be able to view all documents issued in the past and also all future ones. To avoid this traceability problem, fresh pseudonyms can be created for each document exploiting the previously presented properties of HD wallets. Note that only leaves of the pseudonym tree should be used for receiving a document. By doing so, the privacy is preserved by the fact that it is practically impossible to invert a cryptographically secure hash function. Therefore, it is not possible to calculate parent pseudonyms by knowing the corresponding child pseudonyms.

As shown before, the public-private key pairs are deterministically generated out of the random seed S using a HD wallet K_M, as described in Sect. 3.2. This seed is the main secret and is needed for recovering all derived pseudonyms.

Using K_M, the receiver is able to generate child pseudonyms $P_{I_1}, \ldots, P_{I_n}$. Each of those pseudonyms can be used as a new master key for further sub-pseudonyms for a specific issuer. A pseudonym is shared with an issuer using the private channel. From this pseudonym, the issuer is able to generate further sub-pseudonyms by using the master public key property of HD wallets. Note that this can be done without revealing any information about the corresponding private keys.

The ability to derive sub-keys and the fact that the pseudonyms are publicly linked to the documents enables further features, e.g., if an issuer wants to link a document which has dependencies to other already issued ones. This can be the case for a series of educational certificates that build on each other, e.g., required courses for getting a bachelor's degree. Given a parent pseudonym, all descendants are verifiably connected to this parent. If, for instance, pseudonym P_{G_1}, see Fig. 2, represents a Bachelor's diploma, all sub-pseudonyms including $P_{D_1}, \ldots, P_{D_n}$, which may represent particular courses, are permanently and publicly linked to the Bachelor's diploma. We call this property *forced completeness*, since it can be enforced by the issuer and cannot be hidden. Note that a receiver can still share documents $P_{D_1}, \ldots, P_{D_n}$ separately and independently and without revealing the parent pseudonym and thus the corresponding document. If a receiver shares more than one pseudonym that are used for documents issued by the same issuer, which can be avoided by sharing a pseudonym on a higher level of the pseudonym tree, the verifier can conclude that the receiver shows an incomplete information. This is, to the best of our knowledge, a feature that is unique to SPROOF.

The concept of completeness is shown in Fig. 2, where the privacy and completeness property are indicated by arrows. Privacy is provided bottom-up, whereas completeness is achieved top-down.

Note that the pseudonym itself contains no information about the real identity of the receiver, e.g., the name of the person. However, a means of linking a document to the real identity of the receiver needs to be established. Otherwise, receivers may collaborate and share documents among each other by sharing private keys of their pseudonyms. In addition, for attribute-based authentication the identity of the receiver must be split into multiple features.

For this purpose, the real identity is separated into attributes representing, e.g., the name, date of birth, a passport photo or a digital representation of a fingerprint of the person. These attributes are combined by using a hash tree, as shown in Fig. 3. To protect the privacy of the receiver, only the root value of the hash tree is attached to a document. Given the cryptographic hash reference of some data, it is practically impossible to reconstruct the original data. However, cryptographic hash functions are deterministic, hence an attacker who holds a copy of, knows or guesses the identification data of the receiver would be able to reconstruct the hash tree and can then disclose information about the receiver. To avoid this vulnerability, salt values are added to all attributes in order to obfuscate the hash reference [12]. Each attribute consists of a name, a value and a salt value. The hash reference of $attribute_x$ is calculated by $\mathcal{H}(Name_x \| Value_x \| Salt_x)$. The hash reference for all attributes is calculated by the following formula: $attributes = \mathcal{H}(attribute_1 \| \ldots \| attribute_n)$.

Additionally, a validity period represented by two timestamps is added for each receiver of a document. The root value, represented as $Attr_{ID}$, which is publicly available, is calculated by $Attr_{ID} = \mathcal{H}(validFrom \| validUntil \| attributes)$.

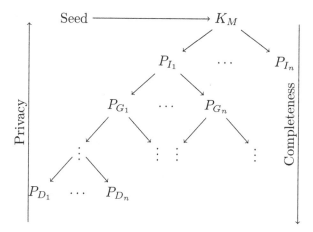

Fig. 2. Pseudonym tree with derived keys and documents in the leaves. Completeness is achieved by a unique, easily verifiable path from the top to the bottom and privacy is achieved by the impossibility to retrieve parent keys from a given leaf key [4].

In Fig. 3, an example attribute tree is illustrated. The construction of the hash tree allows the receiver to selectively disclose chosen attributes.

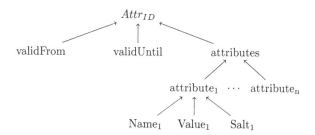

Fig. 3. Attribute tree with a validity time period and multiple attributes. The construction of the tree allows the receiver to selectively disclose specific attributes.

4.3   Document

In this section, the processes to publicly registering a document via SPROOF is described in abstract form. In SPROOF, a document is attached to the registration event. The issuer can decide whether the content of the document is publicly visible nor not. The registration event includes, by embedding it to a transaction, the public key and a signature of the issuer. Additionally, it is possible to attach fields for a validity period, dependencies to other documents, and a list of receivers to a document. In Fig. 4, the possible fields for the registration are illustrated. SPROOF provides three different ways to attach data or digital content the registration event:

Hidden. In the *documentHash* field, hash values of data or digital documents can be entered. The issuer can decide if the referenced file is published on a centralized server or later attached to the document. For verification, the verifier needs the raw data to crosscheck the locally calculated hash reference with the publicly registered one.

Direct. In order to directly attach data to the registration event, the *data* field can be used. This field allows to attach arbitrary JSON objects to the registration event. This data is the publicly available.

Indirect. To enable the attachment of large files or binary files which can not be represent as a JSON objects, the *dhtLocation* field is provided. The *dhtLocation* field represents a location reference to a file stored in a DHT.

In the following the events used to register a document, add a receiver to document and revoke either the receiver of the document or the document itself are described.

```
┌──────── Registration ────────┐
│                              │
│ issuer: publicKey            │
│ validFrom: unixTimestamp     │
│ validUntil: unixTimestamp    │
│ data: jsonObject             │
│ dhtLocation: String          │
│ documentHash: String         │
│ dependencies: List           │
│ receivers: List              │
│                              │
│                              │
└──────────────────────────────┘
```

Fig. 4. A registration object including all possible fields which can be used to register a document via SPROOF.

Register Document. The $E_{\text{Register\_Document}}$ event is then used to publish the information about the registration of a document, as shown in Fig. 4, via SPROOF. Note that it is possible to register a document without adding a receiver. The registration event sealed on the blockchain and the unique ID of the document is calculated out of the hash value of the content in combination with the blockhash.

Add Receiver. To add a receiver to a document, the issuer needs to publish the $E_{\text{Document Add Receiver}}$ event with the unique registration ID. With SPROOF it is possible to add 0 to n receivers for a single document. This enables the feature to group or structure documents. In the case of the document representing a diploma or a driving license, it would be possible to automatically ask for a receiver of a specific document ID in order to enable future services. That document and the representation of the receiver contains additionally a validity range. Hence, it is possible that the document as such may be longer valid than a specific grant to a receiver. The opposite direction is not possible.

In order to add a receiver to a SPROOF registration, the receiver has to register at an issuing institution. For this purpose, the receiver chooses a master pseudonym P_I, which has not already been used by another issuer and which represents a new leaf in the pseudonym tree. The receiver then needs to transmit the necessary identification data that enables the issuer to create the attribute hash tree. This data should be transmitted over a private channel to the issuer. The issuer has to verify if the identification data matches to the real identity of the receiver and check whether P_I is not already used as receiver for another document. Once this process is completed, the receiver is registered at the issuer. Furthermore, by sharing its pseudonym, the receiver permits the issuer to derive new sub-pseudonyms to add the receiver to registered documents. With this approach, the issuer is able to decide the ordering and structuring of the receivers pseudonym tree by deriving new sub-pseudonyms out of the shared master pseudonym. The completeness feature can thus be enforced at the time of adding a receivers' pseudonym to registered documents. A verifier can later check the set of all documents granted to a given pseudonym and all derived sub-pseudonyms. The verifier can thus be sure that no documents were hidden by the receiver. This process is illustrated in Fig. 5.

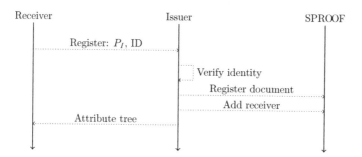

Fig. 5. Process for granting a document in SPROOF. The receiver registers at the issuer and passes the pseudonym which should be used for the new document. The issuer verifies the registration and grants a new document.

Revoke. Documents are not always valid for an unlimited period of time. Sometimes an expiration date is sufficient, e.g., for a first aid course or for a driving license. Additionally, an issuer may also decide to revoke a document or a specific receiver of a document, when, e.g., it detects plagiarism in a graduation paper or for other reasons. Therefore, an issuer which grants a document has the possibility to revoke the whole registration or also to revoke a specific receiver at a later point in time. This is done by adding an $E_{\text{Document Revoke}}$ or the $E_{\text{Document Receiver Revoke}}$ event, which only the issuing institute is allowed to do. This event includes the ID of the registration or the public key of the specific receiver, and a reason to justify the revocation. These event is appended to the public storage and therefore publicly available and accessible by all verifiers.

4.4 Events

Events are the only way to add information to SPROOF and they are sealed in a public blockchain. In this work, only issuers are allowed to add events. The reason is that adding an event requires a transaction on a blockchain. Adding a transaction to a blockchain usually comes at the cost of at least a fraction of cryptographic tokens. We assume that issuers are willing to buy some tokens, but receivers may not. To be considered as valid, each event needs to follow specific rules, as described in Sect. 4.1. Invalid events are ignored. Note that due to the decoupling of the consensus mechanism of the blockchain from the SPROOF protocol, invalid events may become part of the blockchain data, but are not considered by SPROOF users. Therefore, the publicly available data set of SPROOF is a chronologically ordered list of valid events. A blockchain node only needs to check if the blockchain transaction is valid and does not need to validate if the corresponding data represents a valid SPROOF event. This reduces the costs for a transaction to the blockchain.

Since storage space on a blockchain is often limited and expensive, only the hash reference of data is sealed into a transaction. Adding a new transaction for each event would imply that an issuer, which wants to grant n documents, also needs to add n transactions. This is inefficient and expensive. Therefore, events are combined into a chronologically ordered list and the hash reference of this list of events is then registered into a single transaction, as illustrated in Fig. 6. The issuer has to sign this transaction, including the hash reference, and add it to the blockchain as part of a transaction. Once the transaction is included and confirmed, it is traceable and authentic to the issuing institute, integrity-protected and publicly readable.

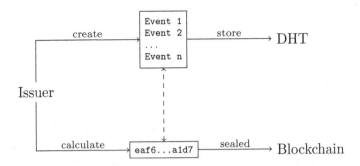

Fig. 6. For adding events to SPROOF, one or more events are collected and written to a DHT. The hash reference of that DHT entry is then sealed in the blockchain and thus publicly visible to all participants [4].

At this point, only the hash reference of events is sealed in the blockchain. The corresponding raw data is stored in a DHT, where the sealed hash value is used to address the raw data. The issuer has to ensure that the raw data is available and complete. A registration of events in the blockchain that does not provide the raw data is transparent visible to all verifiers and would therefore damage the reputation of the specific issuer. A transaction that is considered for the SPROOF data set is always sent to a fixed SPROOF address. Therefore, for validation purposes, a verifier only needs to consider transactions sent to this address.

4.5   Verification

Transactions in SPROOF can be validated by practically anyone in the world. For this purpose, a verifier needs to iterate over all transactions in the blockchain that are sent to the SPROOF address. The verifier then downloads the corresponding raw data from the DHT. After that, the verifier is able to execute each event of the SPROOF protocol and check if it is valid and should be added to a local database. The database represents the precalculated global unique state of SPROOF. Note that this includes also revocation events for documents or receivers. Additionally, this database can then be used to view and validate documents and to authenticate issuers and receivers. This client-side validation process can be done programmatically on a trusted computer that is controlled by the verifier. Since hashes can be assumed to be collision free [8], the data stored in the DHT is immutable. Changing the raw data would results in a different hash reference, not matching the one sealed in the public blockchain.

Receiver. The verifier can validate a receiver by two different approaches. In both approaches, the receiver has to share a pseudonym P_x with the verifier. Using P_x, the verifier is able to find all documents that are granted to P_x or any descendants of P_x. In the first approach the receiver remains anonymous, whereas in the other one the receiver can disclose selected attributes. Both approaches are described in the following.

For the anonymous approach, the verifier has to be convinced by the receiver to be in possession of the private key of a pseudonym P_x. For this purpose, the receiver creates a verification document, which includes the following fields (*Verifier Name, Blockhash*, P_x, *validFrom, validUntil, attributes*) and which is signed using the private key that belongs to P_x. This document is shared with the verifier via a private channel. The verifier is now able to check whether the provided signature matches to P_x and has to check whether the signed *Verifier Name* is correct. In order to check if the receiver is still in possession of a valid document, the verifier additionally needs to check if it is in a valid time period and if the values match the attached $Attr_{ID}$. This can be done by calculating the hash value of ($validFrom||validTo||attributes$). The *Blockhash* acts as a decentralized timestamp to detect outdated signatures. This needs to be done in order to reduce the risk of an attacker reusing the verification document. With this information the verifier can conclude that the receiver knows the private key of P_x, that all documents granted to any derivation path of P_x belong to the receiver, and that the verifier knows the minimum age of the signature by comparing the *Blockhash*. Considering that receivers may cooperate and share pseudonyms, it is not always enough to verify a receiver without identification. For the approach where the receiver additionally discloses, e.g., $attribute_1$ of n attributes, the receiver shares $Name_1, Value_1, Salt_1$ and all n hash references of the remaining attributes with the verifier. The verifier is able to calculate and validate the obfuscated and missing hash value of $attribute_1$ and can thus calculate $attributes$. Finally, the verifier needs to crosscheck the values of the attributes with an official ID-Document to see if it matches to the real identity of the receiver.

Issuer. To decide if an issuer is trustworthy, a verifier can check the publicly available $E_{\text{Identity Evidence}}$ events and decide whether the provided information is sufficient to trust an issuer P_P. Additionally, the linked X.509 certificates can be verified. In case that the $E_{\text{Identity Evidence}}$ events are insufficient, another way is to use the confirmation network to find a path from a known trustworthy party to the issuer.

4.6   Combine Issuer and Receiver

In Sect. 4.1, the process for issuers to create a public profile is described. This process is not limited to issuers, but also allows receivers to create a public account where the receiver has the possibility to disclose privately received documents and attach them to their public profiles. With the use of HD wallets it is possible to generate, out of a single seed S, multiple hierarchically structured public-private key pairs. The first child can be used as the representation for issuers to grant documents and by receivers to publish documents. The second child can be used as the master key for possible pseudonyms, which is illustrated in Fig. 7.

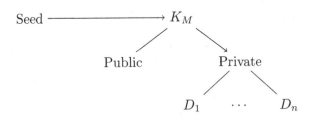

Fig. 7. A SPROOF account can be split into a public and a private part. While the public part is used for granting and receiving documents, whereas the private part is used as a master key for new pseudonyms [4].

To publish a privately received documents to a public profile two signatures are needed. One from the receivers pseudonym and one from the public account. The second signature is implicitly provided by adding the transaction to the blockchain. This is done by triggering an $E_{\text{Link Document}}$ event.

4.7 Summary

In this section, the processes for generating issuers, receivers and processes for register document, add receivers and revoking them later on were presented. The platform is permissionless and therefore provides, for issuers, a decentralized way to add identity claims for bootstrapping accounts. Necessary data to verify the issuer and the document is publicly available without any read restrictions. A privacy-friendly way to generate pseudonyms and link identification data of a receiver to a publicly accessible document has been shown. The generation of pseudonyms enables the platform to fulfill the completeness property. The construction of the attribute tree used to structure the identification data of a receiver allows for selectively disclosure of those. Combining events allows to add data to the blockchain in a scalable way.

5 Implementation

In this section, the fully working prototypical implementation is described. For the implemented prototype the public Ethereum Blockchain and IPFS are used as Blockchain and DHT, respectively. The prototype consists of a smart contract running on the blockchain, a backend implementation referred as to as the SPROOF node and SPROOF client, the client side implementation. In Fig. 8, an overview of all components and their connection is illustrated.

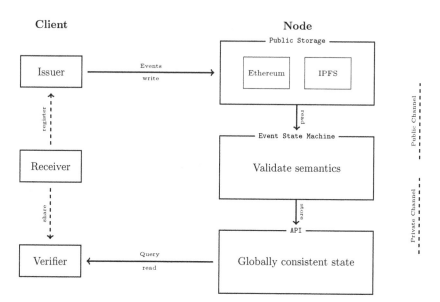

Fig. 8. The implementation consists of a SPROOF client and a node. The node is a combination of three modules: Public Storage, Event State Machine and API which are based on each other.

5.1   Smart Contract

To lock a transaction hash on the blockchain we implemented a very short smart contract in Solidity, see Listing 1.1. Since there are three different ways to lock a hash reference of files stored in IPFS on the public Ethereum blockchain, the smart contract provides three respective public methods. Note, that it is not necessary to use a smart contract to lock a hash reference on a blockchain [1]. By using a smart contract, however, it is possible to seal multiple hash references including a signature verification in one transaction. In the following, the three different ways to seal a hash reference are briefly outlined.

```solidity
 1  pragma solidity ^0.5.1;
 2  contract sproof {
 3      event lockHashEvent(address indexed from, bytes32
            indexed hash);
 4      function lockHash(bytes32 hash) public{
 5          emit lockHashEvent(msg.sender, hash);
 6      }
 7      function lockHashProxy(address _addr, bytes32 hash,
            uint8 v, bytes32 r, bytes32 s) public {
 8          require(ecrecover(hash, v, r, s) == _addr);
 9          emit lockHashEvent(_addr, hash);
10      }
11      function lockHashesProxy(address [] memory _addresses,
            bytes32 [] memory hashes, uint8[] memory vs, bytes32
            [] memory rs, bytes32 [] memory ss) public {
12          for (uint i=0; i < _addresses.length; i++) {
13              require(ecrecover(hashes[i], vs[i], rs[i], ss[i
                    ]) == _addresses[i]);
14              emit lockHashEvent(_addresses[i], hashes[i]);
15          }
16      }
17  }
```

Lock Hash. The *lockHash* function has only one input parameter, a hash reference of files stored in IPFS. The sender signs the transaction, which emits the *lockHashEvent* with the information about the issuers address and the corresponding hash reference. Note that this method can only be executed by the issuer directly, hence the issuer needs to pay the transactions costs, which can be impractical if SPROOF will be used by a wide range of users.

Lock Hash Proxy. In order to avoid the drawback that the issuer needs to acquire cryptographic tokens to pay the transaction cost, the *lockHashProxy* method is provided. This method needs, besides the hash reference of IPFS informations about the issuers address, also a valid signature. The method verifies that the signature over the hash reference is created with the private key corresponding to the issuers address and emits the *lockHashEvent* with the corresponding data. This transaction can be paid by an external party, hence the issuer does not need to acquire cryptographic tokens. However, the additional data and computational steps to verify the signature of the issuer results in higher transaction costs.

Lock Hashes Proxy. To avoid high transaction costs and to improve the scalability, the *lockHashesProxy* method is provided. This methods receives a lists of hashes, issuers and signatures within a single transaction. It iterates over the whole list and emits the *lockHashEvent* for all valid combinations. This transaction can be paid by an external party and has the ability to seal multiple hash references of multiple issuers in a single transaction. This will reduce the cost per transaction by 31.41% in comparison to a Ethereum transaction[7] without additional data.

5.2   SPROOF Node

The SPROOF Node can be seen as blockchain application or as a backend implementation and consists of three main modules: the Public Storage (PS), the Event State Machine (ESM) and an Application Programmable Interface (API). In the following, the three modules are described in detail.

Public Storage. The PS uses IPFS as DHT and the public Ethereum Blockchain. To seal a hash reference in the blockchain a smart contract, as described in Sect. 5.1, is used. The smart contract address is configurable in the PS module. At the first start the PS reads all emitted *lockHashEvents* from the smart contract in a chronological order and fetches the corresponding data stored in IPFS. Additionally, this module verifies the syntax of the data stored in IPFS. If the data is valid and matches predefined JSON schema it will be forwarded to the ESM.

Event State Machine. The ESM module receives all registrations in chronological order including all events sealed by an issuer and validates the semantics. For that purpose it iterates and executes all events. In case, the event is valid, it will be processed as a new state transition and the resulting state is then stored in the local database.

API. To provide easy access from third party applications an API is provided. This API is used to verify issuers, documents and receivers. The SPROOF API only needs hash references of publicly available information about receivers or documents in order to provide the information about the validity of those. Note, that therefore no sensitive information needs to be transfered to a SPROOF node.

---

[7] The cost for a transaction without additional data on Ethereum is 21000 Gas.

5.3 SPROOF Client

The SPROOF Client is a client side module, currently provided in Javascript. This module provides the full functionality for creating seeds, public private keys (HD wallets). Additionally, the issuers are able to create all events and the necessary signatures to interact with the SPROOF protocol locally on the client side. This also includes the generation of the attribute trees for the receivers. The events will be then be uploaded to IPPS and the IPFS hash reference is then signed on the client side. The SPROOF client provides the full functionality to use all methods of the smart contract to lock a hash reference. Additionally, the functionality to verify receivers' attribute trees and the calculation of the root value of the attribute trees is provided to avoid sensitive data to a SPROOF node.

6 Evaluation

In this section the SPROOF protocol is evaluated with respect to maliciously acting issuers, receivers and verifiers. Additionally, general attacks to the SPROOF platform are considered.

A malicious issuer may create a fake profile. Therefore the fake issuer sets up a $E_{Identity\ Claim}$ event and adds numerous $E_{Identity\ Evidence}$ events to strengthen its fake profile. By consistently creating fake social media accounts, a fake website, etc. this makes it hard to identify a true issuer from a fake one. However, the core idea of the WoT is that multiple established and trusted issuers confirm the identity of new issuers. A verifier of a document, attempting to validate the identity of the issuer, can identify such fakes by starting at one or more known trusted issuers and following the paths to the fake issuer. In case there exist no paths or a majority of negatively rated confirmations only, these are strong indications that the document has been created by a fake issuer. Additionally, a verifier can validate the X.509 certificates linked to the issuer. In case that these X.509 certificates are invalid, linked to non-official websites or not available at all, this are also strong indicators of a fake issuer. Issuers may revoke documents with a malicious intent and without justification, or publicly release identification data of documents it has previously issued. While this is a general problem, it would only affect the specific documents from this issuer and not the receivers' whole accounts.

A malicious receiver may attempt to collaborate with other receivers to share pseudo-nyms and thus collecting documents that were issued to another receiver. However, this is prevented by adding $Attr_{ID}$ to documents, which uniquely identifies a specific receiver. Note that this data is not publicly stored in the blockchain, but only the root hash reference is linked to a document in order to protect privacy. In case the receiver wants to remain anonymous at the time of verification, such an attack is feasible, however, it is up to the verifier to allow an anonymous verification at the risk of shared pseudonyms.

A malicious verifier may reuse or publish received documents and the corresponding values of the attribute tree. In the process of sharing a document to a verifier the *Verifier Name* and the *Blockhash* are contained and signed by the receiver. Reusing a document is practically impossible since this would require to change the *Verifier Name* and the *Blockhash* within the signed data. While publishing received documents cannot be prevented in SPROOF it would only affect the specific documents shared with this malicious verifier.

Malicious attackers may add a huge amount of valid or invalid events at once or seal a hash reference where the raw data stored in the DHT is not available or significantly large. However, adding a transaction to the blockchain is only possible with a signature which is linked to a public key. Adding invalid events or hash references where the raw data is not available will downgrade the reputation of an issuer. A timeout for reading data from the DHT and a limit for the number of events which are allowed to be sealed within one transaction can be used to protect the platform from such attacks.

7   Conclusion

In this paper, the extended version of [4], a platform for managing digital documents has been presented. The paper proposes the architectural building blocks, a protocol for issuing, receiving and verifying documents on a public blockchain and a description of a proof of concept. A public blockchain is used to seal hashes of data stored in a Distributed Hash Table. The implemented smart contract for this purpose has been presented. It is further shown how attribute-based authentication can be used by assigning and independently verifying multiple attributes of one receiver. For features such as completeness, i.e., the ability to prevent receivers from hiding certain documents, a Hierarchical Deterministic Wallet is employed for managing the cryptographic keys of receivers and also optionally of issuers. For the verification of issuers a Web of Trust of issuers is sent up and thus provides integrated issuer verification. In summary, the presented platform is fully decentralized, permissionless and provides privacy-friendly attributed-based authentication for receivers of documents. Future work will focus on extending the proposed protocol to be used in other domains, such as digital ID cards or in proofs of ownership and origin.

Acknowledgments. The overall support of Rainer Böhme from the University of Innsbruck as the supervisor of [3] and especially the initial idea of using HD wallets to build pseudonym trees to enable the completeness feature is gratefully acknowledged. The authors also like to acknowledge Michael Fröwis and Pascal Schöttle for discussions about this topic. The financial support by the Federal State of Salzburg is gratefully acknowledged. Funding by the Austrian Research Promotion Agency (FFG) under project number 865082 (ProChain) is gratefully acknowledged.

References

1. Bartoletti, M., Pompianu, L.: An analysis of bitcoin OP_RETURN metadata. In: Brenner, M., et al. (eds.) FC 2017. LNCS, vol. 10323, pp. 218–230. Springer, Cham (2017). https://doi.org/10.1007/978-3-319-70278-0_14

2. Benet, J.: IPFS - content addressed, versioned, P2P file system (DRAFT 3). Technical report, IPFS (2014). https://doi.org/10.1109/ICPADS.2007.4447808, https://ipfs.io/ipfs/QmR7GSQM93Cx5eAg6a6yRzNde1FQv7uL6X1o4k7zrJa3LX/ipfs.draft3.pdf

3. Brunner, C.: Eduthereum: A System for Storing Educational Certificates in a Public Blockchain. Master's thesis, Universität Innsbruck (2017)

4. Brunner, C., Knirsch, F., Engel, D.: SPROOF: a platform for issuing and verifying documents in a public blockchain. In: Proceedings of the 5th International Conference on Information Systems Security and Privacy, pp. 15–25. SciTePress, Prague, Czech Republic (2019)

5. Caronni, G.: Walking the web of trust. In: 9th International Workshops on Enabling Technologies: Infrastructure for Collaborative Enterprises (WET ICE 2000), pp. 153–158. IEEE, Gaithersburg (2000). https://doi.org/10.1109/ENABL.2000.883720

6. Christidis, K., Devetsikiotis, M.: Blockchains and smart contracts for the internet of things. IEEE Access **4**, 2292–2303 (2016). https://doi.org/10.1109/ACCESS.2016.2566339

7. Croman, K., et al.: On scaling decentralized blockchains. In: Clark, J., Meiklejohn, S., Ryan, P.Y.A., Wallach, D., Brenner, M., Rohloff, K. (eds.) FC 2016. LNCS, vol. 9604, pp. 106–125. Springer, Heidelberg (2016). https://doi.org/10.1007/978-3-662-53357-4_8

8. Damgård, I.B.: Collision free hash functions and public key signature schemes. Advances in Cryptology – EUROCRYPT 1987, pp. 203–216 (1988). https://doi.org/10.1007/3-540-39118-5_19

9. Diffie, W., Hellman, M.: New directions in cryptography. IEEE Trans. Inf. Theory **22**(6), 644–654 (1976). https://doi.org/10.1109/TIT.1976.1055638

10. Durumeric, Z., Kasten, J., Bailey, M., Halderman, J.A.: Analysis of the HTTPS certificate ecosystem. In: Proceedings of the 2013 Conference on Internet Measurement Conference (IMC 2013), pp. 291–304. ACM, Barcelona, Spain (2013). https://doi.org/10.1145/2504730.2504755, https://arxiv.org/abs/1408.1023

11. Eyal, I., Gencer, A.E., Sirer, E.G., van Renesse, R.: Bitcoin-NG: a scalable blockchain protocol. In: Proceedings of the 13th Usenix Conference on Networked Systems Design and Implementation, pp. 45–59. NSDI 2016, USENIX Association, Santa Clara, CA (2016)

12. Gauravaram, P.: Security analysis of salt$——$password hashes. In: International Conference on Advanced Computer Science Applications and Technologies (ACSAT), pp. 25–30. IEEE, Kuala Lumpur, Malaysia (2012). https://doi.org/10.1109/ACSAT.2012.49

13. Gräther, W., et al.: Blockchain for education: lifelong learning passport. In: Proceedings of 1st ERCIM Blockchain Workshop 2018. European Society for Socially Embedded Technologies (EUSSET), Amsterdam (2018). https://doi.org/10.18420/blockchain2018

14. Gutoski, G., Stebila, D.: Hierarchical deterministic bitcoin wallets that tolerate key leakage. In: Böhme, R., Okamoto, T. (eds.) FC 2015. LNCS, vol. 8975, pp. 497–504. Springer, Heidelberg (2015). https://doi.org/10.1007/978-3-662-47854-7_31

15. Johnson, D., Menezes, A., Vanstone, S.: The elliptic curve digital signature algorithm (ECDSA). Int. J. Inf. Secur. **1**(1), 36–63 (2001). https://doi.org/10.1007/s102070100002. http://www.cacr.math.uwaterloo.ca

16. Knirsch, F., Unterweger, A., Engel, D.: Privacy-preserving blockchain-based electric vehicle charging with dynamic tariff decisions. J. Comput. Sci. - Res. Dev. (CSRD) **33**(1), 71–79 (2018)

17. Kosba, A., Miller, A., Shi, E., Wen, Z., Papamanthou, C.: Hawk: the blockchain model of cryptography and privacy-preserving smart contracts. In: 2016 IEEE Symposium on Security and Privacy (SP), pp. 839–858. IEEE, San Jose (2016)

18. Nakamoto, S.: Bitcoin: a peer-to-peer electronic cash system. Technical report (2008). https://bitcoin.org/bitcoin.pdf

19. Reid, F., Harrigan, M.: An analysis of anonymity in the bitcoin system. In: Altshuler, Y., Elovici, Y., Cremers, A.B., Aharony, N., Pentland, A. (eds.) Security and Privacy in Social Networks, pp. 197–223. Springer, New York (2013). https://doi.org/10.1007/978-1-4614-4139-7_10

20. Sovrin Foundation: Sovrin : a protocol and token for self- sovereign identity and decentralized trust. Technical Report, January (2018). https://sovrin.org/wp-content/uploads/2018/03/Sovrin-Protocol-and-Token-White-Paper.pdf

21. Unterweger, A., Knirsch, F., Leixnering, C., Engel, D.: Lessons learned from implementing a privacy-preserving smart contract in ethereum. In: 9th IFIP International Conference on New Technologies. Mobility and Security (NTMS), pp. 1–5. IEEE, Paris, France (2018)

22. Vasek, M., Bonneau, J., Castellucci, R., Keith, C., Moore, T.: The bitcoin brain drain: a short paper on the use and abuse of bitcoin brain wallets. In: 20th International Conference on Financial Cryptography and Data Security (FC 2016). Springer, Christ Church (2016)

23. Wood, G.: Ethereum: a secure decentralised generalised transaction ledger. Technical report, Ethereum (2017). https://ethereum.github.io/yellowpaper/paper.pdf

24. Wood, G.: Polkadot: vision for a heterogeneous multi-chain framework. Technical report, Parity.io (2017). https://github.com/w3f/polkadot-white-paper/raw/master/PolkaDotPaper.pdf

25. Wüst, K., Gervais, A.: Do you need a Blockchain. Technical report, International Association for Cryptologic Research (2017). https://eprint.iacr.org/2017/375.pdf

Next Generation Information Warfare: Rationales, Scenarios, Threats, and Open Issues

Roberto Di Pietro[✉], Maurantonio Caprolu[✉], and Simone Raponi[✉]

College of Science and Engineering (CSE), Division of Information and Computing Technology (ICT), Hamad Bin Khalifa University (HBKU), Doha, Qatar
rdipetro@hbku.edu.qa, {mcaprolu,sraponi}@hbku.edu.qa

Abstract. The technological advances made in the last twenty years radically changed our society, improving our lifestyle in almost every aspect of our daily life. This change directly affects human habits, transforming the way people share information and knowledge. The exponential technological advancement, together with the related information deluge, are also radically changing Information Warfare and its scenarios. Indeed, the consequently increase of the digital attack surface poses new challenges and threats for both personal and national security.

In this paper we discuss the motivations behind the need to redefine the Information Warfare according to its new dimensions. Then, we analyze the potential impact of the new threats on the most sensitive targets exposed by every nation: the Society, the Economy, and the Critical Infrastructures. Finally, for every considered scenario, we analyze existing state-of-the-art countermeasures, highlighting open issues and suggesting possible new defensive techniques.

Keywords: Information warfare · Critical infrastructure · Fabric of society

1 Introduction

Information has always played a decisive role in both the wars and the revolutions of the past. The knowledge in advance of a particular move of the adversary could completely overturn the fate of a conflict. In fact, the opponent could be militarily more advanced, but knowing which target he intends to hit gives the defender a significant advantage. At this point, it should not come as a surprise to know that a crucial phase of the war is being fought from the information perspective. Information trusted by a target may be subject to manipulation, without the target's awareness. Thus, making decisions based on this counterfeit information is absolutely against the interests of the victim, that becomes like a puppet at the mercy of the attacker. The manipulation of trusted information takes the name of Information Warfare.

© Springer Nature Switzerland AG 2020
P. Mori et al. (Eds.): ICISSP 2019, CCIS 1221, pp. 24–47, 2020.
https://doi.org/10.1007/978-3-030-49443-8_2

Over the years, we have witnessed an evolution in the transmission of information, starting from the simple chat to the market up to the current Social Media technologies. One of the first revolutions in the field of information transmission was the optical telegraph, invented by Claude Chappe in 1793, at the height of the French revolution. The device was used to connect, in real time, the military bases of Lille and Paris. About 60 years later, in 1854, Antonio Meucci invented the telephone, with which it was possible to overcome many of the limits of the telegraph system. The telephone was based on the transmission of the voice, and therefore it was not limited to the transmission of written documents. Half a century later, in 1895, Guglielmo Marconi had the intuition that radio waves could be used for wireless communications, giving rise to wireless telegraphy via radio waves. The invention of the radio revolutionized the communication systems in force at the time and led to the development of radio communication methods used even today. Many years later, in 1958, General Dwight David Eisenhower created the Advanced Research Projects Agency (ARPA) as a direct response to the Russian launch of Sputnik. The aim of the ARPA project was to provide the United States with a technological advantage over other countries. The project gave birth to Arpanet, a network that linked the supercomputers of the various research centers, and which laid the foundations of the modern Internet. The advent of the Internet has led communication distances to be filled as never before in history, completely revolutionizing the information communication ecosystem. The related introduction of web pages, forums, and Social Media has radically changed many aspects of users' lives from a social point of view, leading to a new logic of information that prefers speed and immediacy to accuracy and reliability. The information during the sharing process undergoes adjustments, enrichments, researching active participation by a dynamic audience until it becomes a heterogeneous collage, from which the original source and opinion can hardly be extracted. People, and Society with them, are not the only potential victims of Information Warfare.

Contribution. In this paper, we first discuss the motivations that lead to redefining the concept of Information Warfare, consequently to the appearance of its new dimensions caused by the advent of new technologies. Each section represents a typical target of the Information Warfare, regarding aspects of the society, the economy, and the Critical Infrastructures of a generic Nation, respectively. For every considered aspect, we build one or more plausible detailed real-world scenarios, showing from which possible threats could be threatened. For each threat, we identified the current state of the art, both in terms of attacks and defenses. In addition, we identified open problems that still affect these fields and the countermeasures that can be implemented, to ensure that readers can have a starting point to enrich the state of the art with innovative and prestigious solutions.

Roadmap. The paper is organized as follows. Section 2 resumes the motivations behind the introduction of the Next Generation of Information Warfare. Sections 3, 4, and 5 introduce innovative scenarios with associated threats, study of the state of the art and open problems, and proposals of countermeasures related to Fabric of Society, Cryptocurrencies, and Critical Infrastructure, respectively. Finally, Sect. 6 draws some concluding remarks.

2   The Need for a Next Generation of Information Warfare

Over the years, new technologies have continually changed society with new discoveries and inventions able to improve human life. The progress machine tirelessly introduces tools and resources that facilitate everyday tasks, since the dawn of humanity.

Usually, processes that radically change the human lifestyle are gradual and take time to complete the revolution. In the past few years, modern technology has made a fast and radical change of our society, modifying our habits with many functional and utility devices like smartphone, smartwatch, and other smart devices, making our lives faster, easier, and funnier. Technology is raising new kinds of habits and addictions, changing every aspect of our society such as personal interactions, education, communication, financial services, entertainment, to name a few, with a wild race to the digitization of information of all kinds, from the most sensitive to the most (apparently) harmless.

Nowadays, almost all our daily activities are held using digital devices, that offer us a huge number of different web-based services through which we manage every aspect of our lives. These services help us to learn, have fun, pay bills and manage our bank accounts, communicate with distant friends and meet with new ones, handle personal agenda, buy items and services, and so on. Such technologies, on one hand, guarantee access to a boundless range of services and information to anyone, on the other hand, allow service providers to access an equally boundless quantity of users' personal information, often harvested without the users' knowledge. Moreover, using online services like Social Media, users voluntary publicly share private information like their personal data, family relations, private multimedia contents, thoughts and experiences, and many others that allow everyone to know a person without ever meeting her. In the era where the wealth is given by information, online Social Media represent real gold mines, in which even without a license anyone can go picketing. Such kind of information represents a big opportunity for different entities such as governments and advertising companies, opening scenarios that would have been unimaginable just a few years ago.

This frenetic technological advancement radically changed Information Warfare scenarios, posing new threats for personal and national security that every nation must take into consideration to safeguard its own security against malicious actors.

The existing contributes related to Information Warfare usually deal with the subject by categorizing the arguments based on the "warfare capabilities and directions" of the most powerful nations (USA, Russia, China, others) or based on the pillars of Information Warfare: Psychological operations (PSY-OPS), Military Deception, Electronic Warfare, Physical destruction, and Operational Security (OPSEC). Unlike these approaches, we will discuss new threats never addressed before in the literature, categorizing them into several macro areas representing the attack surface of a generic nation. Every threat is inserted in a real case scenario and explained in details with their threats and possible impacts. For every scenario, we will also highlight open issues, raising problems that need to be addressed in order to mitigate security threats derived from the technological advance happened in the past few years. Our aim is to spread these new threats with their respective state of the art and existing countermeasures to the community of researcher in the cyber-security field, suggesting also new possible ones when not sufficiently covered in the literature.

3   Fabric of Society

The introduction of new technologies, such as Social Media, Social Networks, Media Sharing services, online forums, and online instant messaging services, make information sharing and propagation extremely fast. The number of Internet users, together with the amount of available information, is growing continuously from day to day. In 2014 there were 3,079 billion Internet users, a number that has grown in the following years up to 4,346 billion Internet users in March 2019 [5]. The number of Internet users has increased by 41.15% in less than five years, leading to a consequent increase in contributions on the web. As an example, Google's search in 2016 knows about over 130 trillion pages [3], but this is only the tip of the iceberg. The Deep Web, also called the hidden or invisible web, represents the part of the World Wide Web whose contents are not indexed by common web search engines, and is estimated to be 500 times the size of the indexed web [2], also known as Surface Web.

People, while surfing the web, have at their disposal this almost infinite amount of information, some truthful, others not. As a consequence, the ideas of individuals are no longer built autonomously (i.e., based on facts obtained independently), but based on hundreds of thousands of opinions read on the web, of which only a negligible part is authoritative. In this way, shifting the attention of the masses and changing individuals' opinion is a breeze, in the first case to make events of national importance go unnoticed, in the other one, to set the agenda. Disinformation grows in step with information, making it difficult to distinguish reliable information from unreliable ones. In addition, people do not use to double check the content found on the web, due to either lack of time or will, resulting in an unintended spread of unreliable information that bounds around the web.

To make matters worse, the concept of the filter bubble comes into play. The filter bubble describes the tendency of social networks such as Facebook and Twitter to lock users into personalized feedback loops, each social network with its own news sources, cultural touchstones, and political inclinations [4]. Users surfing the web will be overwhelmed by a wave of personalized content, based on previous knowledge of their interests, their location, and their browsing history. This phenomenon tends to eventually lower the critical spirit of individuals, placing them in front of a vision of the personalized world, that absolutely does not reflect reality.

In this section, we describe how the Information Warfare could threaten the Fabric of Society, for instance by piloting the elections in democratic states, by running disinformation campaigns to cause unrest and discredit people or governments, and by indoctrinating the population resident in states with Authoritarian governments.

3.1 Scenario: Democratic Election in a Country

In this scenario, we will take into account the political election of a democratic Country. The state promotes transparency and fairness in elections, providing the candidates with a fair media space and controlling their advertising according to principles of equality and correctness. According to the definition of the former U.S. ambassador to the United Nations, "Democratic elections are not merely symbolic. They are competitive, periodic, inclusive, definitive elections in which the chief decision-makers in a government are selected by citizens who enjoy broad freedom to criticize the government, to publish their criticism and to present alternatives [21]. Democratic elections are competitive, because the mere right to participate in the ballot is not enough. Indeed, political (and not political) groups involved in the elections must guarantee fairness, by avoiding censorship and respecting the rules. Both opposition parties and candidates must enjoy the freedom of speech, as well as bringing alternative policies and candidates to the voters. Democratic elections are also definitive, because they determine the leadership of the government. The party leader work has the burden of leading the country, promoting the political program they proposed during the election campaign.

Threat: Inference in Political Election

Political elections within a country are not only reflected in the interests of citizens. Companies and institutions (either local or foreign) may have an interest in illegally interfering with the electoral campaign, with the aim of piloting thus obtaining profits in the short, medium, or long term. Companies and institutions, especially Governments, could use Social Media to profile users and manipulate their attitudes and behaviors through the use of hate speech, fake news, and manipulative campaigns. This user profiling allows companies and institutions to build targeted (possibly fake) advertising, with the aim of manipulating the vote of individuals.

In recent years, several works concerning the interference of bots and actors in the political events have been proposed. In [31], E. Ferrara provided an extensive statistical analysis of the Macron-Leaks disinformation campaign that occurred during the run up to the 2017 French presidential election. A similar study, but on another target, was carried out by Forelle et al, in [33]. The authors study the role of social and political bots in Venezuelan political conversations, together with the relative conditioning of the public opinion. They pointed out that these automatic scripts generated content through Social media platforms, interacting with people, and that most of the active bots have been adopted by Venezuela's radical opposition. Hegelich et al. in [40], investigated whether bots on Twitter have been used as political actors during the conflict between Russia and Ukraine. They pointed out that bots exhibit three distinctive patterns of behaviors: (i) trying to hide their identity, (ii) promoting topics through the use of hashtags, and (iii) retweeting selected tweets and messages. K. Starbird in [70] explored the alternative media ecosystem through the Twitter's magnifying glass. The findings describe a subsection of the emerging alternative media ecosystem and provide insights on how websites that promote conspiracy theories and pseudo-science may function to conduct underlying political agendas. In the primary work [45], Howard et al. studied the use of political bots during the U.K. referendum on EU membership. The authors discovered that political bots had a small but strategic role in the referendum conversation.

In this threat, some of the crucial open problems concern: (i) the detention of illegal political disinformation campaigns, (ii) the reaction after the identification of an illegal disinformation campaign, and (iii) the understanding of the extension of the bots network. The possible countermeasures should take into account the freedom of speech of individuals. Indeed, adopting measures that involve some kinds of censorship would apparently solve the problem, but it would also deprive users of the possibility of expressing their opinion, thus impoverishing the diversity of thought.

Intelligent agents, the result of the artificial intelligence state of the art, could be trained in recognizing both targeted political advertisements and political fake news, with the aim of obscuring the view to the user while navigating a social network, thus safeguarding the user's political opinions. Other agents could be used to analyze in detail the relationship graph, with the aim of isolating content proposed by members of cliques in the graph. Recall that a clique in the graph represents a complete subgraph, i.e., each node in the subgraph is connected through an edge to all the other nodes of the subgraph itself. Bots and misinformers tend to have a high number of contacts, in order to efficiently spread their message, in such a way that it impacts a greater number of people at the first step of communication. After that, each bot, in addition to creating and disseminating its contents, will work to share the information of the other allied bots in order to reach even more viewer. To do this efficiently, the only users in common between two bots should be the bots themselves, and the catchment area reached would be increased with minimal effort and resources. To understand the extent of the bot network there is the need to distinguish bots from normal users. One of the first steps was taken by Chu et al. in [19]. To assist human users in identifying who they are interacting with, the authors focused on the classification of humans, bots, and cyborgs accounts on Twitter. During the study, the considered respectively legitimate bots (i.e., bots that generate a large number of benign tweets delivering news and updating feeds), malicious bots (i.e., bots that spread spam or malicious contents), and cyborgs, that can be either bot-assisted human or human-assisted bot. In [61], the authors studied astroturf political campaigns on microblogging platforms. They represent politically-motivated individuals and organizations that use multiple centrally-controlled accounts to create the appearance of widespread support for a candidate or opinion. The study led to the implementation of a machine learning framework for Twitter, that detects the early stages of the political misinformation viral spreading by combining topological, content-based, and crowd-sourced featured information diffusion networks.

3.2   Scenario: Freedom of Information

This scenario takes into account a State that does not make use of censorship techniques to silence the citizens. People are allowed to publicly express their opinion, in traditional ways as well as with modern means, such as online social networks, blogs, forums, and possibly others. The social platforms do not incur in traffic filtering techniques, that are usually applied to deny access to specific websites, allowing users to freely adopt any communication service like real-time messaging applications and mail services. Moreover, the government has no control over the content of the transmitted and received information, thus allowing users to express their opinion without being incurred in fines or punishments. Citizens are free to express both their thoughts and their opinion about any topic, whatever they are. The information conveying through social media can be of any kind: true or false, trusted or not trusted, accurate or not accurate.

Threat: Disinformation Campaign

One of the first documented examples of supposed Fake news takes us to Ancient Rome in July 64 b.C. The emperor Nero set fire to an entire district of the city to make room for new buildings, accusing the Christian community of the Crime. He created a fake news artfully both to not turn the public opinion against himself, and to continue his persecution campaign against the Christian community. Going forward over the years other famous examples can be found. In 1933, the palace of the Reichstag, seat of the German parliament, was set on fire. The leaders of the Nazi party took advantage of the opportunity to blame the opponents of the Communist party, gaining consensus that led to their final rise to power. These two cases make us reflect on the fact that the invention of news or the alteration of partially true ones makes it possible to maneuver the public opinion, obtaining illicit advantages. The same principle still applies nowadays, with a sounding board that has never been so wide due to the speed of social media information propagation. The study from researchers at Ohio State University finds that fake news probably played a significant role in depressing Hillary Clinton's support on Election Day. The study offers a first look at how fake news affected voters choices, pointing out that about 4% of President Barack Obama's 2012 supporters were dissuaded from voting for Clinton in 2016 because of fake news stories [9]. The lack of truthfulness of information makes the detection of the trustworthiness of content hard for citizens, creating doubts and confusion among the population. Artfully built news usually have mixed with any size fragments of truth over time, escaping the control of the creator, who usually manages to govern the spreading only for a short time. These news then assume realistic contours, becoming in effect truthful news (as accepted by all as such), ignoring denials or not granting replication rights. Foreign governments, as well as terrorist groups and activists, could exploit these uncertainties on Social media to undertake several kinds of disinformation campaigns, to undermine the credibility of the state or to control public opinions, with the aim of generating chaos and destabilizing the population. In the course of history there have been numerous cases in which the use of disinformation campaigns has caused discontent among the population, disagreements, and revolts, giving the history a presumed truth, impossible to ascertain.

There is more information being shared than ever before, and ordinary citizens are playing an active role in the news ecosystem. Among them, there are users that use to run provocative posting intended to produce a large volume of inflammatory and digressive responses, they are called "trolls". Over the past years, trolls played as state-sponsored actors, with the aim of manipulating public opinion on the web, often around major political events. Although the trolls are often involved in spreading disinformation on Social Media, there is still little understanding of how they operate. In [76], the authors proposed a study with the purpose of understanding better the content dissemination and its influence on the information ecosystem. In [50] the authors studied the sockpuppets, i.e., users that create multiple identities and engage in undesired behavior by deceiving other or manipulating discussions. In this work, the authors showed how the sockpuppets differ from ordinary users in term of their posting behavior, linguistic traits, and social network structure.

Trolls are changing the Internet personality. What trolls do to laugh, provoke, and upset, ranges from clever pranks to harassment up to violent threats. Doxxing –publishing personal data, such as social security numbers and bank accounts– and swatting, calling in an emergency to a victims house so the SWAT team busts in, are just two common practices of these individuals. Trolls are turning social media and comment boards into a giant locker room in a teen movie, with towel-snapping racial epithets and misogyny [8]. As if it were not enough, trolls play the role of disinformation diffusers, with the sole purpose of directing the attention of the masses elsewhere and conditioning their judgment. How could these users who, by leveraging their freedom of expression, dangerously influence people's opinions, be stopped? How is it possible to recognize them? How is it possible to protect users from the toxic behavior of other users? Would it be morally right to put them in an Internet quarantine? Several work have been proposed to face these issues. In [32], A. Fokin emphasized the role of hybrid warfare respect to Information Warfare, with a particular focus on the role of hybrid warfare tactics and trolling in Internet media. The author measured how and to what extent certain cyber activities influence the public opinion. The results provided an approach to evaluate the risk potential of trolling and outline recommendations on how to protect the state and society if trolling is used as an instrument of hybrid warfare. The authors in [29] proposed an approach for quantifying the authenticity of online discussions based on the similarity of online social media accounts participating in the discussion, to know abusers and legitimate accounts. The proposed method uses several similarity functions for the analysis and classification of online social media accounts. In [54] the authors discussed the difficulty of recognizing trolls automatically and proposed a pragmatic study. They assume that a user who is called a troll by several people is likely to be one. They experimented with different variations of the definition, and in each case they trained an efficient classifier. Furthermore, there are websites, such as "EU vs Disinfo" [7] that produce weekly disinformation reviews. Their database contains over 3,800 disinformation cases since September 2015 and is the only publicly accessible, international database of disinformation cases.

3.3   Scenario: Authoritarian State

This scenario takes into account a government in an Authoritarian State, that leads the Country without political opponents. In this authoritarian form of government, the power is centralized in a single organ (or in the hands of a single dictator) and is limited neither by constitutions nor by laws. Typically, authoritarian regimes make use of a censorship policy, designed to preserve their political dominance within the State, like North Korea in the past. As a consequence, citizens are not free to talk about political issues conflicting with the ideas of the regime and the main communication channels (such as missives, mail services, messaging apps, even the spoken words) are intercepted, controlled, and censored where necessary. Fundamental rights such as freedom of expression, opinion, and speech, are not guaranteed, allowing the regime to filter contents to make sure to safeguard its own dominance. In this context, the Authoritarian government could take advantage of information control, making use of Social media, forums, blogs, and other communication means, to disseminate information aimed at maintaining political and social supremacy and stability.

Threat: Political Indoctrination of the Population

By controlling and filtering contents in both Social Media and other communication channels, an Authoritarian government is able to control the population by repressing every form of thought contrary to the principles of the dictatorship. The censorship of the conflicting opinions coming from the resident population, together with the filtering of news coming from abroad and the dissemination of appropriately modified contents, makes the population willing to believe that the general situation of the country is flourishing and hard to improve, and that the Government's work is always right and effective. With these assumptions, the population will be unwilling to organize riots or protest actions, blindly trusting the Government, which will continue to cover up and hide the inconvenient truth.

Dictators do not survive because of their use of force or ideology, but because they are able to convince the population, rightly or wrongly, about their competence. The dictator can invest in making convincing state propaganda, censorship independent media, co-opting the elite, or equipping police to repress attempted uprisings. In [38] the authors showed that incompetent dictators can survive as long as economic shocks are not too large, and that repression is used against ordinary citizens only as a last resort when the opportunities to survive through co-optation, censorship, and propaganda are exhausted. In [65] the authors characterize a ruler's decision of whether to censor media reports that convey information to citizens who decide whether to start a revolution. Both the censorship and the propaganda have been studied in several contexts: the authors in [52] studied the censorship and propaganda in the 1991 Gulf War; a similar work has been done in [48] applied to the Canada's Great War, to post-genocide Rwanda [72], to the World War I [35], and to the World War II [43]. The speed of information propagation due to the advent of Social media has allowed dissidents to express their opinion in the face of an ever-increasing public. This enabled the governments of the authoritarian states to adopt more studied and aggressive censorship policies. In [42] the authors claimed that private companies that run Social Media and search engines, despite their free-speech-friendly philosophy, employ terms of service that censor a broad range of constitutionally protected speech. In [44] the authors analyzed in detail the Social Media censorship as well as both the regulations and the new restrictions to protest and dissent. Other work are referred to the Chinese censorship situation: in [14] the authors presented the first large-scale analysis of political content censorship in Social Media, i.e., the active deletion of messages published by individuals, while web articles [11] pointed out how the censorship make the China different from the West, with the list of Social Media that have been replaced by other ones which the government can monitor.

Several technologies have been introduced to allow dissidents to circumvent the censorship imposed by governments. In [23] the authors presented the various techniques and compared the general methods to break through, including Virtual Private Network (VPN), Secure Shell (SSH), IPv6, proxy tools, hosts file modifications, and web proxy. Among the many, two of the most used nowadays are the VPNs and Tor. VPN is a technology that allows safe communication through an encrypted connection over an insecure network, such as the Internet. Applications running across a VPN may therefore benefit from the functionality, security, and management of the private network [53]. In the literature, there are many works that allowed citizens to circumvent censorship policies using VPNs. In [57] the authors worked on VPN Gate. VPN Gate is a public VPN relay service designed to achieve blocking resistance to censorship firewalls such as the Great Firewall (GFW) of China. To achieve such resistance, the authors organized many volunteers to provide a VPN relay service, with many changing IP addresses. In recent years, new technologies such as high-speed Deep Packet Inspection (DPI) and statistical traffic analysis methods had been applied in country-scale censorship and surveillance projects. The traditional encryption solutions do not hide statistical flow properties, and new censoring systems can easily detect and block them "in the dark". The authors of [73] proposed a novel traffic obfuscation protocol, where client and server communicate on random ports. The result of this research is an open-source VPN tool named GoHop and the development of several obfuscation methods, including pre-shared key encryption, traffic shaping, and random port communication. Tor [24], the acronym of The Onion Routing, is one of the most popular anonymity systems. The main idea is that the user selects a circuit that typically consists of three relays –an entry, a middle, and an exit node. The user negotiates session keys with all the relays and each packet is encrypted multiple times, first with the key shared with the exit node, then with the key shared with the entry node (also known as the guard). To send a packet to the final destination anonymously, the packet is first sent to the guard, which removes the outer encryption layer and it relays the packet to the middle node. In turn, the middle node removes its encryption layer and relays the packet to the exit node. Lastly, the exit node removes the last layer of encryption and relays the packet to its final destination [51]. Although Tor is one of the most widely used tools to circumvent censorship [6], some states have implemented mechanisms either to block it, or to make it complex to interact with the platform [74]. Furthermore, many techniques have been introduced over the years to either partially or completely deanonymize users browsing the Dark Web [15,51,67,71].

4   Cryptocurrencies

Nowadays, more and more nations are thinking about establishing a state cryptocurrency that will support or replace the classic currency. This kind of scenario, on one hand, introduces several advantages of practical nature, such as no longer having to print physical banknotes, no longer need banking institutions that keep track of balances and transactions, faster and (supposed to be) more secure transactions, and so on. On the other hand, it could expose the Nation's economy to a new series of cyber-security threats. Indeed, the classical physical currency is vulnerable to several indirect attacks that mainly aim to its devaluation, such as speculative attacks. However, other kinds of attacks such as denial of services are very difficult or not feasible, due to the physical nature of the classical currency. Indeed, an attacker could target the electronic systems that allow virtual transactions, causing a temporary block of this service, but there is no way to stop transactions with cash payments. A cryptocurrency instead, as a virtual asset, is exposed to direct attacks with consequences ranging from blocking the system for a short time to its total destruction. In the first case, malicious entities could prevent legitimate users to join the network, or isolate the peers that validate transactions, leading to the total network paralysis. In this eventuality, no transactions are possible in the network, because users are not able to create them or peers are not able to receive them. If the attacked cryptocurrency is the only currency available in the state, citizens will no longer be able to make transactions of any kind. Consequently, the sale of goods and services among citizens would fall into anarchy, being possible only through the adoption of antiquated forms of exchange such as barter.

4.1 Scenario: Trust in Maths

This scenario takes into account a cryptocurrency that relies on mathematical properties for its protocol security. To guarantee some properties like Confidentiality, Integrity, Authentication, and Availability needed for the security of every communication, the cryptocurrency protocol uses different cryptographic techniques based on mathematical problems. Users trust the system because of the difficulty of the crypto-challenges derived from the aforementioned properties, recognized as computationally hard to solve by the worldwide community.

Threat: Collapse of the Cryptocurrencies Foundation

In this scenario, the major threat is represented by an adversary that reduces the mathematical complexity of the problem on which the cryptocurrency relies on, becoming able to solve it in an optimized way. This knowledge makes the adversary capable to control the cryptocurrency network, exploiting its capabilities (that other peers do not have) to perform illicit activities, like the validation of fake transactions. The same result could happen if an adversary discovers a zero-day vulnerability in the implementation of one cryptographic function used by the cryptocurrency's protocol and develop a methodology to exploit it.

Hash functions are the pillars of the most important cryptocurrencies. Bitcoin, for example, relies on hash functions and their pre-image property to ensure the immutability of the ledger. Several attacks against the most important hash function implementation are discussed in the literature as well as against the compression function they used. The most important are the Chabaud and Joux's attack of SHA-0 [18], and the hash function attack techniques introduced by H. Dobbertin against MD5 [25–28]. These techniques are not applicable against SHA256 and SHA512, used by Bitcoin and other major cryptocurrencies, as investigated by several researchers in [39, 60, 63].

4.2 Scenario: Trust in the Computational Power

In this scenario, the major concern for cryptocurrency security is represented by an attacker with an unexpected high computational power. Possible threats include Quantum Computing that, even if the research is still in its infancy, may be able to efficiently solve problems which are not practically feasible on classical computers. This scenario takes into account a cryptocurrency that relies on the computational power for its security. This is also the case of Bitcoin, which relies on the computational difficulty of calculating hashes for Proof of Work (PoW) security. The protocol provides users with cryptographic challenges to be solved to validate transactions. Users have to spend a certain amount of resources, like CPU cycles, to solve these challenges. Then, peers need to reach a consensus in order to extend the public ledger of transactions. This means that the security of the network is guaranteed as long as the majority of the computational power is owned by honest nodes. Users trust the system because of the difficulty for a single entity to have the 51% of the whole computational power available in the entire network.

Threat: New Technologies

With its huge computational power, a quantum computer could be used to attack cryptocurrencies networks whose security is based on the difficulty for a single entity to hold the majority of the computational power of the entire network. Moreover, if a few single entities control a large part of the total computational power, the risk of joining forces to control the majority cannot be underestimated.

The potential danger posed to IT security by quantum computing was first established in 1994. That year saw the publication of a quantum computer algorithm [68] by the US mathematician and computer scientist Peter W Shor. In his work, he demonstrated how encryption techniques - previously considered secure - could be broken in a matter of seconds by factorization, or reducing a number into its constituent factors. To do so, the Shor algorithm used the computing power of quantum computers [30].

A possible solution for the threats posed by quantum computing and other advances in technologies, is certainly the development of proof of works (or other control protocols) information-theoretically secure. This means that the security of the protocol derives exclusively from Information Theory, rather than depending on other weak assumptions like the computational hardness. In this case, it is impossible for an adversary to break the system, even with unlimited computing power, simply because the attacker does not have enough information to calculate the solution.

Mining pools are a way for cryptocurrencies miners to pool their resources together and share their hashing power while splitting the reward equally according to the number of shares they contributed to solving a block. In some cases, like Bitcoin, very few mining pools control more than the 50% of the total computational power of the network. [1]. In blockchain base systems like cryptocurrencies, game theory can be used to prevents cheating in the network community [16].

4.3   Scenario: Infrastructure

Although anyone can run a cryptocurrency node anywhere on earth, the nodes that compose the network will hardly be physically uniformly distributed around the globe. This means that with high probability most of the nodes are hosted in few Internet Service Providers (ISPs). Consequently, most of the network traffic traverses network devices controlled by these few ISPs. As a direct consequence of this, denial of services attacks could be more easy to perform, by attacking ISPs' infrastructures for indirectly hit the cryptocurrency network availability. Moreover, malicious ISPs could filter the cryptocurrency's network traffic, compromising the overall functionalities or isolating specific nodes.

Threat: Hijacking Cryptocurrency Network

In this section, the threats related to directly attack the network infrastructures will be analyzed. Possible threats include denial of service attacks, in the attempt to disrupt cryptocurrency resources denying crypto coin users access. More specific Routing Attacks such as Border Gateway Protocol (BGP) hijacks, can partition a cryptocurrency network into two or more disjoint components. Another threat consists of delay the delivery of a block to a single specific victim node by several minutes with different impact depending on the victim: if the victim is a merchant, it is susceptible to double spending attacks; if it is a miner, the attack wastes its computational power; finally, if it is a regular node, it is unable to contribute to the network by propagating the last version of the blockchain. The security of Bitcoin to network-based Attacks has been relatively less unexplored compared to other attack scenarios. Heilman et al. in [41] examines the eclipse attack on a single node in the context of Bitcoin's p2p network Gervais et al. [36] consider other aspects of the centralization of Bitcoin and their consequences to the security of the protocol. In [13] authors presented an analysis of the vulnerabilities of the Bitcoin network from the networking viewpoint. Measuring and detecting routing attacks has seen extensive research on BGP hijack [13,66,77] and interception attacks [78].

Some countermeasures has been proposed to secure routing protocols that can prevent the above attacks [17,37,46,58].

5   Critical Infrastructure

Critical Infrastructure represents an umbrella term used by governments to group all those resources that are essential for the economic, financial, and social system of a country. The Presidential Policy Directive 21 (PPD-21): Critical Infrastructure security and Resilience, issued by the President of United States in 2013, advances a national unity of effort to strengthen and maintain secure, functioning, and resilient Critical Infrastructure. PPD-21 identifies 16 Critical Infrastructure sectors: chemical, commercial facility, communication, critical manufacturing, dams, defence industrial base, emergency services, energy, financial service, food and agriculture, government facilities, health-care and public health, information technology, nuclear reactors, materials and waste, transportation system, and water and waste-water system, respectively [10]. The protection of these resources is crucial, because the destruction (or even the partial or momentary inability) could cause significant harm to the society, or worse, could jeopardize human lives. For example, in desert countries such as Qatar, Saudi Arabia, or the United Arab Emirates, attacking the Critical Infrastructures essential for the water supply (i.e., water refineries), would be tantamount to leaving the entire population without drinking water for the entire duration of the fault. The aforementioned Control Systems and protocols were put into operation decades ago, before the global spread of the Internet. At the time, security was not considered of paramount importance, as communication networks were closed and only very few people had access to information. The wide diffusion of the Internet of Things devices, occurred in the following years, made the security issues more sensitive. Indeed, the constant need for connectivity to networks and the interdependence between devices increase the need to make control systems and protocols more robust and resilient [22]. According to the Geneva Conventions of 1949, it is prohibited to attack, destroy, remove, or render useless objects indispensable to the survival of the civilian population, such as foodstuffs, agricultural areas for the production of foodstuffs, crops, livestock, drinking water installations and supplies, and irrigation works, for the specific purpose of denying them for their sustenance value to the civilian population or to the adverse party, whatever the motive, whether in order to starve out the civilians, to cause them to move away, or for any other motive [62]. Nevertheless, the increase of the attack surface due to the technologies has given way to numerous attacks on Critical Infrastructures, aimed at causing extensive damage to the victimized countries. In this section, we will take into account possible attacks related to three real-world scenarios: malware-guided attacks; attacks targeting the Supervisory Control And Data Acquisition (SCADA) systems; and attacks carried forward through the use of drones, respectively.

5.1   Scenario: Cyber Warfare Targeting Critical Infrastructures

This scenario takes into account a Critical Infrastructure located within a country, which manages a critical resource. The Critical Infrastructure can be either a complex set of interconnected electrical components, as in the past, or a set of modern Internet of Things devices that communicate with each other. In both cases, the Critical Infrastructure exposes interfaces on the web, either to remotely receive commands or to show the status of the managed resource. The exposure to the web is necessary, to reduce the amount of dedicated personnel and to monitor the status of the critical resource in real time remotely. At the same time, however, the exposure to the web could lead to an increase of the attack surface, opening the doors to numerous attacks such as malware-base attacks and attacks on the SCADA systems, a subset of the Industrial Control Systems (ICSs).

Threat 1: Malware

The control systems and protocols that protect the Critical Infrastructure are usually a conglomerate of interconnected hardware and software resources. While hardware resources can be physically destroyed, malicious programs can be created to alter the behavior of the software resources. one historical example is Stuxnet, a malicious worm that, back to 2010, is believed to be responsible for causing substantial damage to Iran's nuclear facilities. A more recent example is given by Triton, which exploited a critical switch placed in the wrong position to attack the industrial hardware in the Middle East. In general, old control systems did not take security into consideration because of their presence in restricted environments (i.e., due to the limited diffusion of the Internet). Once the control systems expose their interfaces to the current Internet, however, the danger is around the corner. Simple software errors or carefree third-party software execution can lead to external compromise, causing the temporary (or definitive) malfunction of the control software and jeopardizing the protected critical resource. Even worse, instead of provoking the destruction or the manumission of the control system, an attacker could take control of it from the outside, deceiving security systems and tampering with the critical resource without triggering security alarms.

Modern Critical Infrastructures are continually exposed to new threats due to the vulnerabilities and architectural weaknesses introduced by the extensive use of information and communication technologies (ICT). Of particular significance are the vulnerabilities in the communication protocols used in SCADA systems that are commonly employed to control industrial processes. In [34] authors investigated the impact of traditional ICT malware on SCADA systems, discussing the potentially damaging effects of computer malware created for SCADA systems. In [49] authors, after an introduction of industrial network protocol, design, and architecture, provided methods for risk and vulnerabilities assessment, implementing security and access controls, exception, anomaly, and threat detection that should help to prepare against the more and more sophisticated industrial network malware threats. In June 2017, ESET researchers discovered a malware considered the biggest threat to Critical Infrastructures since Stuxnet, named Industroyer. As its name suggests, Industroyer was designed to disrupt critical industrial processes being capable of doing significant harm to electric power systems. To make matters worse, the malware could also be refitted to target other types of Critical Infrastructures. The 2016 attack on Ukraine's power grid that deprived part of Kiev of power for an hour was caused precisely by a cyber attack. ESET researchers have suggested that the Win32/Industroyer malware would be capable of performing such an attack. Industroyer is a particularly dangerous threat, as it has the ability to control electricity substation switches and circuit breakers directly. According to ESET, it does this by using industrial communication protocols used worldwide in power supply infrastructure, transportation Control Systems, and other Critical Infrastructure systems (such as water and gas) [47].

Ukraine's power grid attack demonstrated that malicious actors seem to have extensive knowledge about Industrial Control Systems and Protocols. Terry Ray, the chief product strategist at Imperva, said "Since the industrial controls used in Ukraine are the same in other parts of Europe, the Middle East, and Asia, we could see more of these attacks in the future. And while these attackers seem to be content to disrupt the system, it is not outside the realm of possibility that they could take things a step further and inflict damage to the system themselves. Many of these industrial control systems have been in operation for years with little or no modification (no anti-virus updates or patches). This leaves them open to a wide range of cyber threats. It is therefore imperative that we find alternative measures to manage the risk." [47]. To mitigate the risk of ICS attacks, first, Critical Infrastructure administrators need to manage their system following the most simple and important best practices. Paul Edon, director at Tripwire, suggests that "security best practice includes selecting suitable frameworks such as NIST, ISO, CIS, ITIL to help direct, manage and drive security programs. It also means ensuring that the strategy includes all three pillars of security; People, Process, and Technology. Protection should apply at all levels; Perimeter, Network, and End Point. Finally, select the foundational controls that best suit your environment. There is a wealth of choice – Firewalls, IDS/IPS, Encryption, Dual Factor Authentication, System Integrity Monitoring, Change Management, Off-line Backup, Vulnerability Management, and Configuration Management to name but a few." [47].

Threat 2: SCADA Systems Attacks

SCADA is a system of software and hardware elements that allows industrial organizations to: (i) control industrial processes locally or at remote locations; (ii) monitor, gather, and process real-time data; (iii) directly interact with devices such as sensors, valves, pumps, motors, and possibly others, through human-machine interface (HMI) software; and (iv) record events into a log file. SCADA systems are crucial for industrial organizations since they help to maintain efficiency, process data for smarter decisions, and communicate system issues to help mitigate downtime. The basic SCADA architecture begins with programmable logic controllers (PLCs) or remote terminal units (RTUs). PLCs and RTUs are microcomputers that communicate with an array of objects such as factory machines, HMIs, sensors, and end-devices, and then route the information from those objects to computers with SCADA software. The SCADA software processes distribute and display the data, helping operators and other employees analyzing the data and make important decisions based on them [12]. The exposure to the network provides the attackers with a wide range of possibilities. SCADA systems could be used to gather a lot of information, such as the facility's layout, critical safety thresholds to be taken into account, and much other critical information.

Academic research centers, after surveyed the most important cyber security problems on SCADA systems, are focusing on forward-looking security solutions. In [55] the authors analyzed several cyber-security incidents involving Critical Infrastructures and SCADA systems. They classified these incidents based on source sector, method of operations, impact, and target sector. Using this standardized taxonomy, they compared current and future SCADA incidents. In [56] the authors surveyed ongoing research and provide a coherent overview of the threats, risks, and mitigation strategies in the area of SCADA security. The research that has been done in this area provides long-term solutions and apply both industry and academic work to the problem. As such, these institutes remain very connected (by interacting regularly) with industry to make sure the research is gauged to provide a positive impact on the national infrastructure.

As already said for ICS in general, SCADA systems were often designed decades ago, when security was of little concern due to the closed nature of the communication networks. As these systems have been modernized, they have become interconnected and have started running more modern services such as web interfaces and interactive consoles (telnet/ssh), by implementing remote configuration protocols. Sadly, security has been left aside during the increased modernization of these systems. Indeed, these systems present very little implementations of standard security mechanisms such as encryption and authentication. The former is sometimes hard in these systems, due to the lack of processing power, the presence of slow links, and the presence of the legacy protocols. The primary issue with the slow links is the byte-time latency (i.e., time to transmit 1 byte) incurred from buffering the data for encryption. Although adding encryption to these systems is generally trivial, maintaining the other properties such as timing and data integrity with the encryption in place is not. Authentication is equally troublesome. Indeed, in the case of authentication, it is fairly common for the devices in the control space to use default passwords for access and control. Most of these default passwords are very easy to find when using search engines. This is a similar issue to network monitoring agents such as SNMP that often come configured by default with known public and private access phrases. The problem is further complicated by the move toward commercial, off-the-shelf (COTS) appliances and systems being integrated with the networks or part of the Control Systems themselves. While cutting costs and eliminating some of the proprietary nature of Control Systems, these appliances and systems bring with them the well-known passwords and vulnerabilities that each product may be subject to. Often these COTS systems may end up providing a point of entry for an attacker into the critical control network [75].

Threat 3: Drones

The advent of drones has introduced a whole new system of attacks aimed at mobile and non-mobile targets. In fact, in addition to the innocent fun related to making it fly to take breathtaking shots, there are some disturbing ways of use. A drone, in the hands of terrorists or malicious users, would make it easier to attack any target, causing massive damage. Strengthened by the fact that its limited size makes it extremely difficult to detect, the drone could be used for multiple purposes: a drone can be equipped with a camera to capture sensitive targets, such as alarm systems of a Critical Infrastructure, with the purpose of carrying out a first recognition useful for both checking security weaknesses and studying a detailed attack plan; a drone could also be equipped with weapons or small bombs, in order to be directly thrown at the target, causing explosions. It is not surprising that drones have been banned in several countries, such as Egypt, North Korea, and Iran, and restricted in others, such as Russia, the United Arab States, and Belgium. The paragraph will describe in detail the use of drones to attack Critical Infrastructures of a Country and analyze real cases, such as the attack of armed drones at the Russian military base in Syria, and Yemen's Houthi drones attack an oil plant in southern Saudi Arabia.

Since their introduction on the retail market, the public opinion, as well as the research community, wondered about the actual danger of drones, opening the debate on what the threats and the benefits of this technology could be. In [69] the author investigated about drones benefit, risks and legal consideration. In [59] authors, considering the significant number of non-military UAVs that can be purchased to operate in unregulated air space and the range of such devices, tested a specific UAV, the Parrot AR Drone version 2, and presented a forensic analysis of tests used to deactivate or render the device inoperative. They found that these devices are open to attack, which means they could be controlled by a third party. In the last few years, several episodes have helped to raise awareness among the institutions of the threat of UAVs against Critical Infrastructures. In December 2014, France revealed that unauthorized and unidentified UAS had breached the restricted airspace over 13 of the Country's 19 nuclear plants during the preceding three months. These UAS were described as highly sophisticated civilian devices, and the flights over nuclear facilities appeared to be coordinated, with most of the violations occurring at night. In light of the increasing security concerns in Europe following terrorist attacks in France and Belgium, there is concern over the possible motives. There have been many notable incidents also in the United States. In early July 2016, the U.S. Department of Energy revealed that its Savannah River Site –which processes and stores nuclear materials– had experienced eight unauthorized flyovers in the span of two weeks. There have been unauthorized flyovers of a U.S. Navy nuclear submarine base, major sporting events, large public gatherings, and national monuments. UAS have crashed into the White House lawn and the New York Capitol, and there has been widespread documentation that they are being used to deliver contraband to prisons [20].

Most traditional radar cannot detect small, low-flying UAS, so this trend is particularly troubling. The majority of previous discussed documented flyovers were only discovered because of human detection –often by vigilant security personnel with keen eyesight. There have been efforts to improve upon the available technology, and a number of companies are marketing drone-detection security systems. However, even when they are detected, there are complications intercepting them and identifying the operators [20]. A possible solution is the design and implementation of anti-drones systems based on Jamming technologies. Recognizing and implementing security practices that meet states regulatory requirements are key to successfully managing potential security incidents associated with UAS. Although no single solution will fully mitigate this risk, there are several measures that can be taken to address UAS-related security challenges [64]: (i) research and implement legally approved counter-UAS technology; (ii) know the air domain around the facility and who has authority to take action to enhance security; (iii) update emergency/incident action plans to include UAS security and response strategies; (iv) build federal, state, and local partnerships for adaptation of best practices and information sharing; and (v) sensitize citizens and institutions to the problem, inviting anyone to report potential UAS threats to local law enforcement agency.

6   Conclusion

In this paper, we extended the classic pillars of Information Warfare to include the new threats posed by changes in our society as a result of technological advances in recent years. We described several real-case scenarios to show the possible impact that the new generation of Information Warfare could have in different aspects of modern society and economy. For each scenario, we identified one or more threats, investigating the state-of-the-art solutions for both the attack and defense methodologies existing in the literature. Finally, we identified open issues that still affect these fields, providing directions that could be useful to the development of more effective countermeasures.

Acknowledgement. This publication was partially supported by awards NPRP-S-11-0109-180242, UREP23-065-1-014, and NPRP X-063-1-014 from the QNRF-Qatar National Research Fund, a member of The Qatar Foundation. The information and views set out in this publication are those of the authors and do not necessarily reflect the official opinion of the QNRF.

References

1. The best bitcoin mining pools. https://www.bitcoinmining.com/bitcoin-mining-pools/. Accessed June 2020
2. The deep web is the 99% of the internet you can't google. https://curiosity.com/topics/the-deep-web-is-the-99-of-the-internet-you-cant-google-curiosity/. Accessed June 2020
3. Google's search knows about over 130 trillion pages. https://searchengineland.com/googles-search-indexes-hits-130-trillion-pages-documents-263378. Accessed June 2020
4. How to escape your political bubble for a clearer view. https://www.nytimes.com/2017/03/03/arts/the-battle-over-your-political-bubble.html. Accessed June 2020
5. Internet growth statistics. https://www.internetworldstats.com/emarketing.htm. Accessed June 2020
6. Breaking through censorship barriers, even when tor is blocked. https://blog.torproject.org/breaking-through-censorship-barriers-even-when-tor-blocked. Accessed June 2020
7. Eu vs disinfo website. https://euvsdisinfo.eu/about/. Accessed June 2020
8. How trolls are ruining the internet. http://time.com/4457110/internet-trolls/. Accessed June 2020
9. A new study suggests fake news might have won donald trump the 2016 election. https://www.washingtonpost.com/news/the-fix/wp/2018/04/03/a-new-study-suggests-fake-news-might-have-won-donald-trump-the-2016-election/?noredirect=on&utm_term=.d6e63f61fa06. Accessed June 2020
10. Presidential policy directive - critical infrastructure security and resilience. https://obamawhitehouse.archives.gov/the-press-office/2013/02/12/presidential-policy-directive-critical-infrastructure-security-and-resil. Accessed June 2020
11. Social media and censorship in china: how is it different to the west? http://www.bbc.co.uk/newsbeat/article/41398423/social-media-and-censorship-in-china-how-is-it-different-to-the-west. Accessed June 2020
12. What is scada? https://inductiveautomation.com/what-is-scada. Accessed June 2020
13. Apostolaki, M., Zohar, A., Vanbever, L.: Hijacking bitcoin: routing attacks on cryptocurrencies. In: 2017 IEEE Symposium on Security and Privacy (SP), pp. 375–392. IEEE (2017)

14. Bamman, D., O'Connor, B., Smith, N.: Censorship and deletion practices in Chinese social media. First Monday **17**(3), 3–5 (2012)
15. Bauer, K., McCoy, D., Grunwald, D., Kohno, T., Sicker, D.: Low-resource routing attacks against tor. In: Proceedings of the 2007 ACM Workshop on Privacy in Electronic Society, pp. 11–20. ACM (2007)
16. Blockgeeks: What is cryptocurrency game theory: A basic introduction. https://blockgeeks.com/guides/cryptocurrency-game-theory/. Accessed June 2020
17. Boldyreva, A., Lychev, R.: Provable security of S-BGP and other path vector protocols: model, analysis and extensions. In: Proceedings of the 2012 ACM Conference on Computer and Communications Security, pp. 541–552. ACM (2012)
18. Chabaud, F., Joux, A.: Differential collisions in SHA-0. In: Krawczyk, H. (ed.) CRYPTO 1998. LNCS, vol. 1462, pp. 56–71. Springer, Heidelberg (1998). https://doi.org/10.1007/BFb0055720
19. Chu, Z., Gianvecchio, S., Wang, H., Jajodia, S.: Detecting automation of twitter accounts: are you a human, bot, or cyborg? IEEE Trans. Dependable Sec. Comput. **9**(6), 811–824 (2012)
20. Dan Shea, A.E., Husch, B.: Drones and critical infrastructure. National Conference of States Legislatures (NCSL). http://www.ncsl.org/research/energy/drones-and-critical-infrastructure.aspx. December 2016. Accessed June 2020
21. Dewey, J.: Democracy in education. Elementary School Teacher **4**(4), 193–204 (1903)
22. Di Pietro, R., Oligeri, G.: Silence is golden: exploiting jamming and radio silence to communicate. ACM Trans. Inf. Syst. Secur. **17**(3), 9:1–9:24 (2015). https://doi.org/10.1145/2699906. http://doi.acm.org/10.1145/2699906
23. Ding, F., Yang, Z., Chen, X., Guo, J.: Effective methods to avoid the internet censorship. In: 2011 Fourth International Symposium on Parallel Architectures, Algorithms and Programming. pp. 67–71. IEEE (2011)
24. Dingledine, R., Mathewson, N., Syverson, P.: Tor: The second-generation onion router. Tech. rep, Naval Research Lab Washington DC (2004)
25. Dobbertin, H.: Cryptanalysis of md4. In: International Workshop on Fast Software Encryption. pp. 53–69. Springer (1996)
26. Dobbertin, H.: Cryptanalysis of md5 compress. Technical report, Presented at the Rump Session of EuroCrypt (1996)
27. Dobbertin, H.: The status of md5 after a recent attack. Crypto-Bytes The technical newsletter of RSA Laboratories, a division of RSA Data Security, Inc. vol. 2, no. (2) (1996)
28. Dobbertin, H.: Ripemd with two-round compress function is not collision-free. J. Cryptol. **10**(1), 51–69 (1997)
29. Elyashar, A., Bendahan, J., Puzis, R.: Has the online discussion been manipulated? quantifying online discussion authenticity within online social media. arXiv preprint arXiv:1708.02763 (2017)
30. Eperiesi-Beck, E.: The threat quantum computers pose to modern security. https://www.scmagazineuk.com/the-threat-quantum-computers-pose-to-modern-security/article/709472/. Accessed June 2020
31. Ferrara, E.: Disinformation and social bot operations in the run up to the 2017 french presidential election (2017)
32. Fokin, A., et al.: Internet trolling as a tool of hybrid warfare: the case of latvia. Technical report, NATO Strategic Communications Centre of Excellence (1996)
33. Forelle, M., Howard, P., Monroy-Hernández, A., Savage, S.: Political bots and the manipulation of public opinion in venezuela. arXiv preprint arXiv:1507.07109 (2015)

34. Fovino, I.N., Carcano, A., Masera, M., Trombetta, A.: An experimental investigation of malware attacks on scada systems. Int. J. Critical Infrastruct. Protect. **2**(4), 139–145 (2009)
35. Gertz, N.: Censorship, Propaganda, and the Production of 'Shell Shock' in World War I. Disciplinary Press, Oxford (2009)
36. Gervais, A., Karame, G., Capkun, S., Capkun, V.: Is bitcoin a decentralized currency? IEEE Secur. Privacy **12**(3), 54–60 (2014)
37. Gill, P., Schapira, M., Goldberg, S.: Let the market drive deployment: a strategy for transitioning to BGP security. In: ACM SIGCOMM Computer Communication Review. vol. 41, pp. 14–25. ACM (2011)
38. Guriev, S.M., Treisman, D.: How modern dictators survive: cooptation, censorship, propaganda, and repression. CEPR Discussion Paper No. DP10454 (2015)
39. Handschuh, H., Knudsen, L.R., Robshaw, M.J.: Analysis of SHA-1 in encryption mode. In: Naccache, D. (ed.) CT-RSA 2001. LNCS, vol. 2020, pp. 70–83. Springer, Heidelberg (2001). https://doi.org/10.1007/3-540-45353-9_7
40. Hegelich, S., Janetzko, D.: Are social bots on twitter political actors? empirical evidence from a ukrainian social botnet. In: Tenth International AAAI Conference on Web and Social Media (2016)
41. Heilman, E., Kendler, A., Zohar, A., Goldberg, S.: Eclipse attacks on bitcoin's peer-to-peer network. In: USENIX Security Symposium, pp. 129–144 (2015)
42. Heins, M.: The brave new world of social media censorship. Harv. L. Rev. F. **127**, 325 (2013)
43. Hilvert, J.: Blue Pencil Warriors: Censorship and Propaganda in World War II. University of Queensland Press, Manchester (1984)
44. Hintz, A.: Social media censorship, privatized regulation, and new restrictions to protest and dissent. Rowman & Littlefield (2015)
45. Howard, P.N., Kollanyi, B.: Bots, #strongerin, and #brexit: computational propaganda during the uk-eu referendum. SSRN **2798311** (2016)
46. Hu, Y.C., Perrig, A., Sirbu, M.: SPV: Secure path vector routing for securing BGP. ACM SIGCOMM Comput. Commun. Rev. **34**(4), 179–192 (2004)
47. Ismail, N.: New malware represents biggest threat to critical infrastructure. https://www.information-age.com/new-malware-represents-biggest-threat-critical-infrastructure-123466733/ June 2017. Accessed June 2020
48. Keshen, J.: Propaganda and censorship during Canada's Great War. University of Alberta, Edmonton (1996)
49. Knapp, E.D., Langill, J.T.: Industrial Network Security: Securing critical infrastructure networks for smart grid, SCADA, and other Industrial Control Systems. Syngress (2014)
50. Kumar, S., Cheng, J., Leskovec, J., Subrahmanian, V.: An army of me: sockpuppets in online discussion communities. In: Proceedings of the 26th International Conference on World Wide Web. pp. 857–866. International World Wide Web Conferences Steering Committee (2017)
51. La Morgia, M., Mei, A., Raponi, S., Stefa, J.: Time-zone geolocation of crowds in the dark web. In: 2018 IEEE 38th International Conference on Distributed Computing Systems (ICDCS), pp. 445–455. IEEE (2018)
52. MacArthur, J.R.: Second Front: Censorship and Propaganda in the 1991 Gulf War. University of California Press, California (2004)
53. Mason, A.: CCSP Self-Study: Cisco Secure Virtual Private Networks (CSVPN). Pearson Higher Education (2004)

54. Mihaylov, T., Georgiev, G., Nakov, P.: Finding opinion manipulation trolls in news community forums. In: Proceedings of the Nineteenth Conference on Computational Natural Language Learning, pp. 310–314 (2015)

55. Miller, B., Rowe, D.C.: A survey scada of and critical infrastructure incidents. RIIT **12**, 51–56 (2012)

56. Nicholson, A., Webber, S., Dyer, S., Patel, T., Janicke, H.: Scada security in the light of cyber-warfare. Comput. Secur. **31**(4), 418–436 (2012)

57. Nobori, D., Shinjo, Y.: {VPN} gate: a volunteer-organized public {VPN} relay system with blocking resistance for bypassing government censorship firewalls. In: Proceedings of the 11th {USENIX} Symposium on Networked Systems Design and Implementation ({NSDI} 14). pp. 229–241 (2014)

58. van Oorschot, P.C., Wan, T., Kranakis, E.: On interdomain routing security and pretty secure BGP (PSBGP). ACM Trans. Inf. Syst. Secur. (TISSEC) **10**(3), 11 (2007)

59. Peacock, M., Johnstone, M.N.: Towards detection and control of civilian unmanned aerial vehicles. SRI Security Research Institute, Edith Cowan University, Perth, Western (2013)

60. Preneel, B., Govaerts, R., Vandewalle, J.: Differential cryptanalysis of hash functions based on block ciphers. In: Proceedings of the 1st ACM Conference on Computer and Communications Security, pp. 183–188. ACM (1993)

61. Ratkiewicz, J., Conover, M.D., Meiss, M., Gonçalves, B., Flammini, A., Menczer, F.M.: Detecting and tracking political abuse in social media. In: Fifth International AAAI Conference on Weblogs and Social Media (2011)

62. Roberts, A.: Documents on the Laws of War. HeinOnline (2000)

63. Saarinen, M.-J.O.: Cryptanalysis of block ciphers based on SHA-1 and MD5. In: Johansson, T. (ed.) FSE 2003. LNCS, vol. 2887, pp. 36–44. Springer, Heidelberg (2003). https://doi.org/10.1007/978-3-540-39887-5_4

64. Security, U.H.: Unmanned aircraft systems (UAS) - critical infrastructure. https://www.dhs.gov/uas-ci. Accessed June 2020

65. Shadmehr, M., Bernhardt, D.: State censorship. Am. Econ. J.: Microecon. **7**(2), 280–307 (2015)

66. Shi, X., Xiang, Y., Wang, Z., Yin, X., Wu, J.: Detecting prefix hijackings in the internet with argus. In: Proceedings of the 2012 Internet Measurement Conference, pp. 15–28. ACM (2012)

67. Shmatikov, V., Wang, M.-H.: Timing analysis in low-latency mix networks: attacks and defenses. In: Gollmann, D., Meier, J., Sabelfeld, A. (eds.) ESORICS 2006. LNCS, vol. 4189, pp. 18–33. Springer, Heidelberg (2006). https://doi.org/10.1007/11863908_2

68. Shor, P.W.: Algorithms for quantum computation: discrete logarithms and factoring. In: 35th Annual Symposium on Foundations of Computer Science, 1994 Proceedings., pp. 124–134. IEEE (1994)

69. Smith, K.W.: Drone technology: benefits, risks, and legal considerations. Seattle J. Envtl. L. **5**, i (2015)

70. Starbird, K.: Examining the alternative media ecosystem through the production of alternative narratives of mass shooting events on twitter. In: Eleventh International AAAI Conference on Web and Social Media (2017)

71. Sun, Y., et al.: {RAPTOR}: routing attacks on privacy in tor. In: 24th {USENIX} Security Symposium ({USENIX} Security 2015), pp. 271–286 (2015)

72. Waldorf, L.: Censorship and Propaganda in Post-Genocide Rwanda. Pluto Press, London (2007)

73. Wang, Y., Ji, P., Ye, B., Wang, P., Luo, R., Yang, H.: Gohop: personal vpn to defend from censorship. In: 16th International Conference on Advanced Communication Technology, pp. 27–33. IEEE (2014)
74. Winter, P., Lindskog, S.: How the great firewall of china is blocking tor. USENIX-The Advanced Computing Systems Association (2012)
75. Yardley, T.: Scada: issues, vulnerabilities and future directions.; login: the magazine of USENIX & SAGE **33**(6), 14–20 (2008) .
76. Zannettou, S., Caulfield, T., De Cristofaro, E., Sirivianos, M., Stringhini, G., Blackburn, J.: Disinformation warfare: Understanding state-sponsored trolls on twitter and their influence on the web. arXiv preprint arXiv:1801.09288 (2018)
77. Zhang, Z., Zhang, Y., Hu, Y.C., Mao, Z.M.: Practical defenses against BGP prefix hijacking. In: Proceedings of the 2007 ACM CoNEXT Conference, p. 3. ACM (2007)
78. Zhang, Z., Zhang, Y., Hu, Y.C., Mao, Z.M., Bush, R.: ispy: detecting ip prefix hijacking on my own. IEEE/ACM Trans. Network. (TON) **18**(6), 1815–1828 (2010)

Information Technology Consulting Firms' Readiness for Managing Information Security Incidents

Christine Große[(⊠)] , Maja Nyman, and Leif Sundberg

Mid Sweden University, 851 70 Sundsvall, Sweden
{christine.grosse,leif.sundberg}@miun.se,
many1307@student.miun.se

Abstract. Because of the increase in the number and scope of information security incidents, proper management has recently gained importance for public and private organizations. Further challenges in this area have resulted from new regulations, such as the General Data Protection Regulation (GDPR) and the Directive on Security of Network and Information Systems (NIS), as well as a tendency to outsource vital services to subcontractors. This study addresses the lack of empirical studies in the field and focuses on information security incident management at information technology (IT) consulting firms. Specifically, it examines challenges due to their exposed position and new regulations. The contribution of the paper is twofold. First, it provides valuable insight into the experiences and challenges of Swedish IT consulting firms. Second, it proposes criteria for classifying an information security incident that can equip decision-makers with a solid and assessable basis for incident management. The results emphasize further improvements in employee awareness, incident classification, and systemic governance, thereby integrating corporate policy making, information security incident management, and information system leadership.

Keywords: Security awareness · Information security incident management · Systemic governance · Incident classification · GDPR · NIS directive

1 Introduction

Recent violations of information security (InfoSec) in Sweden have included leaks of the healthcare hotline 1177 [1] and the Swedish Transport Agency [2, 3] as well as the access of unauthorized persons to the Swedish power grid [4]. The majority of these violations relate to the outsourcing of vital information technology (IT) services and inadequate handling of data by subcontractors. Therefore, the increase in outsourcing and the globalization of service providers have contributed to a growing number of incidents concerning InfoSec. In this context, an incident refers to an event that has the potential to impair the security of information in an unexpected or unwanted manner. Negative consequences pose threats to an organization that might disrupt productivity and lead to economic losses, legal implications, damaged image, and diminished trust among business partners and customers [5]. The risk of becoming the target of an

© Springer Nature Switzerland AG 2020
P. Mori et al. (Eds.): ICISSP 2019, CCIS 1221, pp. 48–73, 2020.
https://doi.org/10.1007/978-3-030-49443-8_3

attack is rising alongside the value and sensitivity of the information that organizations and their subcontractors handle [6–8]. This field of tensions has produced a complicated situation wherein IT consulting firms must confront particular challenges in information security incident management (ISIM) due to their vulnerable position as subcontractors. However, a structured ISIM contains not only operational incident management but also awareness training for employees, mitigation of identified vulnerabilities, and analysis and preparedness activities [6, 9]. Although several standards and guidelines for ISIM have been developed, they have received criticism for their generality, which is a barrier to implementation for organizations [10].

Since subcontractors have access to the data of several customers, they are at higher risk of becoming targets of cyber attacks [11]. However, there is still a substantial lack of research on ISIM at consulting firms in general and IT consulting firms in particular [7]. The few studies that have investigated the implementation and operation of ISIM in practice at public or private organizations have advocated for more specific guidance for organizations and further empirical investigations [12]. Therefore, the present study seeks to address the considerable need for empirical research and a concentration on ISIM in IT consulting firms. It specifically explores challenges that relate to both the subcontractor position of firms and the occurrence of new regulations, such as the General Data Protection Regulation (GDPR) and the Directive on Security of Network and Information Systems (NIS) in 2018. These relatively new regulations reflect significant developments in the fields of InfoSec, data protection, and critical infrastructure protection over the past two decades. Nevertheless, they have also created deep uncertainty among organizations with regard to how to comply with the requirements [13], and they remain poorly understood, as evident from the examples above and the following results of this study. In Sweden, the requirement to report incidents has led to a variety of reporting channels to numerous supervision authorities. Moreover, it has prompted delays ranging from over a week to a month [14, 15].

This paper builds on our previous research [16] by providing further novel content that broadens and enriches knowledge of ISIM in IT consulting firms. The study extends the representation of the interviews with critical quotations from participants. Furthermore, it adds analysis of the survey material and surpasses the scope of the previous research by proposing a model for the classification of InfoSec incidents. The research question of this study is, "which challenges do IT consulting firms encounter with respect to their ISIM, and how can these experiences inform future developments and inter-organizational learning?" The contribution of this paper is twofold. First, it identifies the challenges on the basis of interviews at three Swedish IT consulting firms with more than 20 employees. This information extends and clarifies the body of knowledge with specific insights regarding ISIM in practice. Second, the findings underpin the creation of a conceptual model for the classification of InfoSec incidents. Thus, they provide novel knowledge to enhance future developments of ISIM in theory and practice.

Following this introduction, the paper explains the background and methods of the study. Subsequently, it incorporates experiences of the IT consulting firms to highlight several challenges of ISIM and inform the incident classification model. The study concludes with a discussion of the implications for theory and practice as well as suggestions for further research.

2   Background

2.1   Foundations of InfoSec

InfoSec concerns the preservation of three qualities with regard to data and information: confidentiality, integrity, and availability [17]. The management of InfoSec needs to balance these cornerstones to support daily business operations and avoid interfering with the necessary information flow. However, recent technological developments and the increasing interconnectedness of society have imparted additional complexity to the management of InfoSec. These trends are already underway and continue to dissolve the boundaries of the classical computer system. Thus, the modern information system extends beyond technical artifacts to encompass formal and informal information flows within and between organizations in addition to the technical information transmission paths [18]. Moreover, the modern information system contains increasingly diverse customers. Therefore, InfoSec must address the protection of customers' personal information. The privacy of individuals is emerging as the fourth pillar in InfoSec primarily because of the GDPR, which has applied to the European Union (EU) since May 25, 2018 [11, 19]. The GDPR targets the protection of individuals and the information about them that organizations process. The regulation seeks to unify requirements regarding privacy within the EU and reflect the changed prerequisites of digitalization in society. Since the GDPR focuses on individual rights, it is also applicable outside of the EU if the processed information concerns a citizen of an EU Member State [20]. Organizations must consider the following requirements:

- Establishment of data portability and transparency
- Limitation of data collection and storage to specified purposes
- Assessment of consequences with regard to data breaches
- Appointment of a data protection officer
- Reporting of incidents regarding personal data within 72 h
- Responsibility for processed data and information
- Ability to demonstrate compliance with InfoSec in general and GDPR in particular
- Training of personnel that have access to personal data and information.

The regulation further criminalizes any failure to comply with the requirements and suggests costly penalties for organizations that are in breach of the regulation. Therefore, the content of incident reports must include not only facts about the type, magnitude, and effects of the incident but also details of how the incident has been threatened, which delimits the negative consequences of the security breach [11]. Thus, the responsible national authority can not only assess compliance to regulations but also inform other organizations and customers about breaches and mitigation activities.

Another regulation, the NIS, has the objective of protecting society from failures in InfoSec that can severely disturb important societal services, such as critical infrastructure. The NIS has applied since May 10, 2018 [21]. It targets providers of critical infrastructure, such as digital, finance, and health services, energy, water, and food supplies, and transportation. In contrast to the GDPR, the NIS aims to advance InfoSec in the context of critical infrastructure protection within the EU Member States. Concerned organizations must identify themselves as providers or operators of critical infrastructure and establish measures for the prevention and mitigation of incidents in information systems and networks, which also includes planning for the swift restoration of the societal functionality. To meet the requirements of the recent regulations, an adequate ISIM must complement the systematic InfoSec management, which is now a precondition for public and private organizations. In extension of the GDPR, the NIS more strictly requires providers of critical infrastructure to contend with risks and practice risk-based ISIM. Incidents that are judged to yield serious consequences for the maintenance of critical infrastructure or digital services should be reported to the supervising agency as quickly as possible. The requirements for reporting are similar to those in the GDPR, especially the 72-hour maximum timeline for reporting an incident. In Sweden, the supervision agency recently divided this requirement into three steps of reporting: an initial announcement of the incident within six hours, a concretizing follow-up within 24 h, and a detailed follow-up within four weeks with the possibility of completing the report within one year [22]. Non-compliance can also be subject to penalties; however, in contrast to the GDPR, they are more moderate and depend on the level of non-fulfillment. Meanwhile, the demand for reporting incidents similarly concerns those that occur among subcontractors, such as IT consulting firms. In addition to the reporting requirements of the GDPR, the NIS demands information about both types of measures: those that prevent the incident's spread and reoccurrence as well as those that improve the ISIM at the reporting organization [21].

2.2 Framework for ISIM

Several best practices and guidelines are associated with ISIM, including the international standards ISO/IEC 27035:2016 and NIST SP 800-61 (Rev 2) (hereafter referred to as ISO and NIST, respectively) [8, 23]. Moreover, practical guides are regularly published by, for example, the SANS Institute, CERT Coordination Centre, and ENISA, which are based on the ISO and NIST standards. Gaps between the standards and the new regulations have been identified and encourage further alignment, particularly with regard to privacy [19].

In general, the process of a structured ISIM contains several phases. Specifically, ISO suggests five, while NIST dictates four phases for structuring the strategic and operative work that relates to incidents. Both standards provide organizations with generic principles and content [24] to permit applicability to any type of organization in regard to, for example, operation systems, applications, platforms, or protocols [25]. However, because of the generality of the standards, it is difficult to customize them to the particular settings and demands of organizations. The ISO standard demonstrates a close relationship with consistent quality and InfoSec management, whereas the NIST focuses more heavily on operative incident management, which reduces the synergy effects of two aspects: the integration of ISIM into a strategic management system and the systematic knowledge transfer within and between organizations.

In congruence with [16], this study combines the concepts of ISO and NIST into an adapted ISIM. Four phases constitute the framework for the analysis: planning and preparation in phase one, detection and reporting in phase two, analysis and response in phase three, and learning and improvement in phase four. While phases two and three have a more operative character, phases one and four favor a strategic perspective.

Phase I: Planning and Preparation. During the first phase, organizations establish a solid foundation for systematic ISIM. This basis requires implementing and updating policies regarding InfoSec and ISIM at all organizational levels. The phase specifically considers not only the hardening of the technical part of the information system, which includes devices, applications, and networks, but also the formal rules within and between organizations and the preparation of an incident response team (IRT). Moreover, all employees – whether responsible for ISIM or for other tasks – must be adequately involved and trained to develop proper knowledge of appropriate behavior with regard to InfoSec and ISIM. An organization should consider alternative processes for maintaining critical functionalities, which can interconnect ISIM with continuity management. In addition, this phase implements further tools and rules that are essential for incident detection, analysis, mitigation, and documentation [25]. The phase concludes with proper testing of the functionality of the established means with regard to the technical, formal, and informal parts of the organizational information system.

Phase II: Detection and Reporting. This phase targets the initial phase of an incident, which, apart from the detection of an incident, also includes its initial characterization and reporting. With the aid of the measurements from Phase I, the incident characterization supports the initial estimation of consequences during the first report, which is continuously generated as new results from further activities arise in phase III. The detection of an incident among the large number of warnings that a monitoring system continuously produces requires knowledge and experience within organizations [25]. Achieving an acceptable quality of the information that is manually and automatically collected during this phase facilitates not only further analysis of and response to an incident but also the future development of ISIM. Therefore, comprehensive information should be collected, such as identified vulnerabilities, events, and related decisions. This evidence, apart from enhancing internal ISIM, is also significant for proper reporting of InfoSec-imparing incidents to responsible internal and external stakeholders to inform further decision-making [24]. When the incident type is known, phases II and III are separable in other cases, iterations between these phases can be necessary, particularly when the analyses suggest information that complements the report or detect multiple or subsequent incidents.

Phase III: Analysis and Response. The detected incident undergoes a thorough analysis to determine its character, origin, and consequences. The results of this analysis enable rapid response to the incident and preparation of future routines as well as the improvement of ISIM. A swift reaction can limit the negative consequences and further spread of the incident. In the event that multiple or subsequent incidents arise, the activities of this phase are intertwined and alternate with those of phase II until the incident is finally treated. The policies and processes during phase I constitute the basis of the appropriate proceedings. Similarly, the information that is collected during phase II is input for a proper analysis and response. The analysis assesses the character of the incident and recommends mitigation measures. The response part of this phase then applies those measures and provides feedback about the success or failure of the treatment. Further improvement of ISIM relies on proper documentation of the incident, the analysis and decision-making process, the measurements, and shortcomings that are identified during the activities in all phases. This input facilitates the development of policies and processes, as the classification of an incident is still subject to development [26]. The aforementioned requirements of the new regulations provide areas for improvement in ISIM, relies on the valuable input of the operative ISIM during the analysis and response phase. The documentation of this phase completes the internal data collection and is a vital precondition for the following activities.

Phase IV: Learning and Improvement. In accordance with the concept of continuous quality management, this phase facilitates developments of InfoSec and ISIM. These developments occur mainly within the organization but can also involve external stakeholders, such as subcontractors, suppliers, or business partners. Involvement depends on the role during the ISIM and the interdependency with organizational processes. While NIST recommends attention to key lessons after each large incident, findings from small incidents should be examined on a regular basis [25]. Organizational learning concerns specific knowledge about incidents, such as the causes of their occurrence or the mitigation activities that were successfully applied or ineffective. The purpose is twofold: to protect the entire information system from similar events and to improve its capabilities for coping with incidents in the future. The results of this phase then inform the activities of the next cycle of ISIM, which begins again with phase I [24]. Phase IV updates the procedures that phase I has defined. These routines address each role in an organization and provide guidance for proper action alongside ISIM, which includes rules about the notification of concerned stakeholders, allocation of appropriate resources, suggested treatment, required documentation, and notification of completement, for example. In addition, the phase extends the compiled documentation on ISIM with information on the maturity of ISIM and organizational knowledge management to enhance both the future performance of ISIM and the inter-organizational collaboration before, during, and after incidents.

2.3   Previous Research

Although a few studies have addressed ISIM in practice, empirical research in this area remains underrepresented, particularly in the context of the GDPR. However, case studies have been performed on ISIM in the energy sector [12, 27] and the oil and gas industries in Norway [28]. Other studies have explored practices in large organizations in, for example, Norway [7] and the finance sector [5]. Further research has investigated the challenges of applying technical solutions for the detection and diagnosis of incidents [29, 30]. Another comprehensive study [31] has applied an integrative perspective of the technical, formal, and informal information system to investigate challenges in IT security management. To date, only one study [16] has investigated the ISIM of IT consulting firms in Sweden with regard to the GDPR and NIS. However, the recent regulations and growing tendency to outsource highlight the subcontractor's role in ISIM as the focus of this study.

3 Methodology

3.1 The Swedish IT Consulting Business Consortium

This study investigates ISIM at three IT consulting firms. These firms are part of a Swedish IT consulting consortium that employs about 2,100 individuals in around 70 companies in Europe. The autonomous subsidiaries, which have 30 employees on average, are based in several countries, such as Germany, Norway, Finland, Denmark, and Sweden. From the Swedish part of the consortium, the parent company and two subsidiaries participated in this study. The parent company (PC) is the head of the IT consulting consortium and has 13 employees, while the first subsidiary (S1) is an IT consulting firm with 135 employees, and the second subsidiary (S2) employs 25 individuals. The selection of these firms ensured appropriate variation, as one of the subsidiaries is close to the average size, but the other is four times larger. Meanwhile, the parent company is half of the average size.

To develop a comprehensive understanding of ISIM in IT consulting firms, this study extends the interview study with a survey. The investigation departs from the literature review, which informed the theoretical framework of both the interviews and the survey [32]. In accordance with [33], this study first selected six individuals who are entrusted with InfoSec and ISIM at the IT consulting firms for the interview study. Table 1 presents the participants, their levels of expertise, and their affiliations. The names of the persons are fictive and gender-neutral to ensure the anonymity of the participants. In the second step, the survey involved 80 employees at S1 with a variety of experience in InfoSec.

Table 1. Selection of interviewees for the study.

Firm	Participant[*]	Description
Parent company	Mio	Chief InfoSec officer of the IT consulting business consortium for five years; responsible for InfoSec and safety for the entire group
Subsidiary 1	Alex	Consultant manager for 13 years; responsible for safety, security, InfoSec, and management at S1
	Kim	Senior project manager and expert in customer ISIM for three years
	Sam	Specialist for three years in InfoSec and S1's operations
Subsidiary 2	Elia	Consultant manager and successor of Tove; responsible for InfoSec's management for two years
	Tove	Elia's predecessor; responsible for InfoSec and management from 2011 to 2017

[*] Names are fictive.

3.2   Methods for Data Collection and Analyses

This study employed several methods of data collection and analysis in a mixed methods approach. The initial literature review provided the foundation for the subsequent collection and analysis of empirical material at the IT consulting firms.

The empirical material of this study stems from interviews with the aforementioned individuals, who are responsible for ISIM at their respective companies. In addition, it derives from a survey that was administered to the employees of one of the firms.

In view of the sensitivity of information about InfoSec and ISIM in the work of IT consulting firms, the interviews were conducted individually and in person at each expert's workplace to offer a familiar and comfortable environment for the interviewees. The six interviews lasted nearly one hour on average and were recorded and transcribed with permission to facilitate the subsequent detailed analysis [33]. The semi-structured interviews utilized a questionnaire that departed from the standards and regulations in the ISIM context, which constitutes the theoretical framework of this study. The questionnaire was developed in advance and used open-ended questions to ensure both consistent guidance throughout the interviews and an appropriate openness for encouraging interviewees to describe their experiences from their own point of view and identify challenges that they perceive as particularly important. The classification that emerges from the evidence of this study was also informed by issues that were particularly relevant to ISIM, the GDPR, or the NIS and the position of firms as subcontractors [34].

The survey was created in Google Forms and administered to broaden the knowledge base that resulted from the interview study. The survey addressed employees at IT consulting firms who normally work with tasks other than InfoSec or ISIM duties at their companies. The aim of the survey was to determine the extent of familiarity of the employees with InfoSec and ISIM policies. The survey, which departed from the theoretical framework and results of the interviews, consisted of 11 questions that prompted respondents to grade their knowledge of the variables in Table 2. Four of the survey items were based on a six-point Likert scale ranging from 1 (very limited ability) to 6 (deep knowledge), which forced respondents to opt for one direction by omitting the neutral option [35]. The remaining seven questions were categorical (i.e. yes or no), of which four included an option for ignorance or irrelevance (N/A). The sample of employees was recruited from S1, and the survey was internally distributed by the participant Alex through a link to 80 of the employees. This firm was selected because it has the highest number of employees of the three firms. Forty-seven respondents completed the survey, which translated to a response rate of 58.5%.

During the process of data collection and analysis, the insights from the interviews and survey were mutually supportive and enabled the investigation to achieve proper depth and breadth of understanding of the ISIM of IT consulting firms in light of the new regulations and their particular position as subcontractors. Apart from experiences during the interviews, the analyses were based on recordings, transcriptions, and the answers to the survey questions.

The first part of the analysis concentrated on the evidence of the interview study to clarify the content of the interview material [36] and the challenges with which IT consulting firms must contend in the context of ISIM. The analysis synthesized the results of the interviews with regard to the four phases of ISIM. Issues that apply to each of these four phases were treated separately. To ensure both proper InfoSec for the participating individuals and companies and adequate validity of the study, the interviewees were invited to review the analysis and the results as well as assist with completing comments. Therefore, the insights emphasize the crucial challenges that the IT consulting firms encountered in their work with ISIM and the new regulations of the GDPR and NIS.

Table 2. Survey items.

Question	Theoretical concept	Variable	Scale
Estimate your level of knowledge about how to ...			
... avoid an ISB[*]?	ISIM Phase 1	Avoidance	1–6
... detect an ISB?	ISIM Phase 2	PostKNOW	1–6
... decide whether to report an ISB?	ISIM Phase 2	Decide	1–6
How familiar are you with your company's policies for information security?	ISIM Phases 1 & 4	Policy	1–6
Do you experience that GDPR and NIS make it more difficult to decide whether to report an ISB or not?	ISIM Phase 2	Laws	Yes /No / Undecided
Do you know how to report an ISB to your customer?	ISIM Phase 2	HowExt	Yes /No / not relevant
Do you know how to report an ISB in your company?	ISIM Phase 2	HowInt	Yes /No
Would you prefer anonymous reporting of ISBs?	ISIM Phase 2	Anon	Yes /No / Equal
Do you know where you can gain additional information about routines for information security management in your company?	ISIM Phases 1 & 4	Info	Yes /No
Would you hesitate to report an ISB caused by you or your colleague due to negative consequences?	ISIM Phases 2 & 4	NegCon	Yes /No
Do you think you have sufficient knowledge about information security?	ISIM Phases 1–4	KNOW	Yes /No

[*] (ISB = information security breach)

The survey data were subject to two modes of analysis. First, for the Likert scale items, descriptive data for the total sample were presented in the form of means; for the categorical items, the data were expressed as numbers and percentages of respondents who answered *yes* and *no*. Then, the answers were divided into two parts according to the perceptions of respondents in regard to possessing sufficient knowledge of InfoSec. The *yes* and *no* groups were subsequently compared. Because of the relatively small sample size, the material was subject to a descriptive comparison of means and groups instead of to inferential statistics. The analysis of the dataset reveals the levels of accurate knowledge among the employees with respect to several aspects of ISIM.

4 Experiences and Challenges in Incident Management

4.1 Perceptions of InfoSec Management Experts

The following sections present the results of the interviews in accordance with the idealized ISIM process that has been presented above. The participants' experiences highlight crucial challenges in the context of ISIM at IT consulting firms due to the new regulations and the firm's particular position. Table 3 summarizes the perceived challenges. The names of the participants are gender-neutral and fictive to ensure their anonymity.

Phase I: Planning and Preparation. The majority of the participants noted an increase in incidents as a major challenge that has accompanied the entry into force of the GDPR. Mio, Sam, and Elia identified the requirement of reporting an incident within 72 h as particularly problematic, which illuminated further obstacles for the organizations. For example, Mio acknowledged that the business consortium had no routine for meeting this requirement at the time of the interview. One reason was that only two employees had comprehensive knowledge of ISIM, which caused delays in their absence. This issue reflects the shortage of experts in the field, which is a major challenge in the context of InfoSec and ISIM.

Alex and Sam identified another challenge in the integration of activities that relate to planning and preparation into day-to-day work. Assigning a person to full-time work in ISIM and InfoSec appeared to be particularly difficult. They acknowledged that those who are responsible for these tasks often have to operate in various roles, which results in procrastination. Both participants also reported challenges of prioritization in InfoSec mostly due to a focus on chargeable hours and costs within IT consulting firms.

Sam emphasized that IT-consulting firms and their customers must be equally aware of the meaning and effects of the regulations. The participant illustrated this challenge with the example of the maintenance of databases containing personal data that are stored at the IT consulting firm to improve the test results of the systems of the customer. Without proper information management, such proceeding may no longer be appropriate according to the GDPR. Sam elaborated that *"many organizations have received a large amount of personal data over time that has been stored elsewhere and thereafter has been forgotten."*

Meanwhile, Kim reported difficulties with understanding the GDPR and observed substantial variation in interpretations and implementations with regard to several factors, especially the assessment and classification of an incident and its severity to decide whether to report it. In this context, Mio and Alex emphasized the significance of establishing service agreements that assign responsibility to the customer.

A lack of proper routines for ISIM appeared to be another challenge in this phase. The adaption of existing processes to the GDPR, the implementation of these adaptions, and the usage of the processes by poorly informed employees are particularly obstructive. To mitigate these issues, Mio acknowledged employee training on incident reports as a precondition for the implementation of the adapted routines. Kim and Tove have expressed agreement with the benefits of exercising ISIM; however, they also noted difficulty in the preparation and execution of training opportunities due to highly restricted resource allocation.

Such restriction appeared as a reoccurring problem in the ISIM of the IT consulting firms. Although the participants recognized a higher demand for InfoSec from their customers, the firms still struggled to sell this service to their customers or charge a higher amount for work to account for extended security needs. According to the interviewees, the realization that a higher security level may require extra time could arise late and necessitate post-hoc contract extensions. From the perspective of the interviewees, this challenge is critical for IT consulting firms; for example, if the customer encounters an incident within a computer system that the IT consulting firm developed, the event can yield negative consequences for the reputation of the IT consulting firm.

Moreover, Tove indicated that S2 maintains as few devices as possible and noted that the firm lack tools to monitor devices and networks or record incidents. Elia confirmed this remark and specified that the firm is short on qualified personnel in the area of ISIM and consequently a dedicated team for incident response.

Phase II: Detection and Reporting. The uncertainty about both the characteristics of incidents and the details that the employees must report constitutes a major challenge in this phase, according to all participants. As Alex remarked, this uncertainty results in considerable variation in the content of reports. Such individual interpretations have sometimes led to reports on events that can hardly be considered an incident or failure to report a severe incident. Whereas the former creates a large amount of extra work, the latter introduces further problems for analyzing and responding to the incident as well as for the organizational learning and improvement of ISIM. Elia further emphasized the fear of misjudging an incident and its level of seriousness. In the context of GDPR, many participants worried that an incident would later be revealed to be more malicious then initially judged, which might impose costly penalties on the IT consulting firm.

With regard to costs, Sam viewed restricted resources as a barrier to fulfilling the 72-h requirement and explained that an IT consulting firm would balance the costs for extra personnel against the probability that a severe incident will occur. Sam further explained that IT consulting firms may have considerably less time at their disposal, as their position as subcontractors requires that the concerned customer must be involved first. None of the participants mentioned the tightened requirements in the context of the NIS, which requires an initial report to the supervision agency within six hours.

Many of the interviewees perceived major problems with the routines and processes for the detection and reporting phase. Alex expressed general difficulties in developing a process for detection and reporting that could be easily followed by employees while still addressing all of the significant tasks. Otherwise, employees at the subsidiaries would not employ the process. More specifically, Sam and Elia observed a bottleneck in their current process of incident reporting, as only one individual could access reported incidents, which can lead to a serious problem if that person is absent because of, for example, a holiday. Sam added that employees tended to not self-report a detected incident in the dedicated system and would instead contact Sam to delegate the task of reporting, and Sam would then perform the reporting to ensure a follow-up and later organizational learning. To explain this behavior, Sam referred to a lack of awareness among employees regarding the correct execution of reporting. Kim summarized the behavior of employees at IT consulting firms as follows: '*Often, all employees are so solution-oriented that each solves its own problems but maybe does not report that something has happened.*' According to Kim, such behavior can generate a certain risk if the employee tries to solve the problem in an unsecure manner and is convinced by the result even though the incident actually remains active.

With regard to the GDPR, Mio, Kim, and Elia expected further issues in the detection and reporting phase, as new types of incidents may arise from the extended regulations. Mio imagined two particular obstacles: underreporting because incidents were not identified and overreporting out of fear of making a mistake. Elia reported insufficient clarity of the business consortium's policies, which caused uncertainty among employees with respect to protocol for reporting an incident that concerns customer data. In addition, Tove reported that the PC offers policies that explicitly state that incidents must be reported to the central helpdesk function, which reduces the possibility of handle incidents locally. Tove explained, *"it is some kind of a black hole, because even if we report this way, we do not know if the incident is threatened in an adequate manner."* However, Tove argued that employees should direct questions to their responsible manager and added that employee training has addressed incidents at properties but not InfoSec incidents, which warrant more attention in future employee trainings.

According to Mio, anyone might have to deal with an incident, yet employees may feel embarrassed when they must report an incident. Therefore, the PC seeks to ease this burden for the employees and thereby mitigate the severe consequences that may accompany such behavior. In addition, Sam requested enhanced activities for the detection of incidents that relate to the consortium network. S1 has no possibility of monitoring and controlling the network; therefore, Sam noted that the level of analysis and scan of the network should be heightened, which is ultimately a task of the PC. Mio declared that the PC is generally responsible for ISIM, which applies to all subsidiaries in Sweden. Because of the size of the consortium, its cloud-based data storage is constantly under attack. Therefore, the PC permanently monitors the system of the entire group and filters the incoming warnings, such as those from antivirus software of the clients. Mio acknowledged that it remains uncertain whether the incident will be detected if the antivirus software does not provide an alert. Kim expressed another dimension of the dependency on technology as follows: *"we cannot se if an incident had occurred without an internet connection; we have nothing documented how to act in such situations."*

Phase III: Analysis and Response. The participants revealed immense variation in their perceptions with regard to the analysis and response phase. Mio explained that the PC is responsible for analyzing and mitigating incidents that are manually reported by employees and automatically escalated by the monitoring system. Along with all other issues, the incidents that employees report arise at IT support, which initially assesses the problem. A risk of this proceeding is that it may overlook or delay severe incidents.

Moreover, Mio perceived inadequate experience and knowledge to be other potential threats that can prompt improper decisions, particularly if substitutes must perform the assessment. IT-consulting firms must further contend with their role as subcontractors, as, according to Mio, "*we must always be able to deal with two worlds, our own and our customers' routines.*"

Although S1 has established routines for this phase, Alex identified two major challenges. First, Alex is solely responsible for the initial assessment of an incident, which includes the decisions of to whom to escalate the incident and which stakeholders to involve. The second challenge is to gauge the extent to which the business should be limited. Alex appreciated that S1 never encountered an incident that affected a customer but imagined that the effects would be even stronger, which Kim also feared. The appropriate balance between continuing the day-to-day business and heightening the level of security is a matter of concern that Sam also noted. In this context, the absence of a common classification scheme was repeatedly deemed problematic. Kim and Sam perceived insufficiency in the policies and documentation with regard to prioritization, escalation, and response, and they demanded clarity about the expected response to several types of incidents. Sam emphasized that such clarified policies must be available, well-known, and practiced by the employees and noted, "*you will never reach the optimal level; it is the striving after balance between risk and measures. Just this point is the state that you never reach but always aim for.*" To reduce the dependency on a single individual who is capable of performing the crucial tasks of analysis and response, S1 was training another person in decision-making regarding technical issues during an incident, according to the participants from S1.

Tove explained that S2, in contrast to the larger S1, delegates the tasks of this phase to the PC and blamed an overall disinterest in these issues and inappropriate focus on costs for this approach. Tove criticized the absence of feedback on incidents that S2 has detected and reported, as S2 consequently does not know when, how, and to what extent the PC has mitigated an incident. In contrast, Mio stated that feedback is regularly returned to the reporting instance. However, Tove imagined that local intermediates could improve the ISIM process by concentrating attention on important issues and ensuring a rapid response, which may be of particular interest in the context of the GDPR.

Elia recognized further challenges concerning a lack of proper processes and documentation routines for ISIM. Elia suggested an improved structure and thorough documentation of incidents, including "*what we have done...and not only noticing that something has happened*" as well as who has been or must be involved, the applied mitigation activities, and the level of success.

Many of the interviewees indicated that the IT consulting firms tend to apply a stronger focus on security and requirements in relation to customer data and processes, which entails a faster and more comprehensive analysis of and response to incidents that affect customers; meanwhile, they largely disregard their own business.

Phase IV: Learning and Improvement. In general, Mio claimed that the PC has developed an adequate process to both learn from incidents and improve ISIM. Thereby, minor and major incidents are regularly assessed. Yet Mio highlighted the challenge of deciding whether the information should be available for employees with the same level of details as considered during assessment meetings. According to Mio, the major issue in this regard is to provide an appropriate volume and type of information to ensure that employees continue to take part and do not completely stop reading because the content overwhelms them.

Alex and Kim emphasized the importance of the cross-functional group that S1 has established to discuss incidents during regular meetings. However, they commented that the most thorough discussions focused mostly on major incidents. They both argued that minor incidents or occasional events can provide valuable insight, especially as learning opportunities for avoiding major incidents that can develop from more minor events as well as potential misjudgments in the initial phase. Meanwhile, S2 did not conduct meetings to specifically target incidents or ISIM, according to Tove. Rather, incidents comprised one point of the agenda, which implies insufficient attention to incidents and a lack of organizational learning.

Apart from such meetings, Alex reported the challenge of dedicating time and attention to in-depth learning. Therefore, Alex emphasized an improved flow of information and feedback not only from the meetings to employees but also back. Sam similarly discussed the insufficient feedback from the PC and missed opportunities for learning. Sam also expressed regret that the level of information that is provided about incidents precludes reoccurrences of patterns in attacks on networks. Elia added that inter-organizational communication and the sharing of knowledge about incidents and their mitigation are essential sources of further learning. Tove encouraged a rethinking of systems development: *"When we develop IT systems now so must we have security by default and by design, build in GDPR aspects in the systems and also charging customers for that. So, more focus on all dimensions!"*

Mio perceived another difficulty with regard to knowledge management. Preserving the experiences of an expert in the area of ISIM appeared to be a particular challenge compared to the documentation of external knowledge, such as the detection, analysis, and response to incidents, which Mio considered to be a rather easy task. Mio exemplified the complexities of documenting decision-making during ISIM as follows: *"Why did we made this decision then? Or, why did we this or that? This is much harder to document."*

General Issues. The interviewees emphasized some general issues that can apply to all ISIM phases. All participants acknowledged high awareness among employees and customers as vital for obtaining a proper level of InfoSec and mature ISIM.

The participants reported that employees at IT consulting firms typically possess proper knowledge about InfoSec and technology. However, the majority of the interviewees found it essential to regularly repeat the one-hour InfoSec training, which all new staff members undergo, to maintain awareness and adhere to emerging developments. Tove noted that the content of exercises needs to be updated, and employees should receive reminders on a regular basis; otherwise, InfoSec may be secondary to the core business focus. Sam and Mio imagined that employees' basic knowledge on InfoSec may still be insufficient in regard to contending with advanced and well-performed attacks, which can cause difficulties even for InfoSec experts in detecting an intrusion. According to Mio, the initial assessment and classification of an incident requires appropriate knowledge, especially when it relates to classified customer data, and escalation needs to target the correct stakeholder. Sam complained of a low maturity level among employees at S1 with regard to the usage of open networks in public spaces. Employees tended to ignore the discussed risks, particularly when using mobile phones or other portable devices. Sam added that employees seemed to understand the value and sensitivity of information when using a computer but not when using a mobile device. Kim confirmed the view that mobile devices are considered more insecure than computers. In addition, the participants at S1 described another challenge in sharing sensitive information, which employees may exchange via e-mail within the organization or with customers. Even if S1 were to handle e-mails securely, the IT consulting firm could not ensure that customers take sufficient care in this respect, so it was impossible for employees to delete sensitive information. The interviewees also related proper customer awareness to the content of the provided information and databases, which attracted further attention in light of the GDPR.

Three interviewees discussed the focus of IT consulting firms on chargeable hours. Alex expressed difficulty with prioritizing InfoSec in daily business operations because InfoSec and ISIM are continuous processes yet are not perceived as central to the firm's business. Sam noted that InfoSec may be a lower priority because the firms concentrate on tasks that are in demand and yield a profit. Sam illustrated the situation as follows: *We are permanently busy and customers are hunting us with a blowtorch...There is an infinite demand of operation and support and this implies that I do not prioritize InfoSec...If you go out to 30 IT firms and ask when they got started with their work on InfoSec, so would all 30 reply that it started after "this" incident.* Tove confirmed this perception and shared that InfoSec is recognized as a support process and was therefore underprioritized by S2 because of cost- and time-related restrictions.

A strong customer orientation accompanies the focus on chargeable services. The interviewees indicated that the preoccupation of IT consulting firms with customer demands has led to a neglect of internal InfoSec demands that, in prolongation, will have repercussions for customers. Alex perceived an eagerness of IT consulting firms to support customers in addressing their problems, which may in turn delay internal efforts toward security, especially when individuals must fulfill several roles. The occurrence of the GDPR recently intensified this challenge, as both IT consulting firms and their customers need to ensure their compliance with the regulation. Elia remarked that this enhanced focus on customer demands also applies to the context of ISIM and the mitigation of incidents that affect customers. Kim expressed that S1 aims for higher accuracy in its assessments of customer systems, which S1 considers more critical than its own systems. Because they expect further business opportunities, such imbalance in assessments is widely accepted by IT consulting firms, noted Kim. Nevertheless, the majority of interviewees indicated that the primary emphasis on fulfilling customer demands has actually prompted improvements to internal InfoSec and ISIM. Customers who demand a high level of InfoSec force IT consulting firms to dedicate efforts to the development of InfoSec management, which regards both customers and internal systems. Sam argued that the management of InfoSec becomes a focus only when it is an inevitability due to, for example, the occurrence of an incident. Kim summarized, "*it seems that we have much more to do in the field of IT security, but it is hard to know exactly what before something has happen.*"

Several participants expressed the absence of major incidents as a fortunate circumstance. However, Sam noticed a severe challenge in this lack of experience: employees do not understand the importance of properly reporting incidents for the entire ISIM at S2. Both interviewees from S2 perceived a lack of communication with the PC. For example, Tove emphasized the insufficiency of feedback on how the PC mitigates the reported incidents. In reference to the GDPR, Elia reported ambiguity regarding the extent to which the PC would develop policies for the entire consortium or whether the subsidiaries must create their own.

Table 3. Challenges of ISIM.

ISIM Phase	Challenges perceived by InfoSec managers
I: Planning & Preparation	• Avoiding the growing number of incidents related to the GDPR • Shortage of experts and lack of full-time employees for InfoSec • Integrating routines and processes into daily business operations • Understanding the GDPR both internally and externally • Establishing proper customer contracts regarding the GDPR • Creating routines (related to the GDPR) that all employees know and apply • Failure to dedicate training time or trainings to prepare for incidents • Lack of a computer system to record incidents • Absence of an IRT when no employee is qualified to manage incidents • Convincing customers to pay for InfoSec, especially to account for tightened regulations
II: Detection & Reporting	• Uncertainty, especially after the GDPR, concerning which events constitute an incident and which information employees must report • Fear of misjudging an incident • Adhering to the requirement of timely reporting (e.g. within 72 h) • No easy and adequate process for incident reporting • Bottleneck in the process of incident reporting • Uncertainty over whom employees should contact in the event of an incident that affects a customer • Embarrassment of reporting incidents • Insufficient system scanning from the central level
III: Analysis & Response	• Escalation of incidents • Lack of knowledge and training, especially among substitutes • Gauging the extent to which daily business operations must be tightened in case of an incident and particularly if it affects a customer • Limited policies and routines to guide employees in acting and prioritizing various types of incident • Ensuring that policies about routines and processes are available, known, and practiced • Inadequate documentation of incidents and mitigation activities • No local analysis or response because of costs, which must be changed

(*continued*)

Table 3. (*continued*)

ISIM Phase	Challenges perceived by InfoSec managers
	• Lower security consideration and prioritization of internal data and incidents compared to external issues, i.e. data and incidents that relate to a customer
IV: Learning & Improvement	• Balancing the content and scope of employee information for enhancing awareness of, commitment to, and compliance with policies • Misjudging minor incidents or extraordinary events that have the potential to become an incident • Lack of meetings dedicated solely to incidents • Allotting sufficient time to thoroughly review incidents • Information sharing among all personnel • Lack of feedback from the central level on incidents that relate to networks • Insufficient external communication and knowledge sharing • Organizational knowledge and experience management
General Issues	• Obtaining a high awareness of InfoSec among customers and employees • Focus on chargeable hours, which hampers the implementation of continuous InfoSec work • Excessively strong customer focus, which neglects internal demands • Lack of (experience with) major incidents • Insufficient communication with the parent company

4.2   Knowledge of InfoSec Among Consultants

Tables 4, 5, and 6 contain the results of the survey, which are based on the variables from Table 2 (Y = Yes, N = No, U = undecided, not relevant, equal) in Sect. 3.2. As noted, 47 employees of S1 completed the survey. Of those respondents, only 12 (25.5%) perceived their knowledge of InfoSec to be sufficient. As evident in Table 4, the means of this group ("KnowYES") were higher than those of the other group ("KnowNO") for all Likert scale items.

Table 4. Survey results: means and standard deviations.

Question	Total (n = 47)	KnowYES (n = 12)	KnowNO (n = 35)
Avoidance	4.49 ± 0.9	4.83 ± 0.58	4.37 ± 0.97
PostKNOW	3.77 ± 1.13	4.42 ± 0.52	3.54 ± 1.2
Decide	3.89 ± 1.1	4.33 ± 0.89	3.74 ± 1.12
Policy	3.68 ± 0.96	4 ± 1.2	3.57 ± 0.85

Table 5 reveals that many respondents were undecided on effects of the GDPR and NIS, which might be explained by the relative newness of the laws. Most respondents knew how to report an incident to a customer. A majority were indifferent toward the anonymous reporting of incidents, although 21.3% would prefer anonymous reporting. The "KnowYES" group yielded a slightly higher number of "YES" responses compared to the "KnowNO" group (see Table 5).

Table 6 indicates that a majority of respondents (89.4%) knew where to acquire information about routines for InfoSec management in the IT consulting firm. Moreover, despite potential negative consequences for themselves or their colleagues, the same percentage would not hesitate to report an incident. A majority (93.6%) was also aware of how to internally report an incident. Nevertheless, as the results in Table 5 demonstrate, the respondents indicated lower confidence (70.2%) in regard to incidents that affect customers. The "KnowYES" group displayed slightly higher values compared to the "KnowNO" group with respect to these variables as well.

Table 5. Survey results from questions with three choices.

Question	KnowYES (n = 12)			KnowNO (n = 35)			Total (n = 47)		
Laws	Y	N	U	Y	N	U	Y	N	U
	2	7	3	3	13	19	5	20	22
	16.7%	58.3%	25%	8.6%	37.1%	54.3%	10.6%	42.6%	46.8%
HowExt	Y	N	U	Y	N	U	Y	N	U
	9	1	2	24	9	2	33	10	4
	75%	8.3%	16.7%	68.6%	25.7%	5.7%	70.2%	21.3%	8.5%
Anon	Y	N	U	Y	N	U	Y	N	U
	3	2	7	7	4	24	10	6	31
	25%	16.7%	58.3%	20%	11.4%	11.4%	21.3%	12.8%	66%

Table 6. Survey results from questions with three choices.

Question	KnowYES (n = 12)		KnowNO (n = 35)		Total (n = 47)	
Info	Y	N	Y	N	Y	N
	11 (91.7%)	1 (8.3%)	31 (88.6%)	4 (11.4%)	42 (89.4%)	5 (10.6%)
NegCon	Y	N	Y	N (1m)	Y	N (1m)
	1 (8.3%)	11 (91.7%)	3 (8.6%)	31 (88.6%)	4 (8.5%)	42 (89.4%)
HowInt	Y	N	Y	N	Y	N
	12 (100%)	0 (0%)	32 (91.4%)	3 (8.6%)	44 (93.6%)	3 (6.4%)

5   Characterization of InfoSec Incidents

In the interviews, the decision of whether an incident warrants reporting arose as a reoccurring challenge. The results of the survey further illustrate that IT consulting firms lack knowledge of the character of incidents. The interviewees sought to enhance employee awareness through training scenarios regarding, for example, how to react when a mobile phone is lost or a power failure occurs at the office; still, the timely recognition of incidents remained a challenge. The interviews revealed the following several dimensions that can characterize an incident.

- Organizational level: whose area of responsibility is affected?
- Security level: which level of InfoSec applies, and which requirements exist?
- Knowledge level: which previous knowledge exists about the incident?
- InfoSec attribute: which InfoSec attribute is affected?
- Concerned asset: which asset is affected?
- Time frame: when did the incident start, and how long has it been underway?
- Propagation: how quickly does the incident propagate?
- Impact: what is the scope of effects?
- Mitigation: To what extent must measures must be taken?
- Severity: how serious is the incident?

Comprehensive documentation throughout the ISIM process must collect additional data about mitigation measurements, involved expertise, and the eventual level of success. The evaluation of a finally treated incident should then take account of the consequences, including costs and savings, possible alternative proceedings, and the decision-making process that was applied. Implementing a method for a structured decision analysis could enhance decision-making about future mitigation measures should a similar incident occur.

An incident classification can facilitate a comparison of emerging incidents and their treatments with previously handled instances. Moreover, it can provide a benchmarking tool for IT consulting firms in their ISIM evaluations, which consider not only costs for preventing and mitigating incidents but also possible alternative endings. Thus, such assessments indicate the benefits of vigorously acting InfoSec management and ISIM. The proposed classification scheme in Table 7 assigns several attributes to each dimension of an incident. These attributes constitute a scale from zero to five for each dimension, whereby zero signifies a very mild type of an incident and five represents a worst-case scenario. An incident at zero may concern a public document that fell on the ground on its way to the bin; such case can be easily mitigated and does not require reporting. If one or more dimensions appear to be unknown, then the incident ascends in the ranking. Accordingly, if no dimension is known, then the detected incident would score a five, which would require full efforts – at least initially – for mitigating the incident. An incident's ranking can be adjusted as new information becomes available.

Table 7. Classification scheme of InfoSec incidents.

Dimension	Attributes
Organisational level	0-none, 1-local, 2-subsidiary, 3-business group, 4-customer, 5- N/A
Security level	0-public, 1-internal, 2-restricted, 3-confidential, 4-secret, 5-N/A
Knowledge level	0-very high, 1-high, 2-medium, 3-low, 4-very low, 5-N/A
InfoSec attribute	0-none, 1-availability, 2-integrity, 3-confidentiality, 4-privacy, 5-N/A
Concerned asset	0-property, 1-device, 2-network, 3-human, 4-data, 5-N/A
Time frame	0-seconds, 1-minutes, 2-hours, 3-days, 4-months, 5-N/A
Propagation	0-very slow, 1-slow, 2-medium, 3-quick, 4-very quick, 5-N/A
Impact	0-very limited, 1-limited, 2-serious, 3-major, 4-massive, 5-N/A
Mitigation	0-documented, 1-basic, 2-multiple, 3-advanced, 4-extensive, 5-N/A
Severity	0-marginal, 1-minor, 2-critical, 3-major, 4-catastrophic 5-N/A

In addition to incident classification, IT consulting firms can establish particular thresholds regarding reporting requirements or who is permitted and responsible for mitigating incidents of various levels. Such thresholds could respond to particular dimensions or a cumulative index that specifies the threat level of the incident. For this purpose, the attributes can be cumulated in several ways, including the use of statistical measures, such as the mode, mean, or median, and weighted measures.

The classification of InfoSec incidents can support further opportunities for IT consulting firms. For example, it could allow the compiled documentation of incidents to be searchable for different incident types, which would in turn enable internal and external auditors to assess and evaluate emerging incidents, dedicated mitigation efforts, established policies and routines, and the entire ISIM. Such concentrated assessment could inform improvements to InfoSec in general and ISIM in particular as well as local, internal, and inter-organizational learning (Fig. 1).

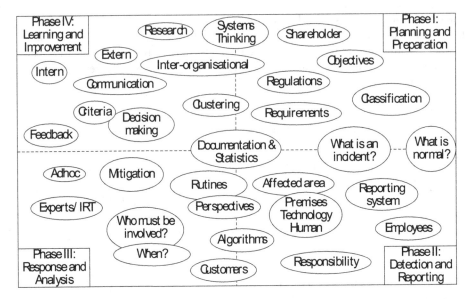

Fig. 1. Activities, means, and stakeholders that can be informed by a structured classification and documentation of InfoSec incidents

Prolonged and widespread use of a similar classification scheme could additionally facilitate the development of an incident database in which incidents and mitigation measures are searchable and comparable. Such database could also contribute local, regional, national, and international statistics about the branch, severity, and types of incidents, for example, which can equip scholars and practitioners to conduct further research and development.

6   Implications

The results of this study demonstrate that ISIM poses a variety of challenges for IT consulting firms. Such challenges have a broad range of possible consequences for the business operations of both IT consulting firms and their customers. This study of Swedish IT consulting firms has identified particular issues that reoccurred in several contexts and thus warrant certain attention:

1. Fixation on costs
2. Trust in technical measurements
3. Lack of documentation
4. Low understanding of and adaption to legal regulations
5. Poor inter-organizational communication and collaboration
6. Insufficient knowledge of the character and proper treatment of incidents.

First, the fixation on costs led to constant oversight of the benefits of proper InfoSec for companies in terms of reducing the negative effects of an incident. Therefore, the findings support the results of [31], which has indicated that costs can easily outrank InfoSec and structured ISIM as a priority. As [27] has also illustrated, such diminished importance of InfoSec further lowered the attention to preparing and executing employee training for improving ISIM. This study noted the consequences of such preoccupation with costs in the smaller subsidiary, S2, which manifested in the insufficiency of documentation, processes, personnel, and technical support for ISIM. Another issue that accompanied the cost focus is that individuals at IT consulting firms valued ISIM of customer systems more highly than that of their own systems. Such imbalance may yield additional severe consequences, such as damage to reputation or customer relations, if an incident propagates across systems. Therefore, the new regulations require more attention to a comprehensive risk analysis for InfoSec.

Second, this study has declined the argument of [30, 31] that the character and number of warnings of monitoring systems cause difficulties. Instead, it is necessary to question the minimization of the number of warnings by filter mechanisms. For example, in the present study, the PC monitored the entire system of the consortium and purchased the filtering of warnings. In combination with a minimized number of system scans, these measures produced a manageable number of warnings. However, this trust in technical measures can be dangerous, as it may allow incidents to proceed undetected for an unwanted period and thereby deliver massive consequences. This study has further indicated that subsidiaries lack knowledge of specific results of the monitoring. Therefore, employee awareness can benefit from improved modes of communication and knowledge transfer with regard to the limitations of automatized monitoring. According to the interviewees, the rarity of experts in InfoSec also represents a challenge, as their well-documented knowledge can become an increasing challenge in a situation that requires specific competence and experience [29].

Third, as noted above, a lack of documentation hampered any structured ISIM within organizations or in inter-organizational cooperation. Previous research, international standards, and best practices have continuously advocated for proper documentation of incidents and the ISIM process. However, this study reveals that the maturity of the documentation remains significantly low, which constitutes a massive challenge in the ISIM of IT consulting firms. Such inadequacy of documentation accompanies the insufficiency of knowledge about the following aspects: the importance of documentation; policies, processes, and regulations; the designation of responsibility within the organization and in cooperation with external stakeholders; how to report and which aspects to include [7]; how to analyze and respond to incidents, especially major ones [28]; and the means of documentation, communication, and feedback.

This study has demonstrated uncertainty among InfoSec experts and employees that may relate to the lack of knowledge and documentation in IT consulting firms. Therefore, the proposed characterization scheme in this study can support improvements. This incident classification can be a catalyst for ISIM in its entirety by facilitating more structured documentation, which involves not only a characterization of the incident but also details about its mitigation and the underlying decision-making process. Comprehensive documentation must include the best treatment and success factors while also elaborating on poor decisions and failures to enhance learning within and between organizations. The results particularly encourage employee trainings that focus on secure practices with respect to mobile devices and their use within public networks. In addition, the model for characterizing incidents can impart structure to meetings for discussing certain events and minor incidents, which reflects another means of enhancing awareness, compliance, and competence.

Fourth, the individuals at IT consulting firms mentioned a major challenge that relates to the tightened regulations of the NIS and GDPR, which amplified uncertainty among both the employees and the individuals who are responsible for ISIM. Despite such ambiguity in interpreting the legal requirements, the policies, routines, and agreements with customers and subcontractors must adapt to current and further developments of the regulations. This study recognizes that IT consulting firms extensively focus on the GDPR as well as the avoidance of costly penalties for inadequate compliance. Moreover, the results of this study reveal an exclusive concentration on the GDPR and complete neglect of the importance of the NIS for the ISIM of IT consulting firms. Apart from the scarcity of experienced personnel in the field, the fixation on costs can be another impactful factor for such orientation, as the GDPR threatens severe penalties, whereas the NIS does not.

Fifth, this study evidences that decision making about serious measures to mitigating an incident, such as the shutdown of a customer system, was perceived as an uncomfortable assignment that requires stable inter-organizational relations. Even though the results emphasize the significance of InfoSec, daily business operations seek to continue service provision with as few disturbances as possible. The inherent ambiguity of this discrepancy complicates decision-making about adequate measures and, when necessary, communication with the concerned customer and supervision agency. Although this study could not investigate such trustful relations in practice, one of the participants acknowledged the potential for inter-organizational sharing of experiences and knowledge. In such context, the proposed characterization scheme could facilitate a structured exchange and offer a benchmark regarding incidents and mitigation measures. Meanwhile, the assignment of corresponding attributes during incident classification can limit access to more detailed documentation. Such enhanced exchange of knowledge through statistics and documentation could improve inter-organizational relations and ISIM at participating organizations.

Finally, uncertainties about the character of an incident and its correct management emerged as central challenges in the ISIM of IT consulting firms. Participants were particularly concerned with the detection of an incident, which includes the realization of a difference from the normal state. Their uncertainty also encompassed knowledge of when, what, how, and to whom an incident should be reported as well as the necessary mitigation measures. Such confusion and lack of knowledge implies that policies and employee training are absent, insufficient, or improperly understood among employees [7, 12]. The findings of this study indicate that employees tended to underpredict seemingly minor incidents [5, 27]. Therefore, such types of incident mitigation could illustrate how to prevent a minor incident from developing into a serious one. The lack of experience with serious incidents at the participating IT consulting firms may have expounded their ignorance of such learning opportunities. In addition, the cost focus may be another reason for this underestimation of minor incidents. The results demonstrate the difficulty of retaining expert knowledge in the organization. In addition to simultaneously involving novices and experts in the mitigation process to learn practices from each other [31], the proposed incident characterization scheme combined with detailed descriptions of concrete activities, including their level of success, could facilitate the establishment of a structured documentation base that allows for knowledge transfer and benchmarking.

7 Concluding Remarks

This study has contributed valuable knowledge to the field of InfoSec and on ISIM at IT consulting firms in particular. First, to address the lack of empirical studies in this context, the results provide insight into experiences and challenges in ISIM at a Swedish consortium of IT consulting firms. The inquiry has particularly examined their specific position as subcontractors. The findings of the interviews with InfoSec experts in the firms and a survey with employees at one of the selected subsidiaries have accentuated practical challenges of ISIM. The main concerns were an obsession with costs, a lack of adequate policies, guidelines, processes, and documentation, and insufficient knowledge of the character of an incident and its proper treatment. The lack of experience with managing major or catastrophic incidents in combination with the recent GDPR and NIS regulations pose a massive challenge for IT consulting firms. The matter of proper interpretation and fulfillment of requirements, such as timely reporting to a supervision agency, the customers of the IT consulting firms, or both, appears to be as critically concerning as the appropriate distribution and balance of responsibilities between the firms and their customers.

This paper has proposed a new classification scheme with 10 criteria, which were substantiated by the findings of the empirical investigation. Applying these criteria to an event provides a solid basis on which decision-makers can assess the incident management. This model for classifying an incident constitutes a tool for comparing emerging incidents and their treatments. Thus, the model can also offer a benchmarking tool for other organisations than IT consulting firms to evaluate their ISIM.

Further developments in theory and practice can support the implementation and improvement of the classification scheme in a variety of contexts and organizations and by involving a larger number of participants. Nevertheless, the enhanced understanding of ISIM challenges for IT consulting firms in regard to their specific position as subcontractors as well as the model to classify InfoSec incidents both provide valuable insights for organizations that seek to improve their ISIM in developing internal and inter-organizational processes.

References

1. Blix, F.: 1177-leak in Sweden: 2.7 million recorded healthcare phone calls leaked online (complete write-up). https://www.linkedin.com/pulse/1177-leak-sweden-27-million-recorded-healthcare-phone-fredrik-blix
2. Sones, M.: Sweden accidentally leaks nearly all citizens' personal details. http://www.israelnationalnews.com/News/News.aspx/233057

3. The Local Sweden: Swedish authority handed over 'keys to the Kingdom' in IT security slip-up. https://www.thelocal.se/20170717/swedish-authority-handed-over-keys-to-the-kingdom-in-it-security-slip-up

4. Olsson, J.: Svenska Kraftnät medger säkerhetsbrister. https://www.svt.se/nyheter/inrikes/svenska-kraftnat-medger-sakerhetsbrister

5. Ahmad, A., Hadgkiss, J., Ruighaver, A.B.: Incident response teams – challenges in supporting the organisational security function. Comput. Secur. **31**, 643–652 (2012)

6. Ab Rahman, N.H., Choo, K.-K.R.: A survey of information security incident handling in the cloud. Comput. Secur. **49**, 45–69 (2015)

7. Hove, C., Tårnes, M., Line, M.B., Bernsmed, K.: Information security incident management. Identified practice in large organizations. In: Freiling, F. (ed.) 8th International Conference on IT Security Incident Management and IT Forensics, pp. 27–46. IEEE, Piscataway (2014)

8. Tøndel, I.A., Line, M.B., Jaatun, M.G.: Information security incident management Current practice as reported in the literature. Comput. Secur. **45**, 42–57 (2014)

9. Cusick, J.J., Ma, G.: Creating an ITIL inspired incident management approach. roots, response, and results. In: Gaspary, L.P. (ed.) 2010 IEEE/IFIP Network Operations and Management Symposium workshops, pp. 142–148. IEEE, Piscataway (2010)

10. Bailey, J., Kandogan, E., Haber, E., Maglio, P.P.: Activity-based management of IT service delivery. In: Kandogan, E. (ed.) Symposium on Computer Human Interaction for the Management of Information Technology. ACM, New York (2007)

11. European Union (EU): Regulation 2016/679 of the European Parliament and of the Council of 27 April 2016 on the protection of natural persons with regard to the processing of personal data and on the free movement of such data, and repealing Directive 95/46/EC (General Data Protection Regulation) (2016)

12. Line, M.B.: A case study. Preparing for the smart grids - identifying current practice for information security incident management in the power industry. In: Morgenstern, H. (ed.) 7th International Conference on IT Security Incident Management and IT Forensics, pp. 26–32. IEEE, Piscataway (2013)

13. O'Brien, R.: Privacy and security. Bus. Inf. Rev. **33**, 81–84 (2016)

14. Swedish Civil Contingencies Agency (MSB): Årsrapport it-incidentrapportering 2018. En sammanställning och analys av de statliga myndigheternas it-incidentrapportering (2019)

15. Swedish Civil Contingencies Agency (MSB): Årsrapport it-incidetnrapportering 2016 (2017)

16. Nyman, M., Große, C.: Are you ready when it counts? IT Consulting firm's information security incident management. In: Proceedings of the 5th International Conference on Information Systems Security and Privacy, pp. 26–37. SCITEPRESS - Science and Technology Publications (2019)

17. International Organization for Standardization (ISO): ISO/IEC 27000:2018

18. Große, C.: Towards an Integrated Framework for Quality and Information Security Management in Small Companies. Luleå (2016)

19. European Union Agency For Network and Information Security (ENISA): Guidance and gaps analysis for European standardisation. Privacy standards in the information security context (2018)

20. Tankard, C.: What the GDPR means for businesses. Netw. Secur. **2016**, 5–8 (2016)

21. European Union (EU): Directive 2016/1148 of the European Parliament and of the Council of 6 July 2016 concerning measures for a high common level of security of network and information systems across the Union (2016)

22. Swedish Civil Contingencies Agency (MSB): Vägledning om rapportering av incidenter för leverantörer av digitala tjänster enligt NISregleringen. MSB 2018-13472 (2018)

23. Swedish Civil Contingencies Agency (MSB): Nationellt system för it-incidentrapportering (2012)
24. International Organization for Standardization (ISO): ISO/IEC 27035:2016. Information technology – Security techniques – Information security incident management (2016)
25. Cichonski, P., Millar, T., Grance, T., Scarfone, K.: NIST 800-61, Revision 2: Computer Security Incident Handling Guide. National Institute of Standards and Technology, Gaithersburg (2012)
26. European Union Agency For Network and Information Security (ENISA): Reference Incident Classification Taxonomy. Task Force Status and Way Forward (2018)
27. Bartnes, M., Moe, N.B., Heegaard, P.E.: The future of information security incident management training. A case study of electrical power companies. Comput. Secur. **61**, 32–45 (2016)
28. Jaatun, M.G., et al.: A study of information security practice in a critical infrastructure application. In: Rong, C., Jaatun, M.G., Ma, J., Sandnes, F.E., Yang, L.T. (eds.) Autonomic and Trusted Computing, 5060, pp. 527–539. Springer, Berlin (2008). https://doi.org/10.1007/978-3-540-69295-9_42
29. Werlinger, R., Muldner, K., Hawkey, K., Beznosov, K.: Preparation, detection, and analysis. The diagnostic work of IT security incident response. Info. Manage. Comp. Secur. **18**, 26–42 (2010)
30. Werlinger, R., Hawkey, K., Muldner, K., Jaferian, P., Beznosov, K.: The challenges of using an intrusion detection system. In: Cranor, L.F. (ed.) Proceedings of the 4th Symposium on Usable Privacy and Security, p. 107. ACM, New York (2008)
31. Werlinger, R., Hawkey, K., Beznosov, K.: An integrated view of human, organizational, and technological challenges of IT security management. Info. Manage. Comp. Secur. **17**, 4–19 (2009)
32. Bryman, A., Bell, E.: Business Research Methods. University Press, Oxford (2015)
33. Denscombe, M.: The Good Research Guide. For Small-Scale Social Research Projects. McGraw-Hill Education, Maidenhead (2014)
34. Johannesson, P., Perjons, E.: An Introduction to Design Science. Springer, Cham (2014). https://doi.org/10.1007/978-3-319-10632-8
35. Croasmun, J.T., Ostrom, L.: Using likert-type scales in the social sciences. J. Adult Educ. **40**, 19–22 (2011)
36. Schutt, R.K.: Investigating the Social World. The Process and Practice of Research. Sage, Thousand Oaks (2015)

Evaluation of Side-Channel Key-Recovery Attacks on LoRaWAN End-Device

Kazuhide Fukushima[1(✉)], Damien Marion[2], Yuto Nakano[1], Adrien Facon[2], Shinsaku Kiyomoto[1], and Sylvain Guilley[2]

[1] KDDI Research, Inc., 2–1–15 Ohara, Fujimino, Saitama 356–8502, Japan
ka-fukushima@kddilabs.jp

[2] Secure-IC S.A.S., 80 Avenue des Buttes de Coësmes Rennes, 35700 Cesson-Sévigné, France

Abstract. IoT devices have come into widespread use. The rapid growth of the IoT market is expected in the field of automobiles and transportation, medical and health care, and industry. Data protection and integrity are critical for IoT-based services in order to maintain the security and privacy of them. Low-power wide-area (LPWA) is a wireless communication technology designed for IoT applications and end-devices requiring low cost, long battery life, wide-area coverage, and high system capacity. LoRaWAN is an open standard for LPWA and achieves data protection and integrity by using encryption and message integrity code (MIC). Many studies have pointed out security issues, and attacks against LPWA protocols and have proposed solutions to improve security against such attacks. However, side-channel analysis techniques can directly recover secret information from a device. In this paper, we evaluate the applicability of a side-channel analysis to a real LoRaWAN end-device. Our experiments attempt to recover AES-128 keys to encrypt frame payload and calculate the message integrity code (MIC) for the encrypted payload based on a correlation power analysis, which is a type of side-channel analysis. The 260 electromagnetic(EM)-leakage traces entirely recover the 16-byte key for the frame payload encryption, and the 140 EM-leakage traces recover the 12 bytes of the 16-byte key for MIC generation. Furthermore, we show that our key recovery attack is applicable in real LoRaWAN protocols. Our attack can entirely recover the root key AppKey in LoRaWAN v1.0 and a root key NwkKey in LoRaWAN v1.1.

Keywords: Internet of things (IoT) · Low-power wide-area (lpwa) · Lorawan side-channel analysis · Correlation power analysis (cpa) · electromagnetic(EM)-leakage · AES

1 Introduction

Rapid growth of the IoT market is expected in the areas of automobiles and transportation, where the use of connected-vehicles is expanding, the medical

A preliminary version of this paper [7] appeared in Proceedings of the 5th International Conference on Information Systems Security and Privacy (ICISSP 2019).

field, where we see growth in the use of digital devices for healthcare, and in industry (including factories, infrastructure, and logistics), where we are witnessing the expansion of smart factories and smart cities. IHS Markit [10] predicts that the number of connected IoT devices worldwide will increase by 12% on average annually.

Low-power wide-area (LPWA) is a term used to describe wireless communication technologies for IoT applications. These technologies are characterized by low cost, long battery life (or low power consumption), wide-area coverage, and high system capacity. LPWA technologies can be roughly categorized into the licensed and unlicensed spectrum. LoRaWAN [17] and Sigfox [21] are typical examples of protocols that run in the unlicensed spectrum, and a license is not needed to build a network and provide services. LoRaWAN and LoRa are open standards designed by the LoRa Alliance. LoRaWAN defines the communication protocol and system architecture in the medium access control (MAC) layer for the network, while LoRa defines the physical layer or wireless modulation that enables wide-area coverage. Everyone can build LoRaWAN network can be built by purchasing equipment similar to a wireless LÀN. Conversely, only one company in each country can build a Sigfox network according to the policy of the Sigfox company. LTE-M [9] and NB-IoT [1] operate over the licensed spectrum, and only mobile operators build a network and provide services. Their advantage is that existing LTE base stations can be used to build a new LPWA network.

Data protection and integrity are critical for IoT-based services. For example, user privacy may be compromised by location information and activity information acquired from a wearable device. As another motivating example, an air conditioner can be manipulated maliciously by modifying the value of the temperature sensor, which can lead to panic in crowded places. In many cases, LPWA technologies achieve data protection and integrity by using encryption and message integrity code (MIC). However, many attacks against the vulnerabilities of LPWA protocols have been proposed, and some of them are potential threats as they can extract the secret keys. Furthermore, side-channel analysis technologies exist that have the capacity to recover secret information from devices by using side-channel information, including timing information, power consumption, electromagnetic leaks, sound, and heat.

Our Contributions. We evaluate the applicability of a side-channel analysis technique to a real LoRaWAN end-device. Our experiments attempt to recover the AES-128 keys from the EM-leakage traces produced by the AES-128 encryption algorithm payload encryption process and MIC generation process for data transmission on a real LPWA end-device. The 350 electromagnetic(EM)-leakage traces of payload encryption process can recover the entire AES key. The required number of EM-traces can be reduced to 260 using a band-pass filtering technique. To the best of our knowledge, this is the first paper that describes a key recovery attack from a real LPWA device with less than 300 EM-leakage traces. The 140 EM-leakage traces of the MIC generation process can recover 12-byte of the AES key, except for the first four bytes. The remaining four bytes can be obtained by brute-force guessing with 2^{32} computational complexity to recover the entire key. Furthermore, we show that our key recovery attack is applicable in real LoRaWAN protocols. Our attack can entirely recover the root key AppKey in LoRaWAN v1.0 and a root key NwkKey in LoRaWAN v1.1.

A preliminary version of this paper [7] appeared in the Proceedings of the 5th International Conference on Information Systems Security and Privacy (ICISSP 2019). This full-version provides a discussion regarding the applicability to real LoRaWAN v1.0 and v1.1 while the previous paper demonstrated potential threats of side-channel key-recovery attacks against payload encryption and MIC generation processes. Furthermore, we add some omitted data in the preliminary paper, including the correlation between the EM-leakage and Hamming weight for all the bytes of the recovered key.

2   Related Work

State-of-art studies have pointed out security issues, and attacks against LPWA protocols and have proposed solutions to improve security against such attacks. Most of them target the LoRaWAN protocol since it is an open standard, and the specification is publicly available. Girard [8] pointed out the issues in key provisioning for LoRaWAN end-devices. Zulian [25] and Tomasin et al. [23] demonstrated the possibility of a replay attack against the join procedure in LoRaWAN. The replay attack is due to the limitation in the variety of the DevNonce generated by an end-device, and theoretically and experimentally showed that random number generators in a real end-device are not secure. Na et al. [20] argued that LoRaWAN was vulnerable to a similar replay attack and described countermeasures, and Lee et al. [15] proposed a bit-flipping attack against an encrypted frame payload using AES-CTR and a countermeasure. Yang et al. [24] discovered several vulnerabilities of LoRaWAN and demonstrated five types of attacks: 1) replay attack leads to a selective DoS attack, 2) plaintext recovery attack, 3) malicious message modification, 4) falsification of delivery reports, and 5) battery exhaustion attack. A selective jamming attack against the LoRa physical layer and its countermeasure is proposed by Aras et al. [2]. Butun et al. [4] demonstrated five types of attacks: 1) RF jamming attack, 2) replay attack, 3) Beacon (Class B) synchronization attack, 4) network traffic analysis and 5) man-in-the-middle (MITM) attack against the latest version: LoRaWAN specification v1.1 released on Oct 11, 2017.

Side-channel analysis can recover secrets of a device based on side-channel information such as sound, heat, timing information, power consumption, and electromagnetic-leakage. Some existing studies target IoT end-devices or resource-constrained devices. Kocher et al. [13] were the first to propose a side-channel attack. They leveraged a device's power consumption on a device and demonstrated that a DES key can be recovered. Their attack contains a simple power analysis (SPA), differential power analysis (DPA), and higher-order DPA (HO-DPA). Messerges et al. [18] theoretically derived the signal-to-noise ratio (SNR) in a DPA attack against DES proposed by Kocher et al., and improved the DPA to d-bit DPA by focusing on multiple bits in the S-Box of DES.

A DPA attack against the scalar multiplication on an elliptic curve-based cryptosystem (ECC) was proposed by Joye and Tymen [12]. Itoh et al. [11] proposed a DPA attack focusing on the register address of an ECC. Brier et al. [3] were the first to study a correlation power analysis (CPA) based on a Hamming distance leakage model. The CPA utilizes the correlation between the leakage model of a sensitive value and its power consumption or electromagnetic(EM)-leakage. The Hamming weight leakage model, proposed by Kocher et al. [13] and Messerges et al. [18], assumes that leakage through the side-channel depends on the number of bits set in the data. The leakage value T_{HW} of data X can be formulated as

$$T_{HW} = a\mathsf{HW}(X) + c + \sigma$$

where a is a coefficient, $\mathsf{HW}(\cdot)$ is the Hamming weight function, c is a constant leakage, and σ is noise. The Hamming distance leakage model assumes that leakage depends on the number of bits switching from one state to another. The leakage for a bit switching from 0 to 1 and from 1 to 0 are assumed to be same. The leakage value T_{HD} in the case where data X change to X' can be formulated as

$$T_{HD} = a\mathsf{HW}(X \oplus X') + c + \sigma.$$

Komano et al. [14] proposed a build-in determined sub-key CPA (BS-CPA) that finds a new sub-key by using the previously determined sub-keys recursively and demonstrated that it can recover a DES key with fewer power traces than the original CPA. Clavier et al. [5] applied a CPA to first-order protected AES implementations and showed that the CPA requires fewer power traces than classical second-order DPA. Dinu and Kizhvatov [6] showed that a DPA can recover a partial AES-CCM key on a wireless microcontroller. Tawalbeh and Somani [22] evaluated the security of AES, ECC, and RSA against timing and fault side-channel attacks and showed countermeasures for IoT implementation. A side-channel evaluation platform for IoT end-devices is proposed by Moukarzel et al. [19].

3   Key Recovery Attack

We propose a key recovery attack based on correlation power analysis, a type of side-channel analysis. Our attack is applicable to general LoRaWAN end-devices. The goal and assumptions are described, and then the details of the attack are explained.

3.1   Goal

LoRaWAN protocol uses Advanced Encryption System (AES), a symmetric encryption algorithm to achieve the security and integrity of transmitted data. Data protection is ensured using AES-CTR, and message integrity is guaranteed by the computing of a message integrity code (MIC) using AES-CMAC. Our key recovery attack thus targets AES-128 keys for payload encryption and

MIC generation stored in an end-device. An attacker can decrypt or forge all messages and commands transmitted between the server and end-devices, or connect malicious end-devices to the LoRaWAN network by abusing these keys.

3.2 Assumptions

An attacker as a security evaluator assumed to be able to access plaintext. The attacker does not have to take control of the plaintext and the corresponding ciphertext. This condition can be met if the attacker knows the data format and the data itself. For example, an end-device sends current temperatures periodically, and the attacker can guess the plaintext using a separate thermometer. Another way to meet the assumption is to access an API for data transmission on an end-device. Some LoRaWAN libraries provide APIs for data transmission that takes plaintext messages or commands as input. Our key recovery attack is based on correlation power analysis and requires multiple pairs of plaintext and ciphertext. This attack is not applicable to fixed messages such as prefixed values in a protocol header since the Pearson correlation coefficient cannot be calculated. However, we can recover the keys and all the messages from a small number of partial plaintext. In our experiments, we modify the source code of a LoRaWAN end-device to set a trigger signal at the first round of AES-128. However, modification of the source code is not essential if different EM-leakage traces can be appropriately aligned along the time axis.

Our proposed attack is focused on the first round of AES-128, using the knowledge of the plaintext and guessing each byte of the AES-128 key independently. Guessing each byte of the first round key allows each byte of the output of the S-Box to be recovered independently at the first round. The first round of AES-128 consists of four operations: AddRoundKey, SubBytes, ShiftRows and MixColumns. Figure 1 shows the detailed processes of the first round of AES-128.

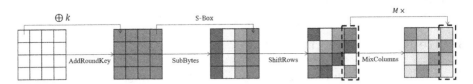

Fig. 1. First round of AES-128.

3.3 Key Recovery Attack

We now describe the key recovery attacks in detail. Our key recovery attack consists of a leakage identification phase and key recovery phase.

Leakage Identification. The first phase of the attack is to identify the EM-leakage traces produced by the AES-128 encryption algorithm. The EM-leakage of hundred executions with the same key and plaintext has been averaged. This process permits an increase in the signal-to-noise ratio (SNR) defined as

$$\text{SNR} = \frac{P_{\text{AES-128}}}{P_{\text{Noise}}},$$

where $P_{\text{AES-128}}$ and P_{Noise} are the power of AES-128 leakage and the noise, respectively. The noise P_{Noise} can be considered to follow a Gaussian distribution $N(\mu, \sigma^2)$ that explains the increase in the SNR by averaging. Figure 2 displays the result of this recording. This graph permits the ten rounds of AES-128 to be identified, and we can delimit each round. This delimitation revealed a repetition of four events in each round (identified by four peaks) and corresponds to AddRoundKey, SubBytes, ShiftRows and MixColumns of AES-128. The x-axis represents time (i.e., the number of samples), and the y-axis represents the electromagnetic range in volts.

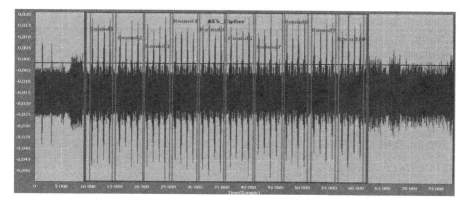

Fig. 2. EM-leakage of hundred AES-128 executions [7].

Key Recovery. The second phase of the attack is to recover the AES-key based on analysis of the EM-leakage traces. Our key recovery attack uses correlation power analysis [3] with the Hamming weight leakage model and focuses on the output of the SubBytes operation in the first round. The Hamming weight leakage model is justified by the fact that it is a software implementation. The following steps describe an algorithm to compute the correlation between the EM-leakage and Hamming weight:

1. Record the EM-leakage traces produced by AES-128 encryption algorithm AES-128$(*, P_i)$ and store them to $X^{d,i}$. Note that $*$ is the unknown AES-128 key, P_i is the plaintext in i-th trace, and $X^{d,i}$ ($0 \leq d < D$ and $0 \leq i < Q$) is the d-th sample in the i-th trace out of Q traces of D samples.

2. Compute the guessed distributions (one by key byte):

$$Y_{i,k}[b] = \mathsf{HW}(\mathsf{SubBytes}(P_i[b] \oplus k))$$

for $0 \leq k < 256$, $0 \leq i < Q$, and $0 \leq b < 16$ where $P_i[b]$ is the b-th byte of P_i, k is the guessed value of the key byte. $Y_{i,k}[b]$ is a (16×256)-guessed distributions of Q elements.

3. Compare $X^{d,i}$ and all the (16×256)-guessed distribution $Y_{i,k}[b]$ using the Pearson correlation coefficient [7]:

$$
\begin{aligned}
r(k,d)[b] \\
= \rho(X^d, Y_k[b]) &= \frac{\mathrm{Cov}(X^d, Y_k[b])}{\sqrt{\mathrm{Var}(X^d)\,\mathrm{Var}(Y_k[b])}} \\
&= \frac{\sum_{i=0}^{Q-1}(X^{d,i} - \bar{X}^d)(Y_{i,k}[b] - \bar{Y}_k[b])}{\sqrt{\sum_{i=0}^{Q-1}(X^{d,i} - \bar{X}^d)^2 \sum_{i=0}^{Q-1}(Y_{i,k}[b] - \bar{Y}_k[b])^2}},
\end{aligned}
\tag{1}
$$

Algorithm 1. Key Recovery Attack [7].

Input: Plaintext P_i $(0 \leq i < Q)$
Output: Recovered key k^*
1 **for** $i \leftarrow 0$ **to** $Q - 1$ **do**
2 | **for** $d \leftarrow 0$ **to** $D - 1$ **do**
3 | | $X^{d,i} \leftarrow$ EM-leakage of AES-128($*, P_i$);
4 | **end**
5 **end**
6 **for** $i \leftarrow 0$ **to** $Q - 1$ **do**
7 | **for** $b \leftarrow 0$ **to** $16 - 1$ **do**
8 | | **for** $k \leftarrow 0$ **to** $256 - 1$ **do**
9 | | | $Y_{i,k}[b] \leftarrow \mathsf{HW}(\mathsf{SubBytes}(P_i[b] \oplus k))$;
10 | | **end**
11 | **end**
12 **end**
13 **for** $d \leftarrow 0$ **to** $D - 1$ **do**
14 | **for** $b \leftarrow 0$ **to** $16 - 1$ **do**
15 | | **for** $k \leftarrow 0$ **to** $256 - 1$ **do**
16 | | | $r_{k,d}[b] \leftarrow \rho(Y_k[b], X^d)$;
17 | | **end**
18 | **end**
19 **end**
20 **for** $B \leftarrow 0$ **to** $16 - 1$ **do**
21 | $k^*[b] \leftarrow \arg\max_{0 \leq k < 256} \{\max_{0 \leq d < D}\{r_{k,d}[b]\}\}$;
22 **end**
23 **return** k^*;

---

where

$$\bar{X}^d = \frac{1}{Q} \sum_{i=0}^{Q-1} X^{d,i} \text{ and } \bar{Y}_k[b] = \frac{1}{Q} \sum_{i=0}^{Q-1} Y_{i,k}[b].$$

for $0 \leq d < D$, $0 \leq b < 16$, and $0 \leq k < 256$.

Algorithm 1 describes all the steps involved in our key recovery attack. The required number of traces to recover b-th byte of the key $N[b]$ is defined as the minimum q such that the recovered key byte $k^*[b]$ using q' traces is identical to that using q traces for all $q' > q$.

4 Experimental Results

We show the result of our experiment of the key recovery attack against a real LoRaWAN end-device. Our experiment setup is sketched in Sect. 4.1 and results of a key recovery attack are shown in Sect. 4.2. Section 4.3 demonstrates a technique to reduce the number of EM-leakage traces to recover AES-128 keys.

4.1 Experiment Setup

We used a LoRa Starter Kit as a target device. This starter kit is composed of two end-devices: an end-device with a plug-and-play LoRa module and an

Fig. 3. EM-leakage measurement from a end-device [7].

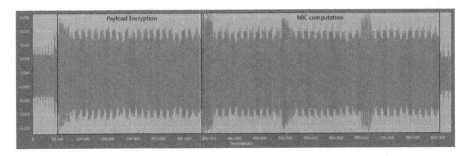

Fig. 4. Identifications of the payload encryption and MIC computation [7].

868 MHz antenna and a gateway equipped with a LoRa module and an 868 MHz antenna. We used an API supplied by the end-device for our experiment to access an implementation of AES-128. The source code of the program provided by the starter kit was modified to add a trigger signal at the first round of the AES-128.

4.2 Key Recovery

We targeted the payload encryption key k_E and MIC generation key k_M in the data transmission process in our experiment. The EM-leakage traces produced by the AES-128 encryption algorithm were recorded according to the following process.

1. The gateway generates a random plaintext P and sends it to an end-device.
2. The end-device generates a ciphertext $C = \text{AES-128}(k_E, P)$.
3. The EM-probe gets the leakage information on k_E, and the oscilloscope records the information.
4. The end-device generates MIC $= \text{AES-CMAC-128}(k_M, \text{DevAddr}\|\text{FCnt}\|C)$ $[0\dots 7]$.
5. The EM-probe gets the leakage information on k_M, and the oscilloscope records the information.
6. The end-device sends a frame including C and MIC to the gateway.
7. Goto step 1 until a sufficient number of traces is captured.

In our key recovery attack, we need to identify the distinct encryption phases in the EM-leakage traces to the first round of AES-128 for the payload encryption or MIC computation. We can find patterns in the EM-leakage traces produced by the AES-128 encryption algorithm. Figure 3 shows the measurement of the EM-leakage from a LoRaWAN end-device.

We can identify two distinct parts; the first part corresponds to the encryption of the frame payload and the second part to the MIC computation. Figure 4 shows 20 similar patterns in the signal part identified as the frame payload encryption. The frame payload is composed of 32 bytes, and AES-128 with ten rounds is executed twice; thus, 20 similar patterns appear. The same pattern can be identified three times in a row within the second part identified as the MIC computation for encrypted payload. The MIC computation for 40-byte data executes the AES-128 encryption algorithm three times. Furthermore, inside each AES-128, the same pattern could be identified ten times, which is corresponding to 10 rounds in AES-128.

Our key recovery attack is applied to the first round of AES-128. Figure 5 shows the result of the attack against the payload encryption process and plots the correlation between the EM-leakage and the Hamming weight for each byte of the recovered key $k[0]$ with the highest correlation. These values with the highest correlation are identical to bytes of the AES-128 key, or $k^\star[b] = K[b]$ for all B. That is, our key recovery attack reveals the entire AES-128 key. In the sixteen traces of correlation, two peaks with an amplitude around 0.4 are identifiable and it suggests that the intermediate value $\{\mathsf{SubBytes}(P[b] \oplus k^\star[b])\}$ $(0 \leq b < 16)$ is manipulated at least twice. The entire AES-128 key for the frame payload encryption can be recovered with 350 electromagnetic (EM)-leakage traces. Table 1 shows the number of required EM-leakage traces $N[b]$ to recover each key-byte. On the other hand, the 140 EM-leakage traces can recover 12 bytes of the MIC calculation key; however, the four bytes from the first byte to the fourth byte of the key never converge in our key recovery algorithm. The first four bytes of the input to the first execution of AES-128 for the MIC calculation are DevAddr and constant. The variances of $\{Y_{i,k}[b]\}$ thus vanish for $0 \leq B < 4$, and we cannot obtain the Pearson correlation coefficient in Eq. (1). One way to recover the four bytes is to use brute-force guessing with 2^{32} computational complexity. Alternatively, another leakage model, such as leakage during the computation of the MixColumns operation, could be used.

4.3 Reduction in the Number of Required Traces

EM-leakage traces contain uncorrelated noise produced by non-cryptographic circuits, and it may increase the required number of EM-leakage traces. The targeted end-device has a frequency of 14 MHz. By computing the spectrogram of the recorded EM-leakage around this frequency, we obtain Fig. 6 where the color gradient indicates the signal amplitude as a function of time (x-axis) and frequency (y-axis). This spectrogram shows activity around 14 to 15 MHz, which corresponds to the activity of the targeted microprocessor. We can thus apply a software-based band-pass filter between 13 and 16 MHz to remove low and high-frequency noise and improve the signal-to-noise ratio. Figure 7 illustrates the effect of the de-noising process, and a raw trace is plotted in blue and the associated de-noised trace in green.

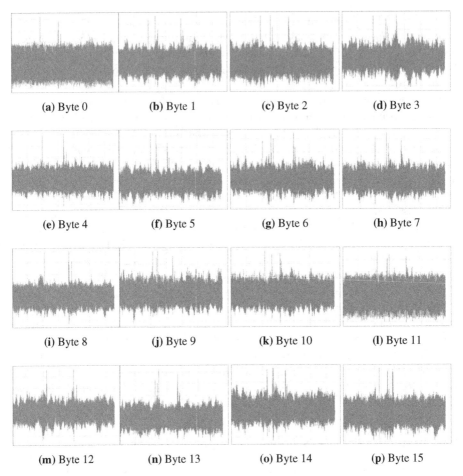

(a) Byte 0   **(b)** Byte 1   **(c)** Byte 2   **(d)** Byte 3

(e) Byte 4   **(f)** Byte 5   **(g)** Byte 6   **(h)** Byte 7

(i) Byte 8   **(j)** Byte 9   **(k)** Byte 10   **(l)** Byte 11

(m) Byte 12   **(n)** Byte 13   **(o)** Byte 14   **(p)** Byte 15

Fig. 5. Correlation between the EM-leakage and Hamming weight for each byte of recovered key $k^\star$.

The application of band-pass filtering on the raw traces used in Sect. 4.2 improves the efficiency of our key recovery attack. We summarized the number of required traces $N[b]$ to recover each key-byte in Table 1 to compare both results. The column "improvement" shows the difference (as a percentage) between the number of traces required to recover each key byte with the raw traces and the de-noised trace. The band-pass filtering technique reduces the number of traces required to achieve the entire key by about 26%.

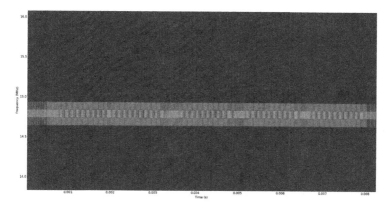

Fig. 6. Spectrum of an EM-leakage trace highlighting the activity of the microprocessor around 14–15 MHz [7]

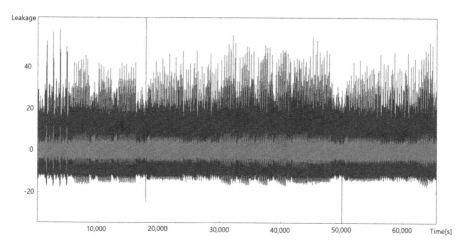

Fig. 7. Band-pass filtered trace between 13 and 16 MHz in green and raw trace in blue [7]. (Color figure online)

5 LoRaWAN Protocol

We provide an overview of the LoRaWAN protocol. The end-device activation to set AES-128 keys for an end-device is described in Sect. 5.1, and data protection and integrity in frame transmission are described in Sect. 5.2 based on LoRaWAN specification v.1.0.3 [16]. We then show the applicability of our attack to the real LoRaWAN protocol v.1.0 in Sect. 5.3 and demonstrate the difference between LoRaWan specification v.1.0 and v1.1 in Sect. 5.4.

5.1 End-Device Activation

We have to personalize and activate the end-devices to connect them to a LoRaWAN network. There are two activation methods for an end-device: over-the-air activation (OTAA) and activation by personalization (ABP).

Table 1. Required number of traces to recover the key [7].

Byte (b)	Raw	De-noised	Improvement
0	140	90	−36%
1	220	130	−41%
2	200	80	−60%
3	310	120	−61%
4	130	70	−46%
5	200	260	+30%
6	150	110	−27%
7	260	110	−58%
8	230	210	−9%
9	320	180	−44%
10	350	130	−63%
11	230	200	−13%
12	180	200	+11%
13	80	80	± 0%
14	300	90	−70%
15	210	260	+23%
Maximum	350	260	−26%

Over-the-Air Activation. In OTAA, an end-device must complete a join procedure to be able to make data exchanges with the network server. The join procedure requires the end-device to be personalized with a globally unique end-device identifier (DevEUI), an application identifier (AppEUI), and an AES-128 key (AppKey).

The join procedure in OTAA is started from an end-device by sending a join-request message. The join-request message contains AppEUI, DevEUI of the end-device, and a nonce of two bytes (DevNonce), or

$$\text{join-request msg} = \text{AppEUI}\|\text{DevEUI}\|\text{DevNonce}$$

AppEUI and DevEUI are a globally unique application ID of an end-device and an end-device ID in the IEEE EUI64 address space, respectively. DevNonce is a random value. The network server needs to keep the list of used DevNonce values for each end-device and ignores join requests with re-used DevNonce values to prevent replay attacks. The MIC for the join-request message is calculated as:

$$\text{MIC} = \text{AES-CMAC-128}(\text{AppKey}, \text{MHDR}\|\text{join-request msg})[0\ldots3].$$

The network server responds to the join-request message with a join-accept message if the server accepts that the end-device can join an LPWA network. No response is sent to the end-device if the network server does not accept the join request. The join-accept message contains an application nonce (AppNonce) of three bytes, a network identifier (NetID), an end-device address (DevAddr), a delay between TX and RX (RxDelay), and an optional list of channel frequencies (CFList) for the network the end-device is joining, or

$$\text{join-accept msg} = \text{AppNonce}\|\text{NetID}\|\text{DevAddr}\|\text{DLSettings}\|\text{RxDelay}\|\text{CFList}.$$

The MIC for the join-accept message is calculated as:

$$\text{MIC} = \text{AES-CMAC-128}(\text{AppKey}, \text{MHDR}\|\text{join-accept msg})[0\ldots3].$$

The join-accept message itself is encrypted with the AppKey as follows:

$$\text{AES-128}^{-1}(\text{AppKey}, \text{join-accept msg}\|\text{MIC}).$$

Note that AES-128 decryption is used to *encrypt* the join-accept message so that the end-device uses only AES-128 encryption to *decrypt* the join-accept message.

The network server and end-device derive the two session keys, NwkSKey and AppSKey, as follows:

$$\text{NwkSKey} = \text{AES-128}(\text{AppKey}, \text{0x01}\|\text{AppNonce}\|\text{NetID}\|\text{DevNonce}\|\text{pad}_{16}),$$
$$\text{AppSKey} = \text{AES-128}(\text{AppKey}, \text{0x02}\|\text{AppNonce}\|\text{NetID}\|\text{DevNonce}\|\text{pad}_{16}).$$

The function pad_{16} adds zero bytes so that the data length is a multiple of 16.

Activation by Personalization. End-devices can be activated by personalization (ABP). ABP directly associates an end-device to a LoRaWAN network without having to use the join procedure needed in OTAA.

NwkSKey, AppSKey, and DevAddr are stored in the end-device directly in ABP, while these keys are derived using the DevEUI, AppEUI, and App-Key in OTAA. The required information is preset to the end-device to connect a LoRaWAN network. Each end-device has a unique set of NwkSKey and AppSKey.

5.2   Data Transmission

Payload encryption using AES counter mode (AES-CTR-128) provides data protection of the frame payload for transmissions in the LoRaWAN protocol. AES-CMAC-128 is used to generate a four-byte message integrity code (MIC) to maintain data integrity in payload transmissions and the OTAA procedure.

Data Protection. FRMPayload is encrypted before the MIC is calculated. The encryption key K depends on the FPort of the data message: If FPort is 0, then NwkSKey is used, and if FPort is in the range of 1, 2, ..., 255, then AppSKey is used. The encryption algorithm defines a sequence of blocks A_i. A block A_i contains one-byte 0x01, followed by four-bytes 0x00000000, one-byte direction field (Dir), four-byte identifier (DevAddr), four-byte FCntUp or FCntDown, one-byte 0x00, and one-byte encoded i, or

$$A_i = \text{0x01}\|\text{0x00000000}\|\text{Dir}\|\text{DevAddr}\|\text{FCntUp or FCntDown}$$
$$\|\text{0x00}\|\text{encode}(i).$$

Dir describes the direction field: 0 for uplink frames and 1 for downlink frames. The DevAddr identifies the end-device in the current network. The frame counter FCntUp, incremented by end-devices, records the number of uplinks to the network server and FCntDown, incremented by the server, records the number of downlink frames from the server. Algorithm 2 shows the procedure of the payload encryption in detail. The function len returns the byte length of the data. device must complete a join procedure

---

Algorithm 2. Payload Encryption in LoRaWAN Protocol [7].

   Input: FramePayload, Encryption key K
   Output: EncrypredPayload
1 pld $\leftarrow$ FRMPayload;
2 $k \leftarrow \lceil \text{len(pld)}/16 \rceil$;
3 **for** $i \leftarrow 1$ **to** k **do**
4 $\quad|\quad S_i \leftarrow \text{AES-128}(K, A_i)$;
5 **end**
6 $S \leftarrow S_1\|S_2\|\ldots\|S_k$;
7 $T \leftarrow (\text{pld}\|\text{pad}_{16}) \oplus S$;
8 EncryptedPayload $\leftarrow$ First len(pld) bytes of T;
   /* Data protection using AES-CTR   */
9 **return** EncryptedPayload;

Data Integrity. All LoRa messages carry a PHY payload (Payload) consisting of one-byte MAC header (MHDR), a MAC payload (MACPayload), and a four-byte MIC. The MAC payload of the data messages starts with a frame header (FHDR) followed by an optional port field (FPort) and ends with an optional frame payload field (FRMPayload). The FHDR consists of the address of the end-device (DevAddr), a frame control byte (FCtrl), a frame counter (FCnt), and frame options (FOpts) to transport MAC commands. The MIC for payload calculated on the entire message is defined as

$$\text{msg} = \text{MHDR}\|\text{FHDR}\|\text{FPort}\|\text{EncryptedPayload}.$$

The block B_0 for the MIC calculation contains one-byte 0x49, followed by four-bytes 0x00000000, one-byte direction field (Dir), four-byte identifier (DevAddr), four-byte FCntUp or FCntDown, one-byte 0x00, and one-byte len(msg), or

$$B_0 = \text{0x49}\|\text{0x00000000}\|\text{Dir}\|\text{DevAddr}\|\text{FCntUp or FCntDown}$$
$$\|\text{0x00}\|\text{len(msg)}.$$

The MIC is calculated as

$$MIC = \text{AES-CMAC-128}(\text{NwkSKey}, B_0 \| msg)[0 \ldots 3].$$

5.3 Applicability to Real LoRaWAN Protocols

The end-device executes AES encryption to calculate MIC for the join-request message, decrypts the join-accept message and verifies its MIC, derives the session keys, encrypts uplink data, calculates the MIC for the uplink data, and verifies the MIC for downlink data. The MHDR, AppEUI, and DevEUI are fixed values and DevNonce is a random value in a join-request message. We can recover up to two bytes of AppKey from the leakage during the MIC calculation for the join-request message since there are fixed values in the input data to AES. The input data to AES is $\text{AES-128}^{-1}(\text{AppKey}, \text{join-accept msg} \| \text{MIC})$ in the decryption process of a join-accept message. The data does not contain fixed values, and we can recover the entire AppKey from the EM-leakage traces produced by the AES-128 encryption algorithm according to our experimental results. The session keys, NwkSKey and AppSKey, can be derived from the NwkKey. The input data to AES contain some fixed values including headers and identifiers in the verification of join-accept MIC, derivation of the session keys, encryption and MIC calculation for transmitted data, and the entire AES key cannot be recovered.

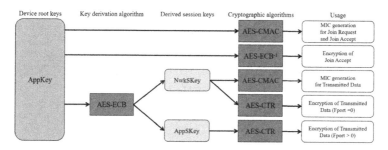

Fig. 8. Key derivation scheme in LoRaWAN v1.0.

5.4 Difference Between LoRaWAN V1.0 and V1.1

The key derivation scheme has been significantly changed between LoRaWAN v1.0 and v1.1. A new root key, NwkKey, and new session keys, NwkSEncKey, NwkSIntKey, SNwkSIntKey, and FNwkSIntKey, were added. The NwkSEncKey encrypts transmitted data where FPort is 0 similar to NwkSKey in LoRaWAN v1.0. The NwkSIntKey is used to calculate the MIC for downlink data. The SNwkSIntKey and FNwkSIntKey calculate the MIC for uplink data. The MIC is calculated as follows:

$$\text{cmacS} = \text{AES-CMAC-128}(\text{SNwkSIntKey}, B_1 \| \text{msg}),$$
$$\text{cmacF} = \text{AES-CMAC-128}(\text{FNwkSIntKey}, B_0 \| \text{msg}),$$
$$\text{MIC} = \text{cmacS}[0,1] \| \text{cmacF}[0,1].$$

The block B_1 is defined as:

$$B_1 = \text{0x49} \| \text{ConfFCnt} \| \text{TxDr} \| \text{TxCh} \| \text{Dir}(= \text{0x00}) \| \text{DevAddr} \| \text{FCntUp}$$
$$\| \text{0x00} \| \text{len}(\text{msg}),$$

where the key derivation schemes of LoRaWAN v1.0 and v1.1 are given in Fig. 8 and Fig. 9, respectively.

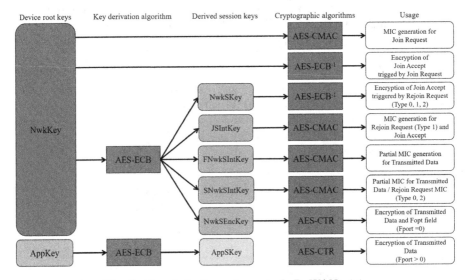

Fig. 9. Key derivation scheme in LoRaWAN v1.1.

However, this improvement makes only a minor contribution to security against our key-recovery attack based on the side-channel analysis. The NwkKey can be recovered in the decryption process of a join-request message. The session keys, JSEncKey, JSIntKey, FNwkSIntKey, SNwkSIntKey, and NwkSEncKey, can be derived from the NwkKey. Some bytes of the AppKey and AppSKey can be recovered.

6   Conclusion

We conducted experiments to extract AES keys that are used to encrypt a frame payload and to calculate the message integrity code (MIC) for the encrypted payload from a real LoRaWAN end-device. Our experiments recovered keys based on a correlation power analysis. The 350 of EM-leakage traces of the payload encryption process can entirely recover the 16-byte payload encryption key while the 140 EM-leakage traces of MIC generation process can recover 12 bytes of the 16-byte MIC generation key. We also achieved 26% of further reduction in the number of traces required to recover keys using a band-pass filtering technique. Furthermore, we showed that our key recovery attack is applicable in real LoRaWAN protocols. Our attack can entirely recover the root key AppKey in LoRaWAN v1.0 and a root key NwkKey in LoRaWAN v1.1. In future work, we will endeavor to recover AES keys from an end-device that supports the real LoRaWAN protocols.

References

1. 3GPP: Standardization of NB-IOT completed, June 2016. http://www.3gpp.org/news-events/3gpp-news/1785-nb_iot_complete
2. Aras, E., Small, N., Ramachandran, G.S., Delbruel, S., Joosen, W., Hughes, D.: Selective jamming of LoRaWAN using commodity hardware (2017). https://doi.org/10.1145/3144457.3144478, http://arxiv.org/abs/1712.02141v1
3. Brier, E., Clavier, C., Olivier, F.: Correlation power analysis with a leakage model. In: Joye, M., Quisquater, J.-J. (eds.) CHES 2004. LNCS, vol. 3156, pp. 16–29. Springer, Heidelberg (2004). https://doi.org/10.1007/978-3-540-28632-5_2
4. Butun, I., Pereira, N., Gidlund, M.: Analysis of LoRaWAN V1.1 security: research paper. In: Proceedings of the 4th ACM MobiHoc Workshop on Experiences with the Design and Implementation of Smart Objects, pp. 5:1–5:6. SMARTOBJECTS 2018, ACM, New York, NY, USA (2018). https://doi.org/10.1145/3213299.3213304
5. Clavier, C., Feix, B., Gagnerot, G., Roussellet, M., Verneuil, V.: Improved collision-correlation power analysis on first order protected AES. In: Preneel, B., Takagi, T. (eds.) CHES 2011. LNCS, vol. 6917, pp. 49–62. Springer, Heidelberg (2011). https://doi.org/10.1007/978-3-642-23951-9_4
6. Dinu, D., Kizhvatov, I.: EM Analysis in the IoT context: lessons learned from an attack on thread. Cryptology ePrint Archive, Report 2018/076 (2018). https://eprint.iacr.org/2018/076/20180118:125926
7. Fukushima, K., Marion, D., Nakano, Y., Facon, A., Kiyomoto, S., Guilley, S.: Experiment on side-channel key-recovery using a real LPWA End-device. In: 5th International Conference on Information Systems Security and Privacy (ICISSP 2019). pp. 67–74, January 2019. https://doi.org/10.5220/0007259500670074
8. Girard, P.: Low Power Wide Area Networks Security, December 2015. https://docbox.etsi.org/Workshop/2015/201512_M2MWORKSHOP/S04_WirelessTechnoforIoTandSecurityChallenges/GEMALTO_GIRARD.pdf
9. GSMA: Long Term Evolution for Machines: LTE-M (2017). https://www.gsma.com/iot/long-term-evolution-machine-type-communication-lte-mtc-cat-m1/
10. IHS Markit: Number of Connected IoT Devices Will Surge to 125 Billion by 2030, IHS Markit Says (2015). http://www.statista.com/statistics/266210/
11. Itoh, K., Izu, T., Takenaka, M.: Address-bit differential power analysis of cryptographic schemes OK-ECDH and OK-ECDSA. In: Kaliski, B.S., Koç, K., Paar, C. (eds.) CHES 2002. LNCS, vol. 2523, pp. 129–143. Springer, Heidelberg (2003). https://doi.org/10.1007/3-540-36400-5_11

12. Joye, M., Tymen, C.: Protections against differential analysis for elliptic curve cryptography – an algebraic approach. In: Koç, Ç.K., Naccache, D., Paar, C. (eds.) Cryptographic Hardware and Embedded Systems – CHES 2001. Lecture Notes in Computer Science book series (LNCS), vol. 2162, pp. 377–390. Springer, Heidelberg (2001). https://link.springer.com/chapter/10.1007/3-540-44709-1_31

13. Kocher, P., Jaffe, J., Jun, B.: Differential power analysis. In: Wiener, M. (ed.) CRYPTO 1999. LNCS, vol. 1666, pp. 388–397. Springer, Heidelberg (1999). https://doi.org/10.1007/3-540-48405-1_25

14. Komano, Y., Shimizu, H., Kawamura, S.: Built-in determined sub-key correlation power analysis. Cryptology ePrint Archive, Report 2009/161 (2009). https://eprint.iacr.org/2009/161/20090803:071855

15. Lee, J., Hwang, D., Park, J., Kim, K.H.: Risk analysis and countermeasure for bit-flipping attack in LoRaWAN. In: 2017 International Conference on Information Networking (ICOIN), pp. 549–551, January 2017. https://doi.org/10.1109/ICOIN.2017.7899554

16. LoRa Alliance™: LoRaWAN™ Specification v1.0.3, November 2018. https://lora-alliance.org/sites/default/files/2018-07/lorawan1.0.3.pdf

17. LoRa Alliance™: LoRaWAN™ Specification v1.1, November 2018. https://lora-alliance.org/sites/default/files/2018-04/lorawantm_specification_-v1.1.pdf

18. Messerges, T.S., Dabbish, E.A., Sloan, R.H.: Investigations of power analysis attacks on smartcards. In: Proceedings of the USENIX Workshop on Smartcard Technology on USENIX Workshop on Smartcard Technology, pp. 17. WOST 1999, USENIX Association, Berkeley, CA, USA (1999). http://dl.acm.org/citation.cfm?id=1267115.1267132

19. Moukarzel, M., Eisenbarth, T., Sunar, B.: μLeech: A side-channel evaluation platform for IoT. In: 2017 IEEE 60th International Midwest Symposium on Circuits and Systems (MWSCAS), pp. 25–28, August 2017. https://doi.org/10.1109/MWSCAS.2017.8052851

20. Na, S., Hwang, D., Shin, W., Kim, K.H.: Scenario and countermeasure for replay attack using join request messages in lorawan. In: 2017 International Conference on Information Networking (ICOIN), pp. 718–720, January 2017. https://doi.org/10.1109/ICOIN.2017.7899580

21. Sigfox: Sigfox Technology Overview (2017). https://www.sigfox.com/en/sigfox-iot-technology-overview

22. Tawalbeh, L.A., Somani, T.F.: More secure Internet of Things using robust encryption algorithms against side channel attacks. In: 2016 IEEE/ACS 13th International Conference of Computer Systems and Applications (AICCSA), pp. 1–6, November 2016. https://doi.org/10.1109/AICCSA.2016.7945813

23. Tomasin, S., Zulian, S., Vangelista, L.: Security analysis of LoRaWAN join procedure for Internet of Things networks. In: 2017 IEEE Wireless Communications and Networking Conference Workshops (WCNCW), pp. 1–6, March 2017. https://doi.org/10.1109/WCNCW.2017.7919091

24. Yang, X., Karampatzakis, E., Doerr, C., Kuipers, F.: Security vulnerabilities in LoRaWAN. In: 2018 IEEE/ACM Third International Conference on Internet-of-Things Design and Implementation (IoTDI), pp. 129–140, April 2018. https://doi.org/10.1109/IoTDI.2018.00022

25. Zulian, S.: Security threat analysis and countermeasures for LoRaWAN™ join procedure. Master's thesis, University of Padova (2016). http://tesi.cab.unipd.it/53210/

Black-Box Attacks via the Speech Interface Using Linguistically Crafted Input

Mary K. Bispham$^{(\boxtimes)}$, Alastair Janse van Rensburg, Ioannis Agrafiotis, and Michael Goldsmith

Department of Computer Science, University of Oxford, Oxford OX1 3QD, UK
{mary.bispham,alastair.rensburg,ioannis.agrafiotis,
michael.goldsmith}@cs.ox.ac.uk

Abstract. This paper presents the results of experiments demonstrating novel black-box attacks via the speech interface. We demonstrate two types of attack that use linguistically crafted adversarial input to target vulnerabilities in the handling of speech input by a speech interface. The first attack demonstrates the use of nonsensical word sounds to gain covert access to voice-controlled systems. This attack exploits vulnerabilities at the speech recognition stage of handling of speech input. The second attack demonstrates the use of crafted utterances that are misinterpreted by a target system as a valid voice command. This attack exploits vulnerabilities at the natural language understanding stage of handling of speech input.

Keywords: Cyber security · Voice-controlled digital assistant · Human-computer interaction

1 Introduction

Speech interfaces as implemented in voice-controlled systems such as Google Assistant and Amazon Alexa represent a new type of attack surface that can be exploited by attackers seeking to gain unauthorised access to a system. Attacks via a speech interface that are not easily detectable by human listeners are particularly pernicious in their potential effects. Various attacks of this nature have been demonstrated in prior work. For example, Carlini et al. [1] have presented results showing it is possible to hide malicious commands to voice-controlled digital assistants in white noise, whereas Zhang et al. [2] have shown that it is possible to hide commands in frequencies that are above the human-audible range. In this paper, we present two new types of attacks via the speech interface that are not detectable by legitimate users of voice-controlled devices. The first

This work was supported by a doctoral training grant from the Engineering and Physical Sciences Research Council (EPSRC).

P. Mori et al. (Eds.): ICISSP 2019, CCIS 1221, pp. 93–120, 2020.
https://doi.org/10.1007/978-3-030-49443-8_5

of these attack types is an attack using nonsensical word sounds to exploit unintended functionality in speech recognition in a voice-controlled system. Specifically, our experimental work demonstrates an attack on speech recognition in Google Assistant using nonsensical word sounds to trigger a set of target commands. The second attack type is an attack targeting unintended functionality in natural language understanding in a voice-controlled system. Specifically, our experimental work demonstrates that it is possible to mislead natural language understanding functionality in Amazon Alexa Skills and in an open-source natural language understanding system to trigger a target action, using utterances that appear to human listeners to have a meaning that is unrelated to the target action. These adversarial utterances are crafted by embedding homophones of target command words in a different sense context.

This paper is an extended version of an earlier paper that presented the results of a pilot experiment and of a proof-of-concept study [3]. The pilot experiment presented in the earlier paper represented initial results on attacks on speech recognition in Google Assistant using nonsensical word sounds. The work presented in the current paper builds on the results of the pilot experiment by generating a new set of results on this type of attack using a refined methodology that achieves a higher attack success rate. The proof-of-concept study presented in the earlier paper represented feasibility tests that demonstrated the potential for attacking natural language understanding in Amazon Alexa Skills using adversarially crafted utterances. The work presented in the current paper builds on the results of the proof-of-concept study by generating a more substantial set of results on this type of attack. The proof-of-concept study presented in the earlier paper included both attacks based on word substitution, in which a word in a target command is replaced with an unrelated word, as well as attacks based on embedding alternate meanings of target command words in new utterances. As stated above, the work presented in the current paper focusses solely on the latter attack method, which we term a 'word transplant' attack. Word transplant represents a novel method for attacking natural language understanding that has to the best of our knowledge not been explored in prior work.

The remainder of the paper is structured as follows. Section 2 describes experimental work demonstrating the feasibility of attacks using nonsensical word sounds. Section 3 describes experimental work demonstrating the feasibility of attacks using unrelated utterances. Section 4 makes some suggestions for future work and concludes the paper.

2   Nonsense Attacks on Google Assistant

2.1   Description and Context

This section presents experimental work showing that it is possible to hide malicious voice commands to the voice-controlled digital assistant Google Assistant in word sounds that are perceived as meaningless by humans. We term this type of attack a 'nonsense' attack, in accordance with a taxonomy published in a previous paper [4], which categorises attacks via the speech interface according to human perceptual categories. The attack can also be characterised as a black-box adversarial learning attack. The idea for this work was inspired by the use of nonsense words to teach phonics to primary school children.[1]

In prior work, Papernot et al. [5] have shown that a sentiment analysis method could be misled by input that was 'nonsensical' at the sentence level, i.e. the input consisted of a nonsensical concatenation of real words. By contrast, the work described here examines whether voice-controlled digital assistants can be misled by input that consists of nonsensical word sounds. Whilst the attack by Papernot et al. targeted a text-based natural language understanding functionality, the attack based on nonsensical word sounds presented here targets the automatic speech recognition component of a voice-controlled digital assistant. The attacks described here represent the first example of an attack of this type targeting speech recognition in a voice-controlled system.

Nonsensical word sounds as understood here are sounds that are composed of the sound units that are used in a given language, but to which no meaning is allocated within the current usage of that language. Sound units used to form words in a given language are known as 'phonemes'.[2] English has around 44 phonemes.[3] The line between phoneme combinations that carry meaning within a language and phoneme combinations that are meaningless is subject to change over time and place, as new words evolve and old words fall out of use (see Nowak and Krakauer [6]). The space of meaningful word sounds within a language at a given point in time is generally confirmed by the inclusion of words in an established reference work, such as, in the case of English, the Oxford English Dictionary.[4] Word sounds that are outside this space can be described as nonsense words. Nonsense words are a grey area between non-speech, i.e. noise, and meaningful speech.

The aim of the experimental work was to develop a novel attack based on nonsensical word sounds that have some phonetic similarity with the words of a relevant target command, using a systematic methodology. Specifically, we tested Google Assistant's response to English word sounds that were outside the space of meaningful word sounds in English, but that had a 'rhyming' relationship with meaningful words recognised as commands by Google Assistant. The term 'rhyme' is used to refer to a number of different sound relationships between words (see for example McCurdy et al. [7]), but it is most commonly used to refer to a correspondence of word endings.[5] For the purposes of the experimental work, rhyme was defined according to this commonly understood sense as words that share the same ending phoneme.

---

[1] See The Telegraph, 1st May 2014, "Infants taught to read 'nonsense words' in English lessons".

[2] See for example https://www.britannica.com/topic/phoneme.

[3] See for example https://www.dyslexia-reading-well.com/44-phonemes-in-english.html.

[4] See for example https://blog.oxforddictionaries.com/press-releases/new-words-added-oxforddictionaries-com-august-2014/.

[5] See https://en.oxforddictionaries.com/definition/rhyme.

The hypothesis behind the experimental work was that nonsensical word sounds represent a category of unexpected input for which current speech recognition systems lack an appropriate handling mechanism, and that this is in contrast to the processing of such input by humans, who perceive such input as having no meaning. Current speech recognition technologies are machine learning-based classifiers that use Hidden Markov Models (HMMs) to map acoustic features in a speech signal to a most likely sequence of words to have produced them (see for example McTear [8]). It was hypothesised that some sequences of nonsensical word sounds with sufficient similarity to a target command might be accepted as that target command at a confidence level higher or equal to the level required for recognition of speech input by the target system's speech recognition system as a legitimate command. It can be assumed that the confidence level required for recognition of speech input will have been set during training of a system such as Google Assistant to achieve optimal recall and precision measures on a test dataset. Setting a higher confidence threshold in order to prevent acceptance of nonsensical word sequences as legitimate commands might therefore lead to rejection by the system of legitimate input, implying an inevitable trade-off between usability and security. The attacks demonstrated in this experimental work thus exploit a vulnerability created by a focus on usability in the implementation of current systems. The attack concept is illustrated in Fig. 1, which shows the alignment of a dummy dataset of nonsense commands and legitimate commands to a higher and to a lower confidence threshold. The figure shows that as some of the nonsense commands are accepted by the system as valid commands with a higher level of confidence than some legitimate commands, it is not possible to prevent acceptance of all nonsense commands whilst ensuring acceptance of all legitimate commands. Implementing the higher

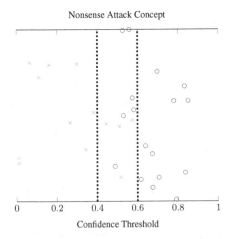

Fig. 1. x = nonsense commands; o = legitimate commands; dummy confidence threshold for ensuring acceptance of legitimate input = 0.4; dummy confidence threshold for ensuring rejection of nonsensical input = 0.6

confidence threshold will result in rejection of some legitimate commands, whereas implementing the lower threshold will result in acceptance of some nonsense commands.

The attacks presented here exploit three related features of speech recognition in voice-controlled systems. One of these features is the delineation of the space of word sounds that the Assistant has been trained to recognise as meaningful. The space of word sounds that a voice assistant such as Google Assistant can transcribe is much larger than the number of words that it can 'understand' in the sense of being able to map them to an executable command. In order to be able to perform tasks such as web searches by voice and note taking, a voice-controlled digital assistant must be able to transcribe all words in current usage within a language. It can therefore be assumed that the speech recognition functionality in Google Assistant is trained to recognise all words in current English usage. Whereas earlier speech recognition systems were vulnerable to potential confusion between out-of-vocabulary words that they did not have a capacity to recognise, on account of only a limited set of in-vocabulary words being included in their phonetic dictionary (see for example Hazen and Bazzi [9]), the potential for this type of confusion has been minimised in current systems. Earlier systems were also vulnerable to confusion between speech and non-speech sounds, but potential for this type of confusion has also been minimised in systems used for wake word detection that are trained using a noise model (see for example Raju et al. [10]). However, whilst the problem of delineating out-of-vocabulary words and non-speech sounds from in-scope words has been minimized in current systems, nonsensical word sounds still represent a type of out-of-scope input that speech recognition functionalities struggle to delineate from in-scope input. The inability of the Assistant to distinguish meaningful from meaningless word sounds is one of the features exploited in the attacks demonstrated here.

Another feature of speech recognition in voice assistants that is exploited in an attack using nonsense syllables is the influence of the language model used in speech recognition. Modern speech recognition technology combines acoustic modelling and language modelling components as parts of HMM-based speech recognition. The acoustic modelling component computes the likelihood of the acoustic features within a segment of speech having been produced by a given word. The language modelling component calculates the probability of one word following another word or words within an utterance. The acoustic model is typically based on Gaussian Mixture Models (GMMs) or deep neural networks (DNNs), whereas the language model is typically based on n-grams or recurrent neural networks (RNNs). Google's speech recognition technology as incorporated in Google Assistant is based on neural networks.[6] The words most likely to have produced a sequence of speech sounds are determined by calculation of the product of the acoustic model and the language model outputs. The language model is intended to complement the acoustic model, in the sense that

---

[6] See Google AI blog, 11th August 2015, 'The neural networks behind Google Voice transcription', https://ai.googleblog.com/2015/08/the-neural-networks-behind-google-voice.html.

it may correct 'errors' on the part of the acoustic model in matching a set of acoustic features to words that are not linguistically valid in the context of the preceding words. This assumption of complementary functionality is valid in a cooperative context, where a user interacts via a speech interface in meaningful language. However, the assumption of complementarity is not valid in an adversarial context, where an attacker is seeking to engineer a mismatch between a set of speech sounds as perceived by a human, such as the nonsensical speech sounds generated here, and their transcription by a speech-controlled device. In an adversarial context such as that investigated here, the language model may in fact operate in the attacker's favour, in that if one 'nonsense' word in an adversarial command is misrecognised as a target command word, subsequent words in the adversarial command will be more likely to be misrecognised as target command words in turn, as the language model trained to recognise legitimate commands will allocate a high probability to the target command words that follow the initial one.

A third feature of speech recognition in voice assistants exploited in covert attacks using this kind of input is the difference between machine and human processing of meaningless speech sounds. Like speech recognition by machines, speech recognition by humans is known also to reference an internal 'lexicon' to match speech sounds to words (see for example Roberts et al. [11]). However, unlike machines, humans also have an ability to categorise speech sounds as nonsensical. This discrepancy between machine and human processing of word sounds was the basis of the attack methodology for hiding malicious commands to voice assistants in nonsense words. Outside of the context of attacks via the speech interface, differences between human and machine abilities to recognise nonsense syllables have been studied for example by Lippmann et al. [12] and Scharenborg and Cooke [13]. Bailey and Hahn [14] examine the relationship between theoretical measures of phoneme similarity based on phonological features, such as might be used in automatic speech recognition, and empirically determined measures of phoneme confusability based on human perception tests. Machine speech recognition has reached parity with human abilities in terms of the ability correctly to transcribe meaningful speech (see Xiong et al. [16]), but not in terms of the ability to distinguish meaningful from meaningless sounds. The inability of machines to identify nonsense sounds as meaningless is exploited for security purposes by Meutzner et al. [15], who have developed a CAPTCHA based on the insertion of random nonsense sounds in audio. This experimental work explores the opposite scenario, i.e. the possible security problems associated with machine inability to distinguish sense from nonsense, and, conversely, human inability to recognise nonsensical input as meaningful.

2.2 Methodology

The experimental work comprised three key stages. The first stage involved generating, from a set of target commands, a set of potential adversarial commands consisting of nonsensical word sequences. These potential adversarial commands were generated using a mangling process that involved replacing consonant phonemes in target command words to create a rhyming word sound, and then determining whether the resulting rhyming word sound was a meaningful word in English or a 'nonsense word', using the Unix word list as a proxy for the space of meaningful words in English. This was done so as to identify nonsensical word sounds that had an acoustic relationship to target command words and thus could be used to create potential adversarial commands. Word sounds identified as rhyming nonsense words were concatenated to create potential adversarial commands. Audio versions of these potential adversarial commands were created using speech synthesis technology. The second stage of the experimental work was to test the response of the target system to the potential adversarial commands, i.e. to test machine 'comprehension'. This was done both via audio file input and via over-the-air input of potential adversarial commands. The third stage of the experimental work was to test the human comprehensibility of adversarial commands that were successful in triggering a target action in the target system. The three key stages of the experimental work are shown in Fig. 2.

Fig. 2. Nonsense Attacks Experimental Stages.

The target system for the experiment was the voice-controlled digital assistant Google Assistant. The Google Assistant system was accessed via the Google Assistant Software Development Kit (SDK).[7] Target commands used in both experiments were selected to represent the generic types of action that can be performed by voice-controlled digital assistants. A voice-controlled digital assistant such as Google Assistant typically performs three generic types of action, namely information extraction, control of a cyber-physical action, and data input. The data input category may overlap with the control of cyber-physical action category where a particular device setting needs to be specified, eg. light colour or thermostat temperature. For this experiment, six target commands corresponding to the three types of action were used. The target commands were:

- "What's my name" (target action: retrieve username, action category: information extraction)
- "Who am I" (target action: retrieve username, action category: information extraction)
- "Turn on light" (target action: turn light on, action category: control of cyber-physical action)
- "Turn off light" (target action: turn light off, action category: control of cyber-physical action)
- "Turn light red" (target action: turn light to red, action category: data input)
- "Turn light blue" (target action: turn light to blue, action category: data input)

In addition to six specific target commands, a further command targeted in the experiments was the wake phrase "Hey Google" used to activate the Assistant.

---

[7] See https://developers.google.com/assistant/sdk/.

Adversarial Command Generation. Potential adversarial wake phrases and commands were created by replacing words in the original wake phrase or target command with a rhyming nonsense word. A set of rhyming nonsensical word sounds for each original word in the wake phrase and in each of the target commands was generated using a word mangling process. This mangling process was based on replacing consonant phonemes in the target command words to generate nonsensical word sounds that rhymed with the original target command word.[8] The target commands were first translated to a phonetic representation in the Kirshenbaum phonetic alphabet[9] using the 'espeak' functionality in Linux. The starting consonant phonemes of each word of the target command were then replaced with a different starting consonant phoneme, using a Python script and referring to a list of starting consonants and consonant blends.[10] Where the target command word began with a vowel phoneme, a starting consonant phoneme was prefixed to the vowel. The word sounds resulting from the word mangling process were checked for presence in a phonetic representation of the Unix word list, also generated with espeak, to ascertain whether the word sound represented a meaningful English word or not. If the sound did correspond to a meaningful word, it was discarded. This process generated for each target command word a number of rhyming nonsensical words to which no English meaning was attached. In the case of the wake phrase 'Hey Google', in addition to replacing the starting consonants 'H' and 'G', the second 'g' in 'Google' was also replaced with one of the consonants that are found in combination with the '-le' ending in English.[11]

For the audio file input tests, potential adversarial wake phrases and potential adversarial commands were generated separately. Original words in the wake phrase and target commands were replaced with one of the rhyming nonsense words for that word identified in the word-mangling process described above. Audio of the potential adversarial wake phrases and commands was created using Amazon Polly speech synthesis.[12] The potential adversarial wake phrases and commands generated for the audio file input tests included both potential adversarial wake phrases and commands in which all of the original words were replaced with nonsense words, as well as potential adversarial wake phrases and commands in which only some words were replaced. Specifically, the experiment included potential adversarial wake phrases and commands in which only one of the original words was replaced, potential adversarial commands in which only two of the three original words were replaced, and potential adversarial wake phrases and commands in which all of the original words were replaced. As the space of potential adversarial wake phrases and commands was quite large,

---

[8] Our approach was inspired by an educational game in which a set of nonsense words is generated by spinning lettered wooden cubes - see https://rainydaymum.co.uk/spin-a-word-real-vs-nonsense-words/.

[9] See http://espeak.sourceforge.net/phonemes.html.

[10] See https://k-3teacherresources.com/teaching-resource/printable-phonics-charts/.

[11] See https://howtospell.co.uk/.

[12] See https://aws.amazon.com/polly/.

a process of filtering and random sampling was used in generating potential adversarial wake phrases and commands in which more than one of the original words was replaced, as described in more detail below. Thus the potential adversarial commands generated for testing covered only a subspace of the full space of potential adversarial commands. The size of the full space of potential adversarial commands in which all of the original words are replaced is shown in Table 1.

Table 1. Space of potential adversarial commands for wake phrase and target commands.

Target Command	No. of Rhyming Nonsense Words	Space of Potential Adversarial Commands
Hey Google	'Hey': 17; 'Google': 395	6715
Who am I	'Who': 18; 'am': 27; 'I': 20	9720
What's my name	'What's': 27 ; 'my': 20 ; 'name': 35	18900
Turn on light	'turn': 40 ; 'on': 38 ; 'light': 28	42560
Turn off light	'turn': 40 ; 'off': 41 ; 'light': 28	45920
Turn light red	'turn': 40 ; 'light': 28 ; 'red': 25	28000
Turn light blue	'turn': 40 ; 'light': 28 ; 'blue': 18	20160

For the over-the-air and human comprehensibility tests, random samples of adversarial wake phrases and adversarial commands that had been successful in the audio file input tests were concatenated in different combinations to generate potential full adversarial commands, i.e. adversarial commands that would both activate the Assistant and trigger a specific target command. Potential full adversarial commands for each of the target commands were generated at different mangling levels. These levels were fully mangled commands, commands in which four of the original words had been mangled (two in the wake phrase and two in the specific target command, or one in the wake phrase and three in the specific target command), commands in which three of the original words had been mangled (one in the wake phrase and two in the specific target command, or two in the wake phrase and one in the specific target command), and commands in which two of the original words had been mangled (one in the wake phrase and one in the specific target command). Two potential adversarial commands were generated at each of the partial mangling levels, one in which the word 'Google' was one of mangled words, and one in which 'Google' was not mangled. This was in order to test the effect of the presence of the unmangled word 'Google' on machine and human comprehensibility of partially mangled adversarial commands.

Machine Comprehensibility Tests. The Google Assistant SDK was integrated in a Ubuntu virtual machine (version 18.04). The reason for accessing the

Google Assistant system via the Google Assistant SDK was that, unlike in the case of accessing Google Assistant using commercial devices such as the Google Home device, this allowed the Assistant's transcriptions of speech input to be retrieved. The transcriptions that could be retrieved using the Google Assistant SDK integrated in a virtual machine included both interim and final transcriptions of speech input to the Assistant. Two separate versions of Google Assistant SDK were integrated in the virtual machine; the Google Assistant Service, and the Google Assistant Library. The Google Assistant Service is activated via keyboard stroke and thus does not require a wake phrase, and voice commands can be inputted as audio files as well as over-the-air via a microphone. The Google Assistant Library, on the other hand, does require a wake phrase for activation, and receives commands via a microphone only. The Google Assistant Service could therefore be used to test adversarial commands for target commands and for the wake phrase separately via audio file input rather than via a microphone. The Google Assistant Library could be used to test the activation of the Assistant and the triggering of a target command by an adversarial wake phrase and adversarial command in combination over the air, representing a more realistic attack scenario. The Assistant's response to plain-speech versions of each target command was tested first to confirm that these target commands triggered the relevant target action.

Audio File Input Tests. For the audio file input tests, the target system's responses to audio versions of potential adversarial wake phrases and commands created using Amazon Polly were tested separately via command line input. The audio file input tests were performed at different levels of mangling using a filtering process for generating potential adversarial wake phrases and commands that built on successes found at a previous level of mangling. The testing process was automated using a Python script that first tested all possible potential adversarial wake phrases and commands in which only one of the original words had been mangled. Potential adversarial wake phrases and commands that were successful at this first level were then combined with one another to create a second level of potential adversarial wake phrases and commands in which two words had been mangled, with potential adversarial wake phrases and commands that were not successful at the first level being discarded. In the case of potential adversarial commands, a third level was also tested consisting of combinations of successful adversarial commands from the first level and successful adversarial commands at the second to generate fully mangled adversarial commands. At the mangling levels subsequent to the first level, the Python script tested up to a maximum of 150 potential adversarial commands at each level using random sampling, with a target of maximum 100 successes. This random sampling process was followed due to the large space of potential adversarial commands. A target action was considered to have been triggered if the Assistant's final transcription of adversarial input matched the target command.

Over-the-Air Tests. For the over-the-air tests, a random sample of adversarial wake phrases and adversarial commands that had been successful in audio file input tests at different levels of mangling were concatenated to form full potential adversarial commands for five of the six target commands (the target command "turn light red" was not included due to a lack of successful adversarial commands being identified in the audio file input tests at higher levels of mangling). These potential full adversarial commands were tested via microphone input using Google Assistant Library. Table 2 shows the concatenations of randomly selected successful adversarial wake phrases and commands at different mangling levels for the target commands that were tested in over-the-air tests.

Table 2. Samples of successful adversarial wake phrases and commands concatenated for over-the-air and human comprehensibility tests.

Target command w. condition	fully mangled command	Level 4	Level 3	Level 2
Hey Google who am I (Google unmangled first)	Z'eI l'Uk@L spl'u: bl'am str'aI ("zhay lookle sploo blam strai")	v'eI g'u:g@L spl'u: bl'am str'aI ("vay Google sploo blam strai")	v'eI g'u:g@L v'u: T'am 'aI ("vay Google voo tham I")	v'eI g'u:g@L h'u: T'am 'aI ("vay Google who tham I")
as above (Google unmangled last)	as above	Z'eI l'Uk@L v'u: T'am 'aI ("zhay lookle voo tham I")	Z'eI l'Uk@L h'u: T'am 'aI ("zhay lookle who tham I")	h'eI g'Ud@L h'u: T'am 'aI ("Hey goodle who tham I")
Hey Google what's my name (Google unmangled first)	T'eI gl'u:s@L D'0ts sn'aI z'eIm ("thay gloosle thots snai zame")	Z'eI g'u:g@L D'0ts sn'aI z'eIm ("zhay Google thots snai zame")	Z'eI g'u:g@L w'0ts gr'aI Z'eIm ("zhay Google what's grai zhame")	Z'eI g'u:g@L w'0ts bl'aI n'eIm ("zhay Google what's blai name")
as above (Google unmangled last)	as above	h'eI w'u:b@L D'0ts sn'aI z'eIm ("Hey wooble thots snai zame")	h'eI w'u:b@L w'0ts gr'aI Z'eIm ("Hey wooble what's grai zhame")	h'eI w'u:b@L w'0ts bl'aI n'eIm ("Hey wooble what's blai name")
Hey Google turn on light (Google unmangled first)	Z'eI fl'Uk@L D'3:n f'0n D'aIt ("zhay flookle thurn fon thight")	Z'eI g'u:g@L D'3:n f'0n D'aIt ("zhay Google thurn fon thight")	Z'eI g'u:g@L t'3:n tr'0n p'aIt ("zhay Google turn tron pight")	Z'eI g'u:g@L br'3:n '0n l'aIt ("zhay Google brurn on light")
as above (Google unmangled last)	as above	h'eI k'u:s@L D'3:n f'0n D'aIt ("Hey koosle thurn fon thight")	Z'eI fl'Uk@L br'3:n '0n l'aIt ("zhay flookle brurn on light")	h'eI k'u:s@L br'3:n '0n l'aIt ("Hey koosle brurn on light")
Hey Google turn off light (Google unmangled first)	v'eI g'u:t@L g'3:n bl'0f j'aIt ("vay gootle gurn blof yight")	v'eI g'u:g@L g'3:n bl'0f j'aIt ("vay Google gurn blof yight")	v'eI g'u:g@L pr'3:n b'0f l'aIt ("vay Google prurn bof light")	v'eI g'u:g@L tr'3:n '0f l'aIt ("vay Google trurn off light")
as above (Google unmangled last)	as above	h'eI k'u:z@L g'3:n bl'0f j'aIt ("Hey koozle gurn blof yight")	v'eI g'u:t@L tr'3:n '0f l'aIt ("vay gootle trurn off light")	h'eI k'u:z@L tr'3:n '0f l'aIt ("Hey koozle trurn off light")
Hey Google turn light blue (Google unmangled first)	Z'eI gl'u:p@L pl'3:n g'aIt v'u: ("zhay gloople plurn gight voo")	T'eI g'u:g@L pl'3:n g'aIt v'u: ("thay Google plurn gight voo")	T'eI g'u:g@L fl'3:n v'aIt bl'u: ("thay Google flurn vight blue")	T'eI g'u:g@L t'3:n Z'aIt bl'u: ("thay Google turn zhight blue")
as above (Google unmangled last)	as above	Z'eI gl'u:p@L fl'3:n v'aIt bl'u: ("zhay gloople flurn vight blue")	h'eI bl'Uk@L fl'3:n v'aIt bl'u: ("Hey blookle flurn vight blue")	h'eI bl'Uk@L t'3:n Z'aIt bl'u: ("Hey blookle turn zhight blue")

Human Comprehensibility Tests. The human comprehensibility tests used the same concatenations of adversarial wake phrases and adversarial commands as were used in the over-the-air tests shown in Table 2. Participants in the human comprehensibility tests were presented with potential full adversarial commands in descending order of mangling on a spectrum from fully mangled adversarial commands to adversarial commands in which only one word in the wake phrase and one word in the target command had been mangled. This approach was taken so as to provide an indication of how many words would need to be mangled in an adversarial over-the-air command in order to escape human comprehensibility. Subjects were asked to indicate whether they had identified any meaning in the audio. If they had identified meaning, they were asked to indicate what meaning they heard. After hearing all of the potential adversarial commands, participants were also presented with a plain-speech version of the full target command, which provided a baseline for the comprehensibility tests, and also served as an attention test.

The potential full adversarial commands were separated into two sets for each target command. In the first set, "Google" was the first word to be revealed to the listener in plain-speech, whereas in the second set, "Google" was the final word to be revealed. The separation of these two conditions enabled an assessment of whether the presence of the specific word "Google" affected listeners' ability to detect the presence of a voice command, and to realise its possible content. Each set of five wake phrase and command combinations for each target command under each of the two conditions was played to six different participants.

Participants were recruited using the survey website Prolific Academic.[13] The experiments with human subjects received ethics clearance through the Departmental Research Ethics Committee of the Department of Computer Science at the University of Oxford. All subjects were native speakers of English.

2.3   Results

Machine Comprehensibility Tests

Audio File Input Tests. Table 3 shows the overall ratio of successes to failures in the audio file input tests, as well as the number of successes for adversarial wake phrases and commands at each level of mangling. The differences between success rates of potential adversarial wake phrases and commands at different levels of mangling are shown to be not very significant. This suggests that the approach of limiting the pool of potential adversarial wake phrases and commands tested at each mangling level to combinations of adversarial wake phrases commands successful at the previous level is effective in maximising the success rates of attacks at each level. With the exception of the "turn light red" target command, successful adversarial commands could be generated for all target commands at all mangling levels, as was also the case for the target wake phrase. Overall success rates for target commands apart from the "turn light red" command

---

[13] See https://prolific.ac/.

ranged from 29.9% to 63.8%. The "turn light red" target command appeared to be an outlier in terms of success rates for potential adversarial commands, with a success rate of only 3.2%; no clear reason for this was apparent. The overall success rate for the adversarial wake phrase was 14.4%.

Figure 3 shows an example of the output to the command line produced by a successful fully mangled wake phrase and two successful fully mangled adversarial commands, showing both interim and final transcriptions of the adversarial input by the Assistant.

Table 3. Success rates of adversarial commands in audio file input tests.

Target command	Overall success rate	Level 1 successes	Level 2 successes	Level 3 successes
Hey Google	14.4%	52	18	n.a.
Who am I	29.9%	46	21	18
What's my name	55.4%	56	52	57
Turn on light	49.2%	44	46	65
Turn off light	56.7%	52	50	83
Turn light red	3.2%	3	none	none
Turn light blue	63.8%	41	62	63

```
ADVERSARIAL WAKE PHRASE FOR "Hey Google": v'eI g'u:t@L ("vay gootle")

WARNING:root:Transcript of user request: "V".
WARNING:root:Transcript of user request: "wake".
WARNING:root:Transcript of user request: "Virgo".
WARNING:root:Transcript of user request: "very good".
WARNING:root:Transcript of user request: "viagogo".
WARNING:root:Transcript of user request: "hey Google".
WARNING:root:Transcript of user request: "hey Google".
WARNING:root:Transcript of user request: "hey Google".
WARNING:root:Playing assistant response.
WARNING:root:Expecting follow-on query from user.
WARNING:root:Finished playing assistant response.
RESPONSE TRANSCRIPTION: hi what can I do for you

ADVERSARIAL COMMAND FOR "who am I": f'u: D'am z'aI ("foo tham zai")

WARNING:root:Transcript of user request: "true".
WARNING:root:Transcript of user request: "through the".
WARNING:root:Transcript of user request: "who am".
WARNING:root:Transcript of user request: "fu Fareham".
WARNING:root:Transcript of user request: "who am I".
WARNING:root:Transcript of user request: "who am I".
WARNING:root:Transcript of user request: "who am I".
WARNING:root:Playing assistant response.
WARNING:root:Finished playing assistant response.

ADVERSARIAL COMMAND FOR "turn off light": n'3:n T'Of j'aIt ("nurn thoff yight")

WARNING:root:Transcript of user request: "no".
WARNING:root:Transcript of user request: "9".
WARNING:root:Transcript of user request: "turn off".
WARNING:root:Transcript of user request: "turn off the".
WARNING:root:Transcript of user request: "turn off  the".
WARNING:root:Transcript of user request: "turn off  my".
WARNING:root:Transcript of user request: "turn off  light".
WARNING:root:Transcript of user request: "turn off light".
WARNING:root:Transcript of user request: "turn off light".
WARNING:root:Playing assistant response.
WARNING:root:Finished playing assistant response.
```

Fig. 3. Audio File Input Tests - Successes.

Figure 4 shows some examples of the output to the command line produced by an unsuccessful fully mangled wake phrase and two unsuccessful fully mangled adversarial commands, showing both interim and final transcriptions of the adversarial input by the Assistant. The unsuccessful examples share one nonsensical word sound with the corresponding successful example in Fig. 3, demonstrating that the success or failure of adversarial wake phrases and target commands in triggering a target action was influenced not only by the probabilities allocated to individual word sounds by the acoustic model used in the Assistant's speech recognition, but also by the probabilities allocated to utterances as a whole by the Assistant's language model.

Over-the-Air Tests. Table 4 shows the results of tests of the Assistant's response to input via microphone of audio versions of the partially mangled and fully mangled adversarial commands listed in Table 2. Specifically, the complete target action was activated by the adversarial commands for the 'what's my name' target command at the fourth, third and second levels of mangling under the condition of the word Google being revealed last, and by the adversarial command for 'turn on light' at the second level of mangling under the condition of the word Google being revealed last. There were also instances where although the target command itself was not triggered, the adversarial command did activate the Assistant by triggering the wake phrase.

Human Comprehensibility Tests. Table 5 shows the results of tests of human comprehensibility of audio versions of the partially mangled and fully mangled full adversarial commands listed in Table 2. The results are summarised according to whether a simple majority of participants identified no meaning, part of the target command meaning, or the full target command meaning in the adversarial audio input. Where different results are identified by an equal number of participants, this is indicated in the table. There were four instances where participants returned a blank test result. In these cases, results are given out of five participants instead of six, as detailed in the table.

A consistent result across all the tests was that, with one sole exception, none of the participants identified any meaning in the fully mangled adversarial wake phrase and target command combinations. Otherwise the results from this small-scale test represent a more mixed picture. Some participants did not hear any meaning in the audio clips prior to hearing the plain-speech command, whereas others picked up some of the adversarial wake phrase and target command words at the lower levels of mangling prior to hearing the plain-speech command. Some participants identified words in adversarial commands that were not actually present in the wake phrase or target command. A few participants believed that they had heard a different language, or tried to transcribe some of the nonsensical word sounds. A couple of participants identified the entire meaning of a target command prior to hearing the plain-speech version in some instances. The condition as to whether the word 'Google' was revealed first or last did not appear to significantly affect the participants' ability to detect the content of the

```
ADVERSARIAL WAKE PHRASE FOR "Hey Google": v'eI gl'u:f@L ("vay gloofle")

WARNING:root:Transcript of user request: "V".
WARNING:root:Transcript of user request: "wake".
WARNING:root:Transcript of user request: "vehicle".
WARNING:root:Transcript of user request: "fake love".
WARNING:root:Transcript of user request: "The Gruffalo".
WARNING:root:Transcript of user request: "The Gruffalo".
WARNING:root:Transcript of user request: "The Gruffalo".
WARNING:root:Playing assistant response.
WARNING:root:Finished playing assistant response.

ADVERSARIAL COMMAND FOR "who am I": spl'u: bl'am z'aI ("sploo blam zai")

WARNING:root:Transcript of user request: "screw".
WARNING:root:Transcript of user request: "play".
WARNING:root:Transcript of user request: "volume".
WARNING:root:Transcript of user request: "who do I am sorry".
WARNING:root:Transcript of user request: "who do I am sorry".
WARNING:root:Transcript of user request: "volume three".
WARNING:root:Finished playing assistant response.


ADVERSARIAL COMMAND FOR "turn off light": n'3:n v'0f tS'aIt ("nurn voff chight")

WARNING:root:Transcript of user request: "no".
WARNING:root:Transcript of user request: "Night by".
WARNING:root:Transcript of user request: "new bar".
WARNING:root:Transcript of user request: "new bath".
WARNING:root:Transcript of user request: "buy a".
WARNING:root:Transcript of user request: "bye bye".
WARNING:root:Transcript of user request: "turn both tried".
WARNING:root:Transcript of user request: "9 Bath Street".
WARNING:root:Playing assistant response.
WARNING:root:Finished playing assistant response.
```

Fig. 4. Audio File Input Tests - Losses.

Table 4. Results of Over-the-Air Tests.

Condition	fully mangled command	Level 4	Level 3	Level 2	Target command
Google unmangled first	wake phrase activated	unsuccessful	unsuccessful	unsuccessful	Hey Google who am I
Google unmangled last	as above	wake phrase activated	unsuccessful	unsuccessful	as above
Google unmangled first	unsuccessful	unsuccessful	unsuccessful	unsuccessful	Hey Google what's my name
Google unmangled last	as above	successful	successful	successful	as above
Google unmangled first	unsuccessful	unsuccessful	unsuccessful	unsuccessful	Hey Google turn on light
Google unmangled last	as above	unsuccessful	unsuccessful	successful	as above
Google unmangled first	unsuccessful	unsuccessful	unsuccessful	unsuccessful	Hey Google turn off light
Google unmangled last	as above	unsuccessful	unsuccessful	unsuccessful	as above
Google unmangled first	unsuccessful	unsuccessful	unsuccessful	unsuccessful	Hey Google turn light blue
Google unmangled last	as above	unsuccessful	unsuccessful	unsuccessful	as above

entire command. A notable result was that the adversarial commands for the 'what's my name' target command at the fourth and third levels of mangling under the condition of the word 'Google' being revealed last that had been effective in triggering the target action in the over-the-air tests were identified as also being successful in evading human comprehensibility. Thus these two partially mangled adversarial commands represent fully effective covert attacks on the target system.

As regards transcription of the plain-speech target commands, these were transcribed correctly by a large majority of participants. There were three instances where transcription of the plain-speech command was incomplete, one where it was incorrect, and one where transcription of the plain-speech was missing.

Table 5. Results of Human Comprehensibility Tests.

Condition	fully mangled command	Level 4	Level 3	Level 2	Target command
Google unmangled first	no meaning (5/6 participants)	no meaning (5/6 participants)	no meaning/partial meaning (3/6 participants)	partial meaning (4/6 participants)	Hey Google who am I
Google unmangled last	as above	no meaning (4/6 participants)	no meaning (4/6 participants)	partial meaning (4/6 participants)	as above
Google unmangled first	no meaning (6/6 participants)	no meaning (4/6 participants)	partial meaning (4/6 participants)	partial meaning (5/6 participants)	Hey Google what's my name
Google unmangled last	as above	partial meaning (4/6 participants)	no meaning/partial meaning (3/6 participants)	partial/full meaning (2/5)	as above
Google unmangled first	no meaning (6/6 participants)	no meaning (5/6 participants)	no meaning/partial meaning (3/6 participants)	partial meaning (5/6)	Hey Google turn on light
Google unmangled last	as above	no meaning (4/6 participants)	partial meaning (4/6 participants)	partial meaning (4/6 participants)	as above
Google unmangled first	no meaning (6/6 participants)	no meaning (4/6 participants)	no meaning/partial meaning (3/6 participants)	partial meaning (5/6 participants)	Hey Google turn off light
Google unmangled last	as above	no meaning (5/6 participants)	no meaning/partial meaning (3/6 participants)	partial meaning (5/6 participants)	as above
Google unmangled first	no meaning (6/6 participants)	no meaning (5/5 participants)	no meaning (3/5 participants)	partial meaning (6/6 participants)	Hey Google turn light blue
Google unmangled last	as above	no meaning (5/6 participants)	partial meaning (5/6 participants)	partial meaning (5/6 participants)	as above

2.4 Discussion

The combined results from the machine response and human comprehensibility tests confirm the hypothesis that voice-controlled digital assistants are potentially vulnerable to covert attacks using nonsensical word sounds. The key finding is that voice commands to voice-controlled digital assistant Google Assistant can be triggered by nonsensical word sounds in some instances, whereby the same nonsensical word sounds are perceived by humans as either not having any meaning at all, or as having a meaning only partially related to the voice commands to the Assistant. This supports the hypothesis that adversarial input consisting of nonsensical word sounds having an acoustic relationship with target command words may be recognised as legitimate commands at a confidence level equal to or higher than that required for speech recognition by the Google Assistant target system as trained for optimal performance in recognition of legitimate commands. The findings further show that it is not always necessary to replace all of the original words in a target command in order to generate an adversarial command that is successful in triggering a target action in a target system. Particularly with regard to over-the-air attacks, replacing only some rather than all of the target command words with nonsense words may increase the success rate of adversarial commands, whilst still preserving the covert nature of the attacks in terms of being hidden from human understanding. This is based on the finding that partially mangled adversarial commands were successful both in triggering a target action over-the-air and in hiding from human recognition in some instances.

The results confirm the influence of the three features of speech recognition in current voice-controlled systems in enabling this type of attack via the speech interface, as discussed above. These three features were thus shown to represent security vulnerabilities in the current generation of voice-controlled digital assistants.

The first of these features was the target system's inability to recognise the true nature of nonsensical word sounds. As envisaged, the attacks demonstrated in this experimental work exploit a vulnerability in the speech recognition functionality of the Google Assistant target system of being unable to recognise nonsensical word sounds as meaningless. In the results of the experimental work, the Google Assistant target system always either indicated incomprehension or attempted to match the nonsensical sounds to real words, rather than transcribing the nonsense word sound. This confirms that the Assistant is vulnerable to being fooled by word sounds that are perceived by humans as obviously nonsensical. The findings are in accord with the hypothesis behind these experiments that as a grey area between speech and non-speech, nonsensical word sounds represent a part of the input space to a voice-controlled system that the current generation of voice-controlled digital assistants struggles to handle appropriately. Whilst the Assistant does reject some of the input from this grey area as incomprehensible, in other instances input from this grey area is treated as meaningful input.

The second of these features was the influence of the language model in enabling the success of some of the attacks. The examples found in the experiment of the same nonsensical word sounds being present in both successful and unsuccessful adversarial wake phrases and commands confirms that the triggering of a target action by adversarial input may be influenced by probabilities allocated by the language model used in speech recognition to an utterance as a whole, as well as by probabilities allocated to individual word sounds by the acoustic model. Thus the aim of language modelling of 'correcting' possible incorrect word recognitions may have the opposite effect in an adversarial context of enabling the success of attacks based on nonsensical word sounds in some instances.

The third feature shown to be exploited in the attacks was discrepancy in human and machine processing of nonsensical input. The machine and human responses to nonsensical word sounds in general were comparable, in that both machine and humans frequently indicated incomprehension of the sounds, or else attempted to fit them to meaningful words. However, in the specific instances of nonsensical word sound sequences that triggered a target command in Google Assistant, human listeners did not hear a Google Assistant voice command in the nonsensical word sounds that had triggered a target command in the majority of instances. In addition to either indicating incomprehension or transcribing the nonsensical sounds as real words, human subjects on occasion attempted to transcribe the nonsensical word sounds phonetically as nonsense syllables. This superior ability of humans to recognise nonsensical word sounds as meaningless paradoxically prevented human listeners from detecting the presence of a malicious voice command, thus enabling the covert attacks.

A notable feature of the results of human comprehensibility tests is their variability between individual experimental subjects. Thus the covert nature of these attacks depends to some extent on individual human perception, i.e. whereas some individuals may hear target command words in an adversarial command based on nonsensical word sounds, others may not. This was seen in the variable results of the human comprehensibility tests described above. Human perception of word sounds is known to be unstable in some instances, seen for example in a widely shared audio recording in which some listeners heard the word "Yanny" whereas others heard the word "Laurel".[14]

3   Missense Attacks on Amazon Alexa and RASA NLU

3.1   Description and Context

This section presents experimental work demonstrating that it is possible to gain unauthorised access to a voice-controlled system using utterances that are

---

[14] See for example The Guardian, "Laurel or Yanny explained: why do some people hear a different word?", 17th May 2018, https://www.theguardian.com/technology/2018/may/16/yanny-or-laurel-sound-illusion-sets-off-ear-splitting-arguments.

accepted by the system as a target command despite having a different meaning to the target command in terms of human understanding. We term this type of attack a 'missense' attack, in accordance with a taxonomy of attacks via the speech interface published in a previous paper [4], which categorises attacks via the speech interface according to human perceptual categories. The attack can also be characterised as a black-box adversarial learning attack. The aim of the attacks of generating adversarial utterances that trigger a target command but that are unrecognisable as such to humans was realised by embedding alternate meanings of target command words in an unrelated utterance to create an adversarial utterance. As stated above, these attacks are termed 'word transplant' attacks.

In prior work, Carlini and Wagner [17] have used crafted audio recordings of speech that is unrelated to voice commands to attack a speech transcription system. Whereas the attacks by Carlini and Wagner target speech recognition functionality, the attacks presented here target natural language understanding. There have been no comparable attacks targeting natural language understanding in voice-controlled systems reported in prior work. There have been some examples of attacks on natural language understanding in related areas, such as sentiment analysis (see for example Kuleshov et al. [18]). However, these attacks have used different attack methods based on word substitution. Word transplant attacks have not been demonstrated in any prior work, and thus represent a novel attack concept.

Linguistically plausible adversarial examples that trigger an action in a voice-controlled system with an utterance of apparently unrelated meaning are difficult to generate using automated, mathematical approaches. As noted by Papernot et al. [5], adversarial learning in the context of natural language understanding technologies that take as input a sequence of words is not a differentiable problem. Papernot et al. concede that their own work on fooling a sentiment classifier with 'nonsensical' sentences generated using a mathematical method has some limitations, in that the nonsensical nature of the adversarial sentences is easily noticeable by humans. They point to the need in future work to address grammar and semantics in adversarial sentence generation, in order to make sentences indistinguishable from innocent utterances by humans. The attacks demonstrated here attempt to do this using a manual, non-mathematical approach for generating adversarial voice commands by manipulating linguistic parameters such as syntactic structures and word meanings, rather than mathematical parameters such as acoustic features or word embedding vector values.

Natural language understanding in voice-controlled systems involves a process of semantic parsing for mapping transcriptions of spoken utterances to a formal representation of the utterances' meaning that the system can use to trigger an action. This usually involves some form of machine learning such as Conditional Random Fields (CRFs) or RNNs (see for example Mesnil et al. [19]). The process of semantic parsing may take into account the syntactical structure of an utterance as well as the presence of individual words to determine the most appropriate action to take in response to a natural language command (see for example McTear [8]). The state-of-the-art in machine natural language understanding is known to fall far short of human abilities (see for example Cambria and White [20]).

The hypothesis behind the attacks presented here is that the deficiencies of natural language functionality in the current generation of voice-controlled digital assistants may render such systems vulnerable to being misled by adversarially crafted input that triggers a target action in the system, whilst being perceived by humans as unrelated to that target action. Specifically, it is hypothesised that word transplant attacks will exploit deficiencies in out-of-domain detection, that is the ability to reliably distinguish between relevant and irrelevant speech input (see for example Tür et al. [21]), as well as deficiencies in word-sense disambiguation, that is the ability to reliably determine the correct meaning of a word in context (see for example Stolk et al. [22]). Current systems identify speech input as in-domain or out-of-domain based the presence or absence of a combination of linguistic features, with word sense disambiguation being performed as part of this process based on co-occurrence of words in a given context. Such methods may be misled by crafted adversarial commands that retain some elements of a target command, as is the case in the word transplant attacks demonstrated here that reuse content words from a target command in a different sense context. Crafted adversarial input of this type is likely to thwart the system's ability to understand the intent of an utterance based on combinations of features, and to determine the intended meaning of individual words based on the context of neighbouring words. Given the crudity of current methods in natural language understanding for distinguishing valid from invalid input, as in the case of the attacks on speech recognition using nonsensical word sounds described above, applying higher confidence levels for the determination of user intent in natural language understanding to thwart such attacks may result in non-acceptance by the system of legitimate input and thus damage usability of the system.

The deficiencies in the current state-of-the-art in natural language understanding in distinguishing relevant from irrelevant input necessitate an assumption in the design principles for systems such as voice-controlled digital assistants of a genuine intent between user and device to communicate as conversation partners. In other words, such systems have no choice but to assume that any speaker interacting with them intends to communicate a relevant meaning. The guidelines for developing Google Conversation Actions, for example, recommend applying a set of conversation rules known as 'Grice's Maxims', the first of which is "only say things which are true".[15] In an adversarial setting, the assumption of shared context does not hold, and thus puts the system at risk of being misled by malicious input in missense attacks.

The covert nature of the attacks depends on unrelated utterances being used for adversarial purposes not being detected as a trigger for a voice-controlled action by human listeners. It is in fact unlikely that human listeners will detect unrelated utterances as covert voice commands, as humans are for the most part

---

[15] See https://developers.google.com/actions/downloads/be-cooperative.pdf.

so proficient at the language comprehension task that a large part of human natural language interpretation is performed automatically without conscious consideration. Miller [23] states that the alternative meanings of a word of which the meaning in context is clear will not even occur to a human listener, claiming the humans hearing the sentence "He nailed the board across the window", for example, will not even notice that "board" has more than one meaning: "Only one sense of "board" (or of "nail") reaches conscious awareness." This suggests that the very proficiency of humans in natural language understanding may hinder victims in identifying attacks that seek to exploit the limitations of automated systems in performing the same task.

The attacks described here were demonstrated on two specific natural language understanding functionalities. The first of these was the natural language understanding functionality behind Amazon Alexa Skills. Skills are third-party applications that can be incorporated in the Alexa digital assistant. Developers of Amazon Alexa Skills can make use of generic templates for actions to be performed by the Skill that are made available in the Amazon Developer Console, the so-called Built-in Intents, and/or create their own Custom Intents using the tools provided in the developer environment (see Kumar et al. [24]). Alexa Skills share speech recognition and natural language understanding functionalities with the core Alexa digital assistant. The natural language understanding functionality in Amazon Alexa uses as a meaning representation structure the so-called Alexa Meaning Representation Language (AMRL), which consists of graph-based structures representing the actions that can be performed by Alexa on different types of entities (see Kollar et al. [25]). Built-In Intents for Alexa Skills are based on pre-existing AMRL structures. Custom Intents in Alexa Skills do not make use of pre-existing AMRL structures as such, however, they do make use of the same natural language understanding models for mapping natural language utterances to meaning representation made available in the developer environment for Alexa Skills, as explained by Kumar et al. As stated by Kumar et al., Alexa's natural language understanding functionality will generate a semantic representation of the Custom Intent based on the sample utterances provided by the user. Various models are used to map natural language utterances to meaning representation in Amazon Alexa Skills, including CRFs and neural networks (see Kumar et al.). Kumar et al. explain that the process of mapping natural language utterances to the semantic representation of an intent, i.e. semantic parsing, has both a deterministic and stochastic element. The deterministic element ensures that all of the sample utterances provided by the user will be reliably mapped to the intent, whereas the stochastic element ensures some flexibility in the parsing of previously unheard utterances.

The second target system used in the experiment was an open source natural language understanding functionality named RASA NLU. RASA NLU is a natural language understanding library made available for use by non-specialist developers.[16] The RASA NLU target system was implemented using the 'spacy sklearn' pipeline option, which incorporates pre-existing generic word embed-

---

[16] https://rasa.com/docs/nlu/.

dings, which are used in combination with training data provided by the user to train a classifier to recognise the intents specified by the developer (as detailed by Bocklisch et al. [26]). This enables users to create bots using a relatively small amount of training data.

The specific setting of the envisaged attacks is a voice assistant used for personal banking. The use of digital assistants in financial services is becoming more common, with some suggestion that such systems are seen as providing better customer service than human agents (as reported by Qi and Xiao [27]). In his book entitled 'Bank 4.0', Brett King claims that voice assistants will assume great signficance in banking and financial advice services in future development of the industry [28].

3.2 Experiment

Methodology. Two target systems were created for the purposes of the experiment. These were an Alexa Skill and a bot based on RASA NLU. Both systems were dummy banking assistants that mimic the capabilities of a real Alexa Skill made available by Capital One bank to its customers.[17] The Capital One Skill enables three types of intents that can be expressed by their customers via voice command, namely Check Your Balance, Track Your Spending, and Pay Your Bill. The dummy assistants created for the purposes of the experiment included mock versions of these three intents, as well as mock versions of two further intents, namely to reset a password that a user had forgotten, and to block a credit card that had been lost or stolen.The dummy Alexa Skill also implemented the pre-built FallBackIntent available in the Amazon Developer Console, which represents a confidence threshold for acceptance of valid input by the Skill. Without implementation of a confidence threshold via the FallbackIntent, an Alexa Skill will treat any utterance as relevant and match the utterance to one of its actions. The RASA NLU target system implemented the same five target intents as the dummy Alexa Skill, and also implemented five generic intents, namely a greeting intent, a thanks intent, a goodbye intent, an affirmation intent, and an intent to provide a name. The generic intents were implemented to improve robustness of the RASA NLU target system. The RASA NLU system further implemented a 'nonsense' intent that was intended to be representative of out-of-scope input, performing a similar function to the FallBackIntent in the Amazon Alexa Skill.

Training data for the five target intents was the same for both the dummy Alexa Skill and for the RASA NLU bot. The training utterances represented a combination of example commands publicised by Capital One for their real Alexa Skill, publicly available training data examples for a third-party banking assistant bot[18], and self-generated training data. The training datasets contained 30 utterances for the account balance, recent transactions and pay bill intents, and 15 utterances for the reset password and block card intents. The five generic

---

[17] https://www.capitalone.com/applications/alexa/.

[18] This was a template for a banking assistant bot made available by IBM at https://github.com/IBM/watson-banking-chatbot.

intents in the RASA NLU target system were trained with sample utterances made available to developers by RASA NLU. The nonsense intent in the RASA NLU target system was trained with a large set of unrelated utterances made available by a third-party developer of another banking bot.[19]

Table 6. Target systems' response to target commands.

Test/Target Intent	Test/Target Command	RASA NLU Test Result	Alexa Skill Test Result
get account balance	tell me the current balance	target intent triggered	target intent triggered
get recent transactions	show me all my transactions	target intent triggered	target intent triggered
pay bill	pay a bill for electricity	target intent triggered	target intent triggered
reset password	can't recall my password	target intent triggered	target intent triggered
block card	think my card is stolen	target intent triggered	target intent triggered

Table 7. Target systems' response to out-of-scope commands.

Control Intent	Control Command	RASA NLU Test Result	Alexa Skill Test Result
be back	I'll get back to you in a moment	nonsense intent triggered	FallBackIntent triggered
be back	be back in 5 min	nonsense intent triggered	FallBackIntent triggered
be back	I'll be back	nonsense intent triggered	FallBackIntent triggered
be back	I promise to come back	nonsense intent triggered	FallBackIntent triggered
be back	I'll be back in a few minutes	nonsense intent triggered	FallBackIntent triggered

After training of the target systems, the systems' responses to utterances not seen in training were tested with respect to both in-scope and out-of-scope utterances. Input to the target systems was text-based. A test utterance for each of the specific intents for triggering the five target actions was inputted. The test utterances were utterances that had not been used in training, but that were clearly within the scope of the given intent. In order to test the systems' ability to reject non-malicious out-of-scope input, the tests also assessed the systems' responses to five other utterances that were unrelated to any of the actions within the scope of the Alexa Skill target system or the RASA NLU target system (these were five training utterances for a 'be back' intent that was part of the sample training data made available to developers by RASA NLU). Details of the tests of the systems' responses to in-scope and non-malicious out-of-scope input are shown in Tables 6 and 7 respectively. The tests confirmed that the target systems were robust in their handling of in-scope input not seen in training and non-malicious out-of-scope input, with all of the test utterances triggering the appropriate intent in both systems, and all of the control utterances triggering the nonsense intent in the RASA NLU target system and the FallBackIntent in the Alexa Skill. The test utterances were thus used as target commands for the missense attacks. Testing of the dummy Alexa Skill was performed in a sandbox environment in the Amazon Developer Console only and was not deployed in the Alexa cloud. Testing of the RASA NLU system was performed locally via a terminal.

---

[19] https://github.com/Twanawebtech/bank-chatbot.

Potential adversarial utterances were generated using the following process. First, a list of content words from the sample utterances for each Custom Intent was extracted (content words are words that give meaning to a sentence or utterance, as distinguished from function words that contribute to the syntactical structure of the sentence or utterance rather to its meaning, examples being prepositions such as 'of', determiners such as 'the', pronouns such as 'he' etc.). This was done automatically using a Python script implementing the Natural Language Toolkit (NLTK).[20] Second, a dictionary API[21] was used to automatically retrieve different word meanings and usage examples for the content words in the target commands. This enabled the identification and use of unusual and outdated word meanings for the target command words, which might be expected to increase the probabilities of successfully misleading natural language understanding systems such as that implemented in an Alexa Skill or RASA NLU bot, which are likely to have been trained to handle only common and current meanings of words. Following the extraction of content words and alternate word meanings, potential adversarial utterances for each Custom Intent were then generated manually, by embedding alternate meanings of words from the target command in new utterances, using as few new content words as possible, to create a potential adversarial command with a different meaning to the target command. The response of both target systems to each potential adversarial utterance was then tested.

Results. Table 8 shows the results of the word transplant attacks. The Amazon Alexa Skill target system was seen to be more vulnerable that the RASA NLU system. All but one of the word transplant attacks on the Alexa Skill target system were successful. On the RASA NLU target system, word transplant attacks were successful in only two out of five instances.

Table 8. Target systems' response adversarial commands generated by word transplant.

Target Intent	Target Command	Adversarial Command (Word Transplant)	RASA NLU Test Result	Alexa Skill Test Result	original content words / total content words
get account balance	tell me the current balance	I kept my balance in the current	target intent triggered	target intent triggered	2 out of 3
get recent transactions	show me all my transactions	the transactions were for show	nonsense intent triggered	target intent triggered	2 out of 2
pay bill	pay a bill for electricity	bill of an anchor	nonsense intent triggered	target intent triggered	1 out of 2
reset password	can't recall my password	we can't recall our product	nonsense intent triggered	FallBackIntent triggered	1 out of 3
block card	think my card is stolen	your card is an ace	target intent triggered	target intent triggered	1 out of 2

---

[20] https://www.nltk.org/.
[21] https://developer.oxforddictionaries.com/.

3.3   Discussion

The results of the experiment confirm the hypothesis that natural language understanding functionality in systems such as Amazon Alexa Skills and RASA NLU is vulnerable to being misled by malicious actors using utterances that are accepted by the system as a valid action trigger, but are unrelated to the relevant target command in terms of their meaning as understood by humans. The results of the experiment support concerns surrounding the implementation of voice control in sensitive areas such as banking.[22]

The results confirm that, whilst measures for enabling voice-controlled systems to reject irrelevant input, such as the FallbackIntent in Alexa Skills or the nonsense intent in the RASA NLU banking bot, do prevent such systems from simply accepting any utterance directed towards them as valid commands, this is not sufficient to prevent voice-controlled systems from accepting irrelevant utterances that have been crafted maliciously so as to mislead natural language understanding functionality. In the case of the Alexa Skill target system, some adversarial commands were identified as the target command with a sufficiently high level of confidence to avoid triggering of the FallBackIntent, whereas in the case of the RASA NLU target system, some adversarial commands were identified as the target command with a higher confidence level than the confidence level assigned to the nonsense intent. The success of some adversarial commands in triggering the target command indicates that the capacities of natural language understanding functionality in current voice-controlled systems to distinguish valid from invalid input and to identify the correct meaning of words in a given context can be easily undermined. These issues represent significant security vulnerabilities, in that they may enable a malicious actor to gain control of a system using utterances that are unlikely to be recognised by the system's human users as a voice command to their system. A notable characteristic of these attacks is that they have the potential to be plausibly deniable, in that a target system's execution of a target action in response to an unrelated utterance vocalised in its environment might be easily explained as being due to an error on the part of the target system, rather than to malicious intent on the part of the source of the utterance.

A clear limitation of the attacks demonstrated here with respect to the Alexa Skill target system is that they do not take into account the need for an attacker to activate the Alexa assistant and the target Skill using a wake-word or activation phrase. However, this limitation should not be viewed as one which cannot be overcome in future work. Due to the known presence of false positives with respect to wake-word recognition, it might be possible to trigger activation of the wake-word by using a single natural language word, other than the wake-word itself, as part of an unrelated utterance, in order to subsequently be able to execute an adversarial learning attack targeting natural language understanding to trigger a specific target command. This possibility was in fact demonstrated in

---

[22] See for example phys.org, 20th June 2018, 'Banking by smart speaker arrives, but security issues exist', https://phys.org/news/2018-06-banking-smart-speaker-issues.html.

an incident in which an Amazon Alexa device misinterpreted a word spoken in a private conversation as the wake-word 'Alexa', and subsequently misinterpreted other words in the conversation as commands to send a message to a contact, resulting in a recording of a couple's private conversation in their home being sent to a colleague.[23] Whilst this transmission of private information occurred as a result of error rather than malicious intent, it highlights the potential for spoofing of wake-word recognition and the inadequacy of wake-word recognition as a security measure.

4   Future Work and Conclusions

The experimental results presented here consolidate initial results presented in our earlier paper, confirming that speech recognition in voice-controlled systems is vulnerable to being misled by adversarial input consisting of nonsensical word sounds that are perceived by legitimate users of voice-controlled systems as having no meaning, and that natural language understanding functionality in voice-controlled systems can be manipulated using crafted utterances that retain elements of a target command, but that are perceived by naive listeners as being unrelated to the action that an attacker is seeking to trigger.

Future work should seek to demonstrate the types of attacks investigated here on different systems and on a broader set of target commands. With respect to the 'nonsense' attacks targeting speech recognition, whilst the target commands used in the experiment performed here were real commands actually executable by Google Assistant, the methodology applied in the experiment described here of assessing the target system's response based on transcription of audio input, rather than an actual performed action, potentially expands the range of target commands beyond actions that are within the scope of a target system's actual capabilities to actions that are currently hypothetical. Therefore it would be possible to investigate the vulnerability of hypothetical target actions to attacks of this type before the actions are actually implemented as part of a live system. The ultimate focus of future work should be to develop defence mechanisms that can make voice-controlled systems more robust to nonsense and missense attacks at a general level.

References

1. Carlini, N., et al.: Hidden voice commands. In 25th USENIX Security Symposium (USENIX Security 2016), Austin, TX (2016)
2. Zhang, G., Yan, C., Ji, X., Zhang, T., Zhang, T., Xu, W. (2017). DolphinAttack: inaudible voice commands. arXiv preprint arXiv:1708.09537
3. Bispham, M. K., Agrafiotis, I., Goldsmith, M.: Nonsense attacks on Google Assistant and missense attacks on Amazon Alexa. In: Proceedings of International Conference on Information Systems Security and Privacy (2019)

---

[23] See BBC News, 24th May 2018, "Amazon Alexa heard and sent private chat", https://www.bbc.co.uk/news/technology-44248122.

4. Bispham, M.K., Agrafiotis, I., Goldsmith, M.: A taxonomy of attacks via the speech interface. In: Proceedings of Third International Conference on Cyber-Technologies and Cyber-Systems (2018)
5. Papernot, N., McDaniel, P., Swami, A., Harang, R.: Crafting adversarial input sequences for recurrent neural networks. In: Military Communications Conference, MILCOM 2016–2016 IEEE, pp. 49–54. IEEE (2016)
6. Nowak, M.A., Krakauer, D.C.: The evolution of language. Proc. Nat. Acad. Sci. **96**(14), 8028–8033 (1999)
7. McCurdy, N., Srikumar, V., Meyer, M.: RhymeDesign: a tool for analyzing sonic devices in poetry. In: Proceedings of the Fourth Workshop on Computational Linguistics for Literature, pp. 12–22 (2015)
8. McTear, M., Callejas, Z., Griol, D.: The Conversational Interface. Springer, Cham (2016). https://doi.org/10.1007/978-3-319-32967-3
9. Hazen, T.J., Bazzi, I.: A comparison and combination of methods for OOV word detection and word confidence scoring. In: Proceedings of 2001 IEEE International Conference on Acoustics, Speech, and Signal Processing, p. 1. 397–400 (2001)
10. Raju, A., Panchapagesan, S., Liu, X., Mandal, A., Strom, N.: Data augmentation for robust keyword spotting under playback interference (2018). Proceedings of arXiv preprint arXiv:1808.00563
11. Roberts, A.C., Wetterlin, A., Lahiri, A.: Aligning mispronounced words to meaning: evidence from ERP and reaction time studies. Mental Lexicon **8**(2), 140–163 (2013)
12. Lippmann, R.P., et al.: Speech recognition by machines and humans. Speech Commun. **22**(1), 1–15 (1997)
13. Scharenborg, O., Cooke, M.: Comparing human and machine recognition performance on a VCV corpus (2008)
14. Bailey, T.M., Hahn, U.: Phoneme similarity and confusability. J. Memory Lang. **52**(3), 339–362 (2005)
15. Meutzner, H., Gupta, S., and Kolossa, D.: Constructing secure audio captchas by exploiting differences between humans and machines. In Proceedings of the 33rd Annual ACM Conference on Human Factors in Computing Systems, pp. 2335–2338. ACM (2015)
16. Xiong, W., et al.: Achieving human parity in conversational speech recognition (2016). arXiv preprint arXiv:1610.05256
17. Carlini, N., Wagner, D.: Audio adversarial examples: targeted attacks on speech-to-text (2018). arXiv preprint arXiv:1801.01944
18. Kuleshov, V., Thakoor, S., Lau, T., Ermon, S.: Adversarial Examples for Natural Language Classification Problems. OpenReview submission OpenReview:r1QZ3zbAZ (2018)
19. Mesnil, G., et al.: Using recurrent neural networks for slot filling in spoken language understanding. IEEE/ACM Trans. Audio Speech Lang. Process. (TASLP) **23**(3), 530–539 (2015)
20. Cambria, E., White, B.: Jumping NLP curves: a review of natural language processing research. IEEE Comput. Intell. Mag. **9**(2), 48–57 (2014)
21. Tur, G., Deoras, A., Hakkani-Tür, D.: Detecting out-of-domain utterances addressed to a virtual personal assistant. In: Proceeding of Fifteenth Annual Conference of the International Speech Communication Association (2014)
22. Stolk, A., Verhagen, L., Toni, I.: Conceptual alignment: how brains achieve mutual understanding. Trends Cogn. Sci. **20**(3), 180–191 (2016)
23. Miller, G.A.: WordNet: a lexical database for English. Commun. ACM **38**(11), 39–41 (1995)

24. Kumar, A., Gupta, A., Chan, J., Tucker, S., Hoffmeister, B., Dreyer, M.: Just ASK building an architecture for extensible self-service spoken language understanding (2017). arXiv preprint arXiv:1711.00549
25. Kollar, T., et al.: The Alexa meaning representation language. In: Proceedings of Proceedings of the 2018 Conference of the North American Chapter of the Association for Computational Linguistics: Human Language Technologies, vol. 3, pp. 177–184 (2018)
26. Bocklisch, T., Faulkner, J., Pawlowski, N., Nichol, A.: Rasa: open source language understanding and dialogue management (2017). arXiv preprint arXiv:1712.05181
27. Qi, Y., Xiao, J.: Fintech: AI powers financial services to improve people's lives. Commun. ACM **61**(11), 65–69 (2018)
28. King, B.: Bank 4.0: Banking Everywhere, Never at a Bank. Marshall Cavendish Business, Singapore (2018)

Proposal and Performance Evaluation of an Order-Specified Aggregate Authority-Transfer Signature

Takuya Ezure[1] and Masaki Inamura[2(✉)]

[1] Graduate School of Science and Engineering, Tokyo Denki University, Tokyo, Japan
17rmd07@ms.dendai.ac.jp
[2] Center for Research and Collaboration, Tokyo Denki University, Tokyo, Japan
minamura@mail.dendai.ac.jp

Abstract. We propose a new order-specified aggregate authority-transfer signature based on the gap Diffie-Hellman group and evaluate the performance of it. In companies, in order to prevent stagnation of the work flow or suspension of operations accompanied by an accident due to concentration of authority to one or a few people, distribution and delegation of authority to multiple persons is performed. Currently, since various operations in a company are performed via a computer network, a mechanism of authority transfer to allow delegation and distribution of authority quickly and properly on this network is needed. In this paper, we propose an authority-transfer signature scheme combining an order-specified aggregate signature and a group signature. In our method, a signature scheme uses a group signature scheme to guarantee authority. Moreover, it transfers the authority owned by the manager to another member of the group. The difference from the group manager of existing group signatures is that this manager not only manages the group but also delegates authority. Regarding this signature, we implement a simulation program and evaluate the performance. As a result, we show that our proposal is practical.

Keywords: Digital signature · Aggregate signature · Authority transfer

1 Introduction

In recent years, a system using a digital signature has been developed as one of the methods for improving the efficiency and security of business activities in companies. For example, in an online system for requesting approval of a proposal, a digital signature is used as proof that authorized managers have approved it. This allows everyone to see if the workflow of the requesting approval is processed correctly. In the existing system, it is assumed that the requesting

Supported by JSPS KAKENHI Grant Number JP16K00192.

P. Mori et al. (Eds.): ICISSP 2019, CCIS 1221, pp. 121–136, 2020.
https://doi.org/10.1007/978-3-030-49443-8_6

approval is processed in one company. Therefore, it is assumed that the managers who can approve the request is in the same company. However, when a plurality of companies jointly works on a project, there is a need for approval of the proposal among the companies, and there are also managers in each company who can process the approval. Assuming such a case, it is necessary to have a new system for requesting approval of a proposal that can be approved among plural companies, and a new digital signature that can be adapted to this system.

In order to realize the digital signature shown the above, it is necessary to have the following three functions, which are to be able to:

- transfer the signer's authority to sign to someone else;
- aggregate multiple signatures and to reduce the size of a signature;
- verify the order of signing.

The first, in a normal digital signature, a private key and a public key are generated, and the signer holds the private key. The public key is published with the certificate of a trusted certificate authority. When signing a document, the signer uses his private key to sign. The verifier obtains the public key and verifies the signature. In this case, because only the signer holds the private key, other person cannot sign on behalf of this signers. Thus, if the signer is absent, the verifier cannot obtain the signature by this signer and must wait until he comes back. If it is possible to delegate the signer's authority to sign without passing his private key to others, it can be a solution to this problem. In this regard, Yao et al. proposed an anonymous-signer aggregate signature [1]. This method can transfer authority using a group signature, which is an anonymous digital signature. By improving this method, it is possible to construct the target digital signature.

The second, under the environment that there are also managers in each company who can process the approval when a plurality of companies jointly works on a project, there are plural signatures by these managers. A method for efficiently processing the plurality of signatures is needed. In this regard, there is a multisignature that aggregates the signatures of the same message by plural signers with a single signature [2], and an aggregate signature that aggregates signatures of different messages by plural signers with a single signature [3]. The above efficiently processing can be realized by applying these methods.

The third, when signing contracts and requesting approvals among plural companies, the order of signing may be important. Therefore, a multisignature or an aggregate signature, which can verify not only who signs the message but also in which order each of signers sign the document is needed.

We have proposed a new order-specified aggregate authority-transfer signature with the above three functions at ICISSP 2019 [4]. First, we have improved the group signature by Yao et al. and have proposed a new signature with a shorter verification time than the signature of Yao et al. Second, we have adapted the idea of structuring method of Yanai et al. [5] to the above new signature, and have realized the order-specified aggregate authority-transfer signature. We have used a graph for the complicated relationships among signers. In addition, we have discussed security analysis of our proposal.

Furthermore, in this paper, we evaluate the performance of our proposal in comparison with existing aggregate signature schemes. We focus on the number of pairing function operations, which dominates the verification time, and show that the number of these operations on our scheme is about as same as or less than those on other existing schemes. In addition, we implement a simulation program and evaluate the performance of our proposal and existing schemes. As a result, although we have added order-specified function to our signature scheme, we show that the performance of our proposal is equivalent to or better than those of other existing schemes.

This paper is structured as follows: Sect. 2 presents related work; Sect. 3 describes aggregate authority-transfer signature, which we have proposed, with discussion of security analysis; Sect. 4 describes expansion of the scheme in Sect. 3 into order-specified aggregate signature; Sect. 5 show the result of performance evaluation; finally, conclusions are drawn in Sect. 6.

2 Related Work

2.1 Aggregate Signature

The gap Diffie-Hellman (GDH) class was defined by Okamoto and Pointcheval [6]. The GDH Class has the following features: the computational Diffie-Hellman (CDH) problem is hard, and the decisional Diffie-Hellman (DDH) problem is easy. The class with these features can be realized on an elliptic curve using a function called pairing.

By using this elliptic curve, Boneh et al. proposed a digital signature scheme that verify the signature with pairing function. This is the Boneh-Lynn-Shacham (BLS) signature scheme [7]. Consider different additive cyclic groups $\mathbb{G}_1$ and $\mathbb{G}_2$ with prime order p. The BLS signature scheme is based on these groups and is structured as follows:

Key Generation: g is a generator of $\mathbb{G}_1$. The private key of the signer is a random element $x \in \mathbb{Z}_p^*$, and his public key is $v = xg$.
Signing: $H{:}\{0,1\}^* \to \mathbb{G}_2$ is a one-way hash function. m is both a plain message and a signing target. The signer computes $h = H(m)$ and returns $\sigma = xh$.
Verification: When the verifier is given (g, v, m, σ), he computes $h = H(m)$ and verifies $e(g, \sigma) = e(v, h)$.

In addition, Boneh et al. proposed an aggregate signature called the Boneh-Gentry-Lynn-Shacham (BGLS) signature [3] based on the BLS signature. It is possible to reduce the signature size and the verification time by aggregating this plurality of signatures. Consider a group U of n signers who contribute to an aggregate signature. Let $i \in U$ $(1 \leq i \leq n)$ be a signer participating in the aggregate signature. Each user i selects a message m_i to be signed and creates a signature σ_i for it. These signatures are then combined into one BGLS signature. The security depends on the co-CDH problem. The algorithm consists of key generation, signature, aggregation, and verification. Also, like the BLS signature, we use the definition of the GDH group on the elliptic curve for $(\mathbb{G}_1, \mathbb{G}_2)$. The algorithm is structured as follows:

Key Generation: g is a generator of $\mathbb{G}_1$. The private key of the signer $i \in U$ is
a random element $x_i \in \mathbb{Z}_p^*$, and his public key is $v_i = x_i g$.

Signing: $H:\{0,1\}^* \to \mathbb{G}_2$ is a one-way hash function. Let m_i be the message of
signer i. The signer i computes $h_i = H(m_i)$ and returns $\sigma_i = x_i h_i$.

Aggregation: Collect all individual signatures σ_i $(1 \le i \le n)$, and calculate
$\sigma = \sum_{i=1}^n \sigma_i$.

Verification: When the verifier is given (g, v_i, m_i, σ) $(1 \le i \le n)$, he computes
$h_i = H(m_i)$ $(1 \le i \le n)$ and verifies $e(g, \sigma) = \prod_{i=1}^n e(v_i, h_i)$.

2.2   Group Signature

A group signature is one of a digital signature scheme, in which a verifier can
confirm only the affiliation of a signer to a group and cannot identify who signed
it. The group signature can protect privacy by preventing identification of the
signer.

Several schemes have been proposed for this group signature, and Chen et al.
have proposed a group signature based on the BGLS signatures [8]. It is proved
that this group signature of Chen et al. is secure if the BGLS signature is secure.
Yao et al. have proposed an aggregate group signature that is an improvement
on this group signature [1]. This aggregate group signature is explained in the
following.

In advance, members create secret keys and public keys, and send the public
key to group manager GM. The GM processes this public key with the group
signature key based on the BGLS signature, and returns it to the member. An
aggregation of the BGLS signature of the message and the group signature key
is released as a group signature. Therefore, group signatures of multiple groups
can be aggregated into one. In addition, information such as an expiry date can
be included in the group signature key of each member issued by the GM, and
this information can be verified. Furthermore, Yao et al. have realized a method
of delegating authority by accompanying the group signature key with authority
information.

An aggregate group signature is organized as follows:

Preconditions:
  – $\mathbb{G}_1$ and $\mathbb{G}_2$ are the additive cyclic group and the multiplicative cyclic
    group of the prime order q, respectively, where $\mathbb{G}_1$ is the GDH group.
  – π is the generator of $\mathbb{G}_1$.
  – A map $e:\mathbb{G}_1 \times \mathbb{G}_1 \to \mathbb{G}_2$ is a bilinear map.
  – $H:\{0,1\}^* \to \mathbb{G}_1$ is a one-way hash function.

Set-Up:
  – A trusted third-party creates the parameter para$(\mathbb{G}_1, \mathbb{G}_2, e, \pi, H)$.
  – Member U chooses a private $s_u \in \mathbb{Z}_q^*$ as his private key and computes
    $P_u = s_u \pi$ as his public key.
  – Similarly, the GM chooses a private key $s_A \in \mathbb{Z}_q^*$ and computes the public
    key $P_A = s_A \pi$.

Join:

- U randomly chooses a number of privates $(x_1, \ldots, x_l \in \mathbb{Z}_q^*)$ and computes one-time signing factors $X_{u,1} = x_1\pi, \ldots, X_{u,l} = x_l\pi$ and one-time signing public keys $K_{u,1} = s_u x_1\pi, \ldots, K_{u,l} = s_u x_l\pi$. Keys P_u, $X_{u,i}$, and $K_{u,i}$ are sent to the GM, for all $i \in [1, l]$.
- The GM tests if $e(K_{u,i}, \pi) = e(P_u, X_{u,i})$ for all i. If the test fails, the protocol terminates. Otherwise, the GM runs the BGLS signing algorithm on inputs s_A and strings $T\|K_{u,i}$ (T is the authority information) to obtain $S_{u,i} = s_A H(T\|K_{u,i})$ for all i. $S_{u,i}$ is the ith one-time signing permit for U and is given to U. The GM adds tuples $(P_u, K_{u,i}, X_{u,i})$ to his record for all i.

Signing:

- U runs the BGLS signing algorithm with private key $s_u x_i$ and message M and obtains a signature $S_u = s_u x_i H(M)$.
- U aggregates signature S_u with one-time signing permit $S_{u,i}$ associated with private $s_u x_i$. This is done by running the aggregation function of the BGLS scheme, which returns a signature $S_g = S_u + S_{u,i}$.

Aggregation:

This is the same as the aggregation algorithm in the BGLS scheme. It takes as inputs n signatures S_{g_k} and the corresponding values P_{A_k} and K_{u_k,i_k} for all $k \in [1, n]$. Set $S_{Agg} = \sum_{k=1}^{n} S_{g_k}$.

S_{Agg} is outputted as the aggregate group signature.

Note that the kth GM public key P_{A_k} for $k \in [1, n]$ does not need to be the same. In other words, signatures from different organizations can be aggregated.

Verification:

- For $1 \leq k \leq n$, compute the hash digest $H(M_k)$ of message M_k and $h_k = H(T_k\|K_{u_k,i_k})$ of the statement on the one-time signing permit.
- S_{Agg} is accepted if $e(S_{Agg}, \pi) = \prod_{k=1}^{n} e(H(M_k), K_{u_k,i_k})e(h_k, P_{A_k})$.

Open:

If S_{Agg} is valid, the GM can easily identify a member's public key P_{u_k} from K_{u_k,i_k} by consulting the record.

3 Aggregate Authority-Transfer Signature

3.1 Motivation for Aggregate Authority-Transfer Signature

When signing for verifiers belonging to different companies to verify, it may be necessary to confirm the signer's identity, affiliation and authority. This requirement can be realized by using the method of Yao et al. as discussed in Sect. 2.2 [1]. Then, strong anonymity such as group signature is not required. Therefore, although aggregate authority-transfer signature is based on group signatures, it has different security requirements than existing group signatures.

Furthermore, the possibility of many people approving a request among plural companies increases the number of signatures to be aggregated and the verification time becomes longer. Therefore, the method of Yao et al. is improved to shorten the verification time.

In addition, unlike the group manager GM in the method of Yao et al. manager M not only manages groups but also delegates authority.

3.2 Security Definition

We describe the security of an aggregate authority-transfer signature. In order for this signature to be secure, the following conditions need to be satisfaction:

Correctness: A signature created by a legitimate member passes verification and identifies the signer.

Unforgeability: Only legitimate members can make valid signatures. Even if an attacker collaborates with another member or manager, it can not forge the signature of a member who is not collusion.

Traceability: The signature that passes the verification can always identify the signer. Even if an attacker collaborates with other members, it is impossible to create a signature that the verification passes but the signer cannot identify.

3.3 Construction

Preconditions:
  - $\mathbb{G}_1$ and $\mathbb{G}_2$ are the additive cyclic groups of the prime order q.
  - $\mathbb{G}_1$ and $\mathbb{G}_2$ are the co-GDH groups.
  - $\mathbb{G}_3$ is the multiplicative cyclic group of prime order q.
  - P is the generator of $\mathbb{G}_1$.
  - Q is the generator of $\mathbb{G}_2$.
  - A map $e{:}\mathbb{G}_1 \times \mathbb{G}_2 \to \mathbb{G}_3$ is a bilinear map.
  - $H_1{:}\{0,1\}^* \times \mathbb{G}_2 \to \mathbb{G}_1$ and
    $H_2{:}\{0,1\}^* \times \mathbb{G}_2 \to \mathbb{Z}_q^*$ are one-way hash functions.

Set-up:
  - A trusted third-party creates the parameter para($\mathbb{G}_1, \mathbb{G}_2, \mathbb{G}_3, P, Q, e, H_1, H_2$).
  - Member U chooses a private $s_u \in \mathbb{Z}_q^*$ as his private key and computes $P_u = s_u P$ as his public key.
  - Similarly, the manager M chooses his private key $s_A \in \mathbb{Z}_q^*$ and computes the public key $P_A = s_A Q$.

Join:
  - U randomly chooses a private $x \in \mathbb{Z}_q^*$ and computes signing factors $X_u = xQ$ and public keys $K_u = xs_u Q$. Keys P_u, X_u, and K_u are sent to the M.
  - The M confirms that P_u is U's public key. The GM tests if $e(P, K_u) = e(P_u, X_u)$. If the test fails, the protocol terminates. Otherwise, the M runs the BGLS signing algorithm on inputs s_A and strings $T_u \| K_u$ (T_u is the authority information transferred by manager) to obtain $S_u = s_A H_1(T_u \| K_u)$. S_u is an authority-transfer key and is given to U. The M adds tuples (P_u, K_u, X_u, T_u) to his record.

Signing:
  U signs message M. U gets an authority-transfer key S_u from the M. U randomly chooses $r \in \mathbb{Z}_q^*$. U computes the following:

$$B = rQ. \tag{1}$$
$$C = S_u + H_2(M\|B)xs_u P + rP. \tag{2}$$
$$K_u = xs_u Q. \tag{3}$$

The signature is $\sigma = \{B, C, K_u, T_u\}$.

Aggregation:

Aggregation takes as inputs n signatures, $\sigma_k = \{B_k, C_k, K_{u_k}, T_{u_k}\}$, and the corresponding values P_{A_k} and K_{u_k} for all $k \in [1, n]$. Only C_k can be aggregated and becomes $C_{Agg} = \sum_{k=1}^{n} C_k$. The aggregate authority-transfer signature is $\sigma_{Agg} = \{B_k, C_{Agg}, K_{u_k}, T_{u_k}\}$ for all $k \in [1, n]$.

Verification:

- For $1 \leq k \leq n$, compute the hash digests $H_1(K_{u_k} \| T_{u_k})$ and $H_2(M_k \| B_k)$.
- σ_{Agg} is accepted if

$$e(C_{Agg}, Q) = \prod_{k=1}^{n}(e(H_1(K_{u_k} \| T_{u_k}), P_{A_k}))$$
$$\cdot e(P, \sum_{k=1}^{n}(H_2(M_k \| B_k)K_{u_k} + B_k)).$$

Open:

If σ_{Agg} is valid, the M can easily identify a member's public key P_{u_k} from K_{u_k} by consulting the record.

3.4 Comparison with Yao et al.'s Method

Th aggregate authority delegation signature in Sect. 3.3 is compared with the method of Yao et al. [1], and we show the advantages and disadvantages of our signature.

The following are the verification formulas of Yao et al.'s method and the aggregate transfer signature when N signatures are aggregated.

The Verification Formula for Yao et al.'s Method:

$$e(S_{Agg}, \pi) = \prod_{k=1}^{n} e(H(M_k), K_{u_k, i_k})e(h_k, P_{A_k}). \tag{4}$$

The Verification Formula for Aggregate Authority-Transfer Signature:

$$e(C_{Agg}, Q) = e(P, \sum_{k=1}^{n}(H_2(M_k \| B_k)K_{u_k} + B_k)) \cdot \prod_{k=1}^{n}(e(H_1(K_{u_k} \| T_{u_k}), P_{A_k})). \tag{5}$$

The number of pairings calculated when verifying the aggregate signature for N signatures for the formula of Yao et al. is $2N + 1$. On the other hand, The number of pairings calculated when verifying the aggregate signature for N signatures for the formula of our proposal. is $N + 2$. From the above, it can be seen that the number of pairings at the time of verification of the aggregate authority-transfer signature is about half of that of Yao et al.'s method if the number of signatures, N, is large. An advantage is that the verification time can be shortened by reducing the number of pairings. A disadvantage is that the number of signatures of a point on the elliptic curve increases by 1 for each message. However, since the points on the elliptic curve are not large, the advantage of shortening the verification time is greater than the disadvantage that the signature size increases.

3.5   Security Analysis

We prove the security of the aggregate authority-transfer signature described in Sect. 3.3. First, we prove the security of a single authority-transfer signature that does not aggregate. Second, we prove the security of the aggregate authority-transfer signature.

Correctness: The correctness of the authority-transfer signature is proved as follows:

$$
\begin{aligned}
e(C, Q) &= e(S_u + H_2(M\|B)xs_u P + rP, Q) \\
&= e(S_u, Q) \cdot e(H_2(M\|B)xs_u P, Q) \cdot e(rP, Q) \\
&= e(s_A H_1(T_u\|K_u), Q) \cdot e(H_2(M\|B)xs_u P, Q) \cdot e(rP, Q) \\
&= e(H_1(T_u\|K_u), s_A Q) \cdot e(P, H_2(M\|B)xs_u Q) \cdot e(P, rQ) \\
&= e(H_1(T_u\|K_u), P_A) \cdot e(P, H_2(M\|B)K_u) \cdot e(P, B) \\
&= e(H_1(T_u\|K_u), P_A) \cdot e(P, H_2(M\|B)K_u + B).
\end{aligned}
\tag{6}
$$

Unforgeability: In the authority-transfer signature scheme, attackers can be either a member or a manager. We do not consider cases where the third party is an attacker because fewer information is available than other attackers.

The Ability to Attack When the Attacker is a Member of the Group:
- Create and register new members.
- Issue authority-transfer authority key A to a new member.
- Collusion between a new member and another member (non-collusion with a manager).

The Attack Target When the Attacker is a Member of the Group:
Passing verification using K for a member other than the member who has colluded or the new member.

The ability to attack when the attacker is a manager:
- Create and Register New Members.
- Issue authority-transfer authority key A to a new member.
- Collusion between a new member and an existing member.

The Attack Target When the Attacker is a Manager:
Passing verification using K for members other than the member who has colluded or the new member.

Security is considered by looking at the signature formula. The signature $C = S_u + H_2(M\|B)xs_u P + rP$ can be divided into the following:

$$
A = S_u = s_A H_1(T_u\|K_u).
\tag{7}
$$
$$
D = H_2(M\|B)xs_i P + rP.
\tag{8}
$$

The respective verification equations are the following:

$$e(A, Q) = e(s_A H_1(T_u \| K_u), Q)$$
$$= e(H_1(T_u \| K_u), s_A Q). \tag{9}$$
$$e(D, Q) = e(H_2(M \| B) x s_i P + r P, Q)$$
$$= e(P, H_2(M \| B) K_u) \cdot e(P, B). \tag{10}$$

The authority-transfer key A of formula (7) and signatures K and T are keys issued during the interaction between the member and a manager. Therefore, there is a possibility that the key information is leaked because of communication leakage or collusion. In addition, old signatures can also be obtained. We set the following attack environment which is favorable to attackers.

Attacker's Environment: An attacker can obtain all authority-transfer keys A, signatures $\sigma = \{B, C, K_u, T_u\}$, and messages M issued, including the forgery target.

For an attacker to forge a signature, they must forge both expression (9) and expression (10). Expression (9) is the same as the BLS signature, where the message is the authority information T_u and the signature K_u. Forging the authority information T_u and the signature K_u corresponding to the message is difficult because of the security of the BLS signature. It is difficult for an attacker who is a member to forge a signature other than the signature K_u. Therefore, the attack target of an attacker who is a member is the same as the attack target of an attacker who is a manager. The attacker tries to forge expression (10) using the signature K_u, where the verification formula of expression (9) is established. There are roughly two methods for forging expression (10).

- Obtain $x s_u$ from the signature $K_u = x s_u Q$ made by the forgery target. Alternatively, obtain r_n from signature $B = r Q$.

  This is difficult because it is a discrete logarithm problem on an elliptic curve.

- Obtain $H_2(M \| B) x s_u P$ or $r P$ from the signature C made by the forgery target. Then, extract $H_2(M \| B)$ from $H_2(M \| B) x s_u P$, find $x s_u P$, and use it for forgery.

  If it is possible to find the same signature $B = r Q$ in multiple signatures, there is a possibility that $x s_u P$ can be obtained, but since the r used for a signature is random, the probability of a match is low.

Unforgeability of the Aggregate Authority-Transfer Signature: The security of the aggregate authority transfer signature will be briefly described. Authority transfer signature and aggregate authority transfer signature indicate that unforgeability is equivalent.

We prove this security using the method of Boldyreva [9,10], which is used in Inamura et al.'s system as the security proof [11,12]. Let A be an attacker who is attempting to forge an aggregate authority-transfer signature C'_{Agg}. Let B be an attacker who forges an authority-transfer signature. If A's attack succeeds, it indicates that B's attack succeeds. If B's attack succeeds, it is obvious that A's attack will succeed, so the proof of this is omitted.

Attacker B has a verification key of the object to be forged $\sigma_1 = \{K_{u_1}, T_{u_1}, P_{A_1}, B_1\}$ and responds to the random oracle and the signature oracle. Attacker B executes A as an honest player. First, B gives σ_1 to A. Attacker A outputs other signature keys and verification keys

$$\left\{ \begin{array}{l} (S_{u_2}, x_2 s_{u_2}, r_2, T_{u_2}, K_{u_2}, B_2, P_{A_2}), \ldots, \\ (S_{u_n}, x_n s_{u_n}, r_n, T_{u_n}, K_{u_n}, B_n, P_{A_n}) \end{array} \right\}.$$

Also, attacker A uses the random oracle and the signature oracle to find C'_{Agg} and the message $(M_1, \ldots, M_n)$ to be signed, and responds to B. Attacker B computes the following using C'_{Agg}:

$$C'_{Agg} - \sum_{i=2}^{n} (S_{u_i} + H_2(M_i \| B_i) x_i s_{u_i} P + r_i P)$$

$$= S_{u_1} + H_2(M_1 \| B_1) x_1 s_{u_1} P + r_1 P.$$

Therefore, the authority-transfer signature corresponding to σ_1 can be computed, and B's attack succeeds.

As described above, it is difficult to forge the aggregate authority-transfer signature if forgery of the authority-transfer signature is difficult.

Traceability: Expression (9) of the verification expression is a BLS signature in which the message is the authority information T_u and the signature K_u. Therefore, it is difficult to make a signature that can pass verification with the signature K_u that cannot be tracked because of the security of the BLS signature, even if a member collaborates with another member.

4   Order-Specified Aggregate Authority-Transfer Signature

4.1   Motivation for Order-Specified Aggregate Authority-Transfer Signature

In order to be able to verify not only who signs the message but also in which order each of signers sign the document, we adapt the structuring method proposed by Yanai et al. [5] to the aggregate authority-transfer signature described in Sect. 3 [4].

By using graphs, we show different types of relationship between signers. When signing, we refer to this graph for showing structure of signers' relationship. A new signer receives the messages of all of the signers before him and signs them in addition to his message. The generated signature and the signatures for the adjacent signers are aggregated, and a new aggregate signature is created.

Note that security of the order-specified aggregate authority-transfer signature conforms to the method of Yanai et al.

4.2   Series-Parallel Graph

Definition of a Series-Parallel Graph: Let G be a set of graphs. A series-parallel graph is a graph generated by applying either a serial graph or a parallel graph recursively in an arbitrary order. Specifically, a series-parallel graph $G(I, T)$, which starts at the initial vertex I and terminates at the terminal vertex T, is defined as follows.

$G(I, T)$ is generated either by following step 1 or step 2.

1. With a unique label i in G, $G_i(I_i, T_i)$ is composed of one edge connecting I_i and T_i. We call such a graph an atomic graph and denote it by $\phi_i \in G$.
2. Either one of the following steps is executed:
   Parallel Graph: Given n graphs $G_i(I_i, T_i)$, for $1 \leq i \leq n$, construct $G(I, T)$ by setting $I = I_1 = I_2 = \cdots = I_n$ and $T = T_1 = T_2 = \cdots = T_n$.
   Serial Graph: Given n graphs $G_i(I_i, T_i)$, for $1 \leq i \leq n$, construct $G(I, T)$ by setting $I = I_1$, $T_1 = I_2, \ldots, T_{n-1} = I_n$, and $T_n = T$.

Intuitively, in the above definitions, constructing $G(I, T)$ means compositions of n atomic graphs $\phi_i \in G$ for $i = [1, n]$ either as a serial one or a parallel one [5].

Graph Composition: For two atomic graphs $\phi_1, \phi_2 \in G$, we define a composition of parallel graphs as $\phi_1 \cup \phi_2$ and the composition of serial graphs as $\phi_1 \cap \phi_2$. In other words, $\phi_1 \cup \phi_2$ means to construct $G(I, T)$ by setting $I = I_1 = I_2$ and $T = T_1 = T_2$, and $\phi_1 \cap \phi_2$ means to construct $G(I, T)$ by setting $I = I_1$, $T_1 = I_2$, and $T_2 = T$. We denote by $T(i)$ a set of graphs connecting to the initial vertex I_i of the ith graph in a way such that

$$T(i) = \{x | I_i = T_x \wedge 1 \leq x < i \wedge G_x(I_x, T_x) \subset \psi_n\},$$

where n is the number of atomic graphs and ψ_n is the whole graph for any n, by $I(i)$ a set of graphs connecting to the terminal vertex T_i of the ith graph in a way such that

$$I(i) = \{x | T_i = I_x \wedge i < x \leq n \wedge G_x(I_x, T_x) \subset \psi_n\},$$

by $\{a_j\}_{j \in T(i)}$, for all a_j for $j \in T(i)$. A whole graph that includes multiple graphs in its terminal vertex T_i can be denoted by $\psi_{I(i)}$. That is, if $\psi_{I(i)}$ includes a single atomic graph ϕ_i in the terminal vertex, then $\psi_{I(i)}$ is equal to ψ_i [5].

Weight of a Graph: We define a weight function $\omega_i(\psi_n)$ that represents a weight of each label i for a graph ψ_n. Intuitively, $\omega_i(\psi_n)$ is the number of paths including an edge with a label i from I_i to T_n for ψ_n. We denote by $\#\psi_n$ the number of edges in ψ_n for any structure ψ_n [5].

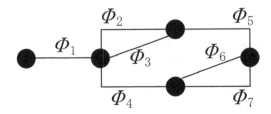

Fig. 1. Toy example of graph ψ_n.

Toy Example: We assume a toy example and show the graphe of this example in Fig. 1. Furthermore, we show the lineage of this example in Table 1 and the series-parallel graph parameters in Table 2.

We call the initial node for the whole graph as "whole initial" and the terminal node for the whole graph as "whole terminal", respectively. In the columns of $T(i)$ and $I(i)$, we give the indexes of corresponding atomic graphs. We also denote by ψ_n as whole graph.

We utilize a series-parallel graph as the signer structure. Here, an edge of a series-parallel graph corresponds to a signer, and a unique edge for the graph corresponds to a unique index that represents the position of each signer in any structure [5].

4.3   Construction

Preconditions:
   The preconditions are the same as those for the aggregate authority-transfer signature in Sect. 3.3.
Set-Up:
   The setup is the same as that for the aggregate authority-transfer signature in Sect. 3.3.
Join:
   The join condition is the same as that for the aggregate authority-transfer signature in Sect. 3.3.

Table 1. Lineage of the toy example.

ψ_i	Graph composition	Indexes $j \in \psi_i$
ψ_1	ϕ_1	1
ψ_2	$\phi_1 \cap \phi_2$	1, 2
ψ_3	$\phi_1 \cap \phi_3$	1, 3
ψ_4	$\phi_1 \cap \phi_4$	1, 4
ψ_5	$\phi_1 \cap \phi_2 \cap \phi_5$	1, 2, 5
ψ_6	$\phi_1 \cap \phi_3 \cap \phi_5$	1, 3, 5
ψ_7	$\phi_1 \cap \phi_4 \cap \phi_6$	1, 4, 6
ψ_8	$\phi_1 \cap \phi_4 \cap \phi_7$	1, 4, 7

Table 2. Series-parallel graph parameters of the toy example.

ϕ_i	$T(i)$	$I(i)$	$\omega_i(\psi_n)$
ϕ_1	Whole initial	2, 3, 4	4
ϕ_2	1	5	1
ϕ_3	1	5	1
ϕ_4	1	6, 7	2
ϕ_5	2, 3	Whole terminal	1
ϕ_6	4	Whole terminal	1
ϕ_7	4	Whole terminal	1

Signing:

U is the ith signer and signs message M_i for ψ_i. U refers to the graph before the signature, and it verifies the signature of the previous signer. We pass (para, $\{P_{A_j}, M_j\}_{j \subset \psi_{T(i)}}, \psi_{T(i)}, \{\sigma_{Agg_j}\}_{j \in T(i)})$ to the verification algorithm. If the verification fails, the protocol terminates. Otherwise, U randomly chooses $r \in \mathbb{Z}_q^*$. U computes the following:

$$B_i = rQ. \tag{11}$$

$$K_{u_i} = x s_u Q. \tag{12}$$

$$h_i = H_2(M_i \| B_i). \tag{13}$$

$$\{h_j = H_2(M_j \| B_j)\}_{j \subset \psi_{T(i)}}. \tag{14}$$

Finally, U computes $C_i = \sum_{j \in T(i)} C_j + S_{u_i} + x s_u (\sum_{j \subset \psi_{T(i)}} h_j + h_i) P + rP$. $S_{u_i} = s_{A_i} H_1(T_{u_i} \| K_{u_i})$ is an authority-transfer key. T_{u_i} is the authority information transferred by the M. The order-specified aggregate authority-transfer signature is $\sigma_{Agg_i} = (\{B_j, K_{u_j}, T_{u_j}\}_{j \subset \psi_i}, C_i)$.

Verification:

Given (para, $\{P_{A_j}, M_j\}_{j \subset \psi_{I(i)}}, \psi_{I(i)}, \{\sigma_{Agg_j}\}_{j \in I(i)})$, we check if $i \leq 3 \frac{\log P}{\log 3}$ holds [13]. If not, the protocol terminates. Next, we check whether all of the authority information $\{T_{u_j}\}_{j \subset \psi_I(i)}$ is appropriate. The verifier computes $C = \sum_{j \in I(i)} C_j$ if $|\{\sigma_{Agg_j}\}_{j \in I(i)}| > 1$. Otherwise, if $|\{\sigma_{Agg_j}\}_{j \in I(i)}| = 1$, we set $C = C_j$. Then, we check if the following equation holds with $H_1(K_{u_j} \| T_{u_j})$ and $H_2(M_j \| B_j)$ for all j:

$$e(C, Q) = e\left(P, \sum_{j \subset \psi_{I(i)}} \left(\left(\sum_{l \subset \psi_{T(j)}} (H_2(M_l \| B_l)) + H_2(M_j \| B_j) \right) \omega_j(\psi_{I(i)}) K_{u_j} \right. \right.$$

$$\left. \left. + \sum_{j \subset \psi_{I(i)}} \omega_j(\psi_{I(i)}) B_j \right) \right)$$

$$\cdot \prod_{j \subset \psi_{I(i)}} e\left(\omega_j(\psi_{I(i)}) H_1(K_{u_j} \| T_{u_j}), P_{A_j} \right).$$

Table 3. The comparison of the verification time of the aggregate signature for one thousand members and the number of the pairing execution.

Signature scheme	Verification time [sec]	The number of the pairing execution (N: The number of members)
BLS [7]	22.92	$2000(2N)$
BGLS [3]	14.27	$1001(N+1)$
YT [1]	21.88	$2001(2N+1)$
Our proposal	14.72	$1002(N+2)$

Open:
    Open is the same as that for the aggregate authority-transfer signature in Sect. 3.3.

5   Performance Evaluation

We show the result of performance evaluation of the simulation program under the protocol in Sect. 4. Furthermore, we show the comparison of our proposal with existing signature schemes. The evaluation environment of simulation is the followings:

PC: Intel Core i3-3120M, Memory 4 GB.
OS: Microsoft Windows10 Home.
Compiler: GCC over Cygwin.
Pairing Library: TEPLA (University of Tsukuba Elliptic Curve and Pairing Library) 2.0 [14].

We assumed that the number of signing members is one thousand and measured the performance of verification of the aggregate signature for one thousand members regarding each signature scheme, BLS [7], BGLS [3], YT [1] and our proposal, over the above environment. The performance comparison of our proposal with other three schemes is shown in Table 3.

In these simulations, the verifying execution time of our proposal is faster than that of BLS and YT, the performance of our proposal is comparable to that of BGLS. This result can be explained by the number of the pairing execution under verification in each signature scheme, because the pairing function is the most heavy processing in the signature schemes on the elliptic curve and have a great effect on the performance.

As a result of the number of the pairing execution, the number in BLS and YT is about four times as many as that in our proposal if there are a large number of signing members. Furthermore, the number of the pairing execution in our proposal is almost the same as that in BGLS if there are a large number of signing members. Therefore, although our proposal scheme has the function of not only aggregation but also order-specification, we can realize our scheme which is not inferior compared to existing schemes in terms of the performance.

6   Conclusions

In this paper, we proposed an order-specified aggregate authority-transfer signature that can be distributed and delegated, and can process signatures efficiently by aggregating while guaranteeing the order of signing. Moreover, with simulation program, we showed that our proposal scheme is practical in terms of the performance compared with existing signature schemes.

The number of pairing executions at the time of verification is smaller than that of the BLS signature and Yao et al.'s method, and is almost equivalent to the BGLS signature. Therefore, it has led to shortening of verification time. For this reason, our proposed method is effective for quick and proper of authority delegation/distribution on computer networks.

On the other hand, our scheme has a large signature size compared to existing schemes, in particular Yao et al.'s scheme. As a future work, we will consider the method to reduce this signature size. In addition, we will consider the security of the order-specified aggregate authority-transfer signatures.

References

1. Yao, D., Tamassia, R.: Compact and anonymous role-based authorization chain. ACM Trans. Inf. Syst. Secur. **12**(3), 15:1–15:27 (2009)
2. Itakura, K., Nakamura, K.: A public-key cryptosystem suitable for digital multisignatures. NEC Res. Dev. **71**, 1–8 (1983)
3. Boneh, D., Gentry, C., Lynn, B., Shacham, H.: Aggregate and verifiably encrypted signatures from bilinear maps. In: Biham, E. (ed.) EUROCRYPT 2003. LNCS, vol. 2656, pp. 416–432. Springer, Heidelberg (2003). https://doi.org/10.1007/3-540-39200-9_26
4. Ezure, T., Inamura, M.: An order-specified aggregate authority-transfer signature. In: International Conference on Information Systems Security and Privacy - ICISSP 2019, pp. 309–318. SciTePress (2019)
5. Yanai, N., Iwasaki, T., Inamura, M., Iwamura, K.: Provably secure structured signature schemes with tighter reductions. IEICE Trans. Fundam. Electron. Commun. Comput. Sci. **E100–A**(9), 1870–1881 (2017)
6. Okamoto, T., Pointcheval, D.: The gap-problems: a new class of problems for the security of cryptographic schemes. In: Kim, K. (ed.) PKC 2001. LNCS, vol. 1992, pp. 104–118. Springer, Heidelberg (2001). https://doi.org/10.1007/3-540-44586-2_8
7. Boneh, D., Lynn, B., Shacham, H.: Short signatures from the weil pairing. In: Boyd, C. (ed.) ASIACRYPT 2001. LNCS, vol. 2248, pp. 514–532. Springer, Heidelberg (2001). https://doi.org/10.1007/3-540-45682-1_30
8. Chen, X., Zhang, F., Kim, K.: New ID-based group signature from pairings. J. Electron. (China) **23**(6), 892–900 (2006)
9. Boldyreva, A.: Efficient threshold signature, multisignature and blind signature schemes based on the gap-Diffie-Hellman-group signature scheme. Cryptology ePrint Archive, Report 2002/118. https://eprint.iacr.org/2002/118. Accessed 26 June 2019

10. Boldyreva, A.: Threshold Signatures, multisignatures and blind signatures based on the gap-Diffie-Hellman-group signature scheme. In: Desmedt, Y.G. (ed.) PKC 2003. LNCS, vol. 2567, pp. 31–46. Springer, Heidelberg (2003). https://doi.org/10.1007/3-540-36288-6_3

11. Inamura, M., Iwamura, K., Watanabe, R., Nishikawa, M., Tanaka, T.: A new tree-structure-specified multisignature scheme for a document circulation system. In: International Conference on Security and Cryptography - SECRYPT 2011, pp. 362–369. SciTePress (2011)

12. Inamura, M., Iwamura, K.: Content approval systems with expansions of a new pair-connected-structured aggregate signature scheme. IGI Glob. Int. J. E-Entrep. Innov. 4(2), 15–37 (2013)

13. Tada, M.: A secure multisignature scheme with signing order verifiability. IEICE Trans. Fundam. Electron. Commun. Comput. Sci. **E86**–**A**(1), 73–88 (2003)

14. TEPLA. http://www.cipher.risk.tsukuba.ac.jp/tepla/. Accessed 26 June 2019

Context-Aware Software-Defined Networking for Automated Incident Response in Industrial Networks

Florian Patzer[1(✉)] , Philipp Lüdtke[2], Ankush Meshram[3] ,
and Jürgen Beyerer[1]

[1] Fraunhofer IOSB, Institute of Optronics, System Technologies and Image
Exploitation, Fraunhoferstr. 1, 76131 Karlsruhe, Germany
{florian.patzer,juergen.beyerer}@iosb.fraunhofer.de
[2] WIBU-SYSTEMS AG, Rüppurrer Str. 52-54, 76137 Karlsruhe, Germany
philipp.luedtke@wibu.com
[3] Vision and Fusion Laboratory (IES), Karlsruhe Institute of Technology (KIT),
Haid-und-Neu-Str. 7, 76131 Karlsruhe, Germany
ankush.meshram@kit.edu

Abstract. Due to the increasing flexibility of processes in modern plants
the need for the respective networks' flexibility rises. Such dynamic networks are already performing well in, for example, data centres where
they are based on the Software-defined Networking (SDN) paradigm.
Because SDN has established itself in flexible, high performance environments, it is currently introduced into industrial networks as well.
With the usage of SDN, a centralized view and controlling is added to
these networks, which enables performing automated responses to network events. Such network events can be classified as incidents to which
SDN can provide timely and, due to the holistic view on the network,
appropriate, automated incident response, like immediate containment,
monitoring or switching to redundancies. However, industrial networks
generally have a high occurrence of availability-, safety- and time-critical
communication which limit the scope for action of such an automated
approach. Nevertheless, SDN-based incident response (SDN-IR) does not
yet take into consideration these limitations, which prevent its application for industrial networks.

This article identifies possible response actions to industrial network
incidents. Furthermore, it presents a concept for SDN-IR where a pre-
defined rule set restricts the response actions based on asset and link
classification. This way, SDN-IR is able to satisfy the before mentioned
requirements of industrial networks. In addition, the article describes a
prototype of this concept and its evaluation, elucidates the perspective
of a device security status in the SDN-IR context and discusses security
issues of the concept.

Keywords: Software-defined networking · SDN security · Automated
incident response · Industrial security · ICS security

© Springer Nature Switzerland AG 2020
P. Mori et al. (Eds.): ICISSP 2019, CCIS 1221, pp. 137–161, 2020.
https://doi.org/10.1007/978-3-030-49443-8_7

1   Introduction

The fourth industrial revolution (Industry 4.0) provides new possibilities which highly flexible industrial processes are supposed to realize. Therefore, modern Industrial Control Systems (ICS) require solutions for highly flexible networks. Such solutions are already well established in other domains, like data centres, where they are realized using the Software-defined Networking (SDN) paradigm. From these domains, the efficiency and advantages of SDN are well known. Therefore, SDN is slowly adopted for industrial networks in order to obtain more flexibility. SDN provides centralized management of data flows which is achieved by separating the control plane from the data plane [8]. The control plane has a logically centralized view of the network containing detailed knowledge of its topology. Utilizing this holistic knowledge of the network, the SDN controller calculates packet forwarding rules and deploys them on the switches. For this, each forwarding rule is added to the target switch's *flow table*. As entries in the flow table, these rules are often called *flow entries*. Once deployed, the switches follow the forwarding rules. If they receive a packet, they look through the flow table trying to find a flow entry matching the meta-data of the packet. A packet not matching any flow entry is sent to the SDN controller, which will react, often resulting in the deployment of new flow entries.

Since the SDN controller manages the data flow within its SDN realm, it can perform automated response to events and classified incidents. As an example, Martins and Campos [11] presented an automated incident response approach using SDN. They proposed a security architecture in which the *Intrusion Detection System (IDS)* Snort sends alerts to an SDN controller which reacts by isolating and blacklisting corrupt devices by deploying respective flow entries. The approach enables a quick reaction to detected events.

The SANS Incident Response Survey 2017 [3] demonstrates the importance of such fast responses. The survey outlines the key time frames of incident response: (1) time from compromising to detection (the "dwell time"), (2) time for containment (e.g. to block activities of the attacker), and (3) time to implement measures for closing the vulnerabilities (remediation time). The survey results clearly indicate that faster containment and short-term remediation help to prevent attack propagation and aid damage regulation. This is especially important in industrial systems, where even primitive attacks can endanger the human safety and additionally cause massive financial damage. Leveraging SDN for automated incident response can contain or even prevent such attacks.

Although leveraging SDN for incident response is still a young research field, researchers have published first results. Koulouris et al. [9] have proposed an interesting concept for *SDN-based incident response (SDN-IR)* called *SDN4S* (SDN for Security). SDN4S includes the concept of *playbooks*, which map triggers (incidents addressed by the playbook) to sets of executable actions (building the response strategy). Thus, playbooks describe the response actions an SDN controller has to perform upon the arrival of an incident alert. Since SDN4S is not designed for industrial environments, it does not meet ICS-specific requirements like time sensitivity, availability, reliability, redundancy and safety. However, these requirements limit the scope for action of SDN-IR within the ICS domain.

Earlier research already addressed SDN-IR specifically for industrial networks. Piedrahita et al. [15] show how SDN and *Network-Function Virtualization (NFV)* can be used for SDN-IR in ICS. The authors propose virtual incident response functions which replace ICS components under attack. These virtual functions consist of a co simulation/emulation environment, where physical processes are simulated, and network and control components are emulated. As an example, if a device is compromised, a virtual function replaces the device, including its physical process like the generation of sensor measurements. As another example, if an attack on SCADA level is identified, the virtual representation is used to create a honeypot of the control system. The attacker assumed in the approach is capable of compromising the real system but not its virtual representation.

Di Lallo et al. [5] address time-sensitivity with SDN-based ICS security and concentrate on monitoring as incident response action instead of the more interfering containment of components. For monitoring, the authors leverage spare of bandwidths to transfer replicas of network packets. The approach demonstrates how SDN can assist in the detection phase of incident response without jeopardizing the network's quality of service guarantees.

During our research we could not identify an SDN-IR concept which is able to support all peculiarities of the industrial domain. Without such a concept SDN-IR is not feasible for SDN-based industrial networks and its advantages cannot be exploited. Therefore, we concluded that a generic concept for SDN-IR in networks with special restrictions is missing.

To close this gap, this work proposes a solution enabling the application of SDN-IR in networks with special restrictions, like industrial networks. This article extends our paper [14] presented at the 5th International Conference on Information Systems Security and Privacy (ICISSP2019) with additional and updated practical insights (especially into the prototype implementation), information about the usage of the solution within a higher-level security infrastructure (cf. Sect. 4.7) and a security analysis of the concept, accompanied by respective countermeasure recommendations (cf. Sect. 8). The solution utilizes the concept of playbooks from SDN4S and introduces the classification of *assets* (here hosts, SDN switches and links, cf. Sect. 3). In order to decide whether an action suggested by a playbook can be performed for a certain asset-classification combination, the solution contains a configurable set of restrictive rules (cf. Sect. 5). These rules also imply preconditions which have to be met before the action is allowed to be executed. Since we focus on incidents occurring in dynamic ICS networks Sect. 4 identifies respective responses an SDN controller is able to perform. If the respective rule allows, the responses are translated into flow entries for reconfiguration of certain SDN switches. The prototype implementation of this SDN-IR concept is presented in Sect. 7. It is based on the open-source SDN platform *OpenDaylight* [13] and the SDN protocol *OpenFlow* [12]. We evaluated the prototype using the Mininet[1] network emulator and explain the evaluation in Sect. 7. Security measures, like the one this article suggests, always have the potential to extend or alter the attack surface. Therefore, as already mentioned, Sect. 8 examines the extension of the attack surface introduced by the here described solution and identifies countermeasures.

2   Incidents

Conventional industrial networks have been built with very specialized, often proprietary components and network protocols. Thus, typical attacks on ICS are very specialized multi-stage attacks like STUXNET [7], Triton [17], Black Energy [10] and many more. However, within the last two decades, industry experienced a massive increase in networking of previously isolated systems, application of enterprise IT operating systems and protocols in the control and field level. This development is generally beneficial, since it supports better maintenance, more flexible processes, unrestricted software development and more. Nevertheless, it introduces a huge amount of new attack vectors to ICS. For example, these systems became vulnerable to typical enterprise IT threats, like WannaCry[2] and Heartbleed[3].

As mentioned in the introduction, the here presented SDN-IR concept is generally applicable for all sorts of software-defined networks. As a consequence the supported incidents and therefore the supported triggering alerts are generic. These alerts are either initiated manually or by any security mechanism, like host-/network-based intrusion detection systems.

We abstractly classify the incidents covered by our approach as *compromised host*, *compromised switch* and *malicious link*. Here, hosts are network participants, switches are SDN switches and a link describes any identifiable end-to-end connection between two hosts (even if that connection is not currently established). Furthermore, in this article, the term *node* is used to abstract from the information whether a host or a switch is addressed.

3   Asset Classification

In this section, we introduce selected basic classes of the previously mentioned assets, namely hosts, switches and links. In various environments the extension of the here mentioned set of classes and their adaptation might be necessary. For this reason, one requirement for the here proposed concept is the configurability of this set of classes. Certain hosts and links are critically important e.g for controlling the production plant or to perform safety functions. Typically, the data transmission between such hosts or via such links may not be interrupted. Such hosts and links are henceforth classified as *functionally-critical*.

---

[1] http://mininet.org.

[2] https://nvd.nist.gov/vuln/detail/CVE-2017-0144.

[3] https://www.us-cert.gov/ncas/alerts/TA14-098A.

Time sensitivity is also an important aspect within ICS. Certain links must meet specified time requirements and adhere to them. We classify these links as *time-critical*.

Redundant network paths are incorporated in ICS for two reasons: to increase the probability that, in case of an attack or disturbance, one of the paths remains functional, and to increase the total bandwidth by adding additional paths. For such redundant paths, it is always important that they contain a disjoint set of physical transmission nodes. Hence redirecting or interrupting redundant links might be undesired. In consequence, instead of paths we classify links and call the respective class *redundant*. If a link is classified as *redundant*, more than one path has to satisfy this link and the respective paths have to be physically disjoint. As a adjustment, we exclude the first and last hop from this requirement.

Additionally, hosts might also be classified as *redundant*. An application for this can be found in the "Virtualization" paragraph of Sect. 5.

Finally, links can belong to more than one class. For example, *functionally-critical* and *time-critical* links are common for safety systems. As a result, whenever this article mentions an asset's classification, it refers to the set of classes it is assigned to.

4   SDN-Based Incident Response

This section presents the identified SDN-based response possibilities to incidents mentioned in Sect. 2. For this, only responses were selected which can be performed by an automated incident response mechanism. According to Cichonski et al. [4] the incident response process can be divided into seven phases: Preparation, Detection, Analysis, Containment, Eradication, Recovery and Post Incident Activity. In research, SDN-IR often only concentrates on the Containment phase. The response actions we identified while researching for this topic, also mainly support the Containment phase, as this is the most feasible phase to automate. However, we also address the phases Detection and Analysis. The following sections summarize the identified response actions.

4.1   Isolate Host

Assuming an alert suggests a host is compromised, an adequate reaction could be to isolate this host from the rest of the network. For this, the SDN controller can deploy high-priority flow entries to the SDN switch the device is directly connected to. Following the flow entries, the switch drops all packages from and to this device. Another strategy is the isolation of communication partners from the rest of the network, but not from each other. More generally, if a host is potentially compromised, it might be necessary to isolate it from the rest of the network but if this host has a functionally critical link to another host, it seems to be a valid strategy to keep the flows enabling this link. The SDN controller might further be able to determine that no links between either of the partners and a third party are functionally critical. Thus, the SDN controller could deduce that the isolation of the two partners from the rest of the network might be a reasonable action. Since flow entries can be defined e.g. for specific TCP/IP connections, this can be achieved by deploying high priority flow entries allowing the critical link and lower priority flow entries dropping all packets from and to the host in question.

4.2 Isolate Switch

Like hosts, SDN switches can be isolated from the rest of the network, if they appear to be compromised. Such an incident response action however has significantly more impact on the rest of the network than isolating a host. Isolating switches can result in isolating other nodes as well. As an example, Fig. 4 depicts a network where the isolation of switch *openflow:1* results in the isolation of *host3* and switch *openflow:6*. Therefore, if any critical link cannot be redirected via paths not containing the compromised switch, the availability of, for example, services is being affected unacceptably. Thus, several conditions have to be checked before isolating a switch (cf. Sect. 5).

4.3 Block Certain Links

Blocking certain links might be an interesting response, especially to Denial-of-Service attacks. For example, if a node within the network is affecting others using a Denial-of-Service attack, the links used for this attack can often be identified very fast and can then be blocked without isolating the whole node, which might be crucial for the system's functionality and safety. This example shows that blocking of links can be chosen as a lighter alternative to the isolation of whole nodes.

4.4 Mirroring/Packet Replicas

One of the arguably most feasible response is the replication of packets, e.g. for monitoring. Whereas in traditional networking mirroring switches or network TAPs with the ability to perform packet replication were needed, SDN can conduct mirroring on every SDN switch by deploying respective flow entries. This response action creates additional traffic, but does not affect the network beyond that. As already mentioned, Di Lallo et al. [5] proposed an approach to minimize this negative effect. If the replication of packets is performed to monitor a host, each SDN switch the host is directly connected to can be selected as replication point. If the monitoring of a switch is desired, the objective is generally a maximization of the amount of monitored links directed over that switch. For links using the respective switch as only hop, trustworthy monitoring is only possible, if the switch is not a suspect of compromising and can therefore replicate the packets itself. Other links' packets can be replicated by other SDN switches along their paths.

4.5   Virtualization

As proposed by Piedrahita et al. [15] it is possible to support a system under attack with several virtualization strategies. According to Piedrahita et al. it is possible to replace a host with its virtual representation. Moreover, this can even be extended towards replacing physical processes with respective simulations. The virtualization approach can therefore be used to considerably improve the resilience of a system. Even though this strategy is very promising and worth more research, its complexity and heterogeneity disqualified it as part of our current research. However, the playbook approach we implemented is sufficient to trigger such incident response actions as well.

4.6   Notification

The SDN-IR solution can create notifications which will be sent to configured contact points, like an administrator's email. The notification action can be beneficial in several states of the SDN-IR progress. It can be sent directly after an alert is received, to inform the administrator and provide first reaction suggestions which, once permission is granted, can be performed automatically. Furthermore, the notification can be enriched with important knowledge about the current network layout (or topology) in order to support analysis and reduce reaction time. In addition, the notification can provide a report about the actions taken during an automated incident response.

4.7   Security Status

As a reaction to alerts, the current security status of hosts, switches, links or whole network slices should be reassessed. Afterwards, the software-defined network and other systems aligning themselves to this status have to act appropriately. Thus, the security status is no typical response action. It is rather a necessary control feature an SDN-IR solution should support, in order to be applicable within a higher-level security architecture. Figure 1 pictures an example for this status dependence. In the picture, an SDN platform is depicted containing an SDN security module managing the security status of an authentication server, a robot module and a workstation. The example depicts the sequence an untrusted device like a new workstation might have to pass until it is successfully authenticated. As can be derived from the red arrows in the picture, the device is not allowed to communicate freely within the SDN domain and is first trusted, when it has successfully performed the authentication. In the first step, the SDN security module learns about the workstation and sets its security status from Unknown to Known but Unauthenticated. In a second step, the authentication server performs the authentication after ensuring that the security status of the workstation does not prohibit this action. If the authentication has been successful, the server suggests to the SDN security module to promote the workstation's security status. Consequently, the SDN security module updates the respective status to Authenticated. At this point in time, the

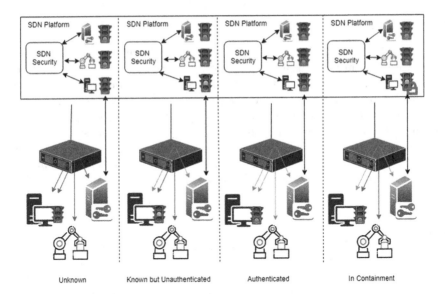

Fig. 1. Four exemplary phases (cf. `Unknown`, `Known but Unauthenticated`, ...) of a device's life cycle in a software-defined network, demonstrating the impact of the device security status (visualized by the traffic light).

SDN lets the workstation and the robot communicate with each other, since they both have the status `Authenticated`. Finally, in this simple example, the SDN security module puts the workstation into quarantine, if a workstation related incident occurs, and updates its status to `In Containment`. Other network participants like the authentication server can then recognize the current state of the workstation and ensure to act accordingly, for example by requesting or denying a re-authentication of the device.

5   Restrictive Rules

In the introduction we already motivated why ICS peculiarities have to be considered during the selection of appropriate automated responses. To enforce this, a rule set has to be available for the SDN-IR instance. We define this set as restrictive, adjustable preconditions for response actions taking into account ICS requirements.

Even without using SDN-IR, industrial SDN controllers need to take such requirements into account, since many of them are also relevant for the regular flow deployment. However, to the best of our knowledge, currently such context-aware controllers are not available. Therefore, the concept described in this article ignores the possibility of using an interface to such context-aware functionality.

The following paragraphs show example rules, including their formal representation wherever reasonable. These formal representations are boolean expressions. If the boolean expression results in the value true, the respective action can be performed and vice versa. For these expressions the following definitions are needed:

- $x \in \mathbb{N}$ describes an index enumerating network participants
- $host_x$ represents a host identifier unique for the SDN domain
- mac_x represents a MAC address
- ip_x represents an IP address
- $port_x$ represents a TCP/UDP port
- $link_{i,j} := \{host_i, host_j, mac_i, mac_j, ip_i, ip_j, port_i, port_j\}$ represents a link between host i and host j
- X represents the set of known links
- $path_{i,j}$ represents a path from $host_i$ to $host_j$ as an ordered set of switches
- $flow_{link}$ represents a deployed flow for $link$
- time_crit$_\tau(link)$ states that $link$ is time-critical with a latency threshold of τ
- meets$_\tau(path)$ states that $path$ can guarantee a latency beneath τ
- funct_crit$(link))$ states that $link$ is functionally critical
- redundant$(link))$ states that $link$ is redundant.

In production, the definition of $link_{i,j}$ might differ. As an example, the ports (and eventually even the IP address) might not be static or the link is more general like *"Any link between $(host_i, mac_i)$ and $(host_j, mac_j)$"*. Thus, in our implementation of $link_{i,j}$ we use a tuple which is variable in length and with the only requirement of containing the host identifiers.

The following paragraphs describe our exemplary rule set:

Blocking a Link: Links should not be blocked if they are functionally critical. Thus, the corresponding rule can be defined as

block_link$(link_{i,j}) := \neg$funct_crit$(link_{i,j})(i \neq j)$

If a link is not functionally critical but redundant, it might be blocked, depending on the severity of the incident.

Isolating a Host: A network participant should not be isolated, if it is marked as functionally critical or if isolation would affect any functionally critical link. This rule can be defined as

iso_host$(host_i) := \neg[$funct_crit$(host_i) \lor \exists link_{k,l} \in X : $funct_crit$(link_{k,l})]$

where $i = k \lor i = l$. If a link is not functionally critical but redundant, it might be still reasonable to isolate the host, depending on the severity of the incident. Furthermore, as mentioned in Sect. 4, isolation of a host with the exception of specific links is also possible.

Isolating a Switch: A switch can only be isolated when each functionally critical, redundant and time-critical link, directed through this switch, can be redirected without using the switch as hop. This includes that new paths for time-critical links have to meet their respective time requirements and redundant links have to be ensured to stay redundant. This rule can be defined as

$$
\begin{aligned}
\mathsf{iso\_switch}(switch) := \quad & link_{i,j} \in X \land switch \in flow_{link_{i,j}} \Rightarrow \\
& [\mathsf{funct\_crit}(link_{i,j}) \Rightarrow \exists path_{i,j} : switch \notin path_{i,j}] \\
& \land [\mathsf{time\_crit}_\tau(link_{i,j}) \Rightarrow \exists path_{i,j} : switch \notin path_{i,j} \land \mathsf{meets}_\tau(path_{i,j})] \\
& \land [\mathsf{redundant}(link_{i,j}) \Rightarrow \exists path_{i,j}, path'_{i,j} : switch \notin path_{i,j} \cup path'_{i,j} \\
& \land \forall n \in path'_{i,j} : n \notin \{switch_i, switch_j\} \Rightarrow n \notin path_{i,j}](i \neq j)
\end{aligned}
$$

For the sake of complexity reduction the above expression assumes that links have only one class assignment. Thus certain practical requirements were omitted. As an example, a link marked as *time-critical* and *redundant* must have an alternative path which meets the time requirements and is disjoint to the current backup path (in order to keep its redundancy). The *iso_switch* expression does not take such combinations into account and has to be expanded in practice. Moreover,

Monitoring a Host: The main issue in replicating host communication for monitoring purposes is the generation of additional traffic between the replication point and the monitoring system. Thus, the SDN management has to verify that no time-critical link looses its real-time assurances when the path between the replication switch and the monitoring system is deployed.

Monitoring a Switch: When monitoring a switch, as many links directed through that switch should be monitored as possible. Assuming the switch cannot be trusted anymore, to monitor its links, their current path (or flow) must contain other switches which can act as replication switches. Just like when monitoring a host, the only time-sensitivity and availability restrictions for this action apply to the path from the replication switch to the monitoring instance. Thus, for the replication path, the same time-sensitivity checks have to be conducted as explained for monitoring a host. Here, we ignore the fact that the deployment of flows introducing additional hops for the purpose of a better monitoring is also possible, which naturally requires additional checks.

Virtualization: Since there are many different possibilities leveraging virtualization for incident response, which all need further research, rules for such techniques are out of scope for this paper. However, a rule for the isolation of a node which is classified as redundant could demand a simulation for the node, which then has to be provided by the NFV environment.

Now that all necessary methods and definitions were presented, the next section describes the overall concept in more detail.

6   Concept

The previous sections described what types of incidents could be reported (cf. Sect. 2), how assets can be classified with respect to ICS peculiarities (cf. Sect. 3), which incident response actions can be executed with SDN (cf. Sect. 4) and what rules could protect critical assets while performing the response actions (cf. Sect. 5). As mentioned in the introduction, Koulouris et al. [9] described a concept called SDN for Security (SDN4S) which is unfortunately not directly applicable for industrial systems, because it does not take domain peculiarities into account. This section extends the SDN4S concept to overcome these issues.

Figure 2 depicts an overview of the extended concept which introduces new components like the *Security Decision Engine (SDE)* and additional libraries and databases to the SDN4S approach. The SDE receives alerts, e.g. from an IDS. Upon receiving an alert, the SDE derives the matching playbook from the *Playbook Library*, which consists of mappings from alert-asset-type combinations to response actions. Since the here described SDE relies on deterministic decisions, the concepts assumes the existence of a matching playbook for every received alert. Given the response actions suggested by the retrieved playbook and the asset type (i.e. host, switch or link) affected by or responsible for the incident, the SDE fetches the respective restrictive rules (cf. Sect. 5) from the *Rule Library*. After interpretation of the rules, the SDE concludes which checks to perform for what assets, in order to decide whether to perform an action

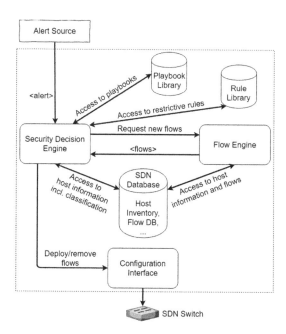

Fig. 2. Concept overview of SDN-IR using classification as additional condition for playbooks. *Source:*[14].

or not. Like our basic rules defined in Sect. 5, most rules will instruct the SDE to perform certain checks on assets with specific classifications. For this, the classification of such assets have to be retrieved from corresponding inventories, namely the *Host Inventory* and the *Link Inventory*. If the SDE comes to the conclusion to perform the response actions, it generates flow entries (if necessary for the response action) either by itself, or by using the SDN's flow engine (cf. *L2Switch* of OpenDaylight, Sect. 7). This depends on the specific implementation. In the latter case, the SDE is able to leverage the existing flow engine's ability to find the best flows for the current topology, e.g. when links have to be redirected. Nevertheless, the SDE can also create straight-forward flow entries, e.g. when a certain link has to be blocked, and does not need the flow engine for the task. The calculated flow entries are then deployed on, or removed from the switches via the *Configuration Interface* (e.g. *NETCONF*[4], OpenFlow [12] or *SNMP*[5]).

Section 7 presents a strategy of flow generation and deployment which leverages the priority attribute of flow entries to enable easy resetting after actions have been performed by the SDE. This is achieved by not having to remove the current flow entries, because they are just overwritten by higher priority security flow entries which can later be removed. After this, the previously deployed flows are immediately reactivated. For most actions, this strategy might be preferable to removing flow entries.

Furthermore, when using network function virtualization an implementation of the SDE concept could leverage existing security controls like firewalls as well. For actions which can be performed by such controls, this is a more consistent approach than directly applying flow entries.

To show the feasibility of the concept and to provide more technical detail, the following section will describe a prototype implementation of the concept.

7   Concept Evaluation

For evaluating the described concept, we built a simple prototype. For this purpose, the OpenDaylight (*ODL*) framework [13] has been applied and extended as SDN management platform. To implement the flow entries generated by the SDE, or in its behalf, the prototype uses the OpenFlow protocol [12]. ODL aims to combine the core concepts of SDN, model-driven software development and model-driven network management. The modular architecture of ODL allowed its extension with customized modules, like the SDE and the additional inventories and libraries (cf. Sect. 6).

A simplified overview of the prototype implementation can be found in Fig. 3. The SDN controller's interface towards SDN switches is called a *southbound interface* for which several protocols are supported by ODL. This interface matches the Configuration Interface of Fig. 2. As mentioned earlier, the prototype uses the OpenFlow plugin as southbound interface. OpenFlow enables

---

[4] https://tools.ietf.org/html/rfc6241.html.
[5] https://tools.ietf.org/html/rfc1157.

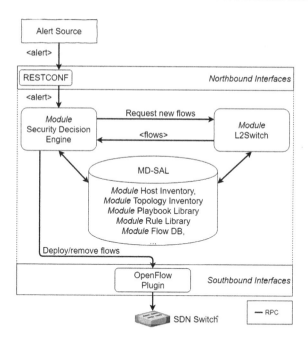

Fig. 3. Simplified overview of the prototype implementing the here proposed SDN-IR concept (cf. Sect. 6). *Source:*[14].

the usage of the SDN switches' statistic functions and the deployment of flow entries on the switches.

ODL's database management is called *Model-driven Service Abstraction Layer (MD-SAL)*[6] which uses the modelling language *YANG* [2] to define database schemes. Listing 1.1 is an example for the scheme representation in YANG, which represents the shortened SDE module's scheme for alert types. The listing shows a scheme defining the priority constants, the components of an alert and a list of alerts called `alerts`. YANG is also used to define interfaces as *Remote Procedure Calls*(see footnote 6) (*RPC*), e.g. the RPC for adding an alert, which is also defined in the listed scheme.

Another important module is earlier mentioned the L2Switch which was already available in ODL. Among other things, this module implements the logic of ISO/OSI layer 2 switches. However, unlike common layer 2 switches, the L2Switch is able to determine layer 2 end-to-end paths, due to its centralized view on the network. To achieve this, the L2Switch uses the network topology, found in the *Topology Inventory*, also stored via MD-SAL, which is automatically generated by ODL once traffic appears on the network. Consequently, in this setup the L2Switch has the role of the earlier mentioned flow engine.

---

[6] https://wiki.opendaylight.org/view/OpenDaylight_Controller:MD-SAL:Developer_
Guide.

Listing 1.1. Scheme of alert categories written in YANG.

```
module sde {
    ...
    typedef priority {
            type enumeration {
                    enum "HIGH";
                    enum "LOW";
            }
    }
    grouping alert {
            leaf id {
                    type int32;
            }
            leaf nodeId {
                    type string;
            }
            leaf name {
                    type string;
            }
            leaf sender {
                    type string;
            }
            leaf watcher {
                    type string;
            }
            leaf priority {
                    type priority;
            }
    }
    ...
    container alerts {
            list alert {
                    key id;
                    uses alert;
            }
    }
    ...
    rpc add-alert {
            description "Adds an alert.";
    }

}
```

Figure 3 also depicts the *northbound interface* which is responsible for the communication between the SDN management and external applications or users. We chose *RESTCONF* [1] for this interface. ODL generates this interface using the module YANG schemes, like the previously briefly described SDE scheme. For this scheme, CRUD (Create, Read, Update, Delete) interfaces for alerts and a special RPC interface for add-alert would be generated. In contrast to the CRUD interfaces, for the RPC, a customized method can be deployed. For example, the add-alert RPC is created to add notifications for received alerts. Unfortunately, ODL does not come with an inventory for hosts. Hence, we developed a host inventory module to store host information. Amongst this information the hosts' classifications are stored (cf. Sect. 6). Furthermore, we added a link inventory to store the earlier mentioned link representations and their respective classifications. In an earlier version of the prototype, we chose to bijectively map links to flows to be able to use the flow database for link classification. However, the assumption that all configured links are represented by persisted end-to-end flow entries turned out to be constrained.

Based on a scenario, this paragraph explains the prototype in greater detail. In the scenario, a COMPROMISED_SWITCH alert is triggered. This alert type was selected as an example, since it has the most impact on the network topology. The exemplary network topology can be found in Fig. 4. Since the prototype offers a REST interface, the alert can simply be triggered manually using the program *curl*[7]. An example is depicted in Listing 1.2.

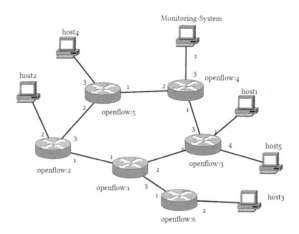

Fig. 4. Example topology we used for evaluating the prototype and respectively the here described SDN-IR concept. The numbers next to the SDN switches index their physical ports. *Source:*[14]

Listing 1.2. Submission of the COMPROMISED_SWITCH alert via REST, using curl.

```
curl -H 'Content-Type:application/json' -X POST -d '
{
    "input": {
        "sde:nodeId":"openflow:1",
        "sde:name":"COMPROMISED_SWITCH",
        "sde:sender":"host2",
        "sde:watcher":"host3",
        "priority":"HIGH"
    }
}
'
-u "admin:admin" 'http://localhost:8181/restconf/operations
    /sde:add-alert'
```

An alert consists of an identifier for the asset the alert belongs to, an alert category, the alert invoking party (**sender**) and a priority. Moreover, the target for packet replicas (**watcher**) should be added, since one of the respective

---

[7] https://curl.haxx.se.

playbooks might define a monitoring action. The priority is an indicator for the severity of the incident and is available as enum value (in the prototype, we only distinguish between HIGH and LOW).

After receiving the alert, an alert object is generated, using the passed parameters and stored to the MD-SAL database together with an identifier.

As can be seen in Listing 1.2, the alert relates to the switch *openflow:1* which seems to be compromised. This incident is furthermore suggested to have the priority HIGH.

After the alert was persisted, the SDE gets invoked and is given the alert's identifier to find it in the database. The SDE retrieves the new alert from the database and queries the playbook library for actions to perform, parametrising the request with the respective alert category and asset type. In the prototype implementation, asset type can be determined via interpreting the asset identifier. The playbook received as the response can be found in Listing 1.3.

Listing 1.3. Example playbook entry for COMPROMISED_SWITCH, which defines response actions for alert priority HIGH.

```
"actioninventory:name":"COMPROMISED_SWITCH",
"actioninventory:priority":"HIGH",
"actioninventory:actions": [
    "ISOLATE", "NOTIFY"
]
```

The playbook entry suggests to perform the actions ISOLATE and NOTIFY. The latter will only send a notification about the alert and the performed actions to a configured email address. The action ISOLATE however, gets sent to a helper called *Feasibility Analyser* which analyses the preconditions to perform the action. First, the Feasibility Analyser retrieves the rules from the Rule Library which are identified by the combination of asset type and action to perform (here, SWITCH and ISOLATE). In this scenario, the result is a rule for switch isolation, which is defined as depicted in Listing 1.4. The only constraints of the rule depicted in Listing 1.4 address the links currently directed through the switch.

Listing 1.4. Rule for switch isolation, which demands checks for each link affected by the isolation. In this case, functionally critical and redundant links have to be checked for being redirectable.

```
SWITCH {
    ISOLATE {
        LINKS {
            functionally-critical {
                redirectable
            },
            redundant {
                redirectable
            }
        }
    }
}
```

The rule states that every link being functionally critical and every link being marked as *redundant* need to be redirectable. The prototype currently only supports Ethernet specific end-to-end flows, which enables the analyser to collect the current flows deployed on switch *openflow:1* from the flow database and to directly determine which links match the flows. Furthermore, it queries the link inventory for the classifications of these links and remembers only the redundant and functionally critical ones. More complex links and flows need a more sophisticated determination of matching between links and flows. However, a respective implementation seems to be easily achievable with some additional effort.

At this point, the remaining task for the analyser is the verification of the feasibility to redirect the identified links without using *openflow:1*. Fortunately, the L2Switch module already provides a method to retrieve a path where a specific node can be excluded (as part of the *NetworkGraphService*). This can be done for both link classes. For redundant links the analyser additionally ensures that the resulting path is disjoint to minimum one alternative path.

If any of the checks fails, the ISOLATE action is not performed. Either way, the results of each test are logged and sent to the configured contact email when the NOTIFY action is executed.

In case the SDE decides to conduct the isolation of the switch, respective flow entries are generated. A shortened example of such a flow entry can be found in the Listing 1.5. This flow entry is deployed on switch *openflow:2* to redirect the traffic from *host2* to *host1* over port 3, hence, redirecting the traffic to *openflow:5*. As typical for Mininet(see footnote 1), in the emulated test network MAC addresses end with the hosts' indexes, e.g. ...00:02 for *host2*.

Another flow entry is deployed on *openflow:2* for the opposite direction and analogous flow entries are generated for the other switches on the redirection path *(openflow:5, openflow:4, openflow:3)*. This is performed for every necessary redirection. Since the flow entries have a higher priority than common flow entries in this SDN realm, old flow entries colliding with the SDE's flow entries are ignored when packets have to be forwarded. This way, the old state of the network can be recovered easily if the isolation gets repealed. For this, it is sufficient to remove the SDE flow entries. Consequently, the old flow entries will be immediately active again.

However, new flow decisions could still take *openflow:1* into account. To prevent this, the security status for this switch is set to In Containment (cf. Sect. 4.7), which leads to the situation that this switch will no longer appear in requests to the Topology Inventory performed by the flow engine. As another important requirement, the SDE ensures that the switch-controller link (management link) is sustained by the isolation.

As mentioned earlier, the prototype was tested using Mininet in version 2.2.0, a network emulator supporting SDN switches and external SDN controllers. Listing 1.6 partially shows how Mininet was configured for the tests. Here, 192.168.56.1:6653 is the endpoint of the ODL implementation.

Listing 1.5. Shortened example flow entry which defines a redirection of packets from *host2* to *host1* via port 3.

```
"id ": "sde-1-forward-host1-host2",
"priority": 100,
"match": {
    "ethernet-match": {
        "ethernet-destination": {
        "address": "00:00:00:00:00:01"
        },
        "ethernet-source": {
            "address": "00:00:00:00:00:02"
        }
    }
},
"instructions": {
    "instruction": [{
        "order": 0,
        "apply-actions": {
            "action": [{
                "order": 0,
                "output-action": {
                    "output-node-connector": "3",
                }
            }]
        }
    }]
}
```

Listing 1.6. Command starting Mininet with our evaluation settings.

```
sudo mn --mac --controller=remote, ip=192.168.56.1, port=6653
    --switch ovs, protocols=OpenFlow13 --custom topo.py
    --topo evaltopo --link tc, bw=10, delay=10ms
```

The parameters configure Mininet with a bandwidth limit of 10 MBit/s, which supports a proper evaluation without packet loss and greater impact of topology changes. Furthermore a latency of 10 ms has been allocated. The file *topo.py* consists of the topology information corresponding to the topology from Fig. 4, by adding switches, hosts and physical links.

Based on this setup, we conducted several tests, namely isolating hosts and switches, redirecting traffic of hosts and switches to the monitoring system as well as blocking various links. We performed these actions with and without classifications.

Despite the qualitative evaluation which demonstrated the functionality of the prototype and respectively the SDN-IR concept (cf. Sect. 6), we measured the latency and bandwidth during the execution of the response actions. Figure 5 depicts the measured latency between *host1* and *host2* when the isolation of switch *openflow:1* (cf. COMPROMISED_SWITCH scenario) is executed in second 12. Before the isolation, the two hosts communicate over path *(openflow:2, openflow:1, openflow:3)*. After the isolation the new path *(openflow:2, openflow:5, openflow:4, openflow:3)* was used. Due to the additional hop in the new path, the picture shows a small latency increase after second 12. In contrast, the bandwidth (cf. Fig. 6) remains unchanged, besides a small slump in second 15. This effect can be traced back to the adaptation to the new path.

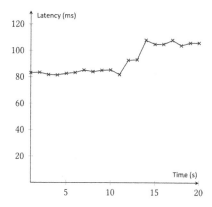

Fig. 5. Latency measurement when isolating switch *openflow:1* in second 12. *Source:*[14]

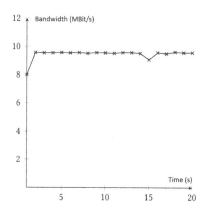

Fig. 6. Bandwidth measurement when isolating switch *openflow:1* in second 12. *Source:*[14]

The latency was measured with the *ping* command which responds with the time in milliseconds from sending an ICMP request packet to receiving the respective response. To measure the bandwidth, however, we needed a traffic generator and another measuring approach. For this, we used the *iPerf* program available in Mininet. Listing 1.7 shows an example of the *iPerf* command. The implementation of the concept using the OpenDaylight SDN platform and the test results clearly showed the feasibility of the here presented SDN-IR concept.

The current prototype is more advanced than its previous version presented in [14]. For example, the playbooks support alternatives, the alerts can include more necessary information (cf. Listing 1.2) and the link definition and classification is detached from the flow specification.

Listing 1.7. Example for *iPerf* execution we used to measure bandwidth.

```
root@mininet -vm :~# iperf -i 1 -s
------------------------------------------
Server listening on TCP port 5001
TCP window size : 85.3 KByte ( default )
------------------------------------------
[ 24] local 10.0.0.2 port 5001 connected
     with 10.0.0.1 port 36720
[ ID] Interval Transfer Bandwidth
[ 24] 0.0 - 1.0 sec 974 KBytes
     7.98 Mbits/sec
[ 24] 1.0 - 2.0 sec 1.14 MBytes
     9.55 Mbits/sec
[ 24] 2.0 - 3.0 sec 1.14 MBytes
     9.57 Mbits/sec
```

Nevertheless, remaining challenges like the implementation of an adequate rule language and more sophisticated endpoint definitions for links and flows have to be addressed in future work.

8   Security Considerations

This section examines the security of the presented SDN-IR concept and its implications for the network. We will only focus on security issues introduced by the concept and will not consider SDN security in general.

For this analysis, we chose an adversary model based on the Dolev-Yao Model [6]. In the Dolev-Yao Model an attacker is defined as a legitimate participant of the network and has the ability to send, receive and modify messages in the network [6]. The attacker, henceforth called Mallory, shall further not be able to add, remove or modify flows. Without this restriction any security analysis of the concept would be unnecessary because Mallory would already control the network and does not have to exploit the concept to achieve her goals.

In the following sections, several attack vectors for Mallory are being analysed.

8.1   Modifying or Dropping Alerts Sent to the SDE

The above described attacker Mallory is able to modify traffic in the network Thus, she has the ability to modify the alerts sent to the SDE. For example, Mallory could change the alert priority from HIGH to LOW, so that less strict actions are performed, or change the sde:nodeID parameter which results in the response actions being applied to the wrong node. With such attacks, Mallory could, for example, gain more time until her intrusion is detected, or she could weaken the incident response actions.

A countermeasure against this attack vector is the application of a communication protocol which offers message authenticity and integrity protection (henceforth called *message authentication*) for the communication between the SDE and the alert sources. With such a mechanism in place, the source of the message can be verified and any modification of messages will be noticed, which in turn can trigger an alert.

As an alternative, Mallory could block an alert which is sent to the SDE. Consequently, no incident response action would be executed. This way, Mallory could execute arbitrary attacks without being disturbed by SDN-IR measures deployed against it. Moreover, the Mallory might even stay undetected if no additional monitoring present within the network.

This attack vector does not exploit an issue or weakness in the SDN-IR concept. However, a possible countermeasure is the tracking of the number of alerts sent by alert sources and the number of alerts registered at the SDE. If a mismatch is detected, there is probably an attack going on. Of course, the transmission of an alert source's alert counter needs to be protected, e.g. using message authentication. Moreover, the counters should be transmitted periodically, so that the absence of a counter update gets recognized.

8.2   Abusing the Automated Flow Deployment

The simplest way for an attacker to abuse the automated incident response is to trigger an alert by purpose, in order to let the SDE perform certain response actions and, as a result, to alter the network topology. Two attack vectors can allow this.

The first one is to generate malicious traffic which will be detected by an alert source, e.g. an IDS. The alert source will then send a respective alert to the SDE.

With this attack, Mallory could, for example, achieve a denial of service, by enforcing actions which will block links or isolate nodes or switches. With knowledge of the playbook and the rule library this is easy to achieve. However, without this knowledge Mallory can only guess and work with the trail and error paradigm. In this case, it is also possible that Mallory triggers an action which will isolate the device under her control.

The possible damage which could be caused by such an attack depends on the actions defined in the playbook and the rule library. If combinations of playbook entries and rules are deployed which allow to isolate critical nodes or block sensitive links the damage could be high. In that case, malfunctioning of the ICS can be provoked which most likely would have dangerous impact on physical processes. The impact of the attack can be minimized, if the rule library contains rules, which ensures that critical nodes are protected from being isolated. Thus, this type of effects can be avoided by properly configuring the SDN-IR instance. The attack exploits the main feature of the SDN-IR concept, namely the automated deployment of flows in response to an incident. Thus, to prevent such attacks, additional security measures have to be deployed following the defence-in-depth paradigm. Moreover, this is an example showing why the automated SDN-IR concept should not fully replace traditional incident response mechanisms. Instead, it should complement and support them.

As the second attack vector, Mallory could impersonate an alert source and send arbitrary alerts to the SDE. This will have the same effect as the first method, but is even easier to perform, because the alerts sources are not involved anymore and constructing arbitrary alerts needs less effort than generating malicious traffic to trigger an alert source.

To prevent the second attack vector, the SDE must be able to verify the alert's source and integrity. As an example, the RESTCONF [1] protocol used in the prototype implementation should apply TLS [16] which would meet this requirement [1].

8.3 Modifying Flow Requests or Flow Engine Responses

In addition to the communication between the alert sources and the SDE, the communication between the SDE and the flow engine is also critical. The ability to modify requests to the flow engine or answers from the flow engine to the SDE would enable Mallory to deploy arbitrary flows in the network. Consequently, Mallory would gain full control over the network. Mallory can achieve this only if SDE and flow engine are communicating over the network. This is not the case for our prototype, where SDE and flow engine are built into one component.

However, with full control over the network, Mallory can, for example, remove or circumvent security measures like Firewalls or IDSs. This can eliminate network boundaries and can be used to modify the behaviour of the ICS, which could cause physical damage.

To prevent this attack vector, the communication between SDE and flow engine must ensure message authentication.

8.4 Manipulating Notifications and Security Status Information

Section 8.2 mentioned that an attacker could impersonate an alert source. In contrast, this section analyses the attack vector at which Mallory impersonates the SDE. In that case, Mallory could manipulate or send fake notifications and, for example, change the incident priorities to low or alter the compromised nodes and attacked targets. This could cause confusion amongst incident responders and increase the time until the attack is correctly identified by an incident response team.

As an alternative, Mallory could manipulate the device security status disclosure, which was introduced in Sect. 4.7. In consequence, security measures relying on this security status could be fooled. Referring to the example from Sect. 4.7 Mallory could inform security measures that a device's security status is `Authenticated` although it might be `Known but Unauthenticated` or even `In Containment`. In this case she could circumvent the authentication measures in the network and could add untrusted devices to the network.

To prevent such an attack, the same countermeasures as suggested in Sect. 8.3 can be applied. Ensuring message authentication will prevent Mallory from sending arbitrary notifications and security status information. If applied, the receivers of notifications or status information should reject the messages if they cannot authenticate the sender.

8.5   Compromise Playbook and Rule Library

Section 8.2 already showed that the playbook and rule library also play a major role in the concept's security considerations. An attacker who can compromise the playbook or the rule library is able to modify the incident response behaviour. Compromising means in this context that an attacker can modify, add or remove entries of these libraries. A requirement for this attack vector is that the SDE communicates with these libraries over the network, e.g. when the libraries are implemented as external databases. In that case, they would provide an interface to apply changes to them. Via such an interface, Mallory could compromise the playbook or rule library to achieve different objectives.

As a first example, the defined incident response actions can be weakened. Assuming Mallory wants to impersonate a switch. Then the attempt could get detected which, according to the playbook entry in Listing 1.3, would result in the switch being isolated and a notification being sent. Thus, as a preparatory step Mallory could modify the playbook entries. For example, she could remove the NOTIFY action and change the ISOLATE action to MONITOR for the HIGH priority playbook (cf. Listing 1.8). As a result Mallory could impersonate the switch, because it will not be isolated and, although the switch is monitored, it will probably take a long time until someone detects the attack, since no one is notified about the incident. Moreover, since the playbook's action list has not only been emptied, it is hard to identify the change in the database.

Listing 1.8. Modified playbook entry for COMPROMISED_SWITCH

```
"actioninventory:name":"COMPROMISED_SWITCH",
"actioninventory:priority":"HIGH",
"actioninventory:actions": [
    "MONITOR"
]
```

As an alternative, by compromising the rule library Mallory is able to execute a denial of service attack on critical network entities, which before were protected from being isolated or blocked by the rules. Assuming Mallory changes the rule from Listing 1.4 in a way that functionally critical links do not have to be redirectable, the switch could get isolated even if such functionally critical links are relying on that switch. The consequences could be fatal up to physical damage to machines or humans.

The here described cases clearly show that the communication between the SDE and the playbook and the rule library must be secured. This can again be achieved with a communication protocol which offers message authentication. Authentication is needed to ensure that only authenticated parties can alter the libraries. Typically, in cases like external databases access control must also be applied, e.g. to protect the entries from being altered by parties only supposed to read them. Moreover, confidentiality of login credentials and other critical information, like playbook entries (cf. Sect. 8.2), has to be ensured, utilizing proper encryption.

8.6 Discussion

The security analysis of the SDN-IR concept showed that the concept needs to be implemented considering security to avoid additional attack vectors being introduced to the SDN realm. Utilizing common security measures like authentication, message integrity and encrypted communication will counter most of the discussed attacks.

The identified attack vectors can damage the network. However, everything an attacker could achieve with these attack vectors, would also be possible without exploiting the here described SDN-IR concept. Since the attacker model of this analyses is a slightly adjusted Dolev-Yao model, the attacker already controls the network and could achieve the same goals with less effort, for example by tampering with sensor data or flooding components to provoke their failure.

To prevent that an attacker can get that much power in an SDN network and to get all benefits from the SDN-IR concept, a more advanced security concept for SDN networks is need, providing the services for building and maintaining trust and controlling the security of devices beyond the deployment of flows. Such a concept is currently developed in the FlexSi-Pro[8] research project.

9 Conclusion

This article describes a context-aware and therefore practical SDN-based solution for automated incident response in software-defined networks with special requirements. As a representative of such networks the article focuses on flexible ICS networks, where time-sensitivity, redundancy, availability and more, represent such requirements. The proposed solution satisfies these requirements by utilising restrictive rules and asset classification which then restrict the automated incident response to adequate response actions. Furthermore, as incident response is a multi-phase process and the knowledge about the phase a compromised node is in is critical for the whole security architecture, the solution provides the management of a node's security state which is dependent of the incident response phase the node is in. For evaluation of the concept, a prototype has been built demonstrating the feasibility of the approach on a common SDN platform (OpenDaylight). Moreover, based on this prototype, remaining issues and starting points for future research were identify. In addition to the prototype implementation, this article presents a security analysis of the concept, concluding that in practice the concept does not increase the SDN network's vulnerability as long as common countermeasures are deployed. We expect that our concept will accelerate the adoption of SDN incident response, and even SDN in general, in environments with the here mentioned peculiarities.

References

1. Bierman, A., Bjorklund, M., Watsen, K.: RESTCONF protocol. RFC 8040, RFC Editor (January 2017). https://tools.ietf.org/html/rfc8040

---

[8] https://www.wibu.com/flexsi-pro.html.

2. Bjorklund, M.: YANG - a data modeling language for the network configuration protocol (NETCONF). RFC 6020, RFC Editor (October 2010). https://rfc-editor. org/rfc/rfc6020.txt
3. Bromiley, M.: The show must go on! The 2017 SANS Incident Response Survey (2017)
4. Cichonski, P., Millar, T., Grance, T., Scarfone, K.: Computer security incident handling guide: recommendations of the national institute of standards and technology. Natl. Inst. Stand. Technol. (2012). https://doi.org/10.6028/NIST.SP.800-61r2
5. Di Lallo, R., Griscioli, F., Lospoto, G., Mostafaei, H., Pizzonia, M., Rimondini, M.: Leveraging SDN to monitor critical infrastructure networks in a smarter way. In: Proceedings of the IM 2017–2017 IFIP/IEEE International Symposium on Integrated Network Management, pp. 608–611. IEEE, Piscataway (2017). https://doi.org/10.23919/INM.2017.7987341
6. Dolev, D., Yao, A.C.: On the security of public key protocols. IEEE Trans. Inf. Theory **29**(2), 198–208 (1983). https://doi.org/10.1109/TIT.1983.1056650
7. Falliere, N., Murchu, L.O., Chien, E.: W32. Stuxnet dossier. Symantec Corp. Secur. Response **5**(6), 29 (2011)
8. Kim, H., Feamster, N.: Improving network management with software defined networking. IEEE Commun. Mag. **51**(2), 114–119 (2013). https://doi.org/10.1109/MCOM.2013.6461195
9. Koulouris, T., Casassa Mont, M., Arnell, S.: SDN4S: software defined networking for security (2017)
10. Lee, R.M., Assante, M.J., Conway, T.: Analysis of the cyber attack on the Ukrainian power grid. Electr. Inf. Shar. Anal. Cent. (E-ISAC) (2016). https://ics.sans.org/media/E-ISAC_SANS_Ukraine_DUC_5.pdf
11. Martins, J.S.B., Campos, M.B.: A security architecture proposal for detection and response to threats in SDN networks. In: Proceedings of the 2016 IEEE ANDESCON, pp. 1–4. IEEE, Piscataway (2016). https://doi.org/10.1109/ANDESCON.2016.7836244
12. McKeown, N., et al.: OpenFlow: enabling innovation in campus networks. ACM SIGCOMM Comput. Commun. Rev. **38**(2), 69 (2008). https://doi.org/10.1145/1355734.1355746
13. Medved, J., Varga, R., Tkacik, A., Gray, K.: OpenDaylight: towards a model-driven SDN controller architecture. In: Proceeding of IEEE International Symposium on a World of Wireless, Mobile and Multimedia Networks 2014, pp. 1–6. IEEE (June 2014). https://doi.org/10.1109/WoWMoM.2014.6918985
14. Patzer, F., Meshram, A., Heß, M.: Automated incident response for industrial control systems leveraging software-defined networking. In: Proceedings of the 5th International Conference on Information Systems Security and Privacy, pp. 319–327. SCITEPRESS - Science and Technology Publications (2019). https://doi.org/10.5220/0007359503190327
15. Piedrahita, A.F.M., Gaur, V., Giraldo, J., Cardenas, A.A., Rueda, S.J.: Virtual incident response functions in control systems. Comput. Netw. **135**, 147–159 (2018). https://doi.org/10.1016/j.comnet.2018.01.040
16. Rescorla, E.R.: The transport layer security (TLS) protocol version 1.3. RFC 8446, RFC Editor (August 2018). https://tools.ietf.org/html/rfc8446
17. Stoler, N.: Anatomy of the triton malware attack (July 2019). https://www.cyberark.com/threat-research-blog/anatomy-triton-malware-attack/

Transparency Enhancing Tools
and the GDPR: Do They Match?

Dayana Spagnuelo[1(✉)], Ana Ferreira[2], and Gabriele Lenzini[3]

[1] Faculty of Science, Vrije Universiteit Amsterdam, Amsterdam, The Netherlands
d.spagnuelo@vu.nl
[2] CINTESIS, University of Porto, Porto, Portugal
[3] Interdisciplinary Centre for Security Reliability and Trust (SnT),
University of Luxembourg, Luxembourg City, Luxembourg

Abstract. The introduction of the General Data Protection Regulation (GDPR) came to further strengthen the need for transparency—one of its main principles—and with it, the users' empowerment to make service providers more responsible and accountable for processing of personal data. The technological infrastructures are not yet prepared to fully support the principle, but changes are bound to be implemented in the very near future. In this work (1) we comprehensively elicit the requirements one needs to implement transparency as stated in GDPR, and (2) we verify which current Transparency Enhancing Tools (TETs) can fulfil them. We found that work still needs to be done to comply with the European Regulation. However, parts of some TETs can already solve some issues. Work efforts need to be put on the development of new solutions, but also on the improvement and testing of existing ones.

Keywords: Transparency · Transparency Enhancing Tools · General Data Protection Regulation · Compliance

1 Introduction

The General Data Protection Regulation (GDPR) is pushing data controllers and processors to review and rethink their procedures. According to the Regulation, data controllers and processors need to ensure data subjects (i.e., whom the personal data are about) that the processing is *lawful, fair* and *transparent*[1].

This paper is about the last of those principles, *transparency*. Differently from lawfulness and fairness, which express legalistic concepts, transparency is a *socio-technical* concept: intended socially, it means to empower data subjects to have the means to know whether their personal data are lawfully and fairly processed, and how; intended technically, means that ways to achieve transparency should be enforced in existing systems whenever appropriate [1].

The interest in a technical implementation of transparency was not born with the GDPR. For example, it was already discussed in cloud computing to enforce

---

[1] GDPR, Article 5.1.(a).

© Springer Nature Switzerland AG 2020
P. Mori et al. (Eds.): ICISSP 2019, CCIS 1221, pp. 162–185, 2020.
https://doi.org/10.1007/978-3-030-49443-8_8

accountability [3], and in this it shares a similar goal to the GDPR. Giving a full overview of the principle's history is beyond the scope of this article, but one important observation is that, simultaneously with the entering into force of the GDPR, there exist already tools for enhancing transparency. They are called Transparency Enhancing Tools (TETs), system-independent apps dedicated to inform her/him about how personal data are handled by an online service she/he is accessing.

Can they help improve a system's transparency according to the GDPR? The answer is unclear; as unclear is whether they can give, to who implements them, a presumption of compliance with the GDPR's legal transparency principle. At least in part, this uncertainty is due to the nature of the GDPR. Its legal provisions are expressed in a way that admits several interpretations. As other regulations, the GDPR has been thought for a broad audience and to be technology independent.

Thus, discussing whether a certain technology, like TETs, helps systems in the task of providing transparency requires a methodology. In this paper we apply one: leveraging on a previous study of ours about transparency for medical data systems [26], we elicit a list of requirements from GDPR Articles and provisions that talk about transparency. Then, we select a few TETs among those recently presented in the literature and we discuss whether they implement the requirements we extracted from the GDPR. In so doing, we systematically analyse transparency in support to identify the GDPR concepts still in need of more development.

This work extends our conference paper [25]: we give more explanation to our methodology, and revisit our results by exploring other technical and legal aspects of transparency. In this extended version, we give focus to the process of eliciting requirements from the GDPR and automatically comparing them with technical requirements. We also give more context to our work by appending the full categorisation of the 27 studied TETs, and the complete list of technical requirements.

2   Transparency and the GDPR

Transparency is a transverse principle in the GDPR, that is, it is referred directly or indirectly in several Recitals and Articles, but there is not a clear characterisation of it in the law. For that, we have to review the Articles of the Regulation, and we did by following a four round approach (see also Fig. 1): 1. Selection; 2. Filtering; 3. Revision; and 4. Validation. These rounds were conducted as follows:

1. Selection. Two of this paper's authors working independently made a list of Articles that, according to their understanding, were about transparency. Both authors had previous experience with transparency and TETs, so the expectation was that the combined knowledge covers the general perception of transparency in different technical domains.

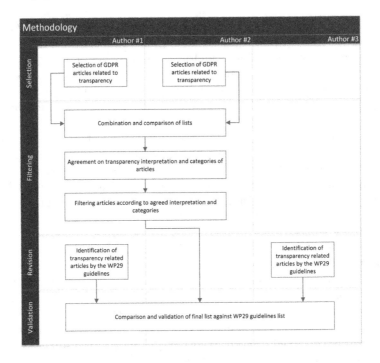

Fig. 1. Methodology for selecting transparency related Articles from the GDPR.

2. Filtering. The two lists selected were compared and combined. One author at least reviewed all the Articles. Both authors defended their interpretation of transparency, agreed on a common understanding, and extracting categories of Articles covering that understanding, including those about properties and arte-facts that support the implementation of the concept. The categories eventually selected by the authors are the following:

1. *Concerning data subjects* – Articles describing the knowledge that should be made available to the data subjects;
2. *Concerning authorities* – Articles describing the knowledge that should be made available to authorities (e.g., Data Protection Officers, or auditors);
3. *Empowerment*[2] – Articles mandating the provision of means for the data subjects to react (e.g., rectification, and erasure);
4. *Quality of transparency* – Articles which qualify transparency and describe how information should be presented to data subjects (e.g., concise, easy to understand);
5. *Certification* – Articles which foresee certification as a means to demonstrate the service's practices;
6. *Consent* – Articles commenting on the need for the data subjects to consent with usage and processing of data.

---

[2] Also know as intervenability [12].

3. Revision. To check whether our selection is in line with the state of the art, we selected one work which is considered authoritative in the matter, the *guidelines* by the Article 29 Working Party [1], and looked into what Articles therein are referred as being about transparency. We did so in the following way. Two authors (but not the same pair that executed the Filtering to reduce the risk of selection bias) independently selected the Articles that, according to their interpretation, are in the *guidelines* mentioned to be related to transparency. Both reviewers produced a very similar list. We believe this happened because the *guidelines* are more explicit about their interpretation of transparency.

4. Validation. The lists from Selection and from Revision were compared. The comparison intended to highlight the relevancy of our selection of Articles by calculating how many Articles mentioned in the guidelines were covered by us (in first and second rounds). We also compared our list with the one presented by the German Standard Data Protection Model (SDM)[3] regarding the protection goals of transparency and intervenability.

2.1 Transparency in GDPR's Articles

As a result, we compiled a list of selected transparency-related GDPR Articles (paragraphs and sub-paragraphs) that comprises 79 items. It can be found in Table 2. Our selection covers approximately 93% of the Articles in the *guidelines*. We consider our list sufficiently relevant. We comment here only on the Articles mentioned in the *guidelines* that we opted not to include in our study. Article 12.5 describes when the charge of a fee may (or may not) be applied when information is provided to data subjects regarding personal data. Even though this Article relates to transparency, it does not describe a technical feature of a TET or system. Article 20 describes the *right to portability*, which contains provisions on the characteristic of the information provided by transparency, and should be verified for compliance in every tool. Articles 25.1 and 25.2 are both regarding the implementation of *data protection by design and by default*. This concept is instead related to the security property of privacy. Hence those Articles were not selected in our list. However, we include Article 25.3, which foresees the use of certification mechanisms to demonstrate compliance with Articles 25.1 and 25.2. We understand that Article defends the right of data subjects to be aware of how their data are processed (in line with data protection principles), and as such, is in line with our interpretation of transparency.

Our selection does not contradict the list presented by the SDM, it is simply more detailed. The majority of Articles listed by the SDM are also considered in our selection. With the exception of Articles 5.1.(d), 5.1.(f), and 20—regarding accuracy of data, security of personal data, and portability of data. These Articles also contain provisions on the quality of the data provided by transparency, and should be verified for compliance in every tool. Article 40, referring to the design of codes of conduct for controllers and processors, which could hardly be

---

[3] https://www.datenschutz-mv.de/static/DS/Dateien/Datenschutzmodell/SDM-Methodology_V1_EN1.pdf.

accomplished through the use of TETs. And Article 42, on certification mechanisms, which are considered in Sect. 3.

2.2   Technical Requirements for Transparency

We match the selected GDPR's Articles with a list of technical requirements for transparency presented in previous work from the authors [26]. Due to space limitations, in Appendix A we present a complete list of requirements to help the reader picture how they look like, but we do not give details on their specification and characteristics, we remand to the original work for full details.

To match the Articles from the GDPR and the technical requirements for transparency in medical systems, we developed a simplified parser based on natural language processing techniques.

Our process consists in (1) the *analysis of the text corpora* (2) *extraction of corpus-based glossaries* and *parsing of the corpora*, and (3) *final adjustments*.

We did not conduct any statistical analysis, nor part-of-speech tagging (techniques applied in more sophisticated natural language processing algorithms). Instead, we iterated a few times realising small adjustments in our glossaries, re-evaluating the results of the parsing and, whenever needed, manually adding or removing a match.

Our approach is indeed only possible as our glossaries are context-based, limited to the terminology found in the GDPR and our requirements. We are aware of existing efforts in interpreting and translating laws, regulations, and other legal documents (e.g., [2,16,30]). We do not mean to compete with them, but rather state that our parser, in the specific problem herein addressed, has given sufficiently accurate results.

Text Corpora Analysis. The first step was carried out manually. We first analysed the two text *corpora*: the Articles and provisions in the GDPR, and a set of technical requirements for transparency in the medical domain (see Appendix A). A text *corpus* is described as a "large body of linguistic evidence typically composed of attested language use", but has been used nowadays for a wide variety of text collections [13]. Our set of requirements is not a text *corpus* in its typical meaning, as they are not composed by standardised terms. In this sense, our requirements constitute a text *corpus* in its modern interpretation: a text collection tailored to one specific domain. The GDPR, on the other hand, represents better a classic text *corpus*, as it is stable, well-established and composed by standard legal terminology.

We analysed the text *corpora* and familiarised with the differences between the terminologies, as one *corpus* comprises technical terms and the other legalistic jargon. The terms found in one *corpus* were interpreted and linked to terms in the other. As a result of this task, we highlighted potential connections between requirements and GDPR Articles and established a preliminary list of matches.

Extraction of Corpus-Based Glossaries and Parsing. To ensure the consistency of our matching procedure, we automated the comparisons by extracting possibly-equivalent terms and structuring them in glossaries. Terms found in the GDPR were matched to their equivalent technical terms, found in the list of requirements. The knowledge base needed for realising this step came from revisiting the preliminary list of matches, from where we extracted the key-terms that seem to have triggered each match. We identify matches according to a few textual elements present in the GDPR Articles: the *information* to be provided to the data subject; the *rights* the data subject must have; the *techniques* described in the Articles; and few selected *keywords*. We organised each of these in hash tables that represent, in a way, simplified *corpus*-based glossaries (see Table 1).

Table 1. Glossary of equivalent terms (*GDPR terms* on the left, and *Technical terms* on the right). Information between brackets are contextual and do not constitute the key-term.

Information	
[action (not)] taken on a request	N/A
[identity] of the controller	Responsible for handling owned data
[identity] data protection officer	Who has the authority to investigate
Purpose of processing	Terms [of use]
Legal basis for processing	Policy; regulation
[conditions for] provision of data	Regulation; terms [of use]
Rights	
Rectification	N/A
Erasure [of personal data]	Revoked consent
Restriction [of processing]	N/A
Copy of the personal data	Mechanisms for accessing [personal data]
Object [process of data]	N/A
Not to be subject [to a decision]	N/A
Exercise his or her rights	N/A
Withdraw his or her consent	Revoked consent
Techniques	
[do not] permit identification	Data privacy; to protect [data]; [data] protection; [data is] protected; separation [of data]
Appropriate security	To protect
Withdraw	Revoke
Not in a position to identify	N/A
Automated decision-making	N/A
Obtaining [personal data]	Gather; infer; aggregate
Copy of personal data	Mechanism for accessing [personal data]
Automated means	N/A
Only personal data which are necessary	Data minimisation
Record of [processing of data]	Accountability; audit
Unauthorised	Without authorisation

(continued)

Table 1. *(contniued)*

Unlawful	Vulnerability; breach
Accidental loss	Data loss; breach
Accidental destruction	N/A
Accidental damage	N/A
Profiling	N/A
Data minimisation	N/A
Existence of the right	Ownership
Shall not apply	N/A
Keywords	
Security	Security
Consent	Consent
Request for consent	N/A
Written declaration	Terms [of use]
Purposes of the processing	Terms [of use]
Concise [information]	N/A
Intelligible [information]	N/A
[information] easily accessible	N/A
[information] using clear [language]	N/A
[information using] plain language	N/A
Icons	N/A
Third party	Third party; third parties; sub-providers; whom it purchases services
Recipients	Who has access; sub-providers; third party; whom it purchases services
International	Other countries; extraterritorial; country
Adequacy decision by the commission	Comply with legal requirements; issues with respect to laws and regulations; legislative regimes
Period	N/A
Categories of personal data	Detailed information [on the data collected]
Source [from where of personal data originate]	[information on] data collected about [the data subject]
Not collected from the data subject	[information on] data collected about [the data subject]
Joint controllers	Different parties
Arrangement	Agreement
Responsibilities	Responsibilities
Respective roles	Responsibilities
Breach	Breach
Without undue further delay	Timely
Document comprising facts [that enables to verify compliance]	Evidence
Able to demonstrate	Evidence
Shall not apply	N/A

Some key-terms were intentionally marked as *not applicable* as they brought almost no contribution to the final list of matches. For example, the term "transparency" found in Article 5.1(a) "Personal data shall be processed lawfully, fairly and in a transparent manner in relation to the data subject ('lawfulness, fairness and transparency')". This Article is comprehensive and should relate to every single requirement from our list, as it mandates data to be processed transparently. To ensure our list had only the most meaningful matches, we decided to explicitly mark this term as not applicable (N/A). The same applies to the term "shall not apply", which is present in Articles (or paragraphs and sub-paragraphs) describing an exception to another Article. In other words, it presents the circumstances in which our requirements do not need to be implemented. Hence, any match with an Article of this sort is likely to be a false-positive. To avoid this, we marked the term as not applicable. It is important to note that terms marked like this are not the same as terms absent from our glossaries. While the first will force a mismatch between a GDPR Article with that term and any possible requirement in our list, the second will just be disregarded when computing the matches.

The matches are based on an automatic parser. Initially, it parses each GDPR Article to identify all the key-terms they contain. Then the requirements are parsed, searching for the ones which present at least one equivalent term for each key-term found. Our criteria for a match between an Article and a requirement is that all key-terms from the first are represented in the second. The matching procedure is abstracted in Algorithm 1.

The computation of matches is realised in steps (as shown in Algorithm 2): we run the same parsing algorithm for each glossary, and later we merge the results of each comparison in one final list. By doing so, we maintained the matching criterion decoupled, which simplified the process of re-evaluation of the terms and their possibly-equivalents. It also helped in balancing the asymmetry between GDPR Articles and our technical requirements, as the Articles are generally more verbose and encompass too many key-terms. Separating the terms into four glossaries ensured our criterion is not too restrictive, and that Articles can be matched by one or several categories of textual elements.

Final Adjustments. After computing the matches based on the glossaries of terms, we reviewed the resulting list and compared with our preliminary list. Each match was analysed, but we focused on the discrepancies between the lists. For those, we semantically interpreted the Article and requirement matched to understand the context in which the key-terms appeared, and whether or not they had the similar meaning. We conducted this procedure in a peer review manner. The matches were adjusted accordingly. We highlight here a few of the manually adjusted matches.

According to our initial list, requirement 111.2 on information about how data are stored and who has access to them, should match with Article 15.1(c), which describes the rights of the data subject in obtaining from the controller the recipients of personal data. The requirement and the Article have a clear relation.

Algorithm 1. Match($articlesGDPR[n], requirements[m], glossary\{\}[]$)

Input: array $articlesGDPR$ with n entries, array of $requirements$ with m entries, hash table of lists representing the $glossary$ of equivalent terms

$keys = glossary$.getKeys()
for each $i \in \{1, \ldots, n\}$ **do**   ▷ For each GDPR Article
    for each key **in** $keys$ **do**
        if $articlesGDPR[i]$.containsString(key) **then**
            $keyTerms[i]$.add(key)
    for each $j \in \{1, \ldots, m\}$ **do**   ▷ For each requirement
    $matchFound = $ **FALSE**
    for each $term$ **in** $keyTerms[i]$ **do**
    $equivalentTerms[] = glossary\{term\}$
    for each $value$ **in** $equivalentTerms$ **do**
        if $requirements[j]$.containsString($value$) **then**
            $matchFound = $ **TRUE**
            break
        $matchFound = $ **FALSE**
    if $!matchFound$ **then**
        break
    if $matchFound$ **then**
        $matchedArticles[i]$.add($requirements[j]$)
Output: $matchedArticles$

Algorithm 2. Init()

Let: $articlesGDPR[n]$ be the list of n selected GDPR Articles, $requirements[m]$ be the list of m technical requirements, $information\{\}[]$ be a glossary of information that should be provided to the data subject, $rights\{\}[]$ be a glossary of the rights the data subject has, $technique\{\}[]$ be a glossary of techniques mentioned in an Article, $keywords\{\}[]$ be a glossary of keywords found in the Articles;

$resultI[] = $ Match($articlesGDPR[], requirements[], information\{\}[]$)
$resultR[] = $ Match($articlesGDPR[], requirements[], rights\{\}[]$)
$resultT[] = $ Match($articlesGDPR[], requirements[], technique\{\}[]$)
$resultK[] = $ Match($articlesGDPR[], requirements[], keywords\{\}[]$)

for each $i \in \{1, \ldots, n\}$ **do**
    $finalMatch[i] = resultI[i] \cup resultR[i] \cup resultT[i] \cup resultK[i]$
Output: $finalMatch$

However, it was being disregarded by our parser as the Article contains the key-term "third countries" which does not appear in the requirement. As this key-term is responsible for several other well-fitted matches, we opted for adjusting this exception manually. Similarly, the matches involving requirement 111.18, on describing the ownership of the data, had to be adjusted. We understand that *describing the ownership* means to clarify what means to be the owner of a piece of data. In other words, to inform and describe the rights the data subjects have regarding the control of their data. In this sense, requirement 111.18 also relates to Articles 13.2.(c), 14.2.(c) and 21.4. Our parser captured a few relevant matches for this requirement, but not all of them. We manually added those remaining.

Some other matches were also considered for adjustments, as they were not present in our preliminary list, but were left untouched after a closer semantic analysis. For example, requirement 111.7, about describing procedures and mechanisms planned in cases of security breaches, matched to Articles 33.3 and 33.5, and requirement 111.15 about informing on who has the authority to investigate any policy compliance, which is also matched with 33.3. These Articles describe the information to be provided to data subjects in case of a data breach. Initially, the match was not considered as the requirements are ex ante (information to help the users understand what will happen to their data beforehand), and the Articles are, in a sense, ex post, as the data breach already happened. However, if the information described in the requirements is made available beforehand, in the event of a data breach, it will facilitate compliance with Article 33 from the GDPR. For this reason, we keep these matches.

Similarly, requirements 221.2,5,8 are matched with Article 5.2 of the GDPR (controller shall be accountable and responsible for demonstrating compliance with the lawfulness, fairness and transparency principles). The requirements, at first glance, seem unrelated to the Article, and to each other. However, the three requirements demand the users to be presented with evidence of security breaches, of recovery from them, and of permission history. As evidence, by definition, is a piece of information or data that is used to prove or disprove something, we understand they contribute to *demonstrate compliance*. Even though these matches were not identified in our initial list, we decided to keep them. Our final list of matches is shown in Table 2.

Table 2. Final list of matches between GDPR Articles and technical requirements. 72% of the requirements are matched (26 out of 36). (Table originally presented in [25])

GDPR	Requirements	GDPR	Requirements
5.1.(a)		14.3.(c)	
5.2	111.16, 111.20, 221.1, 221.2, 221.3, 221.4, 221.5, 221.7, 221.8	14.4	
6.1.(a)	221.7	15.1.(a)	111.19
7.1		15.1.(b)	221.6
7.2		15.1.(c)	111.2, 111.4
7.3	221.7	15.1.(d)	
9.2.(a)		15.1.(e)	111.18
11.2		15.1.(f)	
12.1		15.1.(g)	221.6

(continued)

Table 2. (*continued*)

GDPR	Requirements	GDPR	Requirements
12.3		15.1.(h)	
12.4		15.2	111.4, 111.11, 221.3
12.7		15.3	112.1
13.1.(a)	111.1	16	
13.1.(b)	111.15	17	221.7
13.1.(c)	111.19	18	
13.1.(d)	111.3, 111.4, 111.14	19	111.2, 111.4,
13.1.(e)	111.2, 111.3, 111.4	21.1	
13.1.(f)	111.4, 111.11, 221.3	21.2	
13.2.(a)		21.3	
13.2.(b)	111.18	21.4	111.18
13.2.(c)	111.18	21.5	
13.2.(d)		22.1	
13.2.(e)		22.2.(c)	
13.2.(f)		25.3	
13.3		26.1	111.14
14.1.(a)	111.1	26.2	111.14
14.1.(b)	111.15	26.3	111.14
14.1.(c)	111.19	30.1	221.5, 222.1, 232.1
14.1.(d)	221.6	30.2	221.5, 222.1, 232.1
14.1.(e)	111.2, 111.3, 111.4	30.3	
14.1.(f)	111.4, 11.11, 221.3	30.4	
14.2.(a)		32.3	
14.2.(b)	111.3, 111.4, 111.14	33.1	111.7, 211.1, 211.4, 221.8
14.2.(c)	111.18	33.2	111.7, 211.1, 211.4, 221.8
14.2.(d)	111.18	33.3	111.7, 111.15, 211.1, 211.4, 221.8
14.2.(e)		33.4	211.4
14.2.(f)	221.6	33.5	111.7, 211.1, 211.4, 221.8
14.2.(g)		34.1	111.7, 211.1, 211.4, 221.8
14.3.(a)	211.5	34.2	
14.3.(b)			

3   Transparency and Technology (TETs)

At least at an intuitive level, the most natural technology for transparency is
represented by TETs. According to [18], TETs are tools to "make the underlying
processes [of personal data or a subject] more transparent, and to enable data
subjects to better understand the implications that arise due to their decision
to disclose personal data, or that have arisen due to choices 'made in the past'".

This cited work already provide an extensive list of tools. We also reviewed other survey works about TETs and compiled a drafted list of such tools [4, 7, 17, 22, 31].

Besides, we browsed the literature for "transparency enhancing tools", looking for works that may have referred to the tools indirectly or within text. The search included works published since 2014, the year the GDPR started to be strongly supported by the European Parliament[4]. We selected 27 tools which can be potentially linked to the transparency principle. We categorised them using TETCat [31], a methodology to classify TETs according to their properties and functionalities, for instance, such as among others, *assurance level* (*not trusted*, *semi trusted*, or *trusted*), the *application time* of the tool (*ex ante*, *ex post* or *real time*) and *interactivity level* (*read-only* or *interactive*).

Our categorisation is summarised in Appendix B and described in the next paragraphs. Its full version is made available in [24].

Assertion Tools. Tools are classified as the assertion type whenever the correctness and completeness of the information they provide cannot be verified (*not trusted*), and they can only provide information on the controller's alleged processing practices. The TETCat does not further distinguish assertion tools, so tools of this type have diverse goals.

Examples of assertion tools are third-party tracking blockers, e.g., Mozilla Lightbeam[5] (ML), Disconnect me[6] (DM), and Privacy Badger[7] (PB); and tools that educate users on matters related to privacy protection, e.g., Privacy Risk Analysis (PRA) [5], Me and My Shadow[8] (MMS), Privacy Score[9] (PS) and Access My Info[10] (AMI).

Awareness Tools. This is the first type of tools providing information verifiable for completeness and correctness, for two assurance levels (i.e., *trusted* and *semi trusted*). Awareness tools provide *ex ante* transparency, and interactivity level of *read only*. Tools in this category help the user becoming aware of the privacy policy of the service provider but do not provide the users with controls over the processing of data. Examples of such tools are machine readable or interpreted policy languages, e.g., Platform for Privacy Preferences Project[11] (P3P). Another example of an awareness tool is the Usable Privacy Project[12] [20], which automatically annotates privacy policies. Finally, tools providing certification seals and marks such as the European Privacy Seal (EuroPriSe) [6] or the TrustArc (TArc) [27] are also examples of tools in this category.

---

[4] http://europa.eu/rapid/press-release_MEMO-14-186_de.htm.
[5] https://www.mozilla.org/lightbeam.
[6] https://disconnect.me/.
[7] https://www.eff.org/privacybadger.
[8] https://myshadow.org/.
[9] https://privacyscore.org/.
[10] https://openeffect.ca/access-my-info/.
[11] https://www.w3.org/P3P/.
[12] https://explore.usableprivacy.org/.

Declaration Tools. Only one tool falls under this category: PrimeLife Policy Language (PPL) [10], which is similar to awareness tools, comparable to the P3P tool, but offers some level of interactivity.

Audit Tools. Audit TETs present users with *ex post* or *real time* transparency. Tools in this category include those that allow for access and verifiability of data, but do not provide means for the users to interact and intervene with the data processing (i.e., *read only* tools), such as the Data Track[13] (DT) [9] and Personal Data Table (PDT) [22]. Another tool under this category is The Blue Button[14]. Which is an initiative to standardise the right to access personal medical data in the USA, and display a logo stating that users are allowed to visualise and download their data.

Finally, the Private Verification of Access (PVA) [11] proposes a scheme for *a posteriori* access control compliance checks that operates under a data minimisation principle and provides a private independent audit. This tool also falls under the audit tools category.

Intervention Tools. These tools allow users to verify properties about the processing of their data as well as to interact and control the terms of data collection and usage. Examples are: the Privacy Through Transparency (PTT) [21]—supporting Break-the-Glass (BTG) policies; and Privacy eSuite[15].

Remediation Tools. According to the TETCat these tools comprise functionality to exercise control over data collection and usage, and also to modify and delete personal data stored by a data controller. Tools belonging to this category are, for instance, PrivacyInsight (PI) [4] and GDPR Privacy Dashboard[16] (GPD) [19]—both privacy dashboards; and openPDS (oPDS) [14], and Meeco[17] (Mee) which are examples of data vault/marketplace applications.

4   TETs for the GDPR

Our goal is to select from our list of TETs, those which can presumably help achieve compliance with the provisions of the GDPR. We do this indirectly, by selecting those TETs which satisfy the requirements for transparency that we elicited from the analysis of Articles and Recitals of the GDPR

Methodology. The selected TETs have been compared against the technical requirements for transparency, in search for matches. A match is when a tool satisfies one or more requirements. Here, we first pre-select tools and requirements by their application time, distinguishing between *ex ante* and *ex post/real time*. Then we compared TETs and requirements one by one. We did this work manually, but having categorised TETs helped us to implement this task more systematically.

---

[13] https://github.com/pylls/datatrack.
[14] https://www.healthit.gov/topic/health-it-initiatives/blue-button.
[15] http://hipaat.com/privacy-esuite/.
[16] http://philip-raschke.github.io/GDPR-privacy-dashboard.
[17] https://www.meeco.me/.

4.1   Comparing TETs and Requirements: Results and Discussion

Table 3 summarises the findings (we have put in bold the requirements ex ante (1**), and in slanted those ex post (2**)). A full report of them may be found [24], where we expand the GDPR Articles into the paragraphs and sub-paragraphs relevant to this work.

Looking at the Table, two particular exceptions in this matching—exceptions with respect to what one would expect from the methodology we followed—that stand out and need a comment.

The first is concerning requirement 112.1 on the provision of mechanisms for accessing personal data. In the context of medical systems, data about the patients are typically generated by other users in the system. As a consequence, allowing these patients to access their data can be interpreted as pre-condition for them to anticipate what will happen to their data, hence *ex ante*. However, in the context of TETs, tools which allow for the access of personal data are considered *ex post*. We interpret requirement 112.1 and those tools as closely related, even if their application times do not match. The second is regarding certification seals, which we consider *ex ante*. Certification seals are tools which testifies that a system complies with a given criterion. If the criteria regards the processing of data, these seals can help a data subject to anticipate how their data will be processed. However, from the perspective of the system, when evaluated for the certification, the processing of data is already happening. For this reason, we accept the match between such tools and a few relevant *ex post* requirements.

In what follows, we comment on our findings.

Requirements *vs* TETs: What Matches and What Does Not. Three requirements regarding terms and conditions seem not to be addressed by any TET: 111.1 on information regarding the physical location where data is stored; 111.4 on the existence of third-party services and sub-providers; 111.14 on clarifications of responsibility in case of the existence of third-party services.

We believe this information could be provided together with the terms and conditions of the service. Even though the tool provided by Usable Privacy Project (UP) aims at facilitating the reading of these, we did not identify tags for the requirements above. For this reason, we do not consider these requirements as addressed. There are other relevant developments on this subject, such as the CLAUDETTE project[18], which makes use of artificial intelligence to automatically evaluate the clauses of a policy for clarity and completeness in the light of the GDPR provisions. Another relevant tool in this regard is the Me and My Shadow (MMS), which provides a functionality called Lost in Small Print[19]. It reveals and highlights the most relevant information of a given policy. We do not include those tools in our study as the first only evaluates the quality of the policy, without necessarily easing the understanding of its contents, and the second for only providing few selected examples of policies of popular services.

---

[18] https://claudette.eui.eu/.

[19] https://myshadow.org/lost-in-small-print.

Table 3. From [25]. Transparency Enhancing Tools (TETs), technical requirements, and the GDPR Articles they help realising (* added manually).

TET	Requirements	GDPR Articles
Mozilla Lightbeam	*211.5, 221.6*	14, 15
P3P	**111.2, 111.3, 111.16, 111.18, 111.19**	5, 13, 14, 15, 19, 21
PrimeLife Policy Language	**111.2, 111.3, 111.16, 111.18, 111.19**	5, 13, 14, 15, 19, 21
Data Track	**112.1**, *221.5, 221.6, 221.7*	5, 6, 7, 14, 15, 17, 30
Privacy Insight	**112.1**, *221.4, 221.5, 221.6, 221.7*	5, 6, 7, 14, 15, 17, 30
Privacy Risk Analysis	**111.9, 111.13**	
GDPR Privacy Dashboard	**112.1**, *222.1, 221.4, 221.6, 221.7*	5, 6, 7, 14, 15, 17
Personal Data Table	**112.1**, *211.2, 211.3, 222.1, 221.4, 221.6, 221.7*	5, 6, 7, 14, 15, 17
Disconnect me	*222.1, 221.6*	14, 15
Me and My Shadow	**111.8, 111.13, 111.16, 111.19**	5, 13, 14, 15
EuroPriSe	**111.16**, *221.1, 221.3, 221.4*	5, 13, 14, 15
Privacy Score	**111.6, 111.12, 111.13**	
Google Dashboard	**112.1**, *222.1, 221.6, 221.7*	5, 6, 7, 14, 15, 17
Privacy Evidence	*221.1, 221.4, 221.5, 222.1, 232.1*	5, 30
TAMI Project	*211.2, 211.3, 222.1, 221.1, 221.4, 222.1, 232.1*	5, 14, 30
Privacy Through Transparency	*211.2, 211.3, 221.1, 221.4, 221.5, 222.1, 232.1*	5, 30
Private Verif. of Access	*211.2, 211.3, 221.1, 221.4, 222.1, 232.1*	5, 30
Privacy Badger	*222.1, 221.6*	14, 15
Access My Info	**112.1**, *221.6*	14, 15
TrustArc	**111.16**, *221.1, 221.3, 221.4*	5, 13, 14, 15
openPDS	*222.1, 221.6, 221.7*	5, 6, 7, 14, 15, 17
Digi.me	*221.6, 221.7*	5, 6, 7, 14, 15, 17
Microsoft Dashboard	**112.1**, *222.1, 221.6, 221.7*	5, 6, 7, 14, 15, 17
Privacy eSuite	*221.1, 221.5, 221.7, 222.1, 232.1*	5, 6, 7, 9*, 17, 30
Meeco	*221.6, 221.7*	5, 6, 7, 14, 15, 17
Blue Button	**112.1**, *221.6*	14, 15
Usable Privacy	**111.5, 111.10, 111.11, 111.15, 111.17, 111.19**	13, 14, 15, 33

Nevertheless, they indicate that this matter is already subject of attention. We expect to see a different scenario concerning tools for terms and conditions in the future.

We also observed a lack of tools covering technical aspects of data processing. For example, requirement 111.5 about informing how the system ensures data is not accessed without authorisation, and requirement 111.20 on evidence of separating personal data from metadata, are not addressed by any of the tools we studied. The reason for this is not clear, as other requirements about the use of specific security mechanisms (111.12), and how to protect data (111.13) also cover technical aspects and seem to be the subject of attention of TETs. We speculate this lack of attention may be due to the target audience, which in general has no technical education and would not value such information. Another possible explanation is that this sort of information is provided together with others, and we missed to identify them in our selected tools.

Finally, requirements regarding security breaches and attacks also seem to have gained less attention. They constitute the majority of requirements not addressed by any TET: 111.7, 211.1, 211.4, 221.2, and 221.8. As security breaches are unforeseen events, it does not come as a surprise that there are no tools for aiding the understanding of issues related to them. Nonetheless, it is important to notice that the GDPR reserves two Articles to provisions on personal data breaches (Art. 33 and 34), one of which is dedicated to describing how to communicate such matters to the affected data subjects. Being the health-care industry among the ones with most reported breaches, and being medical data in the top three most compromised variety of data (for more details, see results of the data breach investigation [28]), we consider this to be an area in need of further development.

TETs *vs* Articles: Which Suggests Compliance and Which Does Not.
Only a few Articles from the GDPR are not related to any of the selected transparency tools: meaning that none of its paragraphs or sub-paragraphs is matched to a TET. These concern the Articles about data protection mechanisms and certification. Article 25 regards data protection by design and by default, and Article 32 has provisions on security of processing; both mention that compliance with such Articles may be demonstrated through the use of approved certification mechanisms referred to in Article 42.

Despite having included two certification seals in our list of TETs (i.e., EuroPriSe, and TrustArc), EuroPriSe's criteria catalogue has not been approved pursuant to Article 42(5) GDPR. The reason is that they have not been accredited as a certification body pursuant to Article 43 GDPR yet[20]. While for TrustArc, we cannot confirm it is an approved certification mechanisms, we did not find enough information about this matter.

A few transparency quality and empowerment related Articles are also not addressed by our selected tools. Article 12, for example, qualifies the communications with the data subject and states that it should be concise, easily accessible, using clear and plain language, and by electronic means whenever appropriate. In our understanding, this Article does not match to any specific tool because it is transverse to all of them. This Article has provisions regarding the quality of communications; all tools communicating information to data subjects should be affected by it. In [23] we discuss metrics for transparency which, in line with this reasoning, consider the information provided to final users "being concise", or "being easily accessible" as indicators that transparency is properly implemented.

With regard to empowerment related Articles, while a few Articles do relate to some tools (e.g., Art. 17, 19 and 21), they are either partially addressed by transparency tools, or not addressed at all. In fact, empowerment and transparency are different properties [12,26], and this may explain why only a few of those Articles are addressed by TETs. But at least with regard to Articles describing the rights of the data subject towards the processing of personal data (e.g., Art. 22, and 26), we believe policy, and terms and conditions tools could also address them, but we found no tool addressing those subjects.

There are developments in this topic of empowerment though [12]. In this work empowerment (referred to by the authors as intervenability) is discussed

---

[20] See https://www.european-privacy-seal.eu/EPS-en/Criteria.

as a privacy goal, and it is compared to transparency. In this context, Article 12 relates to their requirement T4 and T5, and Article 17 relates to requirement I10. However, the full implementation of empowerment, as it requires providing ways for users to exercise their rights regarding personal data, may not be suitable for a TET. The analysis of the requirements proposed in [12] and their relationship with TETs falls out of this work's scope.

It is important to notice that a few Articles which appear not to be covered by any TET, are not considered in this analysis because they do not match by key-terms with any of our requirements. We investigate two of them manually: Articles 11, and 9. Article 11 has provisions on processing which does not require identification. We consider this Article in our study as its paragraph 2 states that the controller shall inform the data subjects when it is not in a position to identify them. It also further states that in such a case, Articles 15 to 20 (on the exercise of data subject's rights) shall not apply. In this sense, Article 11 describes a case when empowerment tools (related to Articles 15 to 20) are not required. It does not make sense to discuss the relationship of this Article and TETs in our list.

Article 9, on the other hand, has provisions on data subject's consent for data processing of special categories of personal data, including data concerning health. Privacy eSuite tool (PeS) is a web-service consent engine specifically tailored to collect and centralise consent for the processing of health data. Hence, it is connected with Article 9. In the interest of completeness, we manually added this match in Table 3. However, PeS is a proprietary tool designed in line with the Canadian regulations. We found no means to determine to which extent this tool can help achieving the provisions in the GDPR.

Being *consent* described in the GDPR as one of the basis for lawful processing of personal data, the number of tools addressing this subject seems suspiciously low. This fact does not imply that medical systems and other services are currently operating illegally. We are aware that collecting consent for processing data is a practice. However, we are interested in tools designed to facilitate the task of collecting consent and to help users to be truly informed of the consequences of giving consent.

We investigated this more closely, among our findings there are mostly tools and frameworks aiding the collection of informed consent for digital advertising[21]. We also found mentions to the EnCoRe (Ensuring Consent and Revocation) project, which presents insights on the role of informed consent in online interactions [29]. The project appears finalised, and we found no tool proposed to address the collection of informed consent.

One could claim that tools proposed for terms and conditions, or privacy policies (e.g., P3P, PPL, and UP), can also help collecting consent. While this is a possible solution, special attention is required that the request for consent is distinguishable from other matters (as per GDPR Article 7). It is also important to note that consent to the processing of personal data shall be freely given,

---

[21] See Conversant, IAB Europe, and ShareThis.

specific, informed, and unambiguous[22]. Implicitly collecting consent for data processing is arguably against the provisions in the GDPR [29]. In that work, the authors discuss to which extent terms and policies are even read and understood. In this sense, consent is unlikely to be truly informed and freely given.

5   Related Works

To the best of our knowledge, only a few works discuss matters of compliance with the GDPR principles (i.e., [4,12,19]). In [12], the authors derive technical requirements from the international standard ISO/IEC 291000 and the GDPR. Even though in this work technical (international standard) and legal (GDPR) documents are used, those are not compared. The requirements studied in this work are instead extracted from these documents.

In [4] the authors propose a Transparency Enhancing Tool (TET) in the form of a privacy dashboard. To define the relevant features to be implemented, they derived eight technical requirements from the *right of access* presented by the GDPR, the previous European Data Protection Directive, and the Federal Data Protection Act from Germany. Similarly, Raschke *et al.* propose a GDPR-compliant dashboard in [19]. In this work, however, only four high-level features are extracted from the GDPR: the right to access data, obtaining information about involved processors, rectification and erasure of data, and consent review and withdraw. Both works extract requirements from data protection laws, but do not compare them with any other sources.

Four works review TETs [7,15,17,31]. The work by Murmann and Fischer-Hübner [15] surveys the literature searching for transparency tools, and explores aspects of usable transparency—derived from legals provisions in the GDPR, and well accepted usability principles. The authors identify meaningful categories of tools and propose a classification based on functionalities and implementation, for instance. Although this work is comprehensive in exploring the characteristics of usable TETs, it does not explicitly map technical aspects of the tools with the GDPR provisions they help accomplishing.

There are works, however, which compare and map legal and technical requirements, principles and designs. In particular, [8] reviews usability principles in a few selected TETs. To this aim, the authors gather requirements from workshops and by reviewing documents related to data protection, such as the proposal of the GDPR (document available at the time), and the opinions from the Article 29 Data Protection Working Party. These requirements are mapped to three Human-Computer Interaction (HCI) concepts, which in turn are discussed in the context of the TETs. Even though the mappings presented in this work are thoroughly discussed, the authors do not present a structured procedure followed when defining them. It is our interpretation that those mappings were identified manually.

---

[22] GDPR Article 4 (11).

The SDM[23] also classifies GDPR's provision in terms of *data protection goals* (e.g., availability, transparency, intervenability), and comments on *technical measures* that help to guarantee transparency, such as, documentation of procedures, logging of access and modifications. These measures relate to our requirements, but are more high-level. We believe our requirements could be classified according to them, allowing us to select TETs that can accomplish transparency as described by the SDM. We leave this task to future works.

6   Discussion and Conclusion

Even since before the GDPR entered into force, several activities and initiatives bloomed with the aim to provide advice, guidance, instruments, or all of those services, to enterprises concerned about the high fines that were promised to follow a provable lack of compliance with the Regulation.

In this paper we focus on one particular aspect of the compliance, that about the Regulation's principle of transparency. Despite the principle being only transversely referred in the GDPR—that is, it is not subject of one Article or one Recital in particular, but it is rather referred across many items—compliance with it is a serious matter. In January 2019, this statement could not become clearer, when The French data protection authority, the Commission National de l'Informatique et des Liberte (CNIL), condemned Google to pay an impressively high penalty, in the order of about 50 Million euros, because of lack of transparency. CNIL concluded in fact that users of services like Google Search, YouTube, Google Maps, Play Store etc., are not in the position to have a fair perception of the nature and volume of the collected data[24]. The CNIL also objected the transparency of the consent form that Google offers to its users, arguing that the consent form is not informative enough because it is stated in a way which is unclear and ambiguous, in addition to the fact that users have no choice but to accept it.

Discussing the full extent of this famous legal case is beyond our goal and it is not our business either to speculate on the reasons why Tech Giants like Google fail to be compliant with a Regulation, but at least, in part, one could question whether this might be due to the lack of instruments to inform users. In this paper, we looked into what could be the most natural choice, that is Transparency Enhancing Tools (TETs), while at the same time discussing the technical requirements that emerge from a technical reading of the GDPR's provisions.

This comprehensive analysis of transparency helps identifying current and future developments to better comply with transparency and related GDPR requirements by using TETs. The tools were proposed to protect users' privacy in general and thus not designed specifically for the GDPR; rather they have been tailored for one specific use case or goal, or thought to fulfil a specific legislation or regulation according to what were the priorities of who designed

---

[23] https://www.datenschutzzentrum.de/uploads/sdm/SDM-Methodology_V1.0.pdf.

[24] See https://www.cnil.fr/en/node/25137.

and developed them. Consequently, they cannot be immediately available to be included in most systems nor mindlessly considered ready to interpreting the GDPR's provisions. But our analysis highlights which TETs match the GDPR's requests on transparency, and according to which aspect they do that. However, adapting the tools to become instruments of compliance to the specifics of transparency in GDPR is something that needs to be developed or discussed in a near future. We are not there yet but this paper started to identify and clarify the way towards that goal, so that any future development will not be necessarily built from a blank board, but can be leveraged already by the 12 out of the 21 GDPR Articles that we studied and discussed here. At least partially, those Articles are addressed by the selected/presented TETs.

Acknowledgments. Spagnuelo and Lenzini's research is supported by the Luxembourg National Research Fund (FNR), AFR project 7842804 TYPAMED and CORE project 11333956 DAPRECO, respectively. Ana's research is supported by FCT through the Project TagUBig - Taming Your Big Data (IF/00693/2015) from Researcher FCT Program funded by National Funds through FCT - Fundação para a Ciência e a Tecnologia.

A   Transparency Requirements

(See Table 4).

Table 4. Transparency requirements as originally presented in [26]. IDs refer to the original numbering, those indexed 1** are ex ante, those 2** are ex post.

Req.	Specification
111.1	The system must provide the user with real time information on physical data storage and data storage location of different types of data
111.2	The system must inform the user on how data are stored and who has access to them
111.3	The system must inform the user from whom it purchases services, and about any conflict of interest towards data
111.4	The system, in case of using services from third parties, must inform the user about the existence of sub-providers, where they are located and whether they comply with the legal requirements of the country of the user
111.5	The system must inform the user how it is assured that data are not accessed without authorisation
111.6	The system should make available a document that describes the adopted mechanisms for securing data against data loss as well as data privacy vulnerabilities
111.7	The system should make available a document that describes the procedures and mechanisms planned in cases of security breaches on the user's data
111.8	The system should make available the technical documentation on how data are handled, how they are stored, and what are the procedures for accessing them
111.9	The user must be made aware of the consequences of their possible choices in an unbiased manner
111.10	The system must inform the user about who is responsible for handling owned data

(continued)

Table 4. (*continued*)

Req.	Specification
111.11	The system must inform the user about storage in other countries and compliance issues related to this storage with respect to laws and regulations of both the other country and their own country
111.12	The system should inform the user about the use of specific security mechanisms
111.13	The system must inform the user on how to protect data or how data are protected
111.14	In case of using services from third parties, The system must inform the user on the responsibilities of the different parties involved in the agreement
111.15	The system must inform the user about who has the authority to investigate any policy compliance
111.16	The system must provide the user with evidence of data collection practices
111.17	The system must make available a document explaining the procedures for leaving the service and taking the data out from the service
111.18	The system must make available a document that describes the ownership of the data
111.19	The system must provide the user with disclosure of policies, regulations or terms regarding data sharing, processing and the use of data
111.20	The system must provide the user with evidence of separating personal from meta data
112.1	The system must provide the user with mechanisms for accessing personal data
211.1	The system, in case of security breaches, must inform the user on what happened, why it happened, what the procedures The system is taking to correct the problem and when services will be resumed as normal
211.2	The system must inform the user when the authorities access personal data
211.3	The system must notify the user in case the policy is overridden (break the glass)
211.4	The system must provide the user with timely notification on security breaches (Art. 33 says, within 72 h after one becomes aware of the incident)
221.5	The system must inform the user if and when data is gathered, inferred or aggregated
221.1	The system must provide the user with evidence that policies, regulations and practices have been applied correctly
221.2	The system must provide the user with evidence of the recovery from security attacks
221.3	The system must provide evidence of compliance with respect to extraterritorial legislative regimes
221.4	The system must provide evidence that the data is being maintained in the correct way
221.5	The system must provide the user with evidence regarding permissions history for auditing purposes
221.6	The system must provide detailed information on the data collected about the user, and what information The system has implicitly derived from disclosed data
221.7	The system must provide the user with evidence that revoked consent has been executed
211.8	The system must provide the user with evidence of security breaches
222.1	The system must provide the user with audit mechanisms
232.1	The system must provide the user with accountability mechanisms

B   Transparency Enhancing Tools (TETs)

(See Table 5).

Table 5. Transparency Enhancing Tools (TETs) classified according to their characteristics. (T)TP = (Trusted) Third Party; C = Collection; U = Usage; M = Modification; D = Deletion; A = Analysis; 2^{nd}U = Second Usage.

TET	Applic. time	Exec. envir.	Data type	Auth. level	Interac. level	Assur. level	Transp. dim.	TETCat
Mozilla Lightbeam (ML)	Real-time, Ex-post	Client-side	Obs.	Data-subject	Read-only	Not Trusted	C	Assertion
P3P	Ex-ante	Server-side	Policy	Anonym.	Read-only	(Semi) Trusted	C/U/2^{nd}U	Awareness
PrimeLife Policy Language (PPL)	Ex-ante	Hybrid	Policy	Anonym.	Interac. (C/U)	(Semi) Trusted	C/U/2^{nd}U	Declaration
Data Track (DT)	Ex-post	Hybrid	Volunt., Obs., Incid., Deriv.	Full Id.	Read-only	(Semi) Trusted	C/A	Audit
PrivacyInsight (PI)	Ex-post	Hybrid	Volunt., Incid., Obs., Deriv.	Full Id.	Interac. (C/U/M/D)	(Semi) Trusted	C/A/U/2^{nd}U	Remediation
Privacy Risk Analysis (PRA)	Ex-ante	(T)TP-based	Policy	Anonym.	Read-only	Not trusted	C/A/U/2^{nd}U	Assertion
GDPR Privacy Dashboard (GPD)	Ex-post	Server-side	Volunt., Incid., Obs., Deriv.	Full Id.	Interac. (C/U/M/D)	(Semi) Trusted	C/A/U/2^{nd}U	Remediation
Personal Data Table (PDT)	Ex-post	Server-side	Volunt., Incid., Obs., Deriv.	Full Id.	Read-only	(Semi) Trusted	C/A/U/2^{nd}U	Audit
Disconnect me (DM)	Real-time, Ex-post	Client-side	Obs.	Anonym.	Interac. (C/U)	Not trusted	C/2^{nd}U	Assertion
Me and My Shadow (MMS)	Ex-ante	(T)TP-based	Policy	Anonym.	Read-only	Not trusted	C/A/U/2^{nd}U	Assertion
EuroPriSe	Ex-ante	(T)TP-based	Policy	Anonym.	Read-only	(Semi) Trusted	C/A/U/2^{nd}U	Awareness
Privacy Score (PS)	Ex-ante	(T)TP-based	Policy	Anonym.	Read-only	Not Trusted	2^{nd}U	Assertion
Google Dashboard (GD)	Ex-post	Server-side	Volunt., Incid., Obs., Deriv.	Full Id.	Interac. (C/U/M/D)	(Semi) Trusted	C/A/U/2^{nd}U	Remediation
Privacy Evidence (PEv)	Ex-post	Hybrid	Policy	Full Id.	Read-only	(Semi) Trusted	C/U	Audit
TAMI Project	Ex-post	Hybrid	Volunt., Incid., Obs., Deriv.	Full Id.	Read-only	(Semi) Trusted	U	Audit
Privacy Through Transp. (PTT)	Ex-post	Server-Side	Volunt.	Full Id.	Interac. (C/U)	(Semi) Trusted	C/U	Intervention
Private Verif. of Access (PVA)	Ex-post	Hybrid	Volunt., Obs., Incid., Deriv.	Anonym.	Read-only	(Semi) Trusted	C/U	Audit
Privacy Badger (PB)	Real-time, Ex-post	Client-side	Obs.	Anonym.	Interac. (C/U)	Not trusted	C	Assertion
Access My Info (AMI)	Ex-post	Client-side	Volunt., Incid., Obs., Deriv.	Full Id.	Read-only	Not trusted	C/A	Assertion
TrustArc	Ex-ante	(T)TP-based	Policy	Anonym.	Read-only	(Semi) Trusted	C/A/U/2^{nd}U	Awareness
openPDS	Real-time, Ex-post	Client-side	Volunt., Incid., Obs., Deriv.	Full Id.	Interac. (C/U/M/D)	(Semi) Trusted	C/A/U	Remediation
Digi.me	Real-time, Ex-post	Hybrid	Volunt., Incid., Obs.	Full Id.	Read-only	(Semi) Trusted	C	Audit
Microsoft Dashboard (MD)	Ex-post	Server-side	Volunt., Incid., Obs., Deriv.	Full Id.	Interac. (C/U/M/D)	(Semi) Trusted	C/A/U/2^{nd}U	Remediation
Privacy eSuite (PeS)	Real-time, Ex-post	Hybrid	Volunt., Incid.	Full Id.	Interac. (C/U)	(Semi) Trusted	C/U	Intervention
Meeco (Mee)	Real-time, Ex-post	Hybrid	Policy, Volunt.	Full Id.	Interac. (C/U/M/D)	(Semi) Trusted	C/U	Remediation
Blue Button (BB)	Ex-post	Server-side	Volunt., Obs., Incid., Deriv.	Full Id.	Read-only	(Semi) Trusted	C	Audit
Usable Privacy (UP)	Ex-ante	(T)TP-based	Policy	Anonym.	Read-only	(Semi) Trusted	C/A U/2^{nd}U	Awareness

References

1. Article 29 Working Party: Guidelines on transparency under regulation 2016/679 (April 2018). http://ec.europa.eu/newsroom/article29/item-detail.cfm?item_id=622227. Accessed Aug 2018
2. Bartolini, C., Giurgiu, A., Lenzini, G., Robaldo, L.: A framework to reason about the legal compliance of security standards. In: Proceedings of the 10th International Workshop on Juris-Informatics (2016)
3. Berthold, S., Fischer-Hübner, S., Martucci, L., Pulls, T.: Crime and punishment in the cloud: accountability, transparency, and privacy. In: International Workshop on Trustworthiness, Accountability and Forensics in the Cloud (2013)
4. Bier, C., Kühne, K., Beyerer, J.: PrivacyInsight: the next generation privacy dashboard. In: Schiffner, S., Serna, J., Ikonomou, D., Rannenberg, K. (eds.) APF 2016. LNCS, vol. 9857, pp. 135–152. Springer, Cham (2016). https://doi.org/10.1007/978-3-319-44760-5_9
5. De, S.J., Le Métayer, D.: Privacy risk analysis to enable informed privacy settings. In: 2018 IEEE European Symposium on Security and Privacy Workshops (EuroS&PW). IEEE (2018)
6. EuroPriSe: Europrise certification criteria (v201701) (January 2017). https://www.european-privacy-seal.eu/EPS-en/Criteria. Accessed Oct 2018
7. Ferreira, A., Lenzini, G.: Can transparency enhancing tools support patient's accessing electronic health records? In: Rocha, A., Correia, A.M., Costanzo, S., Reis, L.P. (eds.) New Contributions in Information Systems and Technologies. AISC, vol. 353, pp. 1121–1132. Springer, Cham (2015). https://doi.org/10.1007/978-3-319-16486-1_111
8. Fischer-Hübner, S., Angulo, J., Pulls, T.: How can cloud users be supported in deciding on, tracking and controlling how their data are used? In: Hansen, M., Hoepman, J.-H., Leenes, R., Whitehouse, D. (eds.) Privacy and Identity 2013. IAICT, vol. 421, pp. 77–92. Springer, Heidelberg (2014). https://doi.org/10.1007/978-3-642-55137-6_6
9. Fischer-Hübner, S., Angulo, J., Karegar, F., Pulls, T.: Transparency, Privacy and trust – technology for tracking and controlling my data disclosures: does this work? In: Habib, S.M.M., Vassileva, J., Mauw, S., Mühlhäuser, M. (eds.) IFIPTM 2016. IAICT, vol. 473, pp. 3–14. Springer, Cham (2016). https://doi.org/10.1007/978-3-319-41354-9_1
10. Fischer-Hübner, S., Martucci, L.A.: Privacy in social collective intelligence systems. In: Miorandi, D., Maltese, V., Rovatsos, M., Nijholt, A., Stewart, J. (eds.) Social Collective Intelligence. CSS, pp. 105–124. Springer, Cham (2014). https://doi.org/10.1007/978-3-319-08681-1_6
11. Idalino, T.B., Spagnuelo, D., Martina, J.E.: Private verification of access on medical data: an initial study. In: Garcia-Alfaro, J., Navarro-Arribas, G., Hartenstein, H., Herrera-Joancomartí, J. (eds.) ESORICS/DPM/CBT-2017. LNCS, vol. 10436, pp. 86–103. Springer, Cham (2017). https://doi.org/10.1007/978-3-319-67816-0_6
12. Meis, R., Heisel, M.: Computer-aided identification and validation of intervenability requirements. Information 8(1), 30 (2017)
13. Mitkov, R.: The Oxford Handbook of Computational Linguistics. Oxford University Press, Oxford (2005)
14. de Montjoye, Y.A., Shmueli, E., Wang, S.S., Pentland, A.S.: OpenPDS: protecting the privacy of metadata through safeanswers. PloS One 9(7), e98790 (2014)

15. Murmann, P., Fischer-Hübner, S.: Tools for achieving usable ex post transparency: a survey. IEEE Access **5**, 22965–22991 (2017)
16. Nejad, N.M., Scerri, S., Auer, S.: Semantic similarity based clustering of license excerpts for improved end-user interpretation. In: Proceedings of the 13th International Conference on Semantic Systems, pp. 144–151. ACM (2017)
17. OPC: Privacy Enhancing Technologies - A Review of Tools and Techniques (November 2017). https://www.priv.gc.ca/en/opc-actions-and-decisions/research/explore-privacy-research/2017/pet_201711/. Accessed Aug 2018
18. Murmann, P., Fischer-Hübner, S.: Usable transparency enhancing tools - a literature review (working paper). Universitetstryckeriet, Karlstad 2017 (2017)
19. Raschke, P., Küpper, A., Drozd, O., Kirrane, S.: Designing a GDPR-compliant and usable privacy dashboard. In: Hansen, M., Kosta, E., Nai-Fovino, I., Fischer-Hübner, S. (eds.) Privacy and Identity 2017. IAICT, vol. 526, pp. 221–236. Springer, Cham (2018). https://doi.org/10.1007/978-3-319-92925-5_14
20. Sathyendra, K.M., Wilson, S., Schaub, F., Zimmeck, S., Sadeh, N.: Identifying the provision of choices in privacy policy text. In: Proceedings of the 2017 Conference on Empirical Methods in Natural Language Processing, pp. 2774–2779 (2017)
21. Seneviratne, O., Kagal, L.: Enabling privacy through transparency. In: 12th Annual International Conference on Privacy, Security and Trust, pp. 121–128. IEEE (2014)
22. Siljee, J.: Privacy transparency patterns. In: Proceedings of the 20th European Conference on Pattern Languages of Programs, p. 52. ACM (2015)
23. Spagnuelo, D., Bartolini, C., Lenzini, G.: Modelling metrics for transparency in medical systems. In: Lopez, J., Fischer-Hübner, S., Lambrinoudakis, C. (eds.) TrustBus 2017. LNCS, vol. 10442, pp. 81–95. Springer, Cham (2017). https://doi.org/10.1007/978-3-319-64483-7_6
24. Spagnuelo, D., Ferreira, A., Lenzini, G.: Accomplishing transparency within the general data protection regulation (auxiliary material) (2018). http://hdl.handle.net/10993/37692
25. Spagnuelo, D., Ferreira, A., Lenzini, G.: Accomplishing transparency within the general data protection regulation. In: 5th International Conference on Information Systems Security and Privacy (2019)
26. Spagnuelo, D., Lenzini, G.: Transparent medical data systems. J. Med. Syst. **41**(1), 1–12 (2016). https://doi.org/10.1007/s10916-016-0653-8
27. TrustArc: Enterprise privacy & data governance practices certification assessment criteria (September 2018). https://www.trustarc.com/products/enterprise-privacy-certification/. Accessed Oct 2018
28. Verizon: 2018 data breach investigations report (2018). https://www.verizonenterprise.com/verizon-insights-lab/dbir/. Accessed Oct 2018
29. Whitley, E.A., Kanellopoulou, N.: Privacy and informed consent in online interactions: evidence from expert focus groups. In: ICIS, p. 126 (2010)
30. Wilson, S., et al.: The creation and analysis of a website privacy policy corpus. In: Proceedings of the 54th Annual Meeting of the Association for Computational Linguistics, vol. 1, pp. 1330–1340 (2016)
31. Zimmermann, C.: A categorization of transparency-enhancing technologies. arXiv preprint arXiv:1507.04914 (2015)

User Study of the Effectiveness of a Privacy Policy Summarization Tool

Vanessa Bracamonte[1](✉), Seira Hidano[1], Welderufael B. Tesfay[2],
and Shinsaku Kiyomoto[1]

[1] KDDI Research, Inc., Saitama, Japan
va-bracamonte@kddi-research.jp
[2] Goethe University Frankfurt, Frankfurt, Germany

Abstract. The complexity of privacy policies makes it difficult for users to understand its content. In order to solve this, tools exist that analyze and summarize those privacy policies, and present the results in a standardized visual format. The use of these tools can make it possible to analyze any privacy policy, that is, they have the advantage of scale, unlike processes that require manual classification. However, there is scarce research on their effectiveness and how users perceive them. In this paper, an experimental survey was conducted to evaluate whether one such tool, PrivacyGuide, could communicate risk and increase interest in the content of the privacy policy itself. The survey was conducted in Japan with Japanese participants, and considered two languages of the privacy policy, Japanese and English. The results show that interest in the privacy policy increased after viewing the privacy policy summary. On the other hand, risk communication was limited to the case of an English language privacy policy. In addition, survey participants also provided positive and negative feedback about the tool: there was interest in using the tool in a variety of scenarios, but there was also lack of trust in the results. The findings suggest that privacy policy summarization tools have potential to help users, but that there are barriers for adoption of the tool.

Keywords: Privacy policy summarization tools · User study · Risk · Privacy trust

1 Introduction

There is a continuing expansion of services that take users' data. On the internet, user data is collected by companies in almost every interaction, when a user wants to register for a service of any kind, for example, but also even when only browsing a website. How this data is obtained, processed, transmitted, secured or otherwise handled is usually specified in privacy policies provided by the companies.

The purported objective of privacy policies is to inform users about how the company will handle their data, but they are often complicated and difficult to

© Springer Nature Switzerland AG 2020
P. Mori et al. (Eds.): ICISSP 2019, CCIS 1221, pp. 186–206, 2020.
https://doi.org/10.1007/978-3-030-49443-8_9

read [15,19]. They are also very long, so much that attempting to read every privacy policy that a user encounters would be too costly [14].

There are current regulatory efforts to address this situation. For example, the EU's General Data Protection Regulation (GDPR) [5] states that "data subjects" have a right to information about their collected data "in a concise, transparent, intelligible and easily accessible form, using clear and plain language". There are also research efforts to investigate the use of formats other than a lengthy text to improve the understandability of a privacy policy [6,7]. However, even with these efforts the conciseness and readability of these texts have not improved in many cases.

One challenge for improving this situation is that widely implementing new privacy policy formats represents a considerable effort. Approaches such as the one taken by ToS; DR [21], a project in which volunteers analyze privacy policies of different companies and provide understandable information about them, are difficult to scale because they rely on manual analysis.

To solve this problem of scale, tools that can automatically analyze the content of privacy policies using machine learning techniques and present a summary of results [8,20,22,23] have been proposed and implemented. However, there is very limited research on the effectiveness of these tools and on how users might perceive them.

1.1 Evaluating Privacy Policy Summarization Tools

In this paper, an evaluation of the effectiveness of one of these tools, PrivacyGuide [20], is conducted among Japanese participants. This study focuses on whether PrivacyGuide is effective in communicating a risk level to users and whether it increases interest in the contents of the privacy policy itself, and considers the question of whether Japanese users would be interested in using such a tool and in which circumstances.

In addition, this study considers a particular scenario for the use of privacy policy summarization tools: the case where the privacy policy is written in a foreign language. Due to the cross-border nature of many online services, there are cases where companies target an international audience but provide their privacy policies only in certain languages. For example, the list of top smartphone game apps on Google Play and Apple's App store for Japan regularly includes apps from foreign developers, whose websites only provide an English language privacy policy. Although in general very few users check the privacy policy of the websites they visit [18], this is not an ideal situation from the point of view of providing users the information they need to make good privacy-related decisions. Anecdotal evidence indicates that Japanese users proceed with accepting English language privacy policies that they cannot read, but manifest concern and distrust towards them. This was the case when the GDPR came into effect on May 2018 and Japanese users received privacy policies updates written in English, which they could not read.

If companies offer their services internationally but provide only an English language version of their privacy policy, users in other countries may find it very difficult, if not impossible, to understand the contents of that policy even if they wanted to be informed. Tools that automatically summarize privacy policies and offer the results in a structured format may be useful to address this particular scenario, since a standardized format and pre-defined categorization are suited for translation. This study evaluates whether PrivacyGuide can work to communicate the risk of a foreign language privacy policy, and how users consider its advantages and disadvantages in this context.

This paper is an extended version of the paper "Evaluating Privacy Policy Summarization: An Experimental Study among Japanese Users" presented at the 5th International Conference on Information Systems Security and Privacy (ICISSP 2019) [3]. This revised and extended paper includes additional descriptive data, detailed information on the experiment design and new quantitative data analysis. It also includes detail of the qualitative responses of participants, that serve to illustrate the findings of the study.

2   Related Work

2.1   Understandable Privacy Policy Formats

An important objective of designing understandable privacy policies is whether or not they can effectively communicate risk to users and make them aware of privacy practices. The change in format can be simple: for example, even a shorter text can provide enough information for users to understand risks in privacy policies, compared to longer documents [7]. In addition, presenting information in formats other than purely text can also help users understand the privacy policies of companies. Including graphical information such as icons that indicate the privacy risk level [6] can help users make more privacy-conscious decisions. And standardized formats similar to a nutrition label can be more effective than text in helping users obtain accurate information about a privacy policy [9].

2.2   Privacy Policy Summarization Tools

There are currently proposals and implementations of tools that can analyze the text of existing privacy policies and present a summary of these results [8,20,22, 23]. These tools categorize the content of the privacy policy according to their own criteria, the basis of which is different for each tool. For example, Privee bases its categorization on fair information practices and policies [23]; Polisis bases it on the knowledge of privacy domain experts [8]; PrivacyGuide bases it on an interpretation of the EU GDPR [20].

Of these tools, PrivacyCheck, Privee and PrivacyGuide share some characteristics in terms of their interface elements. The tools all show privacy information categories and a corresponding risk level within that category, according to the contents of the privacy policy. The level is indicated textually and/or with an icon in red, yellow or green. In these tools, the design of the summary, which include icons and short descriptions, was designed to follow the guidelines of previous studies on readable and understandable privacy policy formats [23]. However, there are no user studies that validate whether these tools achieve their goals.

2.3   Privacy Policies in Foreign Languages

As far as could be determined, no studies have been conducted on the scenario evaluated in this paper, where the privacy policy is written in a foreign language. However, it is not so rare to find companies with localized websites that nevertheless only provide a privacy policy in its original language, frequently English, and do not offer a translated version. Translating a privacy policy text may be a complicated task, but the finite combinations of standard information categories and risk levels that are included in the result of a privacy policy summarization tool make translation achievable. Thus, a privacy policy summarization tool with a localized interface may present an option to provide users with information about a foreign language privacy policy.

3   Methodology

3.1   Research Questions

The following main research questions guided this study:

– Will the privacy policy summarization tool results correctly communicate risk level?
– Will the privacy policy summarization tool results increase interest in the contents of the privacy policy itself?
– Will there be interest in using the privacy policy summarization tool and if so, under which circumstances?

In line with the objectives of this study, these research questions were also considered in the scenario where the privacy policy is written in a foreign language.

3.2   Experiment Design

To address these questions, an experimental survey was designed which considered four conditions: a combination of two privacy policy languages (Japanese or English) and risk level (low or high).

The experiment required that participants viewed a fictional website registration page which included a privacy policy and answer some questions about it. Then the participants viewed the results of the privacy policy summarization tool corresponding to the privacy policy risk level and answered further questions on their perception of the website and of the tool. The participants only viewed the website registration page and privacy policy summary corresponding to one of the four combinations (between-subjects design).

The following sections describe the privacy policy summarization tool used and the method for creating the information included in the interfaces corresponding to each experimental condition.

3.3   Privacy Policy Summarization Tool

PrivacyGuide [20], a machine learning-based tool for analyzing and summarizing privacy policies written in English, was used in the study. PrivacyGuide provides information about the risk of the privacy policy, and its stated goal is to support users' understanding of a privacy policy and to elicit interest in the detail of its content [20].

PrivacyGuide classifies the content of the privacy policy into ten privacy aspects, which are based on criteria obtained after an analysis and interpretation of the GDPR[1]. The tool determines a risk level for each privacy aspect and presents the result of this analysis using icons in different colors: one icon for each privacy aspect in green, yellow or red color corresponding to the risk level identified.

3.4   Privacy Policy Summary

In order to construct the PrivacyGuide result screen for the experiment, the PrivacyGuide interface and privacy aspects were first translated to Japanese, as follows. A person fluent in English and Japanese translated the text elements of the interface, such as page title, instructions and button labels. A native Japanese speaker fluent in English, with expert knowledge of Japanese and European privacy regulation, translated the privacy aspects name and description. A second native Japanese speaker reviewed the translated PrivacyGuide interface elements and privacy aspects, focusing on understandability and naturalness. The translation issues identified were addressed at this stage.

Two versions of the PrivacyGuide screen were then constructed, corresponding to the low and high-risk privacy policy. The definition and development of the risk levels is described in Sect. 3.5. In the construction of the interfaces for the experiment, the PrivacyGuide result was simplified as a consequence of feedback received from the Japanese reviewer. In addition to icons, privacy aspect name and description of the identified risk level for the privacy aspect, PrivacyGuide also shows a fragment of the analyzed privacy policy that corresponds to the risk assessment when the user hovers over an icon. The interface was simplified by not including this original privacy policy fragment, since participants were not being asked to read the privacy policy and because it was not possible to ask them to compare the accuracy of those results to the English privacy policy.

---

[1] The explanation of the meaning of each of these privacy aspects is detailed in [20].

3.5   Privacy Policy Risk Level

The PrivacyGuide result screen consists of ten privacy aspects, whose respective risk levels are indicated by icons in three different colors depending on the content of the privacy policy. However, it was determined that it was not feasible to test all combinations of privacy aspects and risk levels, nor was it the goal of this experiment to measure the effect of specific privacy aspects. In order to facilitate distinction, two risk levels—low and high—were defined for the experiment. These levels were not intended to represent an absolute scale, but rather to approximate a risk level that users might realistically encounter in normal circumstances.

The following procedure was used to construct the low and high privacy policies for the experiment. First, a list of the top 50 websites accessed from Japan from the Alexa website [1] was obtained on August 8, 2018. From this list, those websites which provided an English language privacy policy were selected.

Ten privacy policies were identified using these criteria, which were then analyzed using PrivacyGuide. The PrivacyGuide result for each privacy policy consisted of a combination of privacy aspects and corresponding risk levels. A value was assigned to each level (green = 1, yellow = 2, red = 3) and calculated a total risk value for each combination. Higher values were considered to indicate a higher risk privacy policy. The privacy policies with the highest and lowest risk values were removed, and the next values were taken as initial candidates for low and high risk.

The frequency of each risk level for each privacy aspect was counted and a base pattern identified: a group of privacy aspects with the same risk level for most privacy policies in the list. To this base pattern and corresponding risk value were added the remaining privacy aspects at a risk level that would help reach a value corresponding to a low and a high-risk level privacy policy.

To create the text of the experiment privacy policies, fragments from privacy policies of existing websites were used. These privacy policies were obtained from websites which had been used to develop PrivacyGuide and which had both a Japanese and English language privacy policy, for which the Japanese version was a translation of the English version. To minimize any possible influence due to differences in privacy policy length, the privacy policies created had a similar number of lines, and a similar word count for the English version or character count for the Japanese version. Once the fragments were identified, a person fluent in Japanese and English verified that their content was equivalent in both languages.

References to the original website were removed from the fragments and they were put together to create the English and Japanese low and high-risk privacy policies for the experiment. A final review was conducted to verify that the fragments created a coherent privacy policy.

3.6   Experiment Website

A website registration page was developed for the experiment; a fictional company was used to control for reputation effects. The page consisted of a simple online registration form with basic information input fields: first and last name, email address and password. The page also included a scrollable text area with the experiment privacy policy text (created as detailed in the previous section) and a check box to indicate agreement to the privacy policy. The design of the website registration page was the same for all conditions, with the exception of the text of the privacy policy. The website registration page was not functional: the page did not save or send any information even if participants typed it in, which they were not instructed to do.

The page was developed in Japanese and therefore did not go through a translation process; however, the language and design were reviewed for naturalness.

3.7   Questionnaire Design

The online questionnaire instructed participants to imagine a situation where they had found a website and were considering whether or not to register on it. Then the questionnaire provided a link for participants to view the experiment website registration page, indicating that they view it as they would in their normal internet use. The participants were not primed to consider privacy in any way: the instructions did not included any mention of privacy. The participants were not asked to read the privacy policy that was shown in the page. This was done so that participants would view the page as they would normally, which meant that some participants would consider reading the privacy policy but others would not. And in the case of the English language privacy policy, it was not possible to ask every participant to read it since participants were not filtered in any way for their knowledge of English language.

After viewing the website, the participants proceeded to a section to answer questions on their perception of that website. After that, the questionnaire introduced PrivacyGuide as a privacy policy analysis and summarization application, and instructed participants to take some time to check the PrivacyGuide results. The participants then answered the remaining questions. The questionnaire questions were the same for all participants regardless of experimental condition.

Measurement Items. The research question about risk communication was addressed through three constructs: behavioral intention, risk perception and privacy concern using items adapted from previous research on user perception of websites [10]. These questions addressed user perception of the fictional website, rather than of the tool: effective risk communication was defined as a significant difference in these constructs that was consistent with the difference in risk level of the experimental conditions. In addition, behavioral intention questions regarding the tool itself were included to address interest.

A six-point Likert scale was used for the items score; the scales ranged from Completely Disagree to Completely Agree, with the exception of risk items, which ranged from Very Safe to Very Risky. In addition, open-ended questions asking participants about their opinion of the tool and if they were interested in using it to analyze a website's privacy policy, and if so which one, were included.

Likert scale questions about the participants' normal privacy policy-related behavior, whether they would use websites in English and whether they would read privacy policies in English were also included. These two last questions were included as proxy for measuring self-perceived English ability related to these tasks, in order to avoid self-effacing responses.

The number of times a participant viewed the experiment website and PrivacyGuide results, the time they spent viewing those screens and the total time spent on the survey were also measured.

Translation. The survey questionnaire was initially developed in English and then translated to Japanese with the following procedure. First, a native Japanese speaker fluent in English forward translated the questionnaire. Then, a second native Japanese speaker—a person familiar with privacy research—reviewed the translation with the goal of identifying and correcting any inaccuracies. A third native Japanese speaker conducted an additional review of the translation, which focused on understandability and naturalness. The translated questionnaire was then compared with the original English one, by a native Japanese speaker and a person fluent in English and Japanese.

At every stage, identified issues were discussed and addressed by the translators and reviewers until there was agreement about the questionnaire text.

3.8   Data Collection

The survey was conducted online, using a third-party online survey company. The survey company distributed the call for participation among their subscribers. The sample is therefore a convenience sample, although the recruitment process targeted a pool of participants with a distribution of gender and sex similar to that of the Japanese population according to the 2010 census [17].

Each participant was randomly assigned to one of the four conditions, and viewed only one version of the website page—and therefore, only one privacy policy text—an only one PrivacyGuide result screen.

The online survey ran in August 30–31, 2018.

3.9   Methodology Limitations

The methodology had the following limitations. First, a convenience sample was used, obtained from a pool of users that had subscribed to participate in online surveys conducted by the third-party survey company. This may have introduced bias in the analysis; however, the results in the next section show that the sample age distribution followed the Japanese population age distribution and an equal number of male and female respondents was obtained. Second, the website page developed for the experiment as well as the PrivacyGuide result screen were non-interactive, which limited the authenticity of the scenario proposed to the participants.

Third, comprehension of the text of original privacy policy was not measured in any way in the experimental survey. However, the objective of the experiment was to evaluate effectiveness of the tool, and comprehension of the original privacy policy was not considered to be relevant to that objective, since in normal circumstances not all users would decide to read the privacy policy. Fourth, the privacy policies' total risk values were assigned under the assumption that all privacy aspects had equal importance, but users may have different priorities and may consider some privacy aspects more important than others. Finally, although PrivacyGuide was considered suitable for the purposes of this experiment, the study has the limitation of not using a tool specifically designed for Japanese users. Nevertheless, PrivacyGuide was considered adequate due to the compatibility of the EU's GDPR with Japanese privacy regulations, and because the Japanese language privacy policies of international websites are often a direct translation of the English version. Therefore, they share the same structure and content.

4   Analysis and Results

4.1   Data Cleanup

A total of 1040 participant responses were obtained, and each experiment group condition had the same number of respondents (260). Due to the online nature of the survey, the data was first ran through a cleanup process.

The cleanup process consisted of identifying responses with suspicious patterns, that is, respondents who had answered all questions with the highest or lowest score. The questionnaire included reverse-worded questions, therefore this method of data cleanup would identify inattentive participants. Nevertheless, responses that fell under this extreme response invariability criterion were further inspected to decide whether they needed to be dropped from the analysis. The total survey response time for all of these cases was very low, and the decision to eliminate these cases was reached. The sample after data cleanup was 984 cases (English low risk: 243 cases; English high risk: 241 cases; Japanese low risk: 251 cases; Japanese high risk: 249 cases).

4.2   Sample Characteristics

Demographics. The demographic characteristics of the sample are detailed in Table 1. The sample included a similar number of male and female participants. With regards to age, the youngest respondents were 18 years-old and the oldest were 69 years-old. The distribution of gender and age of the participants had been pre-specified in the data collection stage, and the results confirm that the sample's demographic characteristics were similar to that of the Japanese population. In addition, the results of Kruskal-Wallis rank sum tests showed no differences in age or gender between the experimental condition groups.

Table 1. Sample demographics.

		n	%
Total		984	
Gender	Female	490	50%
	Male	494	50%
Age	18 29	181	18%
	30s	185	19%
	40s	223	23%
	50s	184	19%
	60s	211	21%
Job	Government employee	34	3%
	Manager/executive	24	2%
	Company employee	366	37%
	Own business	53	5%
	Freelance	25	3%
	Homemaker	166	17%
	Part time	134	14%
	Student	43	4%
	Other	31	3%
	Unemployed	108	11%

Website Concerns. The survey included questions on the concerns that respondents had on different aspects related to how websites handle users' data. The questions were formulated to correspond to the privacy aspects categorization proposed by PrivacyGuide, although they did not directly mention the name of the privacy aspect. The results are shown in Fig. 1.

The results show that the majority of respondents indicated some concern (Completely agree to Somewhat agree) related to the privacy practices represented by every privacy aspect included in the PrivacyGuide result. Of these, Japanese respondents indicated higher concern about being able to delete their account and about the security of their data. In comparison, they indicated less concern regarding the handling of children's data and whether the website allows changes to the data and to privacy settings.

Privacy Policy Reading Frequency. With regards usual privacy policy reading frequency, approximately half of respondents (52%) indicated that they read the privacy policies of websites at least occasionally. Association tests were conducted to explore whether there was a relationship between the privacy policy reading frequency of respondents and their concerns about websites. As expected, the results show that all types of concerns were positively associated with higher

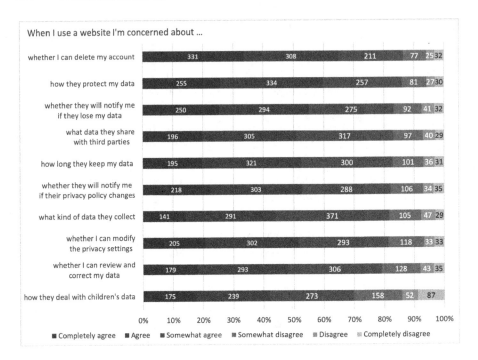

Fig. 1. Respondents concerns regarding how websites handle user data. Each question corresponds to a privacy aspect included in the PrivacyGuide result.

frequency of privacy policy reading. In addition, association tests showed no relationship between the age of participants and their privacy policy reading frequency.

English Language. As mentioned in the Methodology section, the questions on practical use of the English language were included as an indirect measure of English language ability. The majority of respondents indicated they would not use English websites or apps (81%) or read privacy policies in English (88%), which suggest low self-perceived English ability, in particular reading ability. In addition, approximately half (54%) of respondents had encountered privacy policies in languages other than Japanese at least once.

Survey Times. Differences in the time that participants took to view the website registration page and the PrivacyGuide result screen, and the time that it took them to finish the survey were evaluated. The data was highly skewed, and a Kruskal-Wallis rank sum test was used for the test. No significant differences were found for either of these times ($p > 0.05$).

4.3   Construct Validation

Variable distribution was inspected and all variables showed non-normal distributions; therefore, corrections for non-normality were used when conducting construct validation. Confirmatory factor analysis (CFA) using maximum likelihood estimation with robust standard errors was used to evaluate construct validity. The Satorra-Bentler scaled test statistic was used to correct for non-normality [4, 16].

The initial model showed poor fit due to the reverse-worded items. These items were removed and the analysis showed that all items loaded on their respective constructs with a standardized loading higher than 0.7. The revised model showed good fit according to criteria specified in [12]: RMSE $= 0.06$, CFI $= 0.97$, TLI $= 0.97$, SRMR $= 0.03$. All constructs showed good internal consistency, with a minimum Cronbach's alpha value of 0.87. The validated items in each construct were added to create composite variables.

The following sections focuses on the analysis related to the main research questions of this study. As mentioned before, the variables distributions were non-normal; therefore, non-parametric statistical tests were used in addressing the research questions. In addition, the Benjamini-Hochberg procedure for controlling false positives [2] was used. The reported p-values for each test are the adjusted p-values.

4.4   Interest in the Privacy Policy

First, the difference in initial interest in the privacy policy before viewing the PrivacyGuide results was compared between language conditions. The results of a Mann-Whitney U test showed that initial interest in the contents of the Japanese privacy policy was significantly higher ($p = 0.024$) than interest in the English one.

Separate Wilcoxon Signed-Rank tests were used to evaluate interest in the privacy policy after viewing PrivacyGuide, for both risk levels in each language condition. Interest in the contents of the Japanese privacy policy significantly increased for both risk levels (low risk: $p = 0.0004$; high risk: $p = 0.04$). On the other hand, interest in the English privacy policy increased only after viewing the low risk results ($p = 0.0002$), but not for the high-risk results.

4.5   Risk Communication

Risk communication was evaluated by testing for differences in website perception (risk and concern) and behavioral intention between the risk level conditions for both languages. First, differences in website perception before viewing the PrivacyGuide result were evaluated, using Mann-Whitney U tests for the statistical analysis. The results show that there were no differences between the low and high risk levels in each language groups for any of the variables. An additional comparison between languages was conducted: respondents were less willing to register on a website with an English privacy policy than a website with a Japanese privacy policy, although no statistically significant differences were found in perception of risk or privacy concern between these groups.

The effect of PrivacyGuide on perception of the website was then evaluated, using separate Wilcoxon Signed-Rank tests for both risk levels in each language condition. There was a significant increase in behavioral intention (p = 0.0004) and a significant decrease in risk perception (p = 0.004) for the low-risk English privacy policy condition. Considering that behavioral intention towards the websites with an English privacy policy was initially lower than the Japanese ones, the results suggest that PrivacyGuide effectively communicated risk level information to respondents in this condition, whose perception of the website improved for the low risk condition but not for the high-risk condition. However, no significant differences were found for any of the other conditions.

Finally, additional Kruskal Wallis tests were conducted post hoc to evaluate the differences in website perception after viewing the PrivacyGuide results between risk levels for both languages. Significant differences were found between the groups for risk perception (p = 0.021), although a pairwise comparison test did not return significant differences according to the adjusted p-values. Nevertheless, the results suggest the need for additional research, since the unadjusted p-values show that risk perception is lower for the low risk condition compared to the high risk condition, for both languages.

4.6   Interest in PrivacyGuide

There was slightly higher interest in using PrivacyGuide for a low risk English privacy policy, but the difference was not statistically significant ($p > 0.05$). Similarly, the Japanese group showed no statistical difference in interest between the risk levels ($p > 0.05$). In addition, the results of cross-tabulation showed a significant relationship between higher privacy policy reading frequency and positive interest in PrivacyGuide (chi-square = 26.52, df = 2, $p < 0.001$). Respondents who read privacy policies at least some times were more likely to indicate interest in PrivacyGuide.

As an additional way of addressing the question of interest in PrivacyGuide, the responses to the open-ended question of "If you would like to try the privacy policy application, which website would you like to analyze?" were coded. A native Japanese speaker familiar with the goal and structure of the survey coded the responses to the open-ended question on participants' interest in trying PrivacyGuide according to whether they were positive, negative or neutral ("I don't know"). If the answer did not correspond to either of these types, it was coded as "Other". Figure 2 shows the number of comments by type.

The proportion of positive, negative and neutral responses was similar for the same risk level of different language groups. This was validated by quantitatively testing for the difference in interest in using PrivacyGuide between risk levels for each language, using separate one-tailed Mann-Whitney U tests.

Association tests were conducted between the age of the participant and intention of using the privacy policy summarization tool. The results show that

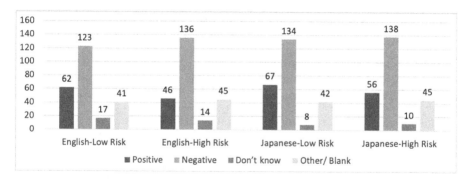

Fig. 2. Responses to the open-ended question on interest in using PrivacyGuide to analyze the a particular website: "If you would like to try the privacy policy application, which website would you like to analyze?".

younger participants (ages 18–39) were positively associated with higher intention, whereas older participants in their 60's were associated with very low intention. Although this association may be mirroring generational attitudes towards technology, it may be important to consider this potential gap when providing these type of tools.

4.7 Qualitative Analysis

In addition to the quantitative analysis, the content of open-ended responses was analyzed qualitatively. Regarding which websites they would be interested in analyzing, respondents in both language groups mentioned a variety of use cases. They gave as an example types of websites ranging from online shopping and SNS website to financial and government websites.

In addition, they indicated interest in trying PrivacyGuide on the privacy policies of websites they frequently used-with mentions of Google, Yahoo and Instagram, among other well known international websites-, but they also mentioned wanting to use it on unfamiliar websites. In particular, they mentioned wanting to use PrivacyGuide when registering on a new website, if they felt the website was asking for too much personal information. Respondents also mentioned personal information in general, only specifying address, phone number and credit card as examples. Interestingly, respondents from the English language groups mentioned an interest on trying PrivacyGuide on Japanese websites; conversely, a respondent from the Japanese language groups mentioned the potential usefulness for analyzing foreign websites' privacy policies. With regards to respondents who indicated no interest in using PrivacyGuide, for the most part they did not specify a reason for their answer.

The answers to the open-ended question about the participants' opinion of the tool, a similar pattern of negative responses as the question on interest was found. Respondents who mentioned that they did not trust the tool (*"I cannot trust (the tool)"*) or had concerns regarding its trustworthiness.

"It can serve as a reference, but I'm not sure about its trustworthiness."
"I don't know how far can the tool be trusted."

Similarly, respondents who answered neutrally mentioned that they would consider using PrivacyGuide if it could be trusted, if it was provided by a well-known company or had some sort of guarantee.

"I have never used this type of application so I cannot trust it immediately. I would search on the internet whether it's safe before using it."
"There is no guarantee that the analysis itself can be trusted. It's easy to say it's safe. If there is a public accreditation system and certification along with it, maybe will think about it."

Negative and neutral respondents also mentioned that they did not know the accuracy of PrivacyGuide, and therefore did not know whether they could rely on its results.

"If the accuracy is high, then maybe it would be ok to use it."
"I'm concerned if this is really correct."

There were also some respondents which mentioned concerns about the impartiality of results.

"I don't know if the application is impartial to the website and the user."

Other respondents indicated that they did not need to use PrivacyGuide because they would not use risky websites in the first place.

5   Discussion

5.1   Goals of a Privacy Policy Summarization Tools

The goals of PrivacyGuide as a privacy policy summarization tool were defined as communicating risk and increasing interest in the privacy policy. The results suggest that these goals are fulfilled partially: interest in the privacy policy increased in all except one condition (the high-risk English privacy policy), but risk communication was only achieved for the English language privacy policy.

In the case of the Japanese privacy policy conditions, the initial intention and risk perception may not have been greatly influenced by the privacy policy itself, but rather by website unfamiliarity. Therefore, although the respondents were more interested about the contents of the Japanese privacy policy, any additional information about the privacy policy did not have significant influence on the website itself. In the case of privacy concern, on which the tool had no effect in any condition, the results are similar to those found by [7]. It is possible that information about the privacy practices of a website by itself cannot ease users' feelings of concern, in particular for an unknown website. In general, though, the results regarding risk communication can be considered inconclusive, and further research is required to validate them.

In the case of the lack of interest in the high-risk English privacy policy, one possibility may be that respondents were completely dismissing the possibility of using the website itself and therefore considering that they no longer have to worry about the contents of its privacy policy.

Finally, the results indicate that the privacy policy summarization tool can also achieve its goals for a foreign language privacy policy.

5.2 Challenges for Privacy Policy Summarization Tools

Although this study has used PrivacyGuide, the findings may help to identify challenges for privacy policy summarization tools in general. In particular, participants indicated in their open-ended comments that they were unsure about whether to trust the results of the tool, and more generally the tool itself. There was a similar pattern for the issue of concern, which was also frequently mentioned in the open-ended comments. Participants' concern about the tool was related to specific aspects such as its accuracy, although participants also manifested generalized concern. The comments that touched upon issues of trust or concern in relation to the results of the tool were often constructed to indicate that the participant's concern or lack of trust was due to lack of information. The information that participants mentioned ranged from performance-related information, for example the reliability or accuracy of results, to information about any bias in the results, for example if they favored the company.

The challenge for privacy policy summarization tools is then how to provide this information to users. This type of information, performance and process of automated systems, are considered the basis of trust in automated systems [13] However, it may not be as easy as adding more information. There is need to consider how much information to provide according to the context and user expectations [11].

An additional challenge that is important to address is related to its potential for foreign language privacy policies. The goal of the privacy policy summarization tool is to provide some information to the user and encourage interest in the content of the privacy policy, not to supplant the privacy policy completely. Although the result format does not give every piece of information about the privacy policy, users can be informed of the risk of a privacy policy without having to read the whole document. However, in the case of a foreign language privacy policy, even if the user has interest in its contents they might not be able to read the text. Future research should consider conducting user studies to evaluate ways to provide further information to those users who require it. For example, fragments of the privacy policy identified as important could be shown in the user's language using translation tools.

6   Conclusions

An experimental survey among Japanese users was conducted to evaluate the effectiveness of a privacy policy summarization tool. The experiment considered four conditions, resulting of the combination of a Japanese or English language privacy policy and a high or low risk privacy policy. The results show that the privacy policy summarization tool can achieve its goal of increasing interest in the content of privacy policy, for both languages, but its effectiveness for risk communication was limited only to the English language privacy policy.

In addition, Japanese respondents indicated in positive comments that they would want analyze the privacy policies of different types of website—familiar and unfamiliar, domestic and foreign. On the other hand, negative comments included mention of concern and lack of trust as barriers for use of the tools.

Future research is planned to evaluate how privacy policy summarization tools could address the challenges identified in this study, and communicate trustworthiness and result reliability.

Appendix

(See Figs. 3, 4 and Tables 2, 3).

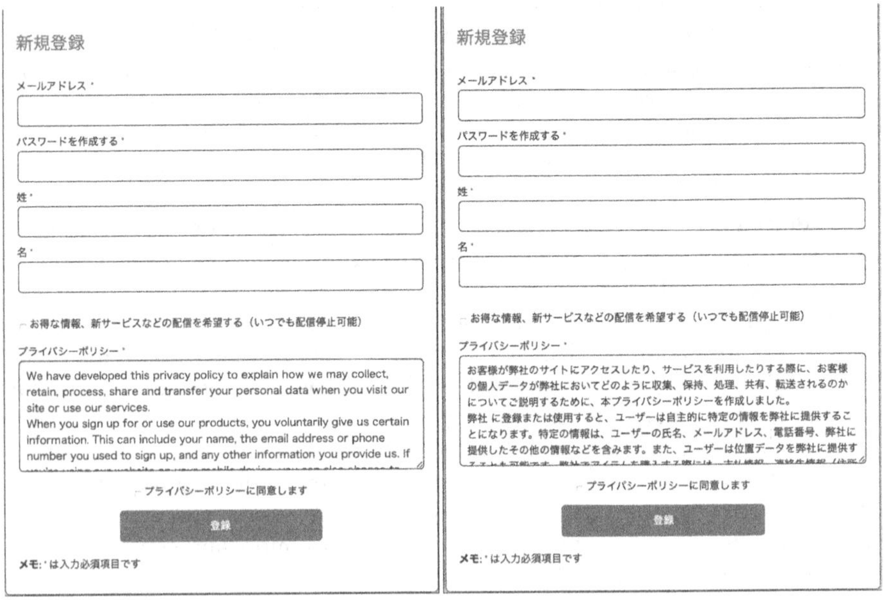

Fig. 3. Experiment website registration forms. Left: registration form showing an English privacy policy. Right: registration form showing a Japanese language privacy policy.

Fig. 4. PrivacyGuide result screens. Top: higher risk privacy policy result. Bottom: lower risk privacy policy result.

Table 2. English text of the information presented in the PrivacyGuide result screen for the high and low risk privacy policies.

Privacy aspect	Privacy aspect description	High risk	Privacy policy	Low risk	Privacy policy
		Level	Description	Level	Description
Data collection	What type of data is collected by the company?	Yellow	Collection of personal information	Yellow	Collection of personal information
Protection of children	Does the company knowingly collect data of children?	Green	Not knowingly collecting information of children	Red	Not mentioned
Third-party sharing	Does the company disclose the data to third parties?	Red	Third party sharing with no further explanation	Red	Third party sharing with no further explanation
Data security	Does the company mention any kind of safeguarding mechanisms?	Green	Security measures mentioned	Green	Security measures mentioned
Data retention	How long does the company store the collected data?	Yellow	Data is kept as long as it is necessary for the intended purpose	Yellow	Data is kept as long as it is necessary for the intended purpose
Data aggregation	Does the company aggregate the collected information?	Red	Sharing of aggregated information with third-parties	Yellow	Data aggregation only for the intended purpose
Control of data	Does the company offer the possibility to review personal information?	Red	Collected data cannot be reviewed, edited or deleted by the user	Green	Full control of personal data (review, edit and deletion)
Privacy settings	Is it possible to choose which privacy related practices will be applied?	Green	User has the option to opt-in for privacy related practices	Green	User has the option to opt-in for privacy related practices
Account deletion	Is it possible to delete an account?	Red	No account deletion possible	Green	Full deletion (no remaining data) possible
Policy changes	Does the company inform their customers in case of a policy change?	Green	Individual notification in case of policy changes	Green	Individual notification in case of policy changes

Table 3. Measurement items. Items adapted from [10].

Construct	Item
Behavioral intention (Website)	I would register my personal information on this website
	I would desist to use this website even if I wanted to use it. (Reverse worded)*
	I would agree with the privacy policy and register on this website

(continued)

Table 3. (*continued*)

Construct	Item
Concern	I would be concerned about using the website
(Website)	I would have no concerns giving my personal information in order to use the website. (Reverse worded)*
	I would be concerned about how this website uses my personal information
	I would be concerned about the security of my personal information
Risk	Interacting with this website would be
(Website)	Giving my personal information to this website would be
	My overall perception is that this website is
Interest in the	I would try to read the privacy policy of the website
privacy policy	I'm curious about the content of the privacy policy of the website
Behavioral intention	I would like to use this application to analyze privacy policies
(Privacy policy summarization tool)	If there was an opportunity, I would like to use this privacy policy analysis tool

* Dropped from analysis

References

1. Alexa: Top Sites in Japan. https://www.alexa.com/topsites/countries/JP
2. Benjamini, Y., Hochberg, Y.: Controlling the false discovery rate: a practical and powerful approach to multiple testing. J. R. Stat. Soc. Ser. B (Methodol.) **57**(1), 289–300 (1995)
3. Bracamonte, V., Hidano, S., Tesfay, W.B., Kiyomoto, S.: Evaluating privacy policy summarization: an experimental study among Japanese users. In: Proceedings of the 5th International Conference on Information Systems Security and Privacy, ICISSP, vol. 1, pp. 370–377. INSTICC, SciTePress (2019). https://doi.org/10.5220/0007378403700377
4. Curran, P.J., West, S.G., Finch, J.F.: The robustness of test statistics to nonnormality and specification error in confirmatory factor analysis. Psychol. Methods **1**(1), 16–29 (1996)
5. European Parliament: Regulation (EU) 2016/679 of the European Parliament and of the Council of 27 April 2016 on the protection of natural persons with regard to the processing of personal data and on the free movement of such data, and repealing Directive 95/46 (2016)
6. Gideon, J., Cranor, L., Egelman, S., Acquisti, A.: Power strips, prophylactics, and privacy, oh my! In: Proceedings of the Second Symposium on Usable Privacy and Security, SOUPS 2006, pp. 133–144. ACM (2006). https://doi.org/10.1145/1143120.1143137

7. Gluck, J., et al.: How short is too short? Implications of length and framing on the effectiveness of privacy notices. In: Twelfth Symposium on Usable Privacy and Security (SOUPS 2016), pp. 321–340. USENIX Association, Denver (2016)

8. Harkous, H., Fawaz, K., Lebret, R., Schaub, F., Shin, K.G., Aberer, K.: Polisis: automated analysis and presentation of privacy policies using deep learning. In: 27th USENIX Security Symposium (USENIX Security 18), pp. 531–548. USENIX Association, Baltimore (2018)

9. Kelley, P.G., Cesca, L., Bresee, J., Cranor, L.F.: Standardizing privacy notices: an online study of the nutrition label approach. In: Proceedings of the SIGCHI Conference on Human Factors in Computing Systems, CHI 2010, pp. 1573–1582. ACM, New York (2010). https://doi.org/10.1145/1753326.1753561

10. Kim, D.J., Ferrin, D.L., Rao, H.R.: A trust-based consumer decision-making model in electronic commerce: the role of trust, perceived risk, and their antecedents. Decis. Support Syst. **44**(2), 544–564 (2008). https://doi.org/10.1016/j.dss.2007.07.001

11. Kizilcec, R.F.: How much information?: Effects of transparency on trust in an algorithmic interface. In: Proceedings of the 2016 CHI Conference on Human Factors in Computing Systems, CHI 2016, pp. 2390–2395. ACM, New York (2016). https://doi.org/10.1145/2858036.2858402

12. Kline, R.B.: Principles and Practice of Structural Equation Modeling, 2nd edn. Guilford Press, New York (2005)

13. Lee, J.D., See, K.A.: Trust in automation: designing for appropriate reliance. Hum. Factors **46**(1), 50–80 (2004). https://doi.org/10.1518/hfes.46.1.50_30392

14. McDonald, A.M., Cranor, L.F.: The cost of reading privacy policies. I/S: J. Law Policy Inf. Soc. **4**, 543 (2008)

15. Proctor, R.W., Ali, M.A., Vu, K.P.L.: Examining usability of web privacy policies. Int. J. Hum.-Comput. Interact. **24**(3), 307–328 (2008). https://doi.org/10.1080/10447310801937999

16. Rosseel, Y.: Lavaan: an R package for structural equation modeling. J. Stat. Softw. **48**(2), 1–36 (2012). https://doi.org/10.18637/jss.v048.i02

17. Statistics Bureau, Ministry of Internal Affairs and Communications: Population and Households of Japan 2010. Tech. rep

18. Steinfeld, N.: "I agree to the terms and conditions": (How) do users read privacy policies online? An eye-tracking experiment. Comput. Hum. Behav. **55**, 992–1000 (2016). https://doi.org/10.1016/j.chb.2015.09.038

19. Sunyaev, A., Dehling, T., Taylor, P.L., Mandl, K.D.: Availability and quality of mobile health app privacy policies. J. Am. Med. Inform. Assoc. **22**(e1), e28–e33 (2014). https://doi.org/10.1136/amiajnl-2013-002605

20. Tesfay, W.B., Hofmann, P., Nakamura, T., Kiyomoto, S., Serna, J.: PrivacyGuide: towards an implementation of the EU GDPR on internet privacy policy evaluation. In: Proceedings of the Fourth ACM International Workshop on Security and Privacy Analytics, IWSPA 2018, pp. 15–21. ACM, New York (2018). https://doi.org/10.1145/3180445.3180447

21. ToSDR: Terms of Service; Didn't Read(2019). https://tosdr.org/

22. Zaeem, R.N., German, R.L., Barber, K.S.: PrivacyCheck: automatic summarization of privacy policies using data mining. ACM Trans. Internet Technol. **18**(4), 53:1–53:18 (2018). https://doi.org/10.1145/3127519

23. Zimmeck, S., Bellovin, S.M.: Privee: an architecture for automatically analyzing web privacy policies. In: 23rd USENIX Security Symposium (USENIX Security 2014), pp. 1–16. USENIX Association, San Diego (August 2014)

A General Framework for Decentralized Combinatorial Testing of Access Control Engine: Examples of Application

Said Daoudagh[1,2], Francesca Lonetti[1]($\boxtimes$), and Eda Marchetti[1]

[1] Istituto di Scienza e Tecnologie dell'Informazione "Alessandro Faedo", CNR, Pisa, Italy
{said.daoudagh,francesca.lonetti,eda.marchetti}@isti.cnr.it
[2] University of Pisa, Pisa, Italy

Abstract. Access control mechanisms aim to assure data protection in modern software systems. Testing of such mechanisms is a key activity to avoid security flaws and violations inside the systems or applications. In this paper, we introduce the general architecture of a new decentralized framework for testing of XACML-based access control engines. The proposed framework is composed of different web services and can be instantiated for different testing purposes: i) generation of test cases based on combinatorial testing strategies; ii) distributed test cases execution; iii) decentralized oracle derivation able to associate the expected authorization decision to a given XACML request. The effectiveness of the framework has been proven into two different experiments. The former addressed the evaluation of the distributed *vs* non distributed testing solution. The latter focused on the performance comparison of two distributed oracle approaches.

Keywords: Access control systems · Testing · Web service · XACML · Oracle

1 Introduction

Nowadays, personal data are subject to different regulations, according to the different contexts in which they are used and stored, then their management becomes a critical activity. To regulate the access to this data, different access control mechanisms are put in place with the aim to grant or deny the access according to subjects and resources attributes as well as to specific environment conditions specified in the access control policies. The eXtensible Access Control Markup Language (XACML) [21] implements the Attribute-Based Access Control (ABAC) model [11] and represents a standard and flexible approach for specifying authorization policies. It leverages a Policy Decision Point (PDP) for evaluating the set of access requests against an XACML policy. To guarantee

Supported by CyberSec4Europe Grant agreement ID: 830929.

P. Mori et al. (Eds.): ICISSP 2019, CCIS 1221, pp. 207–229, 2020.
https://doi.org/10.1007/978-3-030-49443-8_10

the lack of security flaws of the access control systems, testing of the PDP is very important and time consuming activity. It involves: i) the generation of a set of requests, i.e., test cases; ii) the execution of these requests; iii) and the checking of the associated responses against the expected decisions.

In literature, different approaches have been developed to support the generation of XACML requests [5,16]. They are mainly based on combinatorial approaches of the policies values and have been proven to be effective both in detecting faults of the PDP, and enhancing its effectiveness in terms of mutation score or code coverage [7,17]. However, the high number of derived combinations represents the main drawback of combinatorial approaches and prevents their use in real contexts. Specifically, the main issue related to the application of these approaches is the high time/cost due to the execution of a large set of requests and the derivation of the associated oracle, i.e., the correct authorization decision that should be expected from the PDP for each test request.

In the context of XACML-based access control systems, some combinatorial solutions such as X-CREATE [5] are used to reduce the total number of combinations by leveraging the coverage of n-way policy inputs as in AETG [6]. However, due to the complexity and high number of attributes of the XACML policies, the number of derived test cases by these approaches could remain unmanageable.

Parallel and cloud based solutions provide unlimited storage as well as shared virtualized resources useful to reduce the high computational costs needed for executing large sets of combinatorial tests. Specifically, the authors of [24,25] rely on cloud environments to partition the testing activities and allocate these testing activities to different processors in the cloud platform for test execution and results collection.

Following this direction, we propose in this paper an efficient decentralized and cost effective framework for the overall testing process of the access control evaluation engine aiming to improve the quality of the PDP testing[1].

A preliminary version of this framework was presented in [8]. With respect to the solution presented in [8], in this paper we propose the architecture of a general framework for combinatorial testing of access control engine and we show how this framework can be instantiated for different testing purposes, namely test generation, execution of test cases and test oracle derivation. In addition, a new contribution of this paper with respect to the work in [8] is the usage of the framework for an experimental performance comparison of two different automated XACML-based oracle solutions: the former based on a voting mechanism, the latter leveraging a model based approach.

To summarize, the main contributions of our proposal include:

- a general framework able to leverage the available distributed computational resources for exploiting all the power of combinatorial approaches for the generation of XACML requests. Specifically, our solution is able to execute all test sets derived by the application of combinatorial approaches without

---

[1] In this paper, we address testing of both XACML 2.0 and XACML 3.0 based access control engines but our solution can be easily generalized to other access control specification languages.

the need of adopting test suites selection or reduction approaches for cost saving purposes;

- a decentralized framework for the PDP oracle problem. Well-known approaches for automated XACML oracle derivation rely on voting mechanisms such as that of [15]. Our distributed framework leverages these approaches to provide a more efficient oracle solution able to reduce the high computational costs related to the derivation of an authorization response associated to an XACML request;
- a performance comparison of different distributed XACML-based oracle solutions. Specifically, the presented framework has been used to compare an oracle based on voting mechanism such as that of [15] with an automated model based oracle that is XACMET [4]. The comparison has been performed in terms of time/cost for the derivation of the correct authorization decision as well as the required computational resources.

Experimental results show that the proposed framework allows to reduce the time needed of all the main phases of the PDP testing that are: test cases generation, test case execution and oracle derivation, with a final cost saving of the overall testing process. In addition, the framework allows to compare performances of different distributed testing solutions. Furthermore, the proposed framework allows for efficient testing of all possible combinations of the policy values and this might provide reasonably high confidence in the correctness of the PDP.

It is out of scope of the paper to compare the cost reduction of a distributed solution with respect to that of a non-distributed one, neither to show the effectiveness of our solution with respect to the application of test suites selection and reduction techniques.

Outline. Section 2 briefly addresses related work and presents an overview of XACML-based access control systems. Section 3 presents the general distributed architecture of our framework and its instantiation for test cases generation, execution and oracle derivation. Section 4 shows the results of the application of the proposed framework into two different experiments. Finally, Sect. 5 draws conclusions and gives hints for future works.

2   Background and Related Work

This work targets several research topics, including: specification of XACML-based access control model, test case generation based on combinatorial approaches and XACML-based oracle derivation.

XACML-Based Access Control Model. An access control model represents a framework specifying the rights of users in gaining access to a system and preventing unauthorized usage of resources. Well known access control models include Mandatory Access Control (MAC), Discretionary Access Control (DAC), Role Based Access Control (RBAC), Attribute Based Access Control

(ABAC) [12]. Among them, ABAC model [11] is the straightforward and flexible approach for specifying authorization policies. It relies on a set of attributes associated with subjects, resources and actions in order to allow or deny the access to the resources. Security policies specify the attributes that have to be considered for making a decision. In ABAC, permissions are depending on the combination of the subjects and object attribute values that are specified in a given request.

XACML (eXtensible Access Control Markup Language) is a standard language that implements the ABAC model [21]. It is a platform-independent XML-based language for the specification of access control policies. An XACML policy presents a tree structure whose main elements are: PolicySet, Policy, Rule, Target and Condition. The PolicySet contains one or more policies. A Policy contains a Target and one or more rules. The target contains resources, subjects, actions and environments elements to which the policy refers to. The Rule includes a target and a condition element; the latter is a boolean function that is used to specify constraints on target elements.

An XACML request is composed of four elements: subject, resource, action and environment. At evaluation time, if a request is able to satisfy the target of the policy, then the set of rules of the policy is checked, otherwise the policy is skipped.

If the Condition is evaluated to true, the effect of the rule is returned, otherwise a NotApplicable decision is formulated; Indeterminate decision is returned in case of errors. More policies in a policy set and more rules in a policy may be applicable to a given request.

The PolicyCombiningAlgorithm and the RuleCombiningAlgorithm define how to combine the results from multiple policies and rules respectively in order to derive a single access result to a given request. For instance, the deny-overrides algorithm says that Deny takes the precedence regardless of the evaluation result of any other rule (policy). It returns Deny if there is a rule (policy) that is evaluated to Deny.

Figure 1 shows the structure of an XACML policy and request whereas Fig. 3 depicts an example of XACML policy code as explained in Sect. 4.1.

Test Case Generation Based on Combinatorial Approaches. In combinatorial testing, test cases are defined to execute combinations of input parameters [18].

Due to the extremely large number of combinations, providing all the combinations is usually not feasible in practice. Then, combinatorial approaches able to generate smaller test suites for which all combinations of the features are guaranteed, are provided. Among them, common approaches rely on t-way combinatorial criteria of input parameters [6,13,19]. Other approaches rely on crash testing, embedded assertions, and model checker-based test generation [14] for solving the oracle problem for combinatorial testing.

In combinatorial testing, some tools exist [1,22] that use data flow techniques to identify interaction faults in the source code [22]. They are able to generate a test set for the failure triggering interactions aiming to reduce the test set size maintaining the same fault detection capability. Differently from these works, the

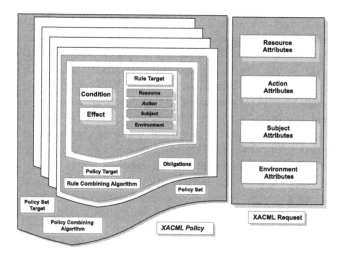

Fig. 1. XACML policy and request structure.

advantage of our proposal is the possibility to leverage parallel computational resources to generate a large set of test cases without applying test suite selection or reduction techniques.

In the context of XACML-based access control systems, combinatorial test cases generation strategies are proposed for testing on the one side the XACML policy specification and on the other the compliance of the PDP behavior with the policy specification. Among them, the Targen tool [16] generates test inputs using combinatorial coverage of the truth values of independent clauses of XACML policy values. A more recent tool is X-CREATE [5] that provides different combinatorial strategies based on combinations of the subject, resource, action and environment values taken from the XACML policy for deriving the access requests. Among the X-CREATE generation strategies, we selected the *Multiple Combinatorial* strategy for deriving test suites in the experiment presented in this paper. This strategy allows for combinations of more than one subject, resource, action and environment values and automatically establishes the number of subjects, resources, actions and environments of each request according to the complexity of the policy. Other works [26,27] focus on model based testing and apply combinatorial analysis to the elements of the model, namely role names, permission names, context names, to derive test cases. Finally, ACPT tool [20] uses combinatorial testing with model checking to derive tests for access control policies. More recent solutions [24,25] leverage cloud computing to overcome the computational cost of combinatorial testing, then a large number of processors and distributed databases are adopted to execute large combinatorial tests in parallel. Differently from our proposal, these approaches are not specifically tailored to access control systems and adopt concurrent test algebra execution and analysis for identifying faulty interactions, reducing combinatorial tests.

XACML-Based Oracle Derivation. Problem of oracle automation has been for long time investigated in literature and still remains a challenging problem [2]. In the context of access control systems, few proposals address PDP testing with the aim to automatically check whether the authorization decision obtained by the evaluation of an XACML request is correct. The authors of [15] propose to simultaneously check the responses of different PDPs on the same request, so that different responses can highlight possible problems. Although effective, this proposal is quite expensive in terms of required computational resources, because it requires using different PDP implementations. Our approach is in line with this proposal, but it uses a distributed solution.

A different approach for oracle derivation proposed in [4,9] is XACMET, which provides a completely automated model-based oracle derivation approach for XACML-based PDP testing. The main idea of XACMET is that, given a generic request, the evaluation of an XACML policy with that request strictly depends on: the request values, the policy constraints as well as the combining algorithm that prioritizes the evaluation of the rules defined in the policy. XACMET is able to derive from an XACML policy, a XAC-Graph and the set of associated evaluation paths, called XAC-Paths. In particular, an XAC-Path is defined as the sequence of policy elements that are exercised by a generic request during its evaluation against an XACML policy and the associated verdict. This set of paths is ordered according to the semantics of the rule combining algorithm, and then according to the verdict associated to each path. For instance, in case of deny-overrides combining algorithm, first the paths having *Deny* are evaluated, then those having *Permit* and finally those having *NotApplicable*. For paths having the same verdict, the evaluation order of the paths is based on their length, namely the shortest path takes the precedence. The ordered set of paths is then used for the requests evaluation and the verdicts association. For each request, the first path for which all the path constraints are satisfied by the request values is identified and the final verdict associated to the request is derived. As described in [9], XACMET is also used for test cases generation and path coverage measuring but these aspects are not considered in this paper.

3   Framework Architecture

We propose in this section the generic architecture of a decentralized framework for the testing of the access control engine. This general framework has been conceived for the generation and execution of test cases as well as for the test oracle derivation with the aim to improve the quality of PDP testing and drastically reduce the computational cost of the testing itself. In particular, we focus on XACML 3.0 based access control engine and we address the application of massive combinatorial testing for assessing the correctness and robustness of the PDP.

As depicted in Fig. 2, the presented architecture includes the following components:

- **XACMLClient:** this component represents the entry point of the proposed architecture. It includes a GUI for user interaction with four distinct operations: i) loading of an XACML policy (or a set of policies) and selection of the test strategy to be used for the generation of test cases, i.e., XACML requests; ii) recovering of already uploaded XACML policies; iii) recovering of the XACML requests associated with a given policy for a specific test strategy; iv) execution of the set of requests and visualization of the obtained results, i.e., the authorization decisions associated with each request, and derivation of the final verdict (pass/fail) of each test case.
- **XACMLTestbedInstantiator:** it is the component in charge of building a different test bed according to a specific testing purpose. This component can be instantiated with one or more components of the proposed framework in the different phases of the testing of the access control engine. Specifically, as depicted in Fig. 2, this component can be instantiated in an *XACML Generator*, an *XACML Executor* and an *XACML Oracle Derivator*. The three different instantiated versions of the framework are described in Sects. 3.1, 3.2 and 3.3 respectively.
- **XACMLComparator WS:** this component is able to compare the test result derived by the *XACML Executor* for each XACML request and the correct authorization decision, computed by the *XACML Oracle Derivator*. If they are equal, a `pass` value verdict is associated to the request, `fail` otherwise. Finally, the final verdicts are stored into a specific database managed by the *XACMLTestingDB* component.
- **XACMLRouter Servlet:** this component is in charge to forward a request to the appropriate web service according to the operation selected by the user through the *XACMLClient* GUI.
- **XACMLTestingDB:** it guarantees the persistency of test data managing the different databases.

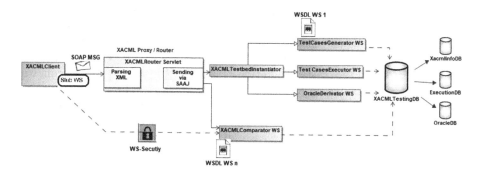

Fig. 2. System architecture (adapted from [8]).

Figure 2 shows the relationships among the different components of the proposed framework. As shown in the figure, the communication between XACML-Client and the services happens through an intermediary node, proxy/router, which forwards the client's request to the appropriate service based on the request content. The framework allows for secure communication among the services able to guarantee the identity of the involved parties. Specifically, interactions with *XACMLTestingDB* database are not exposed to SQL Injection attacks. We adopted the so-called Prepared SQL statement in order to prevent SQL Injection vulnerabilities. Prepared Statements are static techniques that try to prevent SQL Injection by enabling developers to accurately specify the structure of an SQL query, and pass the parameters values to it separately such that any unsanitary user-input is not allowed to modify the structure and the semantic of the query itself. The developed services take SQL Injection attacks into account whereas the interactions with *XACMLTestingDB*, that provide parameters supplied by XACMLClient, are managed via Java *PreparedStatement*.

3.1   Test Cases Generator

The general framework presented in Fig. 2 can be instantiated for improving the cost of the test cases generation in XACML-based access control systems. In this case, using a distributed approach, the instantiated framework is in charge to automatically generate a set of XACML 3.0 requests from an XACML policy according to a combinatorial testing strategy. Specifically, the *XACMLTestbedInstantiator* component is instantiated into the *XACML Generator* component that implements a set of strategies for the derivation of the XACML requests. These strategies can be selected by the user through the *XACMLClient* GUI. They can be integrated in the framework by implementing the corresponding algorithm or by including directly the associated generation tool, wherever possible. The *XACML Generator* component is independent from the specific implemented test generation strategy and it is out of scope of this paper to focus on the validation of the different test cases generation strategies. Different combinatorial strategies able to derive a set of test requests from an XACML policy can be integrated in the *XACML Generator* [3,5,16]. Among them, in the validation proposed in this paper, we used the `Multiple Combinatorial` testing strategy that relies on the combinatorial approaches of subject, resource, action and environment values taken from the XACML policy [5]. Differently from other combinatorial based test cases generation strategies, it is able to derive requests including more than one subject, resource, action and environment targeting the rules of the policy that are applicable only by requests containing more than one subject, resource, action, environment. The *XACML Generator* is also able to recover an available set of test cases already generated by a selected test generation strategy.

3.2   Test Cases Executor

The general framework presented in Fig. 2 can be instantiated for improving the cost of the test cases execution on the XACML evaluation engine. In this case, the *XACMLTestbedInstantiator* component of the general architecture is instantiated into the *XACML Executor* that is able of executing the test cases in a distributed way on the PDP under test. Specifically, leveraging a MapReduce approach, the set of test cases is divided into sub sets of requests having similar complexity and executed over different instances of the policy evaluation engine. The test results, i.e., the authorization decisions, are then collected and stored in the *XACMLTestingDB* component.

3.3 Oracle Derivator

The general framework presented in Fig. 2 can be instantiated for improving the cost of test oracle derivation in XACML-based access control systems. In this case, the *XACMLTestbedInstantiator* component is instantiated into the *XACML Oracle Derivator* that is in charge to derive the correct authorization decision for each request derived by an XACML policy. This component implements a voting mechanism for the derivation of the oracle similar to that presented in [15], in which the same request is evaluated on more than one PDP engine, their responses for the same request are collected, then the most frequent decision value is considered the correct one. Specifically, in the proposed framework, leveraging a map reduce approach, the set of test cases is divided into subsets of similar complexity. Each subset is executed on a cluster composed by an odd number of PDPs, different from the one under test. Each PDP in each cluster receives a set of policies and their associated XACML requests, executes them and derives the associated authorization decision. The *XACML Oracle Derivator* component collects for each request all the authorization decisions derived by the different PDPs in each cluster, and associates the correct authorization decision with the decision value most frequently received. The test results, i.e., all the authorization decisions, are then collected and stored in the *XACMLTestingDB* component. The *XACML Oracle Derivator* is also able to recover an available set of correct authorization decisions for a given policy and a selected test strategy.

4 Experimental Evaluation

Here, we present preliminary results collected during the application of the framework into two different experiments, as detailed more in the following subsections: the evaluation of the distributed *vs* non distributed solution (Sect. 4.1) and the comparison between two distributed oracle approaches (Sect. 4.2).

4.1 Distributed vs Non-distributed Solution

For the evaluation of the distributed *vs* non-distributed solution, we involved some of the students of a secure software engineering course. In particular, we asked four groups of three students to realize a simplified version of a policy evaluation engine. We provided to each group a subset of functionalities for an XACML 3.0 PDP engine that they should implement into Java prototypes; therefore, each group realized a different version of PDP. For the experiment, we randomly selected one of them as a System Under Test (SUT) and we called it SUTPDP. We used the remaining three PDPs as different oracles in the experiment. We called them *Oracle1*, *Oracle2* and *Oracle3* in the remaining of the section.

Additionally, we asked the same students to write down the policy examples useful for testing the SUTPDP during the experiment. The derived policies were different for either the functionalities, the subjects, the resources, the activities or the hierarchical structures they targeted. Finally, the students were able to define a total amount of 100 access policies that we pre-included into XACML-TestingDB. We report in the listing of Fig. 3 one of the developed policies. As in the figure, the policy contains a Target and three XACML Rules with the following meaning:

- the Target specifies that the XACML policy is applicable to the `library` resource;
- the first Rule states that the `read` action can be done by `bob` on resource `library/book`;
- the second Rule says that the `write` action can be done by `alice` on resource `library/journal`;
- and finally, the third Rule denies all the accesses which are not allowed explicitly and represents a default XACML rule.

Because the set of functionalities provided to the students was very simple, the PDPs versions they realized were simple too. However, even if limited in complexity, applying the combinatorial testing to each of them could require considerable amount of time and effort. Hence, a valid compromise for decreasing the testing cost and increasing the final PDP quality and security was the use of a decentralized testing framework.

Three different research questions have been conceived for quantify the cost reduction and better evaluate the proposed approach:

- **RQ1 Generation Cost.** Is the distributed framework able to reduce the time for test cases generation?
- **RQ2 Execution Cost.** Is the distributed framework able to reduce the time for test cases execution?
- **RQ3 Oracle Derivation Cost.** Is the distributed framework able to reduce the time for the correct authorization decisions derivation?

For replying to three research questions we relied on the computational resources available in the University laboratory. Indeed, we used 20 working stations similar in the overall performance, i.e., 10 working stations having a Core i7-4790 (4.0 GHz) Intel processor machine with eight virtual CPUs and 16 GB of memory, running Ubuntu 14.04 (64-bit version) and 10 working stations having a Core i7-4700 (4.2 GHz) Intel processor machine with eight virtual CPUs and 16 GB of memory, running Ubuntu 14.04 (64-bit version).

Because each of the proposed research question follows a different step of the testing process, we decided to divide the experiment into three steps:

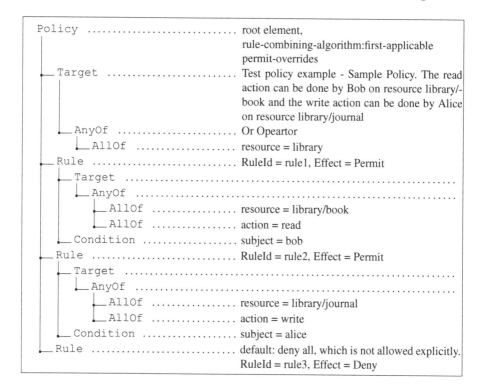

Fig. 3. An XACML policy example (adapted from [8]).

1. *Test Cases Generation:* For each of the policy in the available policies the associated test suite is derived;
2. *Test Cases Execution:* Each test case is executed in parallel on the target SUTPDP, and on the remaining three PDPs (Oracle1, Oracle2 and Oracle3);
3. *Test Cases Evaluation:* The correct authorization decision, i.e., the final verdict, is identified through a voting process by using the replies of Oracle1, Oracle2 and Oracle3.

Details of the evaluation of the above research questions are provided in the remaining of this section.

RQ1: Generation Cost. For evaluating if the distributed framework can be able to reduce the time for test cases generation we customized the proposed testing framework as described in the Fig. 5. Thus the XACML-TestbedInstantiator has been instantiated into 20 XACML Generator components, labelled Generator WS1... Generator WS20 in the figure. Through the XACMLClient GUI, the Multiple Combinatorial testing strategy has be selected on each XACML Generator component and applied in parallel to the policies generated by our students. As in the figure, the XACML-TestbedInstantiator distributes the 100 policies over all the 20 working stations, thus each one received a group of 5 policies to be used for executing the `Multiple Combinatorial` testing strategy. For instance, considering the listing of Fig. 3 a total amount of 945 requests has been generated through the operation GetXacmlRequests. Figure 4 summarizes the obtained results.

Consequently, a set of around 50,000 test requests has been derived considering all the access policies available.

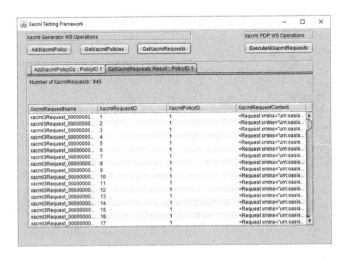

Fig. 4. Result of getXacmlrequests operation (adopted from [8]).

For calculating the overall test generation time, we assumed that each test case has potentially the same impact on the overall testing effort. In such a manner, the generation time was directly connected with the number of test cases generated, i.e., the size of a test suite represents also its cost. Thus, considering the setting of Fig. 5, the test generation phase has been completed in around 5.30 min.

A deeper analysis of experimentation results evidenced that the application of the `Multiple Combinatorial` strategy requires on average from 30 to 80 s; therefore, the execution of a group of 5 policies requires on average from 150 to 400 s. Indeed, the differences were manly due to the complexity of the analyzed policies, the performance of the working stations and the communications delay.

The experimentation results collected can be used for a rough estimation of the time required for test generation if less then 20 parallel working stations were used.

Indeed, repeating the experiment of test cases generation on one randomly selected generation component took around 1.5 h[2].

---

[2] In this case, the test generation time was not affected by communication delay.

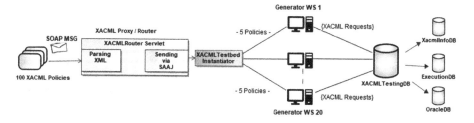

Fig. 5. System architecture for test generation.

The data collected during the comparison of distributed solution with the non-distributed one provided a positive answer to the research question RQ1. Indeed, the distributed framework is able to reduce the time for test case generation.

The threats to validity of the conducted experiment can be summarized into:

- Because of the didactic nature of the experiment, the policies developed by the students were quite simple in the structure and in the number of values used for subjects, resources, actions and environment attributes. Therefore, the computation time required for the test cases generation could be also tolerable for the non-distributed solution even if around 16 times greater than the computation time in the distributed one.
- The test case generation can be performed one and for all the entire policies set. Once available, the test suite can be reused several times in different experimentations. Consequently, the test generation cost would be only the time for test cases retrieval.

RQ2: Execution Cost. For evaluating whether the distributed framework can be able to reduce the time for test cases execution we relied again on the testing framework that we customized as reported in Fig. 6. In this case, the XACML-TestbedInstantiator has been instantiated into 5 XACML Execution components, each one representing the same version of the selected SUTPDP, labelled SUTPDP WS1... SUTPDP WS5 in the figure. Five of the twenty available working stations have been randomly selected and assigned to the SUTPDP testing. Then, in parallel, through the XACMLClient graphical interface and specifically using the operation *ExecuteAllXacmlRequests* (see Fig. 4, each policy and the associated set of test cases have been executed on the SUTPDP. In this case, a total amount of around 10,000 test cases have been assigned to each SUTPDP so as to provide a uniform load balancing.

As an example, in Fig. 7, we report an extract of the derived SUTPDP decisions for the test set relative to the policy of listing in Fig. 3.

Considering the execution cost as in the previous section, we suppose that each test case has potentially the same impact on the overall testing execution time. Again, the execution cost is directly proportional to the size of a test suite. In this case, the test cases execution on the 5 parallel versions of SUTPDP

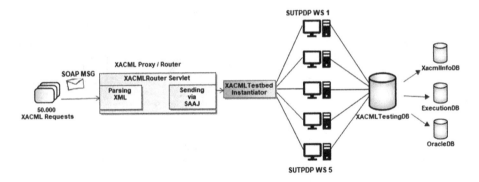

Fig. 6. System architecture for test execution.

required a total amount of around 3.5 min. Of course, this estimation can vary by augmenting or diminishing the number of working stations dedicated to the SUNPDP testing.

From the collected data we also derived the tests executed per second which varies from 40 to 60. Therefore, the total amount of time necessary for executing 10,000 test cases could vary from around 2.8 to 4.20 min. As in the previous section, the differences were mainly due to the complexity of the analyzed policies, the performance of the working stations, and the communications delay.

For aim of completeness, we repeated the experiment of test case generation on a randomly selected working station and it took around 16 min.

The data collected during the comparison of distributed solution with the non-distributed one provided a positive answer to the research question RQ2. Indeed, the distributed framework is able to reduce the time for test cases execution.

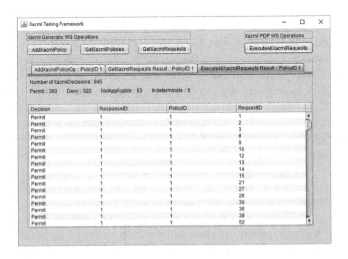

Fig. 7. Result of EvaluateAllXacmlRequests operation (adopted from [8]).

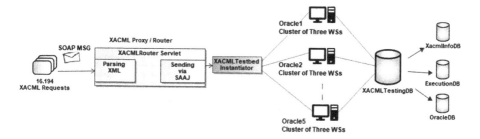

Fig. 8. System architecture for oracle derivation.

RQ3: Oracle Derivation Cost. Finally, for evaluating if the distributed framework can reduce the time for the correct authorization decisions derivation, we customized the proposed testing framework as described in Fig. 8. Thus, the `XACML-TestbedInstantiator` has been instantiated into 5 clusters of `XACML Oracle Derivator` components, labelled `Cluster1... Cluster5` in the figure. In this case, the 15 working stations have been randomly selected and divided into 5 clusters of 3 working stations each. In each cluster, Oracle1, Oracle2 and Oracle3 PDPs have been deployed on one available machines. Then, the 50,000 test cases have been divided into 5 sets of around 10,000 each and executed in parallel in each cluster, i.e., on Oracle1, Oracle2 and Oracle3. Finally, the authorization decisions of the oracles have been collected and compared so as to compute the final verdict for each test case.

Finally, through the XACMLComparator WS, the final verdict for each of the 50,000 test cases has been derived. Due to the simplicity of the operation, a single working station has been used for this task.

Even if the SUTPDP implemented a subset of functionalities, a final amount of 127 fail verdicts have been highlighted. These were due to an incorrect implementation of a rule combining algorithm and a specific set up of the environment condition in the SUTPDP that have been successively corrected.

As in the previous two experiments, we consider the evaluation cost directly connected with the size of a test suite.

Because the number of tests to be executed (i.e., 10,000 XACML requests) and the oracles performance were similar to that of the SUTPDP, the time necessary for the derivation of correct authorization decision for each test case does not evidence important differences from the execution time. Indeed, the total amount was around 3.7 min. In this case, the differences were mainly due the communications delay.

For aim of completeness, we repeated the experiment on a randomly selected working station. We deployed one per time the different oracle versions on the working stations, we collected the authorization decision sets and then we compared them for deriving the correct authorization decisions set. In practice, we repeated the execution of all the 50,000 test cases on an oracle version for three times. Without considering the time necessary for the different oracles instantiation, the total amount of time necessary for the correct authorization decisions set was 49 min.

Comparing the distributed solution with the non-distributed one a positive answer to the research question RQ3 can be collected, i.e., the distributed framework is able to reduce the time for oracle derivation. For aim of completeness, it is important to notice that the correct authorization decisions can be performed one and for all the entire test suite. Once available, correct authorization decisions can be reused several times in different experimentations. Consequently, the test evaluation cost would be only the time for data retrieval.

In the presented experiment, we voluntarily excluded the costs of verdict computation. Indeed, this operation is just a binary comparison between two values: the authorization decision computed by the SUTPDP with the correct one. Due to the simplicity of the operation and the number of data compared, mainly the cost of this operation depends on the data retrieval for the different DBs, therefore it has been ignored.

4.2   Model-Based Oracle vs Voting Mechanism

In this second experiment, we show how our framework is able to compare the time/cost of the oracle derivation approach based on a voting mechanism as described in Sect. 3.3, with the time/cost of a model-based oracle solution. The model-based oracle we selected is XACMET (XACML Modeling & Testing) [4,9] which is a novel model-based approach to support the automation of XACML-based testing.

Testing Environment Set-Up. The subject of the experiment is composed of a set of eight real XACML policies (see Table 1). Specifically, policies *demo-5*, *demo-11* and *demo-26* are taken from the Open Source repository software Fedora [10]; the other five policies released for the pilot application of the TAS3 project [23]). These policies have been included into *XACMLTestingDB*[3]. For each policy, we considered a set of requests generated by adopting the `Multiple Combinatorial` testing strategy as described in [5]. Table 1 shows the number of rules, conditions, subjects, resources, actions and functions for each policy as well as the cardinality of the associated request set.

The object of the experiment is represented by XACMET oracle and a set of five cluster of PDP implementing the voting oracles. In particular, each cluster realizes a multiple implementations testing approach presented in [15], called in this section Automated Voting Oracle (AVO). Similarly to what presented in Sect. 4.1, each AVO is realized by a pool of three XACML PDPs, namely

---

[3] Note that in this experiment we considered XACML 2.0 based policies and PDP implementations.

Table 1. XACML policies subjects.

XACML policy	Functionality						
	#Rule	#Cond	#Sub	#Res	#Act	#Funct	#Req
demo-5	3	2	6	3	2	4	210
demo-11	3	2	4	3	1	5	100
demo-26	2	1	1	3	1	4	40
student-application-1	2	0	4	1	1	2	40
student-application-2	2	0	7	1	1	2	368
university-admin-1	3	0	24	3	3	2	5400
university-admin-2	3	0	24	3	3	2	5400
university-admin-3	3	0	23	3	3	2	4636

Sun PDP[4], Herasaf PDP[5] and Balana PDP[6]. For more details about each AVO implementation we refer to [9].

In [9], we already compared XACMET with an automated voting oracle in terms of effectiveness of the derived authorization decision and we observed that for all requests and policies considered, the XACMET oracle coincided with the automated voting oracle. This confirms that the two oracle approaches are comparable in terms of obtained results. In this experiment, we want to compare the performance of the two automated oracle approaches also in terms of time/cost for deriving the authorization decisions in a distributed execution framework.

For the aim of completeness, we reported in Sect. 2 a brief description of the XACMET oracle, and we refer to [4,9] for more details.

XACMET vs Distributed Voting Mechanism. The architecture we used to compare XACMET and the automated voting oracle is depicted in Fig. 9, where 20 working stations with a similar overall performance are available for the experiment set-up as described in the previous experiment (see Sect. 4.1). In particular, we compare the parallel execution of five versions of the XACMET with five clusters implementing each one an AVO. This experiment is divided into two steps: i) in the fist step, XACMET is running on five of the 20 available working stations; ii) in the second one, AVOs are running on the remaining 15 working stations grouped in five clusters, each cluster including 3 working stations. In this case, in each cluster, the three XACML PDPs, namely Sun PDP, Herasaf PDP and Balana PDP are running on the three working stations respectively.

---

[4] Sun PDP is available at: http://sunxacml.sourceforge.net.
[5] Herasaf PDP is available at: https://bitbucket.org/herasaf/herasaf-xacml-core.
[6] Balana PDP is available at: https://github.com/wso2/balana.

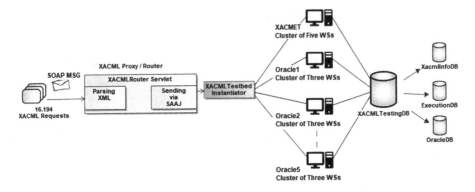

Fig. 9. System architecture for oracles comparison.

Table 2. Experiment results (XACMET): number of XAC-paths and derivation time.

XACML policy	#XAC-Paths	Derivation time (ms)
demo-5	16	281
demo-11	13	253
demo-26	8	235
student-application-1	28	409
student-application-2	106	600
university-admin-1	799	978
university-admin-2	799	868
university-admin-3	757	863

In the first phase, each policy and the associated set of derived XACML requests has been distributed on the set of working stations running XACMET. For instance the 40 requests of *demo-26* have been divided into 5 sets of 8 test cases each; then each set together with the policy itself has been distributed over one of the five working stations running XACMET.

We computed the average times for deriving the authorization decision for each request in the set of requests associated to each policy.

In case of XACMET, the time for deriving an authorization decision is given by: i) the time for deriving the XAC-Graph from the policy and the associated paths. This time is independent by the complexity and cardinality of the evaluated requests; ii) the average time needed for evaluating all the requests on the set of derived paths. Table 2 reports for each policy the number of derived XAC-Paths (column 2) and the average time needed for deriving those paths. Table 3 in the second column reports the total average time for the derivation of the authorization decisions for each policy.

For instance, for *demo-26*, the average time needed for deriving the XAC-Paths is 235 ms whereas the total average time is 261 ms.

As we can see in Table 2, the average time needed for deriving the XAC-Paths is proportional to the number of derived paths. Moreover, as we can observe in Table 3 (column 2), this time greatly impacts on the total time needed for the derivation of the correct authorization decisions for simple policies such as *demo-26*, *demo-11*, *demo-5*, *student-application-1* and *student-application-2*; whereas, for complex policies (for instance *university-admins*), this time is negligible due to both the high number of requests to be evaluated and the number of XAC-Paths involved in the evaluation.

Table 3. Experiment results: average time per test suite in ms.

XACML policy	XACMET	AVO
demo-5	458	177
demo-11	470	217
demo-26	261	36
student-application-1	443	27
student-application-2	1.779	356
university-admin-1	206.516	2.463
university-admin-2	200.084	2.209
university-admin-3	160.111	1.716

To consider the different structure and complexity of the considered policies, we repeated this step for each policy of Table 1 and we computed the overall average time of the XACMET that was 71.265 ms.

In the second phase of the experiment, each policy and the associated set of derived XACML requests has been distributed on the set of the 5 clusters, implementing five instances of AVO. Similarly to the previous phase, for *demo-26*, the 40 requests and the policy itself have been distributed over the 5 oracle clusters, each one receiving a group of 8 requests.

Again, we computed the average times for deriving the authorization decision for each request in the set of requests associated to each policy as reported in Table 3 (column 3). For instance, in case of demo-26, this time was 36 ms. We repeated the experiment for each policy of Table 1 obtaining an overall average time of AVO equal to 900 ms.

We observed that AVO achieves a better performance than XACMET in terms of average time for deriving the correct authorization decision (900 ms *vs* 71.265 ms). The low performance of XACMET is due to the complexity of the policies and consequently to the high number of derived paths and the time need to evaluate each request against all the paths. Table 4 shows the minimum, maximum and average times needed for evaluating each request on the set of paths derived from each policy. We can observe that the average time associated to complex policies is very high and this decreases the overall XACMET performance.

Table 4. Experiment results (XACMET): min, max and average time per test case in ms.

XACML policy	Min	Max	Average
demo-5	2	18	3
demo-11	2	60	4
demo-26	1	12	2
student-application-1	2	7	4
student-application-2	12	43	16
university-admin-1	179	527	190
university-admin-2	170	1279	184
university-admin-3	163	316	171

However, AVO is more expensive in terms of required computational resources (for instance for demo-26 for evaluating the same number of requests, 15 working stations are needed by AVO whereas only 5 working stations are used by XACMET).

Finally, we performed an additional experiment in which the same number of computational resources of AVO (i.e., 15 working stations) has been used for running 15 parallel instances of XACMET for all the policies of Table 1. We observed that the overall average time of XACMET has been reduced of around one third, and only in case of *demo-5* and *demo-11*, XACMET showed a better performance than AVO.

As an important remark of the experiment, even if the five parallel instances of XACMET are less performing than the five AVO instances, exploiting in a better way the available resources of the framework, the parallel execution of XACMET could result a winning solution for simple policies having a small number of paths (for instance *demo-5* and *demo-11*).

Indeed, the choice of the best oracle solution is a trade off between the available computational resources and the performance of the adopted oracle solution.

5   Conclusions

In this paper, we proposed a new general decentralized framework for testing of XACML-based access control engines. The main advantages of the proposed solution include: i) the general architecture of the framework can be instantiated for different testing purposes such as test cases generation based on combinatorial testing strategies, distributed tests execution, decentralized and cost effective automated oracle derivation for the PDP testing; ii) the framework allows to reduce the computational costs of the generation and execution of large combinatorial test suites without adopting test suites selection and reduction techniques; iii) the framework allows for the comparison of different testing solutions.

The proposed framework has been used into two different experiments. In the former, the proposed distributed solution has been applied to a simple application example of PDP testing. The results of this experiment confirmed that our framework was able to reduce the cost of all the main phases of the testing process: test cases generation, test case execution and oracle derivation.

In the latter experiment, the proposed framework has been used to compare the performances in terms of time/cost and required computational resources of two different approaches for the oracle derivation: an oracle derivation approach based on a voting mechanism and a model-based oracle solution implemented in XACMET. This second experiment confirmed the effectiveness of the framework giving good hints on the choice of the best oracle solution and the usage of the available computational resources, according also to the complexity of the policies.

As threat to validity, we have to notice that all the collected time values are related to the computational power of the adopted working stations and to the scheduling time of the test tasks on the different working stations.

In the future, we plan to investigate efficient scheduling algorithms taking into account the power constraints of different working stations as well as the scalability issues of the proposed framework.

Finally, in order to have a better comparison of the oracle derivation approach based on a voting mechanism and XACMET, we plan to implement a distributed XACMET version in which the evaluation of XACML requests against the set of XAC-Paths can be performed in parallel on the different working stations of the proposed framework.

References

1. Aggarwal, M., Sabharwal, S., Dudeja, S.: FTCI: a tool to identify failure triggering combinations for interaction testing. Indian J. Sci. Technol. **9**(38), 1–5 (2016)
2. Barr, E.T., Harman, M., McMinn, P., Shahbaz, M., Yoo, S.: The oracle problem in software testing: a survey. IEEE Trans. Softw. Eng. **41**(5), 507–525 (2015)
3. Bertolino, A., Lonetti, F., Marchetti, E.: Systematic XACML request generation for testing purposes. In: Processing of 36th EUROMICRO Conference on Software Engineering and Advanced Applications (SEAA), pp. 3–11 (2010)
4. Bertolino, A., Daoudagh, S., Lonetti, F., Marchetti, E.: An automated model-based test oracle for access control systems. In: Proceedings of 13th IEEE/ACM International Workshop on Automation of Software Test, Gothenburg, Sweden, 28–29 May (2018)
5. Bertolino, A., Daoudagh, S., Lonetti, F., Marchetti, E., Schilders, L.: Automated testing of extensible access control markup language-based access control systems. IET Softw. **7**(4), 203–212 (2013)
6. Cohen, D.M., Dalal, S.R., Fredman, M.L., Patton, G.C.: The AETG system: an approach to testing based on combinatiorial design. IEEE Trans. Softw. Eng. **23**(7), 437–444 (1997)

7. Daoudagh, S., Lonetti, F., Marchetti, E.: Assessment of access control systems using mutation testing. In: 1st IEEE/ACM International Workshop on Technical and Legal aspects of data Privacy and Security, TELERISE 2015, Florence, Italy, 18 May, 2015, pp. 8–13 (2015)

8. Daoudagh, S., Lonetti, F., Marchetti, E.: A decentralized solution for combinatorial testing of access control engine. In: Proceedings of the 5th International Conference on Information Systems Security and Privacy, ICISSP 2019, Prague, Czech Republic, 23–25 February, 2019, pp. 126–135 (2019). https://doi.org/10.5220/0007379401260135

9. Daoudagh, S., Lonetti, F., Marchetti, E.: XACMET: XACML testing and modeling an automated model-based testing solution for access control systems. Softw. Qual. J. **28**(1), 249–282 (2020)

10. Fedora: Fedora Commons Repository Software. http://fedora-commons.org/

11. Hu, V.C., Kuhn, D.R., Ferraiolo, D.F., Voas, J.: Attribute-based access control. Computer **48**(2), 85–88 (2015)

12. Jayant, D.B., Swapnaja, A.U., Sulabha, S.A., Dattatray, G.M.: Analysis of DAC MAC RBAC access control based models for security. Int. J. Comput. Appl. **104**(5), 6–13 (2014)

13. Kuhn, D.R., Kacker, R.N., Lei, Y.: Introduction to Combinatorial Testing. CRC Press, New York (2013)

14. Kuhn, R., Lei, Y., Kacker, R.: Practical combinatorial testing: beyond pairwise. IT Prof. **10**(3), 19–23 (2008)

15. Li, N., Hwang, J., Xie, T.: Multiple-implementation testing for XACML implementations. In: Proceedings of the 2008 Workshop on Testing, Analysis, and Verification of Web Services and Applications, pp. 27–33. ACM (2008)

16. Martin, E., Xie, T.: Automated test generation for access control policies. In: Supplemental Proceeding of ISSRE (November 2006)

17. Martin, E., Xie, T., Yu, T.: Defining and measuring policy coverage in testing access control policies. In: Ning, P., Qing, S., Li, N. (eds.) ICICS 2006. LNCS, vol. 4307, pp. 139–158. Springer, Heidelberg (2006). https://doi.org/10.1007/11935308_11

18. Nie, C., Leung, H.: A survey of combinatorial testing. ACM Comput. Surv. (CSUR) **43**(2), 11 (2011)

19. NIST: Automated Combinatorial Testing for Software (2016). https://csrc.nist.gov/projects/automated-combinatorial-testing-for-software/downloadable-tools

20. NIST: Access Control Policy Test (ACPT) (2018). https://csrc.nist.gov/projects/automated-combinatorial-testing-for-software/downloadable-tools#acpt

21. OASIS: eXtensible Access Control Markup Language (XACML) Version 3.0 (January 2013). http://docs.oasis-open.org/xacml/3.0/xacml-3.0-core-spec-os-en.html

22. Sabharwal, S., Aggarwal, M.: A novel approach for deriving interactions for combinatorial testing. Eng. Sci. Technol. Int. J. **20**(1), 59–71 (2017). https://doi.org/10.1016/j.jestch.2016.05.008. http://www.sciencedirect.com/science/article/pii/S2215098615303323

23. TAS3 Project: Trusted Architecture for Securely Shared Services. http://www.tas3.eu/

24. Tsai, W.T., Qi, G.: Integrated fault detection and test algebra for combinatorial testing in TaaS (Testing-as-a-Service). Simul. Model. Pract. Theory **68**, 108–124 (2016)

25. Tsai, W.T., Qi, G., Hu, K.: Autonomous decentralized combinatorial testing. In: IEEE Twelfth International Symposium on Autonomous Decentralized Systems (ISADS), pp. 40–47. IEEE (2015)

26. Xu, D., Kent, M., Thomas, L., Mouelhi, T., Le Traon, Y.: Automated model-based testing of role-based access control using predicate/transition nets. IEEE Trans. Comput. **64**(9), 2490–2505 (2015)
27. Xu, D., Thomas, L., Kent, M., Mouelhi, T., Le Traon, Y.: A model-based approach to automated testing of access control policies. In: Proceedings of the 17th ACM symposium on Access Control Models and Technologies, pp. 209–218. ACM (2012)

Protection of User-Defined Sensitive Attributes on Online Social Networks Against Attribute Inference Attack via Adversarial Data Mining

Khondker Jahid Reza[1]([⊠]), Md Zahidul Islam[1], and Vladimir Estivill-Castro[2]

[1] School of Computing and Mathematics, Charles Sturt University, Panorama Avenue, Bathurst, NSW 2795, Australia
{kreza,zislam}@csu.edu.au

[2] Departament de Tecnologies de la Informació i les Comunicacions, Universitat Pompeu Fabra, Roc Boronat, 138, 08018 Barcelona, Spain
vladimir.estivill@upf.edu

Abstract. Online social network (OSN) users share various types of personal information with other users. By analysing such personal information, a malicious data miner (or an attacker) can infer the sensitive information about the user which has not been disclosed publicly. This is generally known as *attribute inference attack*. In this study, we propose a privacy preserving technique, namely *3LP+*, that can protect users' multiple sensitive information from being inferred. We experimentally show that the *3LP+* algorithm can provide better privacy than an existing technique while maintaining the utility of users' data.

Keywords: Attribute inference · Data mining · Online social networks · Privacy protection technique

1 Introduction

Online social networks (OSNs) data can be used to automatically and accurately predict a range of highly sensitive personal attributes including: sexual orientation, ethnicity, religious and political views, personality traits, intelligence, happiness, use of addictive substances, and parental separation [13]. Participants of OSNs may wish to keep some information-items confidential, but the attributes that are made public may enable others to predict the confidential information. The *attribute inference problem* is the possibility that data analyses could infer users' sensitive information [14,19]. Moreover, the malicious attacker has at its disposal all strategies that enable the compromise of users' privacy. However, for the work described here, we only consider a single data mining approach and we propose a privacy-preserving technique to provide privacy against such an attack. We first illustrate the privacy attack considered in this study.

© Springer Nature Switzerland AG 2020
P. Mori et al. (Eds.): ICISSP 2019, CCIS 1221, pp. 230–249, 2020.
https://doi.org/10.1007/978-3-030-49443-8_11

1.1   The Privacy Attack Model

Consider an attacker M who wants to infer the *"Emotional Status"* of an OSN user u who regards this information as sensitive and whose OSN profile does not show it publicly. Here the user u is considered as a target user. In order to launch the attack, M can prepare a training data set D_{tr} by analysing the OSN of a number N of users, A attributes and their friendship information. At first, M may collect some information that u discloses openly on their OSN profile (in this illustration we consider u's settings for the values of the *"Hometown"* and *"Profession"* a public view). M then can select a set of users who disclose their *"Emotional Status"* information as well as the same information (i.e. *"Hometown"*, *"Profession"*) that user u discloses on his/her profile. M may store all this information in D_{tr} and select *"Emotional Status"* as a class attribute and the rest of the attributes as non-class attributes.

Table 1. A hypothetical training data set.

User	Hometown	Profession	Class attribute
a	Sydney	Entrepreneur	Lonely
b	Bathurst	Entrepreneur	Connected
c	Melbourne	Salesman	Connected
d	Sydney	Student	Lonely
e	Melbourne	Salesman	Connected

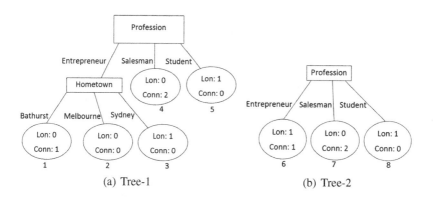

(a) Tree-1   (b) Tree-2

Fig. 1. Decision trees build on the sample data set given in Table 1.

M may include all users for building a training data set D_{tr} that indicates clearly in their profile or recent posts that they are *"Lonely"* or *"Connected"*. A sample of such training data set D_{tr} is shown in Table 1 where rows are records and columns are attributes. This sample data set is an example of what could be prepared with any other set of attributes.

After preparing the training data set D_{tr}, M may apply any data mining algorithms to obtain the rules (or patterns) from D_{tr}. Figure 1 presents a sample decision forest that can be generated from D_{tr}. The rectangular boxes in Fig. 1 are called nodes and ovals are called leaves. The path between a root node (the node at the top) and a leaf presents a logic rule for the leaf. For example, the logic rule for Leaf 3 (see Fig. 1(a)) states that "if the attribute value of "*Profession = Entrepreneur*" and "*Home town = Bathurst*" then the class value is "*Connected*", and 1 record is in the leaf 1 having the class value "*Connected*". Here in this logic rule the condition *Entrepreneur=Profession and "Bathurst = Home town*" is called the antecedent of the logic rule and "*Connected* is called the consequent. By applying the rules derived from the data set containing the information about u, shown in Table 2, M can predict the "*Emotional Status*" of u.

Table 2. A hypothetical test data set.

User	Hometown	Profession	Class attribute
u	Bathurst	Student	?

The existing privacy preserving technique [5] can preserve user u's privacy by suggesting u to suppress some attribute values that appear most frequently in the logic rules. In this example, the attribute "*Profession*" appears in all the logic rules as shown in Fig. 1. If the value of "*Profession*" is suppressed then all the logic rules (shown in Fig. 1) will no longer be applicable to predict u's "*Emotional Status*". This technique appears to be effective to protect user's privacy however it does not consider the friendship information.

OSN is also known as social attribute network (SAN). In an SAN model, both users and their attribute-values are designed as vertices. Therefore, the attacker can take advantage of a metric function as shown in Eq. 1 [1], to incorporate the friendship information into D_{tr} in order to reveal the values of confidential attributes.

$$m(u, A_n = v) = \sum_{t \in \Gamma_{s+}(u) \cap \Gamma_{s+}(A_n=v)} \frac{w(t)}{log|\Gamma_+(t)|}. \tag{1}$$

Here, $\Gamma_{s+}(u)$ is a set of OSN users connected to a user u and $\Gamma_{s+}(A_n = v)$ is the set of users having the attribute-value $A_n = v$. Similarly, $\Gamma_{A_n+}(u)$ is the set of all attribute-value pairs linked to user u. Therefore, the neighbourhood of u is represented as, $\Gamma_+(u) = \Gamma_{s+}(u) \cup \Gamma_{A_n+}(u)$. On the other hand, t is the set of u's friends who have an attribute-value pair $A_n = v$ (i.e. $t \in \Gamma_{s+}(u) \cap \Gamma_{s+}(A_n = v)$) and $\Gamma_+(t) = \Gamma_{s+}(t) \cup \Gamma_{A_n+}(t)$. The $w(t)$ is the weight of each of them and its value is set to 1 in this study. The higher the value of $m(u, A_n = v)$ indicates the higher chance that u has the value v for attribute A_n. An interesting property of this metric is that, if friendship information is available, then $m(u, A_n = v)$

can be calculated for any attribute-value pair $A_n = v$ whether the user u has that value or not.

Table 3. A hypothetical training data set with friendship information.

User	Hometown	m_hometown	Profession	m_profession	m_emotional	Class attribute
a	Sydney	0	Entrepreneur	0	0.56	Lonely
b	Bathurst	0	Entrepreneur	0	0	Connected
c	Melbourne	0.56	Salesman	0	0	Connected
d	Sydney	0.51	Student	0.56	0.56	Lonely
e	Melbourne	0.51	Salesman	0	0	Connected

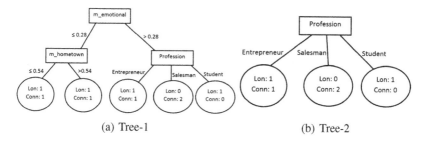

(a) Tree-1   (b) Tree-2

Fig. 2. Decision trees build on the sample data set given in Table 3.

To launch the attack using users' friendship information, M can prepare a training data set D_{tr} by storing u's available information (for example, *Hometown* and *Profession*) and friendship information calculated by using Eq. 1 in it. We present a sample of such training data set in Table 3. The information directly related to OSN users (e.g. *Hometown* and *Profession* as shown in Table 3) are named regular attributes, whereas the information related to the friendship links (such as m_Hometown and m_Profession) are named *link attributes*.

M can consider "*Emotional Status*" as the class attribute and then apply any machine-learning technique to obtain the patterns of the "*Lonely*" and "*Connected*" users from the data set. In Fig. 2, we present a sample decision forest which can be built from D_{tr} (as shown in Table 3). By using these rules, the attacker can predict the emotional status of a new user u (shown in Table 4) even if the user does not disclose the information.

Table 4. A hypothetical test data set with friendship information.

User	Hometown	m_hometown	Profession	m_profession	m_emotional	Class attribute
u	Bathurst	0.51	Student	0.51	0	?

We now argue that OSN users may have diverse preferences on what they consider sensitive. For example, one may consider their *emotional status* as sensitive only while others may consider their *emotional status* and/or *political view* as sensitive. Therefore, a privacy-preserving technique should be capable of protecting all the sensitive information considered by each user. At the same time, the techniques should be capable of providing privacy even if an adversary uses a different classifier (rather than the one used by the privacy preserving technique) to infer the class value of a target user.

Again, privacy is in a constant trade-off with personalization. The more a system (for example, a recommender system) knows about the user, the more it can tailor its services to the users. Therefore, In addition, while protecting users' privacy, a technique must consider maintaining the utility of a data set. A large number of attribute value suppression may provide better privacy, but at the same time, it also defeats the whole purpose of using social network sites for a user. The goal should be to provide privacy by suppressing the minimum number of attribute values.

1.2   Related Work

The existing privacy preserving techniques such as *NOYB* [8], *TOTAL_COUNT* [5], *CUM_SENSITIVITY* [5], and *3LP* [16] can protect users' privacy against the *attribute inference attack*. The basic concept of these techniques are quite similar i.e. to select and suppress users' attribute values which are high predictors of a sensitive attribute [2,3].

A commercially available privacy technique *NOYB* [8] follows a random process to suppress attribute values. Rather than using any classifier to extract the patterns from the training data set, *NOYB* takes a random approach to select and suppress the *regular* attribute values in the testing data set. In an extreme scenario, *NOYB* may obfuscate all the *regular* attribute values for the sake of providing privacy. The random obfuscation may remove a user's *regular* attribute value from public view in an OSN which has no bearing on the sensitive attribute. This unnecessary blocking of a user's profile is undesirable for users but less harmful that the fact that predictors of sensitive information are left for public use. Note that users generally want some information to be public, and hence the goal of a technique is to obfuscate the minimal number of attribute values to reduce the predictability of sensitive information.

TOTAL_COUNT and *CUM_SENSITIVITY* [5] on the other hand identify the influential *regular* attribute values to suppress which are predictors of a sensitive information. These two techniques can suggest the target user to suppress values one by one until the privacy of a sensitive attribute is protected. The functionality of *TOTAL_COUNT* and *CUM_SENSITIVITY* are almost the same except the attribute ranking procedure. Both techniques were shown to be useful and outperform *NOYB*. That is, in order to achieve a security threshold S_t, the required number of attribute value suppression in the case of *NOYB* [8] is much higher than *TOTAL_COUNT* and *CUM_SENSITIVITY* [5].

The data of an OSN can be represented as a social attribute network (*SAN*) model which integrates both users' friendship network and attribute information [20]. However, *TOTAL_COUNT* and *CUM_SENSITIVITY* do not consider the friendship network which can be useful to infer users' sensitive attribute. Using the friendship network an adversary can infer a user's private information [16].

In order to preserve a user's confidential information from being inferred by their friendship information, Estivill-Castro et al. proposed an approach [6,7]. which suggests the target users to un-friend or befriend other users randomly. The number of deletion or addition of friends can often be extensive and the target user may not like such kind of random connection/disconnection.

Heatherly et al. show a Naïve Bayes classifier based protection technique [11], let's call this technique *PrivNB* for short, that can provide privacy by suppressing attribute values and deleting friendship links. The effect of *PrivNB* on data utility of the protected data set was not analysed. Another technique namely *3LP* [16] (three layer of protection) based on decision forests algorithms can protect privacy even if an attacker utilises friendship information(along with the *regular* attributes) to invade privacy.

Similar to *TOTAL_COUNT* and *CUM_SENSITIVITY*, the algorithm *3LP* takes a similar approach to identify the influential attributes in its first layer to suppress predictive attribute values from a victim's profile (*Layer 1*). However, *3LP* goes further to suggests the victim shall delete existing friends from the friend list (*Layer 2*) and add new friends (*Layer 3*). *3LP* can protect privacy for a sensitive attribute (considered by its user) on a single run. However, the OSN users may consider multiple information as sensitive rather than a single information. Hence, *3LP* does not consider the protection policy for multiple attributes on its single run.

3LP assumes the existence of a single sensitive attribute such as the "*Political View*" while in reality a user is likely to have multiple sensitive attributes such as the "*Political View*" and "*Religious View*". To protect the privacy of multiple sensitive attributes *3LP* could be applied multiple times, but every run of *3LP* would be isolated/independent. As a result, they can be counterproductive in the sense that one run (say to protect the "*Political View*") might suggest hiding a friendship information with another user while a subsequent run (say to protect "*Religious View*") might suggest disclosing the same friendship information resulting in the loss of protection of "*Political View*".

1.3   Our Contributions

We propose *3LP+* in this study which is an extension of the existing *3LP* algorithm [16]. *3LP+* aims to provide privacy for multiple sensitive attributes through a co-ordinated approach as opposed to the isolated approach. It uses a matrix to store the history of any friendship being hidden or new friendship being created during a run to avoid a conflicting suggestion in a subsequent run. For example, if the *t*-th run suggests hiding a friendship of the victim user with another user (and the victim user actions on the suggestion), then the matrix stores that information so that a subsequent run does not suggest the victim user creating the friendship with the same user.

Table 5. The major contributions of this study.

Contribution Number	Description of the contributions	Section
1	We propose a privacy preserving technique, namely *3LP+*, that provides privacy for multiple sensitive attributes considered by a user	2
2	We implement the *3LP+* on two OSN data sets and the experimental results indicate the superiority of *3LP+* over an existing technique, even if the attacker uses a set of different classifiers to invade privacy	4.2
3	We also evaluate the data utility of two OSN data sets after applying *3LP+* and compare the results with the previous privacy preserving techniques	4.3

We have three major contributions in this paper and we summarise each of them including their corresponding section number in Table 5. Out of these three contributions, we have previously published Contribution 1 in the International Conference on Information Systems Security and Privacy [18]. In that conference paper we implement the *3LP+* on a synthetically generated OSN data set only whereas in this paper we implement the *3LP+* on a Facebook real users' dataset along with the synthetic data set (see Sect. 3.1).

The rest of this paper is organized as follows. Section 2 presents our proposed technique *3LP+*. We describe the experimental set up in Sect. 3 and the experimental results in Sect. 4. Section 5 gives a concluding remark.

2   The Proposed Technique

The basic idea of *3LP+* is to protect the privacy of all information that a user considers to be sensitive. Users can give the list of attributes they considers sensitive and then, *3LP+* provides three steps (or *layers*) of recommendations:

Step 1: Compute the Sensitivity of Each Attribute for Each User and Suggest to the User Which Attribute Values the User Needs to Suppress.
The pseudo-code for Step 1 is reproduced here within Algorithm 1 from [18], *3LP+* selects a class attribute (from the list of sensitive attributes considered by the *3LP+* User u) randomly, prepares a training data set D, and then applies *SysFor* [12] on D to get a set of logic rules. *3LP+* then uses the support and confidence of each rule to compute its sensitivity (or *Rule Sensitivity*) value in

breaching the privacy of a sensitive attribute. We set this threshold value to 1.006 in order to keep consistence with the previous studies [5, 16]. Similar to previous studies [16, 17], the rules having *Rule Sensitivity* value 1.006 or above are considered Sensitive Rules in this study. We utilize the function *GetSensitiveRules()* in Step 2 of Algorithm 1 to represent the processes of generating the sensitive rule set R^u for u.

After preparing the sensitive rule set R^u, *3LP+* counts the number of appearance of each regular attribute A_n in R^u and store A_n in A^s. Here, A^s stores all the regular attributes and the number of their appearances in R^u. One attribute can appear only once in a sensitive rule R_j^u but more than once in R^u. The regular attribute A_n with the highest number of appearances in R^u is suggested to u for suppression. The decision is then up to u whether to suppress its value or not. If u suppresses the value of A_n, then A_n is no longer available in A^s and all sensitive rules in R^u that have A_n in their antecedent are no longer applicable for u. Regardless whether u suppresses the attribute or not, *3LP+* then identifies A_n with the next highest appearances and suggests u to suppress that. The process continues until R^u or A^s becomes empty.

Step 2: Hide Friendship Links as Necessary If They Are Not Fabricated Previously.

After *Layer 1*, if any sensitive rule remains in R^u such a rule only uses link attributes (i.e. the attribute values can only be altered by using Eq. 1). Therefore, if a link attribute appears as an antecedent of a sensitive rule R_j^u (i.e. $R_j^u \in R^u$), where the value of the link attribute needs to be greater than a constant *SplitPoint* (as mentioned in R_j^u), the *3LP+* explores to reduce its value < *SplitPoint* by hiding some of u's friendship links. By doing this *3LP+* makes the rule unusable to predict the class value of u with certainty.

In Step 2, *3LP+* first identifies the link attribute, A_n, that appears most in the sensitive rule set R^u and compute A_n's value, denoted as V, using Eq. 1. If V is higher than the split point mentioned in R_j^u, then *3LP+* suggests u to hide a friendship link. While choosing a friendship link, *3LP+* selects a friend, t_i, of u who has the smallest degree and has not previously appeared in the friendship matrix F (here F is an $1 \times N$ matrix which stores the *Flag* information for u). The *3LP+* recommends u to hide t_i so that it can reduce V's value the most by hiding a minimum number of friends. If u follows the recommendation, *3LP+* puts a *Flag* up in the ith column of the friendship matrix F and this ex-friend will not be recommended for further hiding or adding. *3LP+* then updates G', F', and recomputes V's value.

This process continues until the value V is lower than the *SplitPoint* mentioned in R_j^u. Once the V is lower than the split point, then the process of hiding friends stops and *3LP+* removes R_j^u and other rules (which have an antecedent with the value V) from R^u as they are no longer be applicable to determine u's class value. At the end of Step 2, if R^u is not empty then only *3LP+* moves to Step 2 i.e. Layer 3.

Step 3: Add Friendship Links as Necessary If They Are Not Fabricated Previously.

Algorithm 1. The Steps of 3LP+

Input	: User u, data set D, friendship network G, total number of records N in D, set of non-class attributes A, set of regular attributes A^r, set of link attributes A^l where $A^r, A^l \subset A$, set of class attributes C.
Output	: Recommendations for u.
Variables	: R = set of sensitive rules, R_j = the jth sensitive rule, A_n = the nth attribute, and F = $1 \times N$ $matrix$ stores $Flag$ information for u /*Initially all values in F are set to $False$ */.

Step 1: Compute Sensitivity of Each Attribute for a User and Suggest the User to Suppress Attribute Values as Necessary.

$R^u \leftarrow GetSensitiveRulesForUser(D, A, C, u)$
  foreach $R_j^u \in R^u$ do
    $n = 0$ /* The value of n is always reset to 0 before the initiation of $While$ loop */
    while $n < |A|$ do
      if $A_n \in A^r$ AND A_n is in the $antecedent$ of R_j^u then
        $A^s \leftarrow A^s \cup \{A_n\}$ /* Add A_n in an array A^s */
        $Counter_n \leftarrow Counter_n + 1$ /* Counts the number of appearance of A_n in A^s */
      end
      $n = n + 1$
    end
  end
  while $R^u \neq \phi$ AND $A^s \neq \phi$ do
    $n \leftarrow maxarg(Counter, A)$ /* Returns the index of the attribute that appears the most */
    $SuggestSuppress(A_n)$ /* Suggest u to suppress the value of A_n */
    if A_n is $suppressed$ then
      $A^s \leftarrow A^s \setminus \{A_n\}$
      $R^u \leftarrow R^u \setminus \{R_j^u\}$ /* Rules using A_n are removed from R^u */
    end
  end
end

Step 2: Hide Friendship Links as Necessary if they are not fabricated previously.

$G' = G$ and $F' = F$
  $n \leftarrow FindIndexMostSensitive(A^l, R^u)$ and $V \leftarrow CalculateValue(A_n, u)$ /* using Equation 1 */
  while $R^u \neq \phi$ AND $A^l \neq \phi$ do
    for $j = 1$ to $|R^u|$ do
      if A_n is in the $antecedent$ of R_j^u AND $V \geq SplitPoint(R_j^u, A_n)$ then
        while $V \geq SplitPoint(R_j^u, A_n)$ AND $MoreFriends(u, G', F', A_n)$ do
          $i \leftarrow FriendWithLeastDegree(u, G', F', A_n)$ /* i is the index of the Friend with least degree when $F_i' \in F'$ is $False$ */
          $SuggestHide(t_i)$ and $G' \leftarrow HideLink(G', u, t_i)$ /* t_i is the ith friend */
          $F' \leftarrow Flag(F', t_i)$ /* F_i' is turned to $True$ */
          $V \leftarrow CalculateValue(A_n, u)$
        end
        $R^u \leftarrow R^u \setminus \{R_j^u\}$ /* Rules using A_n are removed from R^u */
      end
      j=j+1
    end
    $A^l \leftarrow A^l \setminus \{A_n\}$
    $n \leftarrow FindIndexMostSensitive(A^l, R^u)$ and $V \leftarrow CalculateValue(A_n, u)$
  end
end

Step 3: Add Friendship Links as Necessary if they are not fabricated previously.

$n \leftarrow FindIndexMostSensitive(A^l, R^u)$ and $V \leftarrow CalculateValue(A_n, u)$ using Equation 1 */
  while $R^u \neq \phi$ AND $A^l \neq \phi$ do
    for $j = 1$ to $|R^u|$ do
      if A_n is in the $antecedent$ of R_j^u AND $V \leq SplitPoint(R_j^u, A_n)$ then
        while $V \leq SplitPoint(R_j^u, A_n)$ AND $MoreUsers(G', F', A_n)$ do
          $t_i \leftarrow UserWithLeastDegree(G', F', A_n)$ /* i is the index of the User with least degree when $F_i' \in F'$ is $False$ */
          $SuggestAdd(t_i)$ and $G' \leftarrow AddLink(G', u, t_i)$ /* t_i is the ith user */
          $F' \leftarrow Flag(F', t_i)$ /* F_i' is turned to $True$ */
          $V \leftarrow CalculateValue(A_n, u)$
        end
        $R^u \leftarrow R^u \setminus \{R_j^u\}$ /* Rules using A_n are removed from R^u */
      end
      j=j+1
    end
    $A^l \leftarrow A^l \setminus \{A_n\}$
    $n \leftarrow FindIndexMostSensitive(A^l, R^u)$ and $V \leftarrow CalculateValue(A_n, u)$
  end
end

After Step 1 and Step 2, any sensitive rule remains in R^u, that contains link attribute only and tests for a value $V \leq some\ SplitPoint$ in its antecedent. In this case, $3LP+$ suggests u to add new friends so that the V becomes greater than the split point in R_j^u and thus R_j^u is no longer applicable to u. While adding any friend on u's friend list, a user t_i is selected in such a way that a $Flag$ has not been up previously in the ith column of F' matrix and having the smallest $\Gamma_+(t)$ value. If u accepts the recommendation, $3LP+$ then updates the matrix F', friendship graph G', and V increases.

This adding process continues until the value V exceeds the split point value. It is noted that, adding a new friend on a profile is complicated and the fact that two users share the friendship that is not the ownership of either alone [9]. depends on the other users to confirm the friendship on OSN. Hence, $3LP+$ keeps these recommendations as a last resort. Our experimental results also indicate this step is seldom required.

3   Experiments

3.1   Data Set

We implement the privacy preserving techniques on two OSN data sets. The first data set [15], denoted as D_1, contains 1000 records, 11 regular attributes, and 50,397 friendship links among the users. The second data set, denoted as D_2, is prepared by gathering the users' information from Facebook. D_2 contains 616 records, 24 regular attributes, and 1280 friendship links among the users. In order to insert the users' link attribute values into the data set, we calculate metric values for each regular attribute (using Eq. (1)) and therefore, the total number of attributes becomes 22 (i.e. 11 regular attributes and 11 link attributes) for D_1 and 48 attributes for D_2.

We assume the users in the two data sets consider three attributes as sensitive. For the simplicity let's denote them as X, Y, and Z. In the D_1 data set, the sensitive attributes are: X = "Political view", Y = "Religious view", and Z = "Sexual orientation". In the D_2 data set, the sensitive attributes are: X = "Emotional status", Y = "Religious view", and Z = "Political view".

We therefore prepare three versions of each data set for each of the sensitive attribute and in each version we consider a sensitive attribute as a class attribute. We follow 10-fold cross validation method through out our experiments. Therefore, in each fold, a training data set, denoted as D_{tr}, contains 90% of the total records and a testing data set, denoted as D_{ts}, contains 10% of the total records.

For the experimental purpose, we split the 10% test data records into three groups: Group 1 (6% records), Group 2 (3% records), and Group 3 (1% records). We assume the Group 1 users consider any one attribute (i.e. either "X" or "Y" or "Z") as sensitive. On the other hand, we assume Group 2 users consider any two attributes (out of the three attributes) as sensitive. Finally, Group 3 consists of 1% users who consider all the three attributes as sensitive. We

Test data set	$D_{ts,X}$	$D_{ts,Y}$	$D_{ts,Z}$
Group 1 (6% records)	X: 2% records	Y: 2% records	Z: 2% records
Group 2 (3% records)	X, Y: 1% records	X, Y: 1% records	Y, Z: 1% records
	X, Z: 1% records	Y, Z: 1% records	X, Z: 1% records
Group 3 (1% records)	X, Y, Z: 1% records		

Fig. 3. Distribution of 10% test data set records in a fold. Here the different colours indicate the different records and same colour indicates the same records. (Color figure online)

present the three groups and their records distribution in Fig. 3. Here the different cell colours indicate different records and the same colour represents the same records.

While preparing a test data set e.g. $D_{ts,X}$ we select the records who consider X as a sensitive information and return all other records in the training data set $D_{tr,X}$. For example, in case of the first data set D_1, there are 100 records (out of 1000 total records) in a test data set (after applying 10-fold cross validation). We only keep 50 records in $D_{ts,X}$ who consider X as sensitive and return rest of the 950 records in the training data set $D_{tr,X}$. Similarly, for the second data set D_2, we keep 31 records in $D_{ts,X}$ and 585 records in $D_{tr,X}$. On the other hand, when we consider a particular attribute as a class attribute then rest of the attributes are considered to be non-class attributes. For example, in $D_{tr,X}$ and $D_{ts,X}$ data sets, both Y and Z are selected as non-class attributes.

3.2   Experimental Set-Up

We present the entire experimental set-up in three phases for three different sensitive attributes. In Phase I, we first protect the privacy for X, then for Y in Phase II, and finally, for Z in Phase III. We argue that the *3LP+* can protect privacy of all the sensitive information (which are selected by its users) regardless to the sequence of selection as a class attribute. Therefore, we also conduct experiments in an opposite sequence order but for simplicity we only describe the experimental set-up here for first sequence order.

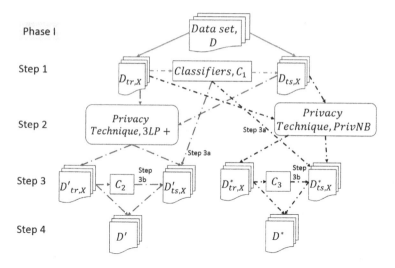

Fig. 4. Phase I of the experiments. (Color figure online)

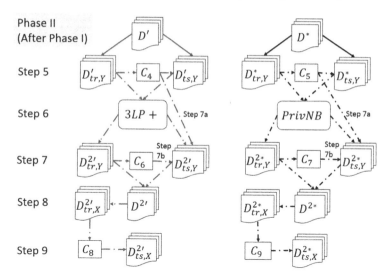

Fig. 5. Phase II of the experiments. (Color figure online)

Phase I. During the first step, illustrated in Fig. 4 taken from [18], we prepare a training data set $D_{tr,X}$, and a testing data set $D_{ts,X}$ from the main data set D by considering users' X as a class attribute. At Step 2, we apply the two privacy preserving techniques, i.e. *3LP+* and *PrivNB*, on the insecure test data sets. Here the term 'insecure' means that the *3LP+* or *PrivNB* have not been applied previously on the test data sets and hence the users' class value can be determined by an attacker easily. The test data sets are then secured by the techniques, as shown in Step 3, denoted as $D'_{ts,X}$ and $D^*_{ts,X}$ respectively. We calculate and compare the number of insecure users exists in the insecure and secure data sets. In order to provide privacy $3LP+$ and $PrivNB$ modifies the data sets by hiding information/friends or adding friends. Therefore, we use two different symbols $'$ and $*$ throughout the experimental set-up to denote the modified data sets by $3LP+$ and $PrivNB$ techniques respectively.

A privacy provider may not determine the classifier which is going to be used by an attacker and therefore, the privacy protecting technique should be able to protect privacy against any machine learning algorithms. In our experiments we explore and compare the performance of $3LP+$ and $PrivNB$ for different classifiers such as Naïve Bayes classifier (NB), Support Vector Machine (SVM), and Random Forest (RF) algorithm. In order to do that we first apply these machine learning algorithms on insecure data set $D_{ts,X}$ in Step 1 and find the number of number of insecure users in the test data set. We name it as classifiers' *accuracy* which refers to the number of users whose class value is identified by the classifiers. The larger the *accuracy* value indicates lower the privacy.

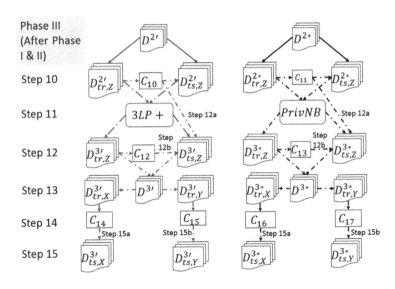

Fig. 6. Phase III of the experiments. (Color figure online)

We then apply the different classifiers on secure test data sets $D'_{ts,X}$ and $D^*_{ts,X}$ in Step 3. By comparing the classifiers' *accuracy* results, in Step 1 and Step 3, we then determine which technique provides better privacy on the test data sets. The results are presented in terms of number of insecure users, denoted as t_0^s and classifiers' *accuracy*, denoted as $t_0^{c_1}$. In Step 3, we also calculate data utility (in terms of number of suppressed attribute values) in $D'_{ts,X}$ and $D^*_{ts,X}$ after applying the two privacy preserving techniques and denoted as t_3^u. We have taken Figs. 4, 5 and 6 from [18]; where different colours of arrows indicate the procedure of two different privacy preserving techniques.

Phase II. After Phase I, we select Y as a class attribute (refer to Fig. 5 taken from [18]). We first prepare training and testing data sets and denote them as $D'_{tr,Y}$ and $D'_{ts,Y}$ which are prepared from D'. Similarly, $D^*_{tr,Y}$ and $D^*_{ts,Y}$ are prepared from D^*. In Step 5, different classifiers are applied on $D'_{ts,Y}$ and $D^*_{ts,Y}$, denoted by C_4 and C_5 respectively, to measure the classifiers' *accuracy*. Then we apply *3LP+* and *PrivNB* on test data sets in Step 7 (in order to secure the users' privacy). Similar to Phase I, the experimental results are analysed and compared in terms of number of insecure users, data utility, and prediction accuracy by different classifiers in Step 7.

After Step 7 we again return all the records to original data set and thus it is modified to $D^{2'}$ and D^{2*} for *3LP+* and *PrivNB* respectively. In Step 9, we again investigate the safety of users (who considered X as sensitive) in $D'_{ts,X}$ due to providing the privacy to users in $D^*_{ts,Y}$.

Phase III. We select Z as a class attribute in this phase and similar to previous two phases, we first prepare training and testing data sets i.e. $D2'_{tr,Z}$ and $D2'_{ts,Z}$ (refer to Fig. 6 taken from [18]) from $D^{2'}$. We also prepared $D^{2*}_{tr,Z}$ and $D^{2*}_{ts,Z}$ are prepared from D^{2*}. In Step 10, we apply different classifiers, denoted by C_{10} and C_{11}, on the two test data sets $D^{2'}_{ts,R}$ and $D^{2*}_{ts,R}$ to find the classification accuracy before and applying any privacy techniques. We then apply *3LP+* on $D^{2'}_{ts,R}$ and *PrivNB* on $D^{2*}_{ts,R}$ in Step 11. We denote $D^{3'}_{ts,R}$ and $D^{3*}_{ts,R}$ to represent the secure test data sets and apply different classifiers, denoted by C_{10} and C_{11}, again on them in Step 12. After securing the test data sets, similar to Phase I and Phase II, we again analyse and compare the number of insecure users (in $D^{3'}_{ts,X}$, $D^{3*}_{ts,X}$, $D^{3*}_{ts,Y}$, $D^{3*}_{ts,Y}$) in Step 15a and Step 15b as shown in Fig. 6. The secured test data sets are analysed and compared in terms of number of insecure users and data utility for both privacy preserving techniques.

4 Results and Discussion

We present the experimental results of our proposed technique *3LP+* in this section. The results are averaged before we present here and then compare with an existing technique *PrivNB* [11]. The results are shown using bar graphs where x-axis represents the step numbers mentioned in Sect. 3.2 and y-axis represents the *Attack Success Rate* percentage. Here the term *Attack Success Rate* indicates the number of users whose class value is correctly predicted by the classifier. Higher *Attack Success Rate* percentage indicates the greater chance for the intruder to infer the class value of a user and vice versa.

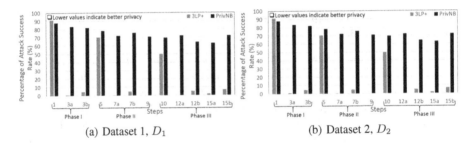

(a) Dataset 1, D_1 (b) Dataset 2, D_2

Fig. 7. Prediction of class value accuracy of two privacy preserving techniques.

4.1 Protection Against the Same Classifier

In Fig. 7 we present the number of insecure users whose class value can still be inferred by applying the same classifier used by the privacy protection technique. As mentioned earlier, *3LP+* uses *Sysfor* [12] decision forests and *PrivNB* uses *Naïve Bayes* classifier to extract the patterns from the data set. We first provide privacy by the two privacy techniques separately as described in the Sect. 3.2. Here y-axis represents prediction probability to classify a record (regardless to correctly or incorrectly classified) by an intruder after the protection techniques are applied. We observe that the probability percentage of records is much higher for *PrivNB* compared to *3LP+* except at Step 1. This is because the privacy preserving techniques are yet to implement at Step 1 as shown in Fig. 4. On the other hand, in Fig. 8(a), the percentage of correctly classified records by *PrivNB* is approximately 70% more than the *3LP+*. We observe a similar results in Fig. 8(b) for the second data set D_2. We also explore the performance of the two privacy protection techniques against different classifiers (not used by the privacy protection technique) and the results are shown in next section.

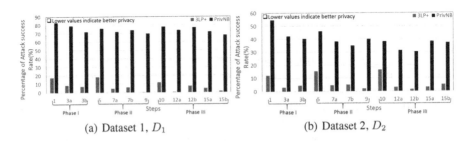

(a) Dataset 1, D_1 (b) Dataset 2, D_2

Fig. 8. Prediction of users' class value(correctly) using the same classifier used by the privacy preserving techniques.

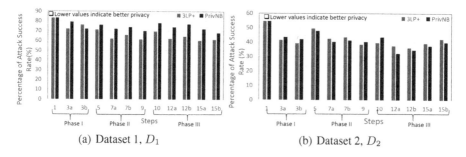

(a) Dataset 1, D_1 (b) Dataset 2, D_2

Fig. 9. Performance of Naïve Bayes in order to breach users' privacy in the test data sets.

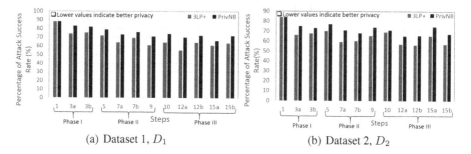

(a) Dataset 1, D_1 (b) Dataset 2, D_2

Fig. 10. Performance of Support Vector Machine in order to breach users' privacy in the test data sets.

4.2   Protection Against Different Classifiers

In order to explore the performance of the two privacy protection techniques, we utilise three conventional classifiers that the attacker may use to invade privacy and they are: *Naïve Bayes* (denoted as *NB*), *Support Vector Machine* (denoted as *SVM*), and *Random Forest* [4] (denoted as *RF*). We use WEKA [10] to implement the classifiers in our experiments. In Fig. 9 we present the results of *3LP+* and *PrivNB* if the attacker uses *NB* classifier to infer the sensitive attributes. We observe in Fig. 9(a) (in D_1 data set) that the provided privacy by *3LP+*is better than *PrivNB* as the classification accuracy drops on average 10% compared to Step 1 to Step 3. However, this accuracy drops is less than 10% in case of *PrivNB*. The similar trend is observed throughout the experimental steps except Step 1. This is because at step 1 the privacy technique was yet to apply on the test data set. Therefore, classification accuracy is similar for *3LP+* and *PrivNB* at this step. For rest of the experimental steps, *3LP+* outperforms *PrivNB*.

In D_2 data set, shown in Fig. 9(b), *PrivNB* performs a bit better than *3LP+*. Unlike *3LP+*, *PrivNB* uses *Naïve Bayes* classifier to extract the pattern from the training data set. Therefore it gets an advantage to suppress the highly predictor attribute values as *Naïve Bayes* consider to correctly predict the class value of a record.

We present the performance of the privacy preserving techniques against *SVM* and *RF* in Fig. 10 and Fig. 11 respectively. Our proposed technique clearly outperforms the existing *PrivNB* technique in both data sets and we can see a *Attack Success Rate* drop for both *SVM* and *RF* classifiers.

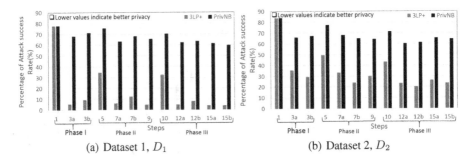

(a) Dataset 1, D_1 (b) Dataset 2, D_2

Fig. 11. Performance of Random Forest Algorithm in order to breach users' privacy in the test data sets.

We observe the prediction accuracy of the classifiers are decreasing as the steps are progressing. The reason is as the number of suppressed attribute values are increasing (to secure from sensitive rules) as the steps are progressing. It is important to note that the classifiers do not consider a missing value in a test data set While predicting a class value and thus reduce the probability for correct classification. We mentioned earlier that the link attribute values can only be modified. Thus it increases the possibility to classify a record correctly by both *SVM*, and *RF*. However, the *3LP+* still performs better in all steps compared to *PrivNB*. It is also noted that we do not consider the attribute *Gender* for suppression in any of the test data sets as We believe *Gender* can be inferred from the user's name or photo.

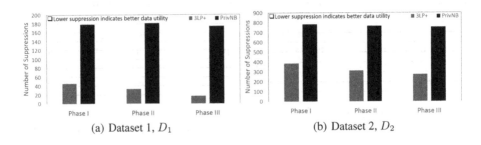

(a) Dataset 1, D_1 (b) Dataset 2, D_2

Fig. 12. Comparison of attribute value suppression.

4.3   Data Utility

We measure the data utility of the test data sets in terms of number of suppressed attribute values. The number of suppressions in test data sets after applying two different privacy preserving techniques are then compared with each other. In Fig. 12 we present and compare the results for Step 3, Step 7, and Step 12 only as the privacy techniques are applied in these steps.

In first data set D_1, each test data set contains maximum 500 *regular* attribute values (i.e. 50 *records* × 10 *regular attribute values* = 500) before applying any privacy preserving techniques. However, some of the records may consider more than one sensitive attribute (as shown in Fig. 3) so, the number of attribute values are varied in different test data sets. As an example, if there are 100 records in a test data set $D_{ts,X}$, then 20 users consider a single attribute (i.e. X) as sensitive, 20 more users consider any 2 attributes as sensitive, and 10 other users consider all the 3 attributes as sensitive. Therefore, the maximum available number of attribute values in $D_{ts,X}$ is ($20 * 10 + 20 * 9 + 10 * 8 = 460$). However, this number is not same for rest of the two test data sets i.e. $D_{ts,Y}$, and $D_{ts,Z}$. Because after applying *3LP+* or *PrivNB* on $D_{ts,X}$, the available number of attribute values will be different on $D_{ts,Y}$, and $D_{ts,Z}$, but it must not exceed the 460.

Similar to D_1 data set, each test data set in D_2, contains maximum 1457 *regular* attribute values (i.e. 31 *records* × 47 *regular attribute values* = 1457) before applying any privacy privacy preserving techniques. However, this number is not the same for rest of the test data sets. In Fig. 12(a) we observe the number of suppressed attribute values by the *PrivNB* technique is almost three times higher than *3LP+*. We see a similar pattern in Fig. 12(b) where the number of suppressions for *PrivNB* is much higher than *3LP+*.

5   Conclusion

We propose *3LP+* in this study to provide users' privacy on social media. Previous privacy preserving techniques can protect users' single sensitive attribute (from being inferred) whereas *3LP+* takes a coordinated approach to protect users' multiple sensitive attributes in one run. Our experimental results indicate that *3LP+* can provide better privacy compared to an existing privacy preserving technique by suppressing less number of attribute values compared to an existing technique. Our experimental results also show that *3LP+* can maintain the high utility of the data set by suppressing less number of attribute values compared to an existing technique.

In this paper, we have considered that an attacker uses *Naïve Bayes, Support Vector Machine, Random Forest* classifiers to invade privacy. If the attacker applies a different set of decision forest algorithms or classifiers to learn the patterns of the data set, then the calculation will be different and it is kept as a direction for further investigation.

References

1. Adamic, L.A., Adar, E.: Friends and neighbors on the web. Soc. Networks **25**(3), 211–230 (2003)
2. Al-Saggaf, Y., Islam, M.Z.: Privacy in social network sites (SNS): the threats from data mining. Ethical Space: Int. J. Commun. **9**(4), 32–40 (2012)
3. Al-Saggaf, Y., Islam, M.Z.: Data mining and privacy of social network sites' users: implications of the data mining problem. Sci. Eng. Ethics **21**(4), 941–966 (2015)
4. Breiman, L.: Random forests. Mach. Learn. **45**(1), 5–32 (2001)
5. Estivill-Castro, V., Hough, P., Islam, M.Z.: Empowering users of social networks to assess their privacy risks. In: 2014 IEEE International Conference on Big Data (Big Data), pp. 644–649. IEEE (2014)
6. Estivill-Castro, V., Nettleton, D.F.: Can on-line social network users trust that what they designated as confidential data remains so? In: Trust-com/BigDataSE/ISPA, 2015 IEEE, vol. 1, pp. 966–973. IEEE (2015)
7. Estivill-Castro, V., Nettleton, D.F.: Privacy tips: would it be ever possible to empower online social-network users to control the confidentiality of their data? In: Proceedings of the 2015 IEEE/ACM International Conference on Advances in Social Networks Analysis and Mining 2015, pp. 1449–1456. ACM (2015)
8. Guha, S., Tang, K., Francis, P.: NOYB: privacy in online social networks. In: Proceedings of the First Workshop on Online Social Networks, pp. 49–54. ACM (2008)
9. Gürses, G., Berendt, B.: The social web and privacy: practices, reciprocity and conflict detection in social networks. In: Privacy-Aware Knowledge Discovery, Novel Applications and New Techniques, pp. 395–429. CRC Press (2010)
10. Hall, M., Frank, E., Holmes, G., Pfahringer, B., Reutemann, P., Witten, I.H.: The weka data mining software: an update. SIGKDD Explor. **11**(1), 10–18 (2009)
11. Heatherly, R., Kantarcioglu, M., Thuraisingham, B.: Preventing private information inference attacks on social networks. IEEE Trans. Knowl. Data Eng. **25**(8), 1849–1862 (2013)
12. Islam, Z., Giggins, H.: Knowledge discovery through SysFor: a systematically developed forest of multiple decision trees. In: Proceedings of the Ninth Australasian Data Mining Conference-Volume 121, pp. 195–204. Australian Computer Society, Inc. (2011)
13. Kosinski, M., Stillwell, D., Graepel, T.: Private traits and attributes are predictable from digital records of human behavior. Proc. Natl. Acad. Sci. **110**(15), 5802–5805 (2013). https://doi.org/10.1073/pnas.1218772110
14. Mislove, A., Viswanath, B., Gummadi, K.P., Druschel, P.: You are who you know: inferring user profiles in online social networks. In: Proceedings of the third ACM International Conference on Web Search and Data Mining, pp. 251–260. ACM (2010)
15. Nettleton, D.F.: Generating synthetic online social network graph data and topologies. In: 3rd Workshop on Graph-Based Technologies and Applications (Graph-TA), UPC, Barcelona, Spain (2015)
16. Reza, K.J., Islam, M.Z., Estivill-Castro, V.: 3LP: three layers of protection for individual privacy in Facebook. In: De Capitani di Vimercati, S., Martinelli, F. (eds.) SEC 2017. IAICT, vol. 502, pp. 108–123. Springer, Cham (2017). https://doi.org/10.1007/978-3-319-58469-0_8
17. Reza, K.J., Islam, M.Z., Estivill-Castro, V.: Social media users' privacy against malicious data miners. In: 2017 12th International Conference on Intelligent Systems and Knowledge Engineering (ISKE), pp. 1–8. IEEE (2017)

18. Reza, K.J., Islam, M.Z., Estivill-Castro, V.: Privacy preservation of social network users against attribute inference attacks via malicious data mining. In: Proceedings of the 5th International Conference on Information Systems Security and Privacy - Volume 1: ICISSP, pp. 412–420. INSTICC, SciTePress (2019). https://doi.org/10.5220/0007390404120420

19. Ryu, E., Rong, Y., Li, J., Machanavajjhala, A.: Curso: protect yourself from curse of attribute inference: a social network privacy-analyzer. In: Proceedings of the ACM SIGMOD Workshop on Databases and Social Networks, pp. 13–18. ACM (2013)

20. Yin, Z., Gupta, M., Weninger, T., Han, J.: LINKREC: a unified framework for link recommendation with user attributes and graph structure. In: Proceedings of the 19th International Conference on World Wide Web, pp. 1211–1212. ACM (2010)

User Behavioral Biometrics and Machine Learning Towards Improving User Authentication in Smartphones

José Torres[1], Sergio de los Santos[1], Efthimios Alepis[2(✉)], and Constantinos Patsakis[2]🆔

[1] Telefónica Digital España, Ronda de la Comunicación S/N, Madrid, Spain
{jose.torres,ssantos}@11paths.com
[2] Department of Informatics, University of Piraeus, Karaoli & Dimitriou 80, Piraeus, Greece
{talepis,kpatsak}@unipi.gr

Abstract. Smartphone and smart devices, in general, have penetrated modern life, accompanying humans in the majority of their daily activities, realizing the era of IoT. This tight bond between mobile devices and humans has introduced numerous solutions and automation in people's everyday living, however, it also comes with a cost, since we are more exposed to security risks and private data leakages. This work extends our previous study on improved user authentication mechanism for smartphones. More specifically, we present a biometric-based approach which utilizes machine learning and the development of a mobile application. The application's evaluation results have shown very large success rates, implying its effectiveness in enhancing user's privacy.

Keywords: Android · Authentication · Biometrics · Machine learning

1 Introduction

About two decades ago, the world witnessed the widespread development of mobile phones, which enabled the communication of people without cables. The first devices came at a high cost and a limited number of basic features which included making phone calls and sending short messages. Almost a decade later, "smart" phones appeared, replacing the majority of "feature" phones, with a large number of sensors integrated and a set of software applications and accompanied services to use. Today, the number of smartphones exceeds in many countries the number of its population, these smart devices have become an indispensable part of most people daily life.

As a result, these smart devices store and process vast amounts of sensitive users' information, collected both directly and also indirectly from them, ranging from personal, to financial and professional data. Consequently, user data protection has grown to become a major concern in all mobile vendors around the

© Springer Nature Switzerland AG 2020
P. Mori et al. (Eds.): ICISSP 2019, CCIS 1221, pp. 250–271, 2020.
https://doi.org/10.1007/978-3-030-49443-8_12

world. Despite the introduction, by a significant number of software companies and also from the mobile OSes, of several biometric-based authentication mechanisms such as fingerprints, iris and face recognition, only a small fragment of users actually uses them, while another percentage of users is using them quite sceptically. The reasons for this lack of adoption can be attributed to several factors. For instance, there is a distrust regarding who may process this unique and personal data, the impact of this data been leaked, as well as their usability and efficiency. Indeed, both fingerprints and eye iris are unique and unchangeable user identifiers which on the one hand accompany humans during their lifetime, while on the other have been proven to be quite easy replicated, e.g. utilizing high-resolution digital cameras. As a result, the vast majority of smartphone users are still using the well-known PIN/Pattern authentication method, with the "pattern" method being the most used user-authentication method for smartphone unlocking to date [18] an action which is performed around 50 times per day [17]. Notably, as Mahfouz et al. note this is performed with at least 95% success rate, where unlocking errors range from 0.6% (PIN) to 2.7% (Pattern) and 3.7% for Password that almost diminished for repeating errors.

An important aspect that has to be considered in this direction is that this authentication method has several drawbacks. The most obvious one is that since users have to authenticate to the device continuously, therefore, many users resort into having a relatively "easy" PIN/Pattern. Moreover, due to the way that users have to perform the authentication, shoulder surfing cannot be avoided. Even by excluding shoulder surfing attacks, other methods could be utilized by an attacker to gain information about the victim's pattern, such as malicious apps by exploiting the "drawing over other apps" permissions and analyzing finger traces on smartphone screens attacks [1].

Such private data rationally involves its protection, thus both smartphone locking and correspondingly unlocking represent mechanisms that have drawn much attention from the research community and the involved industry. In the modern era, private user data is intrinsically connected user rights. In our recent past, in 2016, in what has been known as the "Apple - FBI encryption dispute", [24], the FBI tried to force Apple to develop and electronically sign new software that would enable the FBI to unlock an iPhone 5C. This specific phone has been actually been recovered from one of the shooters of the San Bernardino terrorist attack on December 2015, in California. Both public opinion and also software giants followed the trials that followed, while in most cases the users' privacy has been considered as a "prevailing" and essential right. To this end, it should be noted that modern smartphones have indeed increased their security and privacy levels of their software and in many cases even incorporate the ability to "wipe" (also known as "brick") the mobile device once a number of failed authentication attempts are made, or even remotely according to the device owner will.

Main Contributions. This work is an extended version of the authors' previous work [23]. This paper presents a more thorough overview both on the developed application, which has been already pushed to the market, [11], and also on the evaluation study that has been successfully conducted. Furthermore, we also dis-

cuss about other application domains and IoT devices that could take advantage
of our proposed solution. Our suggested methodology utilizes user behavioural
biometrics through Machine Learning algorithms to improve smartphone locking
security. This approach can be adapted to various other use cases, such as smartphone app, resource locking and two-factor authentication, further discussed in
Sect. 7. The presented evaluation study provides not only clear evidence about
the significance of our proposed approach but also gives further evidence about
the protection levels of categories of lock patterns that are frequently used by
users. Moreover, in contrast to the presented related work, we also detail how the
proposed mechanism can be deployed in stock Android devices without the need
of rooting the devices, which is a usual requirement in other similar approaches.
The latter requirement is very important since it allows the wide adoption of
the method and provides advanced security authentication and authorisations
to devices that do not have, e.g. fingerprint sensors, thus minimising the risks of
user exposure. Finally, as it is outlined, the proposed method, even in the case of
leakage allows the user to change her unlock mechanism, despite the dependence
on biometric measurements.

Organisation of this Work. The rest of this work is structured as follows.
In Sect. 2 the authors present the related scientific literature regarding locking
patterns in smartphones. Section 3 illustrates the problem setting and also details
the specific use case that this paper addresses. Consequently, Sect. 4 follows
illustrating our proposed novel solution. In Sect. 5, the authors discuss about the
Machine Learning backend core of the developed system. Section 6 follows with
an overview of the evaluation experiment that has been conducted, along with its
results, while Sect. 7 gives evidence about possible incorporation of our proposed
approach in other domains where smart devices are also involved. Finally, in
Sect. 8 the authors summarise their contributions and propose future work.

2   Related Work

In the following paragraphs, we provide a brief overview regarding research on
smartphone protection through its locking mechanisms and more specifically
using the locking pattern. The authors have included works that reveal this
topic's scientific significance, in terms of user statistics, studies on the theo-
retic security level of the mechanism in question, as well as attacks focusing on
bypassing secure pattern lock screens.

As stated in [18], to prevent unauthorized access to smartphones, their users
can enable a "lock screen" which may require entering a PIN or password, drawing a pattern, or providing a biometric, such as users' fingerprints. In the survey
conducted by [18], involving more than 8.000 users from eight different countries,
the prevailing method for locking a smartphone is considered the smartphone
pattern, used in almost half of all users of the survey (48% of all locking mechanisms).

Nevertheless, in [3], the authors examine the feasibility of "smudge" attacks on
touch screens for smartphones and focus their analysis on the Android lockscreen

pattern. Alarmingly, their study concludes that in the vast majority of settings, partial or complete patterns are easily retrieved. Indeed, the authors of [3] managed to partially identify 92% of Android patterns and fully in 68% of their attempts, using camera setups.

As stated in [4], Android unlock patterns are considered as the most prevalent graphical password system to date. The same researchers argue that human-chosen authentication stimuli, such as text passwords and PINs, are easy to guess and therefore investigate whether an increase in the unlock pattern grid size positively affects the security level of the mechanism in question.

In [19] two user studies were conducted with a total of 45 participants to investigate the impact of multi-touch behaviours on creating Android unlock patterns. While focusing mainly on the issue of usability, the author proposes increasing the number of touchable points and improving the rules of the unlock pattern creation.

As shown in [12], a mathematical formula for the exact number of patterns is not known yet, even for the simplest case of the unlock patterns, namely, the 3×3 grid. The authors of [14] and [13] respectively calculated in their works the lower and upper bounds of Android unlock patterns, thus providing a theoretical estimation of the unlock patterns' corresponding security level.

Davin et al. [8] demonstrated how a casual observer could easily visually pick up and then reproduce a six-point Android unlock pattern. In their experiment, they conclude that after a single viewing, the evaluated six-point patterns were recreated by about two or three observers from a distance of six feet away from the user who is performing the pattern. Moreover, they evaluate how different angles or perspectives can affect to the observer success and the influence of lines presence in the pattern preview on the lock screen.

In [6], the authors propose a continuous and silent monitoring process based on a set of user-specific features, namely device orientation, touch and cell tower. Other kinds of protection techniques regarding user authentication include the works of [20] where the authors propose authentication token-based mechanisms to identify legal users, [10] where graphical password systems are utilized, and [16] where the authors propose a novel application, where the user draws a stroke on the touch screen as an input password utilizing touch pressure, touch finger size and speed. While this work is the most similar to our work, our experiments have much higher percentages of accuracy, while our approach is based on finger movements on the screen. Arguably, only a very limited number of smartphone devices to date support finger pressure data calculations. For a more detailed analysis of authentication in mobile devices with touch dynamics the interested reader may refer to [22].

After a thorough investigation of the related scientific literature, we have come up with the conclusion that even though there is a growing interest towards the direction of securely locking, and consequently unlock attacks to smartphones, we did not find significant scientific attempts, other than [16] towards improving the already adopted unlock mechanism of the smartphone pattern utilizing machine learning and behavioural biometric user data, as described in this paper. The main drawbacks that we identified in current state of the art is that they either depend on sensors that are not present in all devices (e.g. pressure), they require complete reconstruction of the AOSP unlocking mechanism, or that they imply the use of continuous monitoring of the device hence a wealth of user information and significant resource consumption.

3   Problem Setting

As already mentioned, smartphone locking is very common to the majority of smartphone users to date. In this section, we further analyze the problem of securing sensitive personal data that involve smartphones, going a step further than the actual access to a physical device. We argue that modern smartphone users not only want to secure their mobile device but in many cases, there are also specific applications and data that need to be further strongly secured. In order to understand this argument, a use case is described.

Let us assume that Alice has an Android device which has several applications, some of which require strong authentication, e.g. banking applications. Moreover, Alice may often share her device with her daughter Carol to let her play or browse the Internet. Android may support more than one users; however, this feature is not often used due to usability issues and because in the case of Carol, shoulder surfing cannot be avoided.

Due to her job, Alice comes in contact with many people on a daily basis, and quite often, she has to unlock her device in front of them. Therefore, Alice fears that her unlock PIN/pattern (and possibly other credentials) may have been disclosed through shoulder surfing. Moreover, Alice would like to have control of some web pages and apps to avoid possible issues, from posting something inappropriate on a social network or messing with her bank account.

Based on the above, Alice wants to be able to authenticate on a device easily, avoiding shoulder surfing attacks. Additionally, Alice wants to be able to share her device with Carol, yet lock specific apps and possibly web pages so that her daughter cannot access them. In terms of implementation, we opt for a light solution so that the device must not be rooted but use existing and native mechanisms.

We argue that the above could be solved by providing some *context awareness* to an app that controls access to the device. In this case, context awareness refers to the ability of an app to infer:

- Which user has authenticated.
- Which are the running apps.
- Which web page the user wants to browse.

From the questions above, only the first one can be answered. Regarding running applications, Google has removed the `getRunningTasks` method of `ActivityManager` as of API level 21 to avoid apps surveying users and more importantly to prevent malicious apps from timely overlaying other apps (e.g. banking) and harvesting credentials. While in the literature, there are several ways to determine the foreground app [1,5,7], yet all of them have been depre-cated in AOSP. Nevertheless, Google, as of Android Lollipop, allows developers to use two methods to get usage statistics or detect the foreground app. More precisely, they may either use the UsageStatsManager API which requires the PACKAGE_USAGE_STATS system permission and allows an app to collect statistics about the usage of the installed apps, or use the AccessibilityService API which requires the BIND_ACCESSIBILITY_SERVICE system permission. Notably, both these permissions are "more than dangerous" permissions. In the first case though, Android does not allow apps to derive anything beyond aggregated statistics about the usage of the installed apps. In this regard, an app that has been granted this permission may collect aggregated usage data for up to 7 days for daily intervals, up to 4 weeks for weekly intervals, up to 6 months for monthly intervals, and finally up to 2 years for yearly intervals, always depending on the chosen interval. In the second case, using the AccessibilityService, which includes handling the onAccessibilityEvent() callback and checking whether the TYPE_WINDOW_STATE_CHANGED event type is present, one may deter-mine when the current window changes. It is important to note that Google has warned developers about this permission, that it will remove apps from the Play Store if they use accessibility services for "non-accessibility purposes" [2].

Finally, regarding web pages, it is worthwhile to notice that since Nougat apps may not access any content of /proc/ beyond /proc/[pid]/ where [pid] is their own pid. Therefore, access to /proc/net/tcp6 is not possible, which would allow an app to infer the domain that another app tries to access. Hence, the only available ways to intercept the network usage seem to be by re-routing the network traffic through a local proxy or a VPN. Either of these cases introduces its own security and trust constraints. For instance, the use of a local proxy implies that a self-signed certificate must be installed with the latter triggering a security notification in Android and implying further trust issues. In both cases (local proxy/VPN), one has access to the user's unencrypted traffic.

4   Proposed Solution

In this section, we describe our proposed solution regarding the resulting appli-cation. It should be noted that the backend of our app implements a specific use case of our online service, also called "SmartPattern", which works as an authorization/authentication mechanism of a service that allows protecting any external resource through "Smart Patterns", namely using an API, Oauth2 or JWT. At its first effort to be brought to the real market, the app has focused on securely locking specific apps inside the Android ecosystem. The OS itself could adopt the described underlying approach and use it for locking the Android devices more securely. Indeed, we have developed an Android app that once installed and initialized, can be used as an additional locking mechanism, allow-ing access to smartphone owners in specific resources inside their smartphone and correspondingly denying access to fake ones.

All resources inside the Android OS are handled through corresponding OS apps or third-party apps. In this sense, private resources can also be present within specific apps, such as file-managers, chat applications and photo gallery applications. Our approach utilizes the provided by the OS UsageStatsManager API and handles it to recognize the foreground app successfully. Then, after the app's initialization, its users may choose from a list of installed and pre-installed apps, in their device, that they need to be securely locked.

More precisely, through the UsageStatsManager API, we have managed to successfully recognize the foreground app, contrary to Android documentation that states that this API is used only for "*Usage data that is aggregated into time intervals: days, weeks, months, and years*", [9]. In our approach, we check for newly created lists of UsageStats in regular time intervals, taking only the latest INTERVAL_DAILY records into consideration. Then, looping through the retrieved list, the most recent record in terms of the timestamp is kept which corresponds to the foreground app's package name. Using this approach, we manage to "segregate" the initially "aggregated" results and detect the user's foreground application.

As a next step, the app starts working in the background, as a service, silently monitoring each launched app in predefined short time intervals. Whenever the service recognizes a launched app that is selected by the user to be securely locked, our app presents a full-screen Android activity, "hiding" it, and thus protecting the app in question. This "protecting" screen can only be bypassed if the user authenticates himself, through our novel smart pattern mechanism. As it will be further analyzed in the following section, the pattern mechanism not only checks whether the correct pattern is being drawn, but also whether the user who is drawing the pattern can be authenticated from his behavioural biometric information while drawing the pattern, through the machine learning core underlying module.

The secure screen provided by our app cannot be bypassed, since even when it is minimized or closed, the running service will continuously keep on re-launching it, having detected a "protected" app in the foreground. A possible attack on our app could be an attempt to uninstall it. This can also be easily protected, by additionally monitoring the "settings" of the device through our application, denying the access of non-authenticated users to the app uninstallation panel.

The proposed secure locking/unlocking mechanism has been designed to be as much "lightweight" and "robust" in using it as possible. Both for supporting user experience (UX) and also for providing the end-user with a mechanism that is very close to the one that he is used to. Indeed, after running several experiments with real hardware devices (not emulators), our results have shown that the entire authentication process, after the user has drawn a pattern in the app, is completed within 100–180 milliseconds which can hardly be noticed by the user.

Above all, the work presented in this paper does not focus only to the app being the final "product", but to the underlying approach, which has been made to further secure smartphones and smart devices in general and protect sensitive resources from malicious users. As a result, the proposed solution could be used in an increasing number of even more use cases, such as two-factor authentication with increased levels of security. Thus, its evaluation results, presented in the following sections, are also considered as of great importance in terms of their scientific contribution.

5   Machine Learning Core

To work with drawn patterns, we need to establish an encoding of the associated data initially. Besides, this encoding must include information about how the user enters the pattern; not only the drawing path, that would enable the Machine Learning (ML) system to learn about a set of pattern inputs and allow for successful predictions.

5.1   Pattern Design and Encoding

To encode the information provided by the unlock pattern, we have established an enriched pattern path (pattern + times) as an array of vectors (one by each existing point in the pattern). According to that, the representation of the resulting, "enriched" pattern follows the following structure:

$$[(X_1, Y_1, t_1), (X_2, Y_2, t_2), ..., (X_n, Y_n, t_n)]$$

where X_i represents the row number of the point regarding the virtual matrix where the pattern is entered, Y_i represents the column number and t_i the time elapsed since the last point was reached (it will be 0 for the first point). Clearly, $(X_i, Y_i) \neq (X_{i+1}, Y_{i+1}) \forall i \in (1, n - 1)$. According to this encoding, the pattern presented in Fig. 1 will be encoded as follows:

$$[(1, 1, 0), (2, 2, t_{AB}), (1, 3, t_{BC}), (2, 3, t_{CD}), (3, 3, t_{DE})]$$

5.2   ML Algorithms Selection and Specifications

Once the enriched pattern representation is defined, it should be possible to generate a model for each user to predict whether each one of the future patterns introduced in the application actually belongs to the "genuine" user. Therefore, and after checking the shape of the pattern, the next step focuses mainly on exact "timing" extraction of the drawn pattern, generating a feature vector composed by each point's timestamp representation in the drawn pattern. Continuing with the same example above, we could have different valid inputs for the pattern shown by Fig. 1 such as:

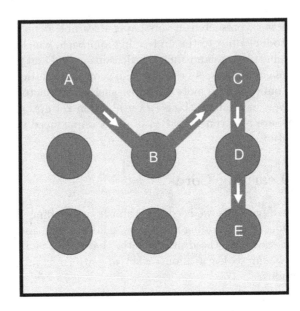

Fig. 1. Example of a pattern input. Adopted from [23].

$$[(1,1,0),(2,2,0.22),(1,3,0.15),(2,3,0.43),(3,3,0.50)]$$

$$[(1,1,0),(2,2,0.17),(1,3,0.15),(2,3,0.41),(3,3,0.57)]$$

$$[(1,1,0),(2,2,0.20),(1,3,0.12),(2,3,0.40),(3,3,0.54)]$$

$$[(1,1,0),(2,2,0.21),(1,3,0.16),(2,3,0.40),(3,3,0.53)]$$

$$[(1,1,0),(2,2,0.23),(1,3,0.14),(2,3,0.42),(3,3,0.53)]$$

After extracting only the time values, the corresponding result will be the following:

$$[0,0.22,0.15,0.43,0.50]$$

$$[0,0.17,0.15,0.41,0.57]$$

$$[0,0.20,0.12,0.40,0.54]$$

$$[0,0.21,0.16,0.40,0.53]$$

$$[0,0.23,0.14,0.42,0.53]$$

Using this known and valid pattern features vectors, it is then possible to generate a dataset to build an ML model, able to predict whether an entered pattern belongs to the real user or not. In this case, it does not seems straightforward to implement a supervised strategy, mainly because it is not possible to learn incorrect pattern inputs. However, it is possible to use some One Class Supervised algorithms (such as One-Class Support Vector Machine, SVM) or another unsupervised ML approaches like clustering. In our case and for the purposes of this study, we have used both, namely a One-Class SVM and also the Clustering approach through the implementation of the K-means algorithm.

One Class SVM Implementation. Using the One-Class SVM algorithm, we managed to learn to distinguish the valid enriched patterns from other invalid ones, using a training dataset only composed by valid samples (only one class). As output, the algorithm will return a binary result (usually 1 and −1), although the result may vary depending on the implementation, language, etc., depending on the sample that has been classified as valid (similar to valid samples used to train the model) or invalid.

K-means Implementation. In this case, after a dimensionality reduction using primary component analysis (PCA), we have used different configurations for the K-means algorithm. Nevertheless, after analyzing the results, we have come up with the findings that the best results have been obtained using 3 and 5 clusters, respectively. The method used for identifying the most representative pattern for the user consists of clustering the training set samples and then selecting the main cluster, that is the one that contains more samples. During the algorithm's final step, we have been able to predict whether an enriched pattern belongs to the user by checking whether it has been positioned into the main cluster of the trained model.

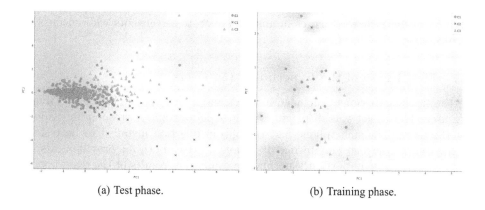

(a) Test phase.   (b) Training phase.

Fig. 2. Clustering samples. Adopted from [23].

Figure 2 illustrates both the training and the testing phase, where the main cluster is "C1".

6 Evaluation Experiment

In this section, we describe the settings of the experiment that has been conducted to evaluate the effectiveness of the resulting app. The experiment involved

64 users, as well as six supervisors in a total of 70 participants, including 2 phases of evaluation. The first phase involved 54 users and the six supervisors, while the second phase involved 10 out of the 54 users and the same supervisors of phase 1.

Specifically, 54 of the evaluation users tested the app's effectiveness of the smart-pattern approach, not being able to be "broken" by other users. Respectively, 10 of the evaluation users tested the app's user-friendliness and focused in its efficiency by considering interaction complexity and minimum false positives.

At this point we should make a short discussion about the different types of user patterns both in terms of complexity that translates into the number of points the users' use and also in terms of complexity that translates in differentiations while drawing the actual pattern, namely quick or slow finger movements and also intended "strategic" pauses of the user in specific parts of the pattern. Our experiment revealed that these criteria are quite significant since both the number of points of the patterns and also the timings involved affect both the effectiveness of the underlying algorithm to reject the false users, but also the system's effectiveness in minimizing false positives of real users. Indeed, as expected, a smart pattern becomes more effective in terms of security as the number of points increases, while users' atomic timings when they are drawing their secure patterns is of equal or even greater importance in terms of app safeguarding.

Figures 3a and 3b represent the initial, simple patterns of the experiment. Of course, the actual patterns that take the timings of the drawn patterns into consideration cannot be visualized in any figure, since for this purpose, video files should be utilized. Figures 4a and 4b illustrate screenshots while using the resulting app.

6.1   First Phase of the Experiment (54 Users)

Settings: The experiment included a tablet and a smartphone for each evaluating user. The tablet was displaying the instructions and corresponding videos for the users. The smartphone had the app in question installed to be tested. A supervisor was also monitoring the whole process, both for providing assisting help and most importantly noting the evaluation results of the experiment. The supervisor was noting for each phase and user attempt, whether the users' attempts were successful (allowing access to the user) or not (denying access to the user). All the supervisors' results were afterwards transferred to a database for further processing and data visualization. Figure 5 illustrates a snapshot of the visualization of users' data involving the five steps/phases of the evaluation that are described following.

Steps: This experiment phase involved five steps, each one corresponding to the four levels of smart-pattern complexity within the evaluation experiment, while there was a fifth step where the users had additional "help" in order to pass the smart pattern test successfully. In each one of the five steps, each user made ten subsequent attempts to bypass the corresponding smart pattern challenge. More specifically, step 1 involved an experiment with the user trying to pass

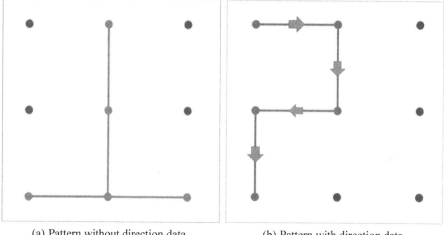

(a) Pattern without direction data.   (b) Pattern with direction data.

Fig. 3. Simple patterns used in the first two steps of the evaluation study. Adopted from [23].

the pattern screen successfully by only seeing an image of the correct pattern, having no motion directions. The reader can imagine a letter that is drawn by the genuine user to unlock a smart device, yet having no clue about the direction of its drawing. Step 2 involved the user trying to pass the smart pattern screen successfully by only seeing an image of the correct pattern, accompanied by small arrows in the image, indicating the correct direction. This step reveals the direction of the patterns, which is hidden in step 1; nevertheless, the users had no indication of the "way" the real users' fingers moved, trying to pass the pattern screen. Step 3 involved the user trying to pass the pattern screen successfully by watching a video of the pattern being drawn by the actual real users of the smartphone, using a common, yet of medium complexity, pattern. Again, Step 3 adds information about the genuine unlock pattern to the user by providing as much information as possible about it. Then, step 4 involved the user trying to successfully pass the pattern screen by watching a video of the pattern being drawn by the actual real users of the smartphone, using a difficult, in terms of higher complexity, pattern. As a result, step 4 is identical to step 3 in terms of information provided to the evaluating users, yet the drawn patterns are considered more "secure". Finally, step 5 was once again similar to the fourth step of the evaluation study, while there was an additional help to the users by giving them the opportunity to watch the video of unlocking the screen one more time to memorize the correct pattern even more.

6.2   Second Phase of the Experiment (10 Users)

Settings: This phase involved ten users using their own mobile, android powered smartphone, where they downloaded, installed and consequently used the app.

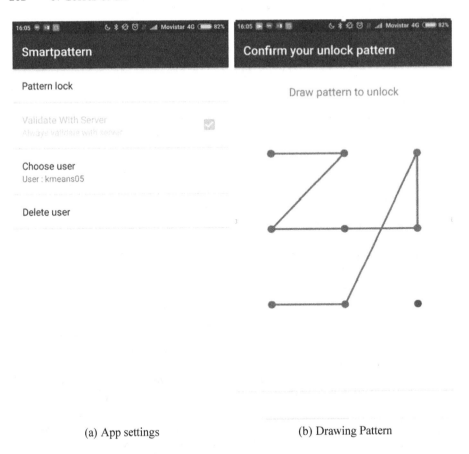

(a) App settings   (b) Drawing Pattern

Fig. 4. Screenshots from the app. Adopted from [23].

The app was downloaded from a web link. A supervisor was also monitoring the whole process, both for assisting purposes and also to note down the results of the evaluation experiment. Correspondingly, all the supervisors' results were again transferred to a database for further processing and result visualization. Phase 1 involved already created user accounts in the smart pattern app, where evaluating users were trying to bypass, as potential attackers. Phase 2 involved genuine users that would use the application in order to successfully authenticate themselves, thus testing the effectiveness of the app from another point of view.

The users followed instructions about how to create their personal pattern and subsequently "train" the model. After successfully creating their patterns, the users made ten subsequent attempts to unlock the app. The supervisor noted the number of successful unlocks by each user.

PHASE 1										PHASE 2										PHASE 3										PHASE 4										PHASE 5									
1	2	3	4	5	6	7	8	9	10	1	2	3	4	5	6	7	8	9	10	1	2	3	4	5	6	7	8	9	10	1	2	3	4	5	6	7	8	9	10	1	2	3	4	5	6	7	8	9	10
F	F	F	F	F	F	F	F	F	F	F	F	F	F	F	F	F	F	F	F	P	F	F	F	F	F	F	P	F	F	F	F	F	F	F	F	F	F	F	F	F	F	F	F	F	F	F	F	F	F
F	F	F	F	F	F	F	F	F	F	F	F	F	F	F	F	F	F	F	F	P	F	F	F	F	F	F	F	F	F	F	F	F	F	F	F	F	F	F	F	F	F	F	F	F	F	F	F	F	F
F	F	F	F	F	F	F	F	F	F	F	F	F	F	F	F	F	F	F	F	P	F	F	F	F	F	F	F	F	F	F	F	F	F	F	F	F	F	F	F	F	F	F	F	F	F	F	F	F	F
F	F	F	P	F	F	F	F	F	F	F	F	F	F	F	F	F	F	F	F	F	F	F	F	F	F	F	F	F	F	F	F	F	F	F	F	F	F	F	F	F	F	F	F	F	F	F	F	F	F
F	F	F	F	F	F	F	F	F	F	F	F	F	F	F	F	F	F	F	F	F	F	F	F	F	F	F	F	F	F	F	F	F	F	F	F	F	F	F	F	F	F	F	F	F	F	F	F	F	F
F	F	F	F	F	F	F	F	F	F	F	F	F	F	F	P	F	F	F	F	F	F	F	F	F	F	F	F	F	F	F	F	F	F	F	F	F	F	F	F	F	F	F	F	F	F	F	F	F	F
F	F	F	F	F	F	F	F	F	F	F	F	F	F	F	F	F	F	F	F	P	F	F	F	F	F	F	F	F	F	F	F	F	F	F	F	F	F	F	F	F	F	F	F	F	F	F	F	F	F
F	F	F	F	F	F	F	F	F	F	F	F	F	F	F	F	F	F	F	F	P	F	F	F	F	F	F	F	F	F	F	F	F	F	F	F	F	F	F	F	F	F	F	F	F	F	F	F	F	F
F	F	F	F	F	F	F	F	F	F	F	F	F	F	F	F	F	F	F	F	F	F	F	F	F	F	F	F	F	F	F	F	F	F	F	F	F	F	F	F	F	F	F	F	F	F	F	F	F	F
F	F	F	F	F	F	F	F	F	F	F	F	F	F	F	F	F	F	F	F	F	F	F	F	F	F	F	F	F	F	F	F	F	F	F	F	F	F	F	F	F	F	F	F	F	F	F	F	F	F
F	F	F	F	F	F	F	F	F	F	F	F	F	F	F	F	F	F	F	F	F	F	F	P	P	F	P	P	F	P	F	F	F	F	F	F	F	F	P	F	F	F	F	F	F	F	F	F	F	F
F	F	F	F	F	F	F	F	F	F	F	F	F	F	F	F	F	F	F	F	P	F	F	F	F	F	F	F	F	F	F	F	F	F	F	F	F	F	F	P	F	F	F	F	F	F	F	F	F	F
F	F	F	F	F	F	F	F	F	F	F	F	F	F	F	F	F	F	F	F	P	P	F	P	P	P	P	P	P	P	F	F	F	F	F	F	F	F	F	F	F	F	F	F	F	F	F	F	F	F

Fig. 5. Visualization of the user evaluation results.

6.3 Results of the Evaluation Experiment

The collected results were merged and analyzed to produce the core of our evaluation experiment. As described above, each user in the first phase made in total 50 attempts to pass each one of the five smart patterns challenges successfully. As for the evaluation results, the 54 evaluation users of the first phase made 2700 attempts in total. After the analysis of the results, from the total of 2700 user attempts, 2530 of them were unsuccessful, meaning that our proposed system had 93.7% success in denying access to unauthorized users. Respectively, in the second phase of the experiment, ten users made ten attempts to unlock the app using their own personal trained model of the smart pattern app. In total, they made 100 attempts, where 86 of them have been successful. As a result, our proposed approach reached 86% in successfully "recognizing" the app's genuine user and consequently accepting his/her access to the app.

For each basic pattern attempt for the attacker, the SmartPattern app blocked the attempts illustrated in percentages in Fig. 6. As a next step of analyzing the results of the evaluation study, each one of the five steps is also discussed. We may easily note that the percentage of the SmartPattern app's security increases, the more "complex" the drawn pattern is. This result might seem expected, however, in our study the complexity level could be translated not only in terms of "more points" but also in terms of "timing pauses", meaning that if the real user had a more "unique" way of drawing the pattern, then this would increase its security level. Another very interesting observation deriving from our study is that malicious users having knowledge only for the "final drawing" and not of the way, in terms of consequent points, that it was drawn did not have much success in "guessing" the correct way of unlocking the pattern. Finally, another significant result of the study is that in the cases of the more complex drawn patterns and consequently their more complex involved timing biometrics, even when the "attackers" had more "help" by watching the pattern being drawn more times in videos, their unlock attempts where still unsuccessful in their vast majority. These results have been quite encouraging, indicating that our research pointed in a good direction, actually providing improvements in the smartphones' unlocking mechanisms.

7   Domains of Application

Our work has been expected to work as the prelude of a more "general" architectural software approach towards better and more securely authenticating users to smart devices. The main reasons for this expectation derive from the fact that more and more smart devices penetrate our daily living, realizing smart environments, smart cities and smart societies. In all these cases, one of the main concerns of people is the protection of their rights. In the digital world, this also denotes their privacy, their security and the control they have on their data. Towards this end, user authentication implies both access to personal data and also, implicitly, user profiling. In this section, we discuss other kinds of smart devices that could incorporate our proposed system, either "as is", or after small changes or calibrations to its structure and algorithms.

To make it accessible and usable for everyone, we have released it as a cloud service for users authentication and processes control as what we have called Block Pattern as a Service (BPaaS). It can be accessed at https://smartpattern. e-paths.com, and can be used through API, Oauth2 or JWT to be integrated into any platform which supports those mechanisms. This, together with a mobile

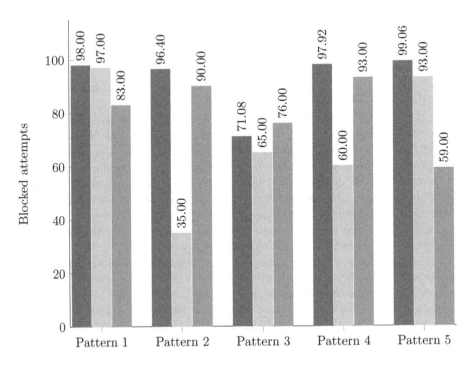

Fig. 6. Attempts blocked by SmartPattern when other users try to unlock the mobile phone. Adopted from [23].

application that requests the user to enter the pattern each time that he needs to login or authorize some operation and send it to the SmartPattern server enables its use in almost any platform which has Internet access, as illustrated in Fig. 7. At the time of writing, we have also published our own SmartPattern mobile application client at Google Play (on the alpha/beta tracks and only accessible through a previous invitation to testers in https://play.google.com/store/apps/details?id=com.elevenpaths.smartpattern). However, everyone could implement her own client using the API specification at https://smartpattern.e-paths.com/apispecification/index.

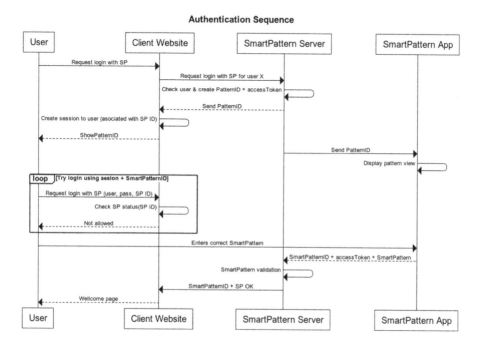

Fig. 7. User authentication example using BPaaS flow diagram.

7.1 Smart Vehicles

With Android Auto being released since 2015 and its corresponding development being realized through a variety of developer tools such as Android Studio, the majority of vehicle vendors have already moved towards the direction of including part of smartphones' functionality into modern vehicles. Both hardware and software in this domain can be compared to a medium-sized tablet included in the vehicle's hardware, which additionally has access to a growing number of vehicle sensors and vehicle-related information.

Since these devices incorporate a touch screen for user-driver interaction, our proposed approach could be incorporated "uncut" under the "light" condition of an established internet connection. Alternatively, a modification of our approach could include the back-end algorithmic model in the hardware device, which would presumably negatively affect its high rates of effectiveness.

7.2 Smart Wearables

Smartwatches and smart wearables, in general, constitute another quite popular domain in smart device technologies, counting tens of millions of installations around the world. Smartwatches and other wearables may incorporate modern OSes such as Wear OS (former Android Wear) which encapsulate quite a large part of Smartphone OS functionalities. In this regard, these devices also include a significant number of sensors that can collect useful information from their physical environment and from the users' context. As a result, other types of user biometric information may be gathered, further processed and, with respect to the proposed architecture, being used for the authentication of their users. Smartwatches incorporate touch screens which are, as expected, much smaller than the ones of the smartphones and thus are not well promoted to be used for complex screen drawn patterns, such as the ones owned by smartphones and tablets. Nevertheless, their accelerometer sensors, as well as other peripheral sensors, such as GPS, can be used by our proposed backend and be calibrated to provide higher levels of user authentication.

7.3 Smart TVs

Smart TVs have also been very popular during the last half-decade, including a number of smart TV OSes such as Android TV and Samsung's Tizen OS. Users are not only buying new Smart TVs, replacing the "older" ones, but they also have the potentiality to add a smart box to almost all older TV terminals, making them smart ones. As a result, a growing number of households and companies around the globe own smart TVs where user authentication is needed for an ever-increasing number of services, either as part of the users' entertainment or even as additional functionalities within the smart home. Nevertheless, security risks exist in these environments too, [21].

Using Smart TVs, our proposed approach can also be beneficial for user authentication. User movement is of course, not captured by touch TV screens in most scenarios; however, this kind of information can be collected through modern smart TV remote controls, operated by users' hands. This information also includes user input timings which are very similar to the information used and processed by our proposed architectural approach.

7.4 Smart IoT Devices

IoT technology is drawing attention from all over the world both in terms of hardware and also in software and its accompanying services. Of course, IoT devices have very large levels of differentiation among them and cannot be easily studied as a whole in terms of user authentication. Nevertheless, smart embedded operating system platforms already exist, e.g. Android Things, which enable the development of software towards user authentication. IoT devices can usually easily embed sensors, sensing the users' environment and correspondingly collect user-specific information. To this end, we argue that IoT devices can also collect useful user biometric-based information, both directly, e.g. direct user interaction, or indirectly, e.g. in cases of capturing user movement through ultra-sonic sensors. The collected data may be further evaluated by machine learning approaches in order to test their effectiveness in successfully authenticating legitimate users, and correspondingly rejecting fraudulent ones.

8 Conclusions

In this paper, the authors have introduced a novel user authentication mechanism for Android smartphones that utilizes Machine Learning using user biometric data. This novel approach can be applied to a significant number of application domains, ranging from general mobile device security, to specifically securing user "sensitive" resources. It can also be used for improving 2FA, while most importantly, there is no need to root users' devices. The evaluation results have been remarkably positive, showing a 93.7% success rate in successfully denying access to unauthorized users and a 86% success rate in successfully allowing access to the "genuine" users of the mobile app. The resulting "lower" success percentage of the proposed approach can be justified, nevertheless. Indeed, it has been the authors' primary objective, when calibrating the ML backend, to maximize user protection, at the expense of lowering the "user-friendliness" level.

The presented evaluation experiments have illustrated strong evidence about our approach's success in correctly "distinguishing" genuine users from malicious users through the way they draw their lock screen patterns. The paper's results also provide the scientific literature with valuable evidence about the efficiency of common lock patterns in securely protecting the smartphones, as well as comparison evidence of current and "newer" smartphone locking approaches that combine biometric data.

As demonstrated in [8], the use of the pattern lock is a very good approach in terms of memorability, but quoting Adam Aviv: "*it is the same as asking people to recall a glyph*". This, together with the conclusions extracted from [15] related with how the mobile phone users statistically define their unlock patterns reinforce the need of a solution like the one proposed in this work, which adds a further dimension to the problem from the attacker's point of view. Some of the aforementioned typical patterns definition rules are the following:

- 77% of Android device users start their pattern on one of the corner dots.
- 44% of Android device users start their pattern from the top-left corner of the first dot.
- Most Android lock screen pattern users use less than five dots, and a significant percentage of them use only four dots.

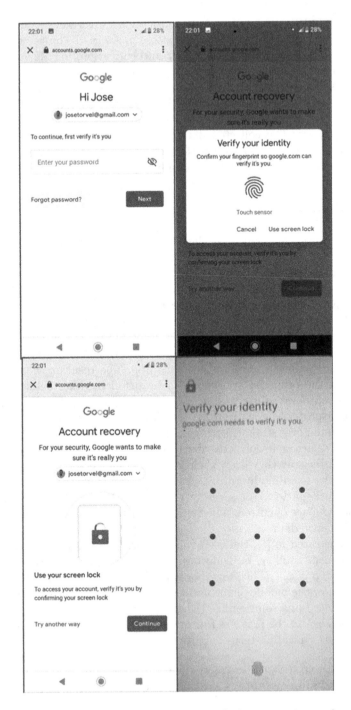

Fig. 8. Remote device account activation using unlock pattern in an already logged phone as account recovery options.

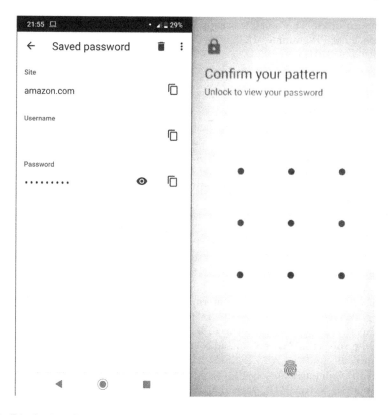

Fig. 9. Displaying Google Chrome saved password using Android device unlock pattern.

– 10% of lock screen patterns are drawn with the shape of a letter of the alphabet, which mostly represents the owners' initial.

An example of the potential of the presented approach is that, after the publication of our paper [23], Google has just started (2019) to use lock patterns as a mechanism to identify the user when performing critical operations, such as unblocking remote devices logged in with the linked Google account (Fig. 8) or access to Google Chrome saved password (Fig. 9). The former is additionally a good example of how the lock pattern can be used at installed applications' level. As expected, as an Android security feature, screenshots are disabled when the user is entering the pattern. However, it is still possible to take a picture of this moment, something that could be avoided by using our proposed technology since even taking a picture of the correct pattern shape it is still impossible to register the user input timings. Of course, our approach is still vulnerable to mobile screen video recording, but even so, it is still difficult to register each finger movement with enough precision to reproduce it without losing anyone.

Acknowledgments. This work was supported by the European Commission under the Horizon 2020 Programme (H2020), as part of the *OPERANDO* project (Grant Agreement no. 653704).

References

1. Alepis, E., Patsakis, C.: Trapped by the UI: the android case. In: Dacier, M., Bailey, M., Polychronakis, M., Antonakakis, M. (eds.) RAID 2017. LNCS, vol. 10453, pp. 334–354. Springer, Cham (2017). https://doi.org/10.1007/978-3-319-66332-6_15
2. Android Police (2017): https://www.androidpolice.com/2017/11/12/google-will-remove-play-store-apps-use-accessibility-services-anything-except-helping-disabled-users/
3. Aviv, A.J., Gibson, K.L., Mossop, E., Blaze, M., Smith, J.M.: Smudge attacks on smartphone touch screens. In: Miller, C., Shacham, H. (eds.) 4th USENIX Workshop on Offensive Technologies, WOOT 2010, Washington, D.C., USA, August 9, 2010. USENIX Association (2010). https://www.usenix.org/conference/woot10/smudge-attacks-smartphone-touch-screens
4. Aviv, A.J., Kuber, R., Budzitowski, D.: Is bigger better when it comes to android graphical pattern unlock? IEEE Internet Comput. **21**(6), 46–51 (2017). https://doi.org/10.1109/MIC.2017.4180833. https://doi.org/10.1109/MIC.2017.4180833
5. Bianchi, A., Corbetta, J., Invernizzi, L., Fratantonio, Y., Kruegel, C., Vigna, G.: What the app is that? deception and countermeasures in the android user interface. In: Proceedings of the 2015 IEEE Symposium on Security and Privacy, pp. 931–948. IEEE Computer Society (2015)
6. Canfora, G., Notte, P.D., Mercaldo, F., Visaggio, C.A.: Silent and continuous authentication in mobile environment. In: Callegari, C., et al. (eds.) Proceedings of the 13th International Joint Conference on e-Business and Telecommunications (ICETE 2016) - Volume 4: SECRYPT, Lisbon, Portugal, 26–28 July 2016, pp. 97–108. SciTePress (2016). https://doi.org/10.5220/0005965500970108
7. Chen, Q.A., Qian, Z., Mao, Z.M.: Peeking into your app without actually seeing it: UI state inference and novel android attacks. In: 23rd USENIX Security Symposium (USENIX Security 2014), pp. 1037–1052. USENIX Association, San Diego (2014)
8. Davin, J., Aviv, A., Wolf, F., Kuber, R.: Baseline measurements of shoulder surfing analysis and comparability for smartphone unlock authentication, pp. 2496–2503, May 2017. https://doi.org/10.1145/3027063.3053221
9. Developers Android (2018). https://developer.android.com/reference/android/app/usage/UsageStatsManager
10. Dunphy, P., Heiner, A.P., Asokan, N.: A closer look at recognition-based graphical passwords on mobile devices. In: Cranor, L.F. (ed.) Proceedings of the Sixth Symposium on Usable Privacy and Security, SOUPS 2010, Redmond, Washington, USA, 14–16 July 2010. ACM International Conference Proceeding Series, vol. 485. ACM (2010). https://doi.org/10.1145/1837110.1837114
11. Elevenpaths (2019). https://play.google.com/store/apps/details?id=com.elevenpaths.smartpattern
12. Kessler, G.C.: Technology corner: calculating the number of android lock patterns: an unfinished study in number theory. JDFSL **8**(4), 57–64 (2013). http://ojs.jdfsl.org/index.php/jdfsl/article/view/243

13. Lee, J., et al.: A visibility-based upper bound for android unlock patterns. IEICE Trans. **99–D**(11), 2814–2816 (2016). https://doi.org/10.1587/transinf. 2016EDL8095

14. Lee, J., Seo, J.W., Cho, K., Lee, P.J., Yum, D.H.: A visibility-based lower bound for android unlock patterns. IEICE Trans. **100–D**(3), 578–581 (2017). https://doi. org/10.1587/transinf.2016EDL8196

15. Loge, M., Duermuth, M., Rostad, L.: On user choice for android unlock patterns. In: Proceedings of the EuroUSEC, January 2016. https://doi.org/10.14722/eurousec. 2016.23001

16. Luca, A.D., Hang, A., Brudy, F., Lindner, C., Hussmann, H.: Touch me once and i know it's you!: implicit authentication based on touch screen patterns. In: Konstan, J.A., Chi, E.H., Höök, K. (eds.) CHI Conference on Human Factors in Computing Systems, CHI 2012, Austin, TX, USA, 05–10 May 2012, pp. 987–996. ACM (2012). https://doi.org/10.1145/2207676.2208544

17. Mahfouz, A., Mahmoud, T.M., Sharaf Eldin, A.: A behavioral biometric authentication framework on smartphones. In: Proceedings of the 2017 ACM on Asia Conference on Computer and Communications Security, pp. 923–925. ACM (2017)

18. Malkin, N., Harbach, M., Luca, A.D., Egelman, S.: The anatomy of smartphone unlocking: why and how android users around the world lock their phones. GetMobile **20**(3), 42–46 (2016). https://doi.org/10.1145/3036699.3036712. http://doi.acm.org/10.1145/3036699.3036712

19. Meng, W.: Evaluating the effect of multi-touch behaviours on android unlock patterns. Inf. Comput. Secur. **24**(3), 277–287 (2016). https://doi.org/10.1108/ICS-12-2014-0078

20. Nicholson, A.J., Corner, M.D., Noble, B.D.: Mobile device security using transient authentication. IEEE Trans. Mob. Comput. **5**(11), 1489–1502 (2006). https://doi. org/10.1109/TMC.2006.169

21. Nikas, A., Alepis, E., Patsakis, C.: I know what you streamed last night: On the security and privacy of streaming. Dig. Invest. **25**, 78–89 (2018). https://doi.org/ 10.1016/j.diin.2018.03.004

22. Teh, P.S., Zhang, N., Teoh, A.B.J., Chen, K.: A survey on touch dynamics authentication in mobile devices. Comput. Secur. **59**, 210–235 (2016)

23. Torres, J., de los Santos, S., Alepis, E., Patsakis, C.: Behavioral biometric authentication in android unlock patterns through machine learning. In: Mori, P., Furnell, S., Camp, O. (eds.) Proceedings of the 5th International Conference on Information Systems Security and Privacy, ICISSP 2019, Prague, Czech Republic, 23–25 February 2019, pp. 146–154. SciTePress (2019). https://doi.org/10.5220/ 0007394201460154

24. Wikipedia (2018). https://en.wikipedia.org/wiki/FBI%E2%80%93Apple_ encryption_dispute/

Threat Modeling and Attack Simulations of Connected Vehicles: Proof of Concept

Wenjun Xiong[✉], Fredrik Krantz, and Robert Lagerström

School of Electrical Engineering and Computer Science,
KTH Royal Institute of Technology, Stockholm, Sweden
{wenjx,fkra,robertl}@kth.se

Abstract. A modern vehicle contains over a hundred Electronic Control Units (ECUs) that communicate over in-vehicle networks, and can also be connected to external networks making them vulnerable to cyber attacks. To improve the security of connected vehicles, threat modeling can be applied to proactively find potential security issues and help manufacturers to design more secure vehicles. It can also be combined with probabilistic attack simulations to provide quantitative security measurements, which has not been commonly used while shown efficient in other domains. This paper reviews research in the field, showing that not much work has been done in the combined area of connected vehicles and threat modeling with attack simulations. We have implemented and conducted attack simulations on two vehicle threat models using a tool called securiCAD. Our work serves as a proof of concept of the approach and indicates that the approach is useful. Especially if more research of vehicle-specific vulnerabilities, weaknesses, and countermeasures is done in order to provide more accurate analyses, and to include this in a more tailored vehicle metamodel.

Keywords: Threat modeling · Attack simulations · Vehicles · Cyber security

1 Introduction

Modern vehicles are often connected to the Internet, and they contain more than 100 Electronic Control Units (ECUs) that control brakes, airbags, parts of the engine, and so on. This combination of ECUs, sensors, and network buses creates a computerized system. Vehicles seem to be vulnerable to exploits in several ways, and a malicious actor getting access to vital ECUs can have dire safety consequences. Vehicle vulnerabilities have been reported numerous times, e.g. in the National Vulnerability Database (NVD)[1]. One famous example of exploiting vehicle vulnerabilities is when two ethical hackers acquired remote control of a 2014 Jeep Cherokee[2].

---

[1] https://nvd.nist.gov/.
[2] https://www.wired.com/2015/07/hackers-remotely-kill-jeep-highway/.

© Springer Nature Switzerland AG 2020
P. Mori et al. (Eds.): ICISSP 2019, CCIS 1221, pp. 272–287, 2020.
https://doi.org/10.1007/978-3-030-49443-8_13

To improve the security of Internet-facing systems e.g. vehicles, one approach is to use methods for modeling and analysis. One can with this understand what parts of the system are the most weak ones, and how they can be secured. Threat modeling is one such way of working with proactive cyber security and security by design [34], moreover, the most recent trend is to combine it with attack simulations to provide quantitative security measurements [13,33], e.g. Time-To-Compromise (TTC) [7,10]. This fairly new approach has been applied successfully in domains like energy [30]. This paper serves as a proof of concept of the approach on connected vehicles.

A threat modeling and risk management tool called securiCAD[3] is used in this work, where users can model e.g. home Local Area Networks (LANs), large corporate networks, and SCADA systems. In securiCAD, different defense strategies are assigned to different assets, and the built-in simulation engine is used to show the probabilities of different attacks succeeding. Some attack types that can be simulated include Denial of Service (DoS), device compromise, and replay attacks [6]. Furthermore, our literature review and practical tests using securiCAD show that threat modeling and attack simulations for vehicles is promising, while some aspects need to be further considered in future research for it be more efficient and successful.

This paper is an extension of the paper presented at the 5th International Conference on Information Systems Security and Privacy in Prague, Czech Republic [33]. The extension includes: 1) related work on vehicle privacy is added in Sect. 2; 2) more detailed vehicle threat modeling steps and one more vehicle model is added in Sect. 3; 3) further described simulation results for the vehicle models in Sect. 4; 4) further discussed proof of concept in vehicle threat modeling and attack simulations in Sect. 5, and more detailed conclusions in Sect. 6.

2   Related Work

2.1   Threat Modeling and Attack Simulations

Threat modeling is proposed as a solution for secure application development and system security evaluations, and it aims to be more proactive and make it more difficult for attackers to accomplish their malicious intents. The work by Shostack [26] and the Microsoft Threat Modeling tool[4] are commonly used in this area. In [31], the authors studied the usefulness of the Microsoft Threat Modeling tool and showed that the tool improved their work on threat modeling. However, it is mainly used for designing secure software applications, and often not for considering the system from a holistic point of view. In [27], SPARTA was proposed to combine Data Flow Diagram (DFD)-based threat modeling with security and privacy solutions. Risk analysis simulations based on concrete element value estimates, countermeasure strengths, and attacker types provide a prioritized list of threats that should be elicited.

---

[3] https://www.foreseeti.com/.
[4] https://www.microsoft.com/en-us/download/details.aspx?id=49168.

Another way of working with threat modeling is to use attack trees or attack graphs [14,23,25]. Attack graphs are widely accepted and used, while there are plenty of known problems. For instance, in [19] the authors stated that previous work on attack graphs has not provided an account of the scalability of the graph generating process, and there is often a lack of logical formalism in the representation of attack graphs, which results in the attack graph being difficult to use and understand by human beings. As a response to these known problems in threat modeling and attack simulations, some approaches have been proposed. For example, pwnPr3d [10] and MAL (the Meta Attack Language) [7] were proposed focusing on providing probabilistic security measures.

2.2   Vehicle Security and Privacy

Previously, vehicle Original Equipment Manufacturers (OEMs) did not consider cyber attacks that much, since an attack was only possible if an attacker had physical access to the vehicle. However, as modern vehicles have multiple wireless connections to both outside networks and devices (e.g. Bluetooth, Internet), they are vulnerable to cyber attacks[5]. Some vehicle vulnerabilities are recorded in NVD, and each of them is associated with a CVE[6] number and CVSS score[7] for analyzing its severity.

To help improving the security of modern vehicles, [32] conducted an empirical study to identify common security vulnerabilities discovered in vehicles. The vulnerability information was gathered for 60 vehicle OEMs and common vehicle components from NVD. The analysis results showed that about 50% of the vulnerabilities fall into the medium severity category, and the three most common software weaknesses reported are protection mechanism failure, buffer errors, and information disclosure.

By using threat modeling for vehicles, the process proposed by [20] starts with defining automotive security use cases, then identifying assets and threats by using the STRIDE method, and finally rating risks and evaluating the threat level and impact level against the found threats. Besides, for assessing the risks of exploiting vehicular on-board networks, [24] automatically generated and analyzed attack graphs, which could aid vehicle development by automatically rechecking the architecture for attack combinations. In [12] the authors adapted two threat modeling methods - TARA and STRIDE from the computer industry to fit the needs of the automotive industry. Also, in [16] an approach to threat modeling to better fit the automotive systems was proposed, a proof of concept implementation of their approach was implemented but without further validation.

Possible security mechanisms to secure vehicles internal communications were addressed in the Holisec project[8], including message authentication codes (MAC)

---

[5] https://www.cpomagazine.com/cyber-security/connected-cars-a-new-and-dangerous-vector-for-cyber-attacks/.

[6] https://cve.mitre.org/.

[7] https://www.first.org/cvss/.

[8] http://autosec.se/wp-content/uploads/2018/04/1.2-holisec-state-of-the-art.pdf.

for traffic integrity, firewalls both for external traffic and for internal traffic implemented in gateway ECUs, use of Intrusion Detection Systems (IDSs) to detect unusual activities on the networks, and certificates for identification of various devices. Security mechanisms were also addressed in [3] to mitigate the threats on assets, which include access control, packet filter firewall, message authentication, etc. Considering the privacy issues of vehicular data, the work by [35] presented a privacy specification for vehicles, which used MAL [7] to assess the security of connected vehicles with a special focus on the privacy aspect.

3   Vehicle Threat Modeling

According to a survey conducted by Miller and Valasek [17], the two most hackable vehicle models are the 2014 Jeep Cherokee and 2015 Cadillac Escalade. Therefore, these two models are used for our proof of concept work.

The threat modeling is done using securiCAD, a tool that can automatically generate probabilistic attack graphs from a given system specification, and serves as an inference engine that produces predictive security analysis results. The threat models can be built by using drag-and-drop functionality with pre-defined assets and associations. Each asset has certain security properties and attack types associated with it. For example, a `Network` asset has e.g. DoS, ARP cache poisoning, and compromise attacks listed.

3.1   Creating Threat Models

For modeling and analyzing vehicles, the first thing is to understand the internal network of a vehicle, and the main assets in it. The main assets in a connected vehicle include `ECU`, `SoftwareProduct`, `Dataflow`, `Protocol`, and `Network`. The most common `Protocols` in vehicle communication include CAN, LIN (Local Interconnect Network), MOST (Media Oriented Systems Transport), and FlexRay.

A `Host` is described as a kernel of an operating system in securiCAD, and is used to represent PCs or servers, thus here it is used to represent ECUs. In order to model the associations between the assets, a `Service` and a `Client` can be connected to each `ECU`, while an `ECU` does not require both of them, e.g. an `ECU` will be connected to a `Client` only if it is required to send data to other ECUs.

The software used on these ECUs is either made entirely by the OEMs, or applies existing architecture standards to define the functions of each ECU, e.g., AUTOSAR[9], which is a standardized software framework for vehicles and offers a multi-level security architecture among others. Many OEMs and third-party developers are members of AUTOSAR today and the number of members is still growing [5,11]. Therefore, a `SoftwareProduct` that represents AUTOSAR is connected to each `ECU`, as well as its `Services` and `Clients`. Moreover, `Dataflow`

---

[9] https://www.autosar.org/.

is connected to each `Network`, and is also connected to `Services` and `Clients` of `ECUs` to represent the communication between them. The communication here denotes the access that `Service` and `Client` have to the commands and function calls in the kernel. The following two examples show how we created the threat models and the reasoning behind it.

2014 Jeep Cherokee Model. The 2014 Jeep Cherokee threat model is created according to its network topology [17]. As is shown in Fig. 1(a), the vehicle network topology contains two CAN `Networks` (CAN-C, CAN-IHS) and one LIN

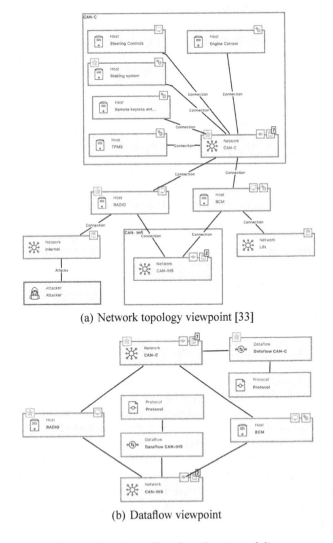

(a) Network topology viewpoint [33]

(b) Dataflow viewpoint

Fig. 1. 2014 Jeep Cherokee threat modeling.

Network. CAN-C is a Low Speed CAN Network that connects ECUs e.g. steering controls, brakes, tire pressure monitoring system (TPMS) that are considered safety-critical. CAN-IHS is an Interior High Speed CAN Network that connects the comfort systems e.g. radio, climate controls. The LIN Network connects ECUs e.g. rear view mirror, and lamps. Also, a RADIO box is connected to these two CAN Networks.

A Body Control Module (BCM) connects both of the two CAN Networks and the LIN Network. It ensures the information exchange in spite of different of data transmission rates in each network. Also, we connect it to Dataflow (see in Fig. 1(b)) as it controls and sends commands to other ECUs, which acts as a gateway among different networks and can be compared to an Ethernet switch.

Besides, the dataflow viewpoint in Fig. 1(b) shows that the network Protocols are connected to their corresponding Dataflows, which regulate the communication between ECUs within the Networks, and also reflect that all messages from ECUs connected to the CAN Network are broadcast.

Furthermore, an Attacker is added to the Internet Network that connects with RADIO to make the threat model complete, with connection type "Compromise" (see in Fig. 1(a)), which indicates the entry point of this attack.

2015 Cadillac Escalade Model. Similarly, the 2015 Cadillac Escalade threat model is created according to its topology [17]. As is shown in Fig. 2, the network topology consists of three CAN Networks (i.e. PT-CAN, Low Speed GMLAN, and High Speed GMLAN), one LIN Network, and one MOST Network, where PT-CAN is the power train CAN protocol, and GMLAN is a CAN protocol for lower layer services.

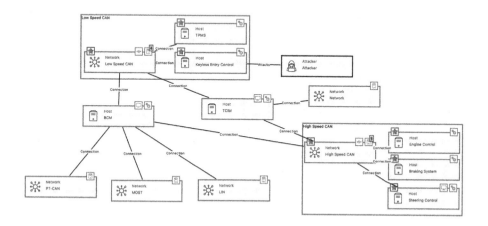

Fig. 2. 2015 Cadillac Escalade threat modeling.

The Low Speed CAN Network connects ECUs e.g. keyless entry control module, and telematics communication interface module (TCIM), etc. The High Speed CAN Network connects ECUs e.g. engine control module, braking system, steering control, etc.

Also, the Clients of both BCM and TCIM are connected to the low and high speed CAN Dataflows (not shown in the figure), because BCM includes ECUs e.g. steering control, pedals, and meters that need to send commands. Besides, we connect the Service of TCIM to both the Low Speed CAN Network and Dataflow (not shown in the figure), as TCIM contains a cellular connection required by the keyless entry control ECU within the Low Speed CAN Network.

Furthermore, we add an Attacker to the keyless entry control ECU, to simulate a scene where an attacker performs a keyless entry attack to gain unauthorized access and manipulate the vehicle. Note that an Attacker can be connected to other assets, modeling different entry points.

3.2 Security Settings

Based on the threat models we created, we assign security settings for each asset. This also includes the consequence for each attack, where the value ranges from 0 to 10 (with 10 being the most severe). Using the system model with security settings and the consequences of attacks securiCAD calculate quantitative measurements, e.g. risks according to the following equation:

$$Risk = Consequence \times Probability \tag{1}$$

As both the two vehicle models apply a SoftwareProduct called AUTOSAR, which also defines the function of the ECUs. Thus, we set the security settings for ECU and SoftwareProduct (i.e. AUTOSAR) of both the two threat models according to AUTOSAR classic documentation[10], and the reasons behind can be seen in Table 1 and Table 2, respectively.

A Network has countermeasures including DNSSec, PortSecurity and Static ARP Tables that are TCP/IP related. For the two CAN Networks, DNSSec settings are disabled. Both Services and Clients connected to ECUs have a countermeasure named Patched that is enabled.

Besides, a Protocol is connected to Dataflow, which gives options to choose different security implementations to apply on the communication over the networks, and the security measurements available are Authenticated, Encrypted and Nonce, where Authenticated is disabled from the security settings of CAN network Protocol[11].

---

[10] https://www.autosar.org/standards/classic-platform/.

[11] https://can-newsletter.org/uploads/media/raw/d904c90ba599c668e9758ae558 dcb845.pdf.

Table 1. ECU security settings.

Defense	Description	Source for decision	Decision
ASLR	Address space layout randomization (ASLR) fortifies against buffer overflow attacks	Not implemented in AUTOSAR classic	Disabled
AntiMalware	It detects, removes and deters malware attacks	Not implemented	Disabled
DEP	Data Execution Prevention (DEP) defends against buffer overflow, by making memory areas non-executable	Not implemented in AUTOSAR classic	Disabled
Hardened	It represents the procedures where unused services, ports and hardware outlets are disabled	The open ports are found by Miller and Valasek in the radio box	Disabled for RADIO in Jeep model; enabled for other ECUs for both two models
HostFirewall	A firewall controls whether dataflow is blocked or allowed between hosts	No public information is available about how OEMs configure their firewalls	Unset
Patched	It means the host has the latest security updates	An Internet connection gives improved software support and patch availability	Patched with probability=50% for BCM in both two models; enabled for other ECUs
Properly Configured	It denotes that the asset is properly configured with regards to access control	No information available	Unset
Static ARP Tables	It means mapping IP address to MAC address to avoid spoofing	Only available for Ethernet	Disabled

2014 Jeep Cherokee Model. Here we assign the consequence for each attack under this model, and their underlying reasons. For example,

– Consequences of compromising Engine control, Transmission and Brake control ECUs are set to 10, because these ECUs are safety-critical, and the compromises of them could lead to fatal road accidents.
– Consequence of compromising RADIO is set to 3, as it is not so safety-critical.
– Consequence of a DoS attack on CAN-C Network is set to 9, because a DoS attack can shut down the access to ECUs of the network, and lead to fatal road accidents.

Table 2. SoftwareProduct security settings.

Defense	Description	Source for decision	Decision
HasVendor Support	Whether the software product is supported and has access to patches	The model has an Internet connection and is assumed to be supported	Enabled
NoPatchable Vulnerability	Whether the software product has no patchable vulnerabilities	No information available	Unset
NoUnPatchable Vulnerability	Whether the software product has no unpatchable vulnerabilities	No information available	Unset
SafeLanguages	The software product is developed in languages that perform checking to reduce the risk of buffer overflow	No information available	Unset
Scrutinized	Whether the software has been thoroughly tested and checked for vulnerabilities	No information available	Unset
SecretBinary	Whether there is an access to the binary by an attacker who can then detect vulnerabilities (no access to the binary makes it impossible to find new vulnerabilities)	No information available	Unset
SecretSource	Whether the source code is a secret source	AUTOSAR is an open-source	Disabled
StaticCode Analysis	Whether there is a code analysis tool to find vulnerabilities and bugs	No information available	Unset

- Consequence of a replay attack on CAN-C Network is set to 10, which represents the actual attack [18].

2015 Cadillac Escalade Model. Similarly, we assign consequences for attacks in the threat model. Since there is no public information showing the exact consequence value we instead provide arguments for our decisions. For example,

- Consequences of compromising Engine control, Braking system and Steering control ECUs are set to 10.
- Consequence of compromising TCIM is set to 3, as it is not so safety-critical.
- Consequence of a DoS attack on Low Speed CAN Network is set to 9, because a DoS attack can shut down the access to ECUs of the network, and lead to fatal road accidents.
- Consequence of compromising the keyless entry control ECU is set to 8, as it (in itself) should not lead to fatal road accidents compared to the former

one. To prevent an attacker accessing the vehicle through compromising the keyless entry control `ECU` and then steal it, we can add `AccessControl` to the `ECU`, and see how it can change the attack path.

4   Vehicle Attack Simulations

After assigning the security settings to the created threat models, we are able to run the attack simulations. The simulation results include risk matrix, attack path, and Time to Compromise (TTC) graph, where the TTC graph presents the probability distribution based on a certain attack path of the expected time for an attacker to compromise an asset.

4.1   Risk Matrix

With the threat model and the security settings of the 2014 Jeep Cherokee Model, when we disable the `HostFirewall` of the `RADIO`, and the resulting risk matrix (shown in Fig. 3(a)) according to Equation (1) shows that the vehicle is not under critical risks. However, when the `HostFirewall` is disabled, the replay attack on CAN-C `Dataflow` is ranked Critical (shown in Fig. 3(b)), which reflects that the firewall is quite important to secure the network.

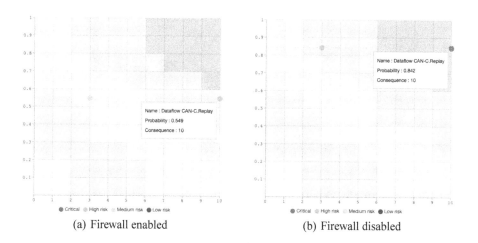

(a) Firewall enabled   (b) Firewall disabled

Fig. 3. Risk matrix from simulations performed on the 2014 Jeep Cherokee model. [33].

Besides, if we change the security setting for `RADIO` from Disabled (see in Table 1) to Enabled, all possible attacks are ranked below Medium according to the simulation results.

4.2 Attack Path

The simulation results also show the attack path of an attack, which represent the possible composition of vulnerabilities used by an attacker. For the 2014 Jeep Cherokee Model, Fig. 4 indicates the attack path of the replay attack on CAN-C `Network`, where the unknown service indicates the D-bus service accessed in an actual attack [18], and they discovered that D-bus was running as root, which enabled them to get access to the vehicle remotely. Also, the green circle shows the countermeasures that could be implemented in this vehicle. We can see that most of the attack steps are related to `RADIO`, and we infer that the `Hardened` setting of `RADIO` is very important as it can be (is) the entry point for an attack. Besides, the width of the lines between attack (defense) steps indicates the likelihood of the attack path.

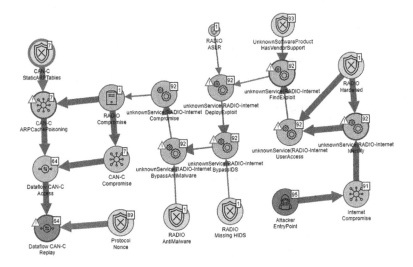

Fig. 4. Attack path of the Jeep replay attack. [33].

Similarly, with the threat model and the security settings, we can get the simulation results for the 2015 Cadillac Escalade Model. For example, the attack path of a keyless entry attack is shown in Fig. 5(a). If we add an `AccessControl` to the keyless entry control `ECU` it will be much more difficult for the attacker to compromise the keyless entry control `ECU` and steal the vehicle, the attack path for this can be seen in Fig. 5(b).

4.3 Time-To-Compromise (TTC)

TTC is used as a measurement of the effort for an attacker to conduct a successful attack. We assume that the attacker will take the shortest path, i.e. the least time-consuming way to the end node. The TTC of the replay attack on CAN-C

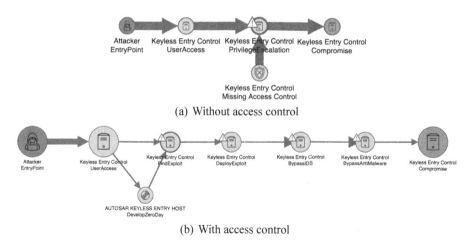

(a) Without access control

(b) With access control

Fig. 5. Attack path of a keyless entry attack on Cadillac Escalade.

`Dataflow` can be seen in Fig. 6, which indicates how many days it takes to reach a certain probability of successfully compromising an asset. In this case, TTC for the replay attack to compromise the `Dataflow` is 20 days with a 50% probability, or is 10 days with a probability above 40%.

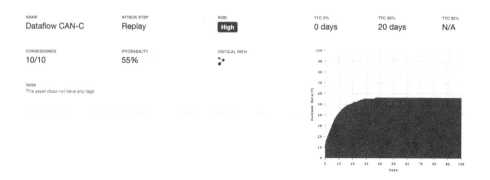

Fig. 6. TTC of a Jeep replay attack. [33].

Overall, the attack simulation results show that the modeled vehicles are not fully secure (as we also know from the real attacks we mimic). According to the risk matrix, we can infer the risk level of the vehicle. Also, we can change the security settings to see how it could influence the overall security level (e.g. Fig. 3). According to the attack path, we know what other countermeasures that can be implemented. At last, TTC provides a measurement of how secure the vehicle is in terms of attack resilience, which provides us a quantitative way of comparing vehicle architecture designs.

5   Discussion

In this paper, holistic threat modeling and quantitative attack simulations are conducted for the two most hackable vehicle models [17]-2014 Jeep Cherokee and 2015 Cadillac Escalade.

The simulation results works as a proof of concept of the approach. As creating large attack graphs for complicate systems manually is time-consuming and error-prone, this approach allows holistic identification and ranking of security-related threats that are likely to affect the vehicles. Also, the set of attack types and associated countermeasures (defenses) related to each asset in a vehicle could be explored and validated further. There are plenty of attacks known to the public for e.g. web applications and Windows-based systems, however, most of them might not be relevant for vehicles [4,28]. On the other hand, there might be certain attacks only related to vehicle systems. When it comes to countermeasures, a vehicle has certain limitations regarding performance, cost, and functionality that might not appear in other larger systems.

It appears that having a firewall is quite important to secure the vehicle [21]. Also, other assets e.g. the keyless entry control ECU can be entry points of attackers and therefore access control could be implemented as a countermeasure [1,2]. Therefore, designing network architectures is also important to vehicle security [9,29].

Furthermore, in order for the approach to be more efficient and for simulation results to be more useful, a metamodel that describes the fundamental assets and their associations of systems [8,15,22] needs to be tailored to fit the internal architecture of vehicles. Also, vehicle-specific statistical studies relating attacks and defenses quantitatively are still needed. This can be realized through hacking exercises or expert studies. Another important step is to validate and test the approach with case studies by modeling vehicles and iteratively enhancing the approach, similar work has been done in the energy domain [30]. Quantitative measures of security (e.g. TTC) require quantitative inputs in order to provide reasonable and useful output. Although it has been done for other system types, vehicle-specific statistical studies relating attacks and defenses are still need to be done.

6   Conclusion

This paper presents a proof of concept of an approach for connected vehicles using threat modeling coupled with attack simulations. Two vehicle models and publicly known attacks were modeled with a tool called securiCAD, showing that the approach is useful in its current state and allows holistic identification and ranking of vehicle security flaws, whereas a more vehicle-specific metamodel would be useful to describe the fundamental assets and associations of vehicles. Future work also includes studying vehicle-specific vulnerabilities, weaknesses, and countermeasures to provide more accurate attack simulation results.

Acknowledgment. This work has received funding from Vinnova, the Swedish Innovation Agency, and the FFI program.

References

1. Alrabady, A., Mahmud, S.: Analysis of attacks against the security of keyless-entry systems for vehicles and suggestions for improved designs. IEEE Trans. Veh. Technol. **54**(1), 41–50 (2005)
2. van de Beek, S., Leferink, F.: Vulnerability of remote keyless-entry systems against pulsed electromagnetic interference and possible improvements. IEEE Trans. Electromagn. Compat. **58**(4), 1259–1265 (2016)
3. Buttigieg, R., Farrugia, M., Meli, C.: Security issues in controller area networks in automobiles. In: 18th International Conference on Sciences and Techniques of Automatic Control and Computer Engineering, pp. 1–6 (2017)
4. Checkoway, S., et al.: Comprehensive experimental analyses of automotive attack surfaces. In: USENIX Security Symposium, San Francisco, pp. 77–92 (2011)
5. Dakermandji, J.: An autosar diagnostic platform. Master's thesis, KTH Royal Institute of Technology, Stockholm, Sweden (2008)
6. Ekstedt, M., Johnson, P., Lagerstrom, R., Gorton, D., Nydrén, J., Shahzad, K.: Securi CAD by foreseeti: a CAD tool for enterprise cyber security management. In: 2015 IEEE 19th International Enterprise Distributed Object Computing Workshop (EDOCW), pp. 152–155. IEEE (2015)
7. Johnson, P., Lagerström, R., Ekstedt, M.: A meta language for threat modeling and attack simulations. In: Proceedings of the 13th International Conference on Availability, Reliability and Security, p. 38. ACM (2018)
8. Johnson, P., Lagerström, R., Ekstedt, M., Österlind, M.: It Management with Enterprise Architecture. KTH, Stockholm (2014)
9. Johnson, P., Lagerström, R., Närman, P., Simonsson, M.: Extended influence diagrams for system quality analysis. J. Software **2**(3), 30–42 (2007)
10. Johnson, P., Vernotte, A., Ekstedt, M., Lagerström, R.: pwnPr3d: an attack-graph-driven probabilistic threat-modeling approach. In: Proceedings of the 11th International Conference on Availability, Reliability and Security, pp. 278–283. IEEE (2016)
11. Karahasanovic, A.: Automotive cyber security: threat modeling of the AUTOSAR standard. Master's thesis, University of Gothenburg, Gothenburg, Sweden (2016)
12. Karahasanovic, A., Kleberger, P., Almgren, M.: Adapting threat modeling methods for the automotive industry. In: Proceedings of the 15th ESCAR Conference, pp. 1–10. Chalmers Publication Library (2017)
13. Katsikeas, S., Johnson, P., Hacks, S., Lagerström, R.: Probabilistic modeling and simulation of vehicular cyber attacks: an application of the meta attack language. In: Proceedings of the 5th International Conference on Information Systems Security and Privacy (ICISSP) (2019)
14. Kordy, B., Mauw, S., Radomirović, S., Schweitzer, P.: Foundations of attack-defense trees. In: Degano, P., Etalle, S., Guttman, J. (eds.) FAST 2010. LNCS, vol. 6561, pp. 80–95. Springer, Heidelberg (2011). https://doi.org/10.1007/978-3-642-19751-2_6

15. Lagerström, R., Johnson, P., Höök, D.: Architecture analysis of enterprise systems modifiability-models, analysis, and validation. J. Syst. Softw. **83**(8), 1387–1403 (2010)
16. Ma, Z., Schmittner, C.: Threat modeling for automotive security analysis. Adv. Sci. Technol. Lett. **139**, 333–339 (2016)
17. Miller, C., Valasek, C.: A survey of remote automotive attack surfaces. In: BlackHat USA (2014)
18. Miller, C., Valasek, C.: Remote exploitation of an unaltered passenger vehicle. In: BlackHat USA (2015)
19. Ou, X., Boyer, W.F., McQueen, M.A.: A scalable approach to attack graph generation. In: Proceedings of the 13th ACM Conference on Computer and Communications Security, pp. 336–345. ACM (2006)
20. Park, J.S., Kim, D., Hong, S., Lee, H., Myeong, E.: Case study for defining security goals and requirements for automotive security parts using threat modeling. In: SAE Technical Paper. SAE International (2018). https://doi.org/10.4271/2018-01-0014
21. Pesé, M.D., Schmidt, K., Zweck, H.: Hardware/software co-design of an automotive embedded firewall. In: SAE Technical Paper. SAE International (2017)
22. Saat, J., Winter, R., Franke, U., Lagerstrom, R., Ekstedt, M.: Analysis of it/business alignment situations as a precondition for the design and engineering of situated it/business alignment solutions. In: 2011 44th Hawaii International Conference on System Sciences, pp. 1–9. IEEE (2011)
23. Saini, V., Duan, Q., Paruchuri, V.: Threat modeling using attack trees. J. Comput. Sci. Coll. **23**(4), 124–131 (2008)
24. Salfer, M., Eckert, C.: Attack graph-based assessment of exploitability risks in automotive on-board networks. In: Proceedings of the 13th International Conference on Availability, Reliability and Security, pp. 1–10. ACM (2018)
25. Salter, C., Saydjari, O.S.S., Schneier, B., Wallner, J.: Toward a secure system engineering methodology. In: Proceedings of the 1998 Workshop on New Security Paradigms, pp. 2–10. ACM (1998)
26. Shostack, A.: Threat Modeling: Designing for Security. Wiley, Indianapolis (2014)
27. Sion, L., Van Landuyt, D., Yskout, K., Joosen, W.: Sparta: security & privacy architecture through risk-driven threat assessment. In: 2018 IEEE International Conference on Software Architecture Companion (ICSA-C), pp. 1–4. IEEE (2018)
28. Välja, M., Korman, M., Lagerström, R.: A study on software vulnerabilities and weaknesses of embedded systems in power networks. In: Proceedings of the 2nd Workshop on Cyber-Physical Security and Resilience in Smart Grids, pp. 47–52. ACM (2017)
29. Van Bulck, J., Mühlberg, T., Piessens, F.: Vulcan: efficient component authentication and software isolation for automotive control networks. In: ACM International Conference Proceeding Series, pp. 225–237 (2017)
30. Vernotte, A., Välja, M., Korman, M., Björkman, G., Ekstedt, M., Lagerström, R.: Load balancing of renewable energy: a cyber security analysis. Energy Inform. **1**(1), 1–41 (2018). https://doi.org/10.1186/s42162-018-0010-x
31. Williams, I., Yuan, X.: Evaluating the effectiveness of microsoft threat modeling tool. In: Proceedings of the 2015 Information Security Curriculum Development Conference, p. 9. ACM (2015)
32. Xiong, W., Gülsever, M., Kaya, K.M., Lagerström, R.: A study of security vulnerabilities and software weaknesses in vehicles. In: Askarov, A., Hansen, R.R., Rafnsson, W. (eds.) NordSec 2019. LNCS, vol. 11875, pp. 204–218. Springer, Cham (2019). https://doi.org/10.1007/978-3-030-35055-0_13

33. Xiong, W., Krantz, F., Lagerström, R.: Threat modeling and attack simulations of connected vehicles: a research outlook. In: Proceedings of the 5th International Conference on Information Systems Security and Privacy (ICISSP) (2019)
34. Xiong, W., Lagerström, R.: Threat modeling - a systematic literature review. Comput. Secur. **84**, 53–69 (2019)
35. Xiong, W., Lagerström, R.: Threat modeling of connected vehicles: a privacy analysis and extension of vehiclelang. In: International Conference on Cyber Incident Response, Coordination, Containment & Control (Cyber Incident). IEEE (2019)

The Security of the Speech Interface: A Modelling Framework and Proposals for New Defence Mechanisms

Mary K. Bispham$^{(\boxtimes)}$, Ioannis Agrafiotis, and Michael Goldsmith

Department of Computer Science, University of Oxford, Oxford OX1 3QD, UK
{mary.bispham,ioannis.agrafiotis,michael.goldsmith}@cs.ox.ac.uk

Abstract. This paper presents an attack and defence modelling framework for conceptualising the security of the speech interface. The modelling framework is based on the Observe-Orient-Decide-Act (OODA) loop model, which has been used to analyse adversarial interactions in a number of other areas. We map the different types of attacks that may be executed via the speech interface to the modelling framework, and present a critical analysis of the currently available defences for countering such attacks, with reference to the modelling framework. The paper then presents proposals for the development of new defence mechanisms that are grounded in the critical analysis of current defences. These proposals envisage a defence capability that would enable voice-controlled systems to detect potential attacks as part of their dialogue management functionality. In accordance with this high-level defence concept, the paper presents two specific proposals for defence mechanisms to be implemented as part of dialogue management functionality to counter attacks that exploit unintended functionality in speech recognition functionality and natural language understanding functionality. These defence mechanisms are based on the novel application of two existing technologies for security purposes. The specific proposals include the results of two feasibility tests that investigate the effectiveness of the proposed mechanisms in defending against the relevant type of attack.

Keywords: Cyber security · Speech interface · Human-computer interaction

1 Introduction

Voice control is becoming an increasingly mainstream modality of human-computer interaction, particularly with respect to the growing popularity of

Supported by a doctoral training grant from the Engineering and Physical Sciences Research Council (EPSRC).

P. Mori et al. (Eds.): ICISSP 2019, CCIS 1221, pp. 288–316, 2020.
https://doi.org/10.1007/978-3-030-49443-8_14

smart speakers such as Amazon Alexa.[1] Voice-controlled systems are being used to perform both virtual actions, such as diary management, and cyber-physical actions, such as controlling devices in a smart home. This new form of human-computer interaction has brought with it new security concerns with regard to attackers exploiting voice commands to perform nefarious actions. Prior research has demonstrated various types of attacks via the speech interface, including attacks in which malicious voice commands are hidden in some form of cover medium so as to make them imperceptible to the legitimate users of voice-controlled devices [14,58]. Whilst there has been a significant amount of prior work demonstrating the various types of attacks that may be executed via a speech interface to gain control of a victim's system, there have been few attempts to conceptualise the security of the speech interface in a comprehensive framework. This paper provides such a framework, using the Observe-Orient-Decide-Act (OODA) loop model that has been used to model adversarial interactions in many contexts.

This modelling framework facilitates a critical analysis of the effectiveness of currently available defences to counter the various types of attacks that can be executed via a speech interface. This critical analysis concludes that attacks that are imperceptible as such by human listeners are particularly dangerous in their potential effects, because of various difficulties in defending against such attacks using currently available defences. Such attacks are made possible by the existence of unintended functionality at various stages of handling of speech input. In accordance with this conclusion of the analysis, the paper further presents proposals for the development of new defence mechanisms to protect voice-controlled systems against attacks that exploit gaps between human and machine perceptions of speech and natural language. These proposals involve the implementation of defence mechanisms at the dialogue management stage of handling of speech input, which would enable a voice-controlled system to block execution of an attack at the dialogue management stage and instead issue a verbal security alert to users via its speech synthesis functionality. This is in contrast to currently available defence mechanisms, which are applied at the voice capture, speech recognition or natural language understanding stages of speech input handling. In support of this high-level defence concept, the paper makes two specific proposals for defence mechanisms to counter attacks exploiting unintended functionality in speech recognition and natural language understanding respectively. Specifically, we propose the novel application of an existing speech recognition system and of machine translation for security purposes in voice-controlled systems.

The remainder of this paper is structured as follows. Section 2 presents some background on human-computer interaction by speech, as well as an overview of prior work on the security of the speech interface. Section 3 maps the various types of attacks via the speech interface described in Sect. 2 to the OODA loop

---

[1] A recent UK government survey, for example, reported that 8% of adults in the UK now own a smart speaker, see https://gds.blog.gov.uk/2018/08/23/hey-gov-uk-what-are-you-doing-about-voice/.

model, and reviews the defence measures currently available to counter such attacks, using the model as a framework. Section 4 presents our proposals for the development of new defence mechanisms, including a high-level concept for a defensive capability at the dialogue management stage of handling of speech input, as well as two specific proposals for defence mechanisms based on the novel application of existing technologies for security purposes. Section 5 concludes the paper and makes recommendations for future work.

This paper is an extended version of a previous paper in which our framework for modelling the security of the speech interface was first presented (see Bispham et al. [7]). The work presented here extends the work in the earlier paper with the proposals for the development of new defence mechanisms referred to above.

2   Background and Prior Work

2.1   Background on Human-Computer Interaction by Speech

The typical architecture of a voice-controlled system consists of a speech recognition component, a natural language understanding component, a dialogue management component, and a response generation component (see for example Lison and Meena [37]). An outline of the processing pipeline is shown in Fig. 1. Following capture of speech input by a microphone, the speech recognition component will transcribe a sequence of words from the captured speech signal, the natural language understanding component will extract from the sequence of words a representation of the user's intent, the dialogue management component will map the representation of user intent to an appropriate response action, and the response generation component will generate a verbal and/or non-verbal response to the user. Both the speech recognition and the natural language understanding components involve some form of machine learning, typically Deep Neural Networks (DNNs) combined with Hidden Markov Models (HMMs) for speech recognition, and Conditional Random Fields (CRFs) or Recurrent Neural Networks (RNNs) for natural language understanding (see for example McTear [41]).

The dialogue management component, as implemented in the current generation of voice-controlled digital assistants, typically maps the representation of user intent outputted by the natural language understanding component to an appropriate action based on a set of handcrafted rules, although there has been some research on the development of more sophisticated dialogue management capabilities based on reinforcement learning (see McTear). The response generation component executes the action determined by the dialogue management component, which might be a virtual action such as an update to a calendar entry or a cyber-physical action such as controlling a smart home device, and/or a verbal response to the user by speech synthesis.

In the current generation of voice-controlled digital assistants like Amazon Alexa and Google Assistant, speech recognition and natural language understanding are performed in the provider's cloud rather than on the user's local device. These devices thus include an additional 'wake-word' functionality to trigger streaming of audio data from the user's environment to the provider's cloud (see for example Chung et al. [16]).

Fig. 1. Spoken dialogue systems architecture.

2.2   Prior Work on the Security of the Speech Interface

The speech interface represents a new type of attack surface for malicious actors seeking to gain unauthorised access to a system. As such it represents a new focus for security research, and various types of attacks via the speech interface have been demonstrated in prior work. Some of the attacks demonstrated in prior work use plain-speech voice commands, as might be spoken by the user themselves. As such attacks will be clearly audible by legitimate users of the target system, they rely on engineering a situation in which a user is not present with their device. An example of this type of attack is described by Dhanjani [18], who hypothesises an attack using plain-speech commands in an audio file which plays when a user is likely to be absent from their PC. Another example is demonstrated by Diao et al. [19], in the form an attack using plain-speech commands which are triggered by a malicious smartphone app during hours when a user can be expected to be asleep. By contrast to these examples, prior work has also demonstrated a number of attacks that are not audible by users of a voice-controlled system, even if they are present with their device. One of these attacks is the so-called 'dolphin' attack demonstrated by Zhang et al. [58]. The attack demonstrated by Zhang et al. shows that it is possible to hide malicious voice commands in audio signals that have a frequency above the range of human hearing. This attack exploits non-linearities in microphone technology that make it possible for the voice capture functionality of voice-controlled systems to be induced to accept non-audible input as a speech signal within human-audible range.

Another type of attack via the speech interface demonstrated in prior work is attacks using adversarial learning to exploit unintended functionality in the speech recognition component of the target system. Adversarial learning can be broadly defined as the process of identifying inputs to a target system that the system misclassifies in some way that is to an attacker's advantage. In the context of voice-controlled systems, this might be done by crafting audio input that, although audible by legitimate users of a voice-controlled device, may not be recognised by them as a malicious voice command to their system. These attacks aim to mislead the target voice-controlled system to accept input that is out-of-scope of the system's intended input space as a valid in-scope voice command. One of the first examples of this type of attack demonstrated in prior work was presented by Carlini et al. [14]. They demonstrated that it was possible, by extracting from voice command recordings the core acoustic features used by speech recognition whilst removing other parts of the speech signal, to create audio input that was perceived by humans as white noise, but that was still recognised by the target system Google Now as a valid voice command. The attack demonstrated by Carlini et al. was a black-box attack requiring no inside knowledge of the target system, and was shown to be effective when played over the air to the Google Now assistant on a smartphone. Bispham et al. [8] demonstrate another type of attack in which malicious voice commands are masked in nonsensical word sounds that rhyme with words of a target command. The authors show that the nonsensical word sounds are recognised by Google Assistant as a valid command, whilst human listeners do not detect the target command in the nonsensical word sounds when hearing them out of context. The attack presented by Bispham et al. is also a black-box attack that is shown to be capable of being executed over-the-air.

A further attack targeting speech recognition is demonstrated by Carlini and Wagner [15], who show that it is possible, using a mathematical adversarial learning technique, to manipulate audio recordings of a spoken text so as to lead the recording to be transcribed by a speech transcription system as an entirely different text chosen by an attacker. Carlini and Wagner also demonstrate that it is possible using the same technique to hide target transcriptions in music recordings. Unlike the attack using white noise presented by Carlini et al. [14] and the attacks using nonsensical word sounds presented by Bispham et al. [8], the attacks demonstrated by Carlini and Wagner are demonstrated in relation to a separate speech transcription system rather than a voice-controlled system as such. Also unlike the other two attacks, these attacks are shown to be effective only as audio file input to the target system rather than as over-the-air input via a microphone, and are white-box attacks requiring inside knowledge of the target system, rather than black-box attacks. As such the attacks presented by Carlini and Wagner might not be seen as representing a real threat at present, given that an attacker is unlikely to have access to the inner workings of a commercial system, and that attacks via audio file input will not be possible in the case of smart speakers that are only accessible by sound. However, Carlini and Wagner claim that their attacks will be capable of execution over the air in future, and research from adversarial learning in image recognition suggests that it might be possible to convert this attack to a black-box attack in future. With respect to the latter, Papernot et al. [43] demonstrate that it is possible to craft adversarial input to an image recognition system using a substitute system that is constructed based on outputs from a target system without requiring details of its inner workings. Such an approach might also be taken in adversarial learning attacks on speech recognition.

In addition to the adversarial learning attacks on speech recognition described above, there has also been some work towards adversarial learning attacks on natural language understanding, albeit that most of this work has been outside the context of voice-controlled systems. Papernot et al. [44] use the forward derivative method, a white-box adversarial learning method, to identify word substitutions that can be made in sentences inputted to an RNN-based sentiment analysis system so as to change the 'sentiment' allocated to the sentence. For example, substituting the word 'I' for the word 'excellent' in an otherwise negative review is shown in the paper to lead to it being classified as having positive sentiment by the target system. Papernot et al. point out that semantically coherent adversarial examples for attacks on natural language understanding are difficult to achieve using purely mathematical adversarial learning approaches. In contrast to adversarial examples in image classification and speech recognition, in which alterations made to the original input are imperceptible to humans, the alterations made to sentences in order to mislead the RNN-based sentiment analysis system targeted in the work by Papernot et al. are easily perceptible by humans as unnatural. Liang et al. [36] demonstrate a linguistically plausible attack on a natural language understanding system. The authors adapt the Fast Gradient Sign Method from adversarial learning in image classification to make human-indetectable alterations to a text passage (by adding, modifying and/or removing words) so as to change the category that is allocated to the passage by a DNN-based text classification system. The attack is not fully automated, but requires human judgement in finding and making changes to parts of the original input identified as significant for text classification by the Fast Gradient Sign Method.

Whilst the attacks on natural language understanding described above were demonstrated outside the context of voice control, Bispham et al. [8] have demonstrated attacks on natural language understanding in voice-controlled systems, using linguistic adversarial learning methods. They present the results of experimental work showing that it is possible to mislead natural language understanding in third-party applications for Amazon Alexa (known as Skills) by replacing words in target commands or by embedding homophones of target command words in a different sense context so as to create apparently unrelated utterances that are accepted by the system as the target command. In an extended version of the original paper, published in this volume, the authors demonstrate further instances of the latter type of attack on Amazon Alexa Skills as well as on open-source natural language understanding technology RASA NLU (Bispham et al. [9]). This type of attack based on embedding homophones of target command words in a different sense context is termed a 'word transplant' attack by the authors.

Bispham et al. [10] have developed a taxonomy of potential attacks via the speech interface that is organised according to the nature of the attack in terms of human perception. The taxonomy divides such attacks into two high-level categories: overt attacks, which aim to take control of a target system using plain-speech voice commands; and covert attacks, in which malicious voice commands are concealed in a cover medium so as to make them imperceptible to human listeners.

Overt attacks are easily detectable by users if they are consciously present with their device, therefore the success of an overt attack relies on a user being distracted or leaving their device unattended. An example of an overt attack might be the activation of a smartphone by a voice command that is delivered via a malicious app whilst a user is away from their device. Covert attacks are by definition not detectable by users, and can therefore be executed even if the user is present with their device. Examples of covert attacks include the high-frequency attacks that hide voice commands in sound that is inaudible to humans demonstrated by Zhang et al. [58], the attacks that hide voice commands via an audio-mangling process that makes them appear to humans as meaningless noise demonstrated by [14], and the targeted use of nonsensical word sounds that trigger target commands in a victim's system despite these word sounds being perceived as meaningless by human listeners, as demonstrated by Bispham et al. [8]. Covert attacks are divided within the taxonomy into five sub-categories namely silence, noise, music, nonsense and 'missense' (missense being defined as the hiding of malicious voice commands in speech that appears to be unrelated to the attacker's intent).

Overt attacks exploit the inherent vulnerability of speech interfaces on account of the difficulty of controlling access to such interfaces. Covert attacks exploit unintended functionality in the handling of speech input by a voice-controlled system that allows it to accept input that is not a valid voice command. The 'silent' attacks demonstrated by Zhang et al. [58] exploit non-linearities in analog-to-digital conversion of speech signals by a microphone, whereas the attacks demonstrated by Carlini et al. [14] are an example of attacks exploiting vulnerabilities in speech recognition. The attacks on Amazon Alexa Skills targeting natural language understanding demonstrated by Bispham et al. [8] are the first examples of attacks on natural language understanding in voice-controlled systems. Regarding the dialogue management and response generation components, as these functionalities are fully dependent on input from the preceding components in the current generation of voice-controlled systems, there are no attacks targeting these functionalities at present.

An attacker's goal in executing an attack via a speech interface will be to gain control of one of the three generic types of action that can be performed via a voice-controlled digital assistant or other speech-controlled system using a sound-based attack. These three types of action are data extraction, data input and execution of a cyber-physical action. Specific attacks on each type of action that might be possible based on the current capabilities of voice-controlled digital assistants include prompting disclosure of personal information such as calendar information as envisaged by Diao et al. [19], instigating a reputational attack by posting to social media in the victim's name as envisaged by Young et al. [56], and causing psychological or physical harm to the victim by controlling a device in their smart home environment as envisaged by Dhanjani [18].

Attacks via a speech interface require a channel through which the sound-based attack is delivered, and in the case of attacks involving theft of information, successful execution also requires a channel for data exfiltration. Sound-based attacks might be delivered through various channels, including natural voice, radio or TV broadcasts, audio files that users are induced to open via a weblink or email attachment, as suggested by Dhanjani [18], or malicious smartphone apps, as suggested by Diao et al. [19]. A further possible attack delivery channel is via an intermediary device under the attacker's control. Some instances of compromise of internet-connected speakers have been reported.[2] Speakers that have been compromised in this way could be used as an attack delivery channel for sound-based attacks on a target voice-controlled digital assistant within the speakers' vicinity. Regarding data exfiltration channels, Diao et al. [19] envisage for example that a system could be prompted to call a phone number linking to an audio recording device, which would then be used to record personal information of the victim that the system might be prompted to disclose by further voice commands.

Attacks via the speech interface have the potential to expand in time by perpetuating over a number of dialogue turns, as well as in space by spreading to other speech-controlled devices. Alepis and Patskakis [3] and Petracca et al. [46] both mention the possibility of attacks by voice 'spreading' from one device to another by hijacking of a device's speech synthesis functionality. An example of an attack via the speech interface spreading through both space and time was seen in an instance in which a Google Home device was prompted to provide data to its user in synthesised speech that was perceived by a nearby Amazon Echo device as a command. This prompted the Echo to provide data that was in turn perceived by the Google Home as a command, the consequence being to set in motion an 'endless loop' between the two devices.[3] This instance represented an example of an 'attack' that spread both in space to another device as well as in time over a potentially endless number of dialogue turns. Whilst this particular instance represents merely a humorous anecdote, it is possible that more malicious actions might be performed using similar mechanisms.

3   Attack and Defence Modelling Framework

There are a number of techniques for attack and defence modelling in cyber security. One of the more well-known modelling techniques for cyber security applications is the cyber kill-chain [2], which is used to analyse the different stages of malware attacks. Other established attack modelling techniques in cyber security include attack graphs [52] and attack grammars [45]. Another type of attack

---

[2] See Wired, 27th December 2017, "Hackers can rickroll thousands of Sonos and Bose speakers over the internet", https://www.wired.com/story/hackers-can-rickroll-sonos-bose-speakers-over-internet/ and Trend Micro report 2017, "The Sound of a Targeted Attack", https://documents.trendmicro.com/assets/pdf/The-Sound-of-a-Targeted-Attack.pdf.

[3] See UPROXX, 12th January 2017 "You Can Make Amazon Echo and Google Home Talk to Each Other Forever", http://uproxx.com/technology/amazon-echo-google-home-infinity-loop/ and cnet.com 15th February 2018, "Make Siri, Alexa and Google Assistant talk in an infinite loop", https://www.cnet.com/how-to/make-siri-alexa-and-google-assistant-talk-in-an-infinite-loop/.

model is the OODA loop. Originally developed for the military context [11], the OODA loop has been applied in many different areas, including cyber defence [31]. The OODA loop method represents the behaviour of agents in adversarial interactions as a continuous cycle through a four-stage loop in a shared environment, the four stages of the loop being observation (Observe), orientation (Orientation), decision (Decide) and action (Act). The four stages of the loop as presented by Klein [31] are shown in Fig. 2. Rule [50] explains that the Observe and Act stages of the OODA loop are the points at which it makes contact with the external world, whereas the Orient and Decide stages are internal processes. Rule further explains that an adversary's aim as modelled by the OODA loop is to interfere with decision-making within their opponent's loop by presenting them with "ambiguous, deceptive or novel" situations, whilst at the same time continuing to execute their own loop independently.

Fig. 2. The four stages of the OODA Loop (from Klein [31]).

For the purposes of this work, the OODA loop was considered to be the most suitable modelling technique. The reason for this was that the OODA model is capable of capturing the cyclical nature of interactions by speech. Therefore the OODA loop model is especially suitable for representing the ways in which the processes of human-computer interaction by speech may be hijacked by adversarial actions. Specifically, the capture of the speech signal by a microphone prior to speech recognition can be mapped to the Observe stage of the OODA loop; the combined functionality of the speech recognition and natural language understanding components can be mapped to the Orient stage; the dialogue management (DM) component can be mapped to the Decide stage; and the response generation and speech synthesis stages can be mapped to the Act stage. Figure 3 shows a mapping of non-malicious user-device interactions via speech to the OODA loop model.

Figure 4 shows a mapping to the OODA loop model of the different types of attacks via the speech interface as categorised in the taxonomy presented by Bispham et al. [10], in which an attacker replaces a legitimate user in interactions with the device. The position of each type of attack in the loop model corresponds to the specific vulnerability exploited by the attack, i.e. the point at which the attacker gains control of the target device's loop. Plain-speech (overt) attacks and silent attacks are positioned at the Observe stage, as these types of attack exploit the inherent vulnerability of the speech interface and unintended functionality in voice capture, respectively. All other types of attack

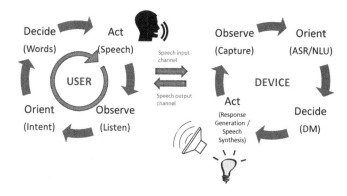

Fig. 3. The OODA Loop in User-Device Interactions (from Bispham et al. [7]).

(noise, music, nonsense and missense) are positioned at the Orient stage, as these types of attack exploit unintended functionality in speech recognition or natural language understanding. The attack model also shows an attack delivery channel for transmission of malicious input by sound, and a data exfiltration channel that is used if the aim of the attack is the extraction of data. The model further indicates the potential expansion of an attack in time over several dialogue turns, as well as the possible expansion in space to a second target. The attacker may be any agent capable of producing sound in an environment shared with a target. In the case of attacks involving extraction of data, the agent will also be capable of recording sound in the shared environment.

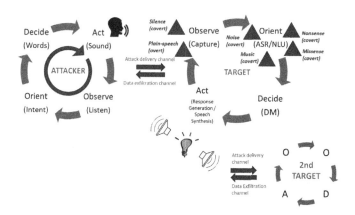

Fig. 4. The OODA Loop in Attacker-Target Interactions (from Bispham et al. [7]).

Figure 5 shows a mapping to the OODA loop model of currently available defence measures. The position of each defence measure in the loop corresponds to the type of system vulnerability that the defence measure aims to patch. Cyber security defence measures are often categorised as either preventive or reactive [39]. Preventive defence measures, such as authentication and access control, prevent malicious payloads from being inputted to a system at all, whereas reactive defence measures, such as anomaly-based or signature-based defences, detect that a malicious payload has been inputted and trigger a response to counteract the attack [22]. In terms of defence measures for human-computer interaction by speech as represented by the OODA loop model, preventive defences are defences that are applied at the voice capture stage of speech input handling, represented by the Observe stage of the loop, whereas reactive defences are applied as part of speech recognition or natural language understanding, represented by the Orient stage of the loop. The preventive measures mapped to the Observe stage of the loop are user presence, access control, audio-technical measures, and voice authentication. Reactive measures mapped to the Orient stage are confidence thresholds, input validation, signature-based defences, and anomaly-based defences. As dialogue management and response generation are fully controlled by input from the preceding components in the current generation of voice-controlled systems, there is currently no scope for additional defences at the Decide stage of the loop.

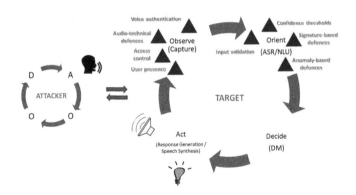

Fig. 5. Defences against attacks via the speech interface in the OODA Loop model (from Bispham et al. [7]).

User Presence. Overt attacks via the speech interface using plain-speech voice commands are easily detectable by users if they are consciously present with their device. Whilst the ability to detect an overt attack may not prevent such attacks from being successful to some extent, as the attack may already be in the process of being executing as the user detects it, the immediate detection of an attack by a user clearly limits the potential effects of the attack, in that the attack is likely to be easily attributable, and the user will be able to prevent any further propagation of the attack. Therefore it is advisable for users to take preventative measures to ensure that overt attacks cannot be executed on their device whilst they are not present with it. Jackson and Orebaugh [27] recommend some basic preventative measures including unplugging a voice-controlled device when leaving the home and not placing a voice-controlled device close to doors and windows to prevent voice commands being inputted to the device from outside a house. User prevention measures such as these apply only to overt attacks and do not represent a defence against covert attacks that are imperceptible to humans and may therefore be executed notwithstanding the conscious presence of the user.

Access Control. Some work has been done on the potential for using formal access control methods to secure interactions via a speech interface and other types of cyber-physical interactions. Agadakos et al. [1] use formal methods to develop a scheme for identifying unintended interactions that may be possible between devices in a smart home environment over 'hidden' physical channels, including voice. Petracca et al. [46] propose a system of access controls to secure audio channels to and from a smartphone. The paper proposes an extension to the Android operating system in smartphones, with the objective of enforcing security policies for communications over three audio channels, namely between the device's speakers and its microphone, between the device's speakers and external parties, and between external parties and the device's microphone. The authors concede that their access control system is based on the assumption of a reliable means of authenticating the legitimate user of a device, which may not be a valid assumption. Gong and Poellabauer [24] argue that the 'Audroid' method developed by Petracca et al. is not effective against adversarial learning attacks.

Audio-Technical Defences. Some defence measures have been presented that are applied at the voice capture stage of the handling of speech input by a voice-controlled device, prior the speech recognition and natural language understanding stages, so as to prevent 'silent' attacks that exploit non-linearity in microphone technology. As mentioned above, such attacks mislead a voice-controlled digital assistant or other voice-controlled device to execute commands that are concealed in high-frequency signals that are outside the human audible range, an example being the attack demonstrated by Zhang et al. [58] mentioned above. Roy et al. [49] present a defence against inaudible attacks based on signal forensics that involves software rather than hardware changes to microphone technology. The applicability of such defence measures is limited to attacks that exploit vulnerabilities in the voice capture functionality of voice-controlled digital assistants; such measures are not effective against attacks that exploit vulnerabilities in the speech recognition or natural language processing functionalities.

Voice Authentication. Biometric voice authentication, also known as speaker recognition, is perhaps the most obvious defence measure that might be implemented to prevent attacks on systems that are accessible via a speech interface. Hasan [26] details how voice biometric authentication is performed using a standard set of acoustic features. In theory, voice biometrics represent a potential solution to all types of attack via the speech interface by ensuring that a speech-controlled device acts only on voice commands from an authorised user. In practice, however, voice biometrics remain vulnerable to spoofing attacks, as stated by Wu et al. [55]. In an overview of the state-of-the-art in speaker recognition, Hansen and Hasan state that unlike in the case of other types of biometrics such as fingerprints, voice is subject to a certain amount of variability within the same individual as well between individuals, implying that some degree of potential for false positives in voice biometric authentication may be inevitable [25]. The potential for false positives is exploited by attackers in voice spoofing attacks.

Confidence Thresholds. Voice-controlled systems generally implement some form of confidence threshold to prevent them from accepting input that cannot be matched to one of their actions with sufficient certainty by the speech recognition or natural language understanding functionalities [30]. Whilst confidence thresholds are implemented as an error prevention measure rather than as a defence measure, they may have some defence functionality in preventing covert attacks via the speech interface, by enabling the system to reject malicious input that is not sufficiently similar to the examples of legitimate input that were used in training the system. However, a confidence threshold is unlikely to be sufficient to prevent all attacks. This was seen for example with respect to the attacks targeting speech recognition in Google Assistant using nonsensical word sounds demonstrated by Bispham et al. [8].

Input Validation. Aside from confidence thresholds, another approach to error prevention for voice-controlled systems has been to restrict in some way the vocabulary that will be recognised by the system as valid input. Controlled Natural Language (CNL) has been used to prevent misunderstandings between machines and humans as to the intended meaning of natural language input. CNL is a general term for various restricted versions of natural language that have been constructed with a restricted vocabulary and syntax in order to enable every sentence in the language to be mapped unambiguously to a computer-executable representation of its meaning [33]. Restricted language models like these have been developed particularly for contexts where avoiding misunderstandings is a critical concern, such as human-robot interactions in military applications [17]. Although primarily an error prevention rather than a security measure, CNL enables natural language input to be validated in the same way as is often done for security purposes in non-speech interfaces [51]. Thus CNL can be seen a defence mechanism against attacks via the speech interface which is implemented as part of the natural language understanding functionality. However, CNL is not likely to be effective in preventing attacks targeting speech recognition. Kaljurand and Alumäe [29] discuss the use of CNL in speech interfaces for smartphones. They point to the additional challenges in using CNL in a speech-based application as opposed to a text-based application, noting the need to avoid homophones within the CNL that can be distinguished in written but not in spoken language. The approach proposed by Kaljurand and Alumäe potentially addresses issues of confusability between user utterances that are within the intended scope of a speech-controlled system. However, it may not be effective in preventing confusion with out-of-vocabulary sounds that are directed to the system by a malicious actor. Thus CNL is unlikely to present a solution to preventing covert attacks that target the speech recognition functionality of a voice-controlled system. Enforcement of a CNL in the design of a speech interface might be effective in preventing some attacks that exploit ambiguities in natural language input. However, such an approach would clearly be contrary to the aim of most providers of voice-controlled systems to enable users to communicate with their devices in as flexible and natural a way as possible [40].

Signature-Based Defences. A potential defence against some types of attacks via the speech interface is detection of attacks based on known attack signatures using supervised machine learning. Carlini et al. [14], for example, propose a machine learning-based defence to their own audio-mangling attack on speech recognition in Google Now, in the form of a machine learning classifier that distinguishes audio-mangled sentences from genuine commands based on acoustic features. Signature-based defences using linguistic features might similarly be used to detect malicious input targeting natural language understanding. Carlini et al. demonstrate that their signature-based classifier is effective against the specific attacks presented in their paper with 99.8% detection rate of attacks. However, the authors themselves note that such defences do not represent a proof of security, and are vulnerable to an 'arms race' with attackers who are likely simply to craft more sophisticated attacks to evade such defences. Attackers have the upper hand in such arms races with respect to machine learning based systems, on account of the vast number of possible inputs to such systems, making it impossible for defenders to prepare systems for all possible input in training.[4]

Anomaly-Based Defences. One possibility for enabling voice-controlled systems to become resistant to previously unseen attacks via the speech interface could be defence measures based on some form of anomaly detection. Anomaly detection-based defences have been applied in other areas of cyber security, such as network defence (see Rieck and Laskov, [48] and Bhuyan et al. [6]). However, anomaly-based defence measures depend on reliable similarity and distance measures in terms of which malicious input can be distinguished as anomalous relative to legitimate input (see Weller et al. [53]). In the context of attacks via the speech interface, such quantifiably measurable indications of suspicious activity may be difficult to identify. Whilst a number of both phonetic and semantic distance measures have been developed (see Pucher et al. [47] and Gomaa and Fahmy [23]), none of these are fully reliable in terms of their ability to separate sounds and meanings that are perceived as different by human listeners. Kong et al. [32] present the results of an evaluative study that indicated significant differences between error rates in human perception of speech sounds and their transcription by different types of automatic speech recognition in terms of a phonetic distance

---

[4] See Cleverhans blog, 15th February 2017, "Is attacking machine learning easier than defending it?", http://www.cleverhans.io/security/privacy/ml/2017/02/15/why-attacking-machine-learning-is-easier-than-defending-it.html.

measure. Budanitsky and Hirst [13] compare different measures of semantic distance with implied human judgements of word meaning via a task that involved detection of synthetically generated malapropisms, finding that none of these measures was capable of alignment with human understanding of word meaning. Thus such distance and similarity measures do not provide a reliable basis for an anomaly detection-based defence against attacks that seek to exploit differences between human and machine perceptions of speech, and may also prevent the system from accepting legitimate input.

4 Proposals for New Defence Mechanisms

This section presents proposals for the development of new defence mechanisms against attacks via the speech interface, grounded in the attack and defence modelling framework presented in the previous section. As concluded in the analysis presented in the previous section, none of the currently available defence mechanisms provide a full solution to prevention of attacks via the speech interface.

The proposals presented here focus on covert attacks. Overt attacks using plain-speech commands are excluded from the scope of the proposals on the basis that the risk of such attacks can be minimised through simple user precautions, such as not leaving devices in listening mode unattended, as discussed in the previous section. Whilst user presence does not remove the risk of overt attacks completely, in that by the time an attack is detected by a user it may already be in the process of being executed, immediate detection by a user implies that an overt attack will be easily attributable, and that any propagation of the attack can be prevented. Thus overt attacks can be considered far less pernicious than covert attacks of which execution can been hidden from user perception.

The scope of the proposals for defence mechanisms is further limited to attacks targeting unintended functionality in speech recognition or natural language understanding. 'Silent' attacks that target unintended functionality at the voice capture stage of speech input handling are excluded on the basis that these are likely to be preventable by audio-technical defences, as discussed in the previous section. By contrast, in the case of covert attacks targeting speech recognition and natural language understanding, none of the currently available defence mechanisms is capable of providing a full solution.

Examples of the attacks falling within the scope of the proposals for defence mechanisms include the attacks targeting speech recognition in Google Now demonstrated by Carlini et al. [14], and the attacks targeting natural language understanding in Amazon Alexa Skills demonstrated by Bispham et al. [8].

Our proposals for the development of novel defence mechanisms against such attacks are presented in three subsections below. The first subsection presents a high-level defence concept envisaging the implementation of defence mechanisms at the dialogue management stage of handling of speech input, separate from the core speech recognition and natural language understanding functionalities. The next two subsections present specific proposals for countering attacks exploiting unintended functionality in speech recognition and natural language understanding respectively, based on novel applications of existing technologies for security purposes. The proposal for a defence mechanism to counter attacks targeting vulnerabilities in speech recognition is presented in the second subsection. We propose the implementation of a knowledge-based speech recognition system in voice-controlled systems, in addition to the core machine learning-based speech recognition functionality, as a security measure. The proposal for a defence mechanism to counter attacks targeting vulnerabilities in natural language understanding functionality is presented in the third subsection. We propose a security measure based on cross-lingual comparison of user intent determination, whereby, in addition to the interpretation by the natural language understanding functionality of a transcription of speech input in its original language, interpretation would also be performed on a machine translation of the transcription, to increase the robustness of the natural language understanding functionality to adversarial learning attacks.

The proposals for new defence mechanisms follow principles of so-called speculative design for ensuring robustness of proposals for the development of future technologies by embedding speculative proposals in a current context. This is done firstly by grounding the proposals for new defence mechanisms in the modelling framework for assessing the security of the speech interface presented above, and secondly by linking the proposals to existing technologies and research, as detailed further below. The principles of speculative design are described in detail by Auger [5].

4.1 High-Level Defence Concept

Our high-level defence concept envisages a defensive capability for voice-controlled systems that would be able to detect potential attacks targeting speech recognition or natural language understanding as part of its dialogue management functionality, and produce security alerts as part of its response generation functionality, using its own speech synthesis capability. In terms of the modelling framework presented in the previous section, the proposed defence concept represents a defence at the 'Decide' stage of the OODA loop, with the security alerts being generated at the 'Act' stage of the loop. This is by contrast to currently available defence mechanisms implemented at the 'Orient' stage of a target system's OODA loop as part of the speech recognition and natural language understanding functionalities.

As explained in the previous section, as dialogue management functionality in current commercial systems responds passively to input from the preceding components, the dialogue management component is not capable of protecting the systems against attacks targeting vulnerabilities in the preceding speech recognition or natural language understanding components. A security-aware dialogue management functionality would conversely be capable of detecting malicious input that has been misrecognised by the speech recognition or natural language understanding functionality as legitimate input. Such a dialogue management functionality would block execution of the command that such input purports to contain, and instead prompt the response generation component to generate an alert to the legitimate user that the system has received input from its environment purporting to be a voice command of which the legitimate user may be unaware. Such security alerts would thus form part of the system's repertoire for interacting with its users. This type of functionality has previously been considered with regard to conversational agents developed specifically for security purposes. Security-aware digital assistants capable of detecting and reporting suspicious events have for example been developed to support analysts in security operation centres, two of these being the Artemis bot developed by Endgame[5] and the Havyn bot developed by IBM.[6] In the case considered here, a voice assistant would report on potential attacks on its own functionality as part of its interaction with users in spoken natural language. Figure 6 shows our concept of implementing a detection capability at the dialogue management stage and an alert capability at the response generation stage in the context of the OODA loop-based attack and defence modelling framework.

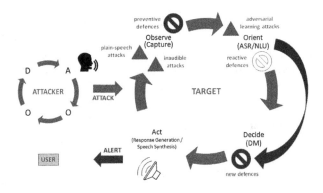

Fig. 6. High-level defence concept.

In order to be able to detect a covert attack and trigger an alert to the legitimate user as envisaged above, a voice-controlled system would need to have a reliable ability to identify input that purports to contain a valid voice command, but that might be perceived by a human as out-of-scope. At an abstract level, a solution to detection of covert attacks on voice-controlled systems that exploit gaps between human and machine perception of speech and language is simply to develop speech recognition and natural language understanding processes that are as similar as possible to human speech and language processing.

---

[5] See Endgame blog 20th January 2017, 'Endgame Announces Artemis: 'Siri For Security' To Transform SOC Operations', https://www.endgame.com/news/press-releases/endgame-announces-artemis-siri-security-transform-soc-operations.

[6] See Medium blog, 13th February 2013, 'Havyn: a cognitive assistant for cybersecurity', https://medium.com/cognitivebusiness/havyn-a-cognitive-assistant-for-cybersecurity-e6580898f49e.

Such improvements would prevent mismatches from being present in the first place. This aim is of course shared to some extent with the more general goal of improving the performance of voice-controlled systems by reducing error rates. However, performance objectives for machine speech recognition and natural language understanding do not require as complete an alignment to human capabilities as security objectives do. From a performance perspective, speech recognition and natural language understanding in a voice-controlled system needs to match human abilities only to the extent that it is able to correctly classify inputs that are within the system's intended scope, relying on the assumption that non-malicious users will not direct input to the system that is not within its scope. From a security perspective, however, the technology needs also to be capable of rejecting maliciously crafted out-of-scope input. The covert attacks via the speech interface considered in the defence proposals made here all represent instances of malicious use of out-of-scope input to attack a voice-controlled system. Securing a voice-controlled system against such attacks requires the system to be capable of matching human capabilities not only in correctly recognising and interpreting in-scope input, but also in identifying out-of-scope input.

Defending voice-controlled systems against malicious out-of-scope input is difficult to achieve as part of machine-learning-based speech recognition and natural language understanding, because the space of out-of-scope input for a given system is likely to be too vast to represent comprehensively in a training dataset to the granularity required to distinguish it from the space of valid speech input to the system. Whilst this is a problem common to all machine learning-based systems, in the context of speech recognition and natural language understanding a particular issue arises on account of the challenges posed by the variability of word sounds and the ambiguity of word meanings in natural language. Due to the presence of variability in word sounds and meaning, some degree of overlap between legitimate and malicious input to a speech interface is likely to be inevitable, at least in as far as they are separable using current techniques. This implies that any measures capable of preventing the speech-controlled system from accepting all malicious input would simultaneously lead it to reject some legitimate inputs, thus damaging the usability of the system. Thus, rather than relying on improvements in speech recognition and natural language understanding technology as such to ensure security of a speech interface, it is necessary to consider additional separate defence mechanisms at the dialogue management stage. Specific proposals for such defence mechanisms to counter attacks on speech recognition and natural language understanding respectively are made in the following subsections.

4.2 Defences Against Attacks on Speech Recognition

Attacks that target speech recognition functionality in voice-controlled systems exploit mismatches between human and machine perceptions of speech sounds. Such attacks include the attacks in noise demonstrated by Carlini et al. [14], the attacks based on nonsensical word sounds demonstrated by Bispham et al. [8], and the attacks in unrelated speech and music demonstrated by Carlini and

Wagner [15]. An effective defence against such attacks would involve removing the potential for mismatches between human and machine speech recognition in the system with respect to out-of-scope input.

One possibility for reducing the potential for mismatches between human and machine speech recognition with respect to out-of-scope input might be to incorporate knowledge from advances in research on human speech recognition in voice-controlled systems. The aim of this would be to filter out input that is unlikely to have been produced naturally by a legitimate human user of a device, and is therefore likely to represent some form of covert attack on the system. The current state-of-the-art in speech recognition technology is dominated by machine learning-based approaches trained with large amounts of speech data. However, from a security perspective, speech recognition technology based on knowledge of human speech recognition might be expected to be more successful than machine learning-based approaches in closing down the space of out-of-scope input in which an adversary can inject malicious voice commands without being detected by a human listener.

One speech recognition system based on knowledge of human speech recognition has in fact been developed. This speech recognition system, named FlexSR, is not in commercial use but is described in a patent application [34]. The system has been developed in the first instance as a language learning tool to help non-native learners of various languages to improve their pronunciation in a target language. Rather than mapping acoustic features such as Mel-frequency Cepstral Coefficients to phonemes in a given language directly, the FlexSR speech recognition technology uses a set of 18 phonological features common to all languages that are linked to the characteristics of the human vocal apparatus (see Lahiri and Reetz [35], Arora et al. [4]). Whereas phonemes are a set of sound units that are specific to a particular language, phonological features are universal, in the sense that all sounds used across all languages can be characterised as some combination of such features. The FlexSR system initially maps acoustic features in a speech sample to a vector that represents the presence or absence of each of the phonological features. The combination of phonological features extracted from the acoustic features is then mapped to phonemes of a given language in a second step, in order to identify spoken words. The aim of the approach to speech recognition incorporated in FlexSR is to achieve high levels of accuracy in speech recognition whilst also accounting for the high levels of variability in the pronunciation of words in natural speech. FlexSR uses the TIMIT system for transcription of phonemes [21].

A speech recognition system based on new insights into human word recognition, such as FlexSR, might have potential security applications in being able to prevent covert attacks targeting speech recognition functionality. This would be achieved by ensuring that input not recognised by humans as a valid pronunciation of a target command is not accepted by a voice-controlled system, whilst simultaneously preserving flexibility and thus usability of the system by allowing for variation in different human pronunciations of the same words. A system such as FlexSR is unlikely to be vulnerable to the same adversarial learning input as the core machine learning-based speech recognition in a voice-controlled system.

Rather than replacing machine learning-based speech recognition in voice-controlled systems, a system such as FlexSR would be applied as a security measure at the dialogue management stage, to filter out input that has been transcribed by the speech recognition component as a voice command, but that is in reality unlikely to have been produced naturally by the human vocal system, and thus might represent a covert attack. The reason for using a speech recognition system such as FlexSR in addition to machine learning-based speech recognition, rather than to replace it, would be that machine learning-based speech recognition may achieve higher levels of accuracy with regard to in-scope input. Thus the two different speech recognition systems would be implemented in tandem as complementary functionalities, with the machine learning-based system being responsible for handling in-scope input, and the knowledge-based system being responsible for excluding out-of-scope input. Rather than performing speech recognition from scratch, a knowledge-based system such as FlexSR would be used to confirm whether a given audio input is likely to represent a genuine attempt to vocalise a voice command that has been transcribed by the core speech recognition system. A voice command identified by the core speech recognition functionality would be executed only if the knowledge-based system recognises the input as a legitimate human-comprehensible input. Such an approach would minimize the potential for covert attacks on speech recognition, by ensuring a closer alignment between machine and human perception of meaningful speech sounds, without affecting the performance of the system in terms of being able to handle variability in human pronunciations of the same words.

In order to investigate the potential defensive capability of FlexSR in a specific context, FlexSR's response to adversarial commands in noise, as demonstrated by Carlini et al. [14], was tested.[7] Specifically, FlexSR's response was tested to five adversarial commands in noise that had been demonstrated by Carlini et al. in black-box attacks on Google Now, as made available by the researchers.[8] The tests used an implementation of FlexSR as a language learning tool on a smartphone. In this implementation, FlexSR provides feedback on pronunciation by advising on how the expression of phonological features in a learner's speech should be changed in order to achieve correct pronunciation. If a learner's vocalisation of a word differs from the correct pronunciation in a way or to a degree that makes the target word unrecognisable, FlexSR may instead identify the insertion, deletion or substitution of a phoneme in the user's speech. Users are required to enter the word or phrase that they are attempting to pronounce, and then speak this word or phrase into the phone's microphone. FlexSR then compares phonological features extracted from the user's speech to the phonological features associated with correct articulation of phonemes in the

---

[7] The authors are grateful to the University of Oxford's Faculty of Linguistics, Philology and Phonetics for providing access to the FlexSR system for the purposes of this work.

[8] See http://www.hiddenvoicecommands.com/black-box.

target word or phrase in order to provide feedback. The example from Table 1 of correction of pronunciation of the word 'Tweet' as "Feature voice should increase for T" indicates that the phonological feature 'voice' in the phoneme transcribed as 'T' should be articulated more clearly to achieve correct pronunciation.

Details of FlexSR's response to the adversarial commands in noise demonstrated by Carlini et al., as well as to a legitimate version of the corresponding target command in live human speech, are shown in Table 1. The table shows FlexSR's judgement as to whether the adversarial and legitimate inputs represented a correct pronunciation of the target command, and, if not, how many features were identified as mispronounced, as well which specific features were identified as mispronounced in what respect. The most significant finding from these tests was that FlexSR did not recognise any of the adversarial commands in noise as correct pronunciations of the corresponding target command. In one case, FlexSR refused to accept the noise command as speech input altogether. This in itself was not sufficient to separate the adversarial commands from the legitimate target commands as spoken by a human, as FlexSR also identified three of the target commands in natural speech as incorrectly pronounced. However, with the exception of the adversarial command for the 'Hey Google' wake phrase, FlexSR did identify a much larger number of mispronounced features for the adversarial commands in noise than for target commands in natural speech for which incorrect pronunciation was identified. This suggests the number of features identified as mispronounced by FlexSR could be used as criteria for distinguishing legitimate 'natural' input from malicious 'unnatural' input in a bespoke implementation of FlexSR for security purposes. Any bespoke implementation of FlexSR for security purposes would need to address the issue of false positives that is evident in the feasibility tests using the implementation of FlexSR as a language learning tool.

The use of two different speech recognition systems with equivalent but different functionality as a security mechanism can be characterised as a cyber mimic defence. Cyber mimic defence involves using redundant alternative processing units of different but equivalent functionality to increase the robustness of a system to adversarial input. This approach has previously been applied in network defence to detect zero-day attacks (see for example Liu et al. [38]). The use of a second speech recognition system to increase the robustness of a voice-controlled system to attack has parallels to this approach.

4.3 Defences Against Attacks on Natural Language Understanding

Attacks that target natural language understanding functionality in voice-controlled systems exploit inadequacies in current methods for representing meaning in such systems. Examples of attacks of this type are the attacks on Amazon Alexa Skills demonstrated by Bispham et al. [8], in which it was shown to be possible to mislead a dummy Amazon Alexa Skill to accept an unrelated utterance as a target command. Current technologies for natural language understanding clearly represent only very crude approximations of the 'true' processes of natural language understanding in the human brain. Defences against attacks

Table 1. FlexSR noise attacks tests - Results.

Target command	human (non-adversarial) / noise (adversarial)	FlexSR correctly pronounced yes/no	FlexSR no. of features mispronounced	Details of FlexSR features mispronounced
What is my current location	human	NO	2	1) Feature voice should decrease for T in what; 2) Feature stop should increase for T in current
	noise	NO	5	1) Feature stop should increase for T; 2) Feature str should increase for z in is; 3) Feature nas should increase for N in current; 4) Feature cor should increase for T in current; 5) Feature nas should increase for N in location
Tweet goodbye	human	NO	1	Feature voice should increase for D
	noise	NO	4	1) Feature stop should increase for T; 2) Feature stop should increase for T; 3) Feature voice should increase for D; 4) Feature labial should increase for B
OK Google	human	NO	1	Feature RTR should increase for AX
	noise	NO	1	Feature cor should increase for EY
Turn on airplane mode	human	YES	0	none
	noise	NO	n.a.	*Not recognised by FlexSR as valid speech input*
Call 911	human	YES	0	none
	noise	NO	6	1) Feature nas should increase for N in nine; 2) Feature nas should increase for N in nine; 3) Feature cor should increase for N in one; 4) Feature rtr should increase for AH; 5) Feature nas should increase for N; 6) Insertion of NG at the end

targeting natural language understanding will need to close the gaps between human and machine understanding of the meaning of utterances that leave the system vulnerable to malicious exploitation.

In theory, similar to defences against attacks on speech recognition based on knowledge of human speech recognition as proposed above, defences against attacks on natural language understanding could be developed based on knowledge of human construction of meaning from spoken utterances, so as to mitigate the threat of attacks that exploit differences in human and machine understanding of natural language. In practice, however, much about the human processes for the construction of meaning remains unknown. At a high level, research from neurolinguistics suggests that the human construction of meaning from sentences emerges from a complex interplay of word meanings and syntax, as shown for example by Fedorenko et al. [20] and Johnson and Goldberg [28]. Such studies confirm the compositional nature of meaning construction in the human brain in general, but do not shed light on this at a level of granularity that might elucidate the process of meaning construction in specific contexts. It is possible that future advances in neuroscience and linguistics may identify features of meaning representation in the human brain that capture the essence of the specific distinctions of meaning made in human natural language understanding, and that are capable of replication in machine natural language understanding. The discovery of such features would enable the natural language understanding of voice-controlled systems to become more closely aligned with human understanding both with respect to in-scope and out-of-scope input, thus minimising the potential for malicious exploitation of gaps between human understanding of spoken language and its imitation in artificial systems. However, this possibility remains futuristic and nebulous at present.

A different approach to defending against attacks targeting natural language understanding is suggested by the work of Navigli and Ponzetto [42] on an approach to word sense disambiguation using multilingual semantic networks. The basis of the approach to word sense disambiguation proposed by Navigli and Ponzetto is that the set of word senses associated with a given word is unlikely to remain constant across different languages. Different senses of the same word in one language are likely to be translated as different words in another language, and thus the translation of a word as used in a particular context can be used to determine the correct word sense. This idea might be adapted to detect covert attacks on natural language understanding in voice-controlled systems by translating utterances inputted to a voice-controlled system and comparing the interpretation of user intent from the utterance in different languages. In the case of a non-malicious command, the interpretation of user intent is likely to remain constant across languages. However, in the case of malicious input aiming to mislead natural language understanding, for example by crafted use of homophones, the interpretation of user intent is unlikely to remain constant in different languages. A defence mechanism based on cross-lingual comparison of natural language understanding outputs could be implemented at the dialogue management stage of handling of speech input by a voice-controlled system. In the event that the intent extracted from a user utterance changes in a different language, execution of the intent would be blocked.

The potential of such an approach to defend against attacks on natural language understanding in voice-controlled systems can be trivially demonstrated in the context of the 'word transplant' attacks on natural language understanding in Alexa Skills and RASA NLU using homophones of target command words demonstrated by Bispham et al. [9], using the readily available machine translation technology Google Translate.[9] Google Translate uses RNNs for sequence-to-sequence mapping of input in one language to output in another language (see

---

[9] See https://translate.google.co.uk/.

Wu et al. [54]). Table 2 shows the successful adversarial commands used in the word transplant attacks on natural language understanding in Alexa Skills and RASA NLU demonstrated by Bispham et al. and their translation by Google Translate into German. It is evident that, with just one exception, the number of content words shared between target command and adversarial command drops significantly in translation, and thus that the interpretation of user intent from adversarial commands is unlikely to remain constant across languages.

The effectiveness of this approach as a potential defence against word substitution attacks on natural language understanding, as also demonstrated by Bispham et al. [8] in relation to voice-controlled systems as well by other researchers in related areas, is difficult to test in the absence of a real multilingual voice-controlled system to use in testing. However, it is reasonable to speculate that this approach might at least minimise the effectiveness of such attacks, as it would be less likely for a word substitution attack to be effective across different languages than in just one language. The defence approach proposed here might also be used to defend against any attacks using non-grammatical and/or meaningless combinations of real words as a cover medium for covert attacks, i.e. nonsense attacks targeting natural language understanding in voice-controlled systems. Again this would be based on the supposition that a nonsensical string of words would be less likely to mislead natural language understanding in two languages than just one.

Similar to the use of two different speech recognition systems as a defence against attacks on speech recognition, performing natural language understanding with respect to two or more languages rather than just one in order to

Table 2. Feasibility test for defence against attacks on NLU based on cross-lingual comparison.

Target Command (original language)	Adversarial Command (original language)	no. of words shared between target and adversarial command (original language)	Target Command (translation)	Adversarial Command (translation)	no. of words retained between target and adversarial command (translation)
tell me the current balance	I kept my balance in the current	2	Sag mir das aktuelle Guthaben	Ich habe mein Gleichgewicht im Strom gehalten	0
show me all my transactions	the transactions were for show	2	Zeig mir alle meine Transaktionen	Die Transaktionen waren für die Show	1
pay a bill for electricity	bill of an anchor	1	Strom bezahlen	Rechnung eines Ankers	0
think my card is stolen	your card is an ace	1	Ich glaube meine Karte ist gestolen	Ihre Karte ist ein Ass	1

increase the robustness of this process against malicious input has some commonality with the cyber mimic defence approach of using equivalent but different functionality as a security mechanism as described for example by Liu et al. [38].

5   Conclusion and Future Work

In this paper, we firstly use a modelling framework based on the OODA loop model to analyse the effectiveness of currently available defences against attacks via the speech interface. The analysis concludes that current defence measures are not adequate to prevent all types of attacks via the speech interface, particularly with respect to attacks that exploit gaps between human and machine perceptions of spoken language. In accordance with this conclusion, the paper further makes proposals for the development of new defence mechanisms against human-imperceptible attacks which exploit unintended functionality in the speech recognition and natural language understanding components of voice-controlled systems. These defence mechanisms would be implemented at the dialogue management stage of speech input handling. To counter human-imperceptible attacks targeting speech recognition, a defence mechanism is proposed based on the use of an alternative speech recognition system as a security measure, whereby the outputs of the core speech recognition functionality and the alternative speech recognition system would be compared at the dialogue management stage. A voice command would be executed only if the alternative speech recognition system confirms that it is legitimate human-generated speech. To counter human-imperceptible attacks targeting unintended functionality in natural language understanding, a defence mechanism is proposed based on cross-lingual comparison using machine translation, whereby the interpretation of an utterance by the natural language understanding functionality in the system's original language would be compared to its interpretation in translation to another language at dialogue management stage. A voice command would be executed only if the same user intent was identified in the translation of an utterance as in its original language. On detection of a potential attack targeting speech recognition or natural language understanding, the dialogue management component of the voice-controlled system would block execution of the command identified by the core speech recognition and natural language understanding components, and instead issue a verbal alert to the legitimate user of the device via its response generation and speech synthesis functionalities. Future work should focus on the further development and testing of the proposals for defence mechanisms outlined in this paper.

References

1. Agadakos, I., et al.: Jumping the air gap: modeling cyber-physical attack paths in the internet-of-things. In: Proceedings of the 2017 Workshop on Cyber-Physical Systems Security and Privacy, pp. 37–48 (2017)
2. Al-Mohannadi, H., Mirza, Q., Namanya, A., Awan, I., Cullen, A., Disso, J.: Cyberattack modeling analysis techniques: an overview. In: IEEE International Conference on Future Internet of Things and Cloud Workshops (FiCloudW), pp. 69–76 (2016)
3. Alepis, E., Patsakis, C.: Monkey says, monkey does: security and privacy on voice assistants. IEEE Access **5**, 17841–17851 (2017)
4. Arora, V., Lahiri, A., Reetz, H.: Phonological feature-based speech recognition system for pronunciation training in non-native language learning. J. Acoust. Soc. Am. **143**(1), 98–108 (2018)
5. Auger, J.: Speculative design: crafting the speculation. Dig. Creativity **24**(1), 11–35 (2013)
6. Bhuyan, M.H., Bhattacharyya, D.K., Kalita, J.K.: Network anomaly detection: methods, systems and tools. IEEE Commun. Surv. Tutor. **16**(1), 303–336 (2014)
7. Bispham, M.K., Agrafiotis, I., Goldsmith, M.: Attack and defence modelling for attacks via the speech interface. In: Proceedings of International Conference on Information Systems Security and Privacy, ICISSP 2019, pp. 519–527 (2019)
8. Bispham, M.K., Agrafiotis, I., Goldsmith, M.: Nonsense attacks on Google assistant and missense attacks on Amazon Alexa. In: Proceedings of International Conference on Information Systems Security and Privacy, ICISSP 2019, pp. 75–87 (2019)
9. Bispham, M.K., Janse van Rensburg, A., Agrafiotis, I., Goldsmith, M.: Black-box attacks via the speech interface using linguistically crafted input. In: Mori, P., et al. (eds.) ICISSP 2019, CCIS 1221, pp. xx–yy, revised and extended paper. Springer, Cham (2020)
10. Bispham, M.K., Agrafiotis, I., Goldsmith, M.: A taxonomy of attacks via the speech interface. In: Proceedings of CYBER 2018: The Third International Conference on Cyber-Technologies and Cyber-Systems, pp. 7–14 (2018)
11. Boyd, J.R.: The essence of winning and losing. Unpublished Lecture Notes **12**(23), 123–125 (1996)
12. Brehmer, B.: The dynamic OODA loop: Amalgamating Boyd's OODA loop and the dynamic decision loop (2005)
13. Budanitsky, A., Hirst, G.: Semantic distance in WordNet: an experimental, application-oriented evaluation of five measures. In: Workshop on WordNet and Other Lexical Resources, vol. 2, p. 2 (2001)
14. Carlini, N., et al.: Hidden voice commands. In: 25th USENIX Security Symposium (USENIX Security 2016), Austin, TX (2016)
15. Carlini, N., Wagner, D.: Audio adversarial examples: Targeted attacks on speech-to-text. arXiv preprint arXiv:1801.01944 (2018)
16. Chung, H., Park, J., Lee, S.: Digital forensic approaches for Amazon Alexa ecosystem. Dig. Invest. **22**, 15–25 (2017)
17. Ciesielski, A., Yeh, B., Gordge, K., Basescu, M., Tunstel, E.: Vocal human-robot interaction inspired by Battle Management Language. In: 2017 IEEE International Conference on Systems, Man, and Cybernetics (SMC), pp. 3379–3384 (2017)
18. Dhanjani, N.: Abusing the Internet of Things: Blackouts, Freakouts, and Stakeouts. O'Reilly Media Inc., Sebastopol (2015)

19. Diao, W., Liu, X., Zhou, Z., Zhang, K.: Your voice assistant is mine: How to abuse speakers to steal information and control your phone. In: Proceedings of the 4th ACM Workshop on Security and Privacy in Smartphones & Mobile Devices, pp. 63–74. ACM (2014)
20. Fedorenko, E., et al.: Neural correlate of the construction of sentence meaning. Proc. Natl. Acad. Sci. **113**(41), 6256–6262 (2016)
21. Garofolo, J.S., Lamel, L.F., Fisher, W.M., Fiscus, J.G., Pallett, D.S.: DARPA TIMIT acoustic-phonetic continous speech corpus cd-rom. NASA STI/Recon technical report (1993)
22. Giraldo, J., Sarkar, E., Cardenas, A.A., Maniatakos, M., Kantarcioglu, M.: Security and privacy in cyber-physical systems: a survey of surveys. IEEE Des. Test **34**(4), 7–17 (2017)
23. Gomaa, W.H., Fahmy, A.A.: A survey of text similarity approaches. Int. J. Comput. Appl. **68**(13), 13–18 (2013)
24. Gong, Y., Poellabauer, C.: An overview of vulnerabilities of voice controlled systems. arXiv preprint arXiv:1803.09156 (2018)
25. Hansen, J.H., Hasan, T.: Speaker recognition by machines and humans: a tutorial review. IEEE Signal Process. Mag. **32**(6), 74–99 (2015)
26. Hasan, M.R., Jamil, M., Rahman, M., et al.: Speaker identification using MEL frequency cepstral coefficients. Variations **1**(4) (2004)
27. Jackson, C., Orebaugh, A.: A study of security and privacy issues associated with the Amazon Echo. Int. J. Internet Things Cyber-Assur. **1**(1), 91–100 (2018)
28. Johnson, M.A., Goldberg, A.E.: Evidence for automatic accessing of constructional meaning: Jabberwocky sentences prime associated verbs. Lang. Cognit. Process. **28**(10), 1439–1452 (2013)
29. Kaljurand, K., Alumäe, T.: Controlled natural language in speech recognition based user interfaces. In: International Workshop on Controlled Natural Language, pp. 79–94 (2012)
30. Khan, O.Z., Sarikaya, R.: Making personal digital assistants aware of what they do not know. In: INTERSPEECH, pp. 1161–1165 (2016)
31. Klein, G., Tolle, J., Martini, P.: From detection to reaction-a holistic approach to cyber defense. In: Defense Science Research Conference and Expo (DSR) 2011, pp. 1–4. IEEE (2011)
32. Kong, X., Choi, J.-Y., Shattuck-Hufnagel, S.: Evaluating automatic speech recognition systems in comparison with human perception results using distinctive feature measures. In: 2017 IEEE International Conference on Acoustics, Speech and Signal Processing (ICASSP), pp. 5810–5814. IEEE (2017)
33. Kuhn, T.: A survey and classification of controlled natural languages. Comput. Linguist. **40**(1), 121–170 (2014)
34. Lahiri, A., Reetz, H., Roberts, P.: Method and apparatus for automatic speech recognition. US Patent App. 15/105,552 (2016)
35. Lahiri, A., Reetz, H.: Distinctive features: phonological underspecification in representation and processing. J. Phonet. **38**(1), 44–59 (2010)
36. Liang, B., Li, H., Su, M., Bian, P., Li, X., Shi, W.: Deep Text Classification Can be Fooled. arXiv preprint arXiv:1704.08006 (2017)
37. Lison, P., Meena, R.: Spoken dialogue systems: the new frontier in human-computer interaction. XRDS: Crossroads ACM Mag. Stud. **21**(1), 46–51 (2014)
38. Liu, W., Chen, F., Hu, H., Cheng, G., Huo, S., Liang, H.: A novel framework for zero-day attacks detection and response with cyberspace mimic defense architecture. In: Proceedings of 2017 International Conference on Cyber-Enabled Distributed Computing and Knowledge Discovery (CyberC), pp. 50–53 (2017)

39. Loukas, G., Gan, D., Vuong, T.: A taxonomy of cyber attack and defence mechanisms for emergency management networks. In: 2013 IEEE International Conference on Pervasive Computing and Communications Workshops (PERCOM Workshops), pp. 534–539. IEEE (2013)

40. McShane, M., Blissett, K., Nirenburg, I.: Treating unexpected input in incremental semantic analysis. In: Proceedings of The Fifth Annual Conference on Advances in Cognitive Systems, Cognitive Systems Foundation, Palo Alto, CA (2017)

41. McTear, M., Callejas, Z., Griol, D.: The Conversational Interface. Springer, Cham (2016). https://doi.org/10.1007/978-3-319-32967-3

42. Navigli, R., Ponzetto, S.P.: Joining forces pays off: multilingual joint word sense disambiguation. In: Proceedings of the 2012 Joint Conference on Empirical Methods in Natural Language Processing and Computational Natural Language Learning, pp. 1399–1410 (2012)

43. Papernot, N., McDaniel, P., Goodfellow, I., Jha, S., Celik, Z.B., Swami, A.: Practical black-box attacks against deep learning systems using adversarial examples. arXiv preprint arXiv:1602.02697 (2016)

44. Papernot, N., McDaniel, P., Swami, A., Harang, R.: Crafting adversarial input sequences for recurrent neural networks. In: Military Communications Conference, MILCOM 2016-2016 IEEE, pp. 49–54 (2016)

45. Patten, T., Call, C., Mitchell, D., Taylor, J., Lasser, S.: Defining the malice space with natural language processing techniques. In: Cybersecurity Symposium (CYBERSEC), pp. 44–50. IEEE (2016)

46. Petracca, G., Sun, Y., Jaeger, T., Atamli, A.: Audroid: preventing attacks on audio channels in mobile devices. In: Proceedings of the 31st Annual Computer Security Applications Conference, pp. 181–190. ACM (2015)

47. Pucher, M., Türk, A., Ajmera, J., Fecher, N.: Phonetic distance measures for speech recognition vocabulary and grammar optimization. In: 3rd Congress of the Alps Adria Acoustics Association, pp. 2–5 (2007)

48. Rieck, K., Laskov, P.: Detecting unknown network attacks using language models. In: Büschkes, R., Laskov, P. (eds.) DIMVA 2006. LNCS, vol. 4064, pp. 74–90. Springer, Heidelberg (2006). https://doi.org/10.1007/11790754_5

49. Roy, N., Shen, S., Hassanieh, H., Choudhury, R.R.: Inaudible voice commands: the long-range attack and defense. In: 15th USENIX Symposium on Networked Systems Design and Implementation NSDI 2018), pp. 547–560. USENIX Association (2018)

50. Rule, J.N.: A Symbiotic Relationship: The OODA Loop, Intuition, and Strategic Thought. US Army War College (2013)

51. Schneider, M.A., Wendland, M.-F., Hoffmann, A.: A negative input space complexity metric as selection criterion for fuzz testing. In: El-Fakih, K., Barlas, G., Yevtushenko, N. (eds.) ICTSS 2015. LNCS, vol. 9447, pp. 257–262. Springer, Cham (2015). https://doi.org/10.1007/978-3-319-25945-1_17

52. Janse van Rensburg, A., Nurse, J.R., Goldsmith, M.: Attacker-parametrised attack graphs. In: 10th International Conference on Emerging Security Information, Systems and Technologies (2016)

53. Weller-Fahy, D.J., Borghetti, B.J., Sodemann, A.A.: A survey of distance and similarity measures used within network intrusion anomaly detection. IEEE Commun. Surv. Tutor. 17(1), 70–91 (2015)

54. Wu, Y., et al.: Google's neural machine translation system: bridging the gap between human and machine translation. arXiv preprint arXiv:1609.08144 (2016)

55. Wu, Z., Evans, N., Kinnunen, T., Yamagishi, J., Alegre, F., Li, H.: Spoofing and countermeasures for speaker verification: a survey. Speech Commun. **66**, 130–153 (2015)

56. Young, P.J., Jin, J.H., Woo, S., Lee, D.H.: BadVoice: soundless voice-control replay attack on modern smartphones. In: 2016 Eighth International Conference on Ubiquitous and Future Networks (ICUFN), pp. 882–887. IEEE (2016)

57. Young, S., Gašić, M., Thomson, B., Williams, J.D.: POMDP-based statistical spoken dialog systems: a review. Proc. IEEE **101**(5), 1160–1179 (2013)

58. Zhang, G., Yan, C., Ji, X., Zhang, T., Zhang, T., Xu, W.: DolphinAttack: inaudible voice commands. arXiv preprint arXiv:1708.09537 (2017)

Hypervisor Memory Introspection and Hypervisor Based Malware Honeypot

Nezer Jacob Zaidenberg[1,2,5](✉) ⓘ, Michael Kiperberg[3,5], Raz Ben Yehuda[2,5], Roee Leon[2,5], Asaf Algawi[2,5], and Amit Resh[4,5]

[1] College of Management Academic Studies, Rishon LeZion, Israel
[2] University of Jyväskylä, Jyväskylä, Finland
[3] SCE, Ashdod, Israel
[4] Shenkar College, Ramat Gan, Israel
[5] TrulyProtect Oy, Tel Aviv, Israel
{nezer,michael,raz,roee,asaf,amit}@trulyprotect.com

Abstract. Memory acquisition is a tool used in advanced forensics and malware analysis. Various methods of memory acquisition exist. Such solutions are ranging from tools based on dedicated hardware to software-only solutions. We proposed a hypervisor based memory acquisition tool. [22]. Our method supports ASLR and Modern operating systems which is an innovation compared to past methods [27,36]. We extend the hypervisor assisted memory acquisition by adding mass storage device honeypots for the malware to cross and propose hiding the hypervisor using bluepill technology.

Keywords: Live forensics · Memory forensics · Memory acquisition · Virtualization · Reliability · Atomicity · Integrity of a memory snapshot · Forensic soundness

1 Introduction

Nowadays, cyber-attacks are so sophisticated that it is almost impossible to perform static analysis on them. Many of the recent attacks have means to detect debuggers and similar dynamic analysis tools. Upon detection of an inspection, the malicious software deviates from its normal behaviour, thus rendering the analysis useless. The malicious software will only activate its destructive parts if no inspection tool is running.

Furthermore, we are often interested in a forensic analysis of such an attack. In some case (such as Wannacry virus [31]) such analysis may locate weakness in the attack. In others (such as Stuxnet [24]) such analysis performed in the post mortem may inform us about the preparators of the attack. Also, in defence oriented cases, the origin of the attack may be another nation. In such cases it is required to know which nation have performed the attack. Furthermore, sometimes false feedback can be provided to the sender which is also required. Since dynamic analysis is doomed to failure, the forensic analysis of is divided into two steps

© Springer Nature Switzerland AG 2020
P. Mori et al. (Eds.): ICISSP 2019, CCIS 1221, pp. 317–334, 2020.
https://doi.org/10.1007/978-3-030-49443-8_15

Memory Acquisition. An acquisition tool (such as [27,36,37,52]) acquires the contents of the system memory (RAM). The tool stores the memory on some file for offline analysis.

Static Analysis. An analysis tool (such as rekall [10] or volatility [26]) is used on the file that was acquired in the previous step. The analysis tools are searching for malware and other anomalies.

During the operating system running time, the operating system updates its data structures and pointers. If the user performs, the memory acquisition while the system is running, the user may acquire an inconsistent image of the system memory. For example we examine the common task of creating a new task. While creating a new task, the operating system performs allocation for the new task memory in one memory region and also updates the task table in another memory region.

If the process table is dumped on one chunk and the process itself is dumped on another chunk them an inconsistency is likely to appear. For example, a task in the task table that does not point to memory or task that exists in memory but does not exist on the task table.

Memory inconsistencies look like anomaly and are likely to confuse the detection process. Therefore, preventing measures must be taken to avoid inconsistencies in the acquired memory image. We present a software hypervisor-based tool for consistent memory acquisition, [22]. The Hypervisor can also be used to create tripwires to detect malicious software. We added this feature to the current work. Furthermore, inspected malicious software can alter its behavior when inspected. Therefore we added blue pill technology to the hypervisor to enable the hypervisor to introspect the system and grab the system memory without being detected.

We use the hypervisor's ability to configure access rights of memory pages to solve the problem of inconsistencies as follows:

1. When memory acquisition is started, the hypervisor configures all memory pages to be non-writable.
2. When any process attempts to write to any memory page (hereby P), the hypervisor is notified.
3. The hypervisor copies the contents of P to an internal buffer and configures P to be writable.
4. The hypervisor performs the dump emptying its internal buffer as first priority. If no data remains to be copied in the internal buffer, then the hypervisor sends other pages and configures them to be writable.
5. Writable pages no longer triggers event in the hypervisor.
6. The hypervisor also serves as an honeypot. The hypervisor is now looking for attacks. The hypervisor is now seducing attacks as some sort of honeypot [32].

Steps 1 through 4 are described in multiple previous works [27,36].

Three problems arise with the described method in modern systems.

Multi-cores. Each processor core has direct access to the main memory. Thus each core can modify any memory page. Therefore, when the hypervisor starts memory acquisition, it must configure all memory pages, *onallprocessors* to be non-writable.

Delay Sensitive Pages. Generally, interrupt service routines react to interrupts in two steps: they register the occurrence of an interrupt and acknowledge the device that the interrupt was serviced. The acknowledgement must be received in a timely manner; therefore, the registration of an interrupt occurrence, which involves writing to a memory page, must not be intercepted by a hypervisor, i.e., these pages must remain writable.

ASLR. Address space layout randomization [45], a security feature employed by modern operating systems, e.g., Windows 10, complicates the delay sensitivity problem even more. When ASLR is enabled, the operating system splits its virtual address space into regions. Then, during the initialization of the operating system, each region is assigned a random virtual address. With ASLR, the location of the delay-sensitive pages is not known in advance.

We solved the problems mentioned above in [22] in the following method. Our hypervisor invokes an operating system's mechanism to perform an atomic access rights configuration on all the processors. Section 4.3 describes the invocation process, which allows our hypervisor to call an operating system's function in a safe and predictable manner.

We solved the delay sensitivity problem by copying the delay-sensitive pages to the hypervisor's internal buffer in advance, i.e., when the hypervisor starts memory acquisition.

We solved the ASLR complication by inspecting the operating system's memory regions map. Thu we have showed how the location of the dynamic locations of the delay-sensitive pages is obtained. Section 4.2 contains a detailed description of ASLR handling in Windows 10 and our solution of the delay sensitivity problem in windows.

The contribution of our work is:

- We showed memory acquisition technique on systems with multiple processors.
- We showed a solution for the delay sensitive data
- We explained how the locations of sensitive pages can be obtained dynamically on Windows 10.

Furthermore, the malware can detect our memory acquisition hypervisor, proposed in [22]. Modern operating systems such as Windows and OSX are using hypervisors as part of the system, however the malware may also detect the hypervisor, suspect an inspection [51] and alter its behaviour.

Therefore, we have add two more contributions to this work

- Summary of recent work on building stealth hypervisors (blue pills) [1].
- we add new feature adding honey pot (trip wire) that will look like an interesting target and attack the malicious code to reveal itself and attack it [4].

2   Related Work

Windows versions before Windows server 2003sp1 contained a special device,

`\\\\Device\\PhysicalMemory`

This device map the entire physical memory. This device could be used to acquire the entire physical memory. However, Microsoft removed this device from modern windows operating systems [29]. This device can be used by malware as means to disrupt the memory acquisition process [9]. Furthermore, this method is not available in recent versions of Windows windows.

One can also use dedicated hardware for memory acquisition. A generic FireWire adapter can be used to acquire memory remotely [52]. A dedicated PCI card, named Tribble, is another option [9]. As well as any RDMA hardware. The advantage of a hardware solution is the ability of a PCI card to communicate with the memory controller directly, thus providing a reliable result even if the operating system itself was compromised. However, hardware-based solutions have three deficiencies:

1. Hardware based solutions require dedicated hardware thus increasing the cost of the implementation
2. Hardware based solution may be faster then software based solution but still do not provide atomic memory dump.
3. Microsoft's device guard [11] prevents using these tools.

Device Guard is a security feature recently introduced in Windows 10. Device guard utilizes IOMMU ([3]; [50]) to prevent malicious access to memory from physical devices [8]. When Device Guard is running, the operating system assigns each device a memory region that it is allowed to access. The DMA controller prevents any attempt to access memory outside this region, including memory acquisition. Recently, researchers proposed several hypervisor-based methods of memory acquisition. HyperSleuth [27] is a driver with an embedded hypervisor. Hyper-Sleuth hypervisor is capable of performing atomic and lazy memory acquisition. Lazy in terms of memory acquisition is the ability of the system to run normally while the memory is acquired. ForenVisor [36] is a similar hypervisor with also act as key logger and monitors hard-drive activity. Both HyperSleuth and ForenVisor works on Windows XP SP3 with only one processor enabled. We show how the idea of HyperSleuth and ForenVisor can be adapted to multi-processor systems executing Windows 10.

3   Background

3.1   Hypervisors

Our primary system component is the hypervisor. We describe the hypervisor design in Sect. 4. We distinguish between two families of hypervisors: full hypervisors and thin hypervisors. Full hypervisors like Xen [2], VMware Workstation

[47], and Oracle VirtualBox [33]. Can run several operating systems in parallel. Almost all hypervisors, including ours and all the hypervisors aforementioned above, use hardware assisted virtualization. Hardware assisted virtualization is an instruct set providing efficient API to run multiple virtual machines. Intel use the term VT-x for their hardware assisted virtualization implementation. Running multiple operating systems efficiently is the primary goal of VT-x [18]. In contrast, thin hypervisors execute only a single operating system. The primary purpose of thin hypervisors is to enrich the functionality of an operating system. The main benefit of a hypervisor over kernel modules (device drivers) is the hypervisor's ability to provide an isolated environment, unlike containers (such as docker [7], kubernetes [16]). Thin hypervisors in the industry have various purposes including for real-time [5,15] and other purposes. We focus on thin-hypervisors use for security. Thin hypervisor can measure operating system's integrity validation [14,43], reverse engineering prevention [6,20] remote attestation [19,21]; malicious code execution prevention [25,38], in-memory secret protection [39], hard drive encryption [44], and memory acquisition [36].

Thin hypervisors perform fewer functions than full hypervisors; therefore, thin hypervisors are smaller than full hypervisors. Thus thin hypervisors are superior in their performance, security, and reliability. Our memory acquisition hypervisor is a thin hypervisor that is capable of acquiring a memory image of an executing system atomically. The hypervisor was written from scratch to achieve optimal performance. Similarly to an operating system, a hypervisor does not execute voluntarily but responds to events, e.g., execution of special instructions, generation of exceptions, access to memory locations, etc. The hypervisor can configure interception of (almost) each event. Trapping an event (a VM-exit) is similar to the handling of an interrupt, i.e., a predefined function executes when an event occurs. Another similarity with a full operating system is the hypervisor's ability to configure the access rights to each memory page through second-level address translation tables (SLAT tables) structure. Intel uses the name EPT for their SLAT implementation and use the terms interchangeably. An attempt to write to a non-writable (according to EPT) page induces a VM-exit and allows the hypervisor to act.

3.2 Lazy Hypervisor Memory Acquisition

Both HyperSleuth and ForenVisor are thin hypervisors and can be summarized as follows. The hypervisor is idle until it receives a memory acquisition command. After the command is received, the hypervisor configures the EPT to make all memory pages non-writable. An attempt to write to a page P will trigger a VM-exit, thus allowing the hypervisor to react. The hypervisor reacts by copying P to an internal buffer and making P writable again. Thus, Future attempts to write to P will not trigger a VM-exit. The hypervisor sends the buffered pages to a remote machine via a communication channel. The required buffer size depends on the communication channel bandwidth and the volume of modified pages. If the communication channel allows sending more data than is the buffer contains, the hypervisor sends other non-writable pages and configures them to be writable. This process continues until all pages are writable.

3.3 Delay-Sensitive Pages and ASLR

We examine Interrupt Service Routines (ISR). Generally, ISR routines react to interrupts in two steps: they register the occurrence of an interrupt and acknowledge the device that the interrupt was handled. The acknowledgement must be received in real-time; therefore, the registration of an interrupt, which involves writing to a memory page, must not be intercepted by a hypervisor, i.e., these pages must remain writable. The authors of HyperSleuth and ForenVisor did not address this issue. We assume that this problem did not occur on single-core Windows XP SP3, which previous works used. Address space layout randomization, a security feature employed by the modern operating system, e.g., Windows 10, complicates the delay sensitivity problem even more. When ASLR is enabled, the operating system splits its virtual address space into regions. Then, during the initialization of the operating system, each region is assigned a random virtual address. This behavior is useful against a wide range of attacks [12] because the address of potentially vulnerable modules is not known in advance. However, for the same reason, the address of the delay-sensitive pages is also unpredictable.

3.4 Honeypots

Honeypots in the network case have been researched for a long time [4]. A Honeypot is a network device that appears vulnerable to an attack. The malicious software reveals itself by attacking the honeypot. The system administrator monitors the honeypot, detect the attack and remove the attacker.

Honeypot (and Anti-Honeypots [23]) are well researched [28] in the network case. Network honeypots are also used in forensics [34].

Our honeypot differs from prior art as we use the hypervisors to create honeypot devices within the machine instead of the network. This innovation allows us to trigger memory collection just as the malware start operating.

4 Design

4.1 Initialization

We implemented the hypervisor as a UEFI application [46]. The UEFI application loads before the operating system, allocates all the required memory, and initializes the hypervisor. After initialization, the UEFI application terminates, thus allowing the operating system boot loader to initialize the operating system. We note that while the UEFI application that started the hypervisor is terminated, the hypervisor remains active.

In order to protect itself from a potentially malicious environment, the hypervisor configures the SLAT such that any access to the code and the data of the hypervisor is prohibited. With this exception, the SLAT is configured to be an identity mapping that allows full access to all the memory pages (Fig. 1).

The hypervisor remains idle until an external event triggers its memory acquisition functionality. The external event might be the reception of a network packet, insertion of a USB device, starting a process, invocation of a system call, etc. In our prototype implementation, we used a special CPUID instruction, which we call FREEZE, as a trigger. CPUID is an Intel assembler instruction that the hypervisor must trap (preform VM-Exit) according to the architecture specification.

When receiving FREEZE, the hypervisor performs two actions:

1. Identifies and copies the delay-sensitive pages.
2. configure the access rights of all memory pages on all cores to be non-writable.

After all pages are marked non-writable the hypervisor reacts to page modification attempts by making the page writable and copying it to an internal buffer. (similar to ForenVisor and Hyper Sleuth) The hypervisor exports the pages stored in the internal buffer in response to another special CPUID instructions, which we call DUMP. (or another trigger as above)

If the queue is not full, then the hypervisor exports other non-writable pages and marks the exported pages writable.

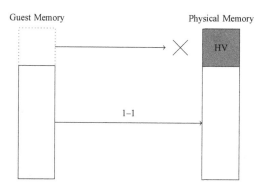

Fig. 1. Mapping between the physical address space as observed by the operating system (left) and the actual physical address space. The mapping is an identity mapping with the exception of the hypervisor's pages, which are not mapped at all. Originally appeared at [22].

Algorithm 1: Memory Acquisition. Originally appeared at [22].

1: file ← Open(. . .)
2: FREEZE()
3: **while** DUMP(addr, page) **do**
4:     Seek(file, addr)
5:     Write(file, page)
6: Close(file)

Algorithm 1 describes how FREEZE and DUMP can be used to acquire an atomic image of the memory. First, the algorithm opens a file that will contain the resulting memory image. Then, FREEZE is invoked, followed by a series of DUMPs. When the DUMP request returns *false*, the file is closed and the algorithm terminates.

The file now contain the entire system memory and can be analyzed by other tools such as volatility [26].

4.2   Delay

We explained in Sect. 3.3 that certain pages cannot not be configured as non-writable. Moreover, due to ASLR, the hypervisor has to discover the location of these pages at run time. The discover process and the Windows 10 data structures that are used are described here.

Table 1. Windows ASLR-related data structures. Originally appeared at [22].

Offset	Field/Variable Name	Type
X	System Call Service Routine	*Code*
...	...	...
+0xFB100	MiState	MI_SYSTEM_INFORMATION
+0x1440	Vs	MI_VISIBLE_STATE
+0x0B50	SystemVaRegions	MI_SYSTEM_VA_ASSIGNMENT[14]
+0x0000	[0]	MI_SYSTEM_VA_ASSIGNMENT
+0x0000	BaseAddress	uint64_t
+0x0008	NumberOfBytes	uint64_t

Windows 10 defines a global variable MiState of type MI_SYSTEM_INFORMA TION. The hypervisor can easily locate this variable as it has a constant offset from the system call service routine, whose address is stored in the LSTAR register (Table 1). The MI_SYSTEM_INFORMATION structure has a field named Vs of type MI_VISIBLE_STATE. Finally, the MI_VISIBLE_STATE structure has a field named SystemVaRegions, which is an array of 15 pairs. Each pair corresponds to a memory region whose address was chosen at random during the operating system's initialization. The first element of the pair is the random address and the second element is the region's size. A description of each memory region is given in Table 2. A more detailed discussion of the memory regions appears in [40]. Our empirical study shows that the following regions contain delay-sensitive pages:

1. MiVaProcessSpace
2. MiVaPagedPool
3. MiVaSpecialPoolPaged
4. MiVaSystemCache
5. MiVaSystemPtes
6. MiVaSessionGlobalSpace

Therefore, the hypervisor never makes these regions non-writable.

Table 2. Memory Regions. Originally appeared at [22].

Index	Name
0	MiVaUnused
1	MiVaSessionSpace
2	MiVaProcessSpace
3	MiVaBootLoaded
4	MiVaPfnDatabase
5	MiVaNonPagedPool
6	MiVaPagedPool
7	MiVaSpecialPoolPaged
8	MiVaSystemCache
9	MiVaSystemPtes
10	MiVaHal
11	MiVaSessionGlobalSpace
12	MiVaDriverImages
13	MiVaSystemPtesLarge

4.3 Multicore

The hypervisor responds to FREEZE, a memory acquisition request, by copying the delay-sensitive pages to an inner queue and configuring all other pages to be non-writable. However, when multiple processors are active, the access rights configuration must be performed atomically on all processors.

Operating systems usually use inter-processor interrupts (IPIs) [18] for synchronization between processors. It seems tempting to use IPIs also in the hypervisor, i.e., the processor that received FREEZE can send IPIs to other processors, thus requesting them to configure the access rights appropriately. Unfortunately, this method requires the hypervisor to replace the operating system's interrupt-descriptors table (IDT) with the hypervisor's IDT. This approach has two deficiencies:

1. Kernel Patch Protection (KPP) [13], a security feature introduced by Microsoft in Windows 2003, performs a periodic validation of critical kernel structures in order to prevent their illegal modification. Therefore, replacing the IDT requires also intercepting KPP's validation attempts, which can degrade the overall system performance.
2. Intel processors assign priorities to interrupt vectors. Interrupts of lower priority are blocked while an interrupt of a higher priority is delivered. Therefore, the hypervisor cannot guarantee that a sent IPI will be handled within a predefined time. Suspending the operating system for long periods can cause the operating system's watchdog timer to trigger a stop error (BSoD).

We present a different method to solve the inter-processor synchronization problem that is based on a documented functionality of the operating system itself. The `KeIpiGenericCall` function [30] receives a callback function as a parameter and executes it on all the active processors simultaneously. We propose to use the `KeIpiGenericCall` function to configure the access rights simultaneously on all the processors.

Because it is impossible to call an operating system function from within the context of the hypervisor, the hypervisor calls the `KeIpiGenericCall` function from the context of the (guest) operating system. In order to achieve this, the hypervisor performs several preparations and then resumes the execution of the operating system. Algorithm 2 presents three functions that together perform simultaneous access rights configuration on all the active processors. The first function, HANDLECPUID, is part of the hypervisor. This function is called whenever the operating system invokes a special `CPUID` instruction. Two other functions, GUESTENTRY and CALLBACK, are mapped by the hypervisor to a non-occupied region of the operating system's memory.

Algorithm 1 begins with a special `CPUID` instruction, called `FREEZE`. This instruction is handled by lines 2–5 in Algorithm 2: the hypervisor maps GUESTENTRY and CALLBACK, saves the current registers' values and sets the instruction pointer to the address of GUESTENTRY. The GUESTENTRY function calls the operating system's KEIPIGENERICCALL, which will execute CALLBACK on all the active processors. The CALLBACK function performs another special `CPUID` instruction, called `CONFIGURE`, which causes the hypervisor to configure the access rights of all (but the delay-sensitive) memory pages on all the processors. This is handled by lines 6–7 of the algorithm, where we omitted the

---

Algorithm 2 : Simultaneous access rights configuration on all the active processors. Originally appeared at [22].

```
 1: function HANDLECPUID(reason)
 2:     if reason=FREEZE then
 3:         Map GUESTENTRY and CALLBACK
 4:         Save registers
 5:         RIP ← GUESTENTRY
 6:     else if reason=CONFIGURE then
 7:         ...
 8:     else if reason=RESUME_OS then
 9:         Restore registers
10:     else if reason=DUMP then
11:         ...
12:     ...
13: function GUESTENTRY
14:     KEIPIGENERICCALL(CALLBACK)
15:     CPUID(RESUME_OS)
16: function CALLBACK
17:     CPUID(CONFIGURE)
```

configuration procedure itself. After the termination of the CALLBACK function, the control returns to the GUESTENTRY function, which executes a special CPUID instruction, named RESUME_OS. In response, the hypervisor restores the registers' values, which were previously saved in line 4. The operation continues from the instruction following FREEZE, which triggered this sequence of events.

5   Honeypot

We augmented the project by creating an honeypot. We create a virtual mass storage device. We assume malware such as stuxnet [24] or computer viruses attempt to detect mass storage device for replication purposes.

We use special device detect device access to the virtual device. In some cases such device access can serve as FREEZE trigger.

The honeypot is made of two main components

Access Identification Component for Storage Components. The component is installed as a Kernel module and extends to a virtual disk operating system that identifies as a physical component and monitors access to it. When a process accesses the storage component, the process data enters the queue of the malicious processes that are waiting for the action of the enforcement component.

Enforcement Component. This component is managed in the user space of the operating system and is waiting to be called, when it is called it invokes the FREEZE and DUMP commands.

6   Blue-Pilling

[41] introduced the blue pill. It was with the concept of the blue pill and red pill that the virtualization concept became so closely related to cybersecurity. The blue pill is a rootkit that takes control of the victim's computer [42]. The blue pill is very hard to detect. Since the blue pill is an hypervisor it is not visible on the standard task manager or even works in the same address space as the operating system. Since our interest is in acquiring reliable memory image that includes any malicious software and since malicious software may hide their presence if a memory acquisition takes place we recommend that blue pill technology will be added to the hypervisor. Rotkowska also coined the term red pill. The red pill is meant to detect and counter the blue pill. The red pill is a hardware or software tool that is designed to detect such malicious camouflaged hypervisor-based rootkit.

Some users start a virtual machine as a sandbox to detect malicious code in contained environment. When using suspected code they install it first on the virtual machine on only if no attacks were spotted they move the software to their physical machine.

To counter the above routine, some malware use simple red pills to detect hypervisors. These malware will not use their offensive features if an hypervisor is present. Therefore, it is vital for the memory acquisition hypervisor to also act as a blue-pill stealth hypervisor.

[1] describes the current status of blue pill hypervisors. We recommend that these methods will be added to this solution as well.

7   Evaluation

We evaluate the performance of the hypervisor and its memory usage. First, we demonstrate the overall performance impact of the hypervisor. (We compare the performance of a normal system to a system with a hypervisor that does nothing)

Next, we analyze the memory usage of the hypervisor. Finally, we evaluate the performance of the memory acquisition process.

All the experiments were performed in the following environment:

- CPU: Intel Core i5-6500 CPU 3.20 GHz (4 physical cores)
- RAM: 16.00 GB
- OS: Windows 10 Pro x86-64 Version 1803 (OS Build 17134.407)
- C/C++ Compiler: Microsoft C/C++ Optimizing Compiler Version 19.00.23026 for x86.

7.1   Performance Impact

We demonstrate the performance impact of the hypervisor on the operating system. We picked two benchmarking tools for Windows:

1. PCMark 10 – Basic Edition. Version Info: PCMark 10 GUI – 1.0.1457 64 , SystemInfo – 5.4.642, PCMark 10 System 1.0.1457,
2. Novabench. Version Info: 4.0.3 – November 2017.

Each tool performs several tests and displays a score for each test. We invoked each tool twice: with and without the hypervisor. The results of PCMark, and Novabench are depicted in Figs. 2 and 3, respectively. We can see that the performance penalty of the hypervisor is approximately 5% on average. This figure is equivalent to similar results achieved by top vendors [17,48,49].

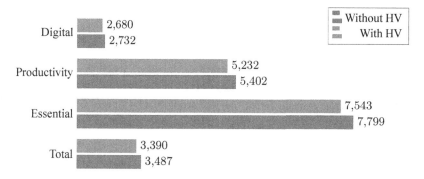

Fig. 2. Scores (larger is better) reported by PCMark in four categories: Digital Content Creation, Productivity, Essential, and Total. Originally appeared at [22].

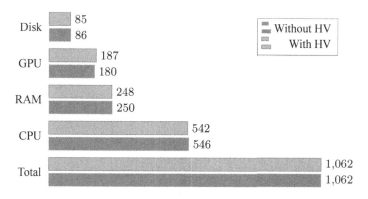

Fig. 3. Scores (larger is better) reported by Novabench in five categories: Disk, GPU, RAM, CPU, and Total. Originally appeared at [22].

7.2 Memory Usage

The memory used by the hypervisor can be divided into three main parts:

1. the code and the data structures of the hypervisor,
2. the EPT tables used to configure the access rights to the memory pages, and
3. the queue used to accumulate the modified pages.

Figure 4 presents the memory usage of the hypervisor including its division.

The size of the queue is mainly dictated by the number of delay-sensitive pages. Table 3 presents the typical size of each memory region.

Pages belonging to the following regions are copied by the hypervisor:

1. MiVaProcessSpace
2. MiVaPagedPool
3. MiVaSpecialPoolPaged

4. MiVaSystemCache
5. MiVaSystemPtes
6. MiVaSessionGlobalSpace

Their total size is ≈60 MB. The size of the queue should be slightly larger than the total size of the delay-sensitive pages because regular pages can be modified by the operating system before the content of the queue is exported. Our empirical study shows that it is sufficient to enlarge the queue by 60 MB.

Table 3. Memory Regions' Sizes. Originally appeared at [22].

Index	Name	Size (MB)
0	MiVaUnused	6
1	MiVaSessionSpace	100
2	MiVaProcessSpace	0
3	MiVaBootLoaded	0
4	MiVaPfnDatabase	0
5	MiVaNonPagedPool	6
6	MiVaPagedPool	0
7	MiVaSpecialPoolPaged	5
8	MiVaSystemCache	52
9	MiVaSystemPtes	0
10	MiVaHal	0
11	MiVaSessionGlobalSpace	0
12	MiVaDriverImages	8

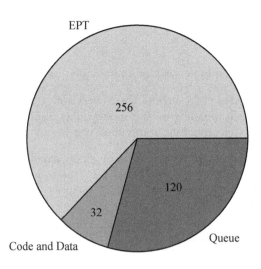

Fig. 4. Hypervisor's Memory Usage [MB]. Originally appeared at [22].

7.3   Memory Acquisition Performance

We examine the correlation between the speed of memory acquisition and the overall system performance. Figure 5 shows the results. The horizontal axis represents the memory acquisition speed. The maximal speed we could achieve was 97920KB/s. At this speed, the system became unresponsive and the benchmarking tools failed. The vertical axis represents the performance degradation (in percent) measured by PCMark and Novabench. More precisely, denote by $t_i(x)$ the *Total* result of benchmark $i = 1, 2$ (for PCMark and Novabench, respectively) with acquisition speed of x; then, the performance degradation $d_i(x)$ is given by

$$d_i(x) = 1 - \frac{t_i(x)}{t_i(0)}. \tag{1}$$

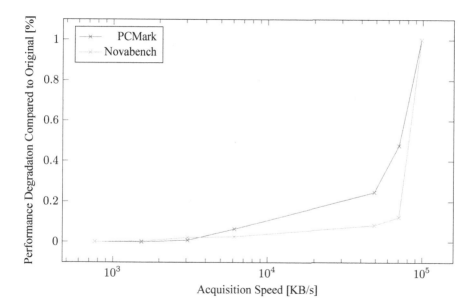

Fig. 5. Performance degradation due to memory acquisition. Originally appeared at [22].

8   Conclusion

Our method is a small improvement over previously described methods with similar design. We describe five improvements over the previously described methods:

1. Our hypervisor supports multiple cores and processors.
2. Our hypervisor supports modern operating systems, e.g., Windows 10 and Linux.

3. Our hypervisor includes honeypot for malicious hypervisors.
4. We have proposed means to use blue-pill techniques so that malware will can not detect the hypervisor.
5. Additionally, our new paper also includes a USB honeypot as trip wire that does not appear in [22].

References

1. Algawi, A., Kiperberg, M., Leon, R., Resh, A., Zaidenberg, N.: Creating modern blue pills and red pills. In: European Conference on Cyber Warfare and Security, pp. 6–14. Academic Conferences International Limited, July 2019
2. Barham, P., et al.: Xen and the art of virtualization. In: ACM SIGOPS Operating Systems Review, vol. 37, pp. 164–177. ACM (2003)
3. Ben-Yehuda, M., Xenidis, J., Ostrowski, M., Rister, K., Bruemmer, A., Van Doorn, L.: The price of safety: evaluating iommu performance. In: The Ottawa Linux Symposium, pp. 9–20 (2007)
4. Ben Yehuda, R., Kevorkian, D., Zamir, G.L., Walter, M.Y., Levy, L.: Virtual USB honeypot. In: Proceedings of the 12th ACM International Conference on Systems and Storage, pp. 181–181, May 2019
5. Ben Yehuda, R., Zaidenberg, N.: Hyplets-multi exception level kernel towards Linux RTOS. In: Proceedings of the 11th ACM International Systems and Storage Conference, pp. 116–117, June 2018
6. Ben Yehuda, R., Zaidenberg, N.J.: Protection against reverse engineering in ARM. Int. J. Inf. Secur. **19**(1), 39–51 (2019). https://doi.org/10.1007/s10207-019-00450-1
7. Boettiger, C.: An introduction to Docker for reproducible research. ACM SIGOPS Oper. Syst. Rev. **49**(1), 71–79 (2015)
8. Brendmo, H.K.: Live forensics on the windows 10 secure kernel. Master's thesis, NTNU (2017)
9. Carrier, B.D., Grand, J.: A hardware-based memory acquisition procedure for digital investigations. Dig. Invest. **1**(1), 50–60 (2004)
10. Cohen, M.: Rekall Memory Forensics Framework. DFIR Prague (2014)
11. Durve, R., Bouridane, A.: Windows 10 security hardening using device guard whitelisting and applocker blacklisting. In: 2017 Seventh International Conference on Emerging Security Technologies (EST), pp. 56–61. IEEE (2017)
12. Evtyushkin, D., Ponomarev, D., Abu-Ghazaleh, N.: Jump over ASLR: attacking branch predictors to bypass ASLR. In: The 49th Annual IEEE/ACM International Symposium on Microarchitecture, p. 40. IEEE Press (2016)
13. Field, S.: An introduction to kernel patch protection (2006). http://blogs.msdn.com/b/windowsvistasecurity/archive/2006/08/11/695993.aspx
14. Franklin, J., Seshadri, A., Qu, N., Chaki, S., Datta, A.: Attacking, repairing, and verifying SecVisor: a retrospective on the security of a hypervisor. Technical report CMU-CyLab-08-008, Carnegie Mellon University (2008)
15. Heiser, G., Leslie, B.: The OKL4 Microvisor: convergence point of microkernels and hypervisors. In: Proceedings of the first ACM ASIA-pacific Workshop on Systems, pp. 19–24. ACM, August 2010
16. Hightower, K., Burns, B., Beda, J.: Kubernetes: Up and Running: Dive into the Future of Infrastructure. O'Reilly Media Inc., Sebastopol (2017)

17. Huber, N., von Quast, M., Brosig, F., Kounev, S.: Analysis of the performance-influencing factors of virtualization platforms. In: Meersman, R., Dillon, T., Herrero, P. (eds.) OTM 2010. LNCS, vol. 6427, pp. 811–828. Springer, Heidelberg (2010). https://doi.org/10.1007/978-3-642-16949-6_10
18. Intel Corporation: Intel© 64 and IA-32 Architectures Software Developer's Manual. Intel Corporation (2018)
19. Kiperberg, M., Resh, A., Zaidenberg, N.J.: Remote attestation of software and execution- environment in modern machines. In: 2015 IEEE 2nd International Conference on Cyber Security and Cloud Computing (CSCloud), pp. 335–341. IEEE (2015)
20. Kiperberg, M., Leon, R., Resh, A., Algawi, A., Zaidenberg, N.J.: Hypervisor-based protection of code. IEEE Trans. Inf. Forensics Secur. **14**(8), 2203–2216 (2019)
21. Kiperberg, M., Zaidenberg, N.: Efficient remote authentication. In: Proceedings of the 12th European Conference on Information Warfare and Security: ECIW 2013, p. 144. Academic Conferences Limited (2013)
22. Kiperberg, M., Leon, R., Resh, A., Algawi, A., Zaidenberg, N.:. Hypervisor-assisted atomic memory acquisition in modern systems. In: Mori, P., Furnell, S., Camp, O. (eds.), ICISSP 2019: Proceedings of the 5th International Conference on Information Systems Security and Privacy, vol. 1, pp. 155–162 (2019)
23. Krawetz, N.: Anti-honeypot technology. IEEE Secur. Privacy **2**(1), 76–79 (2004)
24. Langner, R.: Stuxnet: dissecting a cyberwarfare weapon. IEEE Securi. Privacy **9**(3), 49–51 (2011)
25. Leon, R., Kiperberg, M., Zabag Leon, A.A., Resh, A., Algawi, A., Zaidenberg, N.J.: Hypervisor-based whitelisting of executables. IEEE Securi. Privacy (2019)
26. Macht, H.: Live memory forensics on android with volatility. Friedrich-Alexander University Erlangen-Nuremberg (2013)
27. Martignoni, L., Fattori, A., Paleari, R., Cavallaro, L.: Live and trustworthy forensic analysis of commodity production systems. In: Jha, S., Sommer, R., Kreibich, C. (eds.) RAID 2010. LNCS, vol. 6307, pp. 297–316. Springer, Heidelberg (2010). https://doi.org/10.1007/978-3-642-15512-3_16
28. Mairh, A., Barik, D., Verma, K., Jena, D.: Honeypot in network security: a survey. In: Proceedings of the 2011 International Conference on Communication, Computing & Security, pp. 600–605. ACM, February 2011
29. Microsoft Corporation (2009). Device /PhysicalMemory Object. https://docs.microsoft.com/en-us/previous-versions/windows/it-pro/windows-server-2003/cc787565(v=ws.10). Accessed 02 Nov 2018
30. Microsoft Corporation (2018). KeIpiGenericCall function. https://docs.microsoft.com/en-us/windows-hardware/drivers/ddi/content/wdm/nf-wdm-keipigenericcall
31. Mohurle, S., Patil, M.: A brief study of wannacry threat: ransomware attack 2017. Int. J. Adv. Res. Comput. Sci. **8**(5) (2017)
32. Moore, C.:. Detecting ransomware with honeypot techniques. In: 2016 Cybersecurity and Cyberforensics Conference (CCC), pp. 77–81. IEEE, August 2016
33. Oracle (2018). VirtualBox. https://www.virtualbox.org/
34. Pouget, F., Dacier, M.: Honeypot-based forensics. In: AusCERT Asia Pacific Information Technology Security Conference, May 2004
35. Provos, N.: A virtual honeypot framework. In: USENIX Security Symposium, vol. 173, no. 2004, pp. 1–14, August 2004
36. Qi, Z., Xiang, C., Ma, R., Li, J., Guan, H., Wei, D.S.: Forenvisor: a tool for acquiring and preserving reliable data in cloud live forensics. IEEE Trans. Cloud Comput. **5**(3), 443–456 (2017)

37. Reina, A., Fattori, A., Pagani, F., Cavallaro, L., Bruschi, D.: When hardware meets software: a bulletproof solution to forensic memory acquisition. In: Proceedings of the 28th Annual Computer Security Applications Conference, pp. 79–88. ACM (2012)
38. Resh, A., Kiperberg, M., Leon, R., Zaidenberg, N.J.: Preventing execution of unauthorized native code software. Int. Dig. Content Technol. Appl. **11** (2017)
39. Resh, A., Zaidenberg, N.: Can keys be hidden inside the CPU on modern windows host. In: Proceedings of the 12th European Conference on Information Warfare and Security: ECIW 2013, p. 231. Academic Conferences Limited (2013)
40. Russinovich, M.E., Solomon, D.A., Ionescu, A.: Windows Internals. Pearson Education, London (2012)
41. Rutkowska, J.: Introducing blue pill. The official blog of the invisiblethings. org, 22, 23. http://theinvisiblethings.blogspot.com/2006/06/introducing-blue-pill.html (2006)
42. Rutkowska, J.: Subverting VistaTM Kernel for Fun and Profit. Black Hat Briefings, Singapore (2006)
43. Seshadri, A., Luk, M., Qu, N., Perrig, A.: Secvisor: a tiny hypervisor to provide lifetime kernel code integrity for commodity OSES. In: ACM SIGOPS Operating Systems Review, vol. 41, pp. 335–350. ACM (2007)
44. Shinagawa, T., et al.: Bitvisor: A thin hypervisor for enforcing I/O device security. In: Proceedings of the 2009 ACM SIGPLAN/SIGOPS International Conference on Virtual Execution Environments, VEE 2009, New York, NY, USA, pp. 121–130. ACM (2009)
45. Snow, K.Z., Monrose, F., Davi, L., Dmitrienko, A., Liebchen, C., Sadeghi, A.R.: Just-in-time code reuse: on the effectiveness of fine-grained address space layout randomization. In: 2013 IEEE Symposium on Security and Privacy, pp. 574–588. IEEE. Chicago, May 2013
46. Unified EFI, Inc.: Unified Extensible Firmware Interface Specification, Version 2.6 (2006)
47. VMware: VMware Workstation Pro (2018). https://www.vmware.com/il/products/workstation-pro.html
48. Walters, J.P., et al.: GPU passthrough performance: a comparison of KVM, Xen, VMWare ESXi, and LXC for CUDA and OpenCL applications. In: 2014 IEEE 7th International Conference on Cloud Computing, pp. 636–643. IEEE. Chicago, June 2014
49. Ye, K., Che, J., Jiang, X., Chen, J., Li, X.: VTestkit: a performance benchmarking framework for virtualization environments. In: 2010 Fifth Annual ChinaGrid Conference, pp. 130–136. IEEE, July 2010
50. Zaidenberg, N.J.: Hardware rooted security in industry 4.0 systems. In: Dimitrov, K. (ed.) Cyber Defence in Industry 4.0 and Related Logistic and IT Infrastructures, Chap. 10, pp. 135–151. IOS Press (2018)
51. Zaidenberg, N.J., Khen, E.: Detecting kernel vulnerabilities during the development phase. In: 2015 IEEE 2nd International Conference on Cyber Security and Cloud Computing, pp. 224–230. IEEE, November 2015
52. Zhang, L., Wang, L., Zhang, R., Zhang, S., Zhou, Y.: Live memory acquisition through FireWire. In: Lai, X., Gu, D., Jin, B., Wang, Y., Li, H. (eds.) e-Forensics 2010. LNICST, vol. 56, pp. 159–167. Springer, Heidelberg (2011). https://doi.org/10.1007/978-3-642-23602-0_14

Guidelines and Tool Support for Building a Cybersecurity Awareness Program for SMEs

Christophe Ponsard$^{(\boxtimes)}$ iD and Jeremy Grandclaudon

CETIC Research Center, Charleroi, Belgium
{Christophe.Ponsard,Jeremy.Grandclaudon}@cetic.be

Abstract. Nowadays companies have become highly dependent on digital technology for running their business, regardless their size or domain. Smaller organisations require a specific attention because of their lower level of protection, capability of reaction and recovery while they are increasingly being targeted by cyberattacks. In order to improve their level of cybersecurity and resilience, a first step is to raise awareness. It is however not an easy task because it is highly dependent on human factors, spread across the whole organisation, including managers, business users and IT staff. This paper aims at supporting the development of a cybersecurity awareness program for small and medium enterprises. In order to build the program on strong foundations, the current state of awareness of such companies is presented and a SWOT analysis carried out. Different instruments for efficiently supporting the deployment of the program are then presented. A practical experience carried out in Belgium to implement some of the proposed instruments is also presented and some lessons learned are discussed.

Keywords: Cybersecurity · Awareness · SME · Quiz · Assessment · Toolkit guidelines

1 Introduction

Small and Medium Enterprises (SMEs) are recognised worldwide as the drivers of socio-economic development. In Europe, it is estimated they produce between 50 and 60% of the total value added and they employ about two third of the workforce [46]. Their high level of adaptability and their need for innovation make them big adopters of digital technologies, which increases their exposure to cyberattacks. At the same time, it is well-known that SMEs have a low adherence to procedures and standards as they keep their focus on their business goals [29]. This can result of underestimating the risks related to their cyber security exposure or just think they are not worth being attacked given their size. Unfortunately, this belief is not any more valid nowadays, given a vast majority of attacks are now targeting SMEs. In the past years, the numbers of attacks increased dramatically with estimated around 60% and even 70% of attacked

© Springer Nature Switzerland AG 2020
P. Mori et al. (Eds.): ICISSP 2019, CCIS 1221, pp. 335–357, 2020.
https://doi.org/10.1007/978-3-030-49443-8_16

SMEs [2,41]. Unfortunately, more than half of the hacked SMEs are not able to recover and are going bankrupt within six month after the attack [47].

It is now well-known that technological tools cannot guarantee alone the security of a system involving IT components. It is also required to deal with the human beings within their organisation [34] and thus to consider actions for improving the awareness of all the people across the organisation. The concept of cybersecurity awareness can be defined as "the degree or extent to which every member of staff understands the importance of IT security, the levels of IT security appropriate to the organisation, and their individual security responsibilities" [36]. Awareness is also the first step in building a cybersecurity culture involving everyone within the organisation from the top-level management to low-level employees with each employee responsible for their cybersecurity practices [3].

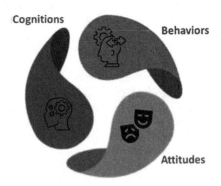

Fig. 1. Attitude, behaviour and cognition dimensions of cybersecurity awareness [61].

Human beings are complex, and their behaviour is quite influenced by organisational norms and habits through the pressure of their peers, even despite their knowledge. For example, even if people are told to use strong passwords and not reuse them, they may not behave like that. While the strength can be enforced at creation time, avoiding reuse generally relies on the people and potentially expose the company through personal social networks. To deal with this, awareness must not only rely on knowledge or cognitive aspects (i.e. teachable and verifiable aspects) but also attitudes (i.e. feelings and emotions in relation to security activities) and behaviours (i.e. actual/intended activities and risk-taking actions directly or indirectly impacting security), as depicted in Fig. 1.

The initial motivation of our work is the deployment of a programme aiming to help Belgian SMEs to better protect themselves against cybersecurity threats through audit and digital transformation actions supported by specific funding aids [19,54]. In order to be successful, such a program must encourage SMEs to realise cybersecurity threats can endanger their business. At this point, they can engage in actions to assess how well their are protected against cyber attacks and ready to react to them. As a consequence, our work also included actions to raise awareness.

This paper is an extended version of our initial report describing our learning path and our experience to setup a cybersecurity awareness programme and to deploy supporting tools matching our local context [53]. This previous work was significantly extended in the following ways across the structure of our paper which is also presented here. In Sect. 2, our study of the SME attitude towards cybersecurity is deeper: our survey on the current awareness was extended based on literature and interaction with specialised European organisation and network [24,62]. It also contains an analysis of barriers and drivers for the adoption of cybersecurity by SMEs under the form of a SWOT analysis (i.e. strengths, weaknesses, opportunities and threats). In Sect. 3, our survey of existing cybersecurity awareness instruments is much more elaborated, especially to guide in the design of an awareness program and to deploy specific instruments like personae and gamification. Next, our own experience to raise awareness in Belgium is reported more extensively in Sect. 4. More lessons learned are also discussed in Sect. 5. Finally, our conclusions and perspectives are also refined based on the knowledge gained both from the literature, our interaction with key players and our practical experience.

2   Current SME Attitude w.r.t. CyberSecurity

This section first reports about the current level of cybersecurity awareness of SMEs in various domains and parts of the world. In a second part, a SWOT analysis is carried out in order to help in identifying drivers and barriers to the adoption of cybersecurity both within the companies (Strengths and Weaknesses) and in their environment (Opportunities and Threats).

2.1   Cybersecurity Awareness in SMEs

We review here different reports carried out over the past few years in various areas to show the global state and evolution of the awareness of SMEs are about cybersecurity threats.

A survey made in 2014 among UK SMEs revealed interesting facts about how SMEs deal with cybersecurity, especially about their perception and awareness [50]. Only 21% of SMEs have shown a low awareness about basic security guidelines, 39% have actually done a global risk analysis which included cybersecurity, and 48% keep the company's risk analysis, policies and backups up-to-date. The main reported barrier is the cost for implementing cybersecurity solutions and standards because they are designed for bigger companies.

In 2016, a survey was carried out by the Zurich Insurance Group across 2,600 SMEs across 13 countries in Europe, the Americas and Asia Pacific [69]. It reported an interesting evolution about the fact of how SMEs think they are protected by their size: they were 17% believing that in 2015 and only 10% in 2016. It also revealed that theft of customer data and reputation damage are the most feared consequences of cyberattacks. Globally only 5% of SMEs have confidence in their cybersecurity measures. The less aware region of the globe seems to be South America, while it is improving quickly in some parts of Asia.

A recent survey carried out in North America by the Better Business Bureau also reported an increase in the awareness to cyberthreats, including the use of proactive security steps [6]. The awareness could be ranked between 76% (for fishing) to 93% (larger variety of threats). However, another survey carried out in Europe and related to the adoption of Big Data, Internet of Things and cybersecurity (BIC) revealed that the lack of understanding and awareness is cited in the top three barriers to the adoption of such technologies. While people in strategic position in SMEs are interested in investing in the right people and technologies, unfortunately, they often lack knowledge of what they need and how to obtain it [22].

Concerning developing countries, the adoption of information technology systems by SMEs has the potential to bring significant benefits and accelerate their growth. However, it will also expose them to online cybersecurity threats. Core cybersecurity characteristics identified in developing countries are poor practices, unique usage patterns (e.g. mobile payments in isolated areas), novice users, use of pirated software and limited understanding of the attacker's motivations. The challenges concern inadequate policies (e.g. limited allowance for encryption), technical specificities (shared computers, offline mode), business aspect (cheaper but less safe solutions and processes) and of course education and awareness [8]. In South Africa, a recent study showed that SMEs do not have to face complex business and legacy system which simplifies the enforcement of cybersecurity. However they are limited in their ability to improve their cybersecurity due to internal organisational factors of budget, management support, and attitudes [38]. A more specific study related to awareness showed that the current initiatives are effective and have been able to address cyber security issues although at a smaller scale [20]. The situation reported in Ghanah is far more worrying with a lack of adherence to standards and best practices, inadequate security solutions and systems protection. This result in about 35% SMEs perceiving the Internet service delivery in Ghana as risky, unsecured and vulnerable to cyber attacks [67].

The bottom line is that even when SMEs seem to have reached a good level of awareness, when looking at attack statistics, they still fail to make it effective. A first explanation is that security measures are perceived by SMEs as too complex, time consuming and requiring a high level of technical knowledge about IT systems. Another reason is the difficulty to transition from a step of initial awareness to the emergence of an internal cybersecurity culture, because of the lack of resources (money, time, expertise). They are also weak at deploying policies and defining responsibilities [57]. This last point is also crucial because security policies are not designed to put burden on the company but to help them protect their business and hence support their development in the long run.

2.2   SWOT Analysis

This section gives a summary of several strengths/weaknesses (internal at the organisation) and opportunities/threats (external to the organisation) that needs to be addressed (for negative factors) or used as drivers (for positive factors) when setting up an awareness program. It is based on a more detailed analysis of the awareness literature sketched in the previous section together with extra references, especially related to opportunities that can be mobilised to foster awareness. For weaknesses and threats, some actions to address them are also identified at this stage.

Strengths. The main strengths of SME were already identified and are further commented here:

- *Agility and Fast Reaction Time:* once SMEs realise securing their business is critical, they can take action quickly. However this should not happen due to an attack because in many cases it will be fatal to the company within a few months [47].
- *Business Alignment:* SMEs are focused on their business, hence all activities are directed towards supporting this objective, meaning that the implementation of cybersecurity will naturally be oriented on minimizing business risks.
- *Accessible Management and Willingness to Improve:* thanks to their flat structure, the management is close to the company operation and able to make the connection with important information being spread in his domain of operation, e.g. through a cybersecurity awareness program.

Weaknesses. A number of weaknesses are depicted in Fig. 2 under the form of a fishbone diagram which actually also includes some threats or opportunities, depending of the environment context. We comment here only SME weaknesses with some possible actions to cope with them.

- *Digital Immaturity:* many SMEs, especially growing startups are early technology adopters. While the technology can support their business growth, it might not be mastered from a security point of view. This could be related to the technology itself (see threats) but also to the lack of analysis of security impact of using a new technology (e.g. moving to smart manufacturing and getting attacked resulting in a costly production interruption).
- *Limited Availability of Resources* of different kinds. The competent people may also be too busy on short term tasks to implement a (see also strategic planning). The SME may lack technical expertise and may not be able to develop this skill internally (see last weakness). Often an external expertise is required, but the company may not have the budget for hiring a specialist or may have trouble in finding such an expert (see threats).
- *Overconfidence:* SMEs think they are protected by their small size and little relative value compared to big corporations. However, this is a wrong belief with estimates as high as 70% of attacks targeting SMEs [41]. The reason is

that attackers can count on a large pool of vulnerable SMEs. They can also be used as entry point to attack larger companies doing business with them, thus compromising relationship. SMEs are also too confident about their recovery capability which takes usually longer than expected, resulting in potentially large business loss.

– *Low Adherence to Standards.* SMEs generally reject standards and norms unless it is required by the market. In order to be successfully adopted, a cybersecurity standard should either be implied by some regulation (see GDPR in opportunities) or be lightweight and with a clear perception of its business benefit. Heavyweight standard like the ISO27K are not recommended.

– *Skill Management w.r.t. Cybersecurity* and more generally emerging technologies. While people in strategic position in SMEs are interested in investing in the right people and technologies, unfortunately, they often lack knowledge of what they need and how to obtain it [22].

Opportunities

– *General Data Protection Regulation (GDPR).* It has become enforceable on 25 May 2018 and has attracted the attention of many companies, including SMEs on the need to secure their IT infrastructure for the purpose of personal data protection. This regulation has a clear positive impact on cybersecurity awareness with many European organisations actually taking actions to improve their security performance over the past year [18]. In Belgium, a 50% increase in requests in some consulting companies in Belgium was reported [7]. For sure, GDPR will remain a strong driver in the next years has many companies are still on their way to achieve full compliance.

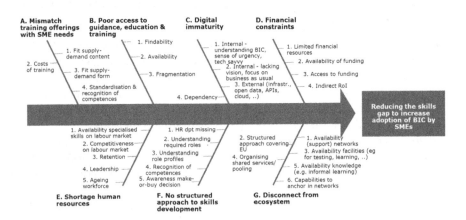

Fig. 2. Main barriers for skills development in SMEs [22].

- *Cyber Security Identified as High Priority in Europe:* improving cybersecurity is now recognised by Europe as a top priority in a world where battles are now carried out on the Internet. Strategic programs are being developed in order to structure the field with a European cybersecurity competence centre relying on networks of national coordination centres [21]. The importance to cope with SMEs and develop a common labelling scheme is also recognised and different organisations like ENISA and ECSO are working on this topic [25, 26]. A wider survey of such initiative is presented in [54].
- *Local Initiatives:* in many countries, cybersecurity and GDPR are also being pushed by many SME association and sectorial federations which are organising specific workgroups and awareness events. Those are interesting instruments for SME managers to engage in an improvement process on those related topics. Specific projects like CYBER are also encouraging the direct sharing of good cybersecurity practices across regions in Europe [35].

Threats. Despite the actions taken to encourage SME to engage into cybersecurity improvement, a number of environmental limitations remain to be addressed:

- *Lack of Cybersecurity Experts:* unfortunately there are too few experts in cybersecurity. Consequently, they are highly demanded and hired by big companies. A solution is to increase the training program both at university level and through dedicated continuing education in cybersecurity. A number of such programs are now being proposed as specialised masters in university or by dedicated international institutes like the SANS Institute [58].
- *Fuzzy Recognition of Experts:* a direct consequence of the lack of cybersecurity experts is that people with insufficient skills can try to access the market to help SMEs looking for those skills. In order to guarantee SMEs can trust some expert, a form of expert certification can be organised, e.g. in the context of specific cybersecurity programs like the cyberessentials in UK [63]. Other similar schemes are reported in [54].
- *Emerging Technologies:* like Internet of Things or Big Data can have complex IT architectures with potential security issues. The general lack of standard in the proposed solution also increases cybersecurity risks. Although such technologies can contribute to the development of a company, the impact on risk should also be evaluated before deploying them.

3 Survey of Cybersecurity Awareness Instruments

This section reviews some interesting instruments for raising SME awareness about cybersecurity. They can be used alone or in combination in the scope of an awareness campaign. Before introducing specific instruments, the notion of campaign is elaborated and integrated in the wider context of a cybersecurity culture (CSC) program. Various awareness instruments are then presented from most introductory to more advanced ones.

3.1 Setting Up and Running an Awareness Program

Cybersecurity needs more than a "one time" effort to be and stay efficient. For this purpose, a specific program should actually be part of a global roadmap to setup a cybersecurity culture and result in the adoption of information security considerations in the day-to-day life of the employees of the targeted organisations. With the right approach, a natural CSC develop over time inside a company by evolving behaviours and attitudes of employees towards information assets, resulting in cybersecurity becoming part of a company's wider organisational culture [26].

Any awareness campaign or more generally CSC program require a global strategy defined through the following key steps depicted in Fig. 3 [3,4,66]:

1. analyse the current situation in the target scope
2. clearly defining the awareness goal, target and means to be used
3. identifying and deploying the necessary instruments
4. communicating over the program
5. monitoring the effectiveness of the program and refine it as required

Those steps are further elaborated here but are also summarised in the compact of ten tactics on a poster by the SANS [59].

Current Situation. Security is not often seen a top priority by most organisations so building a good business case is an important step, even for a small organisation. An initial step is to gather evidence and statistics on cyber threats inside the organisation and in its sector. They can be evaluated in terms of attitude, behaviour and cognition aspects. Different instruments can be used here

Fig. 3. Main steps for developing a cybersecurity culture program [3].

to gather such evidence, like assessment, surveys, quizzes, fishing tests (see relevant sections). A specific SWOT analysis is also useful at this step and can be elaborated based on the generic analysis presented in the previous section.

Defining Goals and Gap Analysis. The long term goal should be to establish a cybersecurity culture. However, progressing towards this goal is a long journey with different maturity milestones. A specific campaign should target the next milestone based on a gap analysis with the current situation. The focus of this paper is essentially the first milestone of reaching awareness.

A framework like Goal-Questions-Metrics can help in structuring a goals more systematically and also to define measurable success criteria [45].

The gap analysis between goals and the current situation can be combined with the SWOT analysis to identify the positive and negative factors that will help to define and conduct the implementation plan.

Implementation Plan. The implementation of specific actions to close the identified gaps can rely on a combination of different instruments proposed later in this section to support awareness raising actions. A balanced CSC program should of course focus on goals with the high priority considering the risks but can also include "quick wins" and actions that can have a good visible return and which can rewards the user for their engagement, keeping them motivated to also pursue their effort of less visible result.

In order to achieve the best results and implement a resilient CSC, a multi-pronged approach is required, involving senior management, key employees and ultimately all employees. A useful technique to build such a plan is the focus group [68]. Specific roadmaps for SMEs have also been defined, e.g. [28].

Communicating Over the Program. Well-defined communication channels should be set up and used to inform about the importance of cybersecurity, to attract attention about specific actions (e.g. passwords, backups, fishing, physical security, etc) and to give feedback about progress as measured. Those means can include: emails, social networks, websites and blogs. They can be company specific or wider but in all cases they need to use trustable channels, especially if external to the company. For wider campaigns, this can also include relays in traditional medias (newspaper, radio, television).

An important message is also to convince employees that improving the company's resilience against most cyber threats does not impose a large burden on key business functions.

Program Evaluation. To be effective, the programme must reach its goals in a measurable way, based on the metrics defined earlier. Considering awareness, it is useful to be able to look for progress in the three key dimensions of attitude, behaviour and cognition. Means used for assessing the initial situation may be reused to measure the improvement on a similar scale of evaluation (e.g.

before/after surveys, observed behaviours) [66]. They can be complemented by data gathered from specific instruments, e.g. participation rate to some security event, number of reads of a security news, etc.

3.2 General Information, Posters and Guides

General information is provided by cybersecurity portals that are often proposed by an organisation supporting the improvement of cybersecurity at different levels: European, national or more local/dedicated security coalitions. At European level, October was selected as the month for cybersecurity, with a specific web site that is always available [23]. An example of national portal targeting the general public is the Belgian SafeOnWeb [56].

Posters are useful introductory material for raising awareness on specific topics, like phishing as shown in Fig. 4. They are easy to produce and can be displayed in a variety of places in workplaces, schools or public areas. Some nice posters are proposed by organisations like SANS and ENISA [27, 60].

Guides aim at providing SMEs with an overview of basic and more advanced cybersecurity measures. Although the implementation depends on specific risks, quick checklists of generic security controls can be provided and are documented by several guides for SMEs, like in Belgium [10], in Germany [9] or in the US [47]. The Center for Internet Security (CIS) developed a set of 20 controls that are easy to implements by SMEs [12]. It also provides a specialised guide to help SMEs to implement the controls [11].

Fig. 4. Example of awareness poster about phishing.

3.3   Personae

Personae are archetypal descriptions of users that embody their goals [13]. Their focus on typical fictional business users helps in elaborating specific user aspects that may be missed by other approaches based on generic roles. Related to cybersecurity, personae can be useful for associating specific threats, vulnerabilities or risks in their environment [42]. Personae have proved very effective and there is psychological evidence about our natural and generative engagement with detailed representations of people [32].

This strong identification can be used both for designing training and communication material for raising cybersecurity awareness. At design time, it helps the trainer to build some concrete cases around the personae with specific characteristics, motivation, business needs, exposure to threads and business impacts. Based on this, the user can more easily imagine what should be done from an external point of view. But at the same time, she can realise (by herself or in a discussion session) that its own case is maybe quite similar to one or several personae and question its own attitude and behaviour. This process naturally leads to improvement decisions. As communication support, a persona can be given some graphical appearance which further allows the end-user identification. They can naturally be used in combination with other instruments, e.g. to illustrate a poster or a quiz.

A key issue is of course the selection process of the relevant personae. The selected archetypes must cover the broad spectrum of people with different backgrounds/experience/roles, more or less exposed and cybersecurity risks. The selected number should be kept minimal (no redundant personae) and low (because the more personae, the less effective the identification process). In practice, a handful of personae is usually used. However different dimensions can be covered independently using combination that makes sense, e.g. a startup company with a young computer literate at his head, a medium company with limited computer support but more aged and less computer literate manager.

Figure 5 shows some personae from an awareness raising web-site proposed in Michigan State, with the support of the U.S. Small Business Administration [61]. It relies on about 10 personae including end users (e.g. a coffee shop owner, a manufacturer and a plumber) with a good coverage of racial and gender diversity.

Fig. 5. Personae for various SME profiles [61].

Those have specific goals related to their business. In addition, some personae are also used to represent "villains", i.e. some hacker possibly oriented to specific kinds of threats related to company data, financial transactions, physical security, etc. This is useful to associate some face and motivation behind threats and attackers that are most of the time invisible and faceless.

3.4   Gamification

A game can be defined as "a system in which players engage in an artificial conflict, defined by rules, that result in a quantifiable outcome" [37]. Gamification is "the use of game-based mechanics, aesthetics, and game-thinking to engage people, motivate action, promote learning, and solve problems" [39]. Gamification fits well the field of cybersecurity awareness because it must adhere to several of rules (i.e. security controls). Game situation can develop quite complex scenarios where the player must identify some threat and be able react in an adequate way. In addition to raising awareness, techniques derived from game-playing can also be used to upskill the staff in order to better cope with cyber threats [49]. Specific offers have developed in this area such as Game of Threats [55].

The rest of this section details a few interesting gamification techniques for awareness purposes: general quizzes and dealing with security threats scenarios. An important point is to encourage the candidate to try the quiz. Different incentives can be used: the fact it is anonymous (for a web-based quiz), playing in teams (group effect) or an attractive graphical design.

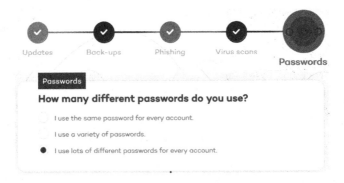

Fig. 6. SafeOnWeb digital health quiz [16].

Quizzes. A quiz is a game or light form of assessment used in education and awareness. Players must try to find the right answer to a series of question, either individually or in team. Quizzes often propose multiple-choice questions usually over a well-defined topic which enable automated correction and support. They are also easy to deploy on-line on a website or as mobile application. Those characteristics make the quiz an interesting tool to propose in a campaign after some introductory material to engage the targeted audience in a first assessment in an entertaining way.

Quizzes generally also provide educational support to help correct wrong answer but also good ones by educating on the topic covered. They can also provide a summary and compare the score w.r.t. global statistics. After completing a quiz, a user might be more aware of the need to learn more and be helped. Pointers and contacts are typically proposed afterwards.

Many cybersecurity quizzes are elaborated in the above spirit. A representative illustration is the SafeOnWeb Belgian campaign which includes two quizzes [61]. One is specifically dedicated to phishing based on different scenarios (email, social networks), while the other, depicted on Fig. 6 is proposing to evaluate its Digital Health Index (DHI) based on questions covering updates, backups, fishing and anti-virus. The results are grouped by categories and globally under the form of a DIH between 0 and 10 which is positioned against the distribution of all collected DIH as shown in Fig. 7.

Fig. 7. SafeOnWeb quiz result analysis [16].

Other examples of interesting quizzes are the Network and Information Security Quiz [23] or the one developed by Lockheed [44], both proposed in the context of 2018 European Cyber Security Month.

Dealing with Security Threats Scenarios. Gamification can also explore common threat scenarios that an employee will have to face, for example dealing with passwords or recognising phishing attempts. Although those can be presented under the form of a quiz, more elaborated gaming supports can be proposed.

For helping the user to learn how easy a weak password can be broken and how to build a strong password, password checkers are available, e.g. the Kaspersky Lab's Secure Password Checker [40] and "How Secure Is My Password?" [17] from Dashlane. Both websites can be trusted and do not advise to use real password. Figure 8 shows the former with some weakness reported as well as the estimated time to crack the password compared to daily human activities.

To deal with phishing, different websites propose quiz-based test mixing legitimate requests and fishing requests through different media (SMS, social net-

Fig. 8. Kaspersky password checker [40].

works, email) e.g. [51,61] A more elaborated gaming scenario is the setup of an internal phishing campaign which will send a fake yet realistic phishing email to employees and check how many employees are able to recognise the threat. Such a campaign must of course be endorsed by the management and different frameworks are available to conduct them, either commercial, e.g. PhishingBox [51] or Open Source, e.g. GoPhish [31] which is depicted in Fig. 9.

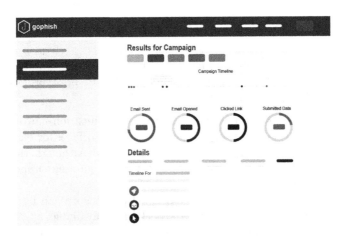

Fig. 9. Typical user interface of a phishing simulator [31].

Of course, after the phishing campaign, awareness activities are organised to explain the risks and to help in better recognising the threat. Statistics typically report 30% of click rate upon a first test campaign but also show it can quickly improve using such actions [33].

3.5 Self-assessments

Assessments are more advanced and structured form of evaluation. In opposition to quizzes which can be partial or even random, they cover a whole field at a certain level of details. They can take some form of audit when performed by a third-party expert in the field. However, like quizzes, it is also possible to propose a lighter and automated form of self-assessment generally based on a dedicated website. The later can be used as introduction for the former.

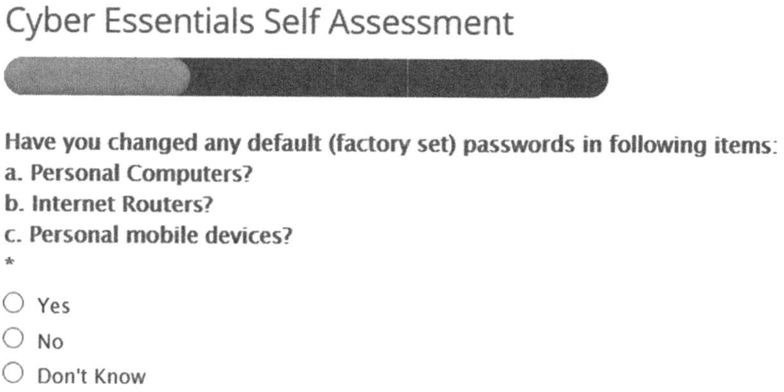

Fig. 10. Cyber essentials self assessment [64].

In the area of SME cybersecurity, several initiatives across Europe propose methods including free self-assessment and/or more advanced assessments [54]. Some examples are the Cyber Essentials in the UK [63] or Vertrauen durch Siecherhiet in Germany [65]. Self-assessments are often quite simple multiple choices quizzes [15,64] as depicted in Fig. 10. They can also be more elaborated and involve personae such Small Business Big Threats [61]. Full assessments which cover classical security controls are paid-for, possibly with some funding aids by the local authorities.

3.6 Training, Courses and Tool Support

At this level, basic awareness is already reached but more specific actions can be taken using on-site training by experts but those can be costly. An alternative is to rely on MOOC (Massive Open Online Courses) which are free and with largely accessible in terms of prerequisites. An example of very successful MOOC is the French SecNumacadémie [1].

More advanced cybersecurity kits are also proposed by various organisations and groups a set of resources like slides, posters, guides, tools, etc. [14,30].

A few specific tools can be recommended to support raising awareness like password strength checkers, web-site vulnerability scanners, phishing simulators.

4 Setup of an Awareness Campaign in Wallonia

4.1 Context and Goals

The target of the cybersecurity campaign is SMEs. The goal is to raise awareness about the importance of deploying adequate cybersecurity measures both at technical and human levels w.r.t. the high impact an attack could have on their business. The awareness program is supported by the regional authorities with the goal to encourage many SMEs to engage in security audits and improvement through a validated network of security experts. In some countries, SMEs can benefit from specific funding for this, like the UK CyberEssentials vouchers.

4.2 Program Design

In order to have a good understanding of the current situation and make sure to have support of the existing actors in the cybersecurity area, specific actions were carried out over a period of roughly one year:

- with the end-users SMEs mainly through relay organisation like incubators for starters, usually relying a lot on IT and through sectoral organisation, dealing with a large variety of SMEs.
- with security experts through a local cybersecurity cluster, typically with quarterly meetings.

To support the launch of the program and encourage SMEs to keep joining it, a variety of instruments among those exposed in the previous sections were used like personae, Frequently Asked Questions (FAQ), a quiz and a self-assessment questionnaire. The rest of this section details them.

4.3 Frequently Asked Questions

In order to identify with each type of organisation, a first step was to try to figure out the reaction of both end-user SMEs and of the security experts that would have to interact with them. This was documented by building a list of questions either anticipated or collected during our interactions. Structuring those questions and building the answers contributed a large part of the program design itself and is still being used as a reference document for evolving it. At some point, a validated and cleaned form of the list resulted in a published Frequently Asked Questions (FAQ) used for communication purposes. This is quite convenient because it splits the description of an elaborated mechanism in progressive set of smaller and easier to explain questions.

Examples of questions from the end users are:

- Why should I ask to be checked for cybersecurity?
- What assurance do I have about being secure ?
- How much does it cost ?
- Can I put this forward to my client or prospects ?
- ...

Examples of questions from security experts are:

- What is the process/cost to join the initiative ?
- What check-list of controls should be enforced ?
- How much can I bill an SME ?
- ...

4.4   Personae

Personae were introduced in a second stage, mainly to segment the wide variety of SMEs. Only two personae were introduced:

- a persona familiar with IT technology from a startup but with little concern about cybersecurity when launching its Minimal Viable Product
- the other persona is the manager of a bigger SME active internationally with a low-tech manager that relies on different IT subcontractors with no idea of how well the business infrastructure is protected against cyber threats.

   The personae are only slightly mentioned in the communication at this stage, but it is our plan to elaborate them. At this point, their main use is for assessing the security expert as it provides a nice way to propose a concrete situation in order to check the people expertise and methodology.

4.5   Quiz and Awareness Event

A quiz was developed initially as a support for a cybersecurity awareness event in the construction sector. The quiz is composed of a set of questions covering the three key dimensions presented previously:

- attitude and behaviour: in situations like managing password, performing backups, updates, etc.
- knowledge: more technical questions about key concepts either theoretical like electronic signature or practical like WIFI protection, what makes a good password, names of recent major attacks.

   The quiz can be configured with a variable number of questions and was deployed both online using [43] and as a mobile application (see Fig. 11). To keep the rules simple, questions have multiple choices with only one correct answer. However, some questions are formulated negatively or can involve a final choice covering previous possibilities. Those where initially developed for supporting a cybersecurity awareness event. The mobile app is also available on the Play Store both in French and in English [52].

Fig. 11. Mobile application featuring a cybersecurity quiz [52].

4.6   Self-assessment Questionnaire

In order to encourage SMEs to engage into a cybersecurity improvement process, we developed a self-assessment questionnaire based on the 20 controls of Center for Internet Security [12] and using Lime Survey [43]. We revisited the grouping into categories based on priority criteria matching some typical SME profiles (through the associated persona). For very small companies relying on general purpose tools, web/email/WIFI aspects are considered first with lower priority on access control. Some organisational issues forming the last part of CIS20 are also considered much earlier to start growing a cybersecurity culture. The result is depicted in Fig. 12 and gives a good idea of what needs to be covered against what is already done.

A more elaborated version of the questionnaire was also used as a checklist to build the requirements and evaluation grid for authorising cybersecurity experts to help SMEs. In this more elaborated version, more structuring was introduced using the functions of the NIST cybersecurity framework (Identify, Protect, Detect, Respond, and Recover) [48].

5   Lessons Learned and Discussion

The feedback collected so far shows a good level of awareness in our SMEs during our interactions. For example, during workshop sessions mixing a dozen of SMEs

Questions	Answers
CIS Control 1: Inventory and Control of Hardware Assets	
Use an active discovery tool to identify devices connected to the company network and update the asset inventory.	Yes
User a passive discovery tool to identify devices connected to the company network and automatically update the device inventory.	Yes
Use Dynamic Host Configuration Protocol (DHCP) logging on all DHCP servers or IP address management tools to update the device inventory.	No
CIS Control 2: Inventory and Control of Software Assets	
Maintain an up-to-date list of all authorized software that is required in the enterprise for any business purpose.	Yes
Ensure that only software applications or OS currently supported are added to the authorized software inventory. Unsupported software should be tagged as so.	Yes
Use software inventory tools throughout the company to automate tracking of all software on business systems.	Yes
The software inventory system should track the name, version, publisher, and install date for all software, including OS authorized within the company.	Yes
The software inventory system should be tied into the hardware asset inventory so all devices and associated software are tracked from a single location.	No
Ensure that unauthorized software is either removed or the inventory is updated in a timely manner	No
CIS Control 3: Continuous Vulnerability Management	
Use an up-to-date SCAP-compliant vulnerability scanning tool to automatically scan all systems on the network on a weekly or more frequent basis to identify all potential vulnerabilities on the organization's systems.	Yes

Fig. 12. Self-assessment summary (updated version of [53]).

active in the construction domain, all the participants scored above the 80% in the quiz with a short cybersecurity reminder. Most SMEs were keen to share their experience, including negative ones (e.g. ransomware with no/corrupted backups). Participants also frequently mentioned having being told about GDPR and of its impact on cybersecurity, confirming the positive impact of GDPR [18].

Our experience is that awareness must be able to rely on bigger initiatives that have a good dynamics, for example the European Cyber Security Month was relayed a lot in national campaigns through emails and social networks [23]. Despite its regional scope, our initiative is not isolated and is actively exchanging with organisations at the Belgian federal level like our national authority (Center for Cybersecurity Belgium) and the federal cluster of companies (Cyber Security Coalition). At European level we have been sharing our practice at the European Cyber Security Organisation (ECSO) [24] and with the CYBER Interreg project [35]. Through those interactions, we can thus learn what is happening in other part of Europe and be part of the process to define a more global and unified way to deal with cybersecurity in Europe, while being able to select the means that best fits our context.

In order to maximise the success for reaching companies, the support of a wider organisation in which the SME is actively involved is really recommended. In our case the workshop co-organised with the construction federation was a success in terms of interactions and experience sharing. A lesson learned here is that campaigns must combine both passive channels to reach a wide audience but also active events where SMEs can meet experts, exchange together and actively engage. As mentioned in the Attitude-Behaviour-Cognition reference framework, focusing on knowledge is far from enough, and more detailed evidence have been reported in the literature that if knowledge and awareness are necessary to initiate a change in behaviour, they are however not sufficient to realise it. Key success factors are a good preparation, not being driven by fear and being actionable in terms of follow-up (including training and feedback) [5].

About the use of personae: although we mainly use it for evaluating our experts, they helped a lot in defining typical usage scenarios and to provide an effective support for elaborating a case. More evolved personae are starting to emerge for people inside companies with specific threats, like having to deal with personal health information. Other usage of personae could also be investigated like complementary profiles inside a company w.r.t. position, level of experience with cybersecurity, using guidelines from [42].

Designing the quiz is an interesting and non-trivial exercise: questions must be clear, have a good technical coverage but also address attitude and behaviour. Our current version does not provide explanation nor introductory material because they were respectively provided through posters and a debriefing. Posters also revealed interesting to make available to SMEs for display in their premises.

6   Conclusion and Future Work

Raising cybersecurity awareness in an organisation is a prerequisite to initiate improvement actions and to start building a cybersecurity culture on top of a good knowledge but also with the right attitude and behaviour. If the staff is known to be a major weakness in cybersecurity, when engaged and correctly trained, it can become the first line of defence against attackers.

In this paper, we focused on the case of SMEs. After reporting about their current state of awareness and performing a general SWOT analysis w.r.t. cybersecurity, we surveyed available guidelines and tools to build a cybersecurity program and implement it through a variety of awareness raising tools. We also reported about our experience in conducting an awareness process in Belgium. This report substantially elaborates over or previous work [53] and although we do not claim to have performed a systematic literature survey, we believe we covered all important dimensions of this problem and that this work can be useful for others engaged in cybersecurity awareness with SMEs.

Our future work will refine the initial and final steps of the building an awareness program by defining more systematically the strategy based on the target audience and identifying more precise success factor that can be collected and monitored on the field over the long term. We also plan to elaborate the communication phase using more detailed personae. Finally, we keep our work evolving in parallel with the definition of European labelling scheme in which we are also actively involved.

Acknowledgements. This research was partly supported by Digital Wallonia and the DIGITRANS project (grant nr. 7618). We thank Infopole and the companies of the cybersecurity cluster for their support and feedback.

References

1. ANSSI: SecNumacadémie (2017). https://secnumacademie.gouv.fr
2. Ashford, W.: SMEs more vulnerable than ever to cyber attacks, survey shows, October 2017. http://bit.do/computer-weekly-SME-cybersecurity
3. Ashik, M.: Building an effective cybersecurity program (2018). https://securereading.com/building-an-effective-cybersecurity-culture
4. Bada, M., Nurse, J.R.C.: Developing cybersecurity education and awareness programmes for small and medium-sized enterprises (SMEs). CoRR abs/1906.09594 (2019)
5. Bada, M., Sasse, A.M., Nurse, J.R.C.: Cyber security awareness campaigns: why do they fail to change behaviour? (2019). http://arxiv.org/abs/1901.02672
6. BBB: State of cybersecurity among small businesses in North America. Better Business Bureau (2017). http://bit.do/2017-state-of-cybersecurity
7. BDO: Forte augmentation de la demande de services de cybersécurité suite au GDPR (2018). http://bit.do/bdo18-cyber-gdpr
8. Ben-David, Y., et al.: Computing security in the developing world: a case for multidisciplinary research. In: Proceedings of the 5th ACM Workshop on Networked Systems for Developing Regions, pp. 39–44. ACM (2011)
9. BSI: Cyber security for SMEs (2018). https://www.bsigroup.com/en-GB/Cyber-Security/Cyber-security-for-SMEs
10. CCB: Cyber security guide for SME (2016). http://www.ccb.belgium.be/en/guide-sme
11. CIS: CIS Controls - Implementation guide for Small and Medium-Sized Enterprises (SMEs) (2017). https://www.cisecurity.org/wp-content/uploads/2017/09/CIS-Controls-Guide-for-SMEs.pdf
12. CIS: CIS control - V7 (2018). https://www.cisecurity.org/controls
13. Cooper, A.: The Inmates are Running the Asylum. Macmillan Publishing Company Inc., New York City (1999)
14. Cyber Security Coalition: Cyber security KIT (2018). https://www.cybersecuritycoalition.be/resource/cyber-security-kit
15. Cyber Security Coalition: SME security scan (2018). https://www.cybersecuritycoalition.be/sme-security-scan
16. CybSafe: Enterprise IT leaders demanding more stringent cyber security from suppliers, July 2017. http://bit.do/cybsafe
17. Dahslane: How secure is my password (2019). https://howsecureismypassword.net
18. Davies, T.: Cybersecurity in Europe is improving: thank you GDPR? (2018). https://gdpr.report/news/2018/12/27/cybersecurity-in-europe
19. Digital Wallonia: Keep IT secure (2018). https://www.digitalwallonia.be/keepitsecure
20. Dlamini, Z., Modise, M.: Cyber security awareness initiatives in South Africa: a synergy approach. Case Stud. Inf. Warf. Secur. Res. Teach. Stud. 1 (2013)
21. EC: Proposal for a European cybersecurity competence network and centre (2017). https://ec.europa.eu/digital-single-market/en/proposal-european-cybersecurity-competence-network-and-centre

356 C. Ponsard and J. Grandclaudon

22. EC: Supporting specialised skills development: big data, Internet of Things and cybersecurity for SMEs. EASME/COSME/2017/007 Interim Report, March 2019
23. ECSM: European cyber security month quiz (2018). https://cybersecuritymonth. eu/references/quiz-demonstration
24. ECSO: European Cyber Security Organisation (2016). https://ecs-org.eu
25. ECSO: European Cyber Security Certification: a meta - scheme approach v1.0 (2017). https://www.ecs-org.eu/documents/publications/5a3112ec2c891.pdf
26. ENISA: Indispensable baseline security requirements for the procurement of secure ICT products and services (2016). http://bit.do/ENISA-baseline-security
27. ENISA: Posters for organisations (2019). https://www.enisa.europa.eu/media/ multimedia/material/awareness-raising-posters
28. Fricker, S.: D2.3 security awareness plan report (2017). https://www.smesec.eu/ doc/SMESEC_D2.3_Security_Awareness_Plan_Report_v1.0.pdf
29. Ghobadian, A., Gallear, D.: Total quality management and organization size. Int. J. Oper. Prod. Manag. **17**(2), 121–163 (1997)
30. Global Cyber Alliance: GCA cybersecurity toolkit for small businesses (2019)
31. GoPhish: Open-source phishing framework (2019). https://getgophish.com
32. Grudin, J.: Why personas work: the psychological evidence. In: The Persona Lifecycle: Keeping People in Mind Throughout Product Design, January 2006
33. Heat, E.: How to improve phishing awareness by 300% in 18 Months. In: RSA Conference, San Francisco, 13–17 February 2017
34. Herath, T., Rao, H.R.: Encouraging information security behaviors in organizations: role of penalties, pressures and perceived effectiveness. Decis. Support Syst. **47**(2), 154–165 (2009)
35. Interreg: Regional policies for competitive cybersecurity SMEs (2018). https:// www.interregeurope.eu/cyber
36. ISF: Effective security awareness. Information Security Forum, April 2002
37. Juul, J.: The game, the player, the world: looking for a heart of gameness. In: Digital Games Research Conference, 4–6 November 2003, University of Utrecht, The Netherlands (2003)
38. Kabanda, S., Tanner, M., Kent, C.: Exploring SME cybersecurity practices in developing countries. J. Organ. Comput. Electron. Comm. **28**, 269–282 (2018). https://doi.org/10.1080/10919392.2018.1484598
39. Kapp, K.M.: The Gamification of Learning and Instruction: Game-Based Methods and Strategies for Training and Education, 1st edn. Pfeiffer & Company, Ablar (2012)
40. Kasperski: Secure password check (2019). https://password.kaspersky.com
41. Keeper Security: 2018 state of cybersecurity in small and medium size businesses study (2018). https://start.keeper.io/2018-ponemon-report
42. Ki-Aries, D., Faily, S.: Persona-centred information security awareness. Comput. Secur. **70**, 663–674 (2017)
43. LimeSurvey: The online survey tool - open source surveys (2017). https://www. limesurvey.org
44. Lockheed Martin: Are you a cybersecurity ninja or n00b? (2018). http://bit.do/ lookheedmartin-quiz
45. Mead, N., Woody, C.: Cyber Security Engineering: A Practical Approach for Systems and Software Assurance. Pearson Education, London (2016)
46. Muller, P., et al.: Annual report on European SMEs 2014/2015. European Commission (2015)
47. NCSA: stay safe online - cybersecurity awareness toolkit for SMB. National Cyber Security Alliance (2018)

48. NIST: Cybersecurity framework (2014). https://www.nist.gov/cyberframework
49. O'Flaherty, K.: How gamification can boost cyber security (2019). https://www.information-age.com/gamification-can-boost-cyber-security-123479658/
50. Osborn, E., et al.: Business versus tech: sources of the perceived lack of cyber security in SMEs. In: 1st International Conference on Cyber Security for Sustainable Society, Feburary 2015
51. PhishingBox: Phishing simulator and test (2019). https://www.phishingbox.com/phishing-test
52. Ponsard, C.: Cybersecurity quizz (Google Play Store) (2018). http://bit.do/QuizzCyberSecurity
53. Ponsard, C., Grandclaudon, J., Bal, S.: Survey and lessons learned on raising SME awareness about cybersecurity. In: Proceedings of the 5th ICISSP, Prague, Czech Republic, 23–25 February, pp. 558–563 (2019)
54. Ponsard, C., Grandclaudon, J., Dallons, G.: Towards a cyber security label for SMEs: a European perspective. In: Proceedingsthe 4th ICISSP, Funchal, Madeira, pp. 426–431 (2018)
55. PwC: Game of threats (2017)
56. SafeOnWeb: Test your digital health (2018). https://campagne.safeonweb.be/en
57. Sánchez, L.E., Santos-Olmo, A., Fernández-Medina, E., Piattini, M.: Security culture in small and medium-size enterprise. In: Quintela Varajão, J.E., Cruz-Cunha, M.M., Putnik, G.D., Trigo, A. (eds.) CENTERIS 2010. CCIS, vol. 110, pp. 315–324. Springer, Heidelberg (2010). https://doi.org/10.1007/978-3-642-16419-4_32
58. SANS: Computer security training and certification (1989). https://www.sans.org
59. SANS: 10 tactics for rolling out a successful awareness program (2018). https://www.sans.org/sites/default/files/2019-04/poster_10-tactics.pdf
60. SANS: Security awareness posters (2018). https://www.sans.org/security-awareness-training/resources/posters
61. SBDC, M.: Small business, big threat (2018). https://smallbusinessbigthreat.com
62. SPARTA: Strategic programs for advanced research and technology in Europe (2019). https://www.sparta.eu
63. UK Government: Cyber essentials (2016). https://www.cyberaware.gov.uk/cyberessentials
64. UK Government: Cyber essentials self assessment (2018). https://www.cyberessentials.ie/self-assessment
65. VDS: A brief assessment for SMEs - quick check for cyber security (2017). http://vds-quick-check.de
66. Veseli, I.: Measuring the effectiveness of information security awareness program. Msc., Department of Computer Science and Media Technology Gjovik University College, South Africa (2011)
67. Yeboah-Boateng, E.O.: Cyber-Security Challenges with SMEs in Developing Economies: Issues of Confidentiality, Integrity & Availability (CIA). Institut for Elektroniske Systemer, Aalborg Universitet, Aalborg (2013)
68. Yunos, Z., Hamid, R.S.A., Ahmad, M.: Development of a cyber security awareness strategy using focus group discussion. In: 2016 SAI Computing Conference (SAI), pp. 1063–1067, July 2016
69. Zurich Inusrance Group: SMEs' cyber risk awareness is on the rise (2016). https://www.zurich.com/en/media/news-releases/2016/2016-1123-01

Analysing the Provenance of IoT Data

Chiara Bodei[1] and Letterio Galletta[2]

[1] Dipartimento di Informatica, Università di Pisa, Pisa, Italy
chiara.bodei@unipi.it
[2] IMT School for Advanced Studies, Lucca, Italy
letterio.galletta@imtlucca.it

Abstract. The Internet of Things (IoT) is leading to a smartification of our society: we are surrounded by many smart devices that automatically collect and exchange data of various kinds and provenance. Many of these data are critical because they are used to train learning algorithms, to control cyber-physical systems or to guide administrators to take decisions. Since the collected data are so important, many devices can be the targets of security attacks. Consequently, it is crucial to be able to trace data and to identify their paths inside a network of smart devices to detect possible threats. To help designers in this threat reasoning, we start from the modelling language IoT-LySa, and propose a Control Flow Analysis, a static analysis technique, for predicting the possible trajectories of data in an IoT system. Trajectories can be used as the basis for checking at design time whether sensitive data can pass through possibly dangerous nodes, and for selecting suitable security mechanisms that guarantee a reliable transport of data from sensors to servers using them. The computed paths are also interesting from an architectural point of view for deciding in which nodes data are collected, processed, communicated and stored.

1 Introduction

We are living the Internet of Things (IoT) revolution: we are surrounded by many interconnected devices (smart objects) equipped with sensors and actuators that automatically collect and transmit huge amounts of data over the net. Actually, a typical IoT system is a production chain that starts from raw data collected by sensors, continues with intermediate devices that perform data aggregation and ends with servers that store and process these data using learning algorithms. The results of the computation made on servers are used to take decisions or to trigger actuator actions in some part of the system.

Partially supported by Università di Pisa PRA_2018_66 *DECLWARE: Metodologie dichiarative per la progettazione e il deployment di applicazioni* and by MIUR project PRIN 2017FTXR7S *IT MATTERS* (Methods and Tools for Trustworthy Smart Systems).

P. Mori et al. (Eds.): ICISSP 2019, CCIS 1221, pp. 358–381, 2020.
https://doi.org/10.1007/978-3-030-49443-8_17

Secure transmission of data becomes even more crucial in IoT systems where devices can be physically attacked and data can be eavesdropped or altered during their communication. Therefore it is important that designers and administrators of such systems are aware of the provenance and the trajectories of data, especially when they are sensitive or when they impact on critical decisions.

Usually, formal methods offer designers tools to support the development of systems. In practice, designers build a mathematical model that describes the system we want to implement at a certain level of abstraction and they use formal verification techniques to reason about properties of the model, and consequently of the system it represents.

In this paper, we follow this approach to enable designers reasoning on data trajectories in IoT systems. Technically, we start from the formal specification language IoT-LySa, a process calculus recently proposed for IoT systems [5,9]. IoT-LySa allows designers to define a model of a system and fosters them to adopt a *Security by Design* development model. Indeed, designers can exploit the language to describe the network architecture of the system and how its components (smart objects or nodes) interact with each other. Furthermore, they can reason about the system correctness and robustness by using the Control Flow Analysis (CFA) of IoT-LySa.

This static analysis without running the system predicts (safely approximates) how data from sensors may spread across the system and how objects may interact. Technically, it "mimics" the behaviour of the system, by using abstract values in place of concrete ones and by modeling the consequences of each possible action. By inspecting the results of this "abstract simulation", designers can detect possible security vulnerabilities and intervene as early as possible during the design phase.

Here, we extend the original IoT-LySa CFA [5] for performing a *data path analysis*. The goal of this analysis is to predict how data travel across the network from specific data source nodes to data consumer nodes, computing all possible paths. Using the analysis results, a designer can investigate whether the trajectories taken from a particular piece of information include nodes that are considered potentially dangerous or that do not have an adequate security clearance for the information they are receiving.

Moreover, the trajectories can be used to make decisions on the architecture of the system by detecting critical nodes where data are collected and stored. Consequently, the information computed by our analysis may help designers in making educated decisions, on the exposure of both raw and aggregated data. Since the CFA over-approximates the behaviour of a given system, if the predicted trajectories do not show dangerous situations, we can be sure that at run time they will never happen. If instead they do, this means that there is a (even small) possibility of these situations to happen, and it can be worthwhile for the designer to carry out further investigations.

A short and preliminary version of the above results have been previously presented in [11]. As new contributions, in this paper, we systematise the full formal development of our data path analysis by presenting all its inference rules together with the formal proofs of its correctness. In addition, we introduce the notion of scored trajectories that enriches the previous notion of simple trajectories with quantitative information. Finally, we apply our analysis on a completely new example, a Closed Circuit Television system, based on a visual sensor network.

Structure of the Paper. The paper is organised as follows. We introduce our approach, in Sect. 2, with an illustrative example that we use as case study. We briefly recall the process algebra IoT-LySa, in Sect. 3. Section 4 defines the CFA for the data path analysis and we show how to compute the data trajectories from the analysis result. In Sect. 5 we enrich the trajectories with the security scores on the involved nodes. Conclusions are in Sect. 6.

2   A Visual Sensor Network

In this section, we illustrate our methodology through a simple yet realistic scenario similar to the ones introduced in [12,13], where we model the problem of tracking some targets moving in the sensing space in the visual sensor network of a building for surveillance aims.

2.1   The Scenario

A Visual Sensor Network (VSN) consists of a large number of interconnected sensor nodes endowed with an imager (photo or video camera) and an embedded processor that communicate via wireless interfaces. Nodes can be different in computing power, amount of memory and energy consumption. Each node (or camera) can directly communicate to the nodes lying in its radio range, here called *physical neighbours*. Moreover, since each camera covers a part of the 3-D space by its conic field of view (FOV), there is a further notion of proximity for nodes: two nodes can collaborate and work on the same data when their FOVs intersect, i.e. the corresponding cameras monitor a common part of the space. Note that they can also be distant from each other. They are here called *logical neighbours*. Many applications of VSN address event detection and estimation of some metrics, based on the combination of different sensor readings, such as light and temperature sensors, or microphones. Since information is more valuable when close to its source and sending it is expensive, distributed approaches are preferable to centralised ones, where visual surveillance tasks are performed by collaborative groups of one or more camera nodes.

We suppose to have, as illustrated in Fig. 1 and as in [12], a Closed Circuit Television system in a building like a university department, with 14 corridor nodes, called of *type 1* and 4 room nodes, called of *type 2*, in the room considered more sensible. Both kinds of nodes are equipped with cameras and, for the sake of simplicity, with just one sensor. Moreover, nodes of type 2 have also alarm buzzers as actuators. According to the given topology both physical and logical neighbours are statically known. In particular, only two corridor nodes with cameras with intersecting FOVs are not physical neighbour, c_0 and c_{13} and cannot communicate directly. In our model we choose w.l.o.g. that the camera nodes 2 and 1 serve as forwarder between the two nodes. Furthermore there are 5 aggregator nodes that collect information on a specific area of the building.

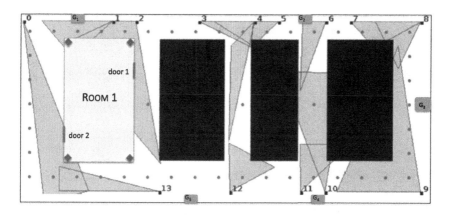

Fig. 1. The organisation of nodes in our Visual Sensor Network (modification of the Fig. 3 in [12]): little rectangles are the nodes with cameras of type 1, having each its FOV rooted in it and represented as a gray triangle, little diamonds are the nodes with cameras of type 2 and alarm actuators. Small orange rectangles are the aggregator nodes. Big rectangles are obstacles, the light green one is Room 1 and little circles are point of interest. (Color figure online)

In this application, corridor nodes detect intruders, in particular close to the sensible room ROOM 1. If one of the corridor nodes detects an intruder and checks that this one is close to one of the doors of the room, the corridor agent sends a warning message to the closest camera node inside the room.

2.2 The IoT-LySa Model

Here, we show how the scenario above can be easily modelled in IoT-LySa and what kind of information our CFA may provide to designers. In our model, the overall behavior of the network depends on the local processing at each node and on the inter-node communication, because the duty cycle of each camera involves only local computations and the exchange of partial approximations with logical and/or physical neighbors. Furthermore, we abstract away from the actual tracking algorithm used to reach a consistent view across nodes, and we model it as collaboration among nodes that exchange information (for further details see e.g. [12]).

The IoT-LySa model, described in Table 1, consists of a finite number of nodes running in parallel (this is the meaning of the parallel composition operator | for nodes). Some of the terms are equipped with annotations (variables

Table 1. Visual Network System N.

Whole Network

$N = N_1^1 \mid ... \mid N_n^1 \mid N_1^2 \mid ... \mid N_s^2 \mid G_1 \mid ... \mid G_k \mid$

Node of type 1 with $i, r1, ..., rt \in [1, n]$

$N_i^1 = \ell_i^1 : [P_i^1 \parallel C_i^1 \parallel S_i^1 \parallel B_i^1]$

$P_i^1 = *[(z_{i1}^{vi1} := 1^{a_{i1}}).(z_{i2}^{vi2} := 2^{a_{i2}}).\langle\!\langle p(z_{i1}^{vi1}, z_{i2}^{vi2})^{p_i}\rangle\!\rangle \triangleright \{L_i^1\} \parallel$

$\quad (; x_{ir1}^{vr1})^{X_i^{r1}} ....(; x_{irt}^{vrt})^{X_i^{rt}}.\hat{P}_i^1$

$\quad detection_{1i}^{v1i} = d(z_{i1}^{vi1}, z_{i2}^{vi2}, x_{ir1}^{vr1}, ..., x_{irt}^{vrt})^{d_{1i}}.$

$\quad detection_{1i}^{v1i}?\langle\!\langle detection_{1i}^{v1i}\rangle\!\rangle \triangleright \{\ell_f^2\}]*$

$\hat{P}_{10}^1 = (; x_{13}')$

$\hat{P}_1^1 = \langle\!\langle fw(x_1^0)^{fw_{11}}\rangle\!\rangle \triangleright \{\ell_{13}^1\}$

$\hat{P}_2^1 = \langle\!\langle fw(x_2^{13})^{fw_{12}}\rangle\!\rangle \triangleright \{\ell_0^1\}$

$\hat{P}_{13}^1 = (; x_0')$

$\hat{P}_i^1 = \tau$ for $i \neq 0, 1, 2, 13$

$C_i^1 = *[(\tau.1_i^1 := k_i^1).\tau]*$

$S_i^1 = *[(\tau.2_i^1 := v_i^1).\tau]*$

Node of type 2 with $j, f \in [1, s]$

$N_j^2 = \ell_j^2 : [Q_j^2 \parallel C_j^2 \parallel S_j^2 \parallel A_j^2 \parallel B_j^2]$

$Q_j^2 = *[(; w_j^{v2j})^{W_j^2}.(w_{2j1}^{v2j1} := 1^{d_{2j1}}).(w_{2j2}^{v2j2} := 2^{d_{2j2}}).$

$\quad confirm_{2j}^{w2j} = check(w_{det}^{v2j}, w^{v2j1}, w^{v2j2})^{c2j}.$

$\quad confirm_{2j}^{w2j}?\langle j, Alarm\rangle.\langle\!\langle 2j, confirm_{2j}^{w2j}\rangle\!\rangle \triangleright \{\ell_l\}]*$

$C_j^2 = *[(\tau.1_j^2 := k_j^2).\tau]*$

$S_j^2 = *[(\tau.2_j^2 := v_j^2).\tau]*$

$A_j^2 = *[(\!|j, \{Alarm\}).\tau]*$

Aggregator 1 with $l \in [1, k]$

$G_l = \ell_l : *[R_l \parallel B_l]*$

$R_l = (21; y_{l1}^{vl1})^{Y_1^l}.R_l^{21} \mid \cdots \mid (2s; y_{ls}^{vls})^{Y_s^l}.R_l^{2s}$

and function applications) and tags (input prefixes) that support the Control Flow Analysis in a way that will be clarified in the next section. Each node, uniquely identified by a label ℓ, consists of control processes and, possibly of camera, a sensor, and an actuator. Communication is multi-party: each node can send information to a set of nodes, provided that they are in the same transmission range. The communication patterns in the described scenario are not too complicate, so the example can serve the aim of illustrating our framework. Outputs and inputs must match to allow communication. In more detail, the output $\langle\!\langle E_1, \cdots, E_k\rangle\!\rangle \triangleright L.P$ represents that the tuple $E_1, \cdots, E_k$ is sent to the nodes with labels in L. The input is instead modelled as $(E_1, \cdots, E_j; x_{j+1}, \cdots, x_k)^X P$ and embeds pattern matching. In receiving an output tuple $E_1', \cdots, E_k'$ of the same size (arity), the communication succeeds provided that the first j

elements of the output match the corresponding first elements of the input (i.e. $E_1 = E'_1, \cdots, E_j = E'_j$), and then the variables occurring in the input are bound to the corresponding terms in the output. Suppose e.g. to have a process P waiting a message that P knows to include the value v, together with a datum that is not known from P. The input pattern tuple would be: $(v; x)$. If P receives the matching tuple $\langle v, d \rangle$, the variable x can be bound to v, since the first component of the tuple matches with the corresponding value.

We first examine the camera nodes N_{1i} of type 1:

$$N_i^1 = \ell_i^1 : [P_i^1 \parallel C_i^1 \parallel S_i^1 \parallel B_i^1],$$

where ℓ_i^1 is the label that uniquely identifies the node, and B_i^1 abstracts other components we are not interested in, among which its store Σ_i^1. Each of these nodes is managed by a control process P_i^1, connected to a camera C_i^1 that covers a given FVO_i^1 and to a sensor S_i^1 that senses the environment in the area close to the node. They run in parallel (this is the meaning of the parallel composition operator $\parallel$ for processes). The node N_i^1 collects the data of its camera and its sensor, elaborates them with the help of a filter and pre-processing function p and then transmits its local result to its physical neighbours in L_i^1. In the meanwhile, the node collects all the local results of its neighbours and analyses them in order to detect a possible intruder in the observed corridors. If this is the case the node sends the camera node of type 2 closest to the intruder a warning message to inform that the intruder may enter the room. In the IoT-LySA jargon, the camera communicates the picture/video to the node by storing it in its reserved location 1_i^1 of the shared store, while the sensor stores the sensed data in the location 2_i^1. The action τ denotes internal actions of the sensor we are not interested in modelling, e.g. adjusting the camera focus. The construct $*[...]*$ denotes the iterative behaviour of processes and of sensors.

The control process P_i^1: (i) stores in the variables z_{i1}^{vi1} and z_{i2}^{vi2} (where $vi1$ and $vi2$ are the variable annotations) the data collected by the camera and the sensor, by means of the two assignments: $(z_{i1}^{vi1} := 1^{a_{i1}})$ and $(z_{i2}^{vi2} := 2^{a_{i2}})$; (ii) elaborates them with the help of a filter and pre-processing function p and (iii) then transmits its local result to its physical neighbours in L_{1i}, with the output $\langle\langle p(z_{i1}^{vi1}, z_{i2}^{vi2})^{p_i} \rangle\rangle \triangleright \{L_i^1\}$, where p_i is the label of the application of the function p. In the meanwhile the node collects all the local results of its neighbours, with the inputs $(; x_{ir1}^{vr1})^{X_i^{r1}} ...(; x_{irt}^{vrt})^{X_i^{rt}}$ (where inputs are enriched with tags X_i^{r1}, ..., X_i^{rt}) and analyses them in order to detect a possible intruder in the observed corridors, with the detection function $d(z_{i1}^{vi1}, z_{i2}^{vi2}, x_{1i}^{r1}, ..., x_{1i}^{rt})^{d_{1i}}$. If this is the case (if $detection_{1i}^{v1i}$ is true) the node sends the value to the camera node of type 2 closest to the intruder to inform that the intruder may enter the room: $\langle\langle detection_{1i}^{v1i} \rangle\rangle \triangleright \{\ell_f^2\}$. The part in blue in the pdf describes the communication for the special nodes N_{10} and N_{13}^1 that cannot communicate directly and that rely on the intermediation of the nodes N_1^1 and N_2^1. In particular, N_1^1 forwards the data received from N_0^1 to N_{13}^1, while N_2^1 forwards the data received from N_{13}^1 to $_0^1$.

In the node N_j^2, the process Q_j^2 waits for possible warning messages from corridor nodes. In case such a message arrives and its is bound to w_j^{v2j}, it collects the data w_{2j1}^{v2j1} and w_{2j2}^{v2j2} of its camera and its sensor, processes them with the help of the function *check* in order to verify the possible presence of intruder inside the room. In case the presence is confirmed, the node activates an alarm buzzer and sends an alarm to its aggregator node, with a label recalling its name. Each aggregator node G_l controls a subset of the camera nodes of both types. Again B_j^2 and B_l abstract other components we are not interested in, among which their stores Σ_j^2 and Σ_l. Some nodes can be attacked and therefore may alter or tamper data passing from there, thus potentially impacting on the whole system and making the building vulnerable.

Since our analysis identifies the possible trajectories of data in the system, we can analyse these trajectories in order to check which are more risky w.r.t. the involved nodes. To this aim we suppose that operators can provide a security score for each node that measures its risk of being attacked. Reasoning on the formal model of the system and on the possible trajectories of data can be exploited to determine possible countermeasures such as redundancy, by introducing some new components that can mitigate the impact of attacks.

3   Overview of IoT-LySa

We now present a briefly overview of IoT-LySa [5,9], a specification language recently proposed for designing IoT systems. It is an adaption of LySa [3], a process calculus introduced to specify and analyse cryptographic protocols and checking their security properties (see e.g. [16,17]).

Differently from other process algebraic approaches introduced to model IoT systems, e.g. [19–22], IoT-LySa provides a design framework that includes a static semantics to support verification techniques and tools for certifying properties of IoT applications.

3.1   Syntax

Systems in IoT-LySa consist of a pool of nodes (things), each of which hosts a store for internal communication, sensors and actuators, and a finite number of control processes that detail how data are to be processed and exchanged among the node. We assume that each sensor (actuator) in a node with label ℓ is uniquely identified by an index $i \in \mathcal{I}_\ell$ ($j \in \mathcal{J}_\ell$, resp). A sensor is an active entity that reads data from the physical environment at its own fixed rate, and deposits them in the local store of. Actuators instead are passive: they just wait for a command to become active and operate on the environment. Data are represented by terms. Annotations $a, a', a_i, ...$, ranged over by $\mathcal{A}$, identify the occurrences of terms. They are used in the analysis and do not affect the dynamic semantics in Table 3. The set of nodes and all the node components are defined by the syntax in Table 2, that completes the one in [11].

Table 2. Syntax.

$\mathcal{E} \ni E ::=$ *annotated terms*		$\mathcal{M} \ni M ::=$ *terms*		
M^a	annotated term	v	value $(v \in \mathcal{V})$	
	with $a \in \mathcal{A}$	i	sensor location $(i \in \mathcal{I}_\ell)$	
		x		
		$\{E_1, \cdots, E_r\}_{k_0}$	encryption with key $k_0 \in \mathcal{K}$	
		$f(E_1, \cdots, E_r)$	function on data	
$\mathcal{N} \ni N ::=$ *systems of nodes*		$\mathcal{B} \ni B ::=$ *node components*		
0	empty system	Σ_ℓ	node store	
$\ell : [B]$	single node $(\ell \in \mathcal{L})$	P	process	
$N_1 \mid N_2$	par. composition	S	sensor (label $i \in \mathcal{I}_\ell$)	
		A	actuator (label $j \in \mathcal{J}_\ell$)	
		$B \parallel B$	par. composition	
$\mathcal{S} \ni S \quad ::=$ *sensors*		$\mathcal{A} \ni A \quad ::=$ *actuators*		
0	inactive sensor	0	inactive actuator	
$\tau.S$	internal action	$\tau.A$	internal action	
$i := v.\,S$	store of $v \in \mathcal{V}$	$(\!|j, \Gamma|\!).\,A$	command for actuator j	
	by the ith sensor	$\gamma.A$	triggered action $(\gamma \in \Gamma)$	
h	iteration var.	h	iteration var.	
$\mu\,h\,.\,S$	tail iteration	$\mu\,h\,.\,S$	tail iteration	

$P ::=$ *control processes*

0	inactive process
$\langle\!\langle E_1, \cdots, E_r \rangle\!\rangle \triangleright L.\,P$	asynchronous multi-output $L \subseteq \mathcal{L}$
$(E_1, \cdots, E_j; x_{j+1}, \cdots, x_r)^X.\,P$	input (with matching and tag)
decrypt E as $\{E_1, \cdots, E_j; x_{j+1}, \cdots, x_r\}_{k_0}$ in P	decryption with key k_0 (with match.)
$E?P : Q$	conditional statement
h	iteration variable
$\mu h.\,P$	tail iteration
$x^a := E.\,P$	assignment to $x \in \mathcal{X}$
$\langle j, \gamma \rangle.\,P$	output of action γ to actuator j

We assume as given a finite set $\mathcal{K}$ of secret keys owned by nodes, exchanged at deployment time in a secure way, as it is often the case [26]. Terms come with annotations $a \in \mathcal{A}$. The encryption function $\{E_1, \cdots, E_r\}_{k_0}$ returns the result of encrypting values E_i for $i \in [1, r]$ under the shared key k_0. We assume to have perfect cryptography. The term $f(E_1, \cdots, E_r)$ is the application of function f to r arguments; we assume given a set of primitive functions, typically for aggregating or comparing values. We assume the sets $\mathcal{V}, \mathcal{I}_\ell, \mathcal{J}_\ell, \mathcal{K}$ be pairwise disjoint.

Each node $\ell : [B]$ is uniquely identified by a label $\ell \in \mathcal{L}$ that may represent further information on the node (e.g. node location). Sets of nodes are described through the (associative and commutative) operator $\mid$ for parallel composition. The system 0 has no nodes. Inside a node $\ell : [B]$ there is a finite set of components combined by means of the parallel operator $\parallel$. We impose that there is a *single* store $\Sigma_\ell : \mathcal{X} \cup \mathcal{I}_\ell \rightarrow \mathcal{V}$, where $\mathcal{X}, \mathcal{V}$ are the sets of variables and of values (integers, booleans, ...), resp.

The store is essentially an array whose indexes are variables and sensors identifiers $i \in \mathcal{I}_\ell$ (no need of α-conversions). We assume that store accesses are atomic, e.g. through CAS instructions [18]. The other node components are control processes P, and sensors S (less than $\#(\mathcal{I}_\ell)$), and actuators A (less than $\#(\mathcal{J}_\ell)$) the actions of which are in Act.

The prefix $\langle\!\langle E_1, \cdots, E_r \rangle\!\rangle \rhd L$ implements a simple form of multi-party communication: the tuple obtained by evaluating $E_1, \ldots, E_r$ is asynchronously sent to the nodes with labels in L that are "compatible" (according, among other attributes, to a proximity-based notion). The input prefix $(E_1, \cdots, E_j; x_{j+1}, \cdots, x_r)^X$ receives a r-tuple, provided that its first j elements match the corresponding input ones, and then assigns the variables (after ";") to the received values. Otherwise, the r-tuple is not accepted. As in [2], each input in the syntax of processes P has a tag $X \in \mathbf{X}$, which is exploited to support the analysis and does not affect the dynamic semantics. A process repeats its behaviour, when defined through the tail iteration construct $\mu h.P$ (h is the iteration variable), intuitively rendered with $*[...]*$ in the motivating example. The process decrypt E as $\{E_1, \cdots, E_j; x_{j+1}, \cdots, x_r\}_{k_0}$ in P tries to decrypt the result of the expression E with the shared key $k_0 \in \mathcal{K}$. Also in this case, if the pattern matching succeeds, the process continues as P and the variables $x_{j+1}, \ldots, x_r$ are suitably assigned.

A sensor can perform an internal action τ or put the value v, gathered from the environment, into its store location i. An actuator can perform an internal action τ or execute one of its actions γ, received from its controlling process. Sensors and actuators can iterate. For simplicity, here we neither provide an explicit operation to read data from the environment, nor to describe the impact of actuator actions on the environment.

Operational Semantics

Our reduction semantics is based on the following *Structural congruence* $\equiv$ on nodes and node components. It is standard except for rule (4) that equates a multi-output with no receivers and the inactive process, and for the fact that inactive components of a node are all coalesced.

(1) $(\mathcal{N}/_\equiv, |, 0)$ is a commutative monoid
(2) $(\mathcal{B}/_\equiv, \|, 0)$ is a commutative monoid
(3) $\mu h . X \equiv X\{\mu h . X/h\}$ for $X \in \{P, A, S\}$
(4) $\langle\!\langle E_1, \cdots, E_r \rangle\!\rangle : \emptyset . 0 \equiv 0$

The two-level *reduction relation* $\rightarrow$ is defined as the least relation on nodes and its components satisfying the set of inference rules in Table 3. For the sake of simplicity, we use one relation. We assume the standard denotational interpretation $[\![E]\!]_\Sigma$ for evaluating terms.

Table 3. Reduction semantics (the upper part on node components, the lower one on nodes), where $X \in \{S, A\}$ and $Y \in \{N, B\}$.

(S-store)

$$\Sigma \parallel i^a := v^{a'}. S_i \parallel B \rightarrow \Sigma\{v/i\} \parallel S_i \parallel B$$

(Asgm)

$$\frac{[\![E]\!]_\Sigma = v}{\Sigma \parallel x^a := E. P \parallel B \rightarrow \Sigma\{v/x\} \parallel P \parallel B}$$

(Cond1)

$$\frac{[\![E]\!]_\Sigma = \text{true}}{\Sigma \parallel E? P_1 : P_2 \parallel B \rightarrow \Sigma \parallel P_1 \parallel B}$$

(Cond2)

$$\frac{[\![E]\!]_\Sigma = \text{false}}{\Sigma \parallel E? P_1 : P_2 \parallel B \rightarrow \Sigma \parallel P_2 \parallel B}$$

(A-com)

$$\frac{\gamma \in \Gamma}{\langle j, \gamma \rangle . P \parallel (\!(j, \Gamma)\!). A \parallel B \rightarrow P \parallel \gamma. A \parallel B}$$

(Act)

$$\gamma. A \rightarrow A$$

(Int)

$$\tau. X \rightarrow X$$

(Decr)

$$\frac{[\![E]\!]_\Sigma = \{v_1, \cdots, v_r\}_{k_0} \wedge \bigwedge_{i=1}^{j} v_i = [\![E_i']\!]_\Sigma}{\Sigma \parallel \text{decrypt } E \text{ as } \{E_1', \cdots, E_j'; x_{j+1}^{a_{j+1}}, \cdots, x_r^{a_r}\}_{k_0} \text{ in } P \parallel B \rightarrow \Sigma\{v_{j+1}/x_{j+1}, \cdots, v_r/x_r\} \parallel P \parallel B}$$

(Ev-out)

$$\frac{\bigwedge_{i=1}^{r} v_i = [\![E_i]\!]_\Sigma}{\Sigma \parallel \langle\!\langle E_1, \cdots, E_r \rangle\!\rangle \triangleright L. P \parallel B \rightarrow \Sigma \parallel \langle\!\langle v_1, \cdots, v_r \rangle\!\rangle \triangleright L.0 \parallel P \parallel B}$$

(Multi-com)

$$\frac{\ell_2 \in L \wedge Comp(\ell_1, \ell_2) \wedge \bigwedge_{i=1}^{j} v_i = [\![E_i]\!]_{\Sigma_2}}{\ell_1 : [\langle\!\langle v_1, \cdots, v_r \rangle\!\rangle \triangleright L. 0 \parallel B_1] \mid \ell_2 : [\Sigma_2 \parallel (E_1, \cdots, E_j; x_{j+1}^{a_{j+1}}, \cdots, x_r^{a_r})^X. Q \parallel B_2] \rightarrow \ell_1 : [\langle\!\langle v_1, \cdots, v_r \rangle\!\rangle \triangleright L \setminus \{\ell_2\}. 0 \parallel B_1] \mid \ell_2 : [\Sigma_2\{v_{j+1}/x_{j+1}, \cdots, v_r/x_r\} \parallel Q \parallel B_2]}$$

(Node)

$$\frac{B \rightarrow B'}{\ell : [B] \rightarrow \ell : [B']}$$

(ParN)

$$\frac{N_1 \rightarrow N_1'}{N_1 | N_2 \rightarrow N_1' | N_2}$$

(ParB)

$$\frac{B_1 \rightarrow B_1'}{B_1 \parallel B_2 \rightarrow B_1' \parallel B_2}$$

(CongrY)

$$\frac{Y_1' \equiv Y_1 \rightarrow Y_2 \equiv Y_2'}{Y_1' \rightarrow Y_2'}$$

The first two semantic rules implement the (atomic) asynchronous update of shared variables inside nodes, by using the standard notation $\Sigma\{-/-\}$. According to (S-store), the ith sensor uploads the value v, gathered from the environment, into its store location i. According to (Asgm), a control process updates the variable x with the value of E. The rules for conditional (Cond1) and (Cond2) are as expected. In the rule (A-com) a process with prefix $\langle j, \gamma \rangle$ commands the jth actuator to perform the action γ, if it is one of its actions. The rule (Act) says that the actuator performs the action γ. Similarly, for the rules (Int) for internal actions for representing activities we are not interested in. The rules (Ev-out) and (Multi-com) drive asynchronous IoT-LySA multi-communications and are explained as follows. In the first rule, to send a message $\langle\!\langle v_1, ..., v_r \rangle\!\rangle$ obtained by the evaluation of $\langle\!\langle E_1, ..., E_r \rangle\!\rangle$, a node with label ℓ spawns a new process, running in parallel with the continuation P; this new process offers the evaluated tuple to all the receivers with labels in L. In the second rule, the message coming from ℓ_1 is received by a node labelled ℓ_2, provided that: (i) ℓ_2 belongs to the set L of possible receivers, (ii) the two nodes satisfy a compatibility predicate $Comp$ (e.g. when they are in the same transmission range), and (iii) that the first j values match with the evaluations of the first j terms in the input. Moreover, the label ℓ_2 is removed by the set of receivers L of the tuple. The spawned process terminates when all the receivers have received the message (L is empty).

The rule (Decr) tries to decrypt the result $\{v_1, \cdots, v_r\}_k$ of the evaluation of E with the key k_0, and matches it against the pattern $\{E'_1, \cdots, E'_j; x_{j+1}, \cdots, x_r\}_{k_0}$. Concerning communication, when this match succeeds the variables after the semicolon ";" are assigned to values resulting from the decryption. The last rules propagate reductions across parallel composition ((ParN) and (ParB)) and nodes (Node), while (CongrY) is the standard reduction rule for congruence for nodes and node components.

4   Control Flow Analysis

Here we present a CFA for approximating the abstract behaviour of a system of nodes and for tracking the trajectories of data. This CFA follows the same schema of the one in [5] and in particular of the one in [8] for IoT-LySa. However, here we use different abstract values. Intuitively, abstract values "symbolically" represent runtime data so as to encode where these data have been introduced. Finally, we show how to use the CFA results to check which are the possible trajectories of these data.

Abstract Values. Abstract values correspond to concrete values for sensors, data, functions, and encryptions, and also record the annotations. Since the dynamic semantics may introduce encrypted terms with an arbitrarily nesting level, we have the special abstract values $\top^a$ that denote all the terms with a depth greater than a given threshold d. During the analysis, to cut these values, we will use the function $\lfloor - \rfloor_d$. Its definition is quite intuitive because we recursively visit the abstract value and cut it when we reach the relevant depth. Formally, abstract values are defined as follows, where $a \in \mathcal{A}$.

$$
\begin{aligned}
&\hat{\mathcal{V}} \ni \hat{v} :: = \ \textit{abstract terms} \\
&(\top, a) && \text{value denoting cut} \\
&(v, a) && \text{value for clear data} \\
&(f(\hat{v}_1, \cdots, \hat{v}_n), a) && \text{value for aggregated data} \\
&(\{\hat{v}_1, \cdots, \hat{v}_n\}_{k_0}, a) && \text{value for encrypted data}
\end{aligned}
$$

For simplicity, hereafter we write them as $\top^a, v^a, \{\hat{v}_1, \cdots, \hat{v}_n\}_{k_0}^a$, and indicate with $\downarrow_i$ the projection function on the ith component of the pair. We naturally extend the projection to sets, i.e. $\hat{V}_{\downarrow_i} = \{\hat{v}_{\downarrow_i} | \hat{v} \in \hat{V}\}$, where $\hat{V} \subseteq \hat{\mathcal{V}}$. In the abstract value v^a, v abstracts the concrete value from sensors or computed by a function in the concrete semantics, while the first value of the pair $\{\hat{v}_1, \cdots, \hat{v}_n\}_{k_0}^a$ abstracts encrypted data. The second component records the annotation associated to the corresponding term. Note that once given the set of encryption functions occurring in a node N, the abstract values are finitely many.

To extract all the annotations of an abstract value, included the ones possibly nested in it, we use the following auxiliary function.

Definition 1. *Give an abstract value* $\hat{v} \in \hat{\mathcal{V}}$, *we define the set of labels* $\mathbf{A}(\hat{v})$ *inductively as follows.*

- $\mathbf{A}(\top, a) = \mathbf{A}(v, a) = \{a\}$
- $\mathbf{A}(f(\hat{v}_1, \cdots, \hat{v}_n), a) = \{a\} \cup \bigcup_{i=1}^{n} \mathbf{A}(\hat{v}_i)$
- $\mathbf{A}(\{\hat{v}_1, \cdots, \hat{v}_n\}_{k_0}, a) = \{a\} \cup \bigcup_{i=1}^{n} \mathbf{A}(\hat{v}_i)$

Trajectories. We now introduce the notion of trajectories of data, in turn composed by micro-trajectories representing a single hop in the communication.

Definition 2. *Given a set of labels* $\mathcal{L}$, *a set of input tags* $\mathbf{X}$, *we define a* micro-trajectory μ *as a pair* $((\ell, \ell'), X) \in (\mathcal{L} \times \mathcal{L}) \times \mathbf{X}$. *A trajectory* τ *is a list of micro-trajectories* $[\mu_1, ..., \mu_n]$, *such that* $\forall \mu_i, \mu_{i+1}$ *with* $\mu_i = ((\ell_i, \ell'_i), X_i)$ *and* $\mu_{i+1} = ((\ell_{i+1}, \ell'_{i+1}), X_{i+1})$, $\ell'_i = \ell_{i+1}$.

In our analysis, trajectories can be obtained, starting from a set of micro-trajectories and by suitably composing them in order. Trajectories can be composed if the head of the second trajectory is equal to tail of the first. In this case the two trajectories can be merged. Technically, we use a closure of a set of micro-trajectories, the inductive definition of which follows.

Definition 3. *Given a set of micro-trajectories* $S \in ((\mathcal{L} \times \mathcal{L}) \times \mathbf{X})$

- $\forall ((\ell, \ell'), X) \in S. \ [((\ell, \ell'), X)] \in Clos_X(S)$;
- $\forall [L, ((\ell, \ell'), X)], \ [((\ell', \ell''), X'), L''] \in S. \ [L, ((\ell, \ell'), X), ((\ell', \ell''), X'), L''] \in Clos_X(S)$.

CFA Validation and Correctness. We now have all the ingredients to define our CFA to approximate communications and data stored and exchanged and, in particular, the micro-trajectories. We specify our analysis in a logical form through a set of inference rules expressing the validity of the analysis results. The analysis result is a tuple $(\widehat{\Sigma}, \kappa, \Theta, T, \rho)$ (a pair $(\widehat{\Sigma}, \Theta)$ when analysing a term), called *estimate* for N (for E), where $\widehat{\Sigma}$, κ, Θ, T, and ρ are the following *abstract domains*:

- the union $\widehat{\Sigma} = \bigcup_{\ell \in \mathcal{L}} \widehat{\Sigma}_\ell$ of the sets $\widehat{\Sigma}_\ell : \mathcal{X} \cup \mathcal{I}_\ell \rightarrow 2^{\widehat{\mathcal{V}}}$ of abstract values that may possibly be associated to a given location in $\mathcal{I}_\ell$ or a given variable in $\mathcal{X}$,
- a set $\kappa : \mathcal{L} \rightarrow \mathcal{L} \times \bigcup_{i=1}^{k} \widehat{\mathcal{V}}^i$ of the messages that may be received by the node ℓ, and
- a set $\Theta : \mathcal{L} \rightarrow \mathcal{A} \rightarrow 2^{\widehat{\mathcal{V}}}$ of the information of the actual values computed by each labelled term M^a in a given node ℓ, at run time.
- a set $\rho : \mathbf{X} \rightarrow \mathcal{L} \times \bigcup_{i=1}^{k} \widehat{\mathcal{V}}^i$ is the sets of output tuples that may be accepted by the input variables X.
- a set $T = \mathcal{A} \rightarrow (\mathcal{L} \times \mathcal{L}) \times \mathbf{T}$ of possible micro-trajectories related to the abstract values.

Note that the component T is new, and also the combined use of these five components is new and allows us to potentially integrate the present CFA with the previous analyses of IoT-LySa.

An available estimate has to be validated correct. This requires that it satisfies the judgements defined according to the syntax of nodes, node components and terms. They are defined by the set of clauses presented in Tables 4 and 5.

Table 4. Analysis of labelled terms $(\widehat{\Sigma}, \Theta) \models_\ell M^a$.

$$\frac{(i,a) \in \Theta(\ell)(a)}{(\widehat{\Sigma}, \Theta) \models_\ell i^a} \qquad \frac{(v,a) \in \Theta(\ell)(a)}{(\widehat{\Sigma}, \Theta) \models_\ell v^a} \qquad \frac{\widehat{\Sigma}_\ell(x) \subseteq \Theta(\ell)(a)}{(\widehat{\Sigma}, \Theta) \models_\ell x^a}$$

$$\frac{\bigwedge_{i=1}^k (\widehat{\Sigma}, \Theta) \models_\ell M_i^{a_i} \wedge}{\forall \hat{v}_1, .., \hat{v}_r : \bigwedge_{i=1}^r \hat{v}_i \in \Theta(\ell)(a_i) \Rightarrow (\lfloor \{\hat{v}_1, .., \hat{v}_r\}_{k_0} \rfloor_d, a) \in \Theta(\ell)(a)}{(\widehat{\Sigma}, \Theta) \models_\ell \{M_1^{a_1}, .., M_r^{a_r}\}_{k_0}^a}$$

$$\frac{\bigwedge_{i=1}^k (\widehat{\Sigma}, \Theta) \models_\ell M_i \wedge}{\forall \hat{v}_1, .., \hat{v}_r : \bigwedge_{i=1}^r \hat{v}_i \in \Theta(\ell)(a_i) \Rightarrow (f(\hat{v}_1, .., \hat{v}_r), a) \in \Theta(\ell)(a)}{(\widehat{\Sigma}, \Theta) \models_\ell f(M_1^{a_1}, .., M_r^{a_r})^a}$$

The judgement $(\widehat{\Sigma}, \Theta) \models_\ell M^a$, defined by the rules in Table 4, requires that $\Theta(\ell)(a)$ includes all the abstract values $\hat{v}$ associated to M^a. In the case of sensor identifiers, i^a and values v^a must be included in $\Theta(\ell)(a)$. According to the clause for the variable x^a, an estimate is valid if $\Theta(\ell)(a)$ includes the abstract values bound to x collected in $\widehat{\Sigma}_\ell$.

The rule for analysing compound terms requires that the components are in turn analysed. The penultimate rule deals with the application of an r-ary encryption. To do that (i) it analyses each term $M_i^{a_i}$, and (ii) for each r-tuple of values $(\hat{v}_1, \cdots, \hat{v}_r)$ in $\Theta(\ell)(a_1) \times \cdots \times \Theta(\ell)(a_r)$, it requires that the abstract structured value $\{\hat{v}_1, \cdots, \hat{v}_r\}_{k_0}^a$, cut at depth d, belongs to $\Theta(\ell)(a)$. The special abstract value $\top^a$ will end up in $\Theta(\ell)(a)$ if the depth of the term exceeds d. The last rule is for the application of an r-ary function f. Also in this case, (i) it analyses each term $M_i^{a_i}$, and (ii) for all r-tuples of values $(\hat{v}_1, \cdots, \hat{v}_r)$ in $\Theta(\ell)(a_1) \times \cdots \times \Theta(\ell)(a_r)$, it requires that the composed abstract value $f(\hat{v}_1, \cdots, \hat{v}_r)^a$ belongs to $\Theta(\ell)(a)$.

The judgements for nodes with the form $(\widehat{\Sigma}, \kappa, \Theta, T, \rho) \models N$ are defined by the rules in Table 5. The rules for the *inactive node* and for *parallel composition* are standard. The rule for a single node $\ell : [B]$ requires that its internal components B are in turn analysed; in this case we the use rules with judgements $(\widehat{\Sigma}, \kappa, \Theta, T, \rho) \models_\ell B$, where ℓ is the label of the enclosing node. The rule connecting actual stores Σ with abstract ones $\widehat{\Sigma}$ requires the locations of sensors to contain the corresponding abstract values. The rule for sensors is trivial, because we are only interested in the users of their values. The rule for actuators is equally trivial, because we model actuators as passive entities. The rules for processes require analysing the immediate sub-processes.

Table 5. Analysis of nodes $(\widehat{\Sigma}, \kappa, \Theta, T, \rho) \models N$, and of node components $(\widehat{\Sigma}, \kappa, \Theta, T, \rho) \models_\ell B$.

$$\frac{}{(\widehat{\Sigma}, \kappa, \Theta, T, \rho) \models 0} \qquad \frac{(\widehat{\Sigma}, \kappa, \Theta, T, \rho) \models_\ell B}{(\widehat{\Sigma}, \kappa, \Theta, T, \rho) \models \ell : [B]} \qquad \frac{(\widehat{\Sigma}, \kappa, \Theta, T, \rho) \models N_1 \wedge (\widehat{\Sigma}, \kappa, \Theta, T, \rho) \models N_2}{(\widehat{\Sigma}, \kappa, \Theta, T, \rho) \models N_1 \mid N_2}$$

$$\frac{\forall i \in \mathcal{I}_\ell . i^\ell \in \widehat{\Sigma}_\ell(i)}{(\widehat{\Sigma}, \kappa, \Theta, T, \rho) \models_\ell \Sigma} \qquad \frac{}{(\widehat{\Sigma}, \kappa, \Theta, T, \rho) \models_\ell S} \qquad \frac{}{(\widehat{\Sigma}, \kappa, \Theta, T, \rho) \models_\ell A}$$

$$\frac{\bigwedge_{i=1}^k (\widehat{\Sigma}, \Theta) \models_\ell M_i^{a_i} \wedge (\widehat{\Sigma}, \kappa, \Theta, T, \rho) \models_\ell P \wedge}{\forall \hat{v}_1, \cdots, \hat{v}_r : \bigwedge_{i=1}^r \hat{v}_i \in \Theta(\ell)(a_i) \Rightarrow \forall \ell' \in L : (\ell, \langle\!\langle \hat{v}_1, \cdots, \hat{v}_r \rangle\!\rangle) \in \kappa(\ell')}{(\widehat{\Sigma}, \kappa, \Theta, T, \rho) \models_\ell \langle\!\langle M_1^{a_1}, \cdots, M_r^{a_r} \rangle\!\rangle \triangleright L. P}$$

$$\frac{\begin{array}{c} \bigwedge_{i=1}^j (\widehat{\Sigma}, \Theta) \models_\ell M_i^{a_i} \wedge \\ \forall (\ell', \langle\!\langle \hat{v}_1, \cdots, \hat{v}_r \rangle\!\rangle) \in \kappa(\ell) : Comp(\ell', \ell) \Rightarrow \\ (\bigwedge_{i=j+1}^r \hat{v}_i \in \widehat{\Sigma}_\ell(x_i) \wedge \\ (\ell', \langle\!\langle (\hat{v}_1, \cdots, \hat{v}_r) \rangle\!\rangle) \in \rho(X) \wedge \forall a \in \mathbf{A}(\hat{v}_i).((\ell, \ell'), X) \in T(a) \\ \wedge (\widehat{\Sigma}, \kappa, \Theta, T, \rho) \models_\ell P) \end{array}}{(\widehat{\Sigma}, \kappa, \Theta, T, \rho) \models_\ell (M_1^{a_1}, \cdots, M_j^{a_j}; x_{j+1}^{a_{j+1}}, \cdots, x_r^{a_r})^X. P}$$

$$\frac{\begin{array}{c} (\widehat{\Sigma}, \Theta) \models_\ell M^a \wedge \bigwedge_{i=1}^j (\widehat{\Sigma}, \Theta) \models_\ell M_i^{a_i} \wedge \\ \forall \{\hat{v}_1, \cdots, \hat{v}_r\}_{k_0}^b \in \Theta(\ell)(a) \Rightarrow \left(\bigwedge_{i=j+1}^r \hat{v}_i \in \widehat{\Sigma}_\ell(x_i) \wedge (\widehat{\Sigma}, \kappa, \Theta, T, \rho) \models_\ell P \right) \end{array}}{(\widehat{\Sigma}, \kappa, \Theta, T, \rho) \models_\ell \text{decrypt } M^a \text{ as } \{M_1^{a_1}, \cdots, M_j^{a_j}; x_{j+1}^{a_{j+1}}, \cdots, x_r^{a_r}\}_{k_0} \text{ in } P}$$

$$\frac{\begin{array}{c} (\widehat{\Sigma}, \Theta) \models_\ell M^a \wedge \\ \forall \hat{v} \in \Theta(\ell)(a) \Rightarrow \hat{v} \in \widehat{\Sigma}_\ell(x) \wedge (\widehat{\Sigma}, \kappa, \Theta, T, \rho) \models_\ell P \end{array}}{(\widehat{\Sigma}, \kappa, \Theta, T, \rho) \models_\ell x^{a_x} := M^a. P} \qquad \frac{(\widehat{\Sigma}, \kappa, \Theta, T, \rho) \models_{n\ell} P}{(\widehat{\Sigma}, \kappa, \Theta, T, \rho) \models_\ell \langle j, \gamma \rangle. P}$$

$$\frac{\begin{array}{c} (\widehat{\Sigma}, \Theta) \models_\ell M^a \wedge \\ (\widehat{\Sigma}, \kappa, \Theta, T, \rho) \models_\ell P_1 \wedge (\widehat{\Sigma}, \kappa, \Theta, T, \rho) \models_\ell P_2 \end{array}}{(\widehat{\Sigma}, \kappa, \Theta, T, \rho) \models_\ell M^a ? P_1 : P_2} \qquad \frac{(\widehat{\Sigma}, \kappa, \Theta, T, \rho) \models_\ell B_1 \wedge (\widehat{\Sigma}, \kappa, \Theta, T, \rho) \models_\ell B_2}{(\widehat{\Sigma}, \kappa, \Theta, T, \rho) \models_\ell B_1 \| B_2}$$

$$\frac{}{(\widehat{\Sigma}, \kappa, \Theta, T, \rho) \models_\ell 0} \qquad \frac{(\widehat{\Sigma}, \kappa, \Theta, T, \rho) \models_\ell P}{(\widehat{\Sigma}, \kappa, \Theta, T, \rho) \models_\ell \mu h. P} \qquad \frac{}{(\widehat{\Sigma}, \kappa, \Theta, T, \rho) \models_\ell h}$$

An estimate is valid for *multi-output*, if it is valid for the continuation of P and the set of messages communicated by the node ℓ to each node ℓ' in L, includes all the messages obtained by the evaluation of the r-tuple $\langle\!\langle M_1^{a_1}, \cdots, M_r^{a_r} \rangle\!\rangle$. More precisely, the rule (i) finds the sets $\Theta(\ell)(a_i)$ for each term $M_i^{a_i}$, and (ii) for all tuples of values $(\hat{v}_1, \cdots, \hat{v}_r)$ in $\Theta(\ell)(a_1) \times \cdots \times \Theta(\ell)(a_r)$ it checks whether they belong to $\kappa(\ell')$ for each $\ell' \in L$. Symmetrically, the rule for *input* requires that the values inside messages that can be sent to the node ℓ, passing the pattern matching, are included in the estimates of the variables $x_{j+1}, \cdots, x_r$. More in detail, the rule analyses each term $M_i^{a_i}$, and requires that for any message that the node with label ℓ can receive, i.e. $(\ell', \langle\!\langle \hat{v}_1, \cdots, \hat{v}_j, \hat{v}_{j+1}, \ldots, \hat{v}_r \rangle\!\rangle)$ in $\kappa(\ell)$, provided that the two nodes can communicate (i.e. $Comp(\ell', \ell)$), the abstract values $\hat{v}_{j+1}, \ldots, \hat{v}_r$ are included in the estimates of $x_{j+1}, \cdots, x_r$. Furthermore, the micro-trajectory $((\ell, \ell'), X)$ is recorded in the T component for each annotation related (via $\mathbf{A}$) to the abstract value $\hat{v}_i$, to record that the abstract value $\hat{v}_i$ coming from the node ℓ can reach the node labelled ℓ', in the input with tag X. For instance, if $\hat{v}_i = (f((v_{i1}, a_{i1}), (v_{i2}, a_{i2})), a_i)$, then the micro-trajectory is recorded in $T(a_i)$, $T(a_{i1})$ and $T(a_{i2})$. Finally, the ρ component records the sets of output tuples that can be bound in the input with tag X.

The rule for *decryption* is similar to the one for communication: it also requires that the keys coincide. The rule for *assignment* requires that all the values $\hat{v}$ in the estimate $\Theta(\ell)(a)$ for M^a belong to $\hat{\Sigma}_\ell(x)$. The rules for the *inactive process*, for *parallel composition*, and for *iteration* are standard (we assume that each iteration variable h is uniquely bound to the body P).

Given a term E annotated by a, the over-approximation of its possible trajectories is obtained by computing the trajectory closure of the set composed by all the possibly enriched micro-trajectories $((\ell, \ell'), X)$ or $((\ell_i, \ell_i'), (\phi(\ell_i), \phi(\ell_i')), X_i)$ in $T(a)$.

$$Trajectories(E^a) = Clos_X(T(a))$$

Therefore, our analysis enables traceability of data. For every exchanged message $\langle\!\langle v_1, \ldots, v_r \rangle\!\rangle$, the CFA keeps track of the possible paths of each of its components v_i and, in turn, for each v_i it keeps recursively track of the paths of the possible data used to compose it.

Example 1. To better understand how our analysis works, we apply it to the following simple system, where P_i' and B_i (with $i = 1, 2, 3$) abstract other components we are not interested in.

$$\ell_1 : [\langle\!\langle v^{a_1} \rangle\!\rangle \triangleright \ell_2. P_1' \parallel B_1] \mid \ell_2 : [(; x_2^{b_2})^{X_2}. \langle\!\langle f(x_2^{b_x})^m \rangle\!\rangle \triangleright \ell_3. P_2' \parallel B_2] \mid \ell_3 : [(; y_3^{c_3})^{Y_3}. P_3' \parallel B_3]$$

Every valid estimate $(\hat{\Sigma}, \kappa, \Theta, T, \rho)$ must include at least the following entries, with $d = 4$.

$$\Theta(\ell_1)(a_1) \supseteq \{v^{a_1}\}$$
$$\kappa(\ell_2) \supseteq \{(\ell_1, \langle\!\langle v^{a_1} \rangle\!\rangle)\}$$
$$\rho(X_2) \supseteq \{(\ell_1, \langle\!\langle v^{a_1} \rangle\!\rangle)\}$$
$$\hat{\Sigma}_{\ell_2}(x^{b_2}) \supseteq \{v^{a_1}\}$$
$$T(a_1) \supseteq \{((\ell_1, \ell_2), X_2)\}$$
$$\Theta(\ell_2)(b_2) \supseteq \{f(v^{a_1})^m\}$$
$$\kappa(\ell_3) \supseteq \{(\ell_3, \langle\!\langle f(v^{a_1}) \rangle\!\rangle)^m\}$$
$$\rho(Y_3) \supseteq \{(\ell_2, \langle\!\langle v^{a_1} \rangle\!\rangle)\}$$
$$\hat{\Sigma}_{\ell_3}(y^{c_3}) \supseteq \{f(v^{a_1})^m\}$$
$$T(a_1) \supseteq \{((\ell_2, \ell_3), Y_3)\}$$
$$T(m) \supseteq \{((\ell_2, \ell_3), Y_3)\}$$

Indeed, an estimate must satisfy the checks of the CFA rules. The validation of the system requires the validation of each node, i.e. $(\hat{\Sigma}, \kappa, \Theta, T, \rho) \models N_i$ and of the processes there included, i.e. $(\hat{\Sigma}, \kappa, \Theta, T, \rho) \models_{\ell_i} P_i$, with $i = 1, 2, 3$. In particular, the validation of the process included in N_1, i.e. $\langle\!\langle v^{a_1} \rangle\!\rangle \triangleright \{\ell_2\}$ holds because the checks required by CFA clause for output succeed. We can indeed verify that $(\hat{\Sigma}, \Theta) \models_\ell v^{a_1}$ holds because $v^{a_1} \in \Theta(\ell_1)(a_1)$, according to the CFA clause for names. Furthermore $(\ell_1, \langle\!\langle v^{a_1} \rangle\!\rangle) \in \kappa(\ell_2)$. This suffices to validate the output, by assuming that the continuation P_1' is validated as well. We have the following instantiation of the clause for output.

$$\frac{v^{a_1} \in \Theta(\ell_1)(a_1)}{(\widehat{\Sigma}, \Theta) \models_\ell v^{a_1}} \wedge (\widehat{\Sigma}, \kappa, \Theta, T, \rho) \models_\ell P_1' \wedge$$

$$\frac{v^{a_1} \in \Theta(\ell_1)(a_1) \Rightarrow (\ell_1, \langle\!\langle v^{a_1} \rangle\!\rangle) \in \kappa(\ell_2)}{(\widehat{\Sigma}, \kappa, \Theta, T, \rho) \models_{\ell_1} \langle\!\langle v^{a_1} \rangle\!\rangle \triangleright \{\ell_2\}. P_1'}$$

Instead $(\widehat{\Sigma}, \kappa, \Theta, T, \rho) \models_{\ell_1} (; x_2^{b_2})^{X_2}. \langle\!\langle f(x_2^{b_x})^m \rangle\!\rangle \triangleright \ell_3. P_2'$ holds because the checks for the CFA clause for input succeed. From $(\ell_1, \langle\!\langle v^{a_1} \rangle\!\rangle) \in \kappa(\ell_2)$, we can indeed obtain that $\rho(X_2) \supseteq \{(\ell_1, \langle\!\langle v^{a_1} \rangle\!\rangle)\}$, $\widehat{\Sigma}_{\ell_2}(x^{b_2}) \supseteq \{v^{a_1}\}$, and that $T(a_1) \supseteq \{((\ell_1, \ell_2), X_2)\}$. The other entries can be similarly validated as well. Finally note that from $T(a_1) \supseteq \{((\ell_1, \ell_2), X_2)\}$ and $T(a_1) \supseteq \{((\ell_2, \ell_3), Y_3)\}$, we can obtain the trajectory $[((\ell_1, \ell_2), X_2), ((\ell_2, \ell_3), Y_3)]$, by applying $\widehat{Clos}_X$ to $(T(a_1))$. Note that the second component of each micro-trajectory records the input in which the communication of the value may take place and can help in statically backtracking the data path. Given the score of each node, the cost of the corresponding scored trajectory amounts to $\phi(\ell_1) + \phi(\ell_2) + \phi(\ell_3)$.

Example 2. Consider now our running example on the visual sensor network in Sect. 2. Every valid estimate $(\widehat{\Sigma}, \kappa, \Theta, T, \rho)$ must include at least the following entries, assuming $d = 4$, and $m \neq i$, with m and i indexes of nodes that are neighbours.

$$\Theta(\ell_i^1)(a_{i1}) \supseteq \{1^{a_{i1}}\}, \ \Theta(\ell_{1i})(a_{i2}) \supseteq \{2^{a_{i2}}\}$$
$$\widehat{\Sigma}_{\ell_i^1}(z^{v_{i1}}) \supseteq \{1^{a_{i1}}\}, \ \widehat{\Sigma}_{\ell_i^1}(z^{v_{i2}}) \supseteq \{2^{a_{i2}}\}$$
$$\kappa(\ell_m^1) \supseteq \{(\ell_i^1, \langle\!\langle p(1^{a_{i1}}, 2^{a_{i2}})^{p_i} \rangle\!\rangle)\}$$
$$\rho(X_m^i) \supseteq \{(\ell_i^1, \langle\!\langle p(1^{a_{i1}}, 2^{a_{i2}})^{p_i} \rangle\!\rangle)\}$$
$$\widehat{\Sigma}_{\ell_m^1}(x_m^i) \supseteq \{p(1^{a_{i1}}, 2^{a_{i2}})^{p_i}\}$$
$$\widehat{\Sigma}_{\ell_j^2}(confirm_{2j}^{w2j}) =$$
$$check(d(1^{a_{i1}}, 1^{a_{i2}}, p(1^{a_{r11}}, 2^{a_{r12}})^{p_{r1}}, ..., p(1^{a_{rt1}}, 2^{a_{rt2}})^{p_{rt}})^{d_{1i}}, 1^{d_{2j1}}, 1^{d_{2j2}})^{c2j}$$
$$T(p_i) \ni ((\ell_i^1, \ell_m^1), X_i^m), ((\ell_m^1, \ell_j^2), W_j^2), ((\ell_j^2, \ell_l), A_j^l)$$
$$T(d_{1i}) \ni ((\ell_i^1, \ell_j^2), W_j^2), ((\ell_j^2, \ell_l), A_j^l)$$

Our analysis respects the operational semantics of IoT-LySa, as witnessed by the following subject reduction result. It is also possible to prove the existence of a (minimal) estimate, as in [5]. The proofs follow the usual schema and benefit from an instrumented denotational semantics for expressions, the values of which are pairs $\langle v, \hat{v} \rangle$, where v is a concrete value and $\hat{v}$ is the corresponding abstract value. The store (Σ_ℓ^i with an undefined $\perp$ value) is accordingly extended. The semantics used in Table 3 just uses the projection on the first component.

The following subject reduction theorem establishes the correctness of our CFA, by relying on the agreement relation $\bowtie$ between the concrete and the abstract stores. Its definition is immediate, since the analysis only considers the second component of the extended store, i.e. the abstract one: $\Sigma_\ell^i \bowtie \widehat{\Sigma}_\ell$ iff $w \in \mathcal{X} \cup \mathcal{I}_\ell$ such that $\Sigma_\ell^i(w) \neq \perp$ implies $(\Sigma_\ell^i(w))_{\downarrow_2} \in \widehat{\Sigma}_\ell(w)$.

Theorem 1 (Subject reduction). *If* $(\widehat{\Sigma}, \kappa, \Theta, T, \rho) \models N$ *and* $N \to N'$ *and* $\forall \Sigma_\ell^i$ *in* N *it is* $\Sigma_\ell^i \bowtie \widehat{\Sigma}_\ell$, *then* $(\widehat{\Sigma}, \kappa, \Theta, T, \rho) \models N'$ *and* $\forall \Sigma_\ell^{i'}$ *in* N' *it is* $\Sigma_\ell^{i'} \bowtie \widehat{\Sigma}_\ell$.

Checking Trajectories. We now show that by inspecting the results of our CFA, we detect all the possible micro-trajectories of the data produced in the system of nodes that, put together, provide the overall trajectories.

The following corollary of subject reduction shows that we do track the trajectories of IoT data. The first item guarantees that κ and ρ predict all the possible inter-node communications, while the second item shows that our analysis records the micro-trajectory in the T component of each abstract value possibly involved in the communication.

Corollary 1. *Let* $N \xrightarrow{\langle\langle v_1, \ldots, v_r \rangle\rangle}_{\ell_1, \ell_2, X} N'$ *denote a reduction in which the message sent by node* ℓ_1 *is received by node* ℓ_2 *with an input tagged* X. *If* $(\widehat{\Sigma}, \kappa, \Theta, T, \rho) \models N$ *and* $N \xrightarrow{\langle\langle v_1, \ldots, v_r \rangle\rangle}_{\ell_1, \ell_2} N'$ *then it holds:*

- $(\ell_1, \langle\langle \hat{v}_1, \ldots, \hat{v}_r \rangle\rangle) \in \kappa(\ell_2) \wedge (\ell_1, \langle\langle \hat{v}_1, \cdots, \hat{v}_r \rangle\rangle) \in \rho(X)$, *where* $\hat{v}_i = v_{i \downarrow_2}$.
- $((\ell_1, \ell_2), X) \in T(a)$, *for all* $a \in \mathbf{A}(\hat{v}_i)$, *for all* $i \in [j+1, r]$.

4.1 Proofs

In this subsection, we provide the formal proofs of the results presented above. The reader not interested in the technical details of this formalisation, can safely skip this subsection without compromising the comprehension of the rest of the paper.

We recall that for the proofs, we resort to an instrumented denotational semantics for expressions, the values of which are pairs $\langle v, \hat{v} \rangle$ where v is a concrete value and $\hat{v}$ is the corresponding abstract value, and that the store and its updates are accordingly extended.

Lemma 1 (Congruence). *If* $N \equiv N'$ *then* $(\widehat{\Sigma}, \kappa, \Theta, T, \rho) \models N$ *iff* $(\widehat{\Sigma}, \kappa, \Theta, T, \rho) \models N'$.

Proof. It suffices to inspect the rules for $\equiv$, since associativity and commutativity of $\wedge$ reflects the same properties of both $|$ and $\|$, and to recall that any triple is a valid estimate for 0. Note that for the case of iteration, the following definition of limited unfolding suffices $\lfloor \mu h. P \rfloor_0 = P\{0/h\}$ and $\lfloor \mu h. P \rfloor_d = P\{\lfloor \mu h. P \rfloor_{d-1}/h\}$.

Theorem 1 (Subject reduction). *If* $(\widehat{\Sigma}, \kappa, \Theta, T, \rho) \models N$ *and* $N \to N'$ *and* $\forall \Sigma_\ell^i$ *in* N *it is* $\Sigma_\ell^i \bowtie \widehat{\Sigma}_\ell$, *then* $(\widehat{\Sigma}, \kappa, \Theta, T, \rho) \models N'$ *and* $\forall \Sigma_\ell^{i'}$ *in* N' *it is* $\Sigma_\ell^{i'} \bowtie \widehat{\Sigma}_\ell$.

Proof. Our proof is by induction on the shape of the derivation of $N \to N'$ and by cases on the last rule used. In all the cases below we will have that (*) $(\widehat{\Sigma}, \kappa, \Theta, T, \rho) \models_\ell \Sigma^i$, as well as that (**) $(\widehat{\Sigma}, \kappa, \Theta, T, \rho) \models_\ell B_1$ and B_2, so we will omit mentioning these judgements.

– Case (Multi-com). We assume

$$(\widehat{\Sigma}, \kappa, \Theta, T, \rho) \models \ell_1 : [\langle\!\langle v_1, \cdots, v_k \rangle\!\rangle \triangleright L.\,0 \parallel B_1] \mid$$
$$\ell_2 : [\Sigma_2^i \parallel (E_1, \cdots, E_j; x_{j+1}, \cdots, x_k)^X.Q \parallel B_2]$$

that is implied by

$$(\widehat{\Sigma}, \kappa, \Theta, T, \rho) \models_{\ell_1} [\langle\!\langle v_1, \cdots, v_k \rangle\!\rangle \triangleright L.\,0 \parallel B_1] \text{ and by}$$
$$(\widehat{\Sigma}, \kappa, \Theta, T, \rho) \models_{\ell_2} [\Sigma_2^i \parallel (E_1', \cdots; x_{j+1}, \cdots)^X.Q \parallel B_2]$$

that have been proved because the following conditions hold:

$$Comp(\ell_1, \ell_2) \tag{1}$$

$$\bigwedge_{i=1}^{k} (\widehat{\Sigma}, \Theta) \models_{\ell_1} v_i \tag{2}$$

$$\forall \hat{v}_1, \cdots, \hat{v}_k : \bigwedge_{i=1}^{k} \hat{v}_i \in \vartheta_i \Rightarrow$$

$$\forall \ell' \in L : (\ell_1, \langle\!\langle \hat{v}_1, \cdots, \hat{v}_k \rangle\!\rangle) \in \kappa(\ell') \tag{3}$$

$$(\widehat{\Sigma}, \kappa, \Theta) \models_{\ell_1} 0 \tag{4}$$

$$\bigwedge_{i=1}^{j} (\widehat{\Sigma}, \Theta) \models_{\ell_2} E_i \tag{5}$$

$$\forall (\ell', \langle\!\langle \hat{v}_1, \cdots, \hat{v}_k \rangle\!\rangle) \in \kappa(\ell_2) : \bigwedge_{i=1}^{j} \hat{v}_i \in \vartheta_i' \Rightarrow \tag{6}$$

$$\bigwedge_{i=j+1}^{k} \hat{v}_i \in \widehat{\Sigma}_{\ell_2}(x_i) \tag{7}$$

$$\forall (\ell', \langle\!\langle \hat{v}_1, \cdots, \hat{v}_k \rangle\!\rangle) \in \rho(X) \tag{8}$$

$$\forall a \in \mathbf{A}(\hat{v}_i).((\ell, \ell'), X, w) \in T(a) \tag{9}$$

$$(\widehat{\Sigma}, \kappa, \Theta, T, \rho) \models_{\ell_2} Q \tag{10}$$

Note that $\forall i\ (\widehat{\Sigma}, \Theta) \models_{\ell_1} v_i$ implies $\hat{v}_i \in \vartheta_i$, where $\hat{v}_i = (\llbracket v_i \rrbracket_{\Sigma_{\ell_2}^i})_{\downarrow 2}$, and that $\ell_2 \in L$ because $N \rightarrow N'$. We have to prove that

$$(\widehat{\Sigma}, \kappa, \Theta, T, \rho) \models, \ell_1 : [\langle\!\langle v_1, \cdots, v_k \rangle\!\rangle \triangleright L'.0 \| B_1]$$
$$\mid \ell_2 : [\Sigma_2^i \{v_{j+1}/x_{j+1}, \cdots, v_k/x_k\} \| Q \| B_2]$$

where $L' = L \setminus \{\ell_2\}$ that, in turn, amounts to prove that

(a) $(\widehat{\Sigma}, \kappa, \Theta, T, \rho) \models_{\ell_1} \langle\!\langle v_1, \cdots, v_k \rangle\!\rangle \triangleright L \setminus \{\ell_2\}.0 \| B_1$
(b) $(\widehat{\Sigma}, \kappa, \Theta, T, \rho) \models_{\ell_2} \Sigma_2^i \{(v_{j+1}, \hat{v}_{j+1})/x_{j+1}, \cdots\} \| Q \| B_2$

We have that (a) holds trivially because of (2–4) (of course $L \setminus \{\ell_2\} \subseteq L$), while (b) holds because of (8). We are left to prove that $\Sigma_{\ell_2}^i{}' \bowtie \widehat{\Sigma}_{\ell_2}$. Now, we know that $\Sigma_{\ell_2}^i{}'(y) = \Sigma_{\ell_2}^i(y)$ for all $y \in \mathcal{X}_{\ell_2} \cup \mathcal{I}_{\ell_2}$ such that $y \neq x_i$. The condition $(\Sigma_{\ell_2}^i(x_i))_{\downarrow 2} \in \widehat{\Sigma}_{\ell_2}(x_i)$ for all x_i holds because of (7).
– The cases (ParN), (StructN), and (Node) directly follow from the induction hypothesis, and the case (CongrN) from Lemma 1.

Corollary 1. *Let* $N \xrightarrow{\langle\!\langle v_1,\ldots,v_r \rangle\!\rangle}_{\ell_1,\ell_2,X} N'$ *denote a reduction in which the message sent by node* ℓ_1 *is received by node* ℓ_2 *with an input tagged* X. *If* $(\widehat{\Sigma}, \kappa, \Theta, T, \rho) \models N$ *and* $N \xrightarrow{\langle\!\langle v_1,\ldots,v_r \rangle\!\rangle}_{\ell_1,\ell_2} N'$ *then it holds:*

- $(\ell_1, \langle\!\langle \hat{v}_1, \ldots, \hat{v}_r \rangle\!\rangle) \in \kappa(\ell_2) \wedge (\ell_1, \langle\!\langle \hat{v}_1, \cdots, \hat{v}_r \rangle\!\rangle) \in \rho(X)$, *where* $\hat{v}_i = v_{i\downarrow_2}$.
- $((\ell_1, \ell_2), X) \in T(a)$, *for all* $a \in \mathbf{A}(\hat{v}_i)$, *for all* $i \in [j+1, r]$.

Proof. By Theorem 1, we have that $(\widehat{\Sigma}, \kappa, \Theta) \models N'$, so we proceed by induction on the shape of the derivation of $N \to N'$ and by cases on the last rule used.

- Case (Multi-com). If this rule is applied, than N is in the form

$$(\widehat{\Sigma}, \kappa, \Theta, T, \rho) \models \ell_1 : [\langle\!\langle v_1, \cdots, v_k \rangle\!\rangle \triangleright L.\, 0 \parallel B_1] \mid$$
$$\ell_2 : [\Sigma_2^i \parallel (E_1, \cdots, E_j; x_{j+1}, \cdots, , x_k)^X.Q \parallel B_2]$$

with $\ell_2 \in L$. Since $(\widehat{\Sigma}, \kappa, \Theta, T, \rho) \models N$ we have $(\widehat{\Sigma}, \kappa, \Theta, T, \rho) \models_{\ell_1} \langle\!\langle v_1, \cdots, v_k \rangle\!\rangle \triangleright L.\, 0$ and the required $(\ell_1, \langle\!\langle \hat{v}_1, \cdots, \hat{v}_k \rangle\!\rangle) \in \kappa(\ell_2)$. From $(\widehat{\Sigma}, \kappa, \Theta, T, \rho) \models_{\ell_2} (E_1, \cdots, E_j; x_{j+1}, \cdots, , x_k)^X.Q$, we can obtain instead the required $(\ell_1, \langle\!\langle \hat{v}_1, \cdots, \hat{v}_k \rangle\!\rangle) \in \rho(X)$, and $\forall a \in \mathbf{A}(\hat{v}_i).((\ell_1, \ell_2), X, w) \in T(a)$.
- Cases (ParN), (StructN), and (Node) directly follow from the induction hypothesis, and for the other rules the premise is false.

5 Scored Trajectories

We now extend the notion of trajectories by associating a *score* $\phi(\ell)$ to each node with label ℓ, representing some quantitative and logical information: in our case with a measure of the risk of node, in a style reminiscent of [1].

Trajectories can be compared on the basis of their overall score.

We assume that a table of scores is known that associates a score $\phi(\ell_i)$ to each node label ℓ_i. As a consequence we can decorate micro-trajectories with the scores of the nodes involved:

$$((\ell_i, \ell_i'), (\phi(\ell_i), \phi(\ell_j)), X_i),$$

resulting in *scored micro-trajectories*. The corresponding *scored trajectories* can be obtained as follows, by using the suitable extended closure function $\widehat{Clos}_X$.

Definition 4.

- $\forall ((\ell, \ell'), (\phi(\ell), \phi(\ell')), X) \in M. \; [((\ell, \ell'), (\phi(\ell), \phi(\ell')), X)] \in \widehat{Clos}_X(M);$
- $\forall [L, ((\ell, \ell'), (\phi(\ell), \phi(\ell')), X)], \; [((\ell', \ell''), (\phi(\ell'), \phi(\ell'')), X'), L''] \in M.$
  $[L, ((\ell, \ell'), (\phi(\ell), \phi(\ell')), X), ((\ell', \ell''), (\phi(\ell'), \phi(\ell'')), X'), L''] \in \widehat{Clos}_X(M).$

We now need a function to extract the overall cost of each trajectory, given the sequence of crossed nodes.

Definition 5.

- $Cost([[((\ell, \ell'), (\phi(\ell), \phi(\ell')), X)]]) = \phi(\ell) + \phi(\ell')$;
- $Cost([L, ((\ell, \ell'), (\phi(\ell), \phi(\ell')), X), ((\ell', \ell''), (\phi(\ell'), \phi(\ell'')), X'), L'']) = Cost(L) + \phi(\ell) + \phi(\ell') + Cost(L'')$.

We can now using the enriched trajectories to reason on which of them are more risky.

Example 3. Back to our example, by using the analysis, we can determine some of the possible trajectories of data, e.g. the ones of the term annotated with d_{1i}, i.e. $Trajectories(d_{1i})$ that includes $[(\ell_i^1, \ell_j^2), W_j^2), ((\ell_j^2, \ell_l), A_j^l)]$. This allows us to check which are the nodes the data may pass from, in this case and which are the corresponding inputs. The communication pattern here is admittedly simple in order to illustrate our approach. It is easy to verify that the above CFA results reflect the dynamic behaviour.

Now, given a security score for each node, we can analyse the trajectories of each piece of data of the analysed system, in order to determine the more vulnerable ones. We can also inspect the paths possibly followed by sensible data and also be suspicious about data produced or passed by unreliable nodes. For the sake of simplicity, we can use only two values for ϕ, by partitioning nodes in less (0) or more (1) secure. The less secure nodes are the ones put in an open and public area of the building, whereas the more secure nodes are the ones placed in areas with restricted access. In our scenario, suppose that all the nodes are secure apart from the node $N_{1\ 13}$ that is in an open area. Under these hypotheses, our analysis points out that the data that arrive to alert the node of type 2 in Room1 use a possibly vulnerable trajectory, i.e. $[(\ell_m^1, \ell_i^1), X_i^m), ((\ell_i^1, \ell_j^2), W_j^2), ((\ell_j^2, \ell_l), A_j^l)]$ with $i = 13$ has a cost 1 whereas with $i \neq 13$ the cost is 0. As a consequence, it could be the case to use a videocamera more difficult to tamper, or, alternatively, to add a new video camera in the restricted area.

We could instead classify links and making a similar reasoning, by associating weights to each of them in micro-trajectories, as in $((\ell_1, \ell_2), X, w)$. Given a classification of the "dangerous" links, we can analyse the trajectories of each piece of data and the way they are transmitted. This is particularly crucial in a setting where encryption and other security mechanisms can be costly and power consuming.

Another possibility to exploit our analysis is to detect possible illegal or bad flows from one point to another based on security levels, by investigating our trajectories, along the lines of [4]. Suppose for instance that nodes are classified according to a hierarchy of clearance levels for nodes (encoded in a value), and that a no read-up/no write-down policy is required. A node classified at a high level cannot send (write) any value to a node at a lower level, while the converse is allowed. The constraint can be restricted to least sensible data. In any case, by inspecting the possible trajectories, we can check for the presence or not of micro-trajectories (ℓ_1, ℓ_2), where the corresponding nodes do not respect the policy.

Note that each kind of enrichment of trajectories with quantitative information can be added after the analysis, making its results useful for different purposes.

6   Conclusions

We proposed a data path analysis, based on the CFA of IoT-LySa specification language, for tracking the propagation of data and for identifying their possible trajectories.

The results of CFA can be exploited in an early phase of system design, as a supporting technique. The analysis is quite general because the underlying idea is that its results can be used as a starting point for many different investigations on a given system behaviour. On the one hand, a designer can answer whether the provenance of the data that are processed or stored in a particular node offers sufficient security guarantees, e.g. these data traveled only along nodes that are considered robust. Furthermore, we can also check whether a system respects policies that rule information flows among nodes, by allowing some flows and forbidding others, e.g. data traveled only across nodes with a certain level of clearance. Answering to these questions can give some confidence to designers about the quality of the data managed by the considered system and how much secure are the data which are essential to take critical decisions. By using this information designers can detect the potential vulnerabilities related to the presence of dangerous nodes, and can determine possible solutions and mitigation.

On the other hand, analysing the trajectories may allow discovering patterns in data, e.g. there are pieces of data that always move together or in a similar way, thus, allowing designers to determine possible emerging features of the system behaviour. Furthermore, we can find which are the paths or segments of paths that are more used, and therefore may need special attention and suitable security mechanisms.

An approach close to the present one is that of [10], where Control Flow Analysis is used to over-approximate the behaviour of KLAIM processes and to track how tuple data can move in the network.

Our approach is quite flexible and can be adapted to different purposes, just by enriching the trajectories obtained from the analysis' results with different kinks of quantitative information. We would like to resort to other possible metrics. An interesting option is the one introduced in [1,23], where each node is associated to a value that quantitatively represents the effort (in terms of cost) required by an attacker to compromise the node. This allows the authors to reason on the dependencies among nodes and to identify the minimal set of nodes that must be compromised in order to impair the functionalities of a given target node. In the same paper, further metrics are proposed. In the first case, they suppose that the edge (or perimeter) nodes are easier to be compromised, and the effort becomes higher while moving to inner nodes of the graph. As a consequence, they assign costs to the nodes based on their depth in a given graph.

The second proposed security metric associates as a priority to the nodes that require utmost attention. In the third one, the metrics includes budget considerations, in order to provide a balance between the efforts required by an attacker to compromise critical nodes and the cost required to fix them.

Another future direction of investigation consists in integrating our present analysis with the taint analysis of [8]. In that analysis, data are marked as tainted when sensitive, and are marked as tamperable when coming from places where they can be tampered. The analysis statically predicts how marked data spread across an IoT system.

We further plan to study how to ensure a certain level of quality service of a system even when in the presence of not completely reliable data, by linking our approach to that used in [24,25]. In those paper authors introduce the Quality Calculus that allows defining and reasoning on software components that have a sort of backup plan in case the ideal behaviour fails due to unreliable communication or data.

Finally, since in many IoT system the behaviour of node adapts to their computational context, we aim at extending IoT-LYSA with constructs for representing contexts along the lines of [14,15], and to study their security following [6,7].

References

1. Barrère, M., Hankin, C., Nicolaou, N., Eliades, D.G., Parisini, T.: Identifying security-critical cyber-physical components in industrial control systems CoRR abs/1905.04796 (2019). http://arxiv.org/abs/1905.04796
2. Bodei, C., Brodo, L., Focardi, R.: Static evidences for attack reconstruction. In: Bodei, C., Ferrari, G.-L., Priami, C. (eds.) Programming Languages with Applications to Biology and Security. LNCS, vol. 9465, pp. 162–182. Springer, Cham (2015). https://doi.org/10.1007/978-3-319-25527-9_12
3. Bodei, C., Buchholtz, M., Degano, P., Nielson, F., Nielson, H.R.: Static validation of security protocols. J. Comput. Secur. **13**(3), 347–390 (2005)
4. Bodei, C., Degano, P., Ferrari, G.L., Galletta, L.: A step towards checking security in IoT. In: Proceedings of ICE 2016. EPTCS, vol. 223, pp. 128–142 (2016)
5. Bodei, C., Degano, P., Ferrari, G.-L., Galletta, L.: Where do your IoT ingredients come from? In: Lluch Lafuente, A., Proença, J. (eds.) COORDINATION 2016. LNCS, vol. 9686, pp. 35–50. Springer, Cham (2016). https://doi.org/10.1007/978-3-319-39519-7_3
6. Bodei, C., Degano, P., Galletta, L., Salvatori, F.: Linguistic mechanisms for context-aware security. In: Ciobanu, G., Méry, D. (eds.) ICTAC 2014. LNCS, vol. 8687, pp. 61–79. Springer, Cham (2014). https://doi.org/10.1007/978-3-319-10882-7_5
7. Bodei, C., Degano, P., Galletta, L., Salvatori, F.: Context-aware security: linguistic mechanisms and static analysis. J. Comput. Secur. **24**(4), 427–477 (2016)
8. Bodei, C., Galletta, L.: Tracking sensitive and untrustworthy data in IoT. In: Proceedings of the First Italian Conference on Cybersecurity (ITASEC 2017), pp. 38–52. CEUR Vol-1816 (2017)
9. Bodei, C., Degano, P., Ferrari, G.L., Galletta, L.: Tracing where IoT data are collected and aggregated. Log. Methods Comput. Sci. **13**(3) (2017)

10. Bodei, C., Degano, P., Ferrari, G.-L., Galletta, L.: Revealing the trajectories of KLAIM tuples, statically. In: Boreale, M., Corradini, F., Loreti, M., Pugliese, R. (eds.) Models, Languages, and Tools for Concurrent and Distributed Programming. LNCS, vol. 11665, pp. 437–454. Springer, Cham (2019). https://doi.org/10.1007/978-3-030-21485-2_24

11. Bodei, C., Galletta, L.: Tracking data trajectories in IoT. In: International Conference on Information Systems Security and Privacy (ICISSP2019). Lecture Notes in Computer Science, vol. 1. ScitePress (2019)

12. Chessa, S., Pelagatti, S., Triolo, N.: Engineering energy efficient visual sensor network applications using skeletons. Int. J. Parallel Program. 42(4), 663–680 (2014). https://doi.org/10.1007/s10766-013-0260-y

13. Concha, Ó.P., Patricio, M.A., Herrero, J.G., Rubiera, J.C., Molina, J.M.: Fusion of surveillance information for visual sensor networks. In: 9th International Conference on Information Fusion, FUSION 2006, pp. 1–8. IEEE (2006)

14. Degano, P., Ferrari, G.L., Galletta, L.: A two-component language for COP. In: Proceedings of 6th International Workshop on Context-Oriented Programming, COP@ECOOP 2014, pp. 6:1–6:7. ACM (2014)

15. Degano, P., Ferrari, G.L., Galletta, L.: A two-component language for adaptation: design, semantics, and program analysis. IEEE Trans. Softw. Eng. 42(6), 505–529 (2016)

16. Gao, H., Bodei, C., Degano, P.: A formal analysis of complex type flaw attacks on security protocols. In: Meseguer, J., Roşu, G. (eds.) AMAST 2008. LNCS, vol. 5140, pp. 167–183. Springer, Heidelberg (2008). https://doi.org/10.1007/978-3-540-79980-1_14

17. Gao, H., Bodei, C., Degano, P., Riis Nielson, H.: A formal analysis for capturing replay attacks in cryptographic protocols. In: Cervesato, I. (ed.) ASIAN 2007. LNCS, vol. 4846, pp. 150–165. Springer, Heidelberg (2007). https://doi.org/10.1007/978-3-540-76929-3_15

18. Herlihy, M.: Wait-free synchronization. ACM Trans. Program. Lang. Syst. 13(1), 124–149 (1991)

19. Lanese, I., Bedogni, L., Felice, M.D.: Internet of Things: a process calculus approach. In: Proceedings of the 28th Annual ACM Symposium on Applied Computing, SAC 2013, pp. 1339–1346. ACM (2013)

20. Lanotte, R., Merro, M.: A semantic theory of the Internet of Things. In: Lluch Lafuente, A., Proença, J. (eds.) COORDINATION 2016. LNCS, vol. 9686, pp. 157–174. Springer, Cham (2016). https://doi.org/10.1007/978-3-319-39519-7_10

21. Lanotte, R., Merro, M.: A semantic theory of the Internet of Things. Inf. Comput. 259(1), 72–101 (2018)

22. Lanotte, R., Merro, M., Muradore, R., Viganò, L.: A formal approach to cyber-physical attacks. In: 30th IEEE Computer Security Foundations Symposium, CSF 2017, pp. 436–450 (2017)

23. Nicolaou, N., Eliades, D.G., Panayiotou, C.G., Polycarpou, M.M.: Reducing vulnerability to cyber-physical attacks in water distribution networks. In: 2018 International Workshop on Cyber-physical Systems for Smart Water Networks, CySWater@CPSWeek, pp. 16–19. IEEE Computer Society (2018)

24. Nielson, H.R., Nielson, F., Vigo, R.: A calculus for quality. In: Păsăreanu, C.S., Salaün, G. (eds.) FACS 2012. LNCS, vol. 7684, pp. 188–204. Springer, Heidelberg (2013). https://doi.org/10.1007/978-3-642-35861-6_12

25. Nielson, H.R., Nielson, F., Vigo, R.: A calculus of quality for robustness against unreliable communication. J. Log. Algebr. Methods Program. **84**(5), 611–639 (2015)

26. Zillner, T.: ZigBee exploited (2015). https://www.blackhat.com/docs/us-15/materials/us-15-Zillner-ZigBee-Exploited-The-Good-The-Bad-And-The-Ugly-wp.pdf

Improving Interoperability in Multi-domain Enterprise Right Management Applications

Luigi Catuogno[✉] and Clemente Galdi

Università di Salerno, Via Giovanni Paolo II, 132, 84084 Fisciano, SA, Italy
{lcatuogno,clGaldi}@unisa.it

Abstract. In this paper we consider the problem of protecting files, possibly stored using remote storage services, on a device running different and independent third party applications. We present a general architecture that, by exploiting the inherent security of Trusted Execution Environments, and by requiring minimal secure storage onboard the device, is able to provide a general purpose, distributed storage system that allows the cooperation among different applications domains. Our system exposes APIs that can be invoked by other trusted applications, using the standard TEE IPC. Furthermore, we discuss a middleware that allows legacy applications to transparently access secured files.

Keywords: Trusted Execution Environments · BYOD · Cloud storage · Secure storage · Enterprise rights management

1 Introduction

An Enterprise Right Management (ERM) system features a set of tools, techniques and practices that allow to share and deploy corporate documents and data while protecting their confidentiality. Such protection is ensured throughout the data lifecycle, regardless to where they are stored or are transferred through, within the corporate's boundaries [12]. To this end, ERM systems specify and enforce fine-grained access control policies over corporate information at fruition time. Such systems typically rely on centralised authorities that are responsible for access control specification while user authentication and policy enforcement are guaranteed by corporate applications installed on trusted devices (*i.e.*, belonging to the company itself and used only for the sake of its internal processes).

In this context, it is becoming a common scenario the one in which: on one hand, the company (the *customer*) may outsource some processes to third party *contractors*, and, on the other hand, such contractors may serve multiple customers at the same time. In such a particular instance of the so-called "Bring Your Own Device" (BYOD) paradigm, contractors use their own mobile equipment to access the internal data repositories and services of every customer. To this end, contractors use the dedicated applications along with the access credential every customer released when the contract was signed.

A preliminary version of this paper appeared as [11].

© Springer Nature Switzerland AG 2020
P. Mori et al. (Eds.): ICISSP 2019, CCIS 1221, pp. 382–402, 2020.
https://doi.org/10.1007/978-3-030-49443-8_18

In the above scenario, it is crucial that the contractor device keeps the workloads of every customer strictly separated from each others. This often entails that every customer requires the contractor to deploy its whole self-contained *ERM workload (i.e.,* the ERM application suite along with user and device credentials, encryption keys, data, etc.) into an isolated partition of the device computational resources.

Due to the traditional "vertical" and "closed" of ERM systems nature, this approach often leads to a considerable waste of resources as several ERM functionalities are made redundant. Amongst such functionalities we identify: (a) secure local storage management and (b) fine grained, data-independent and interoperable mechanisms for Access Control Policy definition and enforcement. In our proposal, such features are provided by the contractor's platform to the installed ERM workloads, as system-wide services.

In a previous work [12], we addressed the ERM scenario by presenting a remote maintenance infrastructure which features secure on-site documentation cross-domain delivery and ensures fine-grained access control throughout the documentation lifecycle. To this end, the infrastructure features an interactive communication protocol for the sake of key management and policy enforcement in which: policy evaluation is up to the data owner while the workload deployed on the local device is in charge of policy decision enforcement and multi-factor user authentication. In [13], we extended the system to allow non-interactive protocols for access control enforcement based on biometric templates [28]. In both cases, data is secured by encryption and its access is granted by unlocking the corresponding decryption key. As pointed out above, every process in the data lifecylce (user authentication, policy decision, data encryption and storage) is accomplished by the manufacturer's ERM applications. The prevention of information disclosure or abuse, on the maintainer devices, is ensured through the confinement of any sensitive information within the boundaries of the manufacturer's ERM workload. The latter aspect is the only which is up to the maintainer device OS.

In [11] we presented a solution for enforcing access control over sensitive data generated by independent third party applications and locally stored on a mobile device. In this paper we extend such a solution and we go one step further. We consider the case in which such data can be locally or remotely stored, and consider the problem of guaranteeing the same security level while improving the scalability in contexts in which multiple content providers deploy their private data through common/shared platforms. In order to do so, we had to rethink the whole solution starting from the high level description of the service to the low level specification of the data structures used in our implementation. Our proposal is to extract common components of every ERM system: secure file storage and policy enforcement, and put them under the "responsibility" of the contractor's device OS while inherently proprietary features (*e.g.,* related to proprietary file format, on-site diagnostic tools) remain still part of the customer's ERM suite.

On the contractor's device, Common ERM components (services) are provided by means of a set of trusted applications. Proprietary ERM applications are designed to access such services by means of a set of *ERM common API.*

Our solution is intended for mobile devices compliant with the GlobalPlatform's Trusted Execution Environments (TEE) specifications [19]. TEE-powered devices provide hardware-based mechanisms to keep separated the untrusted regular "rich" operating system (and its applications) from security-sensitive trusted applications (TAs) which run in a trusted enclave (the TEE itself). Communication between the different components (if allowed) can take place only through strictly defined protocols and APIs. Communication between TAs are accomplished using the *TEE Internal Core API*, while communication between TAs and application running in the "Rich OS" (Rich Applications or RAs) are carried out through the *TEE Client API*.

The core of our system is a number of Trusted Applications (TA) that implement our *ERM service layer*. Provided services are: Policy Management, Key Management and Secure File System. Briefly speaking: the secure file System stores encrypted files along with their security meta-data and access policy. It makes available the files to any requestor through a file system shaped interface. Only authorized entities having the proper key can access files content. The Key manager releases the file encryption keys to the authorized entities. The Policy manager takes file access control decisions for requesting entities according to a set of RBAC policy rules.

Protected data are transferred to the contractor device in encrypted form either over the network, through a secure communication, or by means of mobile storage devices such as "pendrives" and memory cards. Files' encryption key, sticky policy and meta-data are encrypted with the public keys of intended destinations, within a customer domain-wide public key infrastructure.

In certain circumstances the aforementioned transmission mechanisms may not be suitable. This might be the case in which, customers and contractors need to exchange large amounts of data. A possible solution is asking the sender to set up a temporary file sharing facility possibly leveraging any third party (or public) cloud based storage service. This approach is being followed in the design of several mission-critical application including medical record databases and government services due to the high reliability of nowadays cloud providers. Nevertheless, *cloud storage* raises several security issues. Being maintained by a third party, stored data might be subject to theft and fraudulent corruption. In order to mitigate this threat, the *cloud-of-clouds* approach has gained a growing interest. Here, data is somehow split in several portions and stored on multiple clouds. Data encryption and striping algorithms can be used to improve data security and reliability.

Our architecture features *Cloud shared files*. To this end, encrypted files can be split into one or multiple *shares*. Meta-data include the instruction concerning where and how the shares can be retrieved and how the whole file must be rebuilt and/or accessed. With this mechanism, endpoints just exchange (through the "traditional" media) small file portions containing meta-data, whereas the remaining data are made available over the cloud. Our proposal pursues the neutrality with respect the file striping algorithm.

2 Related Works

One of the first solutions presented in the literature for securing data over possibly networked storage systems is represented by cryptographic file systems [6,10,21]. The key idea exploited by cryptographic file systems is to embed the security layer underneath the virtual file system layer. In this way, each application has transparent access to secured files, independently from the specific data type it manages. Although this approach is effective, it is bound to the model "trusted client" versus "untrusted server" and a single security authority enforces essentially discretionary file access control policies. This approach has been extended in several directions, including the capability to store encrypted files on cloud storage facilities and passive mobile storage devices [9, 14, 30, 35].

The Proof-Carrying File System (PCFS) [17, 18, 27] use formal proofs to enforce file access control that can take into account variables like time or current system state. This approach is effective in enforcing access control policies though writing policies turns out to be an error-prone procedure. Furthermore, such systems have a rather invasive interface, making their integration hard to implement.

A full featured cryptographic file system for Android is presented and analysed in [33]. It essentially aims at protecting data stored on micro SD cards exchanged amongst different devices and does not natively support any trusted computing facility to protect encryption keys.

Android OS provides two different possibilities, named Full Disk Encryption (FDE), initially introduced by Android 4.4, and File Based Encryption (FBE), starting from Android 7.0. FDE encrypts the whole user-data partition in a disk using AES-CBC and a randomly generated 128-bit key. The encryption key is password protected. Thus, the user needs to unlock the whole disk partition before any data on it can be read. In contrast, the FBE protects each file independently from the others by using different keys. This allows the apps to unlock each file independently. On the other hand, the usage of FBE requires the applications to be aware of the encryption layer. Both in FDE and FBE, the encryption keys are managed by means of a TEE and may be hardware-backed. In all cases, data stored on external devices such SD cards cannot be encrypted and should be stored unencrypted.

Android is by far the mobile OS that provides the more flexible multi-user support. Starting from Android 5, the OS allows a device to be used by multiple users, each possibly having multiple profiles. There exists three types of profiles, *normal, restricted* and *managed*. A user typically creates a *normal profile*, that allows her to have "complete" access to the device. In a *restricted profile*, typically used for parental control, the profile creator can restrict the capabilities of the user, e.g., deciding which apps can be executed or which contents can be visualized on the device. A *managed profiles* is created and managed by a company and allows the storage of applications and company-sensitive data on the user device. In the latter case, the access control policy to sensitive data is defined by the company.

The combination of trusted computing and virtualization technologies has been used for example in [12, 13] where the authors use biometric identification and key binding in conjunction with workload isolation in order to enforce the security of documents over a system comprising multiple devices owned by different actors.

The architecture of VPFS [34] feature an insecure and a trusted compartment. The former is devoted to run user (untrusted) application whereas the latter offers a trusted environment and secure data storage to sensitive applications. Although encrypted file system lies on the platform's hard disk, it is hidden to the untrusted compartment view by the virtualisation layer.

The ARM TrustZone [3] technology offers hardware support to strongly implement such separation between compartments. DroidVault [22] leverages TrustZone to provide a trusted storage area (suitable to contain small amounts of sensitive data) within an untrusted Android-powered platforms, whereas SBD [20] implements an encrypted block device available to applications running in the normal TrustZone world within the ANDIX OS [16].

Unlike the last two proposals, our solution provides a full featured cryptographic file system for applications running in both trusted and untrusted compartments and is intended to be fully compliant with the GlobalPlaftorm TEE standard [19].

Sharing corporate files through third party cloud based storage services is a practice that has known an impressive success in the last decade, though it still raises several concerns related to data confidentiality [31] and reliability [23]. Plenty of solution have been proposed in order to cope with both. A well established approach consist of introducing an intermediate layer between data owners and data storage which offers to file owners a file system-like interface to their data (front-end) while manages actual files storage on multiple cloud providers (back-ends) by introducing data encryption and redundancy. Amongst the earlier solutions we mention BlueSky [32] and DepSky [5]. These architecture feature a network proxy (aggregator) which uses old-fashioned file sharing protocols such as NFS and CIFS to wrap the back-ends' access API calls. More recent proposals, emphasize the security aspects such as: protecting the data confidentiality with respect to the aggregator (Storekeeper [26]) and hardening the security of the file system front-ends as in RockFS [24].

We highlight that these solutions aim at providing an almost full file system-like interaction. Instead, as we show in the following, the purpose of our proposal is providing occasional file deliverying amongst different entities within the same domain.

3   Preliminars

In this section we describe some preliminary notions that will be used in the following sections.

3.1   Policy Definition

Mobile devices and applications require the possibility of highly flexible, dynamic and extendible access control policy specifications. Flexibility and dynamicity allow the possibility of designing policies that are able to adapt to typical application scenarios that occur when dealing with mobile devices, i.e., situations that may vary over a number of variables like time, location, environmental factors, etc. Extendibility guarantees the possibility of "forward-portability", i.e., to adapt the policy evaluation process without the need of dramatically restructuring the different software components that implement it.

The classical RBAC model has been introduced in [29] and consists, basically, of the following components: A set of users, which we call *entities*, a set of roles, a set of permission and a set of sessions. A user in is a human or artificial agent, that can execute operations in the systems, each of which requires a specific set of permissions. A non-empty set of operations defines a job within an organization. A role can be seen as a set of permissions that are needed to execute a given job within an organization. Finally, sessions associate users to roles. After the authentication phase, the system creates a new session during which the user can require the activation of the roles she is allowed to play. Role activation is successful only if the required role is enabled and the user is entitled to activate it. In this case, the user is granted all the permissions associated to the activated role. The model comprises a number of functions defined below. The user assignment (UA) and the permission assignment (PA) functions are used to associate users and permissions to roles, respectively. As stated above, a user can be associated with many roles and every role can be played by many users. Similarly, a permission can be associated with many roles and a role can include many permissions. In our system access control is modelled by using extensions [2, 4, 8] of the Role Based Access Control (RBAC) model.

3.2   Entities and Roles

In this section we assume that a secure communication infrastructure which comes with a domain-wide PKI and linking all entities for every interaction: mutual authentication, policy enforcement, key management and data transfer. The design of this infrastructure is out of the scopes of this paper. Nevertheless, we point out that several well established solution are on the shelf. In particular, we highlight that naturally fits the scenarios proposed in the IETF's forthcoming model of interaction within TEE ecosystems: the TEEP (Trusted Execution Environment Provisioning) Architecture [25].

Specifically, we aim at implementing a file-level fine-grained access control mechanism. Each access request to any *file* on the file system, submitted by any *entity* running on the device, will be evaluated according to a set of rules specified by the policy. Notice that we explicitly avoid the term *user*, in order to stress that the device might or might not be used by different users but we assume there exist multiple stakeholders, each running, possibly multiple, *entities*. Each entity is the actor that performs access to data and each entity should be considered as a unique user in the standard RBAC model. As usual, each entity can activate multiple roles. Our system defines three default roles, *owner*, *administrator*, and *guest* but allows the definition of new ones. Furthermore, it is possible to refine them per-domain, per-service and/or per-file. This means, for example, that it is possible to define domain administrators or single file administrators (owners). Finally, the set of permissions consists of the classical file read, write and execute. In our terminology, an entity is an instance of an application running on the device on behalf of some *subscriber*. We note that this definition of entity naturally inherits the existence of multiple stakeholders sharing the same device. Each entity is identified by composing a *Domain ID*, that identifies the subscriber, and at least one amongst: (a) the UUID of the application; (b) the unique device identifier (*e.g.* a hardware-bound serial number, the mac-address) the application is running on; and (c) the subscriber credentials of the user is running the application.

Entity and role identifiers are described with a Uniform Resource Name (URN) [15] formed as in Table 1.

Table 1. Entity and role identifiers.

Entity identifier	`urn:entt:<domainID>:<deviceID>:<subsID>:<appUUID>`
Role identified	`urn:role:<domainID>:<deviceID>:<fileID>:<roleID>`

In order to enforce access control, we use public key encryption. Specifically, we associate to every role a public-secret key pair, or *role key pair* in short. Each file is encrypted with a random *file key* and each file key is encrypted using the public keys associated to roles that can access their associated file. Intuitively, a role can perform an operation on a given resource only if it is allowed to sign the associated data structures.

Domains constitute a key ingredient in our architecture. Briefly speaking, a *Domain* defines an unambiguous namespace within which roles and entities are defined. We provide to every *Domain member*, e.g., a device, an application, a subscriber, a unique identifier, the related digital credentials and, possibly, a set of domain-wide role key pairs.

A *user* is a device owner or a device operator. She is registered as *subscriber* and she is associated to a *subsID* and to her authentication credentials, (*e.g.* PIN/password, biometric templates, crypto-tokens, etc.) We note that every device within a domain has its own authentication credentials, typically a digital certificate along with the corresponding secret key. Clearly, the way in which secret information are loaded into a device depend on the specific technology. For example, credentials could be saved on a SIM, or "burnt" as a firmware update. Applications IDs and credentials are assigned according to their registration "scope": either device-wide or domain-wide.

Applications are registered with an *AppID* which pertains to the place they are deployed to (usually, software developers release their applications adopting corporate naming/versioning criteria). This leads to vendor-unique application UUIDs. Similarly, UUIDs of application deployed to the domain's devices (along with their domain-wide credentials) are assume to be "domain-unique". Third party applications (and their UUIDs) should be *registered* to the Domain Authority prior to be deployed.

Role keypairs, IDs and credentials are stored locally on each device at registration time. For certain entities, this choice is inherently static. For example device identifiers and credentials are deployed by the equipment manufacturer in the factory; trusted applications may be installed in the device firmware, along with their private data, once and for all. On the other hand, the choice of subscriber identities and domain-wide roles to be active on any device is likely to change over times. To this end, our architecture provides a mechanism to securely import/export keys and credentials from/to other devices.

Permissions and roles revocation are not straightforward. On one hand, users can trustworthily erase local roles and identities from the device they own. On the other hand, once a role keypair has been deployed on plenty of devices, it is quite hard for the domain authority to force all of them to remove (or possibly update) it. So that, we adopt a *lazy revocation* approach [14]. Whenever certain entities or roles are no longer enabled to access information from any data source, new roles and role-bindings are issued and upcoming data are encrypted using new role keys. So that, new data can be accessed only by new/updated entities whereas, revoked entities can still access old data.

3.3   File System Encryption

In order to guarantee policy enforcement, our system uses symmetric key encryption. Specifically, each file is encrypted with a *file key* that can be recovered only by entities that have activated specific roles, using a mechanism we describe later. Each file has its own access control policy that is stored along with file metadata. Classical security properties of confidentiality, integrity and authenticity are guaranteed by means of standard cryptographic tools, respecitvely, encryption, MAC and digital signatures.

The proposed file system is implemented as a standalone *file server* that stores encrypted files, along with the associated metadata, on a local storage system, on a removable device or on a cloud storage system. Every time an entity needs to access some information on protected file system, it issues a request using a file-system-API shaped IPC protocol, that will be described Sect. 4.3 in details.

Encrypted files are composed of two main parts: the *file header* and the *file envelope*. The former carries information needed to enforce file access control and to verify the file integrity. The latter features: file's general information (*e.g.*, plaintext length, file type, char-set); the instructions to retrieve and compose every (required) file share in order to get the whole file. Finally, the file envelope ends with the original file's *local* share. Figure 1 summarizes the layout of information featured by an encrypted file.

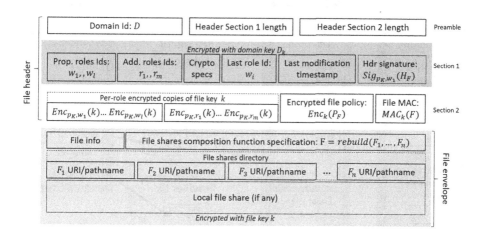

Fig. 1. File format.

File Header. File header is partitioned into three sections: *preamble*, *section 1* and *section 2*. The preamble is in clear and contains the ID of the Domain D the file belongs to and the length (in bytes) of following header sections 1 and 2.

Section 1 contains two sets of role IDs which contain, respectively *proprietary* and *additional* role IDs. Roles of both sets are allowed to access the file according to its access policy. However, only proprietary roles are enable to modify the access policy itself. This part also includes crypto-specs, i.e., the signature, encryption and MAC algorithms specifications and parameters; the ID, say ID_{last}, of the last entity that modified the file, the timestamp of the last modification the whole header's signature which is computed with the private key associated to ID_{last}. Section 1 is encrypted with a *domain key* D_k. Every entity which joined the domain D_k receives such a key. As an example, we can think of the domain D_k as the one associated to a specific *customer* and, thus, each application associated to this customer, belongs to D_k and has access to its domain key.

Section 2 contains a copy of the file key k for every role listed above. Each copy is encrypted with the public key of the corresponding role. When opening the file, entitled roles decrypt k with her own secret key and use it for the sake of any further access to the file contents. The header ends with the file access policy specification and files' Message Authentication Code, encrypted and computed using k.

File Envelope. This part is entirely encrypted with k. It contains a record for file general info; the *file shares directory*, that is the list of references to the shares the file is split into along with the specification of the file reconstruction function. Eventually, if any, local shares follow.

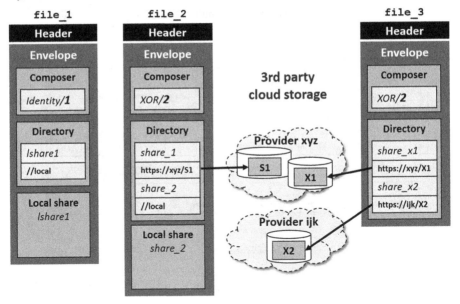

Fig. 2. Cloud "shared" files.

Accessing Cloud Shared Files. In order to open a cloud shared file (both for read or write operations) the terminal needs to retrieve all its share and reconstruct the original file. At the end of this process, the whole encrypted file is present on the local storage.

More precisely, any open invocation is accomplished through the following steps (detalis key mananagent and policy enforcement are discussed in Sect. 4.3). In particular, the system:

1. Extracts from the header: the file shares directory and the file composer function whose description is in the header;
2. fetches each share from its corresponding repository;
3. reconstructs the file from its shares by using the composer;

At this point, a full copy of the encrypted file is present on the device. The File System Backend (see Sect. 4.3) accesses the file on behalf of the requestor.

Nothing particular happens when an unmodified or read/only file is closed. Instead, in case its content has been modified, the file content is split into its shares and, eventually, shares are written back to their respective storage place.

Figure 2 depicts three possible encryption file layouts. File file_1 is entirely stored on the local file system. The composition function we denote with $Identity/1$ returns the same text it received as input. Files file_2 and file_3, both feature two shares each. The former is split in a local and remote share, whereas the latter is composed of two remote shares. In our example, both files are rebuild by computing the bitwise xor of their shares.

We point out that $Identity/1$ and $XOR/2$ are just two possible sample of composition functions. In facts, our architecture is thought to be neutral with respect such a feature.

4 System Architecture

In this section we describe the architecture of the proposed ERM system, whose overall structure is reported in Fig. 3.

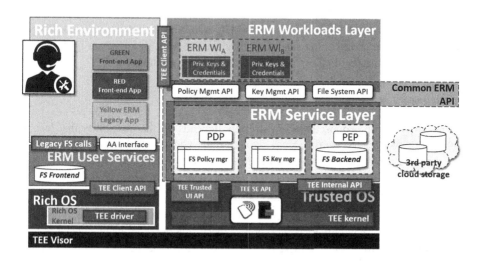

Fig. 3. System architecture of contractors' devices [11].

In our ecosystem we identify two different sets of applications. The first one is a set of applications implementing the system itself. Since our system is built on top of TEE specifications, the ERM system consists of a number of Trusted applications running in the Trusted OS.

The second set of components consist of the applications accessing the protected file system. Each operator uses a *front-end* application, a rich application running in the rich OS, to interact with the resources on the device. These applications can be partitioned into TEE-aware applications and legacy ones. The former, by construction, have been designed with the TEE model in mind. This means that each front-end application has a corresponding *back-end* one, a TA running in the Trusted OS and accessing the component private data. The communications between the front-end and the corresponding back-end occur via TEE APIs. The back-end application can interact directly with the TAs implementing our system by using the TEE Internal APIs. Note that, since these applications are TEE-aware, they *need to know* with whom they communicate and, thus, they need to be aware of the file system they are using and the corresponding interfaces. The latter set of applications are the legacy ones, e.g., browsers, editors, etc. These are rich applications, running in the rich OS, that are *not aware* of the features of the file system they are accessing. In order for these application to properly operate over protected data, we need to intercept the read/write requests issued using standard file system interfaces and redirect them to our ecosystem of TAs. To this aim, we provide a file-system front end through which the application can access protected files after the user/subscribed has been successfully authenticated and authorized. Authentication and Authorization operations are performed by means of an ad hoc interface.

In the following we describe in details the different components of the ERM system.

We recall that in the Trusted OS, access control over private data (*e.g.* keying material) is enforced on the basis of the TA identity. Indeed, private data are cryptographically bound to the TA they belong to, and can be shared between different instances of the same TA while cannot be shared between different TAs. On the other hand, any RA can access the same data only by establishing a session with the appropriate TA, as long the RA is authorized either according its identifier (*e.g.*, its UUID) or by means of an authentication protocol taking place through a trusted channel.

4.1   ERM User Services

The usability of the proposed system strongly depends on the possibility that legacy applications can *transparently* access secured data. Clearly, this possibility conflicts with the need of providing ad-hoc protection mechanisms that may require user interaction for the authentication phase.

The AA Interface. One issue to be addressed is user/operator authentication. Indeed, in the TEE model, TA can only respond to RA requests. On the other hand, since RA cannot be considered to be trusted, there is the need of securely identifying a user/operator to a TA through an insecure RA. To this aim, we can either exploit to different possibilities. On one hand the user can directly entry her PIN or password by means of the TEE Trusted UIs, that creates of a secure channel between the user and the TA. A second option is the usage of cryptographic hardware based authentication systems. Once the user is successfully authenticated, she starts her *session* that lasts until she logs out. Throughout the session, protected data available to the user are made available through the file system front-end, and legacy application access such files enjoying the privileges of the user's active roles.

File System Front-End. Application-wise, transparent access to protected files translates in the need of transparent wrapping of read/write file system operations. In order to provide such type of access, we use a virtual file system layer that intercepts read/write system calls, wraps them properly using the TEE Client APIs, and forwards the requests to the *file system back-end*. In our prototype, this component is implemented with a FUSE file system layer [1].

4.2 ERM Workloads Layer

ERM back-end applications along with their private data take place in the ERM Workloads layer. Such applications are designed to trustworthily interact with their owners' premises in order to carry out their tasks. As TAs, ERM back-ends communicate with the user and remote facilities through the TEE APIs and the secure network protocols and are provided of a private local storage for e.g. temporary data and keying materials. Moreover, such applications handle secured files lying in the File System Backend related services by means the APIs they expose. Through such interfaces, different ERM back-ends are enabled to access and share their secure files with other TAs, according to arbitrary policy rules. Legacy TAs may co-exist with ERM workloads.

4.3 ERM Service Layer

In this section, we describe the TAs that constitute the core of our architecture: the policy manager, the key manager and the file system backend.

The Policy Manager. The first TA in our architecture is the *Policy Manager* (PolicyMGR). As stated in the introduction, we use extensions of the Role Based Access Control (RBAC) policies. Because of the dynamic and mobile nature of the application scenarios, we consider extensions of the basic RBAC model that include temporal, spatial and/or environmental conditions, e.g., [7].

The PolicyMGR maintains a database that stores roles, identities and access policies. At startup time, domain-wide and application-wide roles and identities are loaded into the database. This information is typically static as it can only be modified by the domain administrator is specific cases, e.g., a new version of an application. Applications running on the device are allowed to create new "local" roles and entities by means of a management API. The scope of new entries is limited to the device itself and concerning the definition of policy rules for local files. File access policy specification is contained into file metadata. Whenever a file is opened for the first time, its access policy is loaded into the policy database by the PolicyMGR and it is used for subsequent requests.

The policy manager implements the policy decision point, i.e., it is responsible for granting or denying the access to every received request. For efficiency reasons, PolicyMGR keeps track of the set of roles each entity has activated, i.e., the roles that are *operational* in the current *execution context*. In our implementation, this TA exposes the following APIs:

- check_role(entity-id, role-id): Returns true whenever (a) the entity has activated role-id or (b) the entity is allowed to play that role due to some occurring events or environmental conditions.
- check_policy(policy,role-id): Returns a bit-string denoting the granted access mode (like the unix-like octal digit representing read, write and execute permission) that the policy rules allow to the role *role-id*.

The Key Manager. The Key Manager (KeyMGR) is the TA that handles the cryptographic keys on behalf of every entity and role in the system. Specifically, the KeyMGR uses, on behalf of entities, their private keys for encryption/decryption and signatures. Furthermore, it provides APIs for the generation of key-pairs for locally-defined roles and entities.

Private Key Management. Role keys are physically stored (indexed by role-id) in the *Key Repository*, which is a private storage area cryptographically bound to the KeyMGR. This type of storage guarantees that keys are only accessible through the KeyMGR interfaces.

The KeyMGR provides the APIs needed to manage the whole keys lifecycles, that is key and key pair generation, storage import/export and removal. As stated above, key pair generation is needed in order to provide fresh *locally certifiable* keys to locally created roles. This is typically needed whenever the users are allowed to define new "local roles" and ad-hoc access policies. Of course, there must exists a TEE-aware application that provides this functionality that, on one hand interacts somehow with the user and, on the other hand, properly interacts with the KeyMGR.

The *import* functionality can occur at different times and has the effect of adding new role/role key pairs to the *Key Repository*. At device registration time, domain and device authorities can populate the *Key Repository* with the key pairs related to every pre-defined roles according to every installed application and pre-loaded files and data. In addition, at any time, the user can import a newly generated key pair from an external source. External sources include mainly *Secure Elements* as defined by the GlobalPlatform standard, such as a smart-card, or nearby trusted devices, connected through NFC.

Key Pair Generation. Key pairs generation can be accomplished according different strategies. In the simplest one, the application vendor provides at least the key pair for the domain-wide reserved role of a given application. This guarantees the highest possible portability of encrypted contexts. On the other hand it also allows, in principle, the vendor to access the data generated by every single installation of its application.

Protected files can be transferred between device (*e.g.*, through the network or by means of SD cards). Whenever none of the roles enabled to access the files are present on the receiving device, it is necessary to transfer the related key pairs between the devices. In this case, the endpoints have to establish a trusted channel through which the key are exported.

Rich Applications accessing encrypted files through the file system front-end are collectively identified by a single predefined and reserved *untrusted* role, since we have no way to reliably distinguish and identify different Rich Applications. To this special role the system associates a default pre-loaded key pair and a default file access policy, specifically tailored for untrusted applications.

File Key Recovery. One of the most important functionalities provided by the KeyMGR is the file key extraction from the file header. Access control is implemented by means of a combination of symmetric and asymmetric cryptography. Each file is encrypted using a random file key. Such key is encrypted using the public keys of all the roles that have access to such a file and, as described in the previous Section, encrypted file keys are stored in the file header. Thus, file key needs to be decrypted using the requiring entity private key that is store by the KeyMGR.

Whenever an entity requires to open a protected file the KeyMGR returns to the requesting entity, the file key only if the access policy allow to. In order to so, it receives a request containing the file header and the list of roles activated by the requesting entity. At this point the KeyMGR executes the following steps:

1. Decrypt Sect. 1 of the header using the domain key D_k.
2. Recover the file key from the file metadata using the requesting entity private key. This step is mandatory whenever the entity requires access *for the first time* in order to verify that the requesting entity has indeed access to the specific file.
3. Interact with the PolicyMGR to check whether or not the access should be granted. If access is denied, return an error and stop.
4. Caches the association requesting entity-file key for subsequent requests.
5. Return the ket k to the trusted application that requested the open.

Notice that, since only *trusted* applications can interact with the KeyMGR, file and file key security is guaranteed.

Clearly the KeyMGR always executes steps (3) and (5), while steps (1–2) and (4) are executed only once, for each entity requiring to open the file. In addition, role keypairs are used to sign/verify file data and header. In order to fulfil such tasks, the KeyMGR API provides the following functionalities: *filekey encrypt/decrypt* and *data sign/verify*.

The File System Back-End. The file system back-end (FSB) implements the Policy Enforcement Point, or PEP, in the access control terminology. FSB is a TA that interacts directly with other TAs in the ecosystem, including ERM backends, via a number of interfaces implemented by means of the entry points defined in the TEE internal API. It receives access requests from TAs in the system that use a library which resembles the standard file system calls open, read, write, along with the functions devoted to entity authentication and authorization. Such a library wraps the TA client API and it is intended to provide a high level interface to the FSB for third party TA application developers.

Access requests for encrypted files make the ERM system services components interact each others through the APIs introduced above.

In a nutshell, the FSB works as follows: Upon receiving the request to open a file, the FSB interacts with the KeyMGR to recover the file key. At this point, if the encrypted file is shared among different locations, it is reconstructed locally, by downloading its shares from the different providers and properly recombining them. The handle to the encrypted file is returned after its integrity has been verified. From this point on, each read/write operation is executed by the FSB that properly decrypts/encrypts every file block. Once the requesting entity requires to close the file, the FSB, recomputes the MAC over the encrypted file, reconstructs and signs the header by interacting with the KeyMGR.

Notice that the FSB does not decrypt the file. At the end of the open procedure, there exists an encrypted copy of the original file, locally stored on the device. Furthermore, file integrity is evaluated on the encrypted version of the file. The FSB decrypts a file block only when it receives an access request to the specific block.

We show, as an example, the interaction occurring during a file open (.) operation for a file F. Figure 1 summarizes the metadata involved in serving the call.

1. Retrieves the role set R assigned to the requesting entity.
2. Send a file key extraction request to the KeyMGR, with parameters F and R.
3. If receive an error message, stop.
4. Let k be the received file key.
5. Use the key k to decrypt the file envelop and extract the directory section.
6. If the file is shared among different providers, download its shares and reconstruct it using the composer function.
7. Let H be the handle of the encrypted file.
8. Verify file integrity. On error, stop.
9. Send the triple (F, H, Policy) to the PolicyMGR.
10. Cache the triple (F, H, k).
11. Return H to the requesting entity.

Once the file has been opened, the subsequent read/write requests will force the FSB to interact with the PolicyMGR. Indeed, in a mobile scenario, the response to an access request may depend on the specific context in which the request occurs. Thus, for each read/write operation, the FSB uses the file key only if the access policy grants access to the entity in the specific context.

Finally, whenever the file is closed, the FSB recomputes the file MAC, properly modifies the header and interacts with the KeyMGR to sign the new file header. If needed, the file is shared among the different providers and the triple (F, H, k) removed from the cache.

The open function returns a *virtual file descriptor* to the invoking entity. The entity uses it for every further operation to be done on the file it points to. A virtual file descriptor is a handle which connects the file as it is viewed by the entity (through the filter determined by its roles and the privilege it enjoys) to the same file as it is represented by the FSB.

The FSB features a file system-like interface to encrypted data stored on its *private storage*. Through this layer, data are organized and made available as *logical files*. The way in which any logical file, along with its metadata and status information is structured, handled and made available underneath of such an interface, depends on the nature of the underlying OS (the Trusted OS).

Our FSB mimics some of the data structures currently available in the underlying file system. Specifically, it maintains the *open files table (OFT)* and the *Virtual File Descriptor table (VFD)*.

The OFT keeps track of files that are currently open by at least one entity in the system. Indeed, whenever an entity opens a file, the FSB keeps track of all the information related to the file. Notice that, in the context of operating systems, the only information stored by the OFT are "operational" ones, i.e., the logical file descriptor, the current file offset, flags and a pointer to the data structure containing information on the low level file, e.g., a v-node. In our case, the OFT needs also to store the appropriate header's information including: the file key, the shares directory (to be used at close time).

The second data structure is the Virtual File Descriptor (VFD) table keeps track of the binding between an open file and a specific entity that has opened it. More precisely, this data structure stores a reference to the OFT that points to the low level file, the file key, that has to be used to access the file, the current role-id and credentials of the entity that is using the file and, finally, the access mode information. The information described above are reported in Fig. 4.

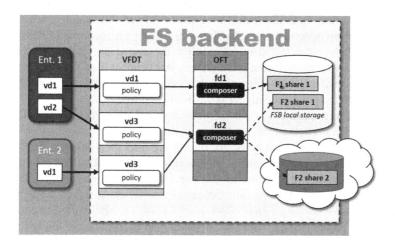

Fig. 4. Filesystem back-end data structures.

5   Prototype Implementation

Our prototype has been implemented over the *OpenTEE* platform. This platform is essentially a software emulator of a GlobalPlatform compliant TEE environment for the Linux operating system. The advantage of developing a prototype using such solution is that it allows to focus only on the feature and the difficulties related to the development of TEE-enabled applications. OpenTEE guarantees a high level of compatibility with real TEE-enabled solutions but it keeps apart the problems related to specific hardware deployment platforms. On the other hand, because it has been thought for being a generic platform for fast prototyping, OpenTEE cannot be taken as a reference w.r.t. performance of the final application.

The Open-TEE environment is composed of two stand-alone servers and a set of dynamic libraries which implements the GlobalPlaftorm APIs. Rich Applications are native Linux Applications written in C/C++, whereas Trusted Applications are dynamic shared objects registered with the launcher and executed in separated threads. It is clear that Open-TEE only reproduces the development environment but does not fulfils any security requirement addressed by GlobalPlatform specifications. This means that TAs execution in the OpenTEE environment is *not secure* whilst their execution in an actual TEE environment is.

6   Performance Evaluation

This section describes the set of experiments we have carried out to verify the feasibility of the proposed solution. We point out that, the tools we have used for setting up the proof-of-concept of our solution, namely OpenTEE and FUSE do not consider optimization a primary concern as they are valuable tools for fast prototyping. Furthermore, the actual running time depends on a number of variables and it is related to the efficiency of different components like file system frontend, mapping of file metadata into underlying filesystem metadata, especially in the case of large policies and so forth. Finally, there exists a variable that is completely independent from the efficiency of the whole solution that is the complexity of the access policy evaluation procedure; the more complex is the policy, the higher is the evaluation time.

Currently, our results are far from the plain ext4 filesystem since (a) we build on top of the filesystem and (b) the tools we have used do not focus on optimization.

In this discussion, the term *block*, (or *allocation block*) will refer to the basic data allocation unit used by the file system. Moreover, *physical block* will refer to the block used by the underlying filesystem (*ext4*, in our case) while *logical block* will refer to the block adopted by our FSB. In our implementation we chose a *logical block* size of 4 KB, coinciding with the *physical block* size of *ext4*. The cipher used to encrypt file content and its policy is AES, while for signature and encryptions of file key we used RSA. For the MACs we used HMAC-SHA1.

In our preliminary evaluation we have measured the impact of the block size over the throughput of the file system. As stated above, we have implemented our system on an ext4 file filesystem by its extended attributes for storing file metadata. The complexity of the access policies is another variable that strongly depends on the specific policy. Since we needed to evaluate the usability of our system, we have run the first experiments using 'flat' spatio-temporal policies, i.e., allow everytime-everywhere. We note that complex access policies verification may have a huge impact on the *open* operation. On the other hand, once the file is opened, the status of the policy condition can be asynchronously monitored by the PDP in order to reduce the response time for each subsequent request.

We have run the following tests:

- Read: This test measures the performance of reading an existing file.
- Randomized Read: This test measures the performance of reading an existing file at randomly selected locations.
- Write: This test measures the performance of writing a new file.
- Randomized Write: This test measures the performance of writing an existing file at randomly selected locations.

Each test only considers the time needed to execute read/write operations in files and does *not* consider the time needed to open or close the file.

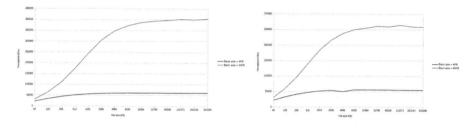

Fig. 5. Performance of read (left) and write (right) operations.

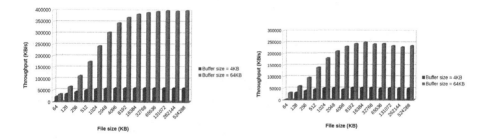

Fig. 6. Performance of random read (left) and random write (right) operations.

In Figs. 5 and 6 we report the performance of our filesystem in for the read, write, random read and random write operations, respectively, into files with size ranging from 64 KB to 512 MB. The performance of the read and write operations are similar to the corresponding randomized versions and are omitted.

7 Conclusions

In this paper we have proposed a general-purpose architecture that simplifies the cooperation among different applications in a multi-domain Enterprise Right Management system

The basic tool we use for this purpose is the integration between the Trusted Execution Environment and the (possibly distributed) underlying file system. On one hand, our system exposes APIs that allow other trusted applications to interact with the secure file system using the standardized TEE communication framework. On the other hand, legacy applications, can transparently interact with our system by means of a middleware that intercepts all classical open/read/write/close systems calls.

Our prototype shows that the proposed architecture is effective in realizing such blending of technologies.

References

1. FUSE: Filesystem in userspace. http://fuse.sourceforge.net
2. Aich, S., Mondal, S., Sural, S., Majumdar, A.K.: Role based access control with spatiotemporal context for mobile applications. In: Gavrilova, M.L., Tan, C.J.K., Moreno, E.D. (eds.) Transactions on Computational Science IV. LNCS, vol. 5430, pp. 177–199. Springer, Heidelberg (2009). https://doi.org/10.1007/978-3-642-01004-0_10
3. ARM Ltd.: ARM TrustZone. http://www.arm.com/trustzone. Accessed 24 June 2018
4. Bertino, E., Bonatti, P.A., Ferrari, E.: TRBAC: a temporal role-based access control model. ACM Trans. Inf. Syst. Secur. **4**(3), 191–233 (2001). https://doi.org/10.1145/501978.501979
5. Bessani, A., Correia, M., Quaresma, B., André, F., Sousa, P.: DepSky: dependable and secure storage in a cloud-of-clouds. ACM Trans. Storage **9**(4), 1–33 (2013). https://doi.org/10.1145/2535929
6. Blaze, M.: A cryptographic file system for UNIX. In: Proceedings of the 1st ACM Conference on Computer and Communications Security, pp. 9–16. ACM (1993)
7. Bonatti, P., Galdi, C., Torres, D.: Event-driven RBAC. J. Comput. Secur. **23**(6), 709–757 (2015). https://doi.org/10.3233/JCS-150539
8. Bonatti, P.A., Galdi, C., Torres, D.: ERBAC: event-driven RBAC. In: Proceedings of the 18th ACM Symposium on Access Control Models and Technologies, SACMAT 2013, Amsterdam, The Netherlands, 12–14 June 2013, pp. 125–136 (2013). https://doi.org/10.1145/2462410.2462415. http://doi.acm.org/10.1145/2462410.2462415
9. Castiglione, A., Catuogno, L., Del Sorbo, A., Fiore, U., Palmieri, F.: A secure file sharing service for distributed computing environments. J. Supercomput. **67**(3), 691–710 (2013). https://doi.org/10.1007/s11227-013-0975-y
10. Cattaneo, G., Catuogno, L., Sorbo, A.D., Persiano, P.: The design and implementation of a transparent cryptographic file system for UNIX. In: USENIX Annual Technical Conference, FREENIX Track, pp. 199–212. USENIX (2001)
11. Catuogno, L., Galdi, C.: A fine-grained general purpose secure storage facility for trusted execution environment. In: Proceedings of the 5th International Conference on Information Systems Security and Privacy - Volume 1: ICISSP, pp. 588–595. INSTICC, SciTePress (2019). https://doi.org/10.5220/0007578605880595
12. Catuogno, L., Galdi, C., Riccio, D.: Flexible and robust enterprise right management. In: IEEE Symposium on Computers and Communication, ISCC 2016, Messina, Italy, 27–30 June 2016, pp. 1257–1262 (2016). https://doi.org/10.1109/ISCC.2016.7543909. http://doi.ieeecomputersociety.org/10.1109/ISCC.2016.7543909
13. Catuogno, L., Galdi, C., Riccio, D.: Off-line enterprise rights management leveraging biometric key binding and secure hardware. J. Ambient Intell. Humaniz. Comput. (2018). https://doi.org/10.1007/s12652-018-1023-9
14. Catuogno, L., Löhr, H., Winandy, M., Sadeghi, A.R.: A trusted versioning file system for passive mobile storage devices. J. Netw. Comput. Appl. **38**, 65–75 (2014)

15. Filament, P.S.A., Klensin, K.: Uniform Resource Names (URNs). RFC 8141, IETF, April 2017. http://www.rfc-editor.org/rfc/rfc8141.txt
16. Fitzek, A., Achleitner, F., Winter, J., Hein, D.: The ANDIX research OS—ARM TrustZone meets industrial control systems security. In: 2015 IEEE 13th International Conference on Industrial Informatics (INDIN), pp. 88–93. IEEE (2015)
17. Garg, D., Pfenning, F.: A proof-carrying file system. In: 2010 IEEE Symposium on Security and Privacy (SP), pp. 349–364. IEEE (2010)
18. Geambasu, R., John, J.P., Gribble, S.D., Kohno, T., Levy, H.M.: Keypad: an auditing file system for theft-prone devices. In: Proceedings of the 6th Conference on Computer Systems, pp. 1–16. ACM (2011)
19. GlobalPlatform: TEE system architecture v1.0, December 2011. http://globalplatform.org
20. Hein, D., Winter, J., Fitzek, A.: Secure block device–secure, flexible, and efficient data storage for ARM TrustZone systems. In: 2015 IEEE Trustcom/BigDataSE/ISPA, vol. 1, pp. 222–229. IEEE (2015)
21. Kallahalla, M., Riedel, E., Swaminathan, R., Wang, Q., Fu, K.: Plutus: scalable secure file sharing on untrusted storage. In: Chase, J. (ed.) Proceedings of the FAST 2003 Conference on File and Storage Technologies, 31 March–2 April 2003, Cathedral Hill Hotel, San Francisco, California, USA, pp. 29–42. USENIX (2003)
22. Li, X., Hu, H., Bai, G., Jia, Y., Liang, Z., Saxena, P.: Droidvault: a trusted data vault for android devices. In: 2014 19th International Conference on Engineering of Complex Computer Systems (ICECCS), pp. 29–38. IEEE (2014)
23. Li, Z., Liang, M., O'brien, L., Zhang, H.: The cloud's cloudy moment: a systematic survey of public cloud service outage. arXiv preprint arXiv:1312.6485 (2013)
24. Matos, D.R., Pardal, M.L., Carle, G., Correia, M.: Rockfs: cloud-backed file system resilience to client-side attacks. In: Proceedings of the 19th International Middleware Conference, pp. 107–119. ACM (2018)
25. Pei, M., Tschofenig, H., Wheeler, D., Atyeo, A., Dapeng, L.: Trusted execution environment provisioning architecture (TEEP). Internet-draft, IETF (2019). https://tools.ietf.org/pdf/draft-ietf-teep-architecture-02.pdf
26. Pereira, S., Alves, A., Santos, N., Chaves, R.: Storekeeper: a security-enhanced cloud storage aggregation service. In: 2016 IEEE 35th Symposium on Reliable Distributed Systems (SRDS), pp. 111–120. IEEE (2016)
27. Peters, T., Gondree, M., Peterson, Z.N.J.: DEFY: a deniable, encrypted file system for log-structured storage. In: 22nd Annual Network and Distributed System Security Symposium, NDSS 2015, San Diego, California, USA, 8–11 February 2014. The Internet Society (2015)
28. Riccio, D., Galdi, C., Manzo, R.: Biometric/cryptographic keys binding based on function minimization. In: 12th International Conference on Signal-Image Technology & Internet-Based Systems, SITIS 2016, Naples, Italy, 28 November - 1 December 2016, pp. 144–150 (2016). https://doi.org/10.1109/SITIS.2016.31
29. Sandhu, R.: Role hierarchies and constraints for lattice-based access controls. In: Bertino, E., Kurth, H., Martella, G., Montolivo, E. (eds.) ESORICS 1996. LNCS, vol. 1146, pp. 65–79. Springer, Heidelberg (1996). https://doi.org/10.1007/3-540-61770-1_28
30. Stefanov, E., van Dijk, M., Juels, A., Oprea, A.: Iris: a scalable cloud file system with efficient integrity checks. In: Proceedings of the 28th Annual Computer Security Applications Conference, pp. 229–238. ACM (2012)
31. Takabi, H., Joshi, J.B., Ahn, G.J.: Security and privacy challenges in cloud computing environments. IEEE Secur. Priv. **8**(6), 24–31 (2010)
32. Vrable, M., Savage, S., Voelker, G.M.: BlueSky: a cloud-backed file system for the enterprise. In: Proceedings of the 10th USENIX Conference on File and Storage Technologies, pp. 19–19. USENIX Association (2012)

33. Wang, Z., Murmuria, R., Stavrou, A.: Implementing and optimizing an encryption filesystem on android. In: 2012 IEEE 13th International Conference on Mobile Data Management (MDM), pp. 52–62. IEEE (2012)
34. Weinhold, C., Härtig, H.: VPFS: building a virtual private file system with a small trusted computing base. ACM SIGOPS Oper. Syst. Rev. **42**(4), 81–93 (2008)
35. Yun, A., Shi, C., Kim, Y.: On protecting integrity and confidentiality of cryptographic file system for outsourced storage. In: Proceedings of the 2009 ACM Workshop on Cloud Computing Security, pp. 67–76. ACM (2009)

Fine-Grained Access Control for Querying Over Encrypted Document-Oriented Database

Maryam Almarwani[(⊠)], Boris Konev, and Alexei Lisitsa

Department of Computer Science, University of Liverpool, Liverpool, UK
{M.almarwani,Konev,A.Lisitsa}@liverpool.ac.uk

Abstract. This paper presents two security models for document-based databases which fulfill three security requirements that are confidentiality, querying over encrypted data, and flexible access control. The first model which we refer to as dynamic is based on a combination of CryptDB [16] and PIRATTE [15] concepts. While CryptDB consists of a proxy between one user and a database for encrypting and decrypting data according to user queries, PIRATTE refers to a proxy wherein encrypted files are shared using a social network between the number of users and the data owner with the files being decrypted using the proxy key on the user side. The second model which we refer to as static is based on CryptDB concepts as well as CP-ABE [6]. CP-ABE is public key encryption which offers fine-grained access control regarding encrypted data and set of attributes that describe the user who is able to decrypt the data provided within the ciphertext. These two models enhance CryptDB security while also helping with data sharing with multi-users using CP-ABE or PIRATTE concept that helps in verifying authentication on the database or application level.

Keywords: Fine-grained access control · Querying over encrypted data · Document database · CryptDB · CP-ABE

1 Introduction

Databases tend to involve sensitive data including government and personal information. For such data, the security must be able to handle threats that are internal as well as external. Although external threats are reduced generally by applying access control, external as well as internal (such as by curious administrators) data leaks can be prevented by encryption. It should be noted, however, that using encryption has its own problems. For querying encrypted data, they either should be decrypted making data leaks possible or special techniques have to be implemented to query encrypted data which have limited querying power and efficiency. According to the authors of [9], there are three requirements for securing databases which are (i) confidentiality, (ii) enforcement access

© Springer Nature Switzerland AG 2020
P. Mori et al. (Eds.): ICISSP 2019, CCIS 1221, pp. 403–425, 2020.
https://doi.org/10.1007/978-3-030-49443-8_19

control, and (iii) querying over encrypted data. There have been numerous systems that have been developed which satisfy one or more of these requirements. Regarding relational databases, the confidentiality and querying over encrypted data requirements are addressed by the CryptDB system [16], whereas all three requirements are addressed by DBMask [18]. In the past few years, numerous NoSQL data models and DBMSs have become popular [1] because they can effectively store as well as process substantial amounts of unstructured and structured information. NoSQL databases can be classified into four types which are key-value store, document-based store, column-based store, and graph-based store. Concerning NoSQL databases security, the first and third requirements are dealt with for example, in [3] (Graph DB) and in [20] (document-based DB), whereas [4](document-based DB) addresses all three requirements and proposes SDDB design that adds more types of encryption methods to securely achieve more queries operations over encrypted data than in [20].

In the paper [4], the *dynamic SDDB* design, (called there just SDDB) utilizes the precise access control functionality provided by PIRATTE approach [15] with a particular benefit of preventing re-encryption data cost in the case of user revocation. This paper expands [4] as follows:

- We present the detailed description of the *dynamic model* from [4].
- We present novel *Static Secure DataBases*(S-SDDB) model. In short, in S-SDDB, PIRATTE is replaced by CP-ABE and in that case, the access control is achieved by using *Attribute-Based Encryption* in the layered encryption onions. This allows decreasing computations cost when applied to fixed data attributes which do not require users revocation feature.
- We compare dynamic and static SDDB models which provide flexible access control at *application* and *database* levels, respectively.
- We describe sets of MongoDB queries supported by two models.
- We report on experiments with an initial prototype of S-SDDB utilizing one layer of Attribute-Based Encryption.

The rest of the paper is organised as follows. Section 2 provides the background of CryptDB, PIRATTE, and CP-ABE systems. Sections 3 and 4 examine the Secure Document Database (SDDB) scheme and SDDB workflow, respectively. Sections 5 and 6 present comparisons between static and dynamic models, and security analysis, respectively. Section 7 defines a case study concerning SDDB scheme application. Section 8 discusses performance and security regarding the SDDB. Section 9 discusses a prototype implementation and Sect. 10 presents the related work. Section 11 provides the conclusion.

2 Background

This section provides the background regarding CryptDB, PIRATTE, and CP-ABE concepts. CryptDB [16] can be considered as the first practical database system supporting SQL queries over encrypted data. It is a proxy between the user and the database as it rewrites a query so that it can execute it over encrypted data on DBMS while not revealing plaintext and passing on the encrypted result it receives from DBMS to the user once decryption is done. Various types of encryption techniques are used based on the type of data and required operations. These include Deterministic (DET) and Random (RND) types of encryption. Onion layers are used to compose these techniques as shown in Fig. 1. CryptDB is unable to implement specific access control regarding columns and cells. It can only use a proxy-based reference monitor to implement row access because of encrypting every column data using one key. Moreover, CryptDB users are unable to share their data with user groups.

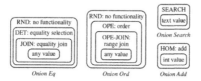

Fig. 1. Onion encryption layers in CryptDB [16].

For reducing CryptoDB limitations as well as adopting for the case of the document-based DB, implementing advanced cryptographic primitives including cipher-policy attributed based encryption (CP-ABE) [6] is that we propose. Attributes Based Encryption (ABE) is a public key cryptographic method in which encryption as well as decryption are based on the attributes. Restrictions on data access as per data owner imposed attributes are defined as access policy. ABE can be classified into Ciphertext-Policy AttributeBased Encryption (CP-ABE) and Key-Policy Attribute-Based Encryption (KP-ABE).

KP-ABE refers to the access policy which is labelled in the private key and the attributes are labelled in ciphertext whereas the reverse is true for CP-ABE. It provides a feature particularly for users who are able to decrypt the data specifically regarding the applications. Hence, it will be implemented in this paper to ensure specific access control for data. CP-ABE refers to public key encryption which offers fine-grained access control regarding encrypted data and can be considered to be similar to Role-Based Access control. Further, it identifies users who are authorized to decrypt data as per Access Policy including a set of attributes provided within the ciphertext. A set of attributes describes the user who is also issued a relevant private key. The user is able to decrypt the data only when private key attributes fulfil access policy regarding the ciphertext. Furthermore, there are four algorithms in CP-ABE as follows:

1. **Setup:** This algorithm includes only the implicit security parameter input while outputting the public parameters PK as well as a master key MK.
2. **Key Generation (MK, S):** This algorithm includes the master key MK as well as a set of attributes S describing the key as input while outputting a private key SK.

3. **Encrypt (PK, A, M):** This algorithm has the public parameters PK, an access structure A, and a message M concerning the attributes as input. The algorithm encrypts M while developing a ciphertext CT because of which only a user who has a set of attributes fulfilling the access structure can decrypt the message. It should be assumed that A is implicitly included in the ciphertext.

4. **Decrypt (PK, CT, SK):** This algorithm includes the public parameters PK, a ciphertext CT containing an access policy A, as well as a private key SK that is a private key regarding a set S of attributes as input. In case of the set S of attributes fulfilling the access structure A, the algorithm is able to decrypt the ciphertext as well as return a message M.

Jahid and Borisov proposed the PIRATTE scheme [12] wherein CP-ABE and user revocation mechanism are integrated through a proxy which takes care of attributes as well as user revocation for enabling dynamic users. While a proxy key and secret keys are issued by the data owner in PIRATTE, only the proxy key regarding user revocation is updated.

3 SDDB Overview

This section provides SDDB's overview concerning both dynamic and static variants, including system requirements, threat model, Entities, and SDDB Models.

As illustrated in Fig. 2, SDDB allows Document DB to perform the queries over encrypted data regarding particular operations depending on access policy restrictions that the data owner imposes. Using user secret key, proxy can decrypt secret keys concerning encrypted data as well as determine encryption layers that can be adjusted.

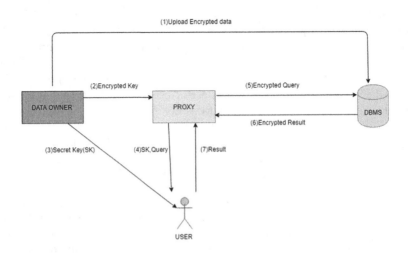

Fig. 2. SSDB design.

There are two models included in SDDB which are a static model a dynamic model [4]. Dynamic principle model is based on CryptDB concept including PIRATTE concept and fulfils fine-grained access control regarding application level that PIRATTE has on the proxy. On the other hand, static principle model is based on CryptDB concept including CP-ABE and fulfils fine-grained access control concerning database level as it encapsulates every onion into CryptDB by CP-ABE. Figure 2 presents four entries whose interactions in both models are as follows:

1. Data Owner (DO) refers to the authority that establishes access privileges concerning her/his data which this paper will call access policy (AP). DO, for example, can be a user sharing their data using applications. They may also use various keys for encrypting diverse aspects of the data based on the AP while uploading them to the DBMS server. This leads to the secret keys being created for every AP which are then distributed to the users. The authenticated user able to access the data is then verified using proxy in dynamic model or using DBMS in static model.
2. User Applications refer to users requesting data sharing regarding the DO. Here, the users' attributes are sent to the DO and their secret keys are received that helps in identifying themselves regarding the DBMS or proxy to gain access to parts of the data and to conduct queries.
3. Proxy refers to the intermediate server existing between DBMS, user application, and DO and helps verify the appropriate access regarding every user when dynamic model as well as rewriting queries should be executed concerning the encrypted data.
4. DBMS server concerns a server that offers database services including storage, retrieval, or verification of access control regarding static model. This also helps in storing encrypted data as well as conducting query while, if possible, not showcasing the plaintext data.

In both models of SDDB, processing query is conducting in six steps. The first step involves the user issuing the query as the data owner obtains the secret key. The second step involves the proxy rewriting the query of the user and replacing the anonymised fields, collection, and documents while encrypting the constants as per the necessary operation. In the third step, the proxy verifies the user query and determines whether it is able to execute regarding the current layer, failing which the proxy issues the update query for decrypting the current layer in case of the user being authorized for accessing such data. The fourth step involves the query being sent by the proxy to MongoDB which then sends the encrypted result to the proxy. In the fifth step, the results are decrypted by the proxy and sent to the user. In the sixth step, proxy re-encrypts the previous layer to ensure further security.

3.1   SDDB Requirements

SDDB design fulfils the requirements [4] given below such that both models fulfil c1–c4 while only the dynamic model fulfils c5–c7.

- **C1: Querying Over Encrypted Data:** This scheme can conduct operations as well as queries over encrypted data while not revealing the data.
- **C2: Flexible Access Control:** This grants users access to data parts as per data owner's policy which can be altered if required.
- **C3: Multi-user Sharing Support:** Depending on the policy of the data owner, numerous users can access data.
- **C4: Security and Performance Trade-off:** This scheme enables better security or performance to be developed.
- **C5: User Revocation Support:** This scheme can, as per requests by data owners, revoke the users and restrict them from accessing data.
- **C6: No Re-encryption Data:** There is no need for data re-encryption when user revocation has occured.
- **C7: No Re-distributed Key:** There is no need for keys to be re-distributed when user revocation takes place.

3.2 Threat Model

- **DO:** This is trusted and is offline following encryption and uploading of the encrypted data. It then distributes the keys to users except when a new user asks for permission or when the owner removes user access rights.
- **User Applications:** This is untrusted, and hence, the proxy has to verify them prior to allowing access and querying data. DO and Proxy and user applications do not share decryption keys.
- **Proxy:** This is semi-trusted and gains encrypted keys as well as is unable to decrypt data by itself.
- **DBMS Server:** This is semi-trusted and hence is unable to gain the keys for decrypting inner layer.

3.3 Document-Aware Encryption

This section examines encryption techniques that layers, security level, and onions use along with their work concept.

1. **Access Control (AC):** Here, encrypted value includes access policy which identifies which users have been authorized for accessing the data in which CP-ABE algorithm is implemented [6]. This does not provide any computation operations regarding the encrypted value. Further, as it does not reveal data information, it ensures optimum security as per Decision Bilinear Diffie-Hellam (DBDH).
2. **Random (RND):** Here, Blowfish-CBC or AES-CBC encrypt the same values regarding various values for numeric or string data, respectively, using a random initialization vector (IV). It appears to be similar to Access control layer which does not provide any computation operations or reveals any information. Further, it grants optimum security as per indistinguishability concerning adaptive chosen-plaintext (IND-CPA) [5].

3. **Deterministic (DET):** Here, AES-CBC and Blowfish-CMC [11] encrypt two equal values as the same value by concerning string and number data, respectively, with zero-IV. It results in leaking equivalent values, and hence, one is able to conduct equality operations on the encrypted data including equality predicate, Count, and Group. Moreover, it grants reduced security compared to AC while being effectively secure.
4. **Order-preserving Encryption (OPE):** Here, data encryption is done an OPE algorithm, such as Boldyreva' algorithm [7], and hence, it leaks data order as well as enables comparisons predicates including Order by, Min, and Max. It also offers less security compared to DET.
5. **Homomorphic Encryption (HOM):** Here, encryption of two same values is done to two different values and is able to conduct arithmetic operations concerning numeric data using Fully Homomorphic Encryption while being expensive and ineffective. On the other hand, partially Homomorphic encryption can support particular operations, such as summation or multiplication, that is less expensive and more effective. For instance, Pailier's algorithm [14] is implemented for supporting summation operations using Further, it provides similar security regarding AC layer.
6. **Word Search (WS):** Here, data encryption is done using Song's protocol [19] which supports LIKE Operator. Song's protocol is used to encrypt keyword in the user's query by proxy, while MongoDB searches aspects of encrypted data which includes the same encrypted keyword. Moreover, it does not leak information to a server, and hence ensures close security concerning AC.

3.4   Adjustable Query-Based Encryption

Every technique can support particular operations that include RND and AC regarding queries with no computations, OPE concerning comparison operations, DET concerning equality operations, WS concerning LIKE operator on string data, and HOM concerning summation (and other arithmetical operations) on numeric data. Every technique can offer different level of security. Hence, such techniques are arranged in the form of layers and onions as per types of data and operations. Further, the outmost layers provide optimum security while inner layers reduced security. For supporting data access restrictions as well as encrypting data using diverse keys using every technique as per who has access to data, AC technique is used to encapsulate the onions in the static model, as shown in Fig. 3(A), or to maintain CryptDB onions in the dynamic model, as shown in Fig. 3(B), while implementing PIRATTE on an application level.

Thus, when adjustable query-based encryption is used, the layers of encryption protecting the data has to be adjusted to allow to perform the required operations. For sharing data as well as restricting data access, the data owner provides a unique encryption key to every layer and onion regarding every access policy. The proxy verifies the access rights as well as clause within the query for identifying the suitable layer, onion, as well as field for encryption. Then, it issues the updated query which includes user-defined functions (UDFs) that should be

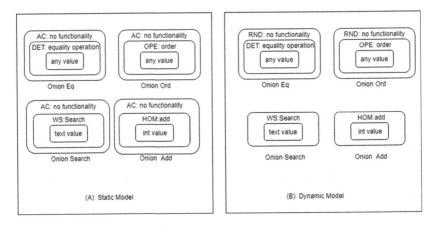

Fig. 3. Layers of onions in models.

executed on document DB. The user, for example, issues the query that includes equality operation, including checking ID = 23. The user also holds access rights with no regard to the query type. Regarding adjustable query-based encryption, the process in both models is as follows. Execution of this query is not possible if the outermost layer RND or AC. To decrypt the ID field's outermost layer concerning Onion Eq, the update query that must be on DET layer is issued. Proxy then rewrites user query which is executed on document DB. Proxy issues the update query to return to the outermost layer such as RND or AC to maintain further security.

3.5 Data Format and Query Language

It is possible to implement SDDB scheme for different document-based DBs, MongoDB environment is regarded as the major target. The data storage format [4] is defined along with the query language concerning MongoDB but we will define it here again with more details to understand the remainder of the paper. A binary coded format known as BSON is used for the representation of MongoDB data. BSON can be regarded as a form of JSON that has further data types, including *binary* and *date*, as well as embedding feature. It offers efficient encoding as well as decoding using various languages, further information for which can be found at http://bsonspec.org. Further, a particular data query language is not used by MongoDB although it adhered to simple query syntax which is appropriate for data representation by JSON which will be referred to as MongoDB Query. MongoDB Query syntax consists of calling database db followed by Collection-name and then operators such as find(), insert() and may be followed by any data condition in the case of request a representative in JSON and maybe also followed by functions such as sort() or count(). An example for this is given below:

```
db.collection-name.find('name':1).sort();
```

Table 1 presents MongoDB queries' common forms as per MongoDB documentation while ensuring the execution on this model's layers and the layers which are possible to adjust to ensure execution.

As shown in Table 1, there are three categories of MongoDB queries that possible in both models.

1. Executing query on the encrypted data while not including adjustable layers. Such as 1, 2 that be executed on the AC layer directly Following is how this group is executed:
   (a) The query is sent by the user to the proxy which is written on the MongoDB query.
   (b) The proxy encrypts the collection name because it is known in the uploading phase and then transfers it to Query router server.
   (c) If there is a find, the encrypted results are sent by the Query router server to the proxy, which then decrypts numerous times as per the number of onions or layers, such as first decrypting RND or AC layer and then the DET layer and providing the user with the result.

Insertion Example:

(a) The user issues I query

db.mycol.insert({'title':'MongoDB'})...(I)

(b) The proxy encrypts 'MongoDB' on onion equal as well as onion order and sends II query to Query router server.

db.mycol.insert({title −eq:'ghftygdyubnbc'},
   {title −ord:'tyuuiiowosak'},
   tilte −search:'xcbvbmnswe')...(II)

(c) The query is executed by the query router by adding a new document which includes three fields as there is a string type title field.

Finding Example without Any Operations:

(a) The user issues I query

db.mycol.find({})...(I)

(b) The query is sent by proxy to Query router server.
(c) Query router server sends fields-eq and Id such as id:7df78ad8902c and title-eq:'ghftygdyubnbc'.
(d) Proxy decrypts the result by first peeling off RND or AC layer followed by DET layer for gaining 'MongoDB' value and forwarding it to user.

2. Query is executed over encrypted data using adjustable layers, including 3, 4, 7, 8, and 9 which are executed on inner layers. Following is how this group is executed:
   (a) The query is sent by the user to the proxy which is written on a MongoDB query.

(b) Proxy peels off RND or AC layer through issuing update query regarding operation field only and then sending to the Query router server for updating this field to make a comparison with the user's query value.

(c) The user query is then rewritten by the proxy and is sent to Query router server.

(d) Encrypted results are sent by the query router server to the proxy which then decrypts numerous times as per the number of onions or layers, and the results are sent to the user.

Finding Example with Equal Operation:

(a) The user issues I query

db.mycol.find({'tittle ':'MongoDB'})...(I)

(b) This query cannot be executed on the current layer (AC), and thus, proxy issues update query (II) for peeling off AC layer.

db.mycol.updateMany({},{\$set:{'tittle −eq'
:decrypt−AC(K,tittle −eq,Ksw))}} in static model...(II)

or

db.mycol.updateMany({},{\$set:{'tittle −eq'
:decrypt−RND(tittle −eq,IV))}} in dynamic model...(II)

This query includes the comparing field as well as key which was used on encrypting value for decrypting this field on DET layer.

(c) The proxy rewrites the existing user query for executing on encrypted data by encrypting ['tittle':'MongoDB'] as per the encrypted data on DET layer as III query.

db.mycol.find({'tittle −eq ':'werwdgdjhhkjiu '})...(III)

(d) Query router server compare the value ('werwdgdjhhkjiu') on tilttle-eq fields and send all field on these documents contain this value to proxy.

(e) The result is decrypted by proxy by first peeling off the RND layer using field-IV or the AC layer using after which the DET layer is peeled off to gain plaintext value which is forwarded to user.

3. Querying is not supported over encrypted data. As existing encryption techniques are unable to support such queries, two solutions are recommended. Following is how this group is executed:

(a) Executing a part of the query that provides support to the existing encryption techniques and eliminates parts which cannot be executed, after which when the results are received by proxy and decrypted, user's queries are executed as per the result to gain the necessary results.

Table 1. Common MongoDB queries.

No	Query type	Executing layer	Adjustable layer
1	- db.collection-name.insert(document)	AC or RND	NO
2	- db.collection-name.find() - db.collection-name.find().pretty()	AC or RND	NO
3	- db.collection-name.find({"key":"value"}).pretty() - db.collection-name.find({"key":{$ne:value}}).pretty()	DET	AC or RND
4	- db.collection-name.find({"key":{$lt:value}}).pretty() - db.collection-name.find({"key":{$lte:value}}).pretty() - db.collection-name.find({"key":{$gt:value}}).pretty() - db.collection-name.find({"key":{$gte:value}}).pretty()	OPE	AC or RND
5	- db.collection-name.find({$and:[{key1:value1}, {key2:value2}]}).pretty()	Not support	-
6	- db.collection-name.find({$or:[{key1:value1}, {key2:value2}]}).pretty()	Not support	-
7	- db.collection-name.update(SELECTION-CRITERIA, UPDATED-DATA)	DET (equal) and OPE (other condition)	AC or RND
8	- db.collection-name.remove(DELLETION-CRITTERIA)	DET and WS	AC or RND
9	- db.collection-name.find().sort({KEY:1})	OPE	AC or RND
10	- db.collection-name.ensureIndex({KEY:1})	Not support	-
11	- db.collection-name.aggregate(AGGREGATE-OPERATION)	Not support	-

4   SDDB Workflow

This section examined how access control can be verified and a query can be executed on SDDB regarding both models. PIRATTE concepts are used by the dynamic [4], model concerning Proxy and DO for verifying access control by allowing decrypting keys which are stored on the proxy. Hence, in case of the user's inability to obtain keys, user query is rejected. CP-ABE as encapsulation is used by the static model on every onion on DBMS. Thus, if the user does not hold right to access, the proxy rejects query. The two models are similar as given below apart from minor differences.

- **DO-DocumentDB Connection:**
  1. DO develops Policy Access (PA) including ((Doctor and L hospital) or Administer).
  2. DO conducts setup function for every encryption technique for gaining symmetric key concerning every policy. This key differs from other access policies.
  3. Regarding the Static Model, DO executes CP-ABE-Setup for gaining public key(pk) as well as master key(mk) for policy access. Regarding Dynamic Model, DO executes PIRATTE-Setup for gaining public key(pk) as well as master key(mk) along with Proxy Key-setup for developing proxy key to ensure policy access.
  4. DO conducts Enc-Layer for encrypting value for every document field through key from step 2.
  5. For Static Model, DO executes Enc-CP-ABE algorithms for encrypting value from step 3 through pk and PA.
  6. DO uploads encrypted documents in DBMS.
- **DO-Proxy Connection:**
  1. DO sends the keys(pk,mk, symmetric keys for encryption techniques, Proxy Key (Dynamic Model)) regarding every policy to proxy which encrypts them using Enc-CP-ABE (Static Model) or Enc-PIRATTE (Dynamic Model) as in case of a proxy attack, the adversary will fail to gain access to data on DBMs.
- **User-DO Connection:**
  1. User sends user attributes to DO.
  2. DO verifies which user attributes belongs to which policy access AP.
  3. DO executes CP-ABE-KeyGen (Static Model) or PIRATTE-KeyGen (Dynamic Model) for gaining secret key (skw) using master key.
  4. Do sends secret key to user.
- **User-Proxy Connection:**
  1. User sends attributes (skw) and Query (Q).
  2. Proxy verifies which attributes belong to which policy access and executes Dec-CP-ABE(Static Model) or Dec-PIRATTE(Dynamic Model) for decrypting keys through skw for gaining secret keys for policy access.
- **Proxy-DocumentDB Connection:**
  1. Proxy verifies whether operation on query is able to be executed on CP-ABE or RND layer. If it can, step 2 is done, and if it cannot, step 3.

2. Proxy alters the outermost layer through issuing update query by skw concerning the intended Onion.
3. Proxy rewrites Q and then replaces the constant with encryption using existing layer for sending query to DocumentDB.
4. DocumentDB forwards encrypted result to proxy.
5. Proxy decrypts the result by conducting Enc-ourmost-layer and then decrypts it again through Enc-inner-layer and forwards the result to user.

5   Static Model VS Dynamic Model

This section focuses on the crucial differences between dynamic and static models. Concerning the static model, every onion's top layer includes Access control technique using CP-ABE, as illustrated in Fig. 3A. For allowing data sharing, diverse keys are provided to inner layers as per the top layer, and only the user who holds the access right can decrypt the data. Hence, if the user does not have access, the user query is rejected. Thus, this model is unable to allow user revocation, in which case re-encryption of data or keys distribution is needed. Regarding the Dynamic model [4], layers and onions regarding CryptDB, as shown in Fig. 3B, are used, and PIRATTE is used for allowing data sharing as well as access enforcement for enabling data encryption using various keys. Hence, data can only be accessed by the user who is from that group. Access control fulfils the application level between the user and proxy with no need for Database sharing. In case the user is not given access, the query is refused by proxy. This model allows user revocation with no need for re-encryption data or keys distribution. The two models are compared in Table 2.

Table 2. Static model VS dynamic model.

	Dynamic model	Static model
AC technique	PIRATTE	CP-ABE
AC level	Application	Database
Onion and layers	As CryptDB	AC technique as outermost layer for onions
Unauthorized user	Rejecting query	Rejecting query
User revocation	YES	NO

6   Security Analysis

Regarding the proposal design, as shown in Fig. 2, as well as the encryption techniques types, the design offers protection against two types of threats:

1. **DBMS Threats:** DBMS threats are intended here ADB curious and external threats against full access and data leaks:

(a) Full access is hindered as encryption keys are not shared with ADB.
(b) On the encrypted data, query is executed for offering confidentiality so that data leaking can be prevented, whereas the leakage level is based on the encryption techniques that are used, as depicted in Table 3. OPE, for example, is the weakest security as it leaks order as well as duplicates and can be part of the plaintext along with DET providing more security which only leaks duplicates. Then are AC, RND, HOM, and WS which have no leakage.

Table 3. Leakage information level for encryption techniques.

Encryption technique	Leakage
AC or RND	None
DET	Duplicates
OPE	Order, duplicates + partial plain-text
HOM	None
WS	None

2. **Arbitrary Threats:** Arbitrary Threats are intended here any attacks on users, proxy and DBMS. If there is an attack on the proxy, the keys will be accessible to the attacker for detecting the stored data while also gaining full access to database. This can be prevented using CP-ABE so that full access to data can be prevented because of various keys being used for data encryption as well as keys encrypted on proxy as per access policy. This, however, does not prevent data leakage of a group which is part of the logged-in user if there is an attack. It also helps in preventing collision resistance threat if users or entities collide.

7   Case Study

This section assumed that the DO includes a data set that has a collection which includes two documents, both of which have two fields, ID and Name, which are integer and string data type, respectively. The execution of Q1 is done using MongoDB querying language to execute query through SDDB model and not using SDDB [4].

```
Q1:(db.collection −1.find({ID:23},
{name:1}))
```

7.1   Without SDDB

This scenario is implemented when the system fails to offer data encryption or access verification. The data is uploaded by DO in DBMS as Plaintext, while it is assumed that access privilege is provided to users by providing them with password (PW). Hence, the Q1 and PW is used by the user through user application which sends it to the DBMS server for execution, the results of which are sent to the user and Name = Alice is matched to ID = 23 [4].

7.2   With SDDB

This scheme can be classified into cases as per computation classes needed by the application's queries. In this case study, for example, because the application needs queries (insert, delete, update, select) that have equality operation, the encryption of data is done using onion equality (DET), as depicted in Fig. 4, in the dynamic model or between DET and AC, as depicted in Fig. 5, in the static model.

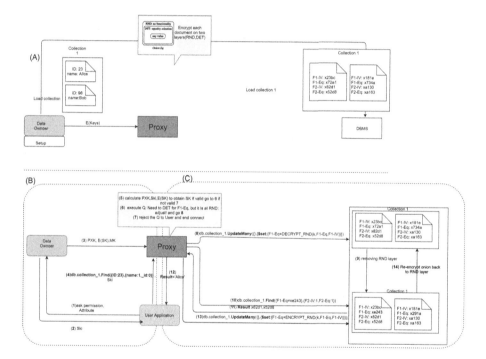

Fig. 4. Dynamic model [4].

There are two major processing stages:

1. Encrypt and upload data
   (a) DO chooses AP for these two documents: AP: (Doctor AND Surgery Department).
   (b) DO runs Setup functions to obtain PK, MK, LK-RND (dynamic model), LK-AC (static model), LK-DET, PXYK (dynamic model).

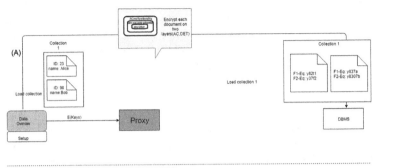

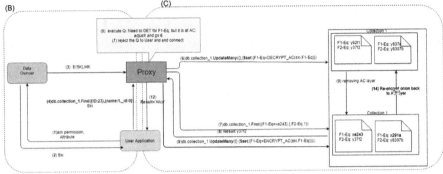

Fig. 5. Static model.

(c) In dynamic, DO encrypts data by LK-RND and LK-DET. While, in static, DO encrypts data by PK, LK-DET.

(d) DO uploads data on DBMS.

(e) DO sends encrypted keys by PK to proxy.

2. Verify access control and execute the query

(a) User sends attributes(Doctor and surgery department) to DO.

(b) Do sends secret key(ski)

(c) User sends ski and attributes and query Q1 to proxy.

(d) in case of dynamic model, Proxy check attributes and decrypt keys if ski is correct, go to next steps, if it is incorrect the query rejects. In case of static model, proxy does to next setps.

(e) Proxy check operation of query in this example is equality operation therefore, outermost layer adjust by LK-RND for dynamic or ski for static model by update query Q2.

$$Q2-\text{dyanimc}:(db.\text{collection}-1.\text{updateMany}(\\\${\},\{\$set=F1-Eq=DECRYPT\_RND(\\k,F1-Eq,F1-IV\}))$$

> Q2−static:(db.collection −1.updateMany(
> ${},{$set=F1−Eq =DECRYPT_AC(
> ski,F1−Eq}))

(f) Proxy rewrites query Q1 to Q3 and sends to DBMS:

> Q3−dynimc:db.collection −1.find({F1−Eq=
> xe243},{F2−IV:1,F2−Eq:1})

> Q3−static:db.collection −1.find({F1−Eq=
> xe243},{F2−Eq:1})

(g) DBMS sends result to proxy which is in dynamic (F2-IV=x82d1, F2,x52d8) or in static (y37f2).

(h) proxy decrypts the result twice in RND and DET (dynamic) or in AC and DET (static) and sends to user.

(i) Proxy come back to outermost layer to more security by issue opposite query in step (e).

> Q4−dyanimc:(db.collection −1.updateMany(
> ${},{$set=F1−Eq =Encrypt_RND(
> k,F1−Eq,F1−IV}))

> Q4−static:(db.collection −1.updateMany(
> ${},{$set=F1−Eq =Encrypt_AC(
> ski,F1−Eq}))

8 Discussion

This section will examine the security as well as performance of the two models in this case study along with the studies that it inspired [4]. This scheme will also be compared with existing works.

Regarding security, in case of the without-SDDB model, in case of the DBMS server's exposure to curiosity or compromise, it will show plaintext data as it is not encrypted. Further, the adversary may also gain the password as well as impersonate the data owner so that they can manipulate the data. Hence, a secure channel is necessary for exchanging it [4].

Concerning the with-SDDB, the information is revealed by the DBMS server only if it is identified as per the encryption algorithm in the existing layer used, including equal in DET. Thus, the decryption layer is sent back to high-security layers except CryptDB. Concerning SDDB, encryption keys also do not need to be shared as various keys are used for user authentication as well as data encryption, as per access privileges except CryptDB. For the user, PIRATTE executes data decryption and cannot be trusted. Hence, this permission is provided to the proxy in the dynamic model, while for the proxy or DBMS, CP-ABE executes data decryption in the static model. If the adversary can gain the keys, they will be unable to impersonate the data owner by connecting the keys with the

Table 4. Comparison of our scheme with some existing work [4].

	[16]	[20]	[3]	[18]	[9]	[15]	Dynamic model [4]	Static model
C1	✓	✓	✓	✓	✓	X	✓	✓
C2	☐	☐	X	✓	✓	✓	✓	✓
C3	X	✓	✓	✓	✓	✓	✓	✓
C4	✓	X	✓	X	X	☐	✓	✓
C5	☐	☐	☐	✓	☐	✓	✓	X
C6	☐	☐	☐	Only users group belong	☐	✓	✓	X
C7	☐	☐	☐	Only users group belong	☐	✓	✓	X
DB	Relational DB	Document DB	Graph DB	Relational DB	Relational DB	☐	Document DB	Document DB
PS	✓	☐	✓	✓	X	☐	In the future	In the future

Notes: Satisfies (✓), Does not satisfy (X), Out of scope (☐).

user attributes or with the Proxy Key. In addition, if the proxy is compromised or is exposed, data leakage will not occur as it is unable to decrypt keys in the dynamic model or gain accurate results in the static model.

Regarding performance, the without-SDDB model is able to execute any query type or computations at a high speed. The with-SDDB model, on the other hand, offers necessary queries as per the algorithm type because of decreased number of layers in CryptDB for attaining the sensitivity level of the data owner as well as the application requirements. Moreover, concerning the dynamic model, the encrypted data size remains constant compared to PIRATTE which increases dependence on AP. In this scheme, the PIRATTE concept is used to verify access and not for data encryption. In the static model, there will be a decrease in the communication cost between the DO and proxy as it will not need a connection for updating the keys which occurs in the dynamic model. Thus, SDDB grants a trade-off between performance and security.

Table 4 [4] depicts the scheme's properties compared to existing works which Section examines in detail. In the reported properties, C1-C7 the database type (DB) as well as practical status (PS) are included which depicts scheme being implemented and evaluated.

9   Implementation

The prototype of the simplified static variant of SDDB has been implemented. It includes a simplified model for data encryption using one layer (CP-ABE) so that flexible access control, querying over encrypted data as well as confidentiality could be ensured and tested in the Document Database. Further, this implementation is written in Java as a monolithic code (no separation between user and data owner components, as yet) and executes on Windows 10. It allows experimenting with the proposed design and assumed workflows. In particular a scenario is implemented in which document fields(name, salary and Credit Card number) and the user name as well as password are first checked, following which user attributes are verified so that they satisfy policy access. Once access is granted, the following list of queries is executed:

- Q1- Insert 100 documents (No computation)
- Q2- Find 100 documents (No computation)
- Q3- Delete 100 documents (No computation)
- Q4- Enter one document (Equality computation)
- Q5-Insert one document (Equality computation)
- Q6- Delete one document (Equality computation)
- Q7- Update one document (Equality computation)

In the query Q4–Q7, the user is asked to enter the value for a particular field to compare encrypted value for it by CP-ABE by data stored then find or delete or update documents in the case of equality. The exeperiments were conducted using Local MongoDB server and a client, implementing user and data owner functionality. Each case was executed 15 times. Then, average execution time is taken as shown in Table 4. As shown in Fig. 6, a significant time increase is observed in Q1, Q2, and Q5, with minimal increase in the remainder of the queries. This performance sacrifice, however, provides enhanced security which will be explored and further verified in the future work (Table 5).

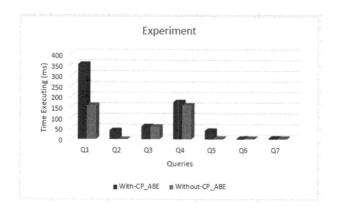

Fig. 6. Result analysis.

Table 5. average execution time of seven queries.

	Q1	Q2	Q3	Q4	Q5	Q6	Q7
With-CP-ABE	350.8	40.9333	60.2667	173.4	40.1333	3.6667	4.5333
Without-CP-ABE	157.8667	0.4667	58.4	157.8667	3.9333	3.1333	4.3333

10   Related Work

CryptDB [16] refers to a secure system that is executed as per relational database concerning SQL queries over encrypted data. Regarding its security, for a proxy attack, only that data is at risk of being leaked which belongs to users logged in then.

Concerning NoSql, CryptMDB [20] refers to a practical encryption system regarding MongoDB using an additive homomorphic asymmetric cryptosystem for data encryption. It implements the proxy concept at MongoDB's top so that it only perform an additive operation concerning encrypted data. Crypt-GraphDB [3] refers to a system which conducts queries over encrypted data that are stored within a graph store, such as Neo4j database, using CryptDB-like technique. Further, it uses dynamically adjusting encryption layers to offer traversal-aware encryption adjustment which is coordinated with the query execution, thus providing enhanced security [2].

Previous studies have examined confidentiality as well as querying concerning encrypted data whereas [9] and [18] emphasise access control regarding relational database. The study by [9] shows that the data owners use SQL-aware encryption regarding CryptDB for data encryption while not requiring a proxy which is then stored as relational database over a cloud. The encryption keys are provided to Database administrator authorised for accessing all the data over the cloud while also passing the keys to users as per legitimate access.

Further, DBmask [18] refers to a system which provides fine-grained access control based on Attribute-Based Group Key Management (AB-GKM) scheme wherein users' attributes fulfil data policies for providing access as well as executing SQL queries over encrypted data according to user permissions. The architecture of the system is based on CryptDB while implementing the proxy which refines clause queries which are unable to execute over encrypted data rather than executing on in-memory concerning the proxy. Two schemas have been used for conducting the DBmask system which are DBmask-SEC providing maximum security and DBmask-PER providing optimum performance. Here, the restriction concerns the access policy groups belonging to every cell being revealed to DBMS. An additional column is added by AB-GKM corresponding to every column in the table for identifying the group which belongs to a cell. For this, a fixed data structure format is needed because relational database and an adversary for database attack helps in determining the cells that are part of the same group. Hence, determining a suitable mechanism is important regarding non-relational database as it offers property for not revealing access control concerning the database. In 2005, however, an attribute-based encryption (ABE) [17] was suggested by Sahai and Waters referring to a form of public key encryption in which user identity is used for data encryption and decryption concerning access control of document data. Moreover, ABE can be classified into ciphertext-policy-ABE (CP-ABE) and key-policy-ABE (KP-ABE). Goyal created KP-ABE [10] in 2006 and noted that there is an association between the ciphertext and a set of attributes that have secret key related to AP. It is possible for a user to decrypt data in case of the ciphertext's corresponding attributes fulfilling the user key AP. Here, the limitation concerning such type of ABE concerns the Data Owner being unable to identify which users are able to decrypt the data. Hence, KP-ABE is inapplicable regarding applications in which data is shared. In 2007, however, Bethencourt created CP-ABE [6] and noted that there is a relationship between cipher-text and AP and the secret key concerns a set of attributes for surpassing the limitations of KP-ABE and further suitable for applications. KP-ABE as well as CP-ABE do not include user revocation mechanism. Although existing studies including [8,13,15] note that revocation mechanism is added to CP-ABE, data re-encryption or key re-distribution is necessary. Moreover, in 2012, the PIRATTE scheme [12] was suggested by Jahid and Borisov concerning the limitations previously stated in the background section.

11 Conclusion

This paper examines the primary idea regarding the Secure Document Database (SDDB) scheme which fulfils three major security database requirements that are flexible access control, confidentiality, and querying over encrypted data regarding a document-based store. The dynamic and static models are used for presenting SDDB. The dynamic model fits dynamic applications which can need changing users' attributes who are able to access data while not re-encrypting data as well as distributing keys. On the other hand, the static model is suitable in static applications which do not alter users' attributes necessary for accessing data. We reported also on the experiments with the simplified prototype implementation of the static model. In future work, we are going to implement both models using MongoDB as a document store, and evaluate trade-offs between performance and security.

References

1. No SQL, RDBMS - explore - Google trends. https://trends.google.com/trends/explore?date=all&q=NoSQL,RDBMS. Accessed 22 June 2019
2. Aburawi, N., Coenen, F., Lisitsa, A.: Traversal-aware encryption adjustment for graph databases (2018)
3. Aburawi, N., Lisitsa, A., Coenen, F.: Querying encrypted graph databases. In: Proceedings of the 4th International Conference on Information Systems Security and Privacy, ICISSP 2018, Funchal, Madeira - Portugal, 22–24 January 2018, pp. 447–451 (2018). https://doi.org/10.5220/0006660004470451

4. Almarwani., M., Konev., B., Lisitsa., A.: Flexible access control and confidentiality over encrypted data for document-based database. In: Proceedings of the 5th International Conference on Information Systems Security and Privacy, vol. 1: ICISSP 2019, pp. 606–614. INSTICC, SciTePress (2019). https://doi.org/10.5220/0007582506060614

5. Bellare, M., Rogaway, P.: Symmetric encryption. In: Introduction to Modern Cryptography (2004)

6. Bethencourt, J., Sahai, A., Waters, B.: Ciphertext-policy attribute-based encryption. In: IEEE Symposium on Security and Privacy, SP 2007, pp. 321–334. IEEE (2007)

7. Boldyreva, A., Chenette, N., O'Neill, A.: Order-preserving encryption revisited: improved security analysis and alternative solutions. In: Rogaway, P. (ed.) CRYPTO 2011. LNCS, vol. 6841, pp. 578–595. Springer, Heidelberg (2011). https://doi.org/10.1007/978-3-642-22792-9_33

8. Boldyreva, A., Goyal, V., Kumar, V.: Identity-based encryption with efficient revocation. In: Proceedings of the 15th ACM Conference on Computer and Communications Security, pp. 417–426. ACM (2008)

9. Ferretti, L., Colajanni, M., Marchetti, M.: Access control enforcement on query-aware encrypted cloud databases. In: 2013 IEEE 5th International Conference on Cloud Computing Technology and Science (CloudCom), pp. 219–219. IEEE (2013)

10. Goyal, V., Pandey, O., Sahai, A., Waters, B.: Attribute-based encryption for fine-grained access control of encrypted data. In: Proceedings of the 13th ACM Conference on Computer and Communications Security, pp. 89–98. ACM (2006)

11. Halevi, S., Rogaway, P.: A tweakable enciphering mode. In: Boneh, D. (ed.) CRYPTO 2003. LNCS, vol. 2729, pp. 482–499. Springer, Heidelberg (2003). https://doi.org/10.1007/978-3-540-45146-4_28

12. Jahid, S., Borisov, N.: Piratte: proxy-based immediate revocation of attribute-based encryption. arXiv preprint arXiv:1208.4877 (2012)

13. Liang, K., Fang, L., Susilo, W., Wong, D.S.: A ciphertext-policy attribute-based proxy re-encryption with chosen-ciphertext security. In: 2013 5th International Conference on Intelligent Networking and Collaborative Systems (INCoS), pp. 552–559. IEEE (2013)

14. Paillier, P.: Public-key cryptosystems based on composite degree residuosity classes. In: Stern, J. (ed.) EUROCRYPT 1999. LNCS, vol. 1592, pp. 223–238. Springer, Heidelberg (1999). https://doi.org/10.1007/3-540-48910-X_16

15. Pirretti, M., Traynor, P., McDaniel, P., Waters, B.: Secure attribute-based systems. J. Comput. Secur. 18, 799–837 (2006)

16. Popa, R.A., Redfield, C., Zeldovich, N., Balakrishnan, H.: Cryptdb: protecting confidentiality with encrypted query processing. In: Proceedings of the Twenty-Third ACM Symposium on Operating Systems Principles, pp. 85–100. ACM (2011)

17. Sahai, A., Waters, B.: Fuzzy identity-based encryption. In: Cramer, R. (ed.) EUROCRYPT 2005. LNCS, vol. 3494, pp. 457–473. Springer, Heidelberg (2005). https://doi.org/10.1007/11426639_27

18. Sarfraz, M.I., Nabeel, M., Cao, J., Bertino, E.: DBMask: fine-grained access control on encrypted relational databases. In: Proceedings of the 5th ACM Conference on Data and Application Security and Privacy, pp. 1–11. ACM (2015)

19. Song, D.X., Wagner, D., Perrig, A.: Practical techniques for searches on encrypted data. In: Proceedings of the 2000 IEEE Symposium on Security and Privacy S&P 2000, pp. 44–55. IEEE (2000)
20. Xu, G., Ren, Y., Li, H., Liu, D., Dai, Y., Yang, K.: CryptMDB: a practical encrypted mongoDB over big data. In: 2017 IEEE International Conference on Communications (ICC), pp. 1–6. IEEE (2017)

Author Index

Printed in the United States
By Bookmasters